Hertfordshire
COUNTY COUNCIL
Community **In**formation

2 5 MAY 2007

0 7 JUN 2007

12/11

2 8 OCT 2001

– 3 MAR 2003

– 4 MAY 2004

Please renew/return this item by the last date shown.

So that your telephone call is charged at local rate,
please call the numbers as set out below:

	From Area codes 01923 or 0208:	From the rest of Herts:
Renewals:	01923 471373	01438 737373
Enquiries:	01923 471333	01438 737333
Minicom:	01923 471599	01438 737599

L32b

ADEN UNDER BRITISH RULE 1839–1967

ADEN

UNDER BRITISH RULE

1839–1967

by

R. J. GAVIN

LONDON

C. HURST & COMPANY

First published in the United Kingdom by
C. Hurst & Co. (Publishers) Ltd., London

© 1975 by R. J. Gavin

ISBN 0–903983–14–1

To Guite Mie

Printed in Great Britain by
Billing & Sons Limited, Guildford and London

Contents

Plates

Maps

Figures

Preface

This study was begun before Aden Colony and Protectorate became the independent People's Democratic Republic of Yemen and was originally intended to present the story of Aden under British rule up to the end of the Second World War. However, the subsequent ending of British rule in 1967 evidently required that the story be carried forward to its logical conclusion and this was done. The form the account therefore takes is not that of a historical preface to the final drama of evacuation and independence, but of a description of Aden's experience while Britain was in control with a final chapter that seeks to establish the historical continuities and discontinuities rather than to plumb the deep complexities of the last phase. Nor is it the author's intention to present a full history of the peoples of South-West Arabia during the period of Britain's occupation of Aden. Such an enterprise would have required a rather different approach from that taken here and will no doubt be undertaken by Arab scholars. My centre of concern is British action in Aden and its hinterland and this study is based above all on the rich documentation available in the India Office Library, the Public Record Office and the Aden Records. It forms a story whose style in large measure reflects the various phases in Britain's attitude and outlook on imperial questions, but whose tempo was determined by more general processes of technological change and their interaction with natural disasters that periodically affected South-West Arabia. The history of Aden under British rule is not simply that of a strategic base functioning more or less according to the directives of British policy-makers in the political context of South-West Arabia. It is also the history of a heterogeneous trading community swelling with the growth of modern industrial society and profiting from its mediatory role between the latter and the less economically advanced societies in its immediate vicinity. The social discontinuities this involved largely determined Aden's function and character – both its prosperity and the harshness in its life. When these discontinuities were eroded in the final years of British rule a profound change began to take place which, together with the dissolution of the British base, forms the conclusion to this account.

I wish to acknowledge the assistance I received in beginning this work from various personalities, British and Arab, whom I met during my stay in Aden in 1959. Their names are too numerous to mention individually but I should like to record my gratitude for their patience with my first fumbling efforts to come to grips with this subject. I am particularly grateful to the librarians and record keepers of the India Office Library and the Public Record Office whose cheerful courtesy and constant solicitude so much assisted me in locating the more recondite sources. The following have kindly accorded me permission to use and to cite manuscripts in their possession: the Controller of H.M. Stationery Office, the British Museum, the Cambridge University Library, the Trustees of the Broadlands Archives Trust, Sir Alan Outram, Bart. and the National Army Museum, Sir Charles Hobhouse, Bart., Lord Elphinstone of Drumkilbo, Viscount Scarsdale, the Marquess of Salisbury, the Earl of Halifax, Baron Northbrook, and Viscount Cross, and to all these I should like to express my sincere gratitude. I am likewise grateful for the help afforded me by Mr. Cheeseman and his staff at the former Colonial Office Library, to Professor R. B. Serjeant upon whose large knowledge of all pertaining to South-West Arabia I was privileged to draw in the early stages of my work, to Sir Bernard Reilly with whom I had a number of illuminating discussions, to Dr. J. B. Kelly, who helped me with some of the intricacies of the India Office Records, to Alix Mac Sweeney who so carefully read the text, and to my colleagues at Ahmadu Bello University and the University of Ibadan who have in a number of ways influenced the direction my treatment of the subject has taken.

R. J. G.

CHAPTER I

The British come to Aden

On the morning of 19 January 1839, a small squadron of British ships, a Royal Navy frigate, an East India Company cruiser, an armed schooner and transports carrying seven hundred British and Indian troops, stood off the town of Aden in South-West Arabia. They were there with instructions to occupy the town and port and they had learned that they could expect resistance. Ashore, about a thousand Arab fighting men crouched behind the mouldering defences along the bay and on the better fortified Sirah Island which commanded the harbour. The defenders were mostly armed with matchlock guns and although some among them knew how to work the thirty-three heavy and light cannon at their disposal, they put their main trust in their familiar hand weapons. At 9.30 a.m. the British flagship swung forward from its anchorage and, holding close to the shore, moved in below Sirah and opened fire at three hundred yards range on the fortified battery on the seafront of the rocky island. For half an hour ship and fort engaged each other with the ship gradually gaining the upper hand. Its weapons were newer and more efficiently handled; the reply from the island was irregular and the shot from the upper defensive works flew harmlessly over the masts. At 10 a.m. the second cruiser moved in on the flank of the lower battery; the two ships pounded down the defences and dismounted five of the guns behind. The defenders fought back tenaciously amid the ruins with their matchlocks but could not hold their ground. The ships' guns then turned on a well-built sixty foot tower which crowned the island's defences and within half an hour reduced it to rubble. By 11 a.m. firing from the shore had become inconsequential and the troops went forward in boats and, landing on the beach, took the town by storm. British casualties were light – only sixteen killed and wounded, and some of those were suffered after the assault, during a quarrel over the disarming of prisoners taken on the island. The British flag was hoisted and Aden became the first colonial acquisition of Queen Victoria's reign.[1]

The spot upon which the victorious East India Company troops stood had been the site of a city for many centuries. The date of the first human settlement at Aden is not known. But there is no doubt of the town's great antiquity, and a glance at its aspect suffices to explain why so many generations had chosen to build their homes and do their business there. What is now the old town of Crater at Aden is a magnificent natural fortress. A semicircle of sheer-sided mountains rise protectingly around it leaving but a few easily-defensible means of access from the land. Beyond the gates the narrow isthmus joining the peninsula to the mainland presents a further obstacle to an invader. In front of the protected town lies a small harbour, one of the very few on the south Arabian coast. The harbour too has its natural defence in the form of Sirah Island, a towering natural fortress guarding the entry and the shipping from marauders in the sea beyond. Modern Aden has sprawled out beyond the Crater; the former natural defences are now a hindrance to communication. The old harbour in Front Bay has been abandoned since the 1860s and the isthmus is an airport and a highway rather than a point of defence.[2] These are all very recent developments; the product of the revolution in the speed and comparative cost of communication and transport of the past hundred years or so. Before then the 50,000 or so inhabitants that the Crater area could comfortably accommodate represented for most of man's history an urban settlement of somewhat more than average size. Likewise the precipitous protection of the Aden mountains was something that city men over the ages appreciated as they piled up their wealthy close-hemmed houses, safe from the prevalent rural poverty. The harbour too was the right size for men's vessels until the use of iron and steel emancipated shipping from the limitations imposed throughout all but the most recent history by wood technology.

The site of the city itself was excellent; the value of its hinterland was more problematical. Travelling beyond the isthmus now, one traverses some twenty miles of semi-desert before reaching the fertile valley of the irrigated Wadi Tuban, and out beyond lie the bare slopes of the South Arabian mountains where a few persons per square mile eke out a living from scattered strips of fitfully watered land. At the head of those slopes about eighty miles northward stands the Yemeni plateau and there at last the land is less inhospitable; fields terrace upward amid rainy slopes and provide sustenance for numerous groups of settled peasantry. This pleasanter land however lies rather far from Aden; the plateau stands nearer to the coast at other points than there. And Aden's remoter hinterland is not entirely well-watered plateau – slightly to the eastward of Aden's longitude the rising hills debouch on the empty desert, not on fertile fields.

For modern Aden the wealth moving through the port and on the seaways is very much greater than anything to be found in the lands behind the town. But this has not always been the case during the town's recorded history. The hinterland has not always been so forbidding. As recently as the beginning of the nineteenth century the mainland immediately behind Aden was described as being largely covered with forest.[3] Further back in time, in the thirteenth and fourteenth centuries A.D. the cultivated lands of Lahej and Abyan appear to have been broader and more extensive than in more recent times.[4] Even earlier, for nearly a thousand years before Islam, the aspect of the whole area was considerably different from what it is at present. What is now the edge of the desert was then the seat of large and wealthy settled populations. The plateau and mountains, which now harbour the bulk of the population, at that time represented less important backlands compared with the richer settlements scattered across the plains. The ruins of the capitals of the great states of Saba, Qataban, Ma'in and Hadhramawt which existed in South-West Arabia before the time of Christ are visited now by only a few herders. Ma'rib, Tumna', Qarnawu and Shabwa are now in the desert. But in their days of glory they were centres of populous districts, like the area around Nisab, the Wadi 'Amd and the country about the ruins of Naqb al Hajr.

Their fame abroad was made by the trade in incense – a commodity of vital importance and great value to the religious élites of the ancient Middle East and Egypt. But valuable as it was, incense could not have built the massive structures whose ruins litter the desert places of South Arabia. The temples and palaces, the walls, irrigation works and paved highways required surplus manpower for their construction, and those men had to be fed. The power and wealth of the ancient South Arabian states was based on a prosperous agriculture and that in turn depended upon large-scale irrigation which the effectively centralised governments of these large political units organised and maintained.[5] The areas around Marib, Tumna' and Shabwa must have been densely settled by sedentary agriculturists who took a pride in their well-furnished cities and in the temples of strongly localised deities, where the sacred business of maintaining the great public works was conducted and where even the export trade in incense was largely transacted.[6] Aden would then have been one possible port among a number on the borders of this civilisation and it is unlikely that any of the seaports were of much consequence compared with the interior cities. Until around the beginning of the Christian era it would appear that the bulk of the incense followed the land route northward to the Hijaz and Syria. As for the movement of the precious commodity along the coast, Aden was not as well placed as Mesala or Qana to the eastward. The main producing area seems to have lain in Dhufar, well to the east, with secondary

Above, H.M.S. *Volage* at Aden, 1839: 'The beginning of the engagement'.
Below, 'The Surrender of the Defenders'. Both watercolours by Captain
Rundle, R.N., who planted the flag in Aden after its capture in
January 1839.

centres in present Somalia and in the Yafi'i mountains to the north of Aden. Since much of the sea traffic represented coastal moving affluents from Dhufar and Somalia to the main great landward stream of northward export in ancient times, and since, as remnants of the old paved highways and other evidence show, that landward stream flowed north from a point well to the east of Aden's longitude, Aden would have stood to profit less than more easterly ports from the trade.

Two broad developments however which took place between the first century B.C. and the third century A.D. created conditions in which Aden's comparative prosperity could be built up. The first of these was the expansion of the trade via the Red Sea between India and China and the growing economies of the western Mediterranean basin. Around the beginning of the first century B.C. Egyptian traders had the Straits of Bab el Mandeb opened to them and somewhat later they discovered and began to use the monsoon system of the Indian Ocean. Thereby it became possible for Egyptian shippers to by-pass the Arabian land routes and enter directly into the newly burgeoning trades in pepper, various nuts and drugs, ebony, ivory and ceramics in the Indian Ocean and beyond. The trade in these commodities provided a most valuable addition to the northward flow of incense through the Red Sea. It also augmented the entrepôt traffic in the coastal ports of South Arabia and made them less dependent on their hinterlands for their trade. The ensuing centuries saw a steady rise in the importance of this seaward trade route both absolutely and by comparison with that by land. At the middle of the first century B.C. ships were sailing direct from Berenice on the Egyptian coast to South Arabian ports and thence to India; toward the end of the same century the merchants of Alexandria had one hundred and twenty vessels at work in the Red Sea bringing vast cargoes from South Arabia and India. The volume of the seaborne traffic appears to have continued to grow to the end of the second century A.D., after which there was a temporary decline.[7] By the early third century the bulk of the commerce had been transferred from land to sea.[8]

The second broad development which affected Aden's comparative importance was the gradual decline of the old centres of power in the South Arabian interior and the emergence of new and looser political systems based closer to the coast. During the first century B.C. the newly risen kingdom of Himyar, whose capital lay in the mountains about one hundred miles due north of Aden, wrested the coastal ports of Mesala and Qana from the ancient states of Qataban and Hadhramawt. The emergence of the new Himyarite political entity as a power in South-West Arabia ushered in a long period of strife between the Himyarite rulers and the rulers of the old kingdom of Saba. During that struggle the centre of gravity in the Sabaean kingdom itself moved westward until from about the beginning of the second century A.D., the Sabaean rulers were being habitually drawn from the tribes inhabiting the mountainous plateau north of the new city of San'a', among whom were the Hashid and Bakil confederations who were to figure prominently in the future history of South-West Arabia. While the struggle between Himyar and Saba continued, the whole area probably underwent a period of great internal turbulence in the second and the greater part of the third centuries A.D. During this period increasing numbers of well-equipped cavalry were incorporated into the ranks of the South Arabian armies. Nomad horsemen from the North Arabian deserts became a vital element in warfare and the military value of the settled peasantry in the old states correspondingly declined. Some of these horsemen were given lands in the settled areas of the old states, as was the case with the old sub-kingdom of Awsan (now the 'Awlaqi area of the Aden hinterland); the former peasantry became bondsmen to the new landowners. The old South Arabian states tottered one after another toward collapse. Ma'in in the north probably succumbed in the first century B.C., Qataban followed suit in the second century A.D. Saba continued to exist but, as has been mentioned above, in a modified form. Power had moved away from the old capital of Ma'rib, and the civilised community in that area began to decline. The first known bursting of the great Ma'rib dam, on which the settled population there absolutely depended, occurred about the beginning of the second century A.D. Ma'rib burst twice in the middle of the fifth century, again in the middle of the sixth century, and the unrecorded final bursting must have occurred not long afterwards.[9] No doubt in the interim the population declined with each catastrophe until the last produced the final dispersal. It is likely that the history of the other settled populations dependent on other closely controlled irrgation systems followed a similar pattern, over a somewhat similar though rather earlier period of time.[10]

Meanwhile South Arabians were being increasingly drawn into the wider Middle Eastern political arena. At the beginning of the second century A.D. Abyssinian rulers acquired territory on the Tihama coast and about the end of the century penetrated as far as Najran. For the next four centuries Abyssinia remained a factor of importance in the politics of the area. Conversely, various South Arabian rulers sought to bring the whole area from Hadhramawt to Hijaz under one sway. When this was attained under Abukarib 'Asad ('Asad Tubba), South Arabians set out on a career of conquest which took them to the confines of Mesopotamia and beyond. This success was shortlived and was followed by the brief Abyssinian conquest which in turn led to the establishment of a distant Persian dominion over South Arabia.[11]

The highly integrated, tightly built societies and economies on the desert fringe with their strongly localised deities and forms of worship were by then becoming things of the past. The new broader and more ambitious political systems were losing touch with parochial communities now predominantly situated in the mountains. The trade routes ran closer to the coast or on the sea itself and those who conducted the trade were now increasingly drawn from the ranks of foreigners with cosmopolitan contacts beyond the region — either Jews or Christian Greeks and Egyptians. The ideas of these two monotheistic religions began to spread more rapidly in the new social situation. A Christian church was erected at Aden in A.D. 346, 'Asad Tubba adopted Judaism in the early fifth century. The scene was set for the coming of the monotheistic, universalist teaching of Muhammad which was adopted during the prophet's lifetime in Aden and spread quickly through the area. Islam reinforced the previous cosmopolitan tendencies in South Arabian society. South Arabians became psychologically citizens of a wider world and this served to strengthen a willingness to migrate which the steady reduction in the agricultural means of subsistence must have already engendered.

Thus by the beginning of the Muslim era the general context within which Aden was to attain the height of its prosperity had been sketched in. The adoption of Islam gave the peoples of South Arabia a religious and, in limited measure, a political affinity with the broader Muslim community which soon spread out from the Middle East to Morocco and Spain, to Central Asia and down the Malabar coast of India. Aden, 'the eye of the Yemen', henceforward had a more important role to play as South Arabia's eye upon this now more interesting outer world. Cosmopolitanism however only operated within a very limited area of the general social consciousness. South Arabia may have been nominally subordinate at various times to this or that Caliphate, but political affiliation seldom went far beyond the ritual mention of the Caliph's name in the Friday prayers. Despite the efforts of the Caliphs to appoint officials and control its government, South Arabia remained for most of its subsequent history politically autonomous in practice. Beneath the surface of declared allegiance to the Caliph or professed solidarity with wider Islamic political movements, dull old political rivalries continued to work themselves out under various forms. Perhaps by a series of political accidents, perhaps owing to the stubborness of inherited tribal antipathies of Kahlanis and Himyarites, the rivalry of Qataban and Saba which had been continued in the first four centuries after Christ as a rivalry between the new Himyarite kingdom and refurbished Saba, reappeared two centuries after the death of Muhammad in the form of a struggle between the Rassite Imams of the north and the Yu'firids of the South. The quarrel had by then become overlaid with sectarian affiliations to Zaydism in the north and, through various deviations, Sunnite Islam in the south.[12] In that form it persisted more or less up to the present day. Beneath this 'party' conflict lay the more basic tendency toward the narrowest parochialism in political and social affairs. Whatever persistent divisions and rivalries there may have been in South-West Arabia, these were not more significant than the fact that its history was punctuated by frequent total breakdowns of government over wide areas which laid bare the basic kinship systems of social control. The kinship organisation of society, the 'clans' and 'tribes', had existed even in the old South Arabian states. But their scope of social and political action had been restricted by the more intense activity of centralised government. In the remoter mountain valleys, however, under the looser governments of the period after the seventh century A.D., the local clan or tribe was often the only operative form of political control; hence the importance of these social elements was enhanced and on occasion fused into large, tribal confederations which took joint action. The principal function of the centralised governments was now largely confined to the preservation of peace, especially on the roads, and the dispensation of justice. The interests of city dwellers and those of the farming peasantry tended to diverge, and this created a dilemma for those who wielded authority. Most of those exercising extensive rule became urban-oriented and spent the greater part of their revenues protecting, adorning and developing mercantile urban settlements which hid from the men of the hills and mountains behind ever stronger fortifications. One might ask: 'What visible return did the farmer receive for the taxes he paid?' The answer would be: 'Not very much', and there was frequent evidence of unwillingness to pay. In any case, the mountain agriculture of most of the Yemen did not produce a large surplus to be taxed. The taxation of urban dwellers, merchants and traders therefore provided a large proportion of government revenue. And this was only just; for it was those classes of the community who benefited most from the services which government offered.[13]

As these developments were taking place in the hinterland, Aden moved more into the limelight. Exactly how and when Aden became a major South Arabian port is still obscure. There is little evidence to support the view that Aden was prosperous in biblical times.[14] There is no unequivocal mention of the town before the fourth century

A.D., although there was an important entrepôt for the traffic between India and the Red Sea established somewhere in the vicinity during and before the second century.[15]

Only when South Arabia was drawn into the arena of wider trading and other rivalries did the commercial stronghold of Aden begin to figure clearly in the records. In A.D. 346 a Byzantine missionary founded one of two Christian churches in the Yemen there. In 540 the Persians singled it out as one of the objectives of a plundering expedition to the Yemen which heralded the establishment of their rule there thirty years later.[16] In Persian hands Aden became a port of some consequence and it may have been at this period that the Khormaksar Bridge at the Isthmus and the cisterns in the Crater were constructed. The prophet's son-in-law, 'Ali, is reported to have preached Islam at Aden in person.[17] By then the town would seem to have become the starting-point of the main overland trade route through the Yemen to the north.[18] In the tenth century it was referred to as the gateway to China. But it was not the only gateway. It had to contend with the competition of rival ports in the Persian Gulf which secured the lion's share of eastern traffic during the period before and after the Prophet's lifetime. Basra, Siraf and later Kish (Qays) were in those days the great entrepôts.[19] Behind them lay the rich culture of Mesopotamia and Persia which had climbed back to pre-eminence in the Middle East–Mediterranean area and reached the height of its splendour under the 'Abbassid Caliphate. Over the same period, the Roman Empire to the west declined and collapsed, producing confusion and a generally lower level of economic activity in the western Mediterranean basin. The centre of gravity of the east–west exchange commerce between south and east Asia and the Mediterranean countries shifted away from the Red Sea to the Persian Gulf and more easterly routes. Aden's fortunes were linked with those of the gradually recovering western countries. The recovery was most marked in the Maghreb and Spain where a new civilisation grew up under the auspices of the Ummayads and their successors. In the tenth century the Fatimid movement began to restore self-confidence among Aden's natural trading partners in Egypt. Trade was connected with politics and that in turn with religion. Subversive movements hostile to the Mesopotamian-based 'Abbasids and inspired by Fatimid ideas became active all along the line from the Maghreb through Egypt and the Yemen to Aden and out to the coasts of western India.[20] As they did so, Aden took the first steps toward the threshold of its greatest period of commercial success.

In 969 Egypt threw off 'Abbassid control and a Fatimid regime was established there. Thenceforward, the balance of political power in the Muslim world, and with it the main flow of trade, swung to the westward. In a determined effort to divert trade away from the 'Abbassids, the Fatimids built up the port of Aydhab, near the present port of Suwakin, as a terminus for the eastern trade. A unified government was secured for south-western Yemen under their Zura'id protégés and Fatimid influence and diplomatic relations with western India were strengthened. By the beginning of the eleventh century there were signs of growing prosperity at Aden and in the Tihama. By the middle of the century Aden had secured a large share of the eastern commerce, and for more than a hundred years afterward, the town was engaged in a bitter struggle for commercial dominance with the ports of the Persian Gulf. The prize at stake was rich, for the goods exchanged were of high intrinsic value. The most valuable of all were spices, and pepper in particular. Commerce in these commodities was strictly controlled and heavily taxed. The trans-shipment charge on pepper at Aden in the twelfth century amounted to a third of its value. Further charges along the route multiplied the original purchase price several times. The articles shipped in the other direction were equally valuable – coral, copper for coinage and the silver and gold which had since Roman times been the West's staple export to the East. In addition there was the backward and forward flow of textiles – for in mediaeval times there was still a market in India for western woven cloth. And there was the transverse and local trades betwen Arabia and Africa. But the rich spice trade and particularly the pepper staple was the most coveted object. For this, men were prepared to put forth great military and political exertions. Once the spices began to flow into Aden, pirates began to hover like vultures round the port. Regular fleets sent by Aden's rivals in the Gulf also made occasional forays. The great corporation of Cairo spice merchants, the Karimi, who dominated the trade, required security and this they found among the fastnesses of Aden. From the second decade of the twelfth century they built their merchant houses in the Crater and made Aden the starting point of their northward trade route through Ta'izz, Zabid and Jedda and thence to Aydhab and Cairo or alternatively by sea direct to the Egyptian coast. In 1175 the first Ayyubid ruler of Egypt gave them added safety by crowning Aden's heights with forts and curtain walls which stood until the nineteenth century. The famous tanks behind the town were possibly also installed at this time. On the sea, Egyptian fleets, operating from Aydhab, protected the port and kept all foreign shipping out of the Red Sea.[21] Thus Aden became in the twelfth century part of a closed and controlled trading system. With the capital invested in its defence and the closure of the Red Sea to Indian shipping, it had little to fear from local rivals within the Red

Sea. The collapse of its competitors to the eastward was to make it the richest entrepôt in the world.

The period of Aden's greatest prosperity is associated with the Rasulid dynasty which began its independent rule in the Yemen in A.D. 1232. The port's legendary biblical glory may only be a legend; its prosperity under the Rasulids is well documented and based on undoubted fact. In 1258 the Mongols swept into Iraq and disrupted the trading system of the Tigris–Euphrates valley. The shippers from India and China who had used that route cast about, seeking a new terminus for their trade. It would appear that some attempted to bend their old commercial system westward round the troubled area by pouring oriental goods into Arabia through Dhufar. But in 1279–80, to the consternation of these merchants, the Rasulid ruler conquered Dhufar and placed his officials in its ports.[22] Under the jealous eyes of the sailor Sinbad's descendants in the Gulf, Aden gathered in the full commerce of India, Ceylon, China and South-East Asia. The variety of spices broadened and to these were added cloths from the West Caspian, Chinese brocades, porcelain and jade, Indian spear-shafts, ewers, trays and censers. The years around the beginning of the fourteenth century saw the first real flush of this new prosperity and the inhabitants of the city watched with amazement the richness of the cargoes being hauled up the beach and through the sea gate.[23] In distant Rome, Aden was now regarded as the principal emporium of Arabia.[24] In the fourteenth and fifteenth centuries embassies came to the rulers of Aden from all parts of the world – from Egypt, from India, from Ceylon and from China.[25] Treasure poured into the Rasulid coffers and poured out again in the form of fine mosques, colleges and other public buildings. The Rasulid period was not one of complete political stability. The chronicles are full of battles and wars, succession disputes and quarrels between rival claimants. Aden was several times taken and retaken during the fourteenth and fifteenth centuries. But politics frothed on the surface of a well-organised and circumscribed state system.[26] Continuity was maintained by a sophisticated administration in which merchants played an important role. Areas of settled cultivation such as Abyan and Lahej and others throughout the Yemen were carefully administered and taxed.[27] Officials at Aden, on regular rotation, paid the proceeds of the customs into the central exchequer and, in case of need, the merchant corporation in the port could be counted on to supply large credits.[28] Behind this stood the slave army organised according to the Egyptian Mamluq model. The army provided the power behind the administration, assisting as required in the collection of land and date taxes in rural areas. It also had the organisation and great siege instruments which alone could break the strong walls of the cities which now stood in opulent dominance over rural Yemen.[29] From the early days of the dynasty, the army stood as a sort of praetorian guard in relation to the Rasulid dynasty and it was associated with the choice of succeeding rulers.[30] The Rasulid system however comprehended only the main cultivated areas of the plains, the cities and the trade routes between them. Beyond, the tribal confederations maintained a semi-autonomous existence, drawn from time to time into the politics of the urban and commercially-oriented state, but mostly standing aloof. Those that stood across the trade routes, like the Jihawf tribes of the Aden hinterland, were alternately visited by punitive expeditions and accorded stipends to keep the peace and let the caravans pass. The others were occasionally recruited as auxiliaries to assist in major campaigns undertaken by the state.[31] In general, the balance of power remained with the forces of the wealthy state and on this basis the system endured.

After the second decade of the fifteenth century there was a break in Aden's period of prosperity. The Rasulid dynasty declined towards its collapse at the middle of the century. The port of Ormuz (Hurmuz) in the Persian Gulf began to rise once more, syphoning part of the trade off eastward while the Sultan of Egypt broke Aden's grip on Red Sea commerce. Between 1422 and 1438 the Egyptian government monopolised the trade through the Red Sea and directed it onto the port of Jedda. Indian shippers were successfully encouraged to sail straight through the Bab el Mandeb and unload their cargoes there. For a short period Aden was by-passed and the landward trade northward out of the port collapsed amid political confusion and civil war.[32] But after 1450 the Tahirid dynasty re-established a now more limited state system in south-western Yemen and brought back prosperity to the port. For the next century Tahirid Aden contested control of the Red Sea commerce with the Egyptian-controlled ports in the upper Red Sea and ports to the eastward in the Hadhramawt. The Tahirids had not the same pretensions to the control of all the Yemen and even the Holy Cities that had been displayed by their predecessors. Their interests and loyalties were more local to Aden and its hinterland. Having a smaller domain, they scattered their munificence less widely than the Rasulids and Aden benefited more from their disbursements. In the last quarter of the fifteenth century Aden's water supply system was overhauled, a cistern and an aqueduct were built to bring water from mainland wells to the city. Two new mosques and a number of schools were founded.[33] At the beginning of the sixteenth century Aden was no longer the dominant Arabian commercial centre it had formerly been. The trading system northward from the Indian Ocean was now more diversified. Aden stood among powerful rivals and its rulers had lost control of Dhufar and even of less distant Shihr which had fallen to the rising Kathiri Sultans in the 1460s. But it was still a magnificent and populous city of 50–60,000 souls and the most strongly defended of all the ports on the southern and western littorals of the Arabian Peninsula.[34] The same cosmopolitan collection of Egyptian, Syrian, Maghrebi, Jewish and Indian merchants still did business in its streets.

The sixteenth century saw the collapse of this continuing prosperity. The collapse was not sudden. It did not result just from the doings of the Portuguese and certainly not simply from a diversion of the eastern trade to the Cape and Atlantic route. For a few years during the first and second decades of the century the Portuguese made a deliberate attempt to cut off the flow of eastern trade through the Red Sea but then they rapidly assimilated themselves to the existing pattern of commerce, taking over the role of plunderers, then 'protectors' of the shipping that plied between India and Arabian ports.[35] For a longer period they managed to swing the bulk of the pepper and other spices consumed in Europe out to the Atlantic route. But even this achievement was not permanent and during the two decades after 1550 Cairo once more supplied pepper to most markets in Europe.[36] The other trades which brought life to Arabian ports went on largely as before except that the Portuguese from their ports in India and the Persian Gulf levied tribute on the merchant shipping and their small warships on the seaways seized all vessels which did not carry a Portuguese pass. This in itself was no new phenomenon. There is every evidence that piracy had always been a common profession along the Indian Ocean shipping routes and that the fleets of Indian and other naval powers policed those routes at a price, confiscating the goods of those who had not paid their dues.[37]

What was new was that the Portuguese had broken into a system in which the naked exercise of power had to some extent at least been mitigated by the ties of accumulated mutual trust and common religion existing between the principal parties. Whereas Muslim rulers in the Indian ports had seen eye to eye with Muslim rulers in Arabian countries on religious, legal and other matters, the Portuguese were avowedly hostile to the religion that underlay Arab society and what deals they made with Arab governments were based strictly on mutual political or commercial advantage.[38] Moreover, the Portuguese presence in the Indian Ocean provoked a strong reaction from Middle Eastern Muslim society united under the leadership of growing Ottoman power. In 1516 Egypt was brought under the rule of the Ottoman Sultans and, after nearly a century of decline, Egyptian power began to revive. In the following thirty years Ottoman forces fought an increasingly successful battle to

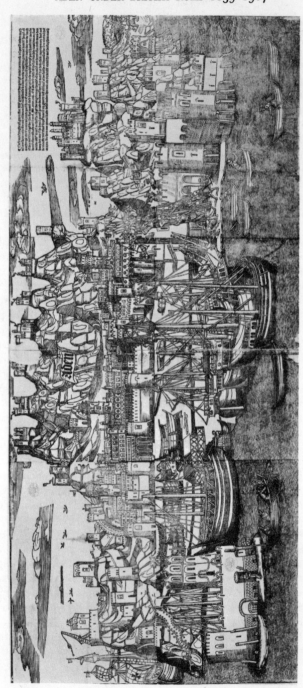

Attempted Escalade of Aden by the Portuguese under Albuquerque in 1513 (reduced from a large contemporary wood engraving in the British Museum).

drive the Portuguese out of the Red Sea and away from the coasts
of Arabia. The war swung back and forth throughout most of the
century, punctuated by periodic truces, with neither party securing
complete victory.[39]

Aden's prosperity was to become one of the main casualties of this
struggle. The Tahirid rulers of Aden, like their counterparts at al
Shihr and Dhufar, were torn between the two contestants and
accommodated themselves as best they could to whichever was currently in the stronger position. Aden withstood two attacks, one by the
Portuguese in 1513, another by Egyptian Mamluqs in 1517. For a
time, indeed, Aden became more prosperous than before, as it
offered greater protection for shipping than its rivals. But ultimately
it was broken between the Portuguese hammer and the Ottoman
anvil. From 1515 onward the Yemen was gradually overrun by
Mamluq and then Ottoman forces using muskets for the first time
in South Arabia with great effect. The major turning-point came in
1535 when a strong Ottoman expedition seized the Tihama and three
years later a Turkish fleet put into Aden and seized and hanged its
Tahirid ruler.[40] Thereafter Aden became part of an increasingly
strong and well-administered Ottoman Province in the Yemen.
Turkish rule in the Yemen reached its period of greatest stability and
prosperity in the last quarter of the sixteenth century and under that
rule Aden was relegated to the role of its southern fortress.[41] Visitors
to the port in the early seventeenth century noted that there appeared
to be more soldiers than merchants in the streets. The impressive
façade remained, but at the back of the town houses were already
beginning to moulder and fall down. Some ships still called at the
port but many of these were only seeking shelter prior to passing the
Bab el Mandeb. The richest port in the vicinity by the end of the
sixteenth century was not Aden but Mocha which stood within the
Ottoman-controlled straits. Mocha harboured the bulk of the Indian
shipping. It was also the terminus of the great annual caravan to
Aleppo and an annual treasure-bearing ship from Suez.[42]

The war between Ottoman and Portuguese was probably the
cause of Aden's downfall. But a more profound transformation in
the whole nature of the Red Sea trade ensured that Aden was kept
down. The key to this transformation was the growth of the commerce
in coffee. Around the middle of the fifteenth century the people of
Aden began to acquire a taste for coffee. Sixty years later coffee was
being drunk in Mecca and in Cairo, by 1537 it was being used in
Syria and in 1554 the first coffee houses appeared in Istanbul.[43] At
first a drink for a few, it quickly became a popular beverage in the
Islamic world. During the two decades after 1570 it came into
general use in Egypt and Syria. By the third decade of the seventeenth

century it was in general use in Persia. By the middle of the seventeenth century every Turkish family, rich and poor, was consuming large quantities.[44] About that time the taste for coffee developed in western Europe. The first coffee houses were opened in London in the early 1650s, in Amsterdam in the early 1660s, in Paris in the early 1670s and in Vienna in the early 1680s. By 1680 London reputedly consumed more coffee than any other city in the world.[45] The European market continued to expand behind that of the Middle East until by the middle of the eighteenth century it began to overtake it. Thus from the early sixteenth century onward there was a continually surging demand for coffee and until the second decade of the eighteenth century there was no significant production of the commodity outside the Yemen. Without reliable statistics it is difficult to assess the volume of the trade in its early stages but it would seem that in the last quarter of the sixteenth century it became a prominent feature of the Red Sea economy. Up to 1573-4 the Egyptian customs at Suez taxed only the trade in spices. But then coffee was made a dutiable article and thereafter the Suez customs became the most lucrative in Egypt.[46] This gives some indication of the value of the coffee trade by this time. It also shows the shift that was taking place in the pattern of commerce. In the early seventeenth century. the Egyptian trade in spices was finally ruined when the more businesslike Dutch sailed round the Cape in force and seized the spices at their source.[47] By the late seventeenth century the spice trade was almost forgotten in the Yemen and people were speaking of coffee as a heaven-given bounty which enabled them to pay for all their necessities.[48]

The replacement of the transit trade in spices by the local production of coffee as the dominant factor in the cash economy brought about a commercial revolution with wide ramifications in South-West Arabia. The commercial relations between the countries of the Mediterranean basin and the Orient were profoundly altered. Instead of being a staging-house between East and West which contributed little besides coral and some semi-precious stones to the general flow of commerce, Yemen became an active, indeed a vital link in the chain of commercial exchange. The Yemen had a huge favourable trade balance with Middle Eastern and later, with the European countries. Yemeni coffee was purchased almost exclusively with silver and gold. Many ships, large and small, were engaged in conveying the chief product of the Yemen from Mocha, Hudayda and a number of other smaller ports to Jedda whence it was dispersed East and West by caravan and ship to Aleppo, to the Maghreb and to Egypt.[49] The return fleets were small and in the early seventeenth century consisted mainly of a single heavily guarded ship from

Egypt bearing treasure. The 'necessities' that Yemen paid for with its crop came principally from India and China and the central item was 'piece goods' – mainly cotton and some silk textiles. The principal trading partner in the seventeenth century was the port of Surat, then at the climax of its prosperity, and Surat acted as the main outlet for the textile industry of Gujerat which was produced largely for the Yemeni market. Textiles were not the only goods imported. Various other commodities were shipped from India including on occasion large quantities of rice from the Malabar ports. But textiles were the main import and the Gujerati weavers demanded in return the silver and other treasure which the Yemenis had earned.[50] There was an immense flow of specie from the Red Sea to western India during the seventeenth century. In 1621 Thomas Mun estimated that the Ottomans sent £600,000 annually to Mocha.[51] In 1695 one of Mun's fellow-countrymen had the opportunity of looking closer at this treasure flow when the pirate Every seized the great ship which sailed annually to Surat. Every's prize was estimated at £500,000 at least – the greatest piratical haul of the century.[52] It was not surprising that such sparkling prey attracted the adventurers of the northern European nations who rushed into the Indian Ocean from 1600 onward. There was scarcely a year during the seventeenth century when some European pirate – English, French, American, Dutch, Danish or of no nation – was not hovering off the Bab el Mandeb hoping to plunder some of the ducats and dollars on their way to India. The Dutch, and more especially the English East India Company, began their careers in the East by plundering and seeking to force their well-paid protection on the Indian fleets.[53] But the East India Companies were unable to control the seaways effectively. The treasure afloat drew too many covetous men, especially during the great age of Red Sea piracy during the thirty years after 1690 when the freebooters of the West Indies, driven from their haunts by the combined European powers, came to the Red Sea to seize the same silver which they could no longer plunder on its way from Havana and Panama.[54] Red Sea silver was the lifeblood of the economic system along the coasts from Western India to China and the European trading companies eagerly sought it to supplement what specie the bullionist legislation of their home countries permitted them to bring direct, to finance their transactions in the East.

The coffee revolution meant also that in South-West Arabia the most valuable streams of trade no longer flowed narrow and deep from guarded port to walled city. The coffee trade flowed shallower and more broadly across the land, especially after Ottoman rule collapsed in the 1630s. The purchasers were mainly Arab and Egypt-ian. From the middle of the seventeenth century European nations also took a hand in the trade but what they exported from Mocha seldom amounted to more than half of what was exported northward throughout the history of the Yemen coffee industry.[55] The Middle Eastern and some Indian merchants bought what they required with silver in the markets below the coffee-bearing mountains and especially in the sprawling town of Bayt al Faqih which soon eclipsed its old, walled former spice-trading neighbour, Zabid. The import trade was a separate institution and was run with Indian capital.[56] The corporations of Cairo spice merchants no longer laced their agencies from port to port in western India. The sale of Indian textiles was financed and pushed from India. The Imams of Yemen depended heavily for revenue on taxes on these Indian imports and received occasional supplementary payments from the rulers of Indian ports such as the Nawab of Surat.[57] In the markets, Indian merchants sold their goods on up to six months credit, and with the growth of coffee production Indian wholesale agents spread from town to town in the Yemen offering their wares for sale. By the eighteenth century, Yemen's markets were dominated by Indian credit – a dominance which however was mitigated by the control which Yemeni officials were able to exercise over the merchants' general activity.[58] The whole commercial system was much more diversified than what had previously been known. The consumption of imported articles was no longer so heavily concentrated in the cities as it had been in the times of the transit trade. The city artisans had to compete with a flood of goods designed for the popular local market.[59] The economic balance was swinging in favour of the rural areas – the rural areas of the coffee-laden hills that is, not the cultivated city hinterlands of the plains.

This new economic situation called for a system of political control more broadly popular and less city-oriented than what had obtained before. Yemeni coffee production was of the order of twenty million lb. per annum by the end of the seventeenth century, that is four to five times the volume of that which eighteenth-century Dutch 'coffee sergeants' carefully cosseted, controlled and taxed in Indonesia. The government had to appeal to the coffee-farmer and plantation-owner standing amid his carefully tended coffee-groves in mountain fastnesses. This the largely foreign and often religiously-deviant Ottoman soldiery and officials in the cities could scarcely do. The Ottoman regime persisted well into the period of the coffee revolution probably because it could compensate for its waning control of general wealth by the superiority of its weaponry. The Ottoman soldiers carried firearms and the sale of these weapons to the Arab population was made punishable by death.[60] Nevertheless muskets filtered into Arab hands. When the great revolt against Ottoman rule began in the late sixteenth century the leaders were equipped with the new firearms. By the time the Ottomans were expelled in the 1630s, large bodies of the Yemeni population were similarly armed and the matchlock was on its way to becoming the Arab's familiar weapon.[61] The overthrow of Ottoman rule represented the overthrow of a system of government in the Yemen which dated from far beyond the sixteenth-century Ottoman invasion. For the imposition of Ottoman rule had involved little more than a change of name and an alteration in the nature of the high command.[62] Ottoman, Mamluq, Tahirid, Rasulid, whichever ruled, the basic elements of the system were the same. The essential power factor dating back to the time of Turan Shah was provided by the foreign slave soldiery and the bedrock of government was the cities. A different disposition of the factors of production made this regime obsolete and a new form of government emerged in the Yemen in the seventeenth century. The rule of the Imams of San'a' involved the continuance of some features of the old regime. The Imam had a standing army; he sought to monopolise the import of munitions and his officials controlled and taxed the trade of the ports and the produce of the soil. But it was altogether a more loosely organised, more popularly oriented and more nationally coloured affair than what had gone before. The Imam sought to govern by political manipulation rather than by command. He emphasised his religious and cultural leadership which could be understood wherever the writings of the active Yemeni literati filtered through to the mass of the population. The Imams had behind them the *elan* of a national rising against the foreigner, their soldiers and officials were mostly local men and the legitimacy of their government derived from within the country and not from the Abbasid Caliph or the Ottoman Sultan.

Against the background of these developments in the Yemen, Aden continued to decline. Its fortunes had been bound up with the old regime; it was unable to share in the prosperity of the new. In 1627 a Yafi'i force broke into the town and expelled the Turks from all but Sirah island, which was vacated eight years later. The port then fell under local rulers who tried with limited success to revive its commerce. Some Indian ships began to discharge their cargoes there in preference to Mocha, many more sought shelter prior to undertaking the dangerous passage through the Bab el Mandeb.[63] But local difficulties with the northward trade route hampered these efforts. The Turks during their latter days had accorded a substantial stipend to the rulers of Dali' to secure the route to San'a'[64] Quarrels between those for and against Imamic rule disturbed these arrangements.[65] In 1644 Aden was conquered by the Imam's forces and thereafter remained more or less under the control of Sana'a.' These were local difficulties.[66] The cardinal reason for Aden's failure to recover even a moderate prosperity was that it was too far from the main coffee-producing areas.[67] These stretched northward from about the latitude of Mocha through the western mountains of the Yemeni massif. Since the bulk of the crop went up the Red Sea, Aden could only hope to share in the smaller export to Persia, India and Europe. This trade however found its outlet through Mocha, which was closer to the major market at Bayt al Faqih and closer too to the centres of Imamic administration. The bulkier less valuable commodities now being exchanged could not afford the transit dues entailed in long-distance land transit and Aden was left to pick up some of the crumbs which fell from time to time from Mocha's table. Apart from that, Aden depended now on a mainly local trade including the eastward export of small quantities of Yafi'i coffee and became increasingly interested in the commerce with Somaliland across the gulf. Meanwhile the traces of decay, seen in the early seventeenth century, began to spread through the town. Neglected fortress walls began to crumble. The houses at the back of the town began to crack and tumble. By the beginning of the eighteenth century half of the town was still active and beautiful but a growing field of rubble was spreading toward the port. By the early nineteenth century the ruin field was engulfing what remained of the town and in 1835 there were less than a thousand inhabitants.[68]

The Yemeni coffee trade reached its apogee in the second decade of the eighteenth century. By then, Middle Eastern and European merchants were scrambling for coffee in the markets, driving the prices to astronomical heights. Then came the decline. In 1723 the Dutch began to import coffee from Java on a substantial scale.[69] Some twenty years later, the French began to import from the West Indies and within a few years West Indian production exceeded that of the Yemen. In 1746 the French began to reverse the former flow of trade by exporting West Indian coffee to the Levant.[70] The Yemeni coffee industry was now feeling the cold blast of competition and, after a long period of buoyancy, prices began to fall back in the middle 1720s.[71] Meanwhile the Imamic state was fraying at the edges. By the early years of the eighteenth century Hadhramawt had regained the independence it had lost some thirty years before and the tribes to the east and north of Aden led by the Yafi'i were defying the Imam. Around 1730 Aden became independent of the Imam's government under the rule of the Sultans of Lahej backed by Yafi'i power in the interior.[72] The Yemen's decline continued throughout the eighteenth century. Strong rulers from time to time drew the energies of the state together but could not arrest the secular weakening of the economic basis of the country's prosperity and the regime's stability. By the late eighteenth century European colonial coffee was invading the Maghrebi market. By the early nineteenth century colonial coffee was even flowing into Egypt. The English East India Company which had marked out coffee as one of the most profitable articles of import in the latter part of the seventeenth century, traded regularly at Mocha up to 1767, but then sent only occasional ships. In 1771 the flow of treasure from the Red Sea ports to India began to dry up.[73] By the last quarter of the eighteenth century production was still substantial, but demand and prices were depressed. The great days of the Yemen coffee trade were over and the Red Sea was fast becoming an economic backwater.

Meanwhile the English East India Company was rising to dominance in India. The latter half of the eighteenth century saw the decisive growth of British power based on their conquest of Bengal and the wealth and military strength which that event afforded them. The Indian states were gradually drawn into subordinate alliances. Toward the middle of the century the British got the upper hand over the other naval powers on the western Indian coast and most of the subcontinent's seaborne trade fell under British control. The merchant company had always had a strongly military character, and by the end of the century had become a major military power. During the same period, the British state lost the major part of its North American empire and turned its eyes eastward to watch with increasing interest and solicitude its rising trade and widening possessions in the Orient.[74] The British possessions in the East were seen now more as a broad, widespread political and commercial system and less as a series of trading establishments each with its own particular interests. Private British business was burgeoning by the side of the Company's trade and as their grip on eastern commerce tightened and their organisations became larger and more sophisticated, they, as well as the Company, became concerned with strengthening and quickening their contacts with the business and political world of Europe. In the last quarter of the eighteenth century serious efforts were made to establish a regular mail communication between India and Europe both by the Red Sea and the Persian Gulf routes, with a fair measure of success.[75]

Mail communication was one thing, the defence of India was another. The shortest route to India from Europe was clearly that from the Mediterranean through the Middle East and the northern Indian Ocean. The Cape route from a geographical point of view was a second best. The reason why it had been used in the first place by the Portuguese was because of the hostility of Middle Eastern powers and that remained the principal reason why other European states continued to use it. While the Ottoman Empire stood power-

fully astride the short routes to the East there was no question of
European states using those routes to build empires in the countries
beyond. In the sixteenth and seventeenth centuries the Ottomans
were feared in Europe, especially in the centre and south of the
continent – they reached the gates of Vienna in 1685. But in the
eighteenth century the Ottomans were in decline and in the last
quarter of the century they suffered a series of resounding defeats
at the hands of the Russians. Central control over outlying provinces,
notably Egypt, began to crumble and European states began seriously
to consider the vivisection of the Empire. The short routes to the East
looked less well guarded than before. From the 1760s the French
government was considering schemes for the conquest of Egypt and
for an advance thence to upset British dominance in India. Some
inklings of these French designs filtered through to London in the
1780s and those concerned with imperial policy shifted uneasily in
their seats. But the matter was not considered urgent and the main
measure taken was to appoint a Consul-General in Egypt, who was
to watch and wait.[76]

Bonaparte's invasion of Egypt in 1798 came as a great shock to the
British government and the East India Company. The ultimate
objective of the expedition was too obvious for any to doubt. Troops
were hastily despatched from India to guard the mouth of the Red
Sea. Perim was chosen as the spot to be garrisoned in order to command the Bab el Mandeb but, contrary to expectation, no water
could be found on the barren island. Water and provisions had to be
brought from Mocha and it soon became clear that they were not
being offered with any goodwill. Indian government bills could not
be discounted and finally a strike by the water carriers forced the
fast sickening garrison to evacuate. The differing attitudes of the
rulers of Mocha and Aden largely decided where the force chose to
go next. While there was evident anti-British feeling in Mocha, the
Sultan of Aden welcomed the idea of stationing British troops in his
port. In the second week of September 1799 the troops transferred to
Aden and remained there until the early months of 1800 when they
were recalled.[77] By this time the French threat had been scotched by
Nelson's victory at Aboukir and the arrest at Acre of the French
advance through Syria toward the Gulf. In 1801 another British
force was sent into the Red Sea to attack the French force in Egypt
but before it arrived the French had capitulated to the army of Sir
Ralph Abercrombie which had invaded Egypt from the Mediterranean. The liquidation of his Egyptian expeditionary force did not
put an end to Napoleon's plans for attacking India. Until 1812 the
Emperor still had at the back of his mind the idea that if Britain could
not be beaten in Europe she could be severely injured in the East.

Intrigues were set on foot in Turkey and in Persia, especially after 1807, with a view to opening the way to another attempt on Britain's Indian possessions.[78] Thus the British authorities were forced to look most carefully to the western defence of India throughout these years, and while improvising strenuously to parry each new immediate threat, they began to work out a strategy for ensuring a more permanent control over the threatened areas.

Their experiences between 1798 and 1801 brought home to them how seriously their commerce with the Red Sea had been reduced. The trade between western India and the Red Sea was no longer so large and prosperous as it once had been and official interest in it had declined. British naval strength in Indian waters had been concentrating on the protection of the rich trade now moving between eastern India, China and England and the shipping in the northern Indian Ocean had been left largely at the mercy of French commerce raiders led by the remarkable Surcouf who operated from the island of Mauritius.[79] What commerce managed to escape French attentions was menaced by the growing fleets of Arab pirates from the Gulf who struck with new Wahhabi zeal along the coasts from the upper Red Sea to the gates of Bombay. The East India Company's passes and the British flag became worse than useless to the ship's captains plying these routes and many accommodated themselves to this fact. By 1800 several large shipping firms from western India had transferred their base of operations and their fleets to friendly Masqat whence they traded under the Arab flag. Arabs from the same port set themselves up in business and by 1803 they were despatching cargoes as far afield as the Bay of Bengal and Indonesia, often using former Indian merchantmen cheaply bought from their captors.[80] Much of the Mocha coffee which had formerly gone to Europe via Bombay was redirected towards Mauritius, and American vessels which began by collecting coffee at that island in the 1790s, took a direct hand in the trade at Mocha in the nineteenth century, exporting coffee and gum and importing 'Merikani' textiles.[81] This diversion of trade had serious military consequences. Any advance from the Middle East to India would require some naval co-operation for the transport of the troops. From ancient times the balance of naval power in the Indian Ocean had normally lain with India where the materials for the construction of ships was to be found. But the abnormal circumstances at the end of the eighteenth century found large fleets of ships in Arabian ports and this represented a threat to India. In the early nineteenth century therefore the major problem of restoring British influence in the Red Sea and Arabian waters generally was tackled. The objective was political but the means used were primarily commercial. Surveying missions were active between 1800 and 1809

charting the waters of the Red Sea and seeking out ways of expanding
trade and spreading British influence in both Arabia and Ethiopia.[82]
The East India Company once more began to buy coffee at Mocha
and a British agent was established there more or less continuously
from 1802 to 1830.[83] Private Indian trade was also encouraged and
escorts were regularly provided for their ships.[84] The Imam was
approached in 1802 to secure a reduction of the duties charged at
Mocha and better treatment for the British Indian merchants. In
the same year a treaty was signed with the Sultan of Aden for the
development of commerce, although it was anticipated that Aden
would supplement rather than supplant the trade at Mocha.[85] During
the ensuing decades the trade between India and the Red Sea was
actively fostered under the British flag. Wahhabi piracy was limited,
driven back into the Gulf and finally suppressed in the 1830s.[86] In
1820 Mocha was bombarded and a commercial treaty thrust upon
the Imam.[87] Berbera was blockaded in 1827 in reprisal for an attack
on a British ship and the blockade was reimposed until satisfaction
was obtained in 1832.[88] Thus a substantial effort was made on behalf
of British–Indian commerce in the Red Sea and Indian traders
were made to feel that they could rely on British protection. There
was to be no return to the days when French influence reigned
supreme in the ports of the Yemen and merchants refused to discount
British bills.

These measures for safeguarding the northern frontiers of India
were regarded as sufficient up the the 1830s. The outcome of the
Napoleonic wars had been satisfactory to Britain. India was thereafter
protected by the new acquisitions at the Cape and Ceylon which
gave it added naval security. The French island of Mauritius, seized
in 1810, remained in British hands after the peace and the small
island of Reunion did not represent a serious threat. The new naval
base at Malta guarded the approaches to the eastern Mediterranean.
Above all, defeated France spent some ten years licking her wounds
and Britain had little to fear from her former colonial rival. Victorious
Russia represented a more serious, though more distant, danger to
Britain's imperial dispositions. In the Middle East however, the
aspect of affairs was not so bright. The buckler which the Ottoman
Empire held up against Europe looked more tattered and work-worn
as time went by and the man behind it appeared to be losing his
nerve. The Greek revolt and the Russian war of the 1820s finally
brought Ottoman fortunes near their nadir when the Tsar forced the
peace of Adrianople on the Sultan at the gates of his capital.
Worse was to come in 1833 when the Sultan's overmighty vassal,
Muhammad ʿAli of Egypt, marched his troops from Syria into
Anatolia and the Sultan had to call on Russian help to save himself.

With these events, a growing chorus of writers on imperial affairs in Britain clamoured for a reassessment of India's defensive position to the north and west and for new measures to reinforce them.[89]

The local situation in the Red Sea and Arabia was scarcely less troubling. In the early nineteenth century the British had watched the extension of Wahhabi power from the cases of Najd in central Arabia with mixed feelings. The anti-commercial practices of the seafaring adherents of the revivalist doctrines aroused anger and dismay. But the presence of a powerful xenophobic force across part of the route to the East was not without its advantages.[90] The Wahhabis however were progressively pushed back by the forces of Muhammad 'Ali's Egypt from 1816 onward, as and when those forces could be released from other Egyptian commitments.[91] In 1818 the Wahhabi capital was temporarily taken and in 1819 Egyptian troops marched into North-West Yemen, releasing the Imam from the Wahhabi threat and forcing him in return to promise tribute to Egypt's ruler. Thereafter Egyptian activity in Arabia lessened until 1831 when Muhammad 'Ali, determined to redeem the Sultan's dishonoured promise of the Syrian Pashalik for Egyptian aid in Greece, directed the full force of the Egyptian army eastward. The Egyptian army was now a formidable instrument. Since his accession to power in 1805 Muhammad 'Ali had reformed and modernised the service, purging it of corrupt Mamluq officers and recruiting the aid of European, largely French, instructors. Its weapons and its drill were vastly improved and behind it stood new war industries monopolistically established by Muhammad 'Ali's government. The army had won its spurs in the first Wahhabi campaigns and had earned the respect of European observers From 1831 this army largely stood on Arabian soil and it was only a matter of time before its attention turned to the Yemen – the most populous land in the Peninsula, with a coffee-producing potential which was ripe for incorporation into Muhammed 'Ali's state-controlled economy.[92] In 1832 the first taste of what was to come was provided by a mutinous group of Egyptian soldiery which under Turki b'al Mas occupied the Tihama ports. Their stay was brief but was followed in 1833 by a regular Egyptian occupation of the Tihama under Muhammad 'Ali's energetic son Ibrahim. During the following four years Egyptian. troops gradually pushed into the mountains with the occasional cooperation of the now very weak Imam. Yemeni politics were in disarray. Only localised resistance slowed the progress of what troops Muhammad 'Ali could spare from other areas for his operations in South-West Arabia.[93]

Muhammad 'Ali's advance into Arabia posed a serious dilemma to those concerned with the making of British policy. His replacement of ineffective and often anti-commercial regimes in the Peninsula was favourable to British commercial interests and Muhammad 'Ali himself constantly stressed this point. He also offered facilities for the transmission of mails through Egypt and when interest grew in the use of steamships for this purpose, as it did from 1822 onward, Muhammad 'Ali was quick to meet British requests for the establishment of coaling depots.[94] There was a substantial current of opinion in Britain favourable to his regime and others saw his modernising system as a force with a promising future which Britain should support rather than seek to hinder. Against this there was the strong suspicion that for all his fair words Muhammad 'Ali was not a friend of Britain. His defeat of a British force which tried to invade his country in 1807 had not been a happy augury. His admiration for France and the presence of Frenchmen in many key posts in his administration was a more substantial reason for doubting his reliability. Worse, his attacks upon his Ottoman suzerain were quite out of tune with what began to emerge in the 1830s as the central theme of British Middle-Eastern strategy – the bolstering up of the Ottoman Empire and the preservation of its integrity as the principal outer bulwark of India's westward defences. All these political reasonings weighed heavily against the countervailing economic calculations.

With regard more specifically to his activity in South-Western Arabia – and eastern Arabia too for that matter – there was now a long-standing British jealousy of any powerful state which might establish itself in those areas. It was perhaps not just the facts of the situation as they stood that induced the political surveyors of the Red Sea at the beginning of the nineteenth century to emphasise the increasing political independence of state after state to the south of Suez. The Sharif of Mecca was decidedly Ottoman; the Imam of Sana'a' was independent of the Sublime Porte. The Sultan of Aden was quite independent of both Porte and Imam.[95] In any case, threats from the north by powerful governments, whether Wahhabi, as in the first decade of the century, or Egyptian, as in the early 1820s, brought suggestions that Aden be set as the limit to their advance and that Britain should tighten its commercial and political grip upon that port. As early as 1825 the British Consul-General in Egypt had begun warning Muhammad 'Ali against interfering with Aden. The extension of Egyptian control within the Bab el Mandeb was perhaps to Britain's interest and perhaps not. But the establishment of a first-rate power so near to India as Aden was not to be countenanced.[96] In the rather tense atmosphere of the 1830s these ideas were restated with greater force and the warnings to Muhammad 'Ali not to pass the Bab el Mandeb and, above all, not to touch Aden, were reiterated in a graver and more forceful tone. In 1837, Captain Mackenzie, one of those British officers who were scurrying ubiquitously round India's outer frontiers from Zanzibar to the Himalayas in the 1830s assessing defensive capabilities, submitted an important memorandum on the condition of South-West Arabia. His main conclusion was that Muhammad 'Ali was intent on the conquest of the whole Peninsula, that he had designs on Aden, and once there, would push through the Hadhramawt to overturn the rule of the Imam of Masqat – the only Arab ruler on whom the British could rely. On the basis of this paper Lord Palmerston, the British Foreign Secretary, expressed the hope that Muhammad 'Ali did not intend to go beyond the Bab el Mandeb. Nine months later, in May 1838, the warning was repeated in more vigorous terms. Further admonitions, specifically mentioning Aden, were issued in the remaining months of that year.[97] By then the content of the warnings had changed. By that time the British were claiming Aden for themselves. Whitehall was no longer warning others off. It had determined to make Aden a British possession. This was to be the major British riposte in the Red Sea to the seriously deteriorating situation in the Middle East.

The decision to occupy Aden was not taken easily by the British government. Much correspondence and hesitation preceded the final decision. Counsels were divided on the matter and even when the occupation had been effected there were many in high places who urged withdrawal. The necessity for a suitable coaling station between Bombay and Suez to fuel the voracious boilers of the steamers which had been carrying mails along that line, since the first voyage of the *Hugh Lindsay* in 1829, played an important role. On this practically everyone was agreed, and powerful interests both in India and the United Kingdom were determined that the overland mail service to India should be effectively established.[98] The Parliamentary Papers published in 1839 to explain why Aden was taken were adroitly selected to suggest that this popular object had been uppermost in the decision-makers' minds.[99] But of course it was not absolutely necessary to occupy the ground on which a coal depot was to be established. Ships could be coaled in ports belonging to other powers as indeed they were and had to be, at Egyptian Suez. The mails themselves passed through Egypt on their way to the Mediterranean. Furthermore, a glance at the map would show that it was not necessary to occupy the whole peninsula of Aden to secure a small coal establishment at Steamer Point. It is remarkable that in the early 1840s the defences of Aden were based on the assumption that no one would wish to plunder or attack the coal depot. Even more remarkable was the fact that this was accepted at Bombay without demur. The Parliamentary Papers damped debate by obscuring the real issues.[100] Aden was not seized simply as a convenient place for a coaling station; it was seized for stategical reasons and its occupation was expected to serve a political purpose.

Aden had been one of the first ports to be used as a refuelling station on the Bombay–Suez run in the earliest days of steam communication. Since 1800 when a first disparaging report on its potential as a harbour had been refuted, it had acquired a favourable reputation among naval officers and its choice to coal the pioneering *Hugh Lindsay* in 1829 was made almost as a matter of course. But the first experience of its use put it out of favour. The *Hugh Lindsay* spent six days coaling in Front Bay and it was found that that vessel's inefficient engine required more than one refuelling stop between Bombay and Suez.[101] The promoters of steam communication turned to other ports. Mukalla and Mocha were used. The possibility of using Kamaran island in the Red Sea was investigated. Perim was considered and in 1835 the island of Socotra was briefly occupied. Socotra might have become a British possession, but the troops suffered from sickness, the ruler refused to sell his island, and the Governor-General of India decided against trying to take it by force.[102] It was at this juncture that Commander S. B. Haines of the Indian Navy, an officer connected with the intensive surveys of the Arabian coasts which had been going on since 1829, came forward with a proposal that Aden be tried again. Haines had been involved in the negotiations for the cession of Socotra; it was suggested in some quarters that his hastiness was responsible for their breakdown.[103] Having failed there, he suggested Aden as a better prospect. In a memoir addressed to the Superintendent of the Indian Navy in 1835 he pointed out that Aden's western harbour was superior to Front Bay and outlined the port's potentiality as a commercial centre at the mouth of the Red Sea. Haines envisaged the outright occupation of Aden. Its Sultan, unlike his friendly predecessor, was in Haines's view little better than a pirate, and he cited two incidents when the Sultan had interfered with shipping, to prove his point. Haines's memoir was laid before the Government of Bombay in March 1837 and it was decided that any further 'outrage' by the Sultan of Aden should be resented.[104] Bombay had not long to wait for this event. At the very moment the Governor was penning his minute, part of the plunder of a vessel flying the British flag was being auctioned in the Aden bazaar. The vessel was the *Duria Dowlat*, an over-insured ship belonging to the Nawab of the Carnatic, which had run aground at Aden in 1837. It was strongly suspected that the supercargo was in collusion with the Sultan of Aden and that he had deliberately wrecked his ship. In any case, the Sultan claimed its freight and some of the passengers were ill-treated by jewel-seeking Adenis. The British authorities could hardly let the plunder of a British-protected vessel pass unnoticed. British protection of Indian merchantmen was now one of the recognised rules of the commercial game. But as it turned out, the plunder of the *Duria Dowlat* was not an ordinary 'outrage', and when news of it reached Bombay in July 1837, the authorities there saw it as an unparalleled opportunity for achieving their broad strategic aims.[105]

The Governor of Bombay at the time was Sir Robert Grant, a former Canningite, now a Whig and very much alive to the new, liberalising, expansive ideas which were broadening industrial Britain's vision of trade and empire during these years.[106] Criticised for lack of attention to the ordinary business of his post, Grant was a man of grand projects rather than a routine administrator.[107] He told the President of the India Board that he intended to draw out the great resources of the Bombay Presidency rather than concentrate on small matters of financial economy. He was very much a law unto himself and was irked by the restraining control of the less energetic Governor-General.[108] Under Grant's rule, a multitude of large-scale projects were pushed forward which were to transform the shape of British policy in the East. He was interested in the opening of the Indus to navigation, in the Euphrates expedition which brought British influence into Iraq and Syria, in the suppression of piracy in the Persian Gulf, in the consolidation of relations with the Sultan of Masqat and Zanzibar, in the surveying work on the coasts of China that was to be a prelude to the Opium War of 1839 and the seizure of Hong Kong. Grant's period as Governor of Bombay was a period of imperial expansion on a large scale.

Grant was naturally closely interested in the cause of overland mail communication. Any man with his finger so closely on the pulse of business interests in Britain and India was bound to be so. But his interest went beyond a mere humdrum concern for rapidity in the exchange of information, to making of the scheme an instrument for attaining larger political and military objectives. In 1836, in the heated discussion over who should pay for the mail steamers and where they should go, he put forward his own plan for converting the Indian Navy to steam and replacing its fleet of sailing vessels by a steam flotilla, whose free and rapid movement would carry British influence to places formerly out of reach during the monsoons.[109] That these steam vessels would also be able to carry the mails to Suez or the Gulf was convenient, since this would induce the less politically-minded Court of Directors of the East India Company to pay for them. Or more exactly, the now impatient business public would make the Court pay for them on such grounds. As for Grant himself, the provision of quicker mail communication was but part of a wider plan to secure political and naval supremacy over the sea frontiers of India from Zanzibar to the mouth of the Indus by means of the new fast vessels. Grant's plan for a steam flotilla came to fruition in 1837 as the question of what should be done at Aden was under discussion. In April the British government and the East India Company came to terms on the question of mail communication, the Treasury agreeing to pay half the cost on the basis of six voyages per year. In August the majority of the Court of Directors came round in favour of purchasing steam vessels for the Indian Navy and two large vessels were bought. In the same month Grant boldly declared that mails would henceforward be sent monthly to Suez despite doubts about the availability of coal.[110]

The establishment of coal depots now became more urgent than before. The question of their security became more urgent too since the steamers were in effect to double as ships of war. At least so Grant thought. By August 1837 he had generally adopted Haines's views about Aden and about its ruler and was advocating that the port be brought under British control.[111] The Governor-General, Lord Auckland, was not wholly convinced. As in the case of Socotra he was in favour of peaceable possession only. He was anxious to avoid a clash with Muhammad 'Ali and he counselled caution. Bombay was authorised to go no further than obtaining satisfaction for the seizure of the *Duria Dowlat* and negotiating with the Sultan an amicable arrangement for the establishment of a coal depot.[112] This was less than what Grant had wanted, but the ambiguity of the Governor-General's instructions left room for manoeuvre and the man sent to negotiate with the Sultan of Aden was Commander Haines, who had already made up his mind that Aden should be British.

Haines's path was smoothed by the fact that the Sultan was not wholly averse to a limited British occupation. His predecessor indeed had made several attempts to get the British to re-establish the garrison they had placed in his port in 1799. He had also negotiated with the Egyptians to secure a like occupation by them.[113] Dual control of the port would have been no new phenomenon. There were precedents in pre-Rasulid times and toward the end of Turkish rule when an Ottoman garrison had held Sirah Island while the rest of the town was ruled from Lahej.[114] Such an arrangement lay in the logic of a situation where local land and naval power rested in different hands. A British presence could attract Indian trade to the Sultan's port. An alliance with the British could be of material assistance against the Sultan's troublesome neighbours and more distant enemies. Sultan Muhsin, whom Haines so decried, was perfectly aware of these possibilities which had for so long been mulled over in the ruling family at Lahej. So when the unpleasant business of the *Duria Dowlat* had been concluded and Haines broached the matter of a British position at Aden, Sultan Muhsin did not answer with a blunt refusal.[115] He began to speak of military aid and asked for six cannon for use against his neighbouring Fadli enemies. The main question that concerned him was what terms could be got from the British and what exact form their presence at Aden would take. The disputes and discussions over the *Duria Dowlat* were not a happy prologue to the negotiations and having been forced to admit some culpability, Sultan Muhsin was uneasy about Haines's intentions.[116] On the other hand he was probably aware that in western India the British were pursuing a liberal policy toward some of the 'Native Princes', while he could expect rather shorter shrift from the Egyptians, who had already shown interest in occupying Aden on their own account.[117] He asked Haines if the British would receive him as an ally on the same terms as the Nawab of Surat (these had been Muhsin's predecessor's terms). He wanted to secure his territory by an offensive and defensive treaty and he wanted an annual subsidy. On these conditions he was prepared to allow the establishment of a British factory with British troops in occupation.

Haines expected much more than this and the draft treaty he put to the Sultan envisaged outright British control of Aden. Yet there was sufficient common ground for discussion and so the detailed negotiations went forward into a morass of intrigue and counter-intrigue, Haines manoeuvring and feeling out the ground through various local agents, the Sultan swaying back and forth under the counsels and pressures of his son Ahmad, his son-in-law Sayyid Muhammad Husayn bin Ways and other politicians. Out of all this emerged, on 22 January 1838, a document affixed with the Sultan's seal, the most important part of which read: 'You can then [when Haines returned to conclude the negotiation in March] make houses or forts or do what you like; the town will then be yours; but consider the money I have to give my neighbours from it, so that when the town is yours, you must answer them all.' This, and a further note sent the following day, was the bond which was to be cited later as one of the bases on which Britain claimed possession of Aden.[118] But it appeared at a time when the negotiation was far from complete. And in the second of the missives, the Sultan said that he did not intend to transfer his jurisdiction over Arabs and Jews in the town. The nature of the British occupation had not been agreed, nor had the price which the Sultan expected them to pay. But at his stage, when Haines was asked to attend a conference with the Sultan and his advisers in Crater town, Haines was told and believed that the Sultan intended to seize his person and recover the bond. Haines thereupon sailed off to Bombay with this fresh 'proof' of the Sultan's unreliability and disrespect for British power.[119] The whole proceedings had that dubious savour that was to characterise most of Haines's subsequent diplomacy. The sultan later denied that he had signed the bond. He said that Haines's servant, Mulla Jaffer, had stolen the seal and forged the document. The bond itself has a ring of authenticity and does not vary much from what the Sultan proposed to Haines in other letters during the negotiation. A more apt criticism of the document would be that it was ambiguous. It reserved much for further negotiation, everything was subject to further consultation – Haines with his superiors, the Sultan with his chiefs – and what it did promise was not very explicit. A forger would have produced a much more helpful document. The affixing of the seal may have been fraudulent. Perhaps a more likely expanation was that he Haines camp decided to welcome its receipt with jubiliation and suggest they already had all they needed, as a means of baffling their opponents and browbeating them into further concessions. However the document was enough to give Bombay a basis for pressing for further action and the attempted seizure of Haines's person was even more useful as a means of persuading the more reluctant among the British authorities to decisive action.

I cannot but hail it as a most happy incident; it settles conclusively the necessity of our holding the port and harbours of Aden in our own hands.

Thus Grant wrote of the alleged attempt on Haines's life. Grant's Chief Secretary, Farish, agreed, and remarked that British prestige was now at stake. Haines's reports from Zden had confirmed their view that this was the naval base they had been seeking and in March 1838 Grant drafted a great minute in which he laid bare the far-reaching nature of his aims.

It is impossible to see France extending her conquests along the coast of Africa [this referred to the extension of the Algerian colony], and at enormous expense covering the Mediterranean with her ships and steamers, without feeling a distinct persuasion that her views are keenly directed toward the possession of Egypt.

Grant surmised that the French hoped to overturn the British position in India by external pressure and social insurrection. He added:

Whether this inference is just or not, there can be no doubt that the gradual approach of France to India by way of Egypt simultaneously with that of Russia by way of Persia is not to be treated as an event beyond the pale of possibility.

Grant's answer to this situation was to seize 'places of strength' in the Red Sea and the Persian Gulf to protect British naval forces in those seas. He had his eye on the island of Kharak in the Gulf; Aden was to be the strong point in the Red Sea area, and, in that case, of course had to be wholly in British hands. The matter was the more urgent because Grant had information which led him to believe that a French agent was on his way to Aden. In any case the Pasha of Egypt's designs on that port were well known, and Grant believed that if Muhammad 'Ali once passed the Bab el Mandeb he would secure control of all Arabia.

The establishment of a potentate thus vigorous and violent at the head of a hundred thousand men on a coast within easy sail of our own shores, forms no bright anticipation for the future fortunes of India.[120]

In a private letter written in May 1838, Grant brought this minute particularly to the attention of the President of the India Board, John Hobhouse. He was somewhat uneasy about what the government at home would say of his doings. 'Perhaps we went too far', he confessed. If so, he asked Hobhouse to 'blame but confirm', as in the time of Lord Wellesley. The home government was too supine, in his opinion, and he intended to send a 'stimulant' to his friend Lord Palmerston.[121] No stimulant was required. Both Palmerston and Hobhouse had views about Aden which fully coincided with those of Grant. Before Grant's letter was written, Hobhouse had already written to him hoping that he would find some pretext for seizing Kharak as well as Aden. Indeed he was under the impression that Aden was already occupied by the despatch of the first Haines mission and was much put out when he heard that Haines had sailed back to Bombay.[122] Palmerston was under a similar impression and in June 1838 he told his Consul-General in Egypt to inform Muhammad 'Ali that Aden was British.

When Palmerston said 'British' he meant entirely so. In the summer of 1838 a project was mooted in British Indian circles for transferring Aden to the Sultan of Masqat, the extension of whose friendly independent power in East Africa was being currently encouraged by the British government. Palmerston and Hobhouse rejected this idea out of hand with sundry uncomplimentary remarks about its advocates. 'Kharrack and Aden would make us very strong in those parts and would ere long become important centres of radiation for our commerce', wrote Palmerston to Hobhouse in August. A year later he reaffirmed his confidence in Aden's military, naval and commercial value.[123] A friendly, enlightened prince was evidently good enough for the second or third line of defence along the East African coast, but not for the strongpoint at Aden.

These were the views of only two members of the Cabinet, but they were the views of the men who counted and between them they engineered the London end of Aden's occupation. The Prime Minister was kept informed of what was happening but that was all.[124] There is no record of a Cabinet meeting being held to discuss the matter, but the Cabinet did spend much time discussing the Persian advance on Herat, and perhaps the matter of the occupation of Aden was brought up in that connection. It is not difficult to imagine how Palmerston would have presented the case if that were so. At the beginning of 1839 he was still representing Egyptian intrigue at Aden as part of a vast Russian plot to break down the northern defences of India.[125] Aden was of course occupied by the East India Company, and after occupation formed part of that organisation's possessions. The Company was in control and the decision to occupy was nominally theirs. But that was as far as it went. In reality the crucial decisions were not taken by the Company. Had the Court of Directors been consulted there is little doubt that they would have pronounced a veto. Three years after the occupation they refused to take any responsibility for what had been done.[126] But in this case it could be argued that the right of decision did not entirely lie within the province of the full Court. The matter was regarded as one of foreign policy, and by the constitution of the Company. matters of this kind were left to the small Secret Committee of the Company, acting in consultation with the supervisory Minister of the Crown – the President of the India Board. The Secret Committee itself was most reluctant, until faced with a virtual *fait accompli*. Its Chairman, Sir James Carnac, afterward condemned the occupation and spoke in favour of withdrawal. But at the time of decision Carnac was an applicant for the lucrative Governorship of Bombay, and was in no position to oppose Hobhouse and Palmerston, who were well placed to influence that appointment.[127] So the voice of the Company was scarcely heard at all and the two ministers carried the day.

In India there was the same pattern of feeble resistance and reluctance overcome by a few determined and strong-minded men. When the Haines reports came through to him with Bombay's request for instructions, Auckland, the Governor-General, put off his decision and said the matter should be referred to the Home Government.[128] Hobhouse sent his own instructions to act in May but throughout the summer no word came to Bombay from Auckland.[129] At Bombay, Grant died at the beginning of July leaving Aden as the most important item of uncompleted business. In his mail was a private letter from Hobhouse urgently requiring him to act, hoping indeed that he had already begun to act.[130] The responsibility of deciding what to do fell to the acting Governor, Farish, who as

Chief Secretary had fully seconded Grant's Aden policy. Farish waited for the necessary authority to come from the Governor-General. But when in September no such instruction had arrived, he decided to take the matter into his own hands. On the basis of the correspondence between the India Board and the Foreign Office, and fortified by the private letters flowing in from Hobhouse, he decided that Bombay should act alone. The other members of his Council gave their consent provided that peaceful means only should be used. On this basis Haines was sent to negotiate once more with the Sultan. He could only be spared one small vessel and a guard of thirty men because the whole Indian army was being mobilised for a march into Afghanistan and Auckland had expressly forbidden the diversion of any troops to Aden[131]

So Haines proceeded to Aden with the fate of that town still very much in the balance. Much depended on his conduct of the negotiation with Sultan Muhsin and more on the sort of policy the Sultan himself chose to follow. Haines had few cards to play. Thirty men were not enough to occupy a fortress of Aden's size and far from sufficient to make a credible offer of British aid to the Sultan against his enemies. The long-term value of British assistance and friendship also looked less convincing than a year before, now that the Indian army was engaged in an adventure of doubtful outcome in Afghanistan while a major crisis was brewing over Muhammad 'Ali's aggressive activity in the Middle East. Sultan Muhsin had to consider what would become of him if British power waned after he had compromised himself with the Egyptians now poised at Ta'izz by treating with their British rivals. Was the Sultan indeed treating with an accredited representative of the Government of India? He had almost been taken in once before by Turki b'al Mas the Egyptian mutineer in 1834. Turki b'al Mas's men had paid with their lives for their imposture; all forty had been killed when they came to take up the Sultan's agreement that they occupy his port.[132] Could Haines be another such man? Sultan Muhsin doubted his credentials. He said that Haines's manner and conduct was unlike that of other Englishmen. Others in Aden believed that Haines spoke only for himself. No doubt the Sultan would have liked to believe that Haines had no authority for he had conceived a strong personal dislike for him. In a long letter to one of Haines's agents, Sultan Muhsin accused Haines of being from the start determined to take Aden by force and concluded: 'That man in his heart wishes to rule Aden, but he never shall until the sword is at our throats.'

In these circumstances there was little likelihood that Haines would be able to negotiate a peaceful cession of Aden. Indeed it is unlikely that those in power at Aden would ever have agreed to such a thing and certainly not in the absolute form that Haines was determined it should take. Even Sultan Muhsin, who had most to gain by securing British aid or money, was adamant on the point of sovereignty. In a letter to the Governor of Bombay of February 1838, he wrote: 'It is an Arabian adage: "Let the body be burnt but do not let the *watan* [fatherland] be pierced through." ' Two years later he stressed the same point: 'The territory belongs to the Arabs and the Muslims." Any form of agreement he would have been prepared to enter into would have stopped short of allowing the British to supplant his own Islamic jurisdiction. However there was no question of his entering into any agreement in October and November 1838. He was not in full control of the situation. His son Ahmad was jealously watching his conduct and at various points in 1838 and 1839 Sultan Muhsin abdicated authority to his son. The ruling house at Lahej was rent by suspicions and mutual fears while the various sections of the 'Abdali tribe were watchfully aware that matters of great import were being discussed, which could affect the balance of power within the community and its status and relationship with the outside world.[133]

Haines therefore spent most of his time aboard the small company cruiser *Coote* from 24 October to the middle of November, while intrigue spread and tempers rose at Lahej and Aden. Matters came to a head after 13 November when the monthly mail steamer arrived from Bombay and departed without bringing any reinforcements.[134] On 20 November a large body of tribesmen entered Aden, and on the same day fifty of them fired on a boat from Haines's vessel. Haines took up the challenge and, placing a nine-pounder gun on Jazirat Faranji, spent a day hurling shot at the Main Pass gate, whence Egyptian-manned guns fired in return. Haines withdrew from the island and for the next two months British and 'Abdalis engaged in blockade and counter-blockade. The 'Abdalis tried to cut off Haines's water supply. Haines seized one Aden boat and prevented trading craft from entering the harbour. The scene was now set for failure or outright conquest and the next development depended upon what new decision the higher authorities in India would take. Once again those who said 'forward' won against those who said 'back'. Once again, as was to happen so often in the future history of the British in Aden, an expansionist subordinate authority acted without, even against, the instructions of its superiors. At the beginning of December, the Government of Bombay had before it a despatch from the Governor-General of India stating that only peaceful means were to be used in seeking to secure Aden. But, hearing of Haines's difficulties, they ignored this caveat and sent two naval frigates and seven hundred men to take Aden by force. What followed at Aden when this force arrived in January 1839 has been described at the beginning of this chapter.[135]

The news of Aden's seizure by force reached Farish at Bombay at the same time as an official instruction from England authorising the action he had already taken on his own responsibility.[136] He had to wait somewhat longer for the Governor-General's approval, which was not despatched until 21 January 1839.[137] The decision to take Aden had been the work of a few energetic men – Grant, Hobhouse, Palmerston and Farish – with Haines acting as the initiator and executor. This was to have an important bearing on the early history of the settlement. One by one, those men were replaced by others who had quite different ideas about Aden's importance. Grant died in July 1838. In June 1839 Farish handed over to Carnac who, from the moment of his arrival until the the autumn of 1840, regarded the new possession as a waste of money and did his best to prevent its being put on a permanent footing.[138] In the summer of 1841 the main architects of the whole new policy in the Indian Ocean – Hobhouse and Palmerston – went out of office. They were replaced by two men of a different stamp, Lords Ripon and Aberdeen who were conciliatory and unaggressive statesmen. They followed a policy of *quietus non movere* in the Indian Ocean and left matters in the hands of the energetic and somewhat bombastic Governor General Lord Ellenborough. Ellenborough had clear-cut views about Aden and Arabia. He had been sent out to India to clear up matters after the disastrous defeat of 1841 in Afghanistan and his censures upon meddling political officers in Central Asia, whom he regarded as largely responsible for that débâcle, were easily extended to those in command of the new settlement at Aden. He could not see the reason for a large garrison. His opinion was: 'We could secure the only rational reason for which Aden can be held, that of maintaining a coal depot there, by the occupation of a restricted position at Steamer Point.'[139] This was to return to the reasons given for the occupation in the Parliamentary Papers. It set out a formula which, had it been presented to Sultan Muhsin in 1838, might very well have secured his willing consent. It was quite out of tune with the expansive ideas of those responsible for the decision to occupy. Ellenborough also ensured that a mission sent to expand trade and political influence in southern Ethiopia in 1841 was not followed up. Ellenborough's ideas about Aden were not fully implemented and he was recalled in 1845. But he and others like him spread an atmosphere of caution in all that concerned Aden and neighbouring countries.

When Palmerston and Hobhouse came back into office in 1846, the latter lamented that he found 'the tone of the Indian Government . . . entirely changed in all that regarded its western policy . . .'. Nor could he hope to bring about an immediate change for he could rely neither on the co-operation of the Governor-General nor on the Directors of the East India Company.[140] This atmosphere of doubt, reluctance and hesitation among those responsible for the development of Aden accounts for much of the neglect with which the settlement was treated in its early years. It had been taken when the threat from Muhammad 'Ali's Egypt had seemed very real. But within two years of its seizure Muhammad 'Ali had been forced out of Arabia, largely through Britain's action in the Mediterranean, and after that the Middle Eastern situation looked much more secure. The strategy out of which British Aden had been born was already in some respects obsolete before the settlement had gathered any momentum. To many Aden was an embarrassment. To many more it was a backwater in which the local officers could be allowed to struggle along on their own resources.

CHAPTER II

Aden under Haines

Of all those who had advocated the occupation, the man who was to have the greatest influence on the subsequent development of the settlement was the man who had actually conducted the negotiations connected with the cession and conquest. While Governors of Bombay and other high officials in the Indian Government came and went, Commander Stafford Bettesworth Haines remained fifteen years in charge of Aden. His long tenure of office reflected indecisiveness in higher quarters on the question of what role Aden should play in British strategy rather than absolute satisfaction with the Political Agent's activity. The control of important stations in India was not normally entrusted to men of Haines's calibre. Such positions were usually reserved for those with the patronage of men in high places and there is no evidence to show that Haines had many influential friends. The appointment of a mere Commander in the somewhat despised Indian Navy signified a demotion of the settlement itself. While Farish had been in charge at Bombay the intention had been that Haines should be replaced by a more senior officer. Further proposals in 1847 for the creation of a powerful government at Aden also involved Haines's replacement. In each case the forward school could not carry their point against those who wanted Aden to remain nothing more than a coaling station. The question of Aden's status raised such controversy that the easiest thing was to do nothing – that is, to leave control in the hands of the man on the spot. Haines himself was a noncommittal candidate who could please both parties. He had advanced ideas about Aden's role but lacked the influence to force those ideas on his superiors. The decision to give him a definitive appointment was taken under Carnac who did not want to see Aden made a permanent settlement.[1] By putting a naval officer in command it seemed that the British had barely decided whether to leave the sea for dry land, and the unimposing title of Political Agent which he was given did nothing to dispel that impression.

His status and the circumstances of his appointment profoundly affected Haines's conduct of the settlement's affairs. He did not have the powers of a Governor and the garrison was left under separate command. Such a division of powers might have worked elsewhere in

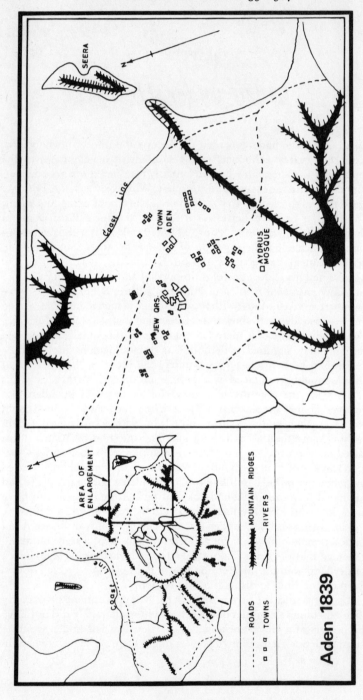

Aden 1839

Commander S. B. Haines, Indian Navy, Political Agent at Aden 1839–54.

India but in a small remote station with a comparatively large military encampment, such an arrangement was almost foredoomed to failure. For the greater part of his period of office Haines had to fight a running battle with the military authorities for control of the settlement. Within six months of Aden's occupation a major controversy arose between him and Captain Baillie, the commander of the garrison.[2] Haines won and a more senior officer, Colonel Capon, was sent to supersede Baillie in the autumn of 1839. Within a few months Capon too had broken off with the Political Agent and, deceived by orders from Bombay to 'take command of Aden', tried to push Haines into a completely subordinate position. A furious dispute ensued and in the spring of 1840 Haines was fighting with his back to the wall against all the officers of the garrison and a coalition of forces which extended to a section of the Arab population in Aden and beyond the walls to powerful groups in the interior. The crisis passed when Bombay intervened and defined more clearly the dividing line between political and military power.[3] But these struggles left a trail of bitterness behind them. Further disputes arose in 1841, 1846 and 1847, all of which were carried to such ridiculous lengths by the parties involved that the ordinary administration of the settlement was dislocated.[4] Again and again Bombay had to intervene and administer censures on both Political Agent and the military, and Aden acquired the reputation of being a troublesome station. In 1849 a visitor to Aden could still comment on the bad relations between the military and political officers.[5] Since Haines was a party to all these disputes while the military officers were constantly changing, it is difficult to avoid the conclusion that there was some defect either in Haines's character or in his mode of handling affairs that led to such incessant conflict. Haines certainly was quick to take offence and very sensitive to personal slights – traits of character which the insecurity of his own position could have done nothing to allay. But most of the disputes were not begun by Haines himself and the reasons for the constant quarrelling must be sought elsewhere. Some light is thrown on the matter by an observation which Lord Dalhousie made after visiting Aden on his way to take up his post as Governor-General. Dalhousie commented that he had seen at Aden things which 'even to my uninstructed eye seemed most strange'.[6] There were indeed many things done at Aden under Haines which would have surprised and shocked any exponent of well-ordered administration. The cold light of utilitarian reform then illuminating other parts of the East India Company's possessions certainly did not shine clearly at Aden in the 1840s. All manner of private arrangements and personal deals falsified what rules and regulations there were. Those with the ear of the Political Agent could do more or less as they pleased while those who fell foul of him or his friends were subject to a variety of vexatious impositions. This was the system which the military men called 'oppressive rule'. They distrusted Haines's agents, were disgusted by their petty tyrannies, and said so, not only in official correspondence, but also through anonymous letters in the Bombay press.[7]

Haines's manner of countering military hostility was not such as to inspire the respect of his opponents. No stratagem seemed too low for Haines to stoop to in vilifying his enemies. In his quest for evidence against one officer Haines called before him a minor official and, alternately smiling and bullying, sought to extract information about the officer's personal conduct with women in the settlement.[8] On another occasion, when he heard through bazaar gossip that two officers had spoken disparagingly of him, he instituted a full-scale inquiry. Various members of the Arab community were called and Haines put to them such leading questions as 'Did it not appear to you that the gentlemen (his military colleagues) were acting in the wrong in speaking of me in the disrespectful manner they did?' He then submitted the whole case to the government. The Governor of Bombay found this an 'extravagant proceeding' and had Haines always been as maladroit he would not have lasted as long as he did.[9] But he could also be a circumspect, crafty adversary. He understood the division between the military and political fields as many of his opponents did not. While rigid army officers like Capon blundered into matters which did not concern them, guided only by their sense of what was right, Haines carefully kept clear of military affairs and only struck when his opponents delivered themselves into his hands. Then he was ruthless in his counter attack – in the Capon case he succeeded on somewhat slender evidence in implicating his opponents among the army officers with all the avowed enemies of the British among the Arabs inside and outside Aden.[10]

Haines's principal argument when he was forced to appeal to Bombay, was that he alone understood the politics of Aden and the hinterland and that his methods were successful.[11] This was in large measure true. He immersed himself in the politics and intrigues of the Arab community at Aden in a fashion which few of his successors were to follow. There was no aloofness in Haines's attitude to the local community. The men others referred to as his 'cronies' were to be found among Arabs rather than among Europeans, at Aden.[12] Other Englishmen might build up friendships at Aden on a basis of mutual respect for one another's culture; when Haines met his 'cronies' he talked of business, contracts and political gossip. Religious and cultural differences seldom entered into the discussion; Haines neither took much interest in, nor even mentioned these subjects, apart from occasional references to the effect of 'religious bigotry' on politics. His prejudices were personal rather than national and he was quite prepared to side with an Arab friend against one of his own countrymen.

There was more in Haines's attitude that was reminiscent of the eighteenth-century exiles who had built the fortunes of the East India Company than of the nineteenth-century administrators who felt themselves part of an essentially British governmental machine. In a sense Haines regarded Aden as his own personal property. He had first seen the port in 1819, twenty years before the occupation and in 1835 when he had first been assigned to the surveying squadron on the South Arabian coasts, he had directed Bombay's attention towards Aden as a potential commercial and naval base.[13] Sultan Muhsin read Haines's mind in 1838 when he said 'that man in his heart wants to rule Aden'. After the occupation Haines settled there with his wife and family. He bought up house property, supplemented the salaries of underpaid clerks out of his own pocket and nurtured the trade of the settlement with a fatherly solicitude.[14] Aden's enemies were Haines's enemies and he pursued such men as Sharif Husayn, the ruler of the rival port of Mocha, with the ruthlessness of a personal vendetta. During his fifteen years of office he never left the settlement except for one period of six weeks' sick-leave and then he had to be practically carried to the steamer.[15] His successors were to regard Aden as a stepping-stone to better things; for Haines it represented the summit of his ambition.

There was something of the eighteenth century also in Haines's methods of administration. For some time his despatches were a headache to the Bombay administration. Only after considerable prodding did he begin to split up the information he sent back under the various required departmental headings. In the somewhat ill-ordered letter-books which were his own records, territorial, judicial and political letters continued to jostle one another in an unsystematic fashion. The cash account books were in little better state and remained so until he left office. This was symptomatic of a general confusion of function that prevailed at Aden during Haines's regime among the minor officials of government. Of course Aden was too small to allow of much departmentalisation of government business. But Haines himself was not the sort of man to encourage such a development. His method of working was such that men were more important to him than departments or measures.

Haines had had considerable experience of Arab politics before he arrived at Aden. Four years surveying the South Arabian coast had enabled him to build up a number of important contacts. But his experience had mostly been gathered among sea-faring *nakhudas* and the cosmopolitan communities of the ports. He could speak Arabic, but his knowledge of the language was somewhat rudimentary. He could not write it and he was therefore more or less at the mercy of the clerks who drafted his letters.[16] He was not a close student of Arab society although he collected a good deal of historical information, and his policy was not based on any scientific examination of its workings. His generalisations about what he saw were well-spiced with catch phrases from the latest works of British political economists. He aimed to draw out the resources of the country by protecting the 'industrious labourers and agriculturists'.[17] Under the existing system he believed that 'the landed proprietor was oppressed and the product of the cultivator's industry taken from him'.[18] The frequent feuds and quarrels he put down to 'the feudal system and its religion'.[19] He believed that the 'merchants and poorer classes' favoured the British.[20] But he did not try to reconcile this with the fact that these same 'poorer classes' were the most enthusiastic supporters of the religious leaders who from time to time attempted to recover Aden from the infidel.[21]

It was possibly this belief in the existence of an oppressed class of merchants and agriculturists that encouraged him to overestimate Aden's commercial potentiality; more probably he was influenced by what he knew of Aden's former commercial greatness. Whatever the reason, Haines was sure throughout his period of office that an era of prosperity lay just beyond the horizon.

One may ask whether Haines really believed that Arab society was differentiated into classes in this fashion or whether he merely repeated these slogans knowing them to be congenial to the ears of like-thinking superiors. Certainly some of his successors, such as Coghlan, wrote in this fashion, while conducting a day-to-day policy which bore little or no relation to their professed social theories. This was not the case with Haines. His theories fitted in well with his own background and experience. Unlike some of his naval colleagues, such as Cruttenden and Wellsted, Haines had never travelled much in the interior of Arabia and had never really come to grips with Arab society away from the coast. What he knew of it he got secondhand from merchants and petty traders. He showed a decided preference for the cosmopolitan Arabs of the coast – the men of every country and of none, men untied by tribal traditions and sceptical of religious beliefs. These were the men Haines liked and trusted. His coterie of friends at Aden included three Persians – Mulla Jaffer, Hajj 'Abd al Rasul and Muhsin Shah Monti – 'Ali Bubakr, the son of the former Governor of Aden and a merchant with connections in Lahej and Fadli territory, Shaykh Tayib Ibramji, one of the principal merchants at Mocha, Sorabji Cowasji, a Parsi merchant, and the Jewish community in Aden. These men were mostly self-seeking and short-sighted businessmen, often corrupt and devious in their methods. But they were interested in trade and so was Haines, and he believed he could rely on them. The 'Aydarus Sayyids impressed the military men as 'gentlemanlike in appearance and manners', in evident contrast to some of Haines's friends, but Haines was not impressed.[22] He never liked the 'Aydarus Sayyids, although at times he accepted their co-operation, and he was generally hostile to the whole Sayyid class of religious learned men. He disliked their interference in political matters and believed they engineered disputes among the tribes in order to profit by offering their services as mediators.[23] He carried this general disposition into his dealings with the tribes. No one knew better than Haines the sinuous subtleties of 'Abdali diplomacy, or the duplicity and deceptions of the Lahej Sultans. But he preferred them to the narrow-minded Fadli. The leaders of Lahej Society were men of business like himself, cosmopolitan and open-minded, and although he knew they disliked him to the point of detestation and would do their utmost to overreach him, he also knew that if he could persuade them that their interests and his were identical they would co-operate with him in his projects. He was aware that he could buy the support of Lahej's Fadli enemies, and if his policy had been based on simple bribery he could no doubt have secured the Fadli Sultan's help. But after a first favourable impression of this warlike man, Haines came to dislike and despise the Fadli Sultan as one who could not see beyond immediate gain and who was always liable to be swayed by religious fanaticism.

Haines's system was reasonably effective up to a point. He had detected a rift in Arab society, and was able to exploit it. Men like Mulla Jaffer disliked Sayyids and chiefs almost as much as Haines, and there was a strong faction in the Arab community at Aden, mostly composed of Mocha men, who could be counted on to back him up. In fact the Arab community at Aden caused the British authorities remarkably little trouble. The various proclamations by would-be invaders from the hinterland caused little or no stir and only on two occasions did some of the inhabitants flee the town, fearing a successful attack. Remarkable too was the fact that Haines was able to secure so much reliable information from the interior. The secret of his success in this respect was that his agents in Aden, such as Jaffer and 'Abd al Rasul, had important connections of their own in the hinterland and the Yemen. The latter had been engaged in the coffee trade from Mocha, and was well known and trusted by the Imams. Jaffer was widely known in southern Arabia and through him Haines engaged the services of the agent of the Lahej Sultan, Hassan 'Abdallah Katif, and a number of other minor agents. Haines's most useful informants, however, were the members of the Jewish community in Aden. These men had relations in San'a', Ta'izz, Lahej and Qa'taba, who acted as cashiers to the authorities in those places, and were therefore able to gather the most confidential information. Haines found their information to be more reliable than that of his other agents, it was also more secret since it was communicated in Hebrew script, which Haines's enemies could not read.[25]

This system was suited to the Political Agent's own nature. For all his social theorising, Haines saw political matters in terms of personalities. He was a man of strong loyalties who gathered round him a small coterie of trusted friends. In them he reposed complete confidence while excluding all others from knowledge of the details of his policy. He was a secretive man and no other European officer at Aden ever fully knew his mind. He picked his own assistants, Jenkins and Cruttenden.[26] They were both Indian Navy men, whom he had known for many years before. But even they were not fully in his confidence. They were given charge of the general order of the towns and Cruttenden spent much of his time settling disputes among the

Somali on the opposite coast. They seldom had anything to do with Haines's Arabian policy. Despite the fact that they worked together for nearly thirteen years, Cruttenden never knew until 1853 of Haines's great secret – the presence of an enormous unexplained deficit in the Treasury.[27]

G. P. Badger, an Arabic scholar who was to be of great assistance to Haines's successor, spent more than seven years at Aden as chaplain under Haines, but was never consulted by the Political Agent on political matters. Even the successive military commanders of the garrison were simply informed that Haines considered that Aden itself was in danger of attack; Haines did not consider it necessary to tell them how he arrived at his conclusions.[28] Haines had to employ European soldiers as part-time clerks in his office, but he hated the system because the soldiers were not fully under his control and might talk elsewhere about what he was doing.[29] Haines had a passion for secrecy.

On the other hand he reposed absolute confidence in his local agents. His policy was to pick a man he thought to be trustworthy and then back him to the hilt. This was the cause of much of the intrigue, corruption and petty tyranny which marked Aden life during his time. In his early days at Aden, Haines chose as his chief assistant Mulla Jaffer, who had been his servant for nine years before the occupation and to whom he believed he owed his life. Jaffer's official position was Native Agent and Interpreter,[30] but in reality he dominated Aden town and was feared by the chiefs in the interior. A visitor to Aden in 1844 could scarcely have doubted Jaffer's power and influence. The largest building in the town, standing six storeys higher than any other, was his.[31] It was well known that the valuable licences to sell liquor could only be obtained through his influence and Arab *nakhudas* trading in the port were careful to curry favour with him.[32] In the bazaar, men hung on his words and a number of minor crises arose from his slighting references to notables in the town and the interior.[33] He was well known not only in Aden but in the whole of South Arabia and on the Somali coast and was in correspondence with the Sultan of Masqat among other prominent personages.[34] His power derived from the fact that he was Haines's channel of communication with the Arab community in Aden and the interior and had Haines's unswerving support.[35] The news of the wreck of the *Duria Dawlat* first came to Haines through Jaffer.[36] Chiefs commonly wrote first to Jaffer before approaching Haines and petitions to the Government of Bombay often ended with the complimentary remark 'Jaffer is a good man'.[37] There can be little doubt that Jaffer made money out of his position. The large properties he owned at Aden could scarcely have been purchased out of his meagre salary of 150 rupees a month and rumours of his financial malpractices were in constant circulation. He was also an overbearing man who ruthlessly pursued his enemies. But Haines trusted him implicitly and risked his own position to defend him. Both Haines's clashes with the military authorities in 1839 and 1840 were occasioned by Jaffer's high-handed actions.[38] In 1841 Haines was reprimanded by Bombay when he tried to brush off in jocular fashion the accusation that Jaffer was giving himself inflated titles in his correspondence with others.[39] On orders from Bombay, Haines was forced to dismiss Jaffer from government service in 1844 for misdemeanours. Nevertheless, Jaffer remained a power at Aden until in 1853, when Bombay intervened once more and ordered his removal from the settlement. Throughout all this, Haines never wavered in his defence of his servant, even when it occasioned considerable risk to his own position.

This dogged loyalty to his Arab friends was the main hallmark of Haines's policy. Others, such as 'Abd al Rasul, the Native Agent at Mocha, benefited in like fashion from his friendship.[40] So also did Hassan 'Abdallah Katif, his agent at Lahej, who was murdered by order of Sultan Muhsin for revealing the time and method of an 'Abdali attack on Aden. Haines secured a pension for the murdered man's descendants from the Bombay Government and made the restoration of his property the chief condition of peace with the 'Abdali Sultan.

Prior to its occupation, Haines foretold a great future for the port under British rule.[42] He continued to make similar optimistic forecasts throughout his period of office and heavily underlined every perceptible sign of progress in his reports to his superiors. But in reality Aden improved only slowly and painfully and when Haines left, the town still bore an air of poverty and impermanence. Not that there were no important changes during the first fifteen years of British rule. The population of the town of Aden did grow enormously. In 1839 there were only 1,289 civilians in the town of Aden; in 1842 there were 16,454 civilians and 3,484 military personnel and camp followers.[43] But there was no corresponding increase in the number of permanent buildings. When Haines arrived in Aden he found behind the wall in Front Bay mound upon mound of ruins among which stood two mosques, dilapidated but intact, and a number of other ruined and half-ruined buildings.[44] Even the Sultan's palace was in such a bad state of repair that shortly after the occupation it began to collapse about the ears of the clerks who were using it as a government office.[45] Some of the inhabitants lived in a few ill-constructed stone houses but most lived in what were called *kutcha* huts.[46] These huts were temporary structures made from reed mats – a type of dwelling very common on the south and west coast of Arabia at the time[47] and one which was reasonably habitable in a climate where rain fell for only a few days in each year. Thus Aden town in 1839 bore the aspect of a temporary encampment among the ruins of ancient greatness. As for Steamer Point, on the other side of the peninsula, it was quite uninhabited. Within the first three years after the occupation there was a rapid influx of settlers from Mocha, the hinterland, Somaliland and India, but the effect of this immigration was merely to extend the temporary encampment. The new settlers were slow to build permanent houses and they accommodated themselves in *kutcha* huts like the bulk of the existing population. They had mostly come to Aden because the British had taken possession, and in those early years, when the future of the settlement was still uncertain, they were loath to invest their capital in shops and warehouses. When new private building did begin in 1842, it began slowly and only after much prodding by the authorities.[48] Haines offered low rents to those who built in stone, and the Engineer's Department cleared the way by removing ruins and levelling the ground.[49] The first structures to go up were the coffee shops owned by Arabs and serving as centres for the coolie population coming in from southern Yemen to work on contract.[50] Not until late in 1845 did the Indian merchants in the town finally have permanent godowns and warehouses to house their goods.[51] By then the nucleus of a new town had begun to emerge from the ruins of the old, a town laid out on a gridiron pattern and wholly constructed in grey stone according to regulations laid down by Haines.[52] Across the mountains at Steamer Point development was even slower due to poor communications with Aden town and the total lack of water there.[53] The first to build was the Agent of the Peninsular and Oriental Steamship Company who established a coalyard there in 1842.[54] Four years later a good road was built from the Main Pass to Ras Tarshyne connecting the two parts of the settlement, and officers began to put up houses on the hills overlooking the western bay.[55] In 1849 a further obstacle was removed when work began on the construction of a watering place on the coast at the foot of the harbour, to provide a regular supply of water for the population at the Point.[56] Yet in the same year there were still only 331 inhabitants there,[57] and in the 1850s Steamer Point remained a small residential suburb for senior officers on the hills with a community of coal coolies huddled round the coalyards below. When Haines left Aden the majority of the population still lived in reed-mat huts. There were stone barracks for the garrison in Front Bay but many soldiers lived in temporary accommodation. Haines himself lived in what seemed to one visitor to be a *kutcha* hut, only distinguishable from the rest by its more elaborate trellis-sing.[58] The main work of making Aden into a permanent well-built, if still unprepossessing, town was left to Haines's successors.

Nevertheless, there was plenty of work for stone-masons and build-ing labourers at Aden during the first fifteen years of the British occupation. Between 1839 and 1851 £175,000 was spent on the construction of fortifications.[59] While Haines was at Aden scarcely a year passed without some addition being made to the settlement's defences. The task of the engineers and masons building walls across precipitous heights far from the nearest supply of water was a difficult one.[60] Scarcely less difficult was the task of those responsible for deciding exactly which type of fortification the settlement required. For every decision on Aden's defences implied a decision about the purpose and value of the settlement itself and on these points there was always great doubt and controversy both in England and India. The first work to be undertaken was the reconstruction of the wall across the flat, sandy isthmus which had served as Aden's chief defence against invaders from the interior since the time of the Turks. The wall was completed in temporary fashion within six months of the occupation.[61] This was intended at first simply as a temporary measure until permanent works were constructed on the heights behind. But when Carnac became Governor of Bombay after Grant and Farish, he showed the greatest reluctance to spend any more on the erection of further works at a port which he still hoped to evacuate. A long argument ensued between Carnac and his Council, until an Arab attack in May 1840 showed the inadequacy of the 'Turkish' wall on the isthmus, and forced him to act.[62] Work accordingly began on a line of forts and walls along the heights in July 1840.[63] They followed the line of earlier forts raised by Aden's former rulers, of which a few remains still survived, but it was remarkable that they only encircled the old town of Aden, and left the new coaling establish-ments at Steamer Point open to attack.[64] The coaling station, supposed to be the principal *raison d'être* of the new possession, was left unprotected except for the blockship lying off the coast. No steps were taken to close this obvious gap in the settlement's defensive system until 1844 when provision was made for a fort on Ras Morbat to protect Steamer Point from seaward attack. This at least was the plan. In fact twelve years of acrimonious debate, consideration and reconsideration passed between the first conception of the plan and the final completion of the works.[65] The last Arab attack on Aden was met in August 1846 at the isthmus wall with the permanent forts on the heights still only half finished.[66] By the time Aden's permanent defences were complete and the temporary wall across the isthmus knocked down, the attitude of Aden's neighbours had so changed that there was little fear that they would ever be tested.

While it took nearly fifteen years to make Aden into a well-fortified naval base, the rebuilding of Aden's commercial prosperity was an even slower process. At the outset the Indian authorities had high hopes that Aden would, like Singapore, develop into a great commercial entrepôt for all the countries around the mouth of the Red Sea. In particular it was hoped that the Egyptian monopoly of the Yemen coffee trade would be broken and the whole of that trade would be redirected to Aden and India.[67] In the first few months of 1839 a rapid influx of supplies of coffee, wheat and jowari into the port gave some colour to these hopes, but it soon became clear that this represented

Jebel Hadid, with the 'Turkish Wall', objective of Arab assaults after the capture of Aden.

only the normal imports of the trading season which had previously been blocked by the hostilities connected with the British occupation. Moreover, the normal imports were somewhat inflated in 1839, since the Hajariya coffee crop, usually exported through Mocha, was directed to Aden by the chief of that district who was then at war with the Egyptian authorities in the latter port.[68] Within a short time Arab hostility to British rule had reduced Aden's inland trade to infinitesimal proportions, while the coasting trade from the Red Sea ports brought virtually nothing but treasure into Aden for re-shipment.

After this first deceptive flirtation with the trade from the Yemen, Aden turned to what had since the early nineteenth century been its main line of commerce, namely that with the opposite coast and the Horn of Africa generally. Among the Indian traders resident in Aden

at the time of the occupation, there were some who had been engaged
in the trade with the Somali coast for more than half a century.[69]
The main centre of business was the annual fair at Berbera – at that
time not a regular town but an annual encampment which was
vacated each year after the thousands of Somalis who frequented it had
disposed of what they had for sale. In 1848 Cruttenden described
Berbera's bustling commerce in the following terms:

The place from April to the early part of October was utterly deserted,
not even a fisherman being found there, but no sooner did the season
change than the inland tribes commenced moving down toward the
coast and preparing huts for their expected visitors. Small craft from
the ports of Yemen anxious to have the opportunity of purchasing
before the vessels from the Gulf could arrive, hastened across, followed
about a fortnight later by their larger brethren from Muscat, Soor
and Ras al Khyma and the valuably freighted *bugalas* from Bahrein,
Bussorah and Graen. Lastly the fat and wealthy Banian traders from
Porebunder, Mandavii and Bombay rolled across in their clumsy
kotias and with a formidable row of empty ghee jars slung over the
quarters of their vessels, elbowed themselves up to the front tier of the
craft in the habour, and by their superior capital and influence soon
distanced all competitors.[70]

Aden's role in relation to this commerce was that of the depository
for the surplus unsold goods which remained on the hands of Indian
merchants when the fair was closed. The 'fat and wealthy Banian
traders' used the services of Indian brokers at Aden in carrying on
their commerce. Among the exports which went out from Berbera
and other similar fairs on the Somali coast was coffee which came from
far inland at Harrar. Haines claimed that two thirds of the coffee
shipped at Mocha came from this source.[71] There was also a rising
export of gum arabic which was much in demand in Europe and the
United States. There were small quantities of those ancient and still
valuable products, myrrh and frankincense. And there were hides and
skins and flocks of sheep and goats for which the Aden garrison
created a substantial demand.[72] In the 1840s this trade was so
important to Aden that when disturbances in Somaliland on occasion
delayed the closing of the Berbera fair until after the end of Aden's
financial year, Haines regarded the trade figures for that year as
totally unreal. And well he might, for no less than 80 per cent of
Aden's revenue as late as 1848 came from duties charged on products
brought in from Berbera.[73] Aden was in effect commercially little
more than an adjunct of the Berbera Fair in those years. Its contribution was to provide a secure base from which the fair could be better
organised. In the course of the 1840s Indian merchants at Aden began
to replace the former system of barter by providing credit to Somali

caravan leaders who then went inland and returned the following year with their purchases.[74] By 1852 Aden merchants were buying up practically everything sold at the Berbera fair and what was not sold there was brought across to them later by Berbera traders.[75]

The occupation of Aden had been coupled with a plan to extend this commerce with North-East Africa. In 1841 a British political mission was sent from India to the King of Shoa in southern Ethiopia. It was associated with the grand plan conceived in England in the late 1830s to draw out the resources of the whole continent of Africa by substituting a trade in commodities required in Europe for the trade in slaves. To support the mission, a British establishment was temporarily set up at Tajura on the Somali coast and the resources of the Aden settlement were used to back up these efforts. But the mission achieved little. It was another of those aggressive, expansive projects which Palmerston and the Whig Ministry (1830–41) conceived in its last years to build up British world trade and throw out defensive bulwarks from Britain's Indian possessions. The Whigs' Tory successors after 1841 recalled the Shoa mission and abandoned Tajura as they cut down most of the commitments which the Whigs had undertaken.[76] But Haines at Aden continued to watch events across the Gulf of Aden and ships were sent each year to supervise the working of the Berbera fair. When, as a result of redistribution of Indian Navy vessels, no ship was available in 1844, Haines got the Indian community at Aden to finance the hire of a vessel to do the work.[77] Haines also sought to work through a Somali leader, Hajj Shermarki, who seized Zayla in 1843 and erected two towers at Berbera in the following year.[78] Cruttenden visited every part of the Somali coast, forming friendly relations with the people and seeking to settle the innumerable disputes between the trading tribes which were one of the principal restraints on commerce. These efforts were not wholly successful, and Somaliland was rent by the quarrels of rival factions, which seemed to become more rather than less severe as time went on.[79] But Aden secured considerable influence along the Somali coast and in the interior. Indeed, during Haines's time Aden had perhaps more influence there than in its own Arabian hinterland.

It is difficult to make any accurate assessment of the nature and rate of development of Aden's trade during Haines's period owing to the lack of reliable statistics. Up to December 1842 the customs accounts were only roughly kept in Arabic and Hebrew. After that date they were more systematically recorded in English, but in 1843 extra articles were included in the list of items and in 1846 the various commodities were revalued according to a new scale.[80] Apart from this there was a considerable amount of smuggling,[81] and Haines, who was eager to prove the commercial value of the new settlement, did his utmost to present the figures in the best light possible. Nevertheless, it is possible to discern certain definite trends. From the end of 1842 there was a steady increase in the total trade of the port up to 1846 and from then it remained more or less at the same level until 1852 when it practically doubled and continued to rise throughout the 1850s.[82] Until the 1850s the amount of goods passing through the port was extremely small, so small that when in 1846 the 'Aqrabi Shaykh's small bandar at Little Aden across the bay was blockaded by the British, the estimated value of the goods stopped up there amounted to a tenth of the total trade of Aden itself.[83] In fact, despite the reference of the Governor-General in 1839 to the creation of another Singapore, Aden was not attractive to foreign merchants until the 1850s. The customs duties imposed at Aden were not substantially lowered after the occupation. The charges on trade from the interior were in reality almost doubled, for the Lahej Sultan sought to collect as much revenue as he had previously received from the port from transit dues which he levied on the roads to Aden while the British collected their own customs at the port. This situation did did not alter until 1850, when the Indian Government made Aden a free port, a measure which immediately brought French and American merchants to Aden and stimulated the great increase in Aden's commerce which took place in the following years.

The attraction of French and American traders to Aden marked the realisation of one of Haines's dearest hopes, namely the acquisition of a substantial share in the Yemen coffee trade. It was the American traders and to a lesser extent the French who carried off most of the coffee exported from southern Yemen.[84] They did not export the whole crop by any means, for the greater part still went northward through Hudayda and Jedda to Egypt and the Middle East. But they did draw a proportion of the Yemen's coffee into Mocha. During Haines's first twelve years as Political Agent he did his utmost to attract the landward coffee trade to Aden.[85] But he faced the greatest difficulties.' Apart from the hostility of the hinterland tribes, particularly the Sultan of Lahej, who for long periods between 1839 and 1844 cut Aden off completely from any contact with the coffee districts in the Yemen, Haines had to contend with the fact that Aden had never really participated in the Yemen coffee trade and that all the normal trading mechanisms in southern Yemen tended to centre on Mocha. Furthermore, the rulers of Mocha in the 1840s were well aware that Aden was a potential rival and they stirred up trouble in the Aden hinterland, prevented coffee brokers at Mocha from transferring residence to Aden and sent agents to contact and divert toward Mocha any American ships which stopped at Aden.[86] It was not simply because the ruler of Mocha insulted the British flag in 1840 that Haines continually begged the Indian Government to order a blockade of that port.[87] Indeed he was anxious that the British flag should never again be raised at Mocha to offer protection to those Indian traders who wished to settle there.[88] He sought by every means to starve Mocha of capital and commercial skill, and generally to create an atmosphere of insecurity at that port. His efforts were in vain. Mocha was reasonably prosperous in the 1840s although substantially less active than in the eighteenth century.[89] Even in time of trouble the merchants of the port were reluctant to leave, and many preferred to return to India rather than to transfer their business to Aden.[90] Only after a prolonged political crisis in 1848 did Mocha fall into decline and the merchants waited more than six months for the return of better times before they finally abandoned the port and began to move in substantial numbers to Aden.[91]

Mocha's rivalry was but one of Haines's difficulties. Linked with this was the fact that until 1850 the flow of traffic from the producing districts was more or less subject to political control. This meant that if Haines was to secure the trade from central Yemen he had to offer political concessions to the Imams or to the chiefs of the Hajariya. On several occasions between 1839 and 1849 agents from San'a' and the Hajariya came to Aden to negotiate with Haines the transfer of the coffee trade from Mocha to Aden. But on each occasion the commercial discussions were linked with political demands, demands which Haines was unable to concede.[92] Haines went as far as he could within the limits of his instructions but he was unable to conclude the sort of politico-commercial agreement which the Imams and their agents evidently sought. No way out of this impasse was found until in 1849 and 1850 the power of the Imam in central Yemen was practically destroyed by an unpopular alliance with the Turks. The ensuing enmity between the Yemenis in the interior and the Turkish occupiers of the Tihama, thereafter diverted a good part of the traffic to Aden without the negotiation of any specific agreement.[93]

The brightening commercial outlook after 1851, however, only meant that Aden was securing a larger share in a generally stagnant if not declining commerce. South-West Arabia had few commodities available at attractive enough prices for the mass-consumption economies of the growing industrial world. The troubled conditions in the Yemen around the middle of the century reduced the total amount of trade, and the external commerce of the whole Red Sea area had for some time been tending to decline rather than expand. Certainly the amount of Indian trade with the Red Sea ports had considerably fallen by 1842.[94] Furthermore, the centre of gravity of the Indian trade in the Red Sea was moving northward as more and more Indian vessels sailed straight for Jedda instead of stopping at the ports on the Yemen coast.[95] Aden therefore managed merely to secure a larger share in what had become a reduced general commerce and the early visions of a great commercial entrepôt at the mouth of the Red Sea, stimulating trade in the area as a whole, were not to be realised until much later in the century.

One of the paradoxical results of the British occupation was that throughout Haines's period the military and naval dispositions which were intended to protect the commerce of the possession became themselves the greatest focus of business activity. Instead of the garrison protecting the Aden business community, a great part of the business community was solely engaged in catering for the needs of the garrison. Between 1839 and 1851 no less than £85,000 was spent each year on maintaining about 2,000 troops at Aden.[96] This was a sum equal to nearly half the gross value of Aden's annual import and export trade.[97] Even though only a portion of this was spent in Aden, it represented a substantial subsidy by the Indian Government to the settlement, and the work of fortification brought in additional money. Not surprisingly, the needs of the garrison accounted for a substantial proportion of Aden's imports, a proportion the more difficult to trace because part of them passed through the Commissariat Department and were therefore not accounted for in the annual returns of trade. Some indication of their importance can, however, be gathered from the fact that the import of the one commodity used by the garrison which was easily identifiable, namely beer and spirits, during the 1840s exceeded in value the total trade in coffee which was Aden's principal import from surrounding countries.[98] The purchase of the Commissariat gave a great fillip to the trade at Berbera where it was the main buyer of livestock. Several thousand sheep were brought in each year to supply the needs of the garrison.[99] The Commissariat also purchased large numbers of donkeys for use on the construction sites, vast quantities of firewood for the manufacture of mortar, large quantities of fodder for draught animals and livestock held in Aden prior to slaughter; after 1846 it also began to purchase vegetables for the troops from the hinterland instead of bringing them from Bombay.[100] The firewood and fodder that the Commissariat bought represented the largest item of trade with the interior in the middle 1840s and thousands of camels were engaged in their transport. In some parts of Fadli country farmers abandoned cultivation of the land and turned *en masse* to the business of providing fodder and provisions for Aden and its garrison.

Inevitably the part played by the Government in the economic life of Aden was very great, and government contracts were much sought after. This was no doubt the reason why a visitor to Aden in 1849 could comment that despite the appearance of free trade there were

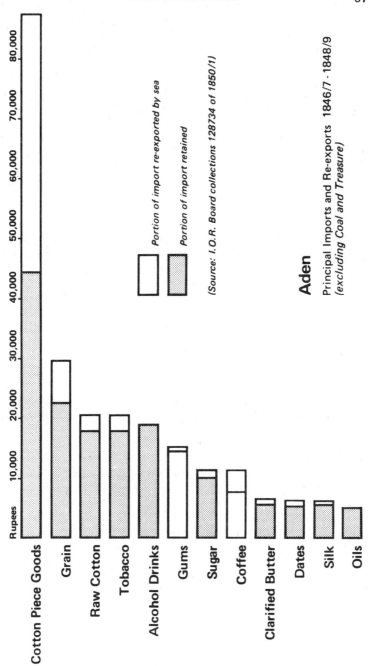

Rupees

80,000
70,000
60,000
50,000
40,000
30,000
20,000
10,000

Cotton Piece Goods
Grain
Raw Cotton
Tobacco
Alcohol Drinks
Gums
Sugar
Coffee
Clarified Butter
Dates
Silk
Oils

Portion of import re-exported by sea

Portion of import retained

(Source: I.O.R. Board collections 128734 of 1850/1)

Aden

Principal Imports and Re-exports 1846/7 - 1848/9
(excluding Coal and Treasure)

a large number of *de facto* monopolies.[101] Apart from the activities of the Commissariat, some of the most valuable businesses were subject to Government licence. The sale of spirits to the troops, for example, was farmed out to a single trader before licences were issued to a number of selected retailers.[102] Likewise the sale of *qat*, a stimulant used largely by the Arab coolies, was restricted to one and later to a small number of sellers licensed by the Government. Both of these trades were exceptionally valuable, sales were heavy and the *qat* contractor, being able to dictate prices to producer and consumer alike, made profits of up to 1,000 per cent.[103]

A case of contract allocation that arose in 1846 provides an outstanding example of how government was involved with business and how the Political Agent sought to manipulate both. In that year when the first great spurt of constructional work began with the building of permanent defence works on a major scale, a dispute developed between Haines and the Army Engineer when the latter decided to by-pass Haines' principal client and give the contracts to a man of his own choosing. At once Haines branded the Engineer his enemy, party lines were drawn and throughout the year the official community was torn by bitterness. All the Political Agent's worst traits of insecure vindictiveness and querulous suspicion of personal betrayal came to the fore. Defectors from the Political Agent's camp were accused of listening to wrong advice, Haines asserted certain knowledge of statements made in the privacy of other officers' homes. Machiavellian schemes, drawing on assistance from unexpected quarters, were laid to obstruct the Engineer.

Haines' attitude and machinations were curiously reminiscent of those used by the Sultan of Lahej—not surprising for Haines was a political broker among the Arab brokers he knew so well. He had the same traits of individualistic alienation from the society from which he came, evident from the superior and somewhat contemptuous tone that the military officers adopted toward him. Against their regimental sense of belonging, reaching back to India and the Queen's army, Haines pitted his knowledge of the law – its letter, not its spirit – and his cosmopolitan connections with others of his type.

What was at stake was no doubt beneath the notice of the new Indian officials graduating from Haileybury, but it was not a marginal issue in Haines's Aden. The contracts in question included a classic one for providing raw ignorant labour from the hills to the stranger infidels – a lucrative engagement for any middlemen's special interpretative skill – and a contract to provide coral or 117 rupees a day. In addition, of course, there were needed donkeys, fodder for the donkeys, water for the labourers – enough to set the Arab brokers of Aden agog with interest. And the personalities involved were no mean figures. Haines's man was his new protégé 'Ali Bubakr, the Sultan of Lahej's former Governor at Aden, while the Engineer had employed an arch-intriguer from the hinterland, Sayyid Muhsin Ways from the village of Saffyan north of Lahej, who had committed the capital offence of betraying Haines' trust on a previous occasion.[104] Merchant brokers at Aden and political brokers in the interior as often as not joined hands; on this occasion two of the principal among them were engaged in deadly rivalry, the subject of dispute being the final destination of the profits from Government expenditures.

This was not the first such dispute nor was it to be the last in the history of British Aden, for as time went on the number of brokers multiplied while their appetite did not diminish. Such was one of the main features of the society that was growing up at Aden, fed by British military expenditure and the growth of the coaling depot with its masses of manhandled coal representing one-third of the port's total imports. Aden did not create the broker. Such men had long flourished in the Red Sea ports, indeed wherever transactions were made between men of different societies and cultures, and the first labour contractors or *Muqaddams* came in the earliest years of the settlement from Mocha. But British Aden gave this social form a peculiar opportunity to flourish and put a political power behind it that it had seldom had before.

The structure of Aden's population during Haines's period of office was also profoundly affected by the activity of the Government. From 1842 onward, fully a quarter of Aden's population were either soldiers in the garrison or their camp followers.[105] The Government's employment policy determined to a considerable extent the composition and character of the community. In 1842, when Haines and the Engineer's Department were employing Arab coolies on the coal depot and various public works, the majority of the population, just over half, was Arab.[106] But when, for a period of fifteen years from the end of 1846, the Government imported Indian labourers instead for the construction of the defensive works, Aden became more an Indian than an Arab town.[107] By 1849 the number of Arabs in Aden had fallen to less than half of what it had been in the early years, while the number of Indians had more than doubled. In 1849 and again in 1856 the Indians formed somewhat over 40 per cent of the total population and were by far the largest national grouping at Aden,[108] followed by Arabs, Somalis and Jews.

As one would expect of a coaling station and garrison town, Aden's population was exceedingly mixed and shifting. Those who settled there, seldom brought their wives and in 1842 women accounted for only 27 per cent of the community.[109] There was a large and growing body of Somalis, few of whom had any regular employment at Aden

but who came there during the off season at Berbera. The Somali
section of the community was inevitably constantly changing and
nearly half left Aden immediately the Berbera fair began.[110] The large
Indian population also fluctuated as Indian Regiments were replaced
and as the labourers on the defence works finished their contracts and
were repatriated. This was also the case with a substantial proportion
of the Arab community especially those who were given the indeterminate name of *Jebelis* (hillmen). These were mostly coolies from the
southern Yemen working on contract for *muqaddams*, and as late as
1856 they still formed the largest single constituent of the Arab
community.[111] At Aden there were Arabs, Indians, Jews, Goans,
Egyptians, Persians, Sudanese and Somalis. The European community was not wholly British since there was always a proportion of
French, Maltese and other nationalities among the commercial
community. The Arab population was likewise mixed. In 1849 only
980 of them were registered as original inhabitants of Aden. For the
rest they came from all parts of South-West Arabia. After the *jebelis*,
the strongest element in the 1840s and 1850s was composed of men
from Mocha who exceeded the number of those registered as Adenis.
Next in number to the Adenis were the immigrants from the
Hadhramawt, and after them the men from Lahej, northern Yemen,
Hajariya and San'a'.[112]

Since the population of the town was so completely lacking in
homogeneity, Haines had little to fear from an internal uprising in
concert with forces outside the town. Yet the character of the population was not such as to guarantee great security of persons and
property. Brawls were not unfrequent and Haines himself never left
his house without two pistols in his belt.[113] The Somalis were
particularly troublesome and were frequently involved in petty
theft.[114] Haines at first attempted to prohibit the sale of alcohol in
deference to the feelings of the original inhabitants, but liquor was
soon being sold in substantial quantities to military and civilians
alike.[115] To keep order, Haines first used Arab peons but soon found
them inadequate, and from 1841 trained men, brought in from
Bombay for the purpose, looked after the policing of the town. This
development was paralleled in other parts of the administration.
Immediately after the occupation, Haines continued to employ many
of those who had served under the Sultan of Lahej in the administration of Aden.[116] But within a few years most of these Arabs and Jews
were replaced by Indians and by the 1850s there were hardly any
Arabs in the subordinate clerical staff of the settlement. The only
position which remained consistently in Arab hands was that of Qadi,
and the Qadi's judicial powers were restricted practically to the field
of marital affairs.

By the time Haines left Aden the town had developed three main centres of life: the old Indian trading community engaged in the commerce of the Red Sea, the garrison and the new Indian community which served it, and the Arab population whose most vital elements were those connected with the British and the garrison. The garrison and the administration with its rules, discipline and its strongly British-Indian character was the main driving force in all aspects of the town's life. The Indian merchants connected with the garrison, especially the Bombay Parsis, were rapidly surpassing those involved in the Berbera trade in wealth and capital.[117] Among the Arabs the old weaving crafts, still in existence in 1839, had died out by 1845 and the craftsmen had turned to labouring in the town and port.[118] Between the garrison community and the Arab population stood Haines, surrounded by a clique of prominent Arabs who had his ear, constantly striving to push the business which the presence of the garrison created into the hands of his friends in order to further the purposes of his general policy in the interior.[119]

CHAPTER III

British Aden and South Arabia: Conflict and Compromise 1839–1854

The political scene in South-West Arabia at the time of the British capture of Aden was one of very considerable complexity. The problem of finding a stable relationship between the British-held port and the shifting network of forces in the hinterland was to tax the ingenuity of British officials throughout the period of British rule. Haines could not have been aware of the full dimensions of the problem. Nevertheless, within a few months of Aden's capture, he began juggling with different powers in the interior spread from the Hadhramawt to San'a'. The men he dealt with were those he had met when engaged on the coastal survey and those who approached him directly or indirectly after Aden's capture. Inevitably his contacts were with men concerned with the control and protection of the movement or shipment of goods from the fertile plateaux to the coast. They were those most interested in what happened at Aden and the commercially-minded Haines was also interested in them. Eastward along the coast from Aden there was the Fadli Sultan, who had his own port at Shuqra which rivalled Aden in the export of coffee, other small-scale commerce and the movement of emigrants from Yafi'i country. The Fadli had been the most bitter enemy of Sultan Muhsin of Lahej. In 1835 his men had broken into and plundered Aden and his sphere of control stretched to within a few miles of the Aden Gate. Further east again along the coast, the Lower 'Awlaqi Sultans controlled the port of Ahwar at the terminus of another caravan route reaching inward toward the Yemen. Closer to Aden lay the territory of the 'Aqrabi Shaykh. He and his few hundred followers claimed the barren land at the foot of Aden's western harbour and the equally barren promontory of Little Aden, on whose western side lay a few small havens where small trading vessels could take on goods. Finally there was the Sultan of Lahej, now deprived of his port with which he had maintained contact along a narrow funnel reaching down to Aden's gate between the largely empty lands of Fadli and 'Aqrabi on either side. When negotiating with Haines in 1838 Sultan Muhsin had mentioned those in the interior

who had enjoyed and who expected payments from the port of
Aden. Sultan Muhsin had pointed out that they would have to be
looked after if the British established themselves there. After the
British occupation these men put their claims forward or had their
claims put forward for them through Sultan Muhsin's son-in-law,
the intriguer from Hawshabi country, Sayyid Muhsin bin Ways.[1]
Among them were the prominent men on the road northward from
Lahej, the Hawshabi Sultan and the 'Amir of Dhali'. Both rulers
were traditionally interested in the control of the movement of
caravans from the grain-producing regions beyond Qa'taba and
from the distant capital of the Yemen at San'a'.

Each of these men who sought contact with Haines possessed small
areas of cultivation around their residences and ruled the subject
farmers who tilled them. These settled areas represented their invested capital, as it were, and gave their rule a certain basis of solidity.
But the amount of land each owned varied greatly. The Sultan of
Lahej had the most, with his fertile irrigated fields in the Wadi Tuban.
Under the pressure of the events of 1839 he lost some of his fields and
the headwaters of his irrigation system to the Hawshabi Sultan, but
he and his family nevertheless remained the largest holders of
permanently cultivated lands in the area. The Fadli Sultan was
considerably poorer than his 'Abdali neighbour. The Abyan irrigation
system had not been so well preserved as that at Lahej. But the Fadli
Sultan had recently extended his property at the expense of his
Yafi'i neighbours to the northward and was a powerful and ambitious
figure in hinterland politics at the time of Aden's capture.[2]

At the other end of the scale from the 'Abdali was the 'Aqrabi
Shaykh with a few acres round Bir Ahmad, while the Lower 'Awlaqi
Sultans and the 'Amirs of Dali' stood midway between the two
extremes. The bulk of the population of the area and its most vigorous
and warlike elements owed little or no allegiance to these 'potentates'.
They were not subject to them. Even in the better-organised dominions of the Lahej Sultans, those who were called "Abdali' did not
always obey the Sultan's command and the popularly chosen heads
of such large sections of the tribe as the 'Uzaybi were virtually a
law unto themselves. The Lahej Sultans seldom took an important
step without securing the support of such men as these. What
authority the Sultanly controllers of ports and trade routes could
command, was dependent upon their wealth and their knowledge
of the world beyond their immediate locality. The correspondence
between Haines and the Lahej Sultans was well-spiced with references to the 'badu' – a word usually coupled with the epithet
'ignorant'. Before a Sayyid, a *badu* was ignorant of religion, science
and learning. Before a Sultan, a *badu* was ignorant of wider political

realities, and the power politics of the world at large. The free tribesman therefore accorded something less than loyalty to the Sultan. What he conceded was respect for the political wisdom and knowledge of the ruling house – a concession which he was more or less at liberty to give or to withdraw as best suited his own material interests. The Sultans on the other hand, spent their lives in a fever of political manipulation, persuasion and calculation, seeking to keep the balance of monetary and military forces constantly in their favour and grasping at any opportunity of securing wealth with which to dazzle their poverty-stricken followers.[3]

Haines was in touch with other leaders in the interior whose position was somewhat different from the 'trade route' Sultans. 'Abdali, Fadli, Hawshabi, and 'Amiri, though commonly referred to as 'tribes' by British officials in the nineteenth century, were in fact only the names given to people who tended to follow the ruling houses which bore those names. Those ruling houses were of fairly recent standing. All seem to date from the sixteenth or seventeenth century. Somewhat different were the Yafi'i and 'Awlaqi peoples. These looked back to a more distant past – the first to Himyar, the second to Ma'in, whence came those who established the kingdom of Awsan in much the same area as that now occupied by the Upper 'Awlaqi.[4] Himyar, Ma'in and Awsan are all pre-Islamic entities. Furthermore these two groups – the Yafi'i and the 'Awlaqi – retained a certain degree of solidarity, and were both numerous and warlike. They could on occasion menace the 'trade-route' Sultans, as the 'Awlaqi had done in 1819 when they attacked Lahej and exacted tribute as the price of their withdrawal. On the other hand, the Sultans sought to use them as mercenaries against their enemies. The Yafi'i in particular hung as an imminent heavy cloud over Aden's immediate vicinity. Yafi'i fighting men had wrested Aden from the Ottomans, and also from the Imams. Sultan Muhsin was careful to make friends with some of them by marrying three of his sons to Yafi'i wives. Haines fell into line and in 1839 accorded a stipend to the Yafi'i Sultan at Qara, who could speak for some of the more southerly members of the group.[5]

To the west and north lay the Yemen. In 1839 Haines could do little in that direction, since Egypt held the coastline and relations with Egypt were a matter for the government in London. But Haines contrived to maintain some contact with the Imams through Hajj 'Abd al Rasul, the British agent at Mocha, and he was in direct touch with the Shaykh of the Hajariya who controlled the politics of a coffee-producing area south of Ta'izz. The agent of the Hajariya Shaykh was indeed the first man of importance to approach the British after Aden's capture. He was anxious for British assistance because his country was threatened by the Egyptians who were now in the town of Ta'izz. He was willing to export his coffee through Aden to avoid it passing through the Egyptian port of Mocha. Behind him the Dhu Muhammad and Dhu Husayn rulers of southern Yemen adjacent to Ta'izz also wrote to Haines and offered him their country in return for assistance against Egypt.[6] Haines sought to pull on all the political strings that came to hand, and between February and July 1839 he made contact with most of the principal 'trade-route' Sultans – the Fadli, the Hawshabi, the 'Amir, and the Lower 'Awlaqi – issuing assurances, stipends and gifts. He provided the Lower Yafi'i Sultan with a stipend and made an agreement with the Hajariya Shaykh.[7] Lahej however remained the linchpin of Aden's relations with the hinterland and some satisfactory arrangement with that Sultanate was vital to the trade and security of the port Lahej could never be a strong ally for Aden but it could be a very dangerous enemy

An arrangement with Lahej was not beyond the realms of possibility in 1839 despite all that had passed. Sultan Muhsin may have hated Haines but he was not entirely anti-British. The presence of British power in the Indian Ocean was one of those 'political realities' which a Sultan who hoped to control the forces beyond South Arabia had to accept. At Lahej this reality had been accepted since the beginning of the century. The important question was how to turn it to 'Abdali advantage. In March 1839 the Sultan treated with Haines and once more brought up a proposal for an offensive and defensive alliance, and treatment equivalent to that of a Nawab or Rajah.[8] Haines went a long way in this direction without conceding the control over the Arabs and Jews of Aden that Sultan Muhsin also wanted. The agreement signed on 18 June 1839 was not an offensive and defensive treaty but it provided that the two parties should make common cause against their enemies and stated that their interests were identical. The Sultan and his family were awarded an annual stipend of 6,500 Maria Theresa dollars in perpetuity and he in turn guaranteed that his people would not interfere with the security of the roads. It is difficult to fathom the reasons for the breakdown of this agreement and the 'Abdali decision to enter upon an unequal struggle by attacking Aden in November 1839. Perhaps the cause is to be found in Sultan Muhsin's capacity for intrigue and continual hope of finding some new winning combination.[9] It is more likely however that the explanation lies embedded in the tortuous plots and counter-plots that went on in Aden and Lahej between 1839 and 1843, glimpses of which appear in the official records. In Aden Haines's position was not entirely secure. He was under criticism from the army officers who disapproved of his friends – notably Mulla Jaffer – and doubted the efficacy of his diplomacy. Rumours of these criticisms reached Lahej from time to time and there is little doubt that Sultan Muhsin hoped to get rid of Haines and Jaffer, and arrange better terms with some other British representative. On the other hand those in power in Lahej were even more divided. Sultan Muhsin was an aged man and he had five sons, all of them young and ambitious, each of them looking forward with hope or anxiety to the time when the old man would die. They were a source of constant anxiety to their father; some of Sultan Muhsin's decisions would seem to have been taken as much with a view to maintaining family unity as for any other purpose. His task was made no easier by his son-in-law Sayyid Muhammad Husayn bin Ways who interfered in and exploited family quarrels while strengthening his own position on the Hawshabi border. Finally a prominent Lahej man and occasional adviser to the family, Hassan 'Abdallah Katif, also intrigued and profited from the confused situation. Haines was soon in touch directly or indirectly with most of the dramatis personae at Lahej.[10] The British stipend was distributed by Sultan Muhsin within his family. The Sultan's eldest son, Ahmad, was engaged as commander of a British-financed camel patrol. Sayyid Muhammad bin Husayn bin Ways was charged with the distribution of stipends to the Hawshabi and other chiefs and was paid a personal monthly fee. Hassan 'Abdallah Katif was made British Agent at Lahej and received a salary. Haines prided himself on the spread of his sources of information; in fact, he was drawn by them into the intrigues for power at Lahej.

During the summer of 1839, Sultan Ahmad, 'Abdallah Katif and Sayyid Ways were certainly engaged in an intrigue to displace Sultan Muhsin. When or how Haines and his circle were, wittingly or unwittingly, drawn into this conspiracy is not clear. But in October 1839, Sultan Muhsin believed that Haines was involved and after Aden had been attacked, Haines himself proposed that Ahmed be placed on the throne by British arms with Katif as his adviser.[11] Had this plot not existed in the background, a robbery on the road to Aden which occurred in August 1839, would no doubt have been handled without injury to Anglo-'Abdali relations. As it was, it led to recriminations and mutual suspicions which finally ended in war.

War between Lahej and Aden opened the floodgates of religious resentment at the presence of infidels on Arab soil. What happened in the port of Aden was normally the Lahej Sultan's business. He owned the port and if the British were established there that was his business. But once Sultan Muhsin began to speak of 'Kafir' invaders the matter became of larger concern. Represented in that light, the occupation was an affront to every Arab. In 1839–40 Sultan Muhsin began to adopt this tone and the call to arms was taken up in more strident terms by the Fadli Sultan who spoke of a *Jihad* or holy war.[12] The raising of the banner of Islam was a symbol of unity. It smoothed over disputes within the Lahej family. It even led to an unprecedented meeting and agreement between the two bitter enemies, Sultan Muhsin and his Fadli counterpart.[13] It gave zeal to the fighting men who assembed at Lahej from the deserts of the Subayhi country and from the wild Rafdan mountains, although these warriors nevertheless had to be paid. But it did not unite all in the Aden hinterland. The Yafi'i Sultan would not join with the Fadli for any purpose. The men of 'Awlaqi were willing to fight either for the 'Abdali or for Haines, but their price was too high for both, and they abstained.[14] The Hawshabi took advantage of Lahej's preoccupation with Aden to built a fort in the Wadi Tuban and diverted some of the 'Abdali waters onto their own fields.[15]

The Arab forces which advanced on Aden in three separate attacks on 11 November 1839, 21 May and 5 July 1840, numbered from three to five thousand men armed with matchlocks. On each occasion their tactics were the same – a skilful enveloping movement in darkness along the exposed beach westward of the main British position at the 'Turkish wall' across the isthmus, followed by a frontal attack by the main force against the wall itself. In each case the wall was successfully outflanked and bodies of Arabs reached the hills, from behind which they fired down on the soldiers facing the attack in front. The British troops were hard put to it to repel the invaders and the inadequate defences had to be bolstered by men and guns from ships in the harbour. During the second attack, in May 1840, which the Arabs accounted a limited success, part of the British baggage was plundered and goods and documents were carried off. But in the end, weight of fire-power carried the day. The fieldpieces at the wall, and gunboats standing offshore, poured shot and shell into the Arab forces, who were completely exposed on the flat stretches of the isthmus. In the third attack of July 1840 the Arabs also had to contend with musketry fire from a newly constructed tower on the hill which they had escaladed with comparative impunity on the two previous occasions. In every case the attacking forces suffered heavy casualties while the British losses were slight, and it was the 'Abdali who bore the brunt of the fighting.[16]

But Aden also suffered severely from Lahej's hostility. The strain told on the troops' morale which was in any case low, since the Indian sepoys did not like expatriation. More serious was the effect of Sultan Muhsins's blockade, which began before the first attack and continued after the third and final failure. Fresh vegetables became virtually unobtainable in Aden; supplies had to be brought from

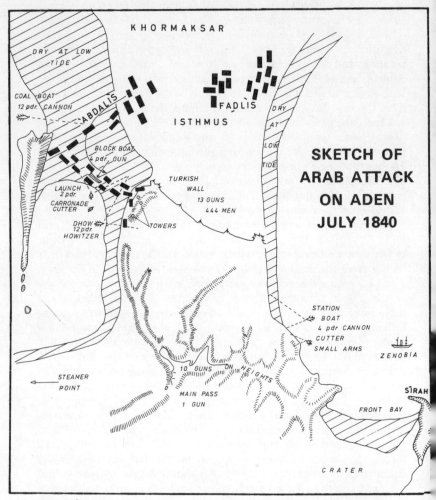

KHORMAKSAR

DRY AT LOW TIDE

COAL BOAT
12 pdr. CANNON

ABDALIS

FADLIS

ISTHMUS

DRY AT LOW TIDE

BLOCK BOAT
4 pdr. GUN

LAUNCH
2 pdr.
CARRONADE
CUTTER

TURKISH
WALL
13 GUNS
444 MEN

DHOW
12 pdr.
HOWITZER

TOWERS

SKETCH OF
ARAB ATTACK
ON ADEN
JULY 1840

STATION
BOAT
4 pdr. CANNON
CUTTER
SMALL ARMS

ZENOBIA

STEAMER
POINT

10 GUNS ON HEIGHTS

MAIN PASS
1 GUN

SÎRAH

FRONT BAY

CRATER

Adapted from Sketch in Haines to Govt. of Bombay 54 of 30 August 1840

Bombay and meanwhile the garrison suffered from scurvy.[17] Fodder
for animals was in short supply and so was wood for firing. During
this period Aden was denuded of the fairly substantial tree cover
which was found there at the occupation.[18] While the prices of
elementary necessities swung violently between high and impossible,
the much looked-for growth in Aden's commerce was hardly worth
thinking of. Men in high places became restive. Carnac warned
Haines in February 1840 that if Aden could not be made valuable

without an expedition to Lahej, it ought to be abandoned.[19] Even
Hobhouse in London began to hesitate.[20]

Sultan Muhsin too experienced difficulties. The blockade of Aden
entailed the renunciation of some glittering opportunities by 'Abdali
farmers and traders. Despite Sultan Muhsin's attempts to maintain
Islamic unity against the 'Franks', men began to slip through with
supplies. The 'Aqrabis had to be coerced at various junctures to
continue their co-operation with the blockaders and ignore Aden's
bribes. Armed patrols were posted to intercept caravans *en route* for
Aden. By the beginning of 1841, even the patience of the 'Abdali
tribesmen was wearing thin. Representations were made to the
Sultan and in April he had to modify his approach and substitute
heavy dues for absolute prohibition on trade with Aden. These dues
were called the 'Aden tax' and at the same time a levy was made on
the Jews at Lahej equivalent to that the Sultan had previously received from their co-religionists at Aden.

For three months the blockade was suspended. But it was reimposed after a dramatic incident at the Aden Gate in August 1841. The
incident involved the Fadli Sultan and one of the sepoy interpreters.
The latter was said to have interfered with some Fadli ladies, and the
Fadli took his revenge in spectacular fashion. Riding up to the Gate
with some members of his family and the chief of the powerful
Marqashi sub-tribe, he summoned the interpreter, who was then
struck down by spears.[21] This bold and somewhat romantic stroke
put new heart into the anti-British party. Enthusiasm for the blockade
was temporarily restored although the lure of profitable business and
mutual suspicion between various groups weakened the resolve of
others.

On 9 August Sultan Muhsin met with the chiefs of the various
'Abdali sections and asked for hostages from each, to ensure respect
for the blockade. On the next day two important chiefs protested that
the order was injurious to their followers' interests and two days later
they escorted a caravan into Aden.[22] The Hawshabi were even more
annoyed and retaliated by blocking the irrigation water to the
'Abdali fields. Nevertheless Sultan Muhsin went on to co-operate
with the Fadli Sultan and the 'Aqrabi Shaykh in building a fort at
Shaykh 'Uthman, which was designed to lock the door finally on Aden
and turn caravans to the rival ports at Shuqra and Little Aden. Once
more Aden became a beleaguered town until 5 October 1841, when
Haines struck a decisive blow. A small force marched out by night
and destroyed the Shaykh 'Uthman fort in a swift action which
caused great alarm at Lahej. The hostile coalition broke up. Simultaneous naval blockades of Shuqra and the 'Aqrabi ports completed
the discomfiture of Aden's enemies. By the end of the year Sultan

Muhsin, the Fadli Sultan and the 'Aqrabi Shaykh were all making overtures to Haines.[23]

The destruction of the forts on the Aden road scotched the last major threat to Aden by blockade. Both the 'Aqrabi and the Fadli made their peace. The Fadli's stipend was renewed and he remained quiet throughout 1842, being more concerned about his failing grip on Dathinah and 'Awdhali to the north-east than with the affairs of Aden.[24] Sultan Muhsin was however unable to come to any settlement with Haines. He could not accept the Political Agent's terms, which included among other things the demand that two of his sons be surrendered as hostages.[25] Haines had formulated this demand in the early months of 1840 and it evidently had a bearing on the vexed question of family politics at Lahej. It faced the Sultan with a most unpleasant choice. Was he to send 'Ali and Fadl, his sons by his favourite wife? Or 'Abd al Karim and his irascible elder full brother 'Abdallah who had a strong following among the slave soldiers, and who in the course of the next year twice faced his father with armed insurrection.[26] If 'Abdallah went, his rival Ahmad's hand would be strengthened, and no doubt this was what Haines had in mind. The complexion of affairs at Lahej had somewhat altered, in that 'Abdallah Katif had been eliminated, after incriminating papers had been found among the British documents captured during the second attack on Aden. His fellow conspirators, Sultan Ahmad and Sayyid Ways, had both had a hand in Katif's killing, and when Haines heard of this at the beginning of 1842 he stopped Sayyid Ways's salary and dismissed him from British service.[27] But the pattern of politics within the ruling house remained the same and Haines's distrust and contempt for Sultan Muhsin continued unabated.

Despite Haines's feelings about Muhsin, an agreement was arrived at in February 1843. One of the key factors in the making of this agreement was the arrival of a troop of fifty irregular horse at Aden in January of that year. Haines had vainly pleaded for three years that such a force be sent to enable him to strike beyond the walls while cautious men in India, fearing involvement in the hinterland, had refused. Haines received firm instructions about their use and was also ordered to drop his demand for hostages from Lahej.[28] Sultan and Political Agent were driven into each other's arms. The arrival of the cavalry at Aden caused alarm at Lahej where there was already apprehension at the hostile attitude recently adopted by the Fadli Sultan. A joint letter was sent by Sultan Muhsin and Ahmad on 20 January seeking friendship. On 29 January, Sultan Muhsin entered Aden, and after discussion a treaty of friendship was signed, under which the Lahej Sultan's schedule of transit dues was recognised and renewal of his stipend promised, provided he kept the peace.[29]

The agreement did not end the feud between Muhsin and Haines's circle. It was renewed in July when Haines's Assistant, Cruttenden, went to visit Lahej and renew his acquaintance with the town which he had first visited in 1836. Cruttenden was well received. But while he was being courteously treated by the Sultan, the subject of Mulla Jaffer's venality was brought up.[30] At Lahej too was 'Alawi bin Zayn, the 'Aydarus Sayyid from Aden, also well received by the Sultan and also interested in his old enemy Jaffer's conduct. Cruttenden, who had heard similar stories about Jaffer on the Somali coast, said he would hear any charges in the Police Court at Aden and on his return Sayyid 'Alawi and others came forward. Things went badly for Jaffer in the court and Haines was hard put to it to save his friend. He delayed remitting the papers to Bombay for two months. When he sent them, he highlighted the corrupt motives of Jaffer's accusers, excused Jaffer's hostile conduct toward Cruttenden in the Court as 'native ignorance' and finally declared Jaffer innocent on all counts. This did not satisfy Haines's superiors. The Political Agent's verdict was accepted but he was ordered to dismiss Jaffer and send him to Bombay by the next steamer.[31] This *cause célèbre* dragged on for most of the year and did not improve relations between Haines and Sultan Muhsin who had submitted one of the most important affidavits in the case. While the case was being studied at Bombay, Haines heard of the mustering of a force at Lahej whose object was reported to be a further attack on Aden, but by the end of the year the men had dispersed and in February 1844 Haines renewed the Anglo-'Abdali agreement.[32]

In the meanwhile relations between the British-held port and the people in its hinterland were steadily improving. Trade was expanding and more tribesmen were finding it in their interest to deal with the settlement. Between 1843 and 1846 the practice of supplying the Aden garrison with fodder and firewood from Bombay was discontinued. These necessities were increasingly brought from the lands behind Aden and provided a considerable amount of employment for poorer tribesmen.[33] By 1844 grain was being brought to Aden down the Hardaba road from areas of surplus north of Qa'taba. In 1845 the first experiments were made in raising vegetables at Lahej for the use of the garrison.[34] Most of these supplies passed through Lahej territory and the Sultan's income from his transit dues exceeded the value of his stipend. By the end of 1843 the presence of British Aden had been accepted, however reluctantly, by the people of its hinterland and the only serious threat to the *status quo* thereafter originated from beyond the mountains to the north.

Throughout the troubled years between 1839 and 1844 the peoples

behind Aden had received encouragement to resist the British from
the rulers of the Yemen coastline. The Egyptians had been somewhat
restrained until the end of 1839 by Muhammad 'Ali's hopes that
Britain could yet be counted on to help him against his suzerain at
Istanbul. Those hopes faded in December 1839 when Palmerston
made his intentions plain by replacing the concilatory Consul
Campbell in Cairo with the fire-eating Hodges.[35] In early 1840
Muhammad 'Ali began to talk of a holy war and opened negotiations
with the Imam of San'a'; he probably had in view an attack on Aden.[36]
But all the Egyptian forces were required to face dangers nearer home
and between March and May their garrisons in the Yemen were
evacuated. This, however, did not seriously diminish the weight of
anti-British pressure from the north. The man to whom the Egyptians
transferred control of the Yemen's seaports was a former employee of
theirs and a member of the powerful Sharifian house of Abu 'Arish who
had formerly ruled over part of the coastline. Sharif Husayn ibn 'Ali
Haydar was a scholar, renowned for piety of a narrow Wahhabi sort.
He had definite views about the integrity of Arabia and did not
hesitate to tell the Governor of Bombay that he wished to see Aden
evacuated.[37] Throughout his period in the Tihama, Sharif Husayn
was an implacable enemy of British Aden and Haines did his best to
pay him back in kind by having the Sharif removed from the Tihama
ports. In the upshot neither succeeded in doing the other serious
injury. The occasional rumours that the much-feared tribesmen of
the Sharif's native 'Asir were marching on Aden never materialised,
and Haines's hopes that the Government would bombard the Sharif's
ports or otherwise injure his interests also came to nothing: England
had too much to fear in the re-awakening French interest in the Red
Sea to allow subversion of existing governments on the coast. British
policy was to spread a safe Ottoman blanket over all parts of the
Arabian coastline not already strongly tied to Britain and Haines
had to watch in frustration as a Turkish Commissioner from Istanbul,
who was supposed to right British wrongs, came to an understanding
with the Sharif and invested him with the cloak of Ottoman integrity
and untouchability.[38]

    The enemies of Haines's enemies tended to become Haines's
friends. It was thus with the Imam of San'a'. The Imams had been at
odds with the Sharifs of Abu 'Arish since the beginning of the century,
when the Sharifs allied with the Wahhabi, breaking shrines and
criticising Sayyids. The Sharifs competed with the Imam for the
allegiance of the tribes of northern Yemen and had seized the Imam's
ports from Hudayda northward. Now that Sharif Husayn was installed along the whole Tihama coastline the Imam was in danger of
being encircled and pushed back to a position of nullity. It was not

difficult to see how Haines could come to a mutually satisfactory agreement with the Imam. Haines wanted the coffee trade of central Yemen, the Imam needed another outlet to the coast. The Imam could mobilise large forces by land but was weak at sea against the guns of Husayn's ports. Haines was strong at sea but could launch no land attack against his enemy at Hudayda and Mocha. The two powers could complement each other's military shortcomings, all that was required was that they concert their actions. Haines had grasped this point almost before Sharif Husayn had come to power and through his friend, the British agent at Mocha, Hajj 'Abd al Rasul, Haines worked toward some understanding with the Imam.[39]

Haines however was limited by his instructions which precluded a direct attack on Sharif Husayn. In 1841 he could do no more than promise that if the Imam would tell him the time of his attack, he would send a vessel simultaneously to Husayn's port 'for the protection of British property'.[40] The other limitation was the extent of Imamic power which was now a simulacrum of what it had been in the seventeenth and eighteenth centuries. Between the beginning of 1841 and mid-1842 the Imam had gathered considerable support, especially among the Dhu Muhammad and Dhu Husayn rulers in the Ta'izz area, and was ready to move against Mocha. During this period six different missions came from the Imam's camp to Haines offering increasingly important concessions – the renewal of the 1821 treaty, the cession of Zayla on the Somali coast, the opening of the coffee trade from San'a' and finally, when the Imam was hard-pressed at Ibb in May 1842, Mocha and the whole Tihama, including Ta'izz and the Hajariya was offered to the British.[41] The next contact was made in March 1843 when the Imam had raised a force to advance on Mocha. Once more envoys came to Aden offering commercial concessions in return for naval co-operation. As on previous occasions, Haines sent a friendly but non-commital reply and wrote to his superiors suggesting that the Imam's proposals be taken up. He got a chilling reply from Lord Ellenborough, the Governor-General, who was now slashing all distant commitments and retreating into fortress India. Ellenborough declared that he had no wish to mix up the British government with the unimportant affairs of the Imam of San'a'.[42]

Haines's protracted negotiations with the Imam could hardly have been regarded with complacency by the Sultans of Lahej. An Anglo-Imamic combination could as easily be repeated nearer at hand, with Lahej as the victim. The harsh references made to the Sultan's obstruction of commerce in conversations between Haines and the Imam's agents were an indication of the way the wind could blow.[43] The treaty with Lahej in 1843 and its renewal in 1844 did not produce a significant change in Haines's attitude toward Sultan Muhsin, and when a new Imam acceded in 1844 and began to put pressure on Lahej and the neighbouring districts, Haines did nothing to stop him. In August the Imam marched south to Qa'taba and demanded tribute from the hinterland rulers. Some of them sent favourable replies but Sultan Muhsin refused, and said that he was tributary to the British.[44] The Imam's emissary then came to see Haines who gave answers to his questions which tended to encourage rather than discourage an Imamic attack on Lahej. This did not please the Bombay Government who only got to know of it after extracting a full report from Haines of what had passed. They said that Haines's letter to the Imam 'encourages him to subject the different chiefs now independent, whereas the interests of the British government would suggest a different policy'. By the time Bombay's reproof reached him, Haines himself had begun to reassess the danger to Aden implicit in the Imam's southward movement. But he was slow to reach the conclusion that Lahej might be a useful buffer and he refused to provide Sultan Muhsin with powder and shot for use in the event of a Yemeni attack. Haines's feud with Sultan Muhsin cut very deep.[45]

Haines had hoped that the Imam intended to continue his predecessor's war against Sharif Husayn. Instead the two veered round toward the end of 1844 and settled their differences to combine against the British. In the first months of 1845 the Imam gave Ta'izz to the Sharif as a base for an attack on Aden. Prayers were said in the mosques for the success of the planned expedition against the port. A composite force was gathered from the Sharif's fighting men, men of the Bani Yam, the Zaydi Dhu Muhammad and Dhu Husayn and the forces of the Hajariya Shaykh — in all some 20,000 men.[46] In Aden the concentration of forces at Ta'izz was regarded as a real danger. Work on the fortifications was speeded up, the garrison was brought to readiness and an extra naval vessel was sent from Bombay.[47] But in April 1845 the Sharif's disparate team broke up as a result of quarrels between him and the Hajariya Shaykh and the threat to Aden passed away as quickly as it had appeared. The men at Ta'izz had received no help from Lahej. Sultan Muhsin had ignored their calls to join them, possibly because the appeal to *jihad* was somewhat blunted by the ambiguity of the Sharif's attitude toward 'Abdali independence.[48]

The state of the Yemen and the whole of Western Arabia during this period was such that in the following year a religious leader came near to succeeding where Sharif Husayn and the Imam had failed. In the summer of 1846 Sayyid Isma'il ibn al Hassan al Husayni began preaching a *jihad* against the infidel in Mocha. Moving southward he gathered followers whom he impressed by his words and promises of immunity from British shells and bullets.[49] As in the case of Faqih Sa'id, another prophet who had arisen in southern Yemen in 1840, calling himself the 'Regenerator of Religion', Sayyid Isma'il's millenarian appeal gathered support from the lower classes in the Yemen. The established leaders of society, such as Sharif Husayn and the Imam, held aloof.[50] The Sultan of Lahej was no more eager than his counterparts in the Yemen to risk involvement, but he was carried forward by a popular upsurge in Sayyid Isma'il's favour among the people of Aden's hinterland. When the prophet arrived in 'Abdali country with 2,000 followers, Sultan Muhsin contrived to avoid the issue by abdicating and handing his Sultanate temporarily to Sayyid Isma'il. Muhsin's sons joined the *jihad* and the 'Aqrabi and Fadli chiefs also brought in their men. On 15 August the large composite *jihadi* force encamped at Shaykh 'Uthman and on the same day a long and damaging blockade of Aden began, which was eventually to reduce the garrison to great straits. On 27 August, after adjuring Haines in due form to change his faith, Sayyid Isma'il and some 2,000 men advanced to Aden's walls without stratagem and with banners flying. There they were met by withering fire from the improved defences and gunboats moored alongside the isthmus.[51] This rebuff weakened the hold of the Sayyid over his followers, although he himself had miraculously escaped from a 68-pounder shell which failed to explode under his horse. On 28 August a meeting was held to discuss a new attempt, and a more sensible plan for a night assault was drawn up. But before the meeting closed, Sayyid Isma'il quarrelled with and tried to arrest the 'Aqrabi Shaykh. The Fadli helped his fellow chief to escape. There was fighting and the camp broke up in uproar. Sayyid Isma'il's spell was broken and his followers gradually dispersed. Their departure was hastened by an outbreak of cholera which, with the sister plague of smallpox, struck at South-West Arabia with devastating frequency in the middle years of the nineteenth century and contributed to the general malaise.[52] After Sayyid Isma'il's failure the blockade of Aden gradually eased and in November it ended after Haines had begun a strict counter-blockade of Shuqra and Bir Ahmad.

The attitude of the hinterland peoples during this episode was a grave disappointment to British policy-makers. Bombay, previously so anxious to conciliate the 'Abdali, contemplated an attack on Lahej. Hobhouse, one of the architects of British Aden, now regarded the place as of 'very questionable value'.[53] Haines thought once more of concluding an alliance with the Imam and letting him overrun the hinterland. The man he now had to deal with, however, was a different character from the weak and dissolute 'Ali Mansur who had threatened Lahej in 1844. The latter had abdicated in July 1845 in favour of Sayyid Muhammad bin Yahya whom Haines adjudged a 'crafty, shrewd politician'. Haines had his eye on the coffee trade and believed that if the Imam once secured Lahej he would push the common enemy, Sharif Husayn, out of Ta'izz and Ibb. Bombay was also interested in the coffee trade but was not prepared to secure it at the price of alienating the hinterland peoples by advising the Imam to subjugate them.[54] Haines adjusted his policy to this instruction. He still sought the coffee trade, but not at the expense of the hinterland tribes. Improved relations with Lahej after Sultan Muhsin's death in 1847 confirmed this attitude and in 1848 Haines suggested that in any future agreement with the Imam Qa'taba should be marked out as the southern limit of his possessions.[55]

By the time Haines had changed his mind, the rulers behind Aden had also changed their opinion about Imamic rule. In 1845, when the new Imam had come to power, he had appeared to be less committed to the Zaydi elements who had traditionally lent strength to Imamic regimes. He gained some popularity in the south and some of the rulers in Aden's hinterland recognised his rule.[56] But in the ensuing years the Imam became more closely identified with the great Hashid and Bakil confederations of the north. His stock in the Aden hinterland fell and, although he still declared that he would right the wrongs of all parties, the chiefs around Aden said that they would never tolerate a Zaydi master.[57] In March 1848 they refused to obey his summons to go to him at Mocha.[58] By that date Mocha was in the Imam's hands. The 'shrewd and crafty politician' had succeeded where his predecessors failed. Sharif Husayn was reeling from his blows and later in the year the Sharif was locked in an Imamic prison after suffering a severe defeat.[59] For a moment it looked as though the Yemen and the Tihama might once again be brought under united rule. But a year's warfare between the Imam and the family of the imprisoned Sharif reduced both sides to a state of exhaustion. Trade was paralysed, mercenaries could not be paid. The whole basis of stable government had been sapped away. In July 1849, making a final tergiversation in a career that had been filled with successful ambiguities, the Imam invited Ottoman forces into the Yemen to support his rule. This time he had gone too far. The entry of the Turkish soldiers into San'a' was greated by a Zaydi uprising. The soldiers were massacred. The Imam himself was deposed and later murdered. The Turks were left holding the seaport towns and little else, while the Yemen highlands slipped into political confusion out of which no stable government emerged until the Turks took over in 1872.[60]

Meanwhile Haines's policy toward the hinterland had undergone a profound change. The death of his old enemy Sultan Muhsin in November 1847 cleared away the major obstacle to an understanding between Haines and Lahej. Before this event Haines had watched the 'Abdali with profound distrust. After Muhsin's death Haines backed the new men at Lahej to the hilt. Haines showed toward Sultans Ahmad and 'Ali the same tenacious loyalty that he bestowed on others whom he regarded as his friends. He became more 'Abadli than the 'Abdali and in his last five years as Political Agent the 'Nawab' policy which the Lahej ruling house had so long hankered after was the order of the day at Aden.

Within a few weeks of Sultan Muhsin's death the new alignment began to emerge and on 24 December 1847 Sultan Ahmad issued a proclamation that he would compel the surrounding tribes to respect his authority. Haines told Bombay that he intended to encourage this line of conduct as the best guarantee of tranquility in Aden's neighbourhood.[61] The pact between Haines and Ahmad was sealed at a conference held at Aden between 29 February and 9 March 1848.[62] Haines personally met the Sultan at the Gate and accompanied him to his house in the town, to the accompaniment of a salute of honour. Ahmad's father had never been welcomed by Haines in this warm-hearted fashion. A new treaty was negotiated providing for a substantial reduction in the transit dues levied by Lahej on goods entering Aden; fodder and provisions for the garrison were exempted altogether. Ahmad apparently accepted Haines's argument that lower rates would lead to a rise in trade and hence that his loss of revenue would be only temporary. In any case the Sultan stood to gain on other counts. The treaty provided that he would encourage the cultivation of vegetables for the garrison. This could involve some profitable transactions. The commissariat contract was a valuable one and it had become more or less part of Haines's patronage. Haines promised to provide seeds; he no doubt also indicated that he would ensure that any vegetables the Sultan offered would be sold at an interesting price.[63] Another item that was most probably negotiated on the side was the fodder contract which the 'Abdali had been trying to secure and which Haines had hitherto kept out of their hands.[64] Sultan Ahmad probably stood to gain as much revenue out of such hidden monopolies as he expected to lose from the reduction of his transit dues.

On the political side Ahmad undertook to stop plundering on the roads and made himself responsible for the acts of his own subjects. At first sight this might seem straightforward. But in fact the men the treaty was referring to were only in a limited sense the Sultan's subjects as had been shown so often in the past. Now Aden recognised them as his subjects, and Ahmad was expected to make the assertion a reality. This would not be easy and Ahmad asked that the Government take his dominions under its protection, send an engineer to reconstruct his capital's walls and provide him with four six-pounder guns. He asked also that the stipends of all the hinterland tribes except the Fadli be paid through him instead of directly by the Aden Government. Finally he wanted a house in Aden to enable him to keep in close touch with the authorities there. Haines recommended that all these points be met except for the provision of cannon.[65]

Bombay took nine months to reply and then it turned down all of Ahmad's requests.[66] But this did not prevent Haines from acting in the spirit of the Sultan's suggestions. There were no further flirtations with the Imams. The other rulers in the hinterland could expect no help from Aden in schemes hostile to the 'Abadli, on the contrary Haines worked hard against anyone who tried to challenge Lahej's growing power. By the time Haines left office the Sultans had come to believe that the treaty itself obliged the British government to protect them against their neighbours.[67] There could be no mistaking the significance of what occurred in Aden in the spring of 1848 as far as the people in the hinterland were concerned. The conference between Haines and Sultan Ahmad was an imposing affair; 160 leaders from the 'Abdali area attended and after the conclusion of the agreement Haines and Ahmad distributed $(M.T.)1,350 among them.[68] On return to his capital Ahmad acted with a firmer hand. In July 1848 he compelled the quarrelling 'Uzaybi and 'Aqrabi to come and settle their differences before him and a council of chiefs. The 'Uzaybi were the largest and most powerful section in 'Abdali territory; the 'Aqrabi were up to this point an entirely independent group and had been so for more than fifty years. In the same month Ahmad took the Hawshabi Sultan under his protection after the latter had been threatened by rebellious tribesmen. He seized and punished men from other tribes who were caught plundering on the roads. By the end of 1848 Sultan Ahmad was the strongest man in the interior. The Fadli Sultan and the Aqrabi Shaykh were coming together in alarm to protect themselves.[69] And then Ahmad died of smallpox on 18 January 1849.

Ahmad's successor was his brother 'Ali, twenty-nine years old, handsome and energetic but already tending to corpulence. 'Ali was in a somewhat weaker position than his predecessor. His right to the Sultanate was challenged by his brother 'Abdallah, who was born about the same time as he from a different mother and who had previously appeared to be the second man in politics at Lahej after Ahmad.[70] 'Ali's election was a rushed affair in the midst of the smallpox epidemic that had produced the vacancy.[71] He claimed the support of two-thirds of the tribe. He claimed also that he was

Sultan 'Ali Muhsin of Lahej.

designated by Ahmad as his successor and had been his father's
favourite son. Whatever 'Ali's claims, 'Abdallah did not accept them,
and this made it more difficult for 'Ali to follow the path that his
predecessor had marked out. Haines however had no doubts about
his right to rule and in May 1849, Ahmad's treaty with Aden was
renewed in 'Ali's name.[72] At the same time the area of co-operation
between the Sultan and the Political Agent was extended by an
agreement concerning a water scheme at the Hiswah. Hiswah lay
at the bottom of Aden's western bay and was a convenient spot from
which water could be brought by boat to the shipping in the harbour
and the growing population at Steamer Point. A tripartite arrangement was arrived at by which Sayyid 'Alawi of Aden leased the
Hiswah wells from Sultan 'Ali, installed the necessary equipment
and undertook a four-year contract with the Naval Department for
the supply of water at a fixed rate. Haines and Sultan 'Ali guaranteed
the installation against marauders.[73] Aden could thus count on a
regular supply of water and 'Ali was cut in on another of Aden's more
lucrative monopolies. The only defect, and it proved a grave one,
was that 'Ali's right to lease had been conjured out of nowhere. If the
land belonged to anyone it belonged to the 'Aqrabi Shaykh in whose
territory it lay.[74] Even Sayyid 'Alawi who was supposed to have
convinced Haines that the 'Aqrabi Shaykh was dependent on Lahej,
covered his investment by a separate secret agreement with the
'Aqrabi in September 1849.[75] The Hiswah contract was to become
both the testing-point and the Achilles heel of the Aden–Lahej
alliance.

Trouble began as soon as work started on the Hiswah depot in
the autumn of 1849. The 'Aqrabi at once made threatening gestures.
Haines said he should be coerced. But conciliatory measures were
taken and matters were smoothed over until May 1850 when a boat
from the Indian Navy vessel *Auckland* landed some sailors at the
Hiswah. Their presence was believed by the 'Aqrabi to be connected
with the land dispute and there was a fight in which one sailor was
killed and another wounded.[76] Haines demanded the surrender of the
murderer, who was well known by name. He also called on Sultan
'Ali to depose Shaykh Haydar of the 'Aqrabis and put another in his
place.[77] Both these demands involved a departure from accepted
behaviour in the hinterland. Muslims had never before been delivered
to the British for punishment and Sultans did not depose Shaykhs of
tribal groups which did not recognise their authority. If Sultan 'Ali
were to meet Haines's demands it would have to be by an act of
violence. In July 'Ali prepared for the struggle by recruiting three
thousand mercenaries from Yafi'i country to add to the Sultanate's
standing force of three to four hundred slave soldiers. In the autumn

he added some 'Awlaqi to these, but was still unable to launch his offensive. Before he could do so he had to deal with those in his immediate vicinity who were resisting the growth of his personal power. Within the ruling family 'Abdallah provided a focus for resistance and various sections of the 'Abdali were up in arms. The long-heralded attack on the 'Aqrabi did not in fact begin until January 1851, when 'Ali had more or less overcome opposition at home and added an eighteen-pounder gun to his armoury with skilled men to work it. Four thousand men then marched on the 'Aqrabi's stronghold at Bir Ahmad and took it by storm.[78]

This pleased Haines and he urged 'Ali to press home his victory. He wanted Bir Ahmad razed to the ground, Shaykh Haydar imprisoned until the murderer was surrendered, and the road between Aden and the Yemen through 'Aqrabi country forced open. But powerful voices were raised in the 'Abdali tribe against any such revolutionary programme. The influential Sayyids of Wahut, who traditionally turbanned the Lahej Sultans, worked against decisive action. Sayyid Muhsin Ways, still spinning intrigues and no friend to Sultan 'Ali, added his weight to the balance. Ali gave way to these pressures and Shaykh Haydar was reinstalled, Bir Ahmad was left intact and the murderer was not apprehended.[79]

While the Bir Ahmad affair was thus petering out inconclusively, an incident occurred which gravely complicated the development of Haines's new policy. On 2 March, Captain Milne of the Aden Garrison, returning from one of those visits to Lahej which officers were now more frequently making under the new regime, was assassinated while spending the night at the 'Abdali village of Wahut. His assassin was a Sayyid who resented the presence of a Christian in his village, and this gave a most serious twist to the affair. For if it was a grave matter to hand over an ordinary Muslim to Christian justice, to do so with a descendant of the Prophet was even worse. But the life of a British officer was valuable too. The official world in India demanded retribution and commanded that no effort should be spared to bring the murderer to book. Haines had to tread with the greatest care for over and above his personal feelings about the fate of a fellow officer, he had to beware the wrath of the military establishment which had never had confidence in his methods. On 15 March Haines demanded from Sultan 'Ali the surrender of the murderer. A month later he insisted that 'Ali either surrender or kill both murderers on pain of being regarded henceforward as an enemy.[80] The suggestion that counter-assassination would suffice represented a concession to 'Ali's difficulties. But even this was too much for the Sultan to perform. It was reported that Milne's assassin had conveniently fled to Fadli country and of course 'Ali could do nothing there. The next step was to seek by bribery to get the man returned. Haines reported that one of the Fadli Sultan's brothers had been won over to the 'Abdali cause in this way. The Fadli Sultan himself received a bribe, but the wanted man remained untouched.[81] Then in July 1851 yet another murder took place. This time the victims were two sailors from a wrecked merchantman and the man responsible was a member of the 'Uzaybi section of the 'Abdali tribe. Again Haines demanded vengeance and Sultan 'Ali managed to seize the culprit. But once arrested, Sultan 'Ali could not decide what to do with the man. Haines suggested a public execution but 'Ali feared this would provoke an 'Uzaybi uprising and possibly an even wider revolt among the tribesmen.[82] It now seemed that direct British action alone would restore lost prestige. By July 1851 Bombay favoured aggressive action while the Governor-General went one better and said that Fadli country should be visited with 'fire and sword'.[83] With these strongly worded despatches from his superiors, Haines began to issue ultimata informing Sultan 'Ali that Fadli country as well as Lahej would be attacked. Still he received nothing more than promises from Lahej. And then came the great deception. The promised reinforcements which were to mete out the general punishment never arrived. Instead Haines received a peremptory order toward the end of August 1851 from the Secret Committee in London prohibiting any sortie from Aden by the garrison.[84]

In the meanwhile the whole business of pursuing the murderers had produced a revulsion of feeling in the hinterland. The spirit of the *jihad* was abroad again, nurtured by food scarcity, cattle disease and social turmoil, as well as by infidel assertiveness. When Haines asked him to surrender the criminals, the Fadli Sultan sent a curt reply asking why 'Franks' should be allowed to roam in his country. In the same vein the Fadli wrote to Sultan 'Ali that 'these *faranj* scorn all other people' and pointed out that by Arab custom a demand could not be made for the surrender of a person.[85] In October a wonder-working seer from the Yemen calling himself the 'righteous delegate' arrived at Lahej. The Sultan was obliged to entertain him; his councillors considered the holy man's proposals and there was a danger of an active renewal of the *jihad*.[86]

The best that Haines could do in the circumstances was to salvage the Aden–Lahej alliance. He had carefully preserved his contacts with Sultan 'Ali throughout the worst period of crisis and contrived to present the Fadli Sultan as the greater villian even though all the murders had occurred on what was nominally 'Abdali territory. Now that there was to be no march inland Haines urged Bombay to renew the 'Abdali's stipend which had been stopped in the summer and asked also that the Sultan be given a three-pounder gun to strengthen his authority. For his part 'Ali had the 'Uzaybi murderer of the seamen done to death secretly on 22 October, after some of the principal 'Abdali chiefs had been bribed to overlook the deed. He also signed a bond promising to deal with the murderer of the sailors from the *Auckland* and Haines accepted this as a satisfactory acquittal by the Sultan of his responsibilities. The stipend was renewed and the Sultan was presented with his gun.[87]

The work of consolidating the Lahej–Aden axis and augmenting 'Ali's authority was resumed. The expected clash with the 'Uzaybi followed closely on the private execution of their arrested man and they were dealt with harshly by the Sultan. The section was split up, five of their principal men were imprisoned and forty tribesmen fled to Fadli country.[88] Aden added its own contribution. The port had now been declared free of customs duties and the immediate effect of this measure was to throw the lion's share of the trade with the interior into Adeni and 'Abdali hands. The small competing 'Aqrabi ports and the Fadli port of Shuqra were severely hit. Haines drove the lesson home by blockading the 'Aqrabi's ports – ostensibly in retaliation for the murder of the *Auckland* seamen. The 'Aqrabi Shaykh depended heavily for his revenue on the dues levied at his ports. The Fadli somewhat less so. Both were likely to be ompoverished by the diversion of trade to Aden. Both could see that while they were becoming poor, their neighbour at Lahej was flourishing financially from his close connection with Aden.

This situation set the pattern for politics in the hinterland during the next ten years. At the heart of the violent and confused struggle that developed stood the mercantile communities of Aden and Lahej which were determined to grasp control of the really profitable long-distance trades, particularly the trade in coffee. The two communities understood each other very well for both in Aden and in Lahej the traditional trading networks and many of the crafts were predominantly in the hands of the Jewish community. The similarly oriented Jewish ghettoes that were strung out along the routes towards the heart of Yemen no doubt represented the remnant of a formerly more active trading system. Their religion and their race ensured that these merchants would remain politically quiescent. They needed protection and this was supplied by 'Ali Bubakr and Haines at Aden and Sultan 'Ali at Lahej. For this protection the Sultan expected a return in higher tax revenue and *ad hoc* aids. It was for him to beat down or buy off competitors and disappointed transporters who had not been incorporated into the system. In the summer of 1851 Sultan 'Ali had bought the Fadli off. In July 1852 he did so again, and then marched on the fort at Bir Ahmad in August. Bir Ahmad did not fall but the 'Aqrabi was sufficiently frightened to make gestures of fealty and discuss the transfer to 'Ali of half his revenue, previously pledged to the Fadli. This brought the Fadli Sultan back to the charge and the closing months of 1852 were filled with rumours that the Shuqra chief was bringing the hillmen down on to the fertile fields at Lahej. For his part, Sultan 'Ali abortively schemed with Haines to pay back the Fadli in his own coin by bribing the 'Awlaqi to attack the fields at Abyan.[89]

During all this scheming of combinations and counter-combinations, Sultan 'Ali was gradually consolidating his grip on Aden's economic links with the hinterland. In August 1852 he profited from 'Aqrabi weakness to build a fort at the Hiswah with Haines's assistance. In February 1853 he erected another fort at Shaykh 'Uthman[90] These strongpoints enabled him both to protect his own traffic to Aden and to control the movement of 'Aqrabi and Fadli caravans toward the port. He set up a customs post at Shaykh 'Uthman and levied transit dues on traffic making for Aden. At once the other chiefs were up in arms. The Fadli sought to mobilise his own men and all the tribes on the major roads running inward to Aden from the Yemen. Plundering on the roads reached a new pitch. During the spring and summer of 1853, prices of necessities fluctuated wildly at Aden as the struggle burgeoned and subsided in the interior and at times the blockade conditions of 1840 were repeated.[91] Sultan 'Ali built up a large permanent mercenary force which numbered four hundred or more, specifically assigned to the protection of the roads. By June 1853 a proportion of the caravans were moving in armed convoy and on 3 June a particularly valuable caravan of 686 camels entered Aden under the protection of no less than 500 mounted 'Abdali men and 1,500 foot.[92] During the next year the battle for the roads swayed back and forth between Sultan 'Ali and his Fadli and 'Aqrabi opponents. Each sought to involve the hill tribes, and this time the rumours of their movement were confirmed: 3,000 'Awlaqi matchlockmen and 2,000 armed with other weapons swept down through Dathinah into Fadli country and pursued their devastating path as far as Assala before the Fadli Sultan succeeded in arresting their progress by the desperate expedient of filling the wells.[93] The 'Abdali were able to harvest in peace, supplies flowed into Aden and Haines took the opportunity to arrange a general truce to last two months. Haines congratulated himself on having usurped the Sayyids' usual function. But his truce, unlike theirs, was a barbed arrangement and the 'Aqrabi was once more to be made the victim of circumstances. The 'Aqrabi elders were called together and it was hoped that they would agree to renounce the Fadli alliance and admit 'Abdali suzerainty. When this did not transpire, Haines gave a firm promise to the Lahej Sultan that before the truce ended he would induce the Bombay Government to destroy once and for all the plundering base at Bir Ahmad.[94]

Haines was not destined to redeem that promise, or even to see the end of the truce. By April 1854, when the truce was due to end, Haines was at Bombay faced with charges of malversation of government funds. Haines's last five years at Aden had been far from happy. He had had the unpleasant experience of finding that his earlier sanguine hopes of expanding Aden's trade had been misplaced. The constant resurgence of anti-British feeling in the hinterland and the difficulty of breaking through the tangled net of inter-tribal politics confused and depressed him. He was in fact involved in a war that was eventually to shift in a substantial fashion the basic trade patterns and social relationships in the Aden hinterland. Those that would lose by such a transformation inevitably resisted his efforts to replace the diverse trading networks of the area with a dominant Aden–Lahej axis and to establish a power constellation that would ensure that the bulk of the new surpluses generated would flow into the hands of Aden merchants and 'Abdali Sultans. For Haines the growth of Aden trade was the prime consideration; who should control and profit from that trade was uppermost in the minds of his allies. For those outside the magic circle, what Haines and his friends were doing represented a major threat to their social and political positions and their resistance prevented the full establishment of the new system in Haines's time. In the meanwhile Aden paid in terms of plundering, special taxes and 'Abdali monopolies for Haines's efforts to put Sultan 'Ali into a commanding political position.[95] Nevertheless Haines remained true to the 'Abdali alliance. He provided shot for Sultan 'Ali's guns, he kept the 'Aqrabi's port under blockade, he facilitated the 'Awlaqi–'Abdali alliance and at one critical moment he moved in gunboats to cover the Hiswah.[96] He therefore watched with growing disappointment the repeated failures of the Lahej Sultan to consolidate his authority. He could not understand how Sultan 'Ali allowed the 'Aqrabi chief to slip free when he had him in his grasp in January 1851. He entreated 'Ali to crush Bir Ahmad but without avail.[97] At each stage when the dust of conflict subsided, the Lahej Sultan still seemed no more than a political *primus inter pares* among the hinterland chiefs and Aden's trade was still subject to frequent and damaging attacks.

While Haines could report little apparent progress in the war to transform hinterland society, his own position as Political Agent became increasingly uneasy. An adjustment in the auditing system at Aden in 1852 revealed a large deficit in the cash balances in the Treasury and rumours of Haines's displacement began to circulate.[98]

He was given time to find the error or the missing funds and the matter dragged on for another year until in September 1853, when no satisfactory explanation had been offered, a Special Commission was sent to Aden to help him with his enquiries. The Commissioners found the Aden accounts in a chaotic state and Haines's answers to their enquiries were evasive and unco-operative. They were however able to learn enough to realise that the deficiency was not the result of a mere accounting error. The Treasury had in fact been robbed of some £28,000 and all the evidence seemed to point to Haines as the man responsible.[99] He was recalled and on 8 April 1854 he arrived in Bombay to face charges of fraud and embezzlement of public funds.

Haines could hardly have fallen foul of Government on such a count at a more inopportune moment. In the spring of 1854, Bombay was seething with intrigue. Major James Outram, a man with powerful connections who seemed to thrive on controversy, had in the previous year unearthed a mass of corruption in the State of Baroda and his efforts to stamp out this so called system of khutput involved him in a violent dispute with the Government of Bombay. Charges and counter-charges were flung about in official correspondence and the press. Government officials entered fully into the combat; the then Governor, Lord Falkland, proved quite incapable of controlling the situation.[100] Doubt was cast on the integrity, financial or otherwise, of men in the highest places, and two of the four members of the Bombay Council fell under suspicion.[101] Towards the end of 1853, Lord Falkland left Bombay under a cloud, and his successor, Lord Elphinstone, took office with a firm determination to restore discipline in the Presidency. He was backed by Sir Charles Wood at the India Board, who told him to 'spare no man who deserves rebuke or punishment. . . . If a man is amenable to any tribunal which exists or can be created, let him be fairly and openly tried.'[102] These words were written before Haines's case broke upon the public scene, but they were in the Governor's mail when the Aden Commissioners' report was brought before him.

Apart from the new Governor's desire to restore standards of public rectitude, there was no initial prejudice against Haines on other grounds. Both Elphinstone's and Wood's first reaction to the news that Haines was under suspicion was one of dismay. Both regarded him as a satisfactory officer who was doing his job well.[103] But as they became acquainted with the evidence their attitude hardened, for it would be difficult to scrutinise the papers without coming to the conclusion that Haines's financial stewardship at Aden left practically everything to be desired.[104] It would be unjust to say that Haines had deliberately embezzled public funds. But what he had done amounted to very much the same thing. Under Haines's regime the Aden Treasury had not been an ordinary depository of public funds. Without any authority he had made it into something in the nature of a central bank for the settlement. Since it was open only three days a month, the Treasury was seldom used for the ordinary transaction of public business. Most of the money received and disbursed went through the hands of Veerchund Ameerchund, the Indian brokers to the Aden Government. Veerchund Ameerchund discounted bills drawn on the Bombay Government by Haines for the payment of public accounts and held the proceeds in their coffers. Haines then authorised disbursements on public account by notes of hand to these brokers.[105] This proceeding may have been irregular but was not criminal. More suspicious was Haines's practice of buying bills on financial institutions in Bombay, London and Marseilles, and using this means to transmit savings from his own salary out of Aden. In return for certain of those bills he gave notes of hand authorising payments in dollars from Veerchund Ameerchund's general pool, and in at least one case there was no record of his having paid in an equivalent sum from his own resources. Furthermore over certain periods he remitted monies to England in excess of his own total salary during those periods.[106] This also was suspicious, but was certainly not the reason for the enormous deficiency of £28,000, which exceeded Haines's total salary during the whole of his period of office. Nor, in all probability, was it the reason for any substantial part of that deficiency.

Under Haines the Aden Treasury was a bank and acted as a bank. It therefore issued loans in addition to its brokerage business. Some of these loans were easily traced. A prominent Parsi merchant, Sorabji Cowasji, was lent money to improve his hotel. Haines himself borrowed money to build a house.[107] But the largest borrower, and almost certainly the one responsible for a major part of the deficiency, was 'Ali Bubakr, the son of the former Governor of Aden.[108] By 1854 this man had become a key figure in Haines's political and commercial system and filled part of the place left by Mulla Jaffer. His commercial activities extended to most of the lucrative branches of Aden's trade and particularly to those which were connected with politics. He was a labour contractor to the Government and supplier of vegetables from the interior for the Commissariat.[109] He was a party to the Hiswah water agreement and he was the man who signed the agreement to provide water at Steamer Point with his friend Sayyid 'Alawi acting as a sort of sleeping partner in the business.[110] He claimed to have great influence over the trade to the Fadli country and it was probably he who was the Aden merchant who helped Sultan 'Ali to subsidise the Fadli in 1851.[111] He had played a major part in bringing about the downfall of Mulla Jaffer, which would have made him *persona grata* at Lahej and his influence there was secure.[112] He must also have taken part in the export trade to the interior, for he exchanged dollars for rupees at the Aden Treasury.[113] Finally he was heavily involved in the coffee trade and acted as broker to the French and American firms at Aden which bought up the crop.[114] In 1850 Haines had complained that the expansion of the coffee trade was being hampered by the fact that the Aden merchants had insufficient capital to provide cargoes for the American vessels.[115] He apparently used Treasury funds to fill the breach for large short-term advances were made to 'Ali Bubakr to enable him to fulfil his coffee contracts. Haines's relations with 'Ali Bubakr were, if anything, more compromising than those he had with Veerchund Ameerchund. After his trial it was discovered that Haines had actually been selling water from the wells in his own garden to 'Ali Bubakr to enable the latter to fulfil his contract with the Government, while Government departments were paying extortion-ate prices for water brought from outside the settlement.[116] More serious was the fact that 'Ali Bubakr's accounts, unlike those of Veerchund Ameerchund, never came to light. He said that as Haines's advances were short-term he had made no note of them.[117] It was therefore difficult to determine how far 'Ali Bubakr was indebted to the Aden Government and what use he had made of the funds. There can be little doubt however that a large part of the deficit was due to 'Ali Bubakr's failure to pay his debts. Such a defalcation would not have been surprising in view of the fact that 'Ali Bubakr's fortunes must have been closely tied to those of the settle-ment as a whole and in 1852 and 1853 troubles in the interior had brought the latter to a low ebb. Haines's providing him with water to enable him to maintain his contract may have represented an attempt to shore up a failing concern. It was the opinion of the well-informed Chaplain at Aden, G. P. Badger, that Haines's involvement with 'Ali Bubakr was the main cause of his downfall.[118]

Haines's position in 1854 therefore was essentially that of a banker whose creditors had secured a foreclosure order and found an un-favourable balance in the accounts. Haines himself seemed to regard his plight in these terms. When the deficit had first been discovered he had asked for time to regulate his affairs; when faced with the charges he promised to repay the money out of his own resources.[119] But of course he had no right to be in the banking business, and the money he had been using had not been his. The Bombay Government can hardly be blamed for determining to bring him to book. It was however far from easy to see how this could effectively be done. Haines was a Government officer but was not in India; he was a naval captain but not on marine duty. It appeared that a court-martial was not legally possible and in any case this method of trial had its dangers, since Haines was the most senior officer but one in the whole Indian Navy.[120] Finally it was decided that he should be tried on criminal charges of fraud and embezzlement before a Bombay jury. The decision was made with considerable misgivings for the leniency of Bombay juries in cases of this nature was well known. Nor was the invitation of the alleged criminal to a sailing party by the Commander in-Chief of the Indian Navy a very encouraging sign of public impartiality.[121] The prestige of the Bombay Government was not high, and there was a powerful current of feeling in Haines's favour.

Haines's trial took place in July 1854 and was followed with the greatest interest by all classes of the community. The Prosecution marshalled the facts with convincing logic and confined its case to the surest ground – Haines's unrepaid withdrawals from the Treasury through Veerchund Ameerchund. The Defence on the other hand made little attempt to present a factual refutation of what the Prosecution had said. Instead, it stressed Haines's great services to the Government, and without producing much in the way of concrete evidence, asked the jury to consider whether there might be some element of doubt. The Prosecution's case was exceptionally strong and was such as would have convinced most juries even though the bald term 'embezzlement' would have been a bad characterisation of Haines's activities. Nevertheless two Grand Juries acquitted Haines completely on two of the three counts and the Government in despair dropped the third charge.[122] Opinion at Bombay was generally in favour of Haines's acquittal and when the verdict was delivered 'one loud burst of approbation broke out among the crowds who thronged the court', and the prisoner himself was 'unable to control his feelings'.[123]

But Lord Elphistone had no intention of letting Haines go scot-free.[124] Much had been made during and before the trial of Haines's willingness to make good the deficiency. The Governor therefore called on him to honour his pledge and pay. But Haines had probably meant that he would pay if he could remain in the service and settle the debt by instalments. When faced with a demand for immediate payment he began to back out. This convinced Elphinstone that he was a 'rascal', and by order of Government Haines was cashiered from the service and thrown into a debtor's prison.[125] Further negotiations ensued and the Government moderated its demands, dropped the requirement for full payment and offered to release Haines if he would surrender all his property as part payment. But Haines refused, kept his property and remained in gaol until 1860, when he was released a few days before his death.[126]

In many quarters the Government's conduct was regarded as unduly harsh. At the time charges of victimisation were bandied about and five years later, when Haines died shortly after his release, articles appeared in the Bombay Press castigating the Government for its severity towards a man who had rendered such signal services to the State. Certainly there seemed to be a great deal of ingratitude in what had been done. But it must be borne in mind that many a Company promotor in the mid-nineteenth century who rendered equally important services to the public, ended up in similar fashion. Haines was in fact bankrupt, but he sought to evade the consequences of bankruptcy. Nor was opinion at the time unanimously favourable to his case. During the trial most seemed to hope for his acquittal. But many did so with reservations. One newspaper, *The Englishman* of Calcutta, put its finger on the main weakness in the pro-Haines argument by citing the case of Lord Breadalbane, who in the reign of George II had been sent by the Government with large sums to calm the Highlanders in Scotland. On his return, when asked to render an account of his disbursements, that magnate had cried: 'Account! the money is spent and the Highlands are quiet, what more do you want?' Unfortunately Haines could not even claim to have pacified the area to which he was sent.

CHAPTER IV

Shares in Prosperity

The removal of Haines ushered in a new era in the history of Aden under British rule. The days of pioneering uncertainty were over and a period of organised consolidation and growth began. The defences of the settlement were practically complete, interior trade had taken an upward turn and the free port was attracting the larger merchant ships which visited the Red Sea. The appointment of Colonel James Outram as Haines's successor indicated that the authorities in India had become more aware of the constructive role Aden could play in British strategy. For Outram was no ordinary Political Officer. Prior to taking up his Aden appointment he had held one of the highest political posts under the Bombay Government. From Aden he went to Lucknow, the most coveted Residency in the gift of the Governor-General.[1] The contrast between Haines and Outram was striking. The Indian Navy Captain had had few fast friends of any standing even in the Bombay Presidency. Outram could look beyond Bombay to the Governor-General and his influential friends in East India House for support. At the time of his appointment to Aden he was already a political figure of such stature that the Governor of Bombay himself had to handle him carefully.[2] While Haines had been sitting in isolated secretiveness in Aden, Outram had been moving easily in the highest social and political circles in London and Calcutta expounding his views on Middle Eastern strategy and reflecting on the information he had gathered in Egypt during two visits to that country in 1848–9 and 1852. A memoir he had written on the defences of Egypt and the invasion of India from the westward had won him fame and was to have an important influence on British strategic thinking in the mid nineteenth century.[3]

Outram's appointment had the effect of integrating Aden more closely into the administrative system of the East India Company. Before his arrival Aden had been regarded as a backwater, its interests had been neglected, its politics largely misunderstood and the views of those in charge often ignored. Outram was able to replace muddle with some sort of ordered policy largely because he personally carried such weight that his views had to be accepted by Bombay as final.[4] He did not resolve the dilemma concerning the murders in the interior but he forced the superior authorities to admit that the dilemma existed and thus cleared the way for a solution in the future. Outram's clarification of tribal policy was the most obvious instance of the greater consideration which was now given to the views of the Aden authorities. But the same applied in smaller ways to other departments of governmental activity.[5] Funds flowed more freely, administrative reorganisation was facilitated and the Aden authorities began to play a more constructive role in forming policy toward the states bordering on the Red Sea.

Perhaps the most important legacy left by Outram after his very short stay in the settlement was the staff which he managed to recruit for the higher offices of government. The new men, like Outram himself, although on a lower plane, had contacts in high places outside Aden through whom they could make their views known and respected. R. L. Playfair, chosen by Outram as Assistant Resident before his arrival at Aden, belonged to an influential family and had the ear of John Murray, British Ambassador to Persia from 1855 and later Permanent Under-Secretary at the Foreign Office.[6] G. P. Badger, already Chaplain at Aden, was called on by Outram in 1854 to participate in the formulation and conduct of policy. The two quickly struck up a close friendship. Once described by an India Office official, as 'one of the finest diplomatists in the world, strangled by a white choker', Badger had the same breadth of vision and ready pen as Outram. Within five years he was corresponding privately with the Governor of Bombay and the President of the India Board. By the 1860s he was acknowledged in England as an expert on Middle Eastern affairs, advising Ministers and publishing his views frequently in the main political journals.[7] The third of the new appointees was Hormudz Rassam, a Christian from Iraq whom Outram had met in London society where he was being lionised as one of the participants (Outram said, the major participant) in the recent Assyrian archaeological discoveries. Rassam also could carry weight outside Aden as the protégé of the up-and-coming Henry Layard, his employer in Assyria, who passed from an archaeological to a political and diplomatic career.[8] Outram did not pick his successor but the Resident who followed him, Colonel William Coghlan, was as it were, forced to open up his own avenues of influence to keep up with his powerful subordinates. He knew of, and in some cases resented, the contacts they kept up outside the settlement and he relied on the close relationship he was able to forge with the Governor of Bombay to have his own views known and given due weight. At no other time in the nineteenth century did Aden, which, in the army at least, came to be regarded as a punishment posting, attract such a team of able and influential men.[9]

Each was given ample opportunity to show his talent. The movement of events and ideas was gradually bringing Aden back into focus as a key point in British strategy. By the 1850s the tide of European expansion was once more flowing strongly in the direction of the Red Sea and was creating a number of non-European cross-currents and counter-currents which called for the closest attention by the men in London, Bombay and Calcutta. The increasing use of the steamship turned the attention of other countries to the possibility of establishing mail communication on the short route to the East. The invention of the telegraph, and the proof of its value during the Crimean War, suggested the possibility of connecting Europe with India by cable via the Red Sea. And in 1854 the visionary project of connecting Europe with the East by a great maritime canal across the isthmus of Suez became a realistic proposition when the new ruler of Egypt, Sa'id Pasha, granted a concession for that purpose to Ferdinand de Lesseps.[10] Anglo-French rivalry in the Middle East had been one of the reasons for Aden's occupation and, while the two powers had been at daggers drawn during the Muhammad 'Ali crisis, Aden played an important role in countering French schemes in North-East Africa and Arabia. But the improvement of relations between Britain and France during the Tory government between 1841 and 1846 had led to a tacit understanding on both sides to avoid creating causes of conflict in the Middle East.[11] This mutual forebearance continued after Palmerston's return to the Foreign Office, partly because that statesman's incorrigible restlessness was curbed by the East Indian Company's reluctance to depart from a policy of caution.[12] The Orléans monarchy wished to avoid a quarrel with Britain, and Egypt – the key country in the whole area – was ruled by men who had no wish to clash with Britain again. Muhammad 'Ali – had learned his lesson in 1840. The only change he made in his dispositions in the Red Sea area after 1840 was to agree to remove his troops from Massawa in 1848 and hand over the so-called Pashaliq of Abyssinia to the Ottoman Sultan. Muhammad 'Ali's successor, Abbas, was, if anything, more favourable to Britain than to France, and was indisposed to resume the modernising expansive policies of his predecessor.[13] With France reasonably quiescent, and the situation in Egypt stable and more or less favourable to British interests, Aden had tended to become a backwater. If not exactly considered strategically superfluous, it was at least strategically inactive.

The new threat to Ottoman integrity posed by the Russo–Turkish discord which led up to the Crimean War transformed the situation. Once Russia and Turkey were involved in hostilities it was impossible to tell what turn events might take. Until the Anglo–French declaration of war against Russia in the summer of 1854 there could be no certainty that the sick man of Europe might not be brought to a speedy demise and his inheritance in Egypt as well as Europe disposed of in a manner unfavourable to Britain. It was for this reason that Outram was asked to watch the volatile situation at close quarters from Aden. By the autumn of 1854 however, when the European powers were fully engaged in the struggle, it became clear that the Black Sea was to be the main area of conflict. Outram became restless, the climate at Aden did not agree with him, and in November he bustled off to Lucknow to prepare the annexation of Oudh.[14] In the same month Sa'id Pasha granted the fatal Suez concession, and within three months the stage was set for a new and more bitter Anglo–French dispute over the control of the Red Sea route to India.[15]

Lord Palmerston said of the Suez Canal project in 1864: 'This whole scheme is one of the most audacious, but at the same time, subtle and ingenious plans of ambitious inroad into a coveted country that was ever recorded.'[16] This was his final verdict at the end of his life on a plan which for the previous ten years he had opposed with every weapon at his disposal. Whereas some other British statesmen were attracted by the vision of uniting East and West by a new waterway, Palmerston refused to see in it anything more than a cunning trick to promote French power at Britain's expense and, as he was in a position to make his views prevail, the whole power of the British diplomatic machine was developed against the Suez scheme.[17] De Lesseps dismissed Palmerston's objections as 'insane' and 'contradictory'. He said Britain opposed the scheme out of commercial jealousy and a fear that the new sea route would undermine the established British trading position in the East.[18] In fact Palmerston's objections were based on political and military grounds and were largely founded on Colonel Outram's assessment of the strategic situation in the Middle East. In the early 1850s Outram had revived Sir Robert Grant's fears of a French approach to India by way of Egypt and the Red Sea. In his memorandum on the defences of Egypt and the invasion of India from the westward he refurbished Grant's arguments and added new evidence to show that France had by no means abandoned her schemes to undermine the British position in India. The new evidence was the construction of fortifications at Alexandria and the raising of an irrigation barrage on the Lower Nile, both undertaken in the last years of Muhammad 'Ali's reign, allegedly with technical and financial aid from the French Government. The object of these works in Outram's view was to make Egypt immune from attack by either the British Mediterranean fleet or by forces from India approaching by way of the Red Sea. Outram's

memorandum was circulating in 1854 prior to the granting of the de
Lesseps concession; as soon as Palmerston heard that the concession
had been made he was convinced that the proposed canal was merely
a means of completing the Egyptian system of fortifications. He
persistently maintained that whether or not the Canal project was a
viable technical and commercial proposition (and he had doubts
on that point too), the effect of it would be to sever Egypt from
Turkey militarily by the excavation of a defensible ditch across the
isthmus. Egypt would then be the more able to declare her independence of Turkish control, being fully protected from invasion from
all quarters except the west, where the French in Algeria were the
nearest power of any consequence.[19]

Just as Grant's surmises concerning French advances in the
Middle East in 1838 had played a major part in framing the policy
which led to Aden's occupation, so now, Outram's strategic arguments re-emphasised the importance of Britain's base at the mouth
of the Red Sea. Anglo–French quarrels over Egypt, now focused on
the fortunes of the Suez project, led to sporadic efforts to seize options
on other ports and islands in the diplomatically more vulnerable
area of the Red Sea. The first decisive consequence of this new state
of affairs was the British occupation of the island of Perim. Outram
while at Aden, believed that Kamaran Island would be the most
likely object of French intentions,[20] but in 1855 and 1856 the attention
of the British authorities gradually turned toward Perim, waterless
but well placed at the very mouth of the Red Sea and endowed with a
commodious harbour. Care was taken to find some convenient pretext to cloak British strategic designs. The possibility of setting up a
telegraphic station was first considered, then it was decided that a
lighthouse was what was wanted, and in December 1856 a detachment
was sent from Aden to survey the island and prepare to set up a light.
There was no doubt that Perim was a proper site for a lighthouse;
even when the light was in place, the tricky waters around the island
claimed more than their fair share of the vessels wrecked in the Red
Sea. But the British authorities in their secret correspondence were
but slightly concerned about the interests of navigation and the light
was not finally raised until six years after the occupation of the
island. The interim period was spent in controversy over whether
the light or a gun battery should be placed on the highest point.
Perim was occupied to forestall the French whose agents had surveyed
the island; the decision to do so was taken in London and formed
part of the general diplomatic manoeuvring in connection with the
Suez project.[21]

During the five years following the occupation of Perim the British
were constantly disturbed by rumours that the French intended to

occupy positions in the Red Sea. There were reports in 1857 that a French company had purchased land at the barren roadstead of Edd opposite Perim. In 1859 Socotra seemed to be the object of French designs. In the following year Disseh Island, opposite Massawa, was surveyed by a French naval officer and rumour had it that they were interested in other points on the Abyssinian coast. [22] None of these French moves had any permanent effect. But others nearer to Aden did. The first notable extension of Aden's territory followed upon reports received in November 1862 that the French had been negotiating for the purchase of Little Aden – the promontory across the bay from Aden itself. In this case the British reaction was immediate and positive. The Aden Government was ordered first to buy an option on the territory and ultimately to purchase it outright. [23] After prolonged negotiations Little Aden became British in 1869, an event which had wide repercussions on hinterland politics as will be seen later. Similarly pregnant with future possibilities was the French purchase of the island of Obokh on the Somali coast in 1862. for the claim asserted then was to be used again by the French in 1884 to secure their claim to the port of Djibouti opposite the island. [24]

In terms of actual territory occupied, the alarms and excursions of the 1850s and 1860s left few traces on the map of European empires. Two practically barren islands and an equally barren promontory were but small increments in the account of general European expansion. Yet the occupation of territory, however useless, anywhere in the world is never a slight matter; it passes judgement on the relative power of those who gain and those who lose and it is the latter who are usually most seriously affected. The seizure of Perim and of Obokh caused much heart-searching in the Ottoman Empire and directed the attention of men in the Mediterranean heartland to the situation at the Empire's southern extremities. [25] Was the Empire adequately fulfilling its role as protector of the Muslim peoples in the Red Sea? These and other events suggested it was not. The Holy Cities, that sounding board of Islamic opinion, were in a state of constant turmoil and at times open revolt against Ottoman authority from 1854 onward. The main cause of disturbance was the struggle for power between two rival families with competing claims to the Sharifate of Mecca. But the pilgrimage brought to the Holy Cities men from India, the Sudan, the Maghreb, Central Asia and the East, with reports of universal European encroachment at the expense of political Islam, while distorted echoes of events in the Crimea yielded conflicting impressions of the Ottoman Sultanate's attitude to these hostile powers. In 1855 came a shock when the Sultan, in deference to the wishes of the British Government, abolished the slave trade, which many said was sanctioned by the Qur'an.

This caused a commotion in Mecca and Jedda where slaves were being imported from the opposite coast. During the 1850s European merchants had begun to elbow their way into the carrying trade of the Red Sea and, to the dismay of the Muslims, the system of capitulations which elsewhere in the Ottoman Empire were making non-Muslims an over-privileged rather than an under-privileged class, began to take effect in the Turkish Red Sea ports. Seething unrest culminated in a massacre of Christians in Jedda in 1858 and this was followed by a British bombardment of the port and the execution by the Turkish authorities of two prominent Muslims who were found guilty of instigating the incident.[26] None of this was calculated to improve the Sultan's prestige in this politically sensitive area. All the more reason then that attempts by European powers to occupy land should be forestalled. In 1861 and 1862 the Ottoman Government raised its flag or secured a loose protectorate over the Dahlac islands, Disseh, Adulis, Amphilla and Edd, a string of un-inhabited or barely habited points on the inhospitable coastline of Eritrea, all of which had been threatened by European encroachment in one form or another in the previous three years. In 1862 the Turkish Governor of Massawa announced that it was Ottoman policy to extend its control to the Bab el Mandeb.[26] [27]

Neither Britain nor France were much upset by this new Turkish expansiveness, but the Christian Emperor Theodore of Ethiopia was, and he expected his co-religionists in Europe to take action on his behalf. The British Government need not have been involved in the imbroglio that ensued, had it not been seeking during the previous twelve years to expand its own influence with the Ethiopian state and to keep the French out. The British Consul, and the missionaries and technicians who had been helping Theodore, now fell foul of him and ended up in prison. And so this remote area of activity, where Britain had been working to obtain very long-term options, suddenly swung into immediate focus, as an officer of the Crown languished in captivity, with consequent damage to British prestige. Great exertions were made to secure the Consul's release and Aden became the centre of the activity directed to this end. In July 1864 Rassam was sent to negotiate with the Emperor, in April 1865 he was joined at Massawa by another Assistant Resident from Aden, Lieutenant Prideaux. In the spring of 1867 the Resident himself went up as diplomacy began to give place to preparation for war. There followed the Abyssinian expedition of 1867–8, a lavishly organised affair in which the military men were given practically a blank cheque to drive in and secure the Consul's release at no matter what expense. Aden was made the forward base for the enterprise and thus became the scene of unprecedented activity – the harbour was full of ships, equipment of all kinds passed across its wharves, and large numbers of troops were temporarily quartered here and there in the town.

Thus by one of those ironic paradoxes with which the history of the British connection with Aden is so liberally strewn, British Aden for the first time fulfilled one of the main purposes for which it was occupied and fortified, not to meet a threat from some first-class European power, but to give a costly quietus to a minor British policy which had failed. Yet, futile and unprofitable as the Abyssinian expedition was from the British point of view, it brought Aden into the limelight, its passage gave a much needed stimulus to Aden's economy and when the expeditionary force withdrew it left Aden marginally better off in terms of harbour installations and general equipment.[28]

The Aden seen by the troops passing through for the Abyssinian expedition of 1868 was very different from the Aden which met Outram's eye on his arrival in July 1854. The intervening period was one of rapid building development during which the main lines of modern Aden began to emerge. Assistant Resident Playfair, charged in 1855 with responsibility for the town, took up where Haines had left off and administered the regulations with a new severity. By 1859 his zealous energy had earned him the unpopularity of all sections of the Aden population, but stone structures were springing up on all sides. Reed huts were torn down and the occupiers were offered frontages for stone houses which they were compelled to build within a specified period on pain of losing their plots. A fire in August 1856, which swept through the town destroying soldiers' quarters, the bazaar and officers' houses, showed the danger of buildings constructed of combustible materials and was the occasion for a further tightening-up of the rules.[29] Thus prompted, private individuals bent to the task. All the available skilled carpenters and bricklayers at Mocha and Hudayda had been attracted to Aden by 1858 and were fully engaged in constructing the rapidly extending town.[30] The Government was unable to compete for their services and public works were held up for lack of artificers. Nevertheless Playfair found the means to push forward a heavy programme of Government construction. Skilled European sailors serving sentences in the gaol were pressed into service; they were used to begin the task of clearing out Aden's famous water tanks which at that time were entirely useless, being choked with rubble in some places and broken down in others. The first of them was ready by the end of 1856 but the whole work was spread over a period of years. In 1856 also, the Police building was completely reconstructed after the former building had been blown down in a gale. In the following year a new Treasury building was completed to accommodate the Treasury and the Residency Offices in the Crater. Meanwhile the military were at work on barracks for the troops at the isthmus.[31]

This first period of rapid construction in the latter half of the 1850s was followed by another in the middle '60s. By then, the deterioration of Anglo–French relations and the progress of works at Suez had created new concern at the state of Aden's fortifications. The Indian Government was prepared to put more money into the perfection of the fortress, while at Aden the Resident was anxious to provide employment to alleviate distress in the interior. The result was the erection of a number of structures which until recently were still prominent festures of the Aden landscape. In the spring of 1866 the lighthouse on Ras Marshag was built and its light was installed in the following year. In 1867 and 1868 four upper-storied barrack buildings, facing Front Bay, were completed. The fortified bridge gate in the gorge of the Main Pass, was begun in January 1867 and completed in the following year. In 1868 the Anglican church in Crater, began to take on its jagged, mock-Gothic shape as work was pushed forward to complete what had been begun and abandoned during Playfair's first building phase. At Steamer Point, storied Barrack buildings, which a century later still housed the Aden Secretariat, were completed in 1868. The main road from Crater to Steamer Point was extended to Ras Tarshyne after a fatal accident with a heavy gun on the 1 in 7 gradients at the approaches to the Tarshyne fort.[32]

The largest work of all, begun by Merewether and completed by his successor, Russell, in 1869, was the Shaykh'Uthman water scheme comprising pumps at the Shaykh 'Uthman wells, reservoirs at the isthmus and a six-mile aqueduct between the two. This scheme was financed by the military but was in fact one of those plans for economic development and social welfare which engaged so much of Resident Merewether's attention. Its main purpose was to relieve the chronic shortage of water at Aden which the clearing out of the tanks and the installation of five sets of condensers between 1857 and 1867 had only partly mitigated.[33] Before the completion of the scheme, water was still rationed out to the troops as if they were aboard ship while the civil population was forced to pay prices so high that with his whole weekly wage a coal coolie would have been able to purchase less than fifty gallons.[34]

Water was indeed the Achilles' heel of the Aden fortress; the lack of an adequate supply within the settlement gave a certain air of unreality to the walls and forts which encrusted the hills and the heavy guns which pointed at the country beyond the isthmus from which most of Aden's water now had to come. Aden could hardly

Above, view of Aden in 1867; below the same view 1900.

have sustained a prolonged siege and therefore good relations with the neighbouring Sultanate of Lahej were a necessity rather than a matter of choice. The recognition of this fact partly prompted Merewether's undertaking the Shaykh 'Uthman scheme. The Sultan of Lahej was to profit from it by sharing in the revenues it would earn. Beyond this, the water scheme and the other public works undertaken in the settlement were intended as the Aden Government's main contribution to the alleviation of distress in the interior in the famine years of the middle '60s.[35] Conditions were at their worst in 1865 when Merewether first conceived the plan. Three years of rinderpest, which had decimated the numbers of draught animals needed to build the irrigation bunds, were followed in 1865 by drought and locusts, and the famine which ensued affected the whole of South-West Arabia, including the Yemen. Everywhere there was poverty. Those who had renewed their cattle three or four times over no longer had the funds to buy anew and profit from the rains when they did come in 1866. Thousands of poverty-stricken tribesmen poured into Aden; in July 1865 between three and four hundred were engaged on public works. By September the number had risen to over a thousand. Grain prices soared. On the eve of the arrival of a grain ship hastily sent by the Bombay Government in August 1865, 2 lbs. of grain cost a coolie's normal daily wage. A relief fund raised by the Government and the business community eased the situation, but some of those fed were already so weak that they died on eating their first meal. The Shaykh 'Uthman scheme therefore offered much-needed employment at a critical moment. Together with the other public works and the Abyssinian expedition, it ensured the rapid recovery of Aden and its hinterland once the famine had abated.[36]

Aden itself was little affected by the famine years of the 1860s. It had its own sources of income and these were rapidly expanding in the period from 1855 to 1870. This was for Aden the period of rising prosperity for which Haines had looked in vain. In the early 1850s Aden's total trade amounted to between 5 and 8 million rupees; in the early 1870s it stood between 22 and 33 million rupees.[37] Commerce played its part in this expansion. That barometer of Aden's general trade, the cotton piece goods import, which underpinned most branches of the settlement's commerce, remained set fair throughout the period. Worth some 773,000 rupees in 1854-5, the piece goods import had risen to over 2 million rupees in 1865-6.[38] The coffee trade fluctuated but remained buoyant; in 1871 the import of coffee by land alone was double the value of the import by land and sea in 1854. The gum trade held its own, while the trade in hides and skins increased greatly during the 1860s.[39] The pearl fisheries of the Red Sea, notably those around the island of Perim were also exporting their product through Aden by the end of the period and at that time formed a sizeable part of Aden's export trade.[40] There was reason for optimism in commercial circles in Aden in the 1860s, for the steady expansion of that decade was but a foretaste of what was to come in the 1870s and 1880s, when Aden became the true entrepôt for the Red Sea and East Africa.

Trade was still organised on what might be termed traditional lines during this period. The steamer had not yet ousted the sailing ship as a carrier of goods and while this was the case, trade remained in the hands of a few specialist shippers. The Americans were still prominent in the trade up to the 1860s, followed closely by French firms and Oswald and Co. of Hamburg. All of these plied their commerce at Zanzibar, Berbera and the southern Somali ports as well as Aden. Most carried supercargoes aboard who bought and sold and performed a number of other functions which might otherwise have fallen within the sphere of business houses at Aden. The ships themselves lay at anchor for a month or more in the upper harbour waiting for a cargo to be collected.[41] The trading system of the 1850s however involved one important deviation from traditional methods. For centuries trade had been conducted in Front Bay, in the harbour lying between Sirah island and the town. This harbour was still used in 1839 and an observer then remarked 'the bunder or wharf in East Bay is the most frequented part of the town where merchandise and passengers are hourly landed.'[42] But Haines in the 1840s reported that Front Bay was silting up and in any case the larger merchant vessels of the nineteenth century could not use a port which was suited to the needs of the smaller ships of an earlier age. The square-rigged merchantmen thenceforward used Back Bay and the local dhows began to follow suit. Nevertheless the town of Crater remained the commercial centre and an outport grew up on Ma'alla beach opposite the Main Pass leading over the hills into the town. From here goods were shipped out to the vessels in Back Bay. Here too the Somalis landed their livestock and began to build a shanty town for themselves. In 1855 three prominent merchants sought to organise the handling of goods there by building a pier. In the following year the Government supported their endeavour by granting them landing rights on the adjacent beaches. After preliminary difficulties this project prospered and the wharves there are still the main cargo-handling sector of Aden's port.[43] In 1864 the dominance of the Ma'alla outport was recognised when the old Customs House in Front Bay was closed down and replaced by an office in Ma'alla itself.[44] The town, which had not figured at all in Haines's earlier census reports, became a sizeable settlement of over 4,500 people with 506 stone houses by 1883.[45]

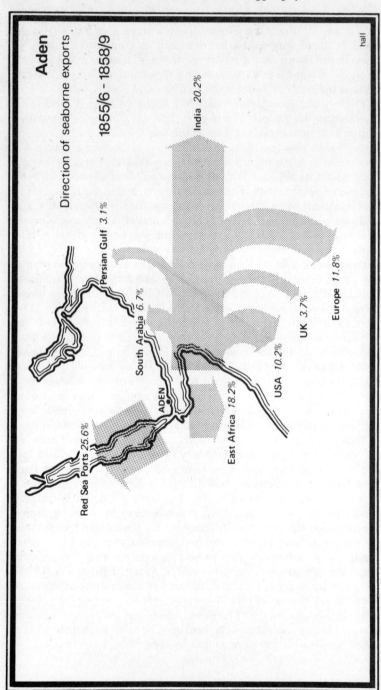

Aden

Direction of seaborne exports

1855/6 - 1858/9

Red Sea Ports 25.6%

Persian Gulf 3.1%

South Arabia 6.7%

ADEN

India 20.2%

Europe 11.8%

UK 3.7%

USA 10.2%

East Africa 18.2%

hall

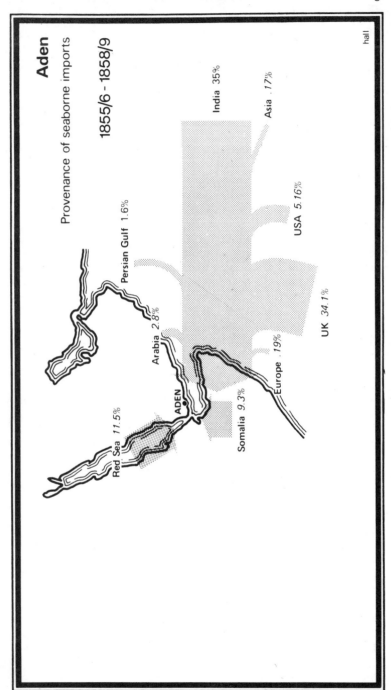

Aden

Provenance of seaborne imports

1855/6 - 1858/9

India 35%

Asia .17%

USA 5.16%

Persian Gulf 1.6%

Arabia 2.8%

UK 34.1%

Europe .19%

Red Sea 11.5%

ADEN

Somalia 9.3%

hall

Further to seaward the other western town, Steamer Point (Tawahi), was also prospering. By 1881 the 331 inhabitants of 1849 had multiplied themselves to over 4,000.[46] A good deal of this expansion took place in the 1870s with the enormous increase in the coal bunkering business in that decade. But even before the Suez Canal was opened in 1869 there was a considerable expansion in this branch of activity at Aden. The value of Aden's coal import more than doubled between 1855 and 1865.[47] This was due to the establishment and development of mail steamship lines operating through Aden. The Peninsular and Oriental Company, which had pioneered the monthly Suez–Calcutta line through Aden in 1842, took over from the Indian Navy the branch line to Bombay in 1855, although the Indian Navy continued to run a regular troopship service from Aden to Bombay.[48] A few years later, the P. and O. extended their Calcutta service to Australia and by the late 1860s two P. and O. steamers a week were calling at Aden for coal and other services.[49] In 1856 a shortlived competitor sprang up to challenge the P. and O.'s dominance of the Eastern mail lines. The European and Australian Royal Mail Company opened its service through Aden in that year, but two years later the Company collapsed and its business fell into the hands of the P. and O.[50] In 1856 the foundations were also laid for the establishment of the future Messageries Maritimes Company, with the opening of an Anglo–French service to the island of Mauritius. A French agent opened a coal depot next to that of the P. and O., and this served first the French share of the traffic to Mauritius, then the monthly French Government steamers which carried troops to and from Indo-China from 1860 onward, and finally the regular mail steamers of the Messageries Impériales which replaced the troopships, and converted its monthly service to a fortnightly service in 1869.[51]

Most of these vessels carried passengers. They therefore required a greater variety of services than the ordinary merchant steamer which later made use of Aden's bunkering facilities. They needed water, they began to demand ice and they needed all types of provisions. In the months of May, June and July 1870, the three principal Parsi firms at Aden supplied 261 dozen fowls, 2,866 eggs and 13,192 lb. of vegetables to the 88 steamers and 18 sailing vessels using Aden harbour. They supplied also 20,019 lb. of beef, 14,957 lb. of mutton, 1,022 sheep and 69 bullocks. All these were procured locally. In addition, flour and other provisions were imported into the settlement specifically for the use of the passenger vessels.[52] The harbour arrangements had to be reorganised in 1853 and again in 1857 to deal with the increasing number of ships. All this confirmed the role of Steamer Point as the focus for the mail and passenger business, for the berths in the deep water opposite the Point were reserved for Government vessels and the mail steamers. Other vessels either found their way down to the holding ground opposite Ma'alla or remained in the outer harbour.[53]

Important as commerce and the bunkering business now were, Government subventions and the presence of the garrison remained one of the main supports of the settlement's economy. The recurrent expenditure from Imperial funds on Aden stood at £160,000 per annum in 1884, and in addition to this, money was laid out from time to time on fortifications and public works of various descriptions.[54] Contracting for Government was still the most profitable line of business. An illustration of this may be found in the careers of three men described by Merewether in 1865 as the 'most influential men in Aden'.[55] Of these, two, Edulji Manockji and Cowasji Dinshaw had been prominent enough in 1854 to be among the principal signatories of an address to Haines at the time of his departure.[56] Both had come to the settlement after the arrival of the British and Cowasji Dinshaw had started business at Aden selling milk to the soldiers of the garrison.[57] Both were members of a Parsi community which since 1841 had been engaged in selling beer and liquor to the troops, and buying vegetables and firewood from the interior for the garrison.[58] They also dealt in Somali livestock for the garrison and by 1870 they had extended this activity to the provisioning of ships.[59] Hassan 'Ali Rajab 'Ali, the third of the trio, was a Persian. He also was connected with the livestock trade from an early date, for, with Manockji and one other, he built the Ma'alla pier, one of whose main purposes was to organise the landing of Somali cattle and sheep.[60] Hassan 'Ali was even more closely connected with Government than the Parsis. In 1857 he took up the contract for provisioning the garrison at Perim. In the 1870s he held the contract for supplying meat to the garrison and in 1875 he constructed two mess houses at a cost of 60,000 Rs. as a private venture to sell meals to the troops. About the same time he took over the messing arrangements at the Government Guest House for visiting chiefs – a contract which he held until the end of the century. He was also from 1870 the agent of the newly formed Ottoman Steamboat Company and unofficial representative of the Turkish Government at Aden.[61] All three had family ties with Government servants. The Head Accountant and Treasurer from 1856 was a Manockji. Dinshaw had relatives in the Ordnance and Municipal Departments, while Hassan 'Ali established ties through marriage with the Jaffer family.[62]

With the development of the town and its commerce, the system of government was becoming more sophisticated and better-organised. The new men in 1854 reorganised the finances of the settlement and

established clear-cut, self-sufficient departments. A separate municipal fund was created in 1855 to be financed by the payment of a
quit rent of one pie per square yard on town property. In 1856 this
was differentiated from the gaol fund and became fully autonomous
in 1861 when quit rents were raised to two pies. In addition there was
the Port Fund based on the payment of harbour dues and this too
was augmented in 1870 by an increase in harbour dues.[63] But
appearances were deceptive. The neat division of the Aden budget
hid a number of anomalies. Local funds were consistently used to
finance offices which should have been paid for by Bombay. From
1859 the post of Registrar of Trade became a sinecure used to finance
an underpaid Head Accountant partly from Port Fund money. The
salary of this underpaid official was once more increased in 1863
by paying him cash saved by transferring the salary of the Town
Overseer to be drawn from the Municipal Fund.[64] In 1871 the
reorganisation and enlargement of the Trade Registration Department was only effected by making the whole Department a charge
on the Port Fund.[65] These were some of the contrivances successive
Residents at Aden had to use to retain good men in the face of Bombay's systematic parsimony and refusal to alter their own rigid rules
to fit the special requirements of a settlement with a high cost of
living. The career of Cranfield, the first Superintendent of the
Secretariat Office, provides an outstanding example of these contor-
tions. Cranfield arrived at Aden in 1875 and soon made himself
indispensable as organiser of the business of the Office, a chore which
had kept many a former Assistant Resident deskbound. By 1878 he
began to chafe at his low salary, and as India would pay no more,
the purely nominal post of Auditor of the Municipal Accounts was
created to augment his emoluments. Fortunately the Abkari Act was
extended to Aden in the following year and one of the anomalies it
created was the post of Superintendent of Abkari, a sinecure which
was immediately passed to Cranfield. Not until 1886 did Government
sanction the post of Office Superintendent which Cranfield thereupon filled, passing on his sinecures as Superintendent of Abkari
and Salt to another underpaid Official. Before he left Aden in 1904,
Cranfield had had his salary increased twice more in irregular fashion.
In 1897 he received an allowance for house rent and a further allowance for work in connection with Somaliland which he continued
to receive after 1899 when this work was removed.[66] Cranfield,
through length of service and his difficult intermediary position
between the upper and lower scales of Government service, was an
outstanding example of an irregularly paid Aden official. But few
men, from the Resident himself to the lowest peon or messenger,
were untouched by this unsystematic system. During his first two

years at Aden, Coghlan spent much of his time struggling for the brevet colonelcy which he believed should appertain to his office.[67] For over a year Rassam lived and worked at Aden on loans from Playfair, who was himself grossly underpaid. Thereafter Rassam's position as Interpreter was sanctioned but he also performed the function of Postmaster to eke out his salary. In 1857 he was superseded as Postmaster and new efforts were required to reestablish his income.[68] The story of the staffing of the Aden settlement is the story of a constant struggle against authorities with little knowledge of the special problems of the place and one main concern, namely to reduce as far as possible the expenses of a costly commitment. In these circumstances it was difficult to escape from the irregularities of the Haines era or to dispel the atmosphere of intrigue, backbiting and petty corruption which continued to hang over the settlement.

There was still little specialisation of function among the officers. The First Assistant, Playfair, acted mainly as Magistrate in Aden but he also saw to all matters concerning the Municipality. Rassam was part in charge of the Police, part Postmaster and largely involved in the nascent Arabic Department. Badger, although officially the Chaplain, concerned himself with education and the business of the Arabic Department.[69] Goodfellow and Prideaux, who became Assistant Residents in the 1860s, both graduated to their positions through preliminary service as Interpreters, although both had a closer real connection with the duties of the Arabic Department after than during their tenure of the latter post. In 1856 the former Head Accountant became Chief Gaolor. In 1859 the Trade Registrar became Harbour Master.[70] Everyone in the administration down to the level of peon was likely to be called on at any time to perform a multitude of quite different functions. Thus the staff was much less a bureaucracy than a group of men sharing between them the many duties of a port and garrison town. Moreover leaves, frequent secondments and the normally fairly rapid turnover of personnel, helped to create an increasingly dangerous discontinuity in the upper echelons of the service. In 1856–7 Badger and Playfair were called away to serve with the Persian expedition, and in 1860 Coghlan and Badger were deputed to settle a dispute between the Sultanates of Masqat and Zanzibar, while at the same time Rassam was sent to act as Agent at Masqat. Coghlan remained nominally Resident until 1863. But in his last three years he spent only a few months in the settlement, and others acted in his place. His successor, Merewether, likewise spent much of his tour of service away from Aden, preparing the ground for and serving with the Abyssinian expedition. Rassam, appointed First Assistant Resident in 1863, was even more heavily involved in the Abyssinian affair and spent less than two of his remaining six years of service in Aden itself. These frequent absences put a heavy strain on the remaining staff and business was only kept going by constantly borrowing the services of officers of the garrison.[71] More serious than this was the constant sweeping by new brooms, particularly in the sphere of tribal affairs, where personalities and personal relationships were of paramount importance. Each officer tended to have his own approach to hinterland policy, each tended to ignore the lore and personal contacts built up by his predecessor. The result was a serious lack of consistency and long-term purposeful action in the conduct of relations with the peoples of the hinterland.

In spite of these shortcomings, Aden's administration was greatly improved by Haines's successors. Although the personnel was constantly changing there was decidedly less confusion of function as between the different departments of government. The creation of separate funds did something to straighten out the finances. In 1854 the post of Town Overseer was abolished and Haines's old Judicial establishment was separated from the general secretariat to become the nucleus of a municipal administration.[72] In 1856 the gaol was hived off under a European gaoler.[73] The new buildings constructed by Playfair and his successors assisted the process. In 1856 the fourteen N.C.O.s and 130 peons of the police force were given permanent stone-built accommodation. In the following year a new Treasury was completed and the records and the Residency Office were moved there.[74] In 1863 the decision of the Indian Government to make payments by cheque led to the opening of the Treasury every day instead of three times a month, to facilitate cheque payments and to act as a savings bank and issuer of remittance receipts. The consequent increase in financial transactions promoted the differentiation of function between the Treasury and Secretariat staff which had not existed in the time of Haines.[75] In the following year the Trade Registration department was moved away from Crater to Ma'alla and it too became a more autonomous body.[76] In 1870, following the application of the Indian Court Fees Act to Aden, the post of Registrar of the Residency Court was created and thereafter legal and judicial business had a new and separate focus.[77]

Perhaps the most important of these administrative developments was the gradual emergence of an Arabic Department for handling tribal affairs. The appointment of Rassam to the post of Interpreter with the duty of translating and writing Arabic letters was the first move in this direction. Rassam became the specialist in tribal politics. It was he who went on missions to 'Abdali and Fadli country and along the coast to the capital of the Lower 'Awlaqi Sultans. He always accompanied Coghlan on his visits to the interior and to the Hadhrami coast.[78] Coghlan retained general control of policy and regarded these political duties as the major part of his work. But Coghlan could not speak Arabic and he did not exercise the same detailed supervision as Haines. The frequent shifts in tribal affairs baffled him. As he once remarked: 'There was war betwixt Jeroboam and Rehoboam all their days, and so it is with Jeroboams and Rehoboams of this wretched country but we must do our best to make matters up amongst them.'[79] It was not he but Rassam who usually 'made matters up'. Just as Coghlan left Rassam to 'unravel' the Sultan of Lahej's relations with his neighbours in 1859, so he delegated most of what seemed to him unimportant minutiae, but were in fact very important diplomatic initiatives.[80] Aden's policy in the hinterland in the period between 1854 and 1864 therefore was very largely the policy of the unassuming but persistent Iraqi Interpreter. In accordance with his character it was a period of frequent and ingenious diplomatic initiatives and a sparing use of force. An Arab himself, Rassam was the more easily able to make contact with and win the confidence of the South Arabian chiefs even though in their eyes he was an Englishman.[81] Much the same might be said of the Chaplain Badger, who also played a prominent part in the formation of tribal policy. Badger was an Arabic scholar with a wide interest in Arab society and culture. Author of an Arabic Lexicon and collector of manuscripts, he took a much wider view of the problems of tribal policy than Haines had done.[82] In practical terms, Badger's scholarly proclivities and those of the archaeologist and Oxford graduate, Rassam, drew them towards the intellectual Sayyid 'Alawi bin Zain al 'Aydarus. While Rassam and Badger were at Aden, therefore, Sayyid 'Alawi reached the peak of his influence as mediator between the tribes and the Aden Government. This combination of learned men with some sympathy for Arab culture and their friendship with the leading religious personality in Aden did much to take the sting of religious and cultural fanaticism out of relations between the British and the South Arabian tribes. It was reported that the Sharif of Mecca said that the British ascendancy over the tribes of South Arabia was due to the influence of Sayyid 'Alawi.[83] The Fadli Sultan began to use the term *Inklis* rather than the opprobrious *Faranj*, with its religious overtones, in describing the British.[84] Men even began to venture beyond a realistic acceptance of the British presence to take an interest in the language and culture of Aden's rulers.[85] The most forward in this respect were the members of the 'Abdali ruling family. From the time that 'Ali Muhsin had accepted the presence of the British in Aden as an unalterable fact, the consistent object of the Lahej Sultans was to seek the friendship of the Aden authorities and thereby monopolise the political and commercial advantages which the presence of a strong and rich power offered to its neighbours. This was one of the few constant factors in the politics of South Arabia, for the House of Muhsin pursued this policy with greater persistence and judgement than the Aden Government itself. On both the occasions in the 1850s when the Aden–Lahej alliance was temporarily broken, responsibility for the breach lay with Aden rather than Lahej.

These rifts in the Anglo-'Abadli alliance are worth examining in some detail. They were important in themselves as representing decided though temporary shifts in British policy. They reveal the real texture of hinterland politics at mid century – the tenacity of inter-tribal rivalry, the complex intensity of intrigue, the pitfalls set by mutual ignorance and lack of communication. They also partly explain, in a negative fashion, why, for the greater part of the period, Aden and Lahej remained at one.

The first rupture in March 1854 followed from the fall of Haines and his temporary replacement by the narrow-minded, humourless commander of the garrison, Brigadier Clarke – a man quite lacking in diplomacy. Clarke, with evident contempt for Haines and all his doings, believed it his duty to undo all his predecessor's policies, and so his first measure on assuming office was to open negotiations with the Fadli Sultan.[86] This constituted a clear affront to the 'Abdali, who had been leagued with Haines against the Fadli. There was an agitation in Aden by the pro-'Abdali party there against the change of policy and Sultan 'Ali, who was informed by spies in Government offices of all that passed, unceremoniously turned down Clarke's suggestion that he should meet the Fadli to work out a compromise. This snub was quickly followed by other evidence that the 'Abdali was a dangerous man to cross.[87] On the other hand the Fadli proved himself an impossible ally. Although the Fadli Sultan was as eager as the 'Abdali to share in, indeed to monopolise, the economic opportunities offered by British Aden, he seemed to think that he could do this while continuing to insult and humiliate Aden's rulers. He replied to Clarke's initiatives sourly, congratulated him on 'deposing' Haines but indicated that his friendship could only be bought at a price.[88] Clarke, now in a false position after rebuffing the 'Abdali, swallowed these affronts and persisted fruitlessly until Outram arrived and immediately threw over the Fadli negotiation in favour of restoring relations with the more reasonable Sultan of Lahej.[89]

When one considers the completeness of Clarke's failure, it is the more difficult to understand how three years later Coghlan fell into the same error and substituted Fadli for 'Abdali friendship. Yet it is difficult also to examine the circumstances of the 1857 breakdown of Anglo-'Abdali relations without modifying the strictures on Sultan

'Ali's behaviour contained in Playfair's *History of Yemen*, which subsequent authors gradually turned into a bald accusation of 'treachery'.[90] The breach was not heralded by any noticeable worsening of relations between Aden and Lahej. Indeed the train of events which ultimately led to the crisis may be traced back to a particularly cordial visit paid by Coghlan to Lahej in the company of Playfair, Rassam, and a party of horse, on 16 December 1856. 'That is the way to pacify the country' commented Coghlan on the visit.[91] The cordiality was maintained by a return visit from Sultan 'Ali in January 1857 and three further visits to Lahej by Rassam in the following month. On 23 February Rassam wrote that the whole interior was peaceful and the 'Abdali Sultan especially kind.[92] But a month later Coghlan concluded an agreement with the Fadli Sultan which undermined the alliance with Lahej and from that point relations steadily deteriorated until March 1858, when an expedition was mounted against the 'Abdali.

What did the agreement with the Fadli entail? The answer, strangely enough, is practically nothing. The old matter of Milne's murderer was still involved and the Fadli merely certified that this man, whom no British officer could have recognised, had left the Fadli country, which no officer then at Aden had ever visited. In return for this and an unsolicited bond not to molest Aden-bound caravans, Coghlan re-established friendly relations and renewed the Fadli's stipend.[93] This sort of agreement could have been conjured out of the air at any time since the end of 1855 when Fadli attacks on Aden traffic has ceased. Why did it come to pass in March 1857? The explanation partly lies in Coghlan's growing disillusion with his former policy. He had spent most of the previous two years concocting alliances with the 'Awlaqi and others to protect Lahej and crush the Fadli. Like Haines he had sought a solution of the Hiswah question and like Haines he had failed, owing to the general disinclination at Lahej and elsewhere to use extreme measures. No tangible results had been produced and Coghlan was uneasily aware that his superiors disliked the system of creating tribal combinations in support of Lahej and only tolerated it for want of a viable alternative.[94] This provides a motive but does not adequately explain the timing. A clue to the latter is to be found in a statement by Sultan 'Ali's brother, Fadl Muhsin, ten years later, to the effect that the breakdown in Anglo-'Abdali relations in 1857–8 was due to a disagreement between Sultan 'Ali and Sayyid 'Alawi. Fadl Muhsin's statement should not be taken at face value, since his object at the time was to discredit Sayyid 'Alawi in the eyes of the British.[95] But an examination of the sequence of events in 1857 reveals that there was much truth in his remark.

There were indeed grounds for a serious disagreement between the two men in the winter of 1856-7. Coghlan's visit to Lahej on 26 December 1856 was his first to the 'Abdali capital. Previous encounters had taken place at Aden or the Hiswah under Sayyid 'Alawi's watchful eye; now the British officers met the Sultan alone, and the latter was evidently so impressed by the value of such direct contact that he and his brothers asked to send their sons to Aden for education.[96] Coghlan also benefited from the experience. A conducted tour of the 'Abdali country revealed to him the fertility of the Wadi Tuban, and on his return he sat down and penned an enthusiastic despatch cancelling his former proposal to develop vegetable production at the Hiswah, and recommending that experiments be begun at Lahej instead.[97] Four months later the gardens at Lahej were flourishing and Sultan Fadl Muhsin had the contract for providing vegetables for the garrison.[98] Sayyid 'Alawi stood to gain nothing and lose much by this euphoria; he had been by-passed by Sultan 'Ali and the cancelled gardens at the Hiswah were his.

In the midst of the exchange between Aden and Lahej, however, some strange and contradictory things were happening. On his way back from the Hiswah, Coghlan visited the 'Uzaybi chief who told him that Sultan 'Ali stood in the way of a settlement with the Fadli.[99] Then in January 1857 an unfamiliar figure, the black sheep of the House of Muhsin, Sultan 'Abdallah, appeared at Aden and to his own astonishment was enthusiastically received by Coghlan. Former strictures on this personality were forgotten. He was an intelligent man, clearly the heir-apparent to the Lahej Sultanate and above all, influential with the Fadli and likely to be able to induce that recalcitrant chief to settle his differences with the British.[100] Both the 'Uzaybi and Sultan 'Abdallah of course were members of the old opposition party at Lahej, and both were in league with the Fadli Sultan. During the first three months, Coghlan drew steadily closer to them with Sayyid 'Alawi acting as his go-between and it was through their agency that the Fadli Sultan was brought to the conference table on 30 March.[101] Two years before this, Sayyid 'Alawi had warned Coghlan against any negotiation with the Fadli to which Sultan 'Ali was not a party.[102] Now, with Sayyid 'Alawi's advice, Coghlan brushed aside Sultan 'Ali's last-minute offer to bring the Fadli to terms and Sayyid 'Alawi was entrusted with the conclusion of a unilateral agreement. Within a few days the 'Aqrabi chief had also come to Coghlan with loud expressions of friendship.[103]

At this point Coghlan believed that he had finally emancipated his Government from dependence on any group in the interior, was now pursuing a neutral policy and Aden was at peace with all. He

proudly remarked that he was the 'confidant of all parties'.[104] Looked
at from another point of view however, all confided in him in the
hope of making him their dupe. Suffering from overwork and
shortage of staff, he was more deeply immersed in tribal intrigue
than ever while his own shift in policy was, by the uncertainty it
created, intensifying the struggle for power in the interior.[105] Following the Fadli agreement, disputes at Lahej reached a new intensity.
Sultan 'Ali turned on the 'Uzaybi chief, and Sultan 'Abdallah flew
to the latter's aid. 'Abdallah seized an important watercourse, Sultan
Fadl Muhsin sent a force to dislodge him and seven were killed in the
affray. Meanwhile the Fadli was collecting forces for an attack on
Lahej.[106] As tempers rose in the interior, Coghlan's neutral policy
wore thin. He complained that it was impossible to get at the truth.[107]
Yet from April onward his reports were full of 'facts' new and stale
which were obviously fed to him by the 'Alawi–'Abdallah–Fadli
faction while his correspondence with Sultan 'Ali grew steadily more
acrimonious.[108] It is difficult to see what positive gain Coghlan derived
from the Fadli agreement but it certainly earned him the enmity
of Sultan 'Ali who now seemed to regard him as part of a hostile
coalition. In June 'Ali struck a blow calculated to injure both Aden
and Sayyid 'Alawi when he raised a tax on Shaykh 'Uthman water.
This forced Coghlan further into the arms of the Sultan's enemies
for he had to line up with the 'Uzaybi to force 'Ali to retract.[109] A few
days after this incident the Mutiny broke out in India, Aden was
denuded of troops and Coghlan became even more dependent on
his new allies. Throughout the autumn, disputes and drought sent
Aden water prices rocketing. 'Abdali pinpricks continued and
Coghlan, always fearful of criticism by his superiors, became ultra-
sensitive and blackballed Badger when he heard that the Chaplain
had written to the Governor of Bombay about Aden affairs.[110]

In March 1858 matters came to a head. Sultan 'Ali stopped a
particularly valuable caravan from the Yemen accompanied by an
embassy from the Imam *en route* for Aden. When Coghlan held up his
stipend in protest, Sultan 'Ali followed up by sending a force to
Shaykh 'Uthman to blockade the Aden road. 'Ali boasted that
Coghlan would not dare attack him and waited for the Aden Government to come to terms.[111] There was some reason for this over-
confidence, for Coghlan required a good deal of moral courage to
strike. Although he had been reinforced with troops since the
Mutiny had abated, he had the strictest instructions not to use them
beyond Aden's walls.[112] But Coghlan was by this time so exasperated
that he threw caution to the winds and on 18 March he led out 650
men of the Aden garrison to attack the 'Abdali force at Shaykh
'Uthman. He found his enemy much larger and more resolute than

he expected. He was also surprised by their tactical skill for they engaged the British force in front and then sought to turn both flanks. Nevertheless the troops of the garrison carried the day and drove the 'Abdali from the field.[113] Both parties left the scene of battle with a greater appreciation of the other's power. Sultan 'Ali became more accommodating and a reconciliation was effected in July, when Coghlan visited Lahej accompanied by Rassam and Sayyid 'Alawi.

One of the most promising features of this July meeting in Coghlan's view was the engagement which then took place between Sayyid 'Alawi and the Lahej Sultan's sister.[114] This political marriage was carefully promoted by the Aden authorities and when it was duly solemnified in the following February ten British officers were among the distinguished company of guests.[115] The Anglo-'Abdali crisis ended as it had begun with Sayyid 'Alawi playing a prominent role. Coghlan could claim with some justice that the Aden Government had attained a position of paramountcy in the country; it now had direct relations with each of the tribes. But Sayyid 'Alawi was the agent and mouthpiece of both the Fadli and the 'Aqrabi in their dealings with the British, he had now forced himself on the 'Abdali, and to crown all he received a pension from the Indian Government 'for services rendered during the Mutiny'.[116] In fact it appeared when the smoke of battle had cleared that it was Sayyid 'Alawi, not Coghlan, who had diversified his alliances and strengthened his influence in the interior, and Sultan Fadl Muhsin's remark in 1867 assumes a further meaning.

The clearing away of the multiple misunderstandings of the years 1857 and 1858 restored the even tenor of Anglo-'Abdali friendship, albeit on a slightly altered footing. It also ushered in a period of peacable relations between Aden and the tribes, which freed Coghlan's hands to deal with other problems in the Red Sea and on the northern coasts of the Indian Ocean. Coghlan was satisfied with the outcome. He was prepared to let sleeping dogs lie and he had confidence in Sayyid 'Alawi. The next major upturn in South Arabian politics came after his departure when other men with other ideas had taken control of Aden's policy.

From 1861 onward, the business of the Arabic Department began to shift into new hands. Rassam's frequent absences in the early 1860s, Badger's departure from the settlement and finally Rassam's long secondment to deal with Abyssinian affairs in 1864 left a vacuum which others stepped in to fill. The newcomers, Goodfellow and the more junior Prideaux, were political officers of a more orthodox type. Their vision was in a sense narrower, their political activity more thrusting and self-reliant than that of their predecessors. Much the same might be said of Merewether, who replaced Coghlan as

Resident in 1864. Not that Merewether was in any way hidebound. He had served for many years during the pioneering days in Sind, when unorthodoxy had been the rule rather than the exception. But he tended to make facile comparisons between Sind and South Arabia and what Coghlan and Badger saw as a sensitive point of contact between the British and the Arab world was to him a poverty-stricken province waiting for development. Force and persuasion had made the desert bloom in Sind; a similar prescription might have like effects at Aden. Merewether therefore tended to assume the role of forceful pacifier and promoter of social progress in the lands within his reach.[117] In terms of ultimate goals he did not basically differ from Coghlan. Coghlan, like Haines, believed the objective of British policy to be the release of the energies of the agricultural and productive classes in South Arabia. This sort of underlying conception was fundamental to the thinking of all mid-Victorian colonial administrators and Coghlan was no exception.[118] But during Coghlan's regime this general policy was subordinated to a desire to avoid offending Arab susceptibilities by over-zealous independent activity. The offer of British friendship and economic and other co-operation was kept open, but Badger and Rassam believed that the Arabs themselves should be left to accept or refuse. This was not Merewether's view and Badger and Rassam became increasingly critical of this aspect of his policy.[119] Merewether believed that the passive approach had failed to stimulate progress and wanted more positive, British-directed, action to force reform in Aden's immediate hinterland. His assistant Goodfellow agreed with him and Goodfellow communicated these ideas to Merewether's successors.[120] The new policy thus endured for nearly a decade and culminated in a proposal to take the whole of the Lahej Sultan's territory under a form of direct British administration.

It so happened that at the time of Merewether's arrival at Aden, the situation was ripe for a fresh departure such as that which the new Resident had in mind. The death of Sultan 'Ali of Lahej in April 1863 brought on a political crisis which weakened the 'Abdali and made them more receptive to British influence. 'Ali's twenty-year-old son, Fadl bin 'Ali, was turbanned on his father's death, but quarrels between his powerful uncles made his position impossible, and within three months he had resigned office, leaving the two other principal candidates, Fadl Muhsin and 'Abdallah Muhsin, to fight it out.[121] In this case Merewether did not have to take the initiative; Aden was called on to mediate in the dispute. Rassam had a long acquaintance with the internal politics of the House of Muhsin, had mediated before, and had the confidence of most members of the family. At the same time British recognition and the payment of the stipend was essential to any new Sultan who wished to remain solvent. The final decision on the succession was taken at Aden at a meeting attended by Merewether and three of the brothers – 'Abdallah, 'Abd al Karim and Muhammad Muhsin. 'Abdallah's strong claim as the eldest brother was set aside and Fadl Muhsin, the dead Sultan's favourite and a man who was much better known and liked by the Aden authorities, was offered the title. British intervention in the Lahej succession dispute however could not be regarded as decisive. 'Abdallah had personal faults, notably unreliability and lack of balance, which told against him in the eyes of all, his party at Lahej was weak and at the Aden meeting he concurred in his brother's appointment.[122] Nevertheless, the fact that the British had helped to choose him strengthened the ties between them and the new Sultan and this initial connection was to be reinforced by Fadl Muhsin's awkward financial position, which made him increasingly dependent on British aid.

Fadl Muhsin had to pay a heavy price for his office. In effect he bought his accession by distributing largely among the ruling family the wealth proper to the Sultanate. 'Abdallah Muhsin and Fadl bin 'Ali were both left with portions of the land revenue. The annual subsidy from the Aden Government was divided up among the sons of Muhsin, and state monopolies were granted to his supporters.[123] In addition to this, Lahej, together with the rest of South Arabia, suffered from an unparalleled series of natural disasters in the first nine years of Sultan Fadl's reign. Successive rinderpest epidemics, long droughts, plagues of locusts, hurricanes and attacks of cholera produced famine, misery and political disruption from the Yemen to the Hadhramawt in the years between 1863 and 1872.[124] The Lahej Sultan's weakened finances were given no opportunity to recover and Fadl Muhsin was driven to a number of desperate expedients in his attempt to augment his income and cut his losses. Almost all of these expedients required British aid or acquiescence to make them work, and while Fadl Muhsin was under pressure, the ties between Aden and Lahej were drawn steadily tighter.

The dependence of the Lahej Sultanate on good relations with Aden can be best understood by reference to the content of its budget at the time of Fadl Muhsin's accession. By then, only one third of the Sultan's revenue originated from within his dominions. Of his total annual income of some $M.T. 45,000, only 15,000 came from the land taxes and tithes assessed in accordance with the permanent land settlement made at the time of the 'Abdali assertion of independence in the eighteenth century. The land was held by individual proprietors, subject to the demands of the Sultan and to the control of those charged with supervision of the irrigation of the Wadi. The rest of the Sultan's revenue came from monopolies and taxes on trade. Of these the most important was the levy of transit dues on the roads to Aden. This accounted for one ninth of his income and it was a tax that frequently created friction with his neighbours. The rulers of the coffee-producing areas said that the levy of transit dues was contrary to religion and that only land taxes were legitimate.[125] Without Aden's backing the Sultan could have experienced difficulty in maintaining his charges.

The centres of production of the most valuable articles in demand at Aden lay beyond the immediate hinterland in the rich highlands of the Yemen. The coffee coming into the Aden market at the end of the 1860s came almost exclusively from the district of Hajariya to the south of Ta'izz. In 1870 over 6,000 camel loads of this commodity came into Aden and the value of the import at 323,000 Rs. or some $160,000 represented nearly a third of Aden's total landward import.[126] To the south eastward of Hajariya, on the trade route from there to Aden, was the qat-producing Maktari district. Hence came the cheaper varieties of qat consumed by the lower classes of the Aden populace. These and other commodities of lesser importance coming into Aden from this direction were subject from time to time to taxation by the Mansuri, Makhdumi or Rija'i branches of the nomad Subayhi. The trade routes through the Subayhi country were subject to alteration depending on the state of politics in that wild area, but the exactions of one or other of these small but dangerous sub-tribes could hardly be avoided. The Sultan of Lahej interfered widely in Subayhi politics to keep the traffic in motion but could exert little coercive authority over those whose villages were difficult of access and who could choose one of many suitable spots to levy their duties. Having passed the Subayhi plain, the caravans from the Hajariya entered the territory of the 'Aqrabi Shaykh where they were once more taxed before they reached Aden. The caravans did not pass through 'Abdali territory proper until they reached the small strip of 'Abdali land between 'Aqrabi country and Aden itself. Nevertheless they were heavily taxed by the Lahej Sultan, at Shaykh 'Uthman or later, at his customs house at Aden.

The second principal area of production lay to the south of San'a'. From this district came the loads of saffron, one of Aden's second-rank imports, and madder and beeswax. By 1870 little of the coffee from the rich district of Udayn came to Aden, but in the 1850s it provided a substantial portion of Aden's coffee import. Further south the Mawiya district to the west of Hawshabi country provided the better quality qat which was consumed by the richer classes in Aden and Lahej. These and other commodities came to Aden via western Hawshabi country and Lahej. At Lahej the cara-

vans from this direction met those coming down the Wadi Hardaba
from the 'Alawi lands and the territory of the 'Amirs of Dali'. These
latter bore the large quantities of grain (Aden's second largest
import in 1870) which in normal years came from the Dali' Plateau
and the Wadi Bana further north. A third inland area producing a
surplus for export lay further eastward, and found most of its outlets
beyond 'Abdali territory. The coffee, aloes and madder produced in
the fertile highlands of Upper and Lower Yafi' found their way to
the coast through Fadli country and were shipped either at Aden or
at the Fadli port of Shuqra, where the greater part of the Yafi'i
coffee crop was purchased for sale in the Hadhramawt.[127] Thus,
apart from the provenance of the Yafi'i country, the Lahej Sultans
were in a position to tax every commodity coming from a distance
into the Aden market. The only effective check upon the level of
dues charged was the willingness or otherwise of the Aden government
to tolerate variations from an agreed schedule of charges fixed by
treaty with Sultan 'Ali in 1849. Aden's co-operation therefore was
of some importance to Sultan Fadl Muhsin, who wished to expand
his revenue from this source.[128]

This was even more the case with a multitude of other means
which the Lahej Sultans used to augment their income. Contracts
for the provision of vegetables for the garrison, monies derived from
the sale of Shaykh 'Uthman water at Aden and indirectly from the
sales of grass and fodder, these and of course the British stipend of
$19,000 per annum were dependent on the goodwill of the Aden
authorities.[129] There were yet other ways in which the 'Abdali
Sultans could make money out of Aden. Lahej did not actually raise
livestock for the Aden market, but Somali sheep and cattle were
held there for fattening during the eight months of the year when
communication with the Somali coast was impossible. Thence they
were sold to the Parsi merchants at the port and the Lahej Sultans
imposed a brokerage charge on every animal so handled.[130] The
Sultans were also involved in the lucrative business of labour
contracting.[131] Sultan Fadl Muhsin monopolised the sale of potash
used for detergent purposes by Aden labourers and the sale of a
sweet-scented flower also much in demand among them. He disposed
of the monopoly of the salt from the pans at the Hiswah which yielded
a 300 per cent profit on sale in the Aden market. He also taxed the
trade in the other direction. The exclusive right to supply the
inhabitants of Lahej with fish, meat, ghee, tobacco, and the leaves
of wild almond trees used as wrappers, were all sold by the Sultan to
the highest bidder. Had there not been strong protest, Sultan Fadl
Muhsin would have extended the system of monopolies even further.
In the 1870s he tried to assert his seignorial rights over mineral oils

in the western portion of his Sultanate. Rumour had it that he would also have monopolised the sale of toddy from the palms at Hiswah to the soldiers of the Aden garrison, but for the religious feelings of his people.[132]

For Sultan Fadl Muhsin therefore, as for a great number of his subjects, the connection with British Aden had become an indispensable feature of his financial arrangements. Two-thirds if not more of the Sultanate's revenue was dependent on the preservation of the

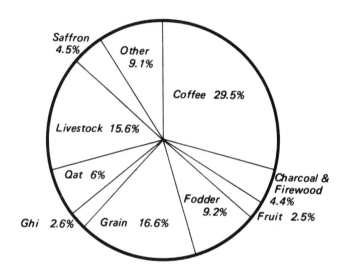

Aden

Landward imports 1867/8 - 1869/70   by Value

links with the port and its government. Moreover, as Lahej and the rest of South Arabia were wasted in the '60s by drought and disease, Sultan Fadl had to harness his fortunes more closely to the rising prosperity of the Aden community and its wealthy government if he were to hold his income steady. The extent of the agricultural disaster was such, however, that he was unable to balance gains against losses. His income fell and he had to cut his expenditure – a difficult operation which also required the assistance of the Aden government to effect. The charges on the 'Abdali exchequer were heavy and some were incapable of reduction. The greater part of the land revenue, the British stipend, and the income from some of the monopolies, never even reached the Sultan's personal coffers, for they had been granted away either at Sultan's Fadl's accession or later, to other members of the House of Muhsin and to heads of sub-tribes.[133] Sultan Fadl in fact had been handed a poisoned cup when offered the Sultanate, for he received it minus some two-thirds of its revenue. Out of what remained to him he had to maintain the state administration and the slave guards, employ mercenaries in time of need and pay customary subsidies to other tribes. The first two were more or less fixed charges but the last two were variable and in a sense interchangeable items. The extent of the subsidy offered, depended on the ability of the beneficiary to enforce it; non-payment of a subsidy as often as not required the engagement of mercenaries to resist attack from the disappointed party. The principal subsidies owing were those to the Fadli Sultan which Lahej had paid intermittently under duress since before the arrival of the British, and to the 'Awlaqi tribe paid in similar fashion since the 1820s. In addition, douceurs were offered from time to time to the Hawshabi and Subayhi as part of the general system of protecting trade routes and regulating transit dues. The penalty for non-payment was war, and this was where the British came in. If the Aden Government could be induced in the interests of peace either to suppress the 'Abdali's enemies or offer the Sultan money enough to worst them, then he could withhold these subsidies with impunity.

These financial and political considerations set the pattern for Sultan Fadl Muhsin's political manoeuvres during the first ten years of his reign. From the start he cultivated the friendship of Merewether and his Assistant Goodfellow. The British officers were invited on several occasions to the Hiswah, to Shaykh 'Uthman and to Lahej, and Sultan Fadl himself paid two long visits to Aden in 1864 and 1865. Merewether soon became familiar with the problems of the Sultanate. Sultan Fadl flatteringly offered several times to put his country under the British, and after each interview Merewether became more thoroughly convinced of the Sultan's ability and of the necessity to accord him support.[134] Seeds were provided for the development of vegetable production at Lahej. The Shaykh 'Uthman water scheme was embarked upon as a joint Anglo-'Abdali effort, part of whose profits were to prop up the weakened Lahej finances. Then, in 1864, Sultan Fadl refused to pay the Fadli subsidy, and withheld it again the following year. When the inevitable Fadli reaction came in the form of plunder on the roads and forays into 'Abdali territory, Merewether immediately branded the Fadli Sultan as a disturber of the peace. A $5,000 loan, later converted to a gift, was accorded to Sultan Fadl in 1864 to raise mercenaries, and with these he held off attacks by both the Fadli and 'Awlaqi.[135] At the end of the following year, Merewether was so incensed that, in co-operation with the ʿAbdali, he led out the most powerful British force yet seen beyond the Aden walls into Fadli country. This force of 500 infantry and four guns first dispersed a Fadli force eight miles north of Shaykh ʿUthman, then marched along the beach to the heart of Fadli territory, where during an eleven-day occupation it destroyed buildings belonging to Fadli leaders at al Khor and Amudiyah and pulled down a considerable part of the declining but still large trading town of Assala. Further plundering by the Fadli in the spring of 1866 led to another sortie, this time by sea to Shuqra, where 300 British troops with two guns blew up the Fadli Sultan's residence and two other houses.[136] The old Fadli Sultan remained defiant for another year, indeed one might say until his death in 1870, for it was his sons who patched up a peace with the British in May 1867, after a vain attempt to seek Turkish aid.[137] The old warrior was anything but a pliant individual. In his ninetieth year he was in the saddle at the first encounter between his forces and the British. He was one of the few who still spoke of *jihad*, he wrote insulting letters to the Resident even when nominally at peace, and when called on to surrender after the first punitive expedition, replied by demanding compensation for the destruction wrought by the British troops.[138]

Sultan Ahmad bin ʿAbdallah did not know when he was beaten, for beaten he was. The eleven-day occupation by Merewether's force crushed the Fadli Sultanate and ruined the Sultan's life-work. Some of the Fadli sub-tribes defected to the ʿAbdali. Some Hawshabi sections formerly attached to him turned away. The Lower Yafiʿi seized the opportunity to occupy the hamlet of Juwalla and secured the headwaters of what was left of the Abyan irrigation system. The Fadli ruling family was riven by disputes and disagreements and Sultan Ahmad's successors were to find difficulty in controlling tribal sections formerly regarded as undoubtedly Fadli.[139] As for the ʿAbdali Sultan, his policy of cultivating British friendship had paid great dividends. He had rid himself of his most troublesome enemy and by 1867 he was looking round for new fields to conquer.

His next move was made to the northward against his neighbours the Hawshabi. That tribe had occupied the strategic village of Zaʾida in the Wadi Tuban together with the fertile land around it, the key to the whole ʿAbdali irrigation system, in 1839. They had since exacted payment from the ʿAbdali for the use of the waters and when the latter defaulted in 1868 they diverted the water into the desert. At this Sultan Fadl struck and, beating the Hawshabi in a short campaign, recovered Zaʾida and its waters.[140] He then consolidated his hold by interesting the Aden Government in a plan to extend the Shaykh ʿUthman scheme by tapping the sweet water

at its Za'ida source and conveying it thence direct to Aden.[141] Thus
when the Hawshabi sought later in 1868 and again in 1869 to recover
what they had lost, the British regarded this as an attack on their own
interests. Sultan Fadl once more received strong backing from Aden.
During 1868 the Sultan invited a troop of Aden horse to recover from
scurvy at Lahej – a neat way of menacing his neighbour. In 1869 the
British cut off the Hawshabi stipend in retaliation for attacks on
Aden-bound caravans.[142] Once more Sultan Fadl had contrived
to extend his power and increase his wealth by exploiting his
friendship with the British.

While the Hawshabi trouble was still unsettled, Sultan Fadl got
word of a transaction between the British and the 'Aqrabi Shaykh
which offered the opportunity of glittering gains. In April 1869 the
Aden authorities purchased the promontory of Little Aden from the
impoverished 'Aqrabi Shaykh for the substantial sum of $30,000.
Negotiations to this end had begun seven years before, when rumours
that the French had offered a price for the 'Aqrabi's land had raised
fears for the integrity of Aden harbour and loosened British purse
strings. The British were eager to buy, the 'Aqrabi was less eager to
sell. The Aden Government therefore entrusted Sayyid 'Alawi with
the task of bringing him round and arranging the deal. This proved
a lengthy business. Alleged Fadli claims had to be disposed of. The
exact limits of the purchase had to be agreed on. So had the price.
Yet at no time did Sayyid 'Alawi say anything of any 'Abdali lien
on the territory. Sultan Fadl however had a claim – a claim to
suzerainty over the 'Aqrabi which could be embarrassing to both the
British and Sayyid 'Alawi, who had recognised it several times in the
past.[143] Had he heard in time of what was happening, the 'Abdali
could have expected a share in the deal. But he did not. He only
heard the news after the agreement had been signed and the money
delivered.

Sultan Fadl was therefore left with two possible courses of action.
He could either blackmail the British into buying out his interest
or he could force the 'Aqrabi to disgorge a portion of his gains. Neither
of these offered an inviting prospect. The Aden authorities who had
just wound up the case with satisfaction and relief were ready to be
stubborn, and the history of 'Abdali–'Aqrabi relations indicated that
the 'Aqrabi would not be less so on such a point. But there was a
third way. Sultan Fadl could concentrate his full attack on Sayyid
'Alawi who had made the agreement, persuade the British that they
had been misled and mulct the Sayyid of some of the $10,000 he had
reputedly received from the 'Aqrabi on the conclusion of the negotiation.[144] This solution would have the additional advantage of weakening the architect of Coghlan's 'neutral policy' and strengthening

Sultan Fadl's own influence at Aden. Of course there was a risk, for Sayyid 'Alawi could be a formidable opponent, as Sultan Fadl's predecessor had found to his cost. But the Sayyid's fortunes were on the wane. He was growing old, his friends Rassam and Badger had left the settlement and his inability to handle the Fadli Sultan at the time of the expedition in 1865 had damaged his prestige.[145] Moreover, his place in the counsels of the Aden Government was being gradually usurped by a rising young official, Salah Jaffer, and during the discussion of the case, Sultan Fadl was able to count on the latter's invaluable assistance.[146]

The 'Abdali Sultan brought matters to a head in August 1869 by following up a protest against the agreement with an armed occupation of the Hiswah. At first the Resident, Russell and his Assistant, Goodfellow, were indignant. But then Sultan Fadl paid another of his prolonged visits to Aden. He cultivated Goodfellow as he had done Merewether. He produced documents showing that Sayyid 'Alawi had agreed in 1853 to pay rental to Lahej for the supposedly 'Aqrabi-owned Hiswah lands and with Jaffer's help he soon had Goodfellow completely converted. Sayyid 'Alawi was called on to explain and at a painful meeting in the presence of the Sultan, the Sayyid made the great mistake of letting it appear that he thought Goodfellow to be ignorant and incompetent. From that point, Sayyid 'Alawi was lost. Sultan Fadl brought a case against him for ten years' arrears of rent on his Hiswah property and faced by a hostile Aden Qadi, he was forced to settle for $6,000.[147] Having disposed of Sayyid 'Alawi, Sultan Fadl offered the Hiswah to the Aden Government as a gift. He also offered to recognise the Little Aden transfer. But at the same time he said that he expected some compensation for the large sums disbursed by the Lahej Sultanate in subjecting the 'Aqrabi to 'Abdali control in the late 1840s and early 1850s. In this, despite strong backing from Aden for a generous *ex gratia* payment, he was less successful. Whether or not the Sultan was the legal suzerain of the 'Aqrabi was one of those open questions which yields a different answer each time it is posed, to the lucrative bafflement of lawyers. A decision could not be arrived at easily and after two years of internal discussion the Indian Government finally decided to grant $2,500, less than half what the Sultan had expected to receive.[148]

On their way through the Indian machinery of government, the papers on the Hiswah case crossed and intermingled with those concerning a more startling project set on foot by Sultan Fadl. In 1871 he proposed to occupy Ta'izz and the fertile coffee districts of the Hajariya, in southern Yemen, in alliance with the British. In return for the provisions of troops, arms and a guarantee against outside attack, he offered to share the government and revenues of the

province with his allies.[149] Since 1869 he had been fomenting
rebellion by the Shafi'i people of the area against their Zaydi overlords.[150] Then and in the following year he secured loans amounting
to some $125,000 to finance his scheme from Muhsin al 'Awlaqi, an
Arab *jemadar* at the Nizam of Hyderabad's Court. Plans were laid
for the raising of 'Awlaqi mercenaries and intrigues were set on foot
among the Subayhi to win them to the 'Abdali side.[151] Here was an
ambitious scheme of conquest. But there was also another side to the
picture. Since 1865 the Zaydi rulers of the Hajariya had been
protesting at the steadily mounting transit dues which the im-
pecunious 'Abdali had been levying on the Yemen–Aden traffic.
Several times they threatened to attack Lahej if the Sultan would not
desist. They appealed to the Aden Resident to intervene, contemplated seizing Mocha from the Turks to provide an alternative outlet, and entered into a negotiation with a group of French merchants
who conceived the idea of bypassing Lahej and Aden altogether by
opening a port at Shaykh Sa'id, opposite Perim.[152]

The Aden Government was touched by all this feverish activity
at a number of points. Sultan Fadl's meddling in the Hajariya could
not be ignored. The imminent threat of a Zaydi attack on Lahej
had to be countered by the issue of powder and shot to the Sultan in
September 1870.[153] The Zaydi protest against rising transit dues was
taken seriously – Aden too was suffering – and a plan for offering a
fixed subsidy in return for their abolition was contemplated.[154] As
for the French Company's designs on the strategic point of Shaykh
Sa'id, this gave the whole business an international slant and diplomatic machinery was set in motion to have them ousted.[155] Out of
all this and Sultan Fadl's multiple monetary claims grew a counter
British scheme as startling as Sultan Fadl's own. In March 1871 a
well-matured plan was gravely put forward by the Bombay Government for the occupation of the whole of the 'Abdali territory. The
Lahej Sultan's many offers, especially that made in writing in 1870
that 'Government should either look on me with the eyes of kindness
and should strengthen my hands and my property and establish my
name, or should take my territory from me and give me a sufficiency
for myself, my brothers, followers and children . . .' were taken to
mean literally what they said. Sultan Fadl had had in mind his
Yemeni project and his relations with his neighbours. But the officers
of the forward school at Bombay were thinking in terms of hill stations
for the garrison, safer and cheaper provisions for Aden and the
preservation of British ascendancy in the Red Sea after the opening
of the Suez Canal. Lahej was to be brought under direct British
administration and there was wild talk of 'very little tact' being
required to make the Arabs of the far interior fast friends of the

British. In a sense the scheme lay in the logic of events in the Aden hinterland during the reign of Sultan Fadl, but it was received with something approaching shock by the Indian Central Government and flatly turned down.[156]

While the Aden authorities were thus half by intent, half by the intent of others, being drawn into hinterland politics, they were at the same time improving the apparatus for dealing with their extended commitments. During the 1860s the Arabic Department grew from the one-man affair it had been in Rassam's time to one of the largest and most costly agencies of Aden's Government. At one period in the 1860s the amount of correspondence increased tenfold in five years and at the end of the decade the Department had a sizeable staff and a separate office. In 1869 a large house in Crater was purchased by Government for the entertainment of official guests from the hinterland. Previously, visitors to Aden had been accommodated by the British officers or were lodged in private houses in the town.[157] Now, to encourage such friendly contacts and cope with increasing numbers, Government decided on a more regular arrangement.[158] So the Guest House was established, and quickly became the focal point in the conduct of tribal policy. In the 1870s the numbers of official visitors leapt upward and in the financial year 1880–1 no less than 1,395 were received. These people were lodged and catered for during their stay at Aden; on their departure they were, as the phrase went, 'dismissed with presents'. The expenditure on presents substantially exceeded that on entertainment and the two taken together reached the sizeable sum of 46,000 Rs. in 1880–1.[159] Thus what had been a small *ad hoc* arrangement in the time of Coghlan became a powerful and important organisation. The role it played in British relations with the tribes may be gathered from the sums of money spent and the fact that a carefully graded hospitality was offered. Tribesmen were divided into three categories for the purpose of entertainment. Two rupees 4 annas per day was the allowance for first-class guests. Half that sum was allowed for those who fell into the second class and only half a rupee for the lowest class. In addition, lists were drawn up of the number of adherents each chief was entitled to bring with him, and in the 1870s the practice grew up of allowing chiefs to send in men with letters of recommendation for entertainment at Government expense.[160] The whole system was geared to the pattern of social relationships in the hinterland, modified by the degree of friendliness of the individuals concerned toward the British authorities. Here was a fertile field for offering slights or flattery to tribal potentates.

The transformation of the Arabic Department was connected with the rise to power of Salah Jaffer, a descendant of Haines's agent

Mulla Jaffer and the founder of a dynasty of interpreters. Salah Jaffer and his son were to run the Arabic Office for the next thirty years, and others among his descendants were to hold analogous posts in the Aden administration to the time of the British withdrawal in 1967.[161] A man of exceptional intelligence, Jaffer was at once a bureaucrat and a skilful navigator through the tricky waters of Arab diplomacy. He could draw up a concise informative report in a civil service style equal to that of any of his British superiors; he could also overreach the astute politicians of the Hadramawt. A succession of Residents commended him to Government. He ultimately reached the rank of Native Interpreter with the title of Khan Bahadur and indeed he served the interests of his masters well, while not neglecting to look equally well after his own.[162] Yet he started with few advantages. He entered government service in 1855 in the humble position of Arabic writer at the Residency Court just two years after Mulla Jaffer's deportation. He served there for ten years until his opportunity came with Rassam's departure and the transfer of the Arabic Department to the inexperienced hands of Captain Goodfellow. Thenceforward his rise was rapid. In 1865 he was made Arabic Writer in charge of reservoirs. Three years later he was given the combined offices of Supervisor of Waterworks, Town Overseer and Summons Writer in the Police Court.[163] These were merely typical Aden devices for increasing his salary. The duties of his new offices were largely nominal and in fact he was playing an increasingly notable role in the conduct of hinterland policy. When Goodfellow went on leave in 1867 Jaffer was almost solely responsible for the running of the Arabic Department. Two years later he pushed out his rival, Sayyid 'Alawi, by helping Sultan Fadl over the Little Aden and Hiswah affairs.[164] Sayyid 'Alawi's defeat on that occasion was as much a victory for Jaffer as it was for Lahej; thenceforward little was done in the hinterland without his having some say.

Jaffer was by this time Interpreter and Superintendent of the Guest House. He had five Arab assistants under his control and they looked after the tribal visitors.[165] Jaffer drew up the lists of those eligible for entertainment for the approval of the First Assistant Resident and recommended the size of the present to be proffered on departure.[166] The ever-changing British personnel could not hope to rival his accumulated knowledge of the names and significance of all those entertained and in consequence this department of tribal policy fell more and more into his hands with the passage of time. It was he therefore who really determined the social status of Aden's guests, and the fact that some 'very powerful' chiefs later inexplicably became relatively unimportant suggests that his social measuring-stick was not always free from personal bias.[167] Thus with the Guest

House the Aden Government furnished itself with a well-developed and flexible instrument for influencing tribal politics. But like the rest of the machinery of nineteenth-century Aden Government, it was less exact, less responsive to 'official' and bureaucratic commands than would seem from first appearances.

To back up this organisation, Aden was by the end of the decade also able to dispose of a small but effective force specially designed for use in the hinterland. One of the bequests left to Aden by the Abyssinian Expedition was a troop of irregular horse raised among Baluch tribesmen from the Sind frontier and armed with carbine and sabre. Since the time of Haines, Aden officials had persistently sought to overcome the well-founded fears of superior authorities that the establishment of such a force would invite military adventures in the interior and made Aden more than a mere naval base. Haines had secured a troop of horse for a short period but it was soon withdrawn. In 1855 Outram's team, thanks to the confidence it could command in higher circles, temporarily overcame the opposition of the Court of Directors and had a troop of horse raised in Sind. But this force never reached Aden. It was diverted to serve with the Persian expedition and thereafter was drawn into the vortex of the Mutiny. Coghlan tried a Camel Corps as a substitute but quickly disbanded it when it failed to hold its own against Arab cameleers. Coghlan then lost confidence in the whole scheme and it was left to the more aggressive Merewether to take it up once more in 1865 as part of his larger policy of promoting social improvement in the interior. Merewether expected that a hundred horse at Aden would produce another Sind miracle. In a few years, he optimistically wrote, 'the rich plain would once more be covered with fields of waving corn, and the villages filled with a happy and wealthy population'.[168] Others were more sceptical. Lawrence, the Viceroy, and Wood, the Secretary of State, foresaw a grim future of frontier wars and political embroilments if Merewether were given too much scope. But the Governor of Bombay, Bartle Frere, another Sind veteran, was enthusiastic and offered persuasive guarantees. Two years' argument wore down the opposition to the scheme and the troop was formed in 1868, with the strict proviso that it be used only in the immediate vicinity of the settlement.[169]

Conscious of jealous eyes in London and Calcutta, the Aden authorities seldom used the force on offensive operations. Yet the presence of these cavalrymen at their Khormaksar base, just outside the Aden walls, had an important effect on British relations with the tribes. They represented a constant threat to those tribes which were near at hand. Their frequent peaceful reconnaissances yielded a mass of exact information about the terrain if not the inhabitants of the country within a forty-mile radius of Aden. The grosser geographical blunders which still occurred at the end of the 1860s were avoided thereafter as the troop's mapping operations got under way. British officers could now make more impromptu visits to the interior than had been the case when the provision of an effective tribal escort had required elaborate diplomatic preparation. Reports were now based less on hearsay and more on personal knowledge. And in the early 1870s wide horizons began to open up as it became possible to see more effectively beyond the little group of 'Abdali, Fadli and 'Aqrabi tribes which had previously loomed so large in the considerations of Aden Residents.

CHAPTER V

Turkish Intervention and
the Beginning of the Protectorate

Whatever blunders and tergiversations may have marked the conduct of relations with the hinterland tribes in the 1850s and 1860s there could be no doubt that the half-expressed basic objectives of British policy were being attained. The undertow of economic forces was drawing Aden's neighbours into close relations with the settlement. Lahej was already by 1870 inextricably connected with British Aden. Other parts of the hinterland, notable Fadli country, were following in its wake. The British had become an accepted, even an essential part of the political system and their activity was intensifying and extending beyond Aden's immediate neighbourhood.

This forward movement was in full flood when an entirely new situation was produced by the sudden appearance of a powerful new force on the frontiers of the hinterland. From 1850 to 1872 the authorities at Aden had been able to pursue their ends in South-West Arabia without fear of disturbance from the north. The threats of invasion by outside forces which had complicated Haines's relations with the tribes had ceased as the Yemen itself passed through what may be described as the worst years of its recent history. Economically, the whole region was in a state of chronic depression.[1] Coffee was no longer a great source of wealth. The Yemeni producer had to compete with the lower-priced product of better organised planters in Ceylon, the West Indies, Java, and later in the century, Brazil. The reliable old outlets in the Middle East were lost and even in the neighbouring province of the Hijaz, the main coffee import came from Java. Exporters could only stay in business as the purveyors of a rare variety sought by a few connoisseurs. When the Turks rehabilitated the trade toward the end of the century only a tenth of the crop went to Egypt, the rest was absorbed by the luxury trade of Europe and the United States.[2] In the interior the long-suffering Banian merchants who swarmed there in the great days of the country's prosperity had abandoned the cities of the Yemen; only three were to be found in San'a' in 1855 and a year later two of those had left.[3] What

little external commerce there was took place at Hudayda and
Aden. By the mid-1850s Mocha lay silent and dead, a town of the
past which had lost its trade, its merchants, its donkeymen and casual
labourers to Aden.[4]

The weakness of the economic base set all organised government
at a discount, and the competition of Aden's free port did not help
seaport Governors balance their budgets. The lack of financial and
political stamina on both sides, which characterised the last phases
of the struggle for supremacy between the Imams and the Sharifs of
Abu 'Arish in the 1840s, was repeated in the next decade in the
desultory contests between Imamic pretenders and the Turkish
occupiers of the Tihama ports. From time to time their forces clashed
as the Turks sought to extend their rule. But the real enemy of both,
as some far-sighted Imams came to see, were the forces of political
disintegration which were reducing the country to a congeries of
independent units. From 1850 onward one might say that the
Imamate had to all intents and purposes ceased to exist. Those who
claimed that title in this period were little more than the creatures
of one or other of the great tribal confederations which in fact ruled
the land. One *soi-disant* Imam spent several poverty-stricken years
neglected and ignored in his native village.[5] Another, elected by
the townsmen of San'a' from among their number, ruled effectively
no further than the city walls.[6] The panoply of jurisdiction erected
by the Imams in their heyday had fallen into desuetude and when the
Turks and later Imam Yahya began to reimpose their Qanun and
the Shari'a code, they had to contend with the widespread dominance
of tribal courts and tribal law.[7]

The decade of the 1860s was if anything worse than that which
preceded it. The Aden hinterland was not the only part of South-
West Arabia to be visited by famine and disease. Cholera, rinderpest,
drought and locusts also struck at the Yemen, with the same political
results as at Lahej. In 1863 Merewether reported that the Yemen
had become a barren wilderness – an exaggeration no doubt, but also
a reflection of what his informants thought about the existing
situation.[8] The British had little to fear from such a distracted land.
But by 1870 political and economic weakness had reached the point
where the Yemen had become a political vacuum inviting the intervention of outside forces. Indeed the whole of South Arabia was in a
similar state. The days when the Wahhabis of Najd could threaten
Syria and Mesopotamia, and Masqat could usurp the commerce
of the Indian Ocean, were decidedly past. Arabia was fast becoming a
backward area in a developing world – backward that is, not only in
relation to Europe but also in relation to Egypt, Turkey, India and
the coastal communities in East Africa. In all those countries,

expatriate Arabs and others were beginning to use the money and the new technical devices such as steamships, steel cannon and rifles, which their place in richer and more modern societies afforded them, to interfere decisively in the affairs of Arabian states. The purchase of tribal mercenaries, the buying up of bankrupt governments, the destruction by gunfire of formerly impregnable strongholds, all by foreigners or by Arabs backed by foreigners, was beginning to become a common feature of the South Arabian scene. The Sultan of Lahej's schemes of conquest in the Yemen, backed by money from Hyderabad and arms from Aden, was not an isolated case. Hyderabad Arabs were pursuing similar schemes on their own account with greater success on the coast and in the interior of the Hadhramawt.[9] Further east at Masqat, Sayyid Turki, a contender for the Sultanate, ousted his rival in 1870 with the help of Zanzibar money and British arms.[10] The resources of these adventurers were puny compared with those which the rulers of Egypt and Turkey could command. For centuries Arabia had been more or less protected from the interference of those powers by the poor communications across the deserts stretching from Cairo to the Shatt al 'Arab. But in 1869 the main arsenals at Istanbul and Alexandria were suddenly brought thousands of miles closer when the Suez Canal opened a short route from the Mediterranean to Arabian waters. The tribes of Arabia were now brought face to face with states which, though weak in relation to European neighbours, were giants in comparison with themselves. Moreover, those states, especially Egypt, had augmented their means of action by drawing capital from the world financial market. Both were in process of re-equipping their armies with the best weapons which modern technology could provide. All that was required was a sufficient motive for them to launch their forces southward.[11]

In its impoverished state, Arabia offered no inviting prospect to anyone interested in commercial gain. But in the world of Islam it was still a powerful political symbol. Control of the Holy Places and the people of the Prophet carried with it a claim to the leadership of the followers of the Muslim faith. Such a claim may have been of marginal political value in the past but events in all parts of the world were increasing its apparent worth. The collapse of Muslim governments in Africa and the East before advancing European Empires was setting many Muslims in search of another focus for their religious loyalty. Nor did this only mean the mention of some other secular ruler in the Friday prayers. In many places Muslim revivalism was the forerunner of later secular nationalism in its resistance to European encroachment, and while Muslim governments were falling, a series of underground religio-political movements were in process of full expansion.[12] None could tell what dividends the leadership of such forces could pay, and in the 1860s theorists in the heartland of the Ottoman Empire, such as Sayyid Jamal al din al Afghani, were beginning to perceive the possibilities of a programme of Islamic unity under the Ottoman Sultan-Caliph.[13]

Other factors of a less speculative nature made the preachings of such pan-Islamic enthusiasts appeal to a wider public among those concerned with the running of the Ottoman Empire. The new military schools were producing an increasing number of young men who, having imbibed modern ideas on politics and administration and seen what nationalism could do in Europe, were dissatisfied with the irrational, pragmatic and uninspiring structure of the Ottoman Empire.[14] Yet, for such a heterogeneous, multinational system, European-type nationalism meant only precipitate dissolution into its several Turkish, Egyptian and Arab components, none of which would be able to compete with powerful European rivals. On the other hand the creed of Islamic unity under the Caliphate could fuse the many racial elements of the Empire into one and also enable the state to swing over to the offensive by attracting the loyalty of Muslim subjects of European powers in Africa, India and Central Asia. Within a narrower field it was becoming evident that the Christian subjects in the Balkans were hopelessly disaffected, and elsewhere in the Empire they were systematically seeking the protection of European Consulates. They were a wasting asset if not an incubus. The Empire was being steadily thrust out of Europe. On the other hand by the use of modern arms and modern methods it was tightening its hold on Mesopotamia. By the same means Egypt was pushing its rule southward through the Sudan to Central Africa. All these facts indicated that there was a brighter future for the Empire as an Islamic state in Africa and Asia rather than as a secular power poised uncomfortably on either side of the Bosphorus.

While such ideas were gaining currency in Istanbul, the Ottoman Sultanate seemed on the point of being cut off from its Afro-Asian destiny. In the late 1860s and early 1870s the ambitious Khedive Isma'il was working hard to secure complete independence of the Porte. Egyptian intrigue in Arabia concomitantly raised the fear that he would carry the Arabs with him, leaving the Empire a truncated and meaningless entity confined to Anatolia and the Balkan remnants. In 1869 a rising of the 'Asir tribe on the Yemen–Hijaz border which threatened to push the Turks from their narrow foothold on the west Arabian littoral dramatised this problem. Egyptian complicity was suspected, and as the fate of Arabia suddenly appeared to be in the balance, the pan-Islamic enthusiasts came to the forefront of the Ottoman political scene. The patriotic Grand

Vizier, 'Ali Pasha, an administrative reformer hitherto suspicious of advocates of political change, now began to patronise them. Their idealism was needed while the Khedive, who could command more capital than his Suzerain, was suborning high and low at Istanbul. Thus the policy which launched two expensive but successful expeditions in 1871 against 'Asir and Najd, also brought to power those influenced by the ideas of pan-Islam. From that time forward the new doctrine and the south- and eastward-thrusting strategy which it entailed was a powerful factor in Ottoman policy. Under Sultan 'Abd al Hamid II it became the dominant factor. The effects of this was to refurbish and modernise the political symbolism of Arabia. To the enthusiasts who were now to be found in all parts of the Ottoman political structure, on the frontiers as well as at the Porte, the possession of the Holy Places and a few of the more lucrative seaports was not enough. The logic of their doctrine pointed to complete control of the whole peninsula, and whoever stood in the way of this was met with the assertive intransigence later to be the hallmark of more straightforward nationalists.[15]

These were the changes in the general situation in the Middle East which led to the invasion of Arabia and the transformation of the conditions in which Britain exercised its influence in the Aden hinterland. The troops sent against the 'Asir in 1871 were not re-called when their task was done.[16] In the following year they were switched southward to Hudayda and from there they marched inland to the Yemen highlands. This was the most formidable Otto-man force the Yemen had seen since the seventeenth century. It numbered 8,000 infantry and a thousand cavalry, was well led by a dedicated, energetic commander, Ahmad Mukhtar Pasha, and its array of rifles and mountain guns were handled by skilled artillerists who knew how to use them. With their matchlocks and smooth-bore weapons the Arabs would have had difficulty in resisting such an onslaught, even in their mountain fastnesses. But the Yemen was ripe for conquest. There was no co-ordinated opposition and the Turks were able to reduce the country to submission piecemeal. Strangely enough the toughest struggle was put up not by the Imams but by the Bani Yam adherents of the eclectic Isma'ili sect who held the strategic natural fortress of Manakha on the edge of the highlands. As for the citizens of San'a', they surrendered their city and submitted to the Turks without a shot being fired. Such was the chaos and misery in the land that the invaders appeared as harbingers of peace to a city beleaguered by the badawin, and among the deputation which welcomed Ahmad Mukhtar in April 1872 were included the descendants of those who rose against the Turks in 1849, and some of the leaders of the future Imamic rebellion against Ottoman rule. Within the space of six months the greater part of the country had accepted the new regime. Ahmad Mukhtar was appointed Governor-General of the new Ottoman province; he proclaimed a policy of economic development and social improvement under the rule of the Sultan Caliph, and set about introducing the new style *Vilayet* system of Ottoman administration.[17]

By the summer of 1872 the main lines of the new situation in the Middle East had been sketched in. How were those responsible for the making of British policy to deal with it? One possible course of action was to permit or even encourage the extension of Ottoman rule over Arabia and come to an agreement with the Porte for the preservation of vital British interests in South Arabia, including the tenure of the Aden base. This would greatly simplify the task of handling the whole area, and anything which would simplify British relations with Arabia at that particular time had much to recommend it. The declining strength of South Arabian society and its openness to outside influence was creating a number of new and complicated situations in which it was not clear what Britain's objectives were or how they could be attained. Controversy was heated, government departments were often at cross purposes. The Bombay Government's projected annexation of Lahej in 1871, together with similar adventurous schemes concerning Zanzibar and Masqat, had generated such friction between Bombay and Simla that the Supreme Government had taken control of Indian Ocean policy out of the hands of its subordinates. Yet Bombay could argue with some justice that it was merely trying to maintain the *status quo*.[18] Thus Britain's policy, for quite independent reasons, was in a state of flux when the Turks first appeared and many officials were inclined to watch their progress with a favourable eye. Certainly each new Turkish move was met with questions, threats and admonitions from India.[19] This was an obvious reaction. No politician intent on negotiation would throw away his bargaining counters before he reached the conference table. The Indian authorities had not decided on negotiation, but the Viceroy, Northbrook, toyed with the idea in 1872. In April of that year he expressed the view that he would prefer to have a '*quasi*-civilised power' to deal with in the Persian Gulf and near Aden than the Arab chiefs 'who shift and change as often as the sands of their deserts'.[20] Likewise at Aden the Resident, Schneider, was at first impressed by the vigour and progressive disposition of Ahmad Mukhtar Pasha. While wrestling in 1872 with the intricacies of Subayhi politics, he looked forward to the day when 'the Turks sweep these rascals [i.e. the Subayhi] off the face of the earth'.[21] Another of those who played a large part in determining what should be done at Aden, namely Bartle Frere, former Governor of Bombay and now a member of the Indian Council, was also aware of the possibility of safeguarding fundamental British interests while permitting an extension of Ottoman rule.[22] On the other hand if it were decided that the Turks were not to be trusted then the obvious course was to determine just how much of Aden's hinterland was needed for the free functioning of the base, and establish a protectorate over it. This would have clarified the British position and prevented much misunderstanding with the Porte. It would also have given the tribes a clearer idea of where they stood.

Either of these courses, however, involved large issues of policy which could not be decided by the Indian Government alone. The Ottoman Empire was not another tribe to be dealt with according to the requirements of the local situation. It was a great power, closely involved in the complexities of European diplomacy. To surrender to the Porte the guardianship of Aden's sources of supply required an assessment of future Turkish friendliness which the Indian Government was not competent to make. Likewise the declaration of a protectorate in South Arabia might sour Anglo-Ottoman relations and have a deleterious effect on British interests elsewhere. The final decision therefore could only be made by the cabinet in London. Unfortunately the Home Government was at that time in no condition to offer constructive leadership. A multitude of problems, foreign and domestic, assailed the Ministry, some issues endangered its majority in the House, others provoked violent dispute within the cabinet itself. Under Gladstone's influence the keynote of the Government's foreign policy was peace, the preservation of the 'Concert of Europe' and the cessation of Palmerstonian aggressiveness in the world at large. But it was the tragedy of the Ministry that while it wished only to be on good terms with all and to maintain the *status quo*, dynamic forces in other countries were transforming the world picture, creating new causes of conflict and threatening British positions which even Gladstone was unwilling to sacrifice. In Western Europe Bismarck crushed France, in Eastern Europe Russia re-armed its Black Sea ports, in Central Asia the Russians were at last approaching the frontiers of Afghanistan, the United States claimed compensation for the Alabama depradations, the Ashanti descended on the British-protected Gold Coast tribes, and in East Africa the Sultan of Zanzibar threatened to throw off the long-exercised British tutelage.[23] Ottoman extension in Arabia was just one more burden which the overladen machinery of government had to carry. To pursue a quiescent policy in such circumstances was impossible. New problems required new solutions. But in most cases the new solutions offered, savoured of that expansionism which Gladstone and a dominant group in the Liberal Party were deter-

mined to renounce. Beneath all ran strong undercurrents of doubt
which extended widely within British political society; doubt about
religion, doubt about the viability of the existing social order and its
values, doubt about the universal improvability of man darkened by
a growing tendency to divide mankind into a hierarchy of un-
changeable racial categories. Such heartsearchings did not help
provide constructive statesmanship. They only served to reinforce
the normally strong forces of inertia. Thus the stream of appeals for
instructions from India and Aden petered out in the sands of indecision at London and the only intelligible reply which came back
was to keep on doing what had been done before.[24] With all its other
troubles, the Gladstone government went out of office in 1874 without
ever having seriously considered what its Arabian policy should be,
and in consequence British policy toward the Aden hinterland was
allowed to emerge in a hand-to-mouth fashion in response to the
pressure of local forces.

The local forces were represented on the one hand by the south-
ward-advancing Turkish battalions and on the other by the political
system of Aden's tribal hinterland with all its factions, disputes and
alliances. Had the Turks met with universal acceptance or universal
hostility on the part of the tribes, the British Government might have
had its problem settled for it. But this was not to be. Tribal disputes
and old factional quarrels loomed larger in the minds of the tribesmen
than either the appeal of pan-Islam or the fear of Turkish invasion
and soon the Turks were to find themselves enmeshed in the same net
as the Aden authorities, being able neither to cut through nor to
disentangle themselves. The Ottoman officials were not helped by
the fact that at the outset in Yemen itself they had to work through
local co-operators. On paper Yemen might be a *Vilayet*, with its
Wali and its *Mutasarrifs* ruling the various neat administrative
districts.[25] But in fact Turkish rule in 1872 meant little more than
that those local potentates whom the Turks decided to back, now had
the power of the Ottoman army and Ottoman resources behind them.
On the western borders of Lahej the Turkish authorities chose to
rule through those old enemies of the 'Abdali Sultan, the Zaydi Dhu
Muhammad tribe. In consequence the Dhu Muhammad were able
to accomplish with Turkish aid what in 1871 Sultan Fadl Muhsin
had hoped to do with British support. In the last months of 1872,
backed by 2,000 Turkish regular troops at Ta'izz, they overran the
'Abdali Sultan's former Shafi'i allies in the Hajariya and began to
push down to the borders of Subayhi country.[26]

This was not likely to predispose Sultan Fadl in favour of the
newcomers, nor was the fact that the first call to declare his allegiance
to the Sultan-Caliph came to him as to a subordinate authority,

through the medium of one of the Yemeni Imams.[27] In any case Sultan Fadl had for some time been receiving at Lahej refugees from the Turkish invasions further north, and since as early as February 1871 he had been seeking to turn the attention of sceptical Residents to the dangers involved in the presence of large Ottoman forces in the Red Sea.[28] As the invaders marched southward he became increasingly alarmed, and in May and July 1872 he sought assurances from Aden of continued British support. His first fear was of a Turkish revival of the Zaydi scheme of diverting the coffee trade away from Lahej. As the Turks came nearer he was given cause for further alarm. In October the hinterland tribes received a direct summons from Ahmad Mukhtar to accept Ottoman suzerainty and while the 'Abdali, on British advice, refused, his enemy the Hawshabi agreed, and went to Ta'izz. There was no need to seek far for the Hawshabi's reason for submission. He hoped to repoen the question of the Za'ida lands which Lahej still held with a large measure of British support, and his hopes were not in vain, for after his interview at Ta'izz the Turks began to take an interest in the case, with a strong bias in favour of their new-found friend. In December 1872 Sultan Fadl received a peremptory summons to appear before the Turkish authorities and this sent him rushing in panic to Aden, where he implored the Resident to take his state under British protection.[29]

Up to this point the British authorities had regarded what was happening in the Yemen with some equanimity. Even the Aden Residents had tended to regard the Lahej Sultan as an alarmist, until Sultan Fadl's visit to Resident Schneider in October with the Pasha's letter.[31] This interview converted Schneider. He forgot his ruminations on the blessings of Turkish rule and urgently recommended the reassertion of Palmerston's 1838 objection to the extension of Ottoman rule beyond the Bab el Mandeb.[31] The Resident's superiors were slower to take alarm. They did not lose their complacency and were inclined to blame Schneider for losing his.[32] No further instructions had reached Aden when Sultan Fadl came again in January 1873 with the second Turkish summons. Only then did the wheels of government begin to turn, and that largely because Bartle Frere was there to help Schneider sound the tocsin. The former Governor of Bombay happened to be at Aden at that moment *en route* for Zanzibar. Ostensibly he was commissioned to deal only with the East African slave trade, but he had virtually forced his services on the Government and in his own mind the purpose of his mission was to break the administrative deadlock which was paralysing Britain's Arabian policy. He and his lieutenant Badger therefore went to work with a will, by-passing official channels, and warning all and sundry in the upper echelons of government of the seriousness of the Aden situation.[33] Thus when attention was first focused on the problem posed by Turkish encroachment it was not some outlying bulwark of British influence which was in question but Aden's most immediate and vital hinterland. The argument of those who called for strong action was made easy and the Porte was asked to stop interfering with Lahej.[34] Istanbul agreed, but in such terms as to reserve a claim to suzerainty over all the hinterland tribes.[35] On the Secretary of State for India's insistence this claim was resisted, but the situation on the spot steadily worsened. With the Turks now firmly established at Ta'izz and Qa'taba the struggle for power on the western borders of the Aden hinterland was now fully engaged. Every forward move in the Hajariya could now be represented as an advance on Lahej. The Hawshabi became more assertive and defiant toward the Aden Government. To the north the 'Alawi Shaykh was forced to surrender his son as a hostage to the Turks and the British-recognised 'Amir, 'Ali Muqbil, was ousted in favour of a rival. All these events were carefully reported to Schneider by Sultan Fadl and his friends and in the light of the Porte's assurances, what was happening began to look more and more like a case of Turkish duplicity.[36] The Indian authorities became restive and by March they were beginning to think in terms of extending formal protection to the tribes within the British sphere of influence.[37]

The fact that Sultan Fadl Muhsin was unwilling to make any concessions in the face of Turkish pressure was a cardinal factor in the Anglo-Ottoman diplomatic crisis which now ensued and which lasted for over a year. For the previous eight years he had been exercising the greatest influence over Aden's hinterland policy; now as the British were forced to decide how much of the hinterland was essential to Aden's wellbeing, their decision was coloured as much by 'Abdali needs as by Aden's requirements. In simple economic terms, Lahej, the 'Aqrabi and the Fadli country alone were really vital to the Aden base. Thence came the fodder, vegetables and water consumed by the garrison. Beyond that, the trade routes in the Wadi Hardaba and Subayhi country were no more necessary than the centres of coffee, qat and corn production in the Yemen proper, without which they were economically meaningless. Thus when in May 1873 the British Government listed the 'Abdali, Fadli, 'Awlaqi, Yafi'i', Hawshabi, 'Amiri, 'Alawi, 'Aqrabi and Subayhi tribes as those whose independence it wished the Porte to respect, it was delineating a political rather than an economic entity.[38] The western tribes among them could be said to be the controllers of the incoming trade routes from the Yemen, but this did not apply to the Yafi'i' and ʿAwlaqi, whose trading system was independent of Aden.[39] The only feature common to all was that they each formed part of a political system, and the hub of that system was Lahej rather than Aden. Apart from trading ties, the ʿAqrabi were bound to Lahej politically by their state of unresolved semi-dependence. The Subayhi too were subject to ʿAbdali influence, and often provided Lahej with mercenaries. To the north the Hawshabi still claimed the headwaters of the ʿAbdali irrigation system, and the ʿAlawi had helped to mediate in that dispute.[40] Daliʿ was also indirectly involved in the matter and in 1872 Sultan Fadl Muhsin mediated between the various claimants to the ʿAmirate. To the east the Fadli challenged the ʿAbdali right to control the Aden roads. The Yafiʿi were linked by marriage with Lahej, and were obvious allies against the Fadli. The ʿAwlaqi, the blackmailers of the east, still regarded Lahej as their tributary, and were a fertile source of mercenaries. The tribes met each other not for trade but for purposes of war and politics; the common meeting-place of all was the ʿAbdali Sultan's capital.

The Indian Government's justification for claiming more interest in the independence of these tribes than in that of those in the rest of the Yemen was that the Aden Government had for some time been interfering to settle their disputes, and had treaty and stipendiary arrangements with them.[41] This was indeed true, but Aden's connection with some was of a minimal nature and with others did not extend far into the past. Some only of the Subayhi Shaykhs received Aden stipends. Until 1870 they had been regarded as dependent on the ʿAbdali and in 1871 the first attempt to interfere directly in their affairs had come to grief as a result of Sultan Fadl's opposition.[42] The Aden authorities had only a nodding acquaintance with the ʿAlawi Shaykh and no direct treaty or stipendiary relationship.[43] The ʿAmirs of Daliʿ had received a small stipend since the occupation of Aden but they had seldom visited the settlement and the British had only the vaguest knowledge of their power and the extent of their dominion. Coghlan had secured an agreement not to engage in the slave trade from the Lower ʿAwlaqi in 1855, but his main interest in them and their northern neighbours at the time of signature was their ability to stop the Fadli attacking Lahej, not their ability to stop the import of slaves.[44] The Lower Yafiʿi had only entered into close relations with Aden after the Fadli expedition of 1866, and the Upper Yafiʿi' were practically unknown. It was possible by reference to Aitchison's compendious collection of treaties to see all these tribes mentioned either in the texts or in the commentary, but the mere mention of a name did not necessarily mean the exercise of continuous influence. In many cases tribal leaders had been accorded stipends in 1839 after the occupation of Aden and had scarcely been seen since. Even their stipends were often claimed by agents on their behalf.[45] Most of the old stipendiary commitments had been taken over *en bloc* from the Aden-Lahej Sultanate. They had not been acquired in the course of a new, independently-developed hinterland policy. Thus Aden's connection with the tribes in question was recent and rudimentary compared with that of the old and active political centre at Lahej.

Had the extent of British interests in the hinterland been worked out on a careful, rational basis by reference to the economic facts of the situation alone, a quite different set of boundaries would have been arrived at. But the confusion in governing circles and the failure to come to an agreement with the Turks before a series of diplomatic clashes had hardened attitudes on all sides ensured that this did not happen. Instead, most of the really important choices were made in the Aden Residency, where Sultan Fadl's views were well represented, and where there was a natural tendency to preserve intact the whole political system of the settlement's premier ally. The result was old and 'Abdali rather than new and British.[46] For this very reason however, what it lost in economic rationality it gained in terms of political viability. The nine tribes in which the British Government declared its interest may not all have been vital to the Aden base but they did represent in some sense an historic political entity. Owing to geographical facts and the curious political conservatism which endured through the constantly frothing factional disputes in southern Arabia, the 'Abdali Sultanate in 1872 still maintained its closest relations with those tribes which had taken part in the late-seventeenth-century revolt against Imamic rule, and later helped the first 'Abdali Sultan establish his independence. By identifying their interests so closely with those of the Lahej Sultan, the British, albeit unwittingly, were strengthening their links with Aden's past.

The May 1873 notification to the Porte was less important at the time than it was to become in the future as a point of reference for officials wrestling with the complexities of the Aden boundary question, as a description of a largely mythical *status quo*. Diplomatically, it was not irrevocable in that the British Government expressed a desire only that the Porte respect the independence of the nine listed tribes; it did not establish a British Protectorate over them. As far as the local situation was concerned, it changed nothing. At Istanbul the British Ambassador received conciliatory replies to his frequent protests at Turkish interference with the tribes, but on the spot Turkish activity intensified.[47] In May Turkish regular troops moved in toward Lahej from Ta'izz and Qa'taba, and after

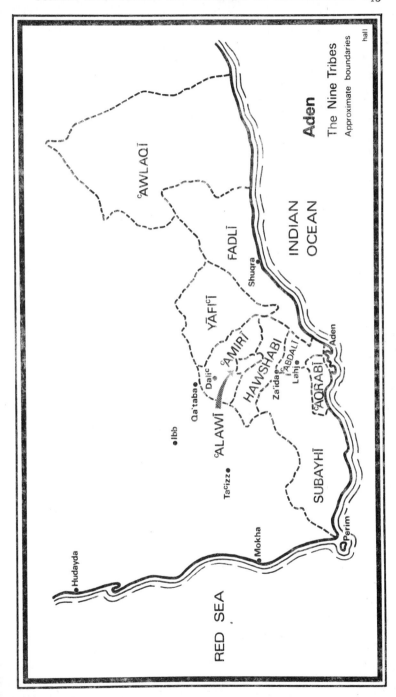

a military demonstration in Subayhi country and the Wadi Hardaba, they installed a garrison of irregulars, first at the Hawshabi capital and then at Shuka in the Za'ida lands.[48] Sultan Fadl was stripped of his allies and the Hawshabi began to intrigue with members of the 'Abdali tribe itself.[49] It was not long before the old leader of the opposition party at Lahej, 'Abdallah Muhsin, and his brother 'Abd al Karim, went over to the Turks and now, with a rival claimant at hand, the Turks were able to threaten Sultan Fadl Muhsin with deposition, as well as the loss of his Za'ida lands. The 'Abdali struggled on against mounting odds, but he came near to the end of his tether when in October 1873 clashes took place at the town of Lahej itself, and the Turks sent regular troops to protect 'Abdallah Muhsin's house from reprisals.[50] By this time the patience of the Indian Government had almost run out. The Viceroy, Northbrook, realised that if something positive were not done to check the Turkish authorities, the British would be faced with a *fait accompli*. He therefore conceded Schneider's request that British troops be sent to Lahej to protect the 'Abdali Sultan.[51] On 24 October, fifty sabres of the Aden Troop went to Lahej and were followed three days later by the Resident at the head of 328 infantry and artillery of the garrison. Despite this, the small Turkish force held its ground. Rumours spread that reinforcements were marching in from Ta'izz, and while Turks and British faced each other in the 'Abdali capital, two Turkish troopships, with 1,200 troops aboard, entered Aden harbour and were delayed there for unknown reasons. H.M.S. *Wolverine* was hastily ordered up from Trincomali to counteract the effect of this Turkish naval demonstration, and for more than a month Aden hung on the brink of war.[52]

London was forced toward decisive action. The Duke of Argyll, the impulsive, Palmerstonian Secretary of State for India, became rapidly more excitable. For some time he had been chafing at the weak foreign policy the Ministry under Gladstone's and Granville's guidance had been pursuing elsewhere in the world.[53] He refused to have one of India's vital northern bastions treated like some unimportant colony.[54] When diplomatic action failed to yield results he threatened to use the Indian army to force the Turks from their position. Granville and Gladstone, thoroughly alarmed at the prospect of a 'departmental war' by the India Office against what the Foreign Office was still treating as a friendly power, managed to restrain him by sending stiffer orders to Ambassador Elliott at the Porte.[55] The Turkish authorities at Istanbul were warned that if they failed to restrain their local subordinates, war would ensue.

At this, the Turks in turn went through a period of stress. Like Schneider at Aden, Turkish officials in the Yemen were committed to their Arab allies. Unlike him, they had backed the weaker party and knew that their withdrawal would entail the downfall of their friends. Yet they were convinced that their friends had justice on their side. After all, Sultan Fadl's claim to the Za'ida lands was based on little more than the right of recent conquest, and even his tenure of the Sultanate could easily be challenged in terms of strict legality.[56] As the Turks had only heard the arguments of one party there was no reason for them to doubt the rightness of their cause. Not only did withdrawal seem morally wrong, it was also politically inexpedient.[57] In the rest of the Yemen Turkish rule depended largely on their reputation for invincibility; a defeat at that stage could have had the widest repercussions. As far as the Turkish authorities in the Yemen were concerned, disengagement from the political imbroglio in which they had so incontinently involved themselves was unthinkable, and two successive Governors-General had plunged deeper in. They could count on the support of the Ministry of War which was responsible for Yemeni affairs,[58] while behind the scenes the Russian Ambassador was urging the Porte to stand its ground.[59] On the other hand the Grand Vizier and the Foreign Minister were not enthusiastic, and Egyptian money was still circulating at the Porte, backing arguments for the transfer of the Yemen to the Khedive's control. The new province was already an expensive item in the Ottoman budget. If to that were added the cost of a war with Britain, one of the possible sources of a new Turkish loan, the case for abandoning the whole of the Yemen to Egypt could have become overwhelming. The Sultan himself was worried by the amount of money spent.[60] Thus the expansionist party lost the day and definitive instructions were finally sent to the Governor-General to withdraw his troops from Lahej and Hawshabi country, and on the 6 December they accordingly departed.[61]

Schneider, exultant, was left in command of the field and immediately set about crushing Sultan Fadl's opponents. 'Abdallah Muhsin was unceremoniously summoned to Aden and confined there, together with his brother and their families and followers – one hundred and sixty-one persons in all. At Lahej his house, proving too strong for gunfire, was dismantled by British troops. The Hawshabi Sultan, fearing similar treatment, fled. But his lands at Za'ida fell once more into 'Abdali hands and three months later he too submitted to the Aden Government.[62] Never before had the British acted so decisively in the hinterland. The purge at Lahej had been severe and thorough. The expeditionary force stood for two months in 'Abdali territory – six weeks longer than Merewether had kept his troops in Fadli country in 1866 – and when the main body returned to Aden in January 1874 the Aden Troop remained at

Lahej to support the Sultan. The traumatic experience of having Turkish soldiers within twenty miles of Aden had produced a new acerbity in Aden's attitude to those who resisted its authority in the hinterland. Tribal politics no longer consisted of so many factions whose disputes the British should seek to mediate. In addition to the normal pressures which warped British impartiality there was now the belief in the existence of a 'loyal' party and a 'disloyal' party among the various tribes affected by Turkish encroachment. The primary British interest in the hinterland which had been peace and the steady flow of supplies to Aden now began to give place to a new interest in the rooting-out of Turkish influence within the limits of the May 1873 notification to the Porte. No more *faits accomplis* were to be permitted. International complications must be stopped at source before they began. And so, the Hawshabi, the 'Alawi and Dali' began to feel more strongly the weight of British influence exercised from Aden.

These long-term results of the Anglo-Turkish clash would very likely have surprised and annoyed Gladstone. At the height of the crisis he had brusquely rejected Argyll's and Northbrook's proposal to extend formal protection to the threatened tribes, on the grounds that it would bind Britain to support people whose conduct towards others it would be unable to control. The analogy he set with Gold Coast–Ashanti relations, at that time forcing Britain into war, might not have been entirely appropriate, but his prognosis was remarkably accurate.[63] Gladstone could see what was going to happen, what indeed was already happening. But he did not know how to stop it. The refusal to declare a protectorate amounted to little more than denying the name of something which was already coming into existence. There were fewer illusions at Dali' where a year later the Shaykhs were arguing with the British-supported 'Amir about whether their country should 'go under the English government'.[64] Yet the possibility that the crisis could have produced another result, given slightly different circumstances, was vividly illustrated by what was taking place on the other side of the Gulf of Aden.

The British at Aden could put forward almost as strong a claim to control the politics of the Somali tribes as those of the Aden hinterland. In terms of strict treaty rights the Somalis were more closely bound to the British than the Arabs of South Arabia. At different times since 1827, various authorities on the Somali coast had been induced to engage themselves to protect British commerce, to enter no agreements with other European powers, to abstain from the slave trade and to protect wrecked vessels. Up to the mid-1850s these engagements had been backed up by constant British interference to enforce their implementation.[65] Haines's assistant,

Cruttenden, had spent much of his time dealing with Somali affairs, and until 1855 the annual Berbera fair was supervised by one or more naval vessels. After 1855, however, when the Aden Government no longer had a flotilla of Indian Navy ships permanently at its disposal, it was unable to exercise the same direct and continuous control over the politics of the opposite coast. The dissolution of the Indian Navy in 1863 further weakened Aden's grip, for the officers of the Royal Navy were less co-operative and less experienced than the old hands of the local Service. In 1868 Aden began to press the Indian Government to allow them to station a man of their own at Berbera to preserve Aden's declining influence.[66] The Aden authorities, nevertheless remained in touch with what was going on. Every official with Magisterial or Police duties in the settlement was in all too frequent contact with members of the Somali community living down the beach at Ma'alla. One of the *subehdars* of Police at Aden was a Somali who wielded the greatest influence among his people on both sides of the Gulf, and through him the Residency essayed to act indirectly on Somali politics.[67] Then there was the Commissariat, still a large purchaser of Somali livestock and therefore able, if it wished, to make or break the men it dealt with. In any case, however much British political influence may have been on the wane, the economic links between Aden and the opposite coast were if anything becoming stronger and closer. Aden and its garrison were decidedly more dependent on the opposite coast for food supplies than they were on the Arabian hinterland. If Lahej was in this sense vital to the security of the base, by the same token so was Berbera and the other ports across the Gulf.[68]

The first serious external challenge to British influence in Somaliland came simultaneously with Turkish encroachment on the British position in the Aden hinterland. As the Ottoman forces pushed forward along the western littoral of the Red Sea, the Egyptians were advancing *pari passu* down the opposite coast. Khedive Isma'il was building up his Sudanese empire in the Nile valley; he was also determined to buttress and strengthen it by establishing his power on the African coasts. In 1866 he induced the Porte to transfer Massawa to his authority, and in the following year an Egyptian official engaged on a survey of the Khedive's new acquisition visited Berbera and helped to arrange one of the perennial disputes between the two Somali factions there. Three years later the Egyptians visited Berbera again, strengthened their control over Somali politics and prepared the way for a definitive occupation, which took place in the autumn of 1873, when Schneider had his hands full with the Turks in Lahej. Several hundred troops were landed, forts were built, a new permanent town was laid out, and work was begun on an aqueduct to provide a regular supply of water. Within two years the whole aspect of affairs had changed. The Egyptians were firmly established, an attempt by the Ayal Yunus to divert Berbera's trade in protest against Egyptian backing of their Ayal Ahmad rivals was crushed by the closing of the port of Bulhar and the interior city of Harrar was brought under Egyptian control. In the process, Aden's *subehdar* had been squeezed out, and by 1875 his influence over Somali politics had vanished.

Each stage of this Egyptian take-over of Aden's Somali preserves was watched with growing alarm at Aden. Every Resident between 1867 and 1875 believed that Egyptian control of Berbera and the adjoining coast would be highly detrimental to Aden's interests, and urged their superiors to take action.[69] In 1870 the Government steamer *Sind* followed the Egyptian *Khartum* into the Berbera road-stead and the *subehdar* went ashore in a vain attempt to dissuade the people of the town from recognising Egyptian authority.[70] Schneider would have made a similar move in 1873 had he not been fully engaged in dealing with the Turks. The Residents believed that the Egyptians would monopolise Berbera's trade and cripple a large part of Aden's commerce, that their garrisons would consume the livestock otherwise destined for the troops at Aden, and that if allowed to stay they would have a stranglehold on the British if at any time they wished to exercise it. The rough handling which the Aden *subehdar* received at Berbera in 1870 and his loss of control thereafter provided additional grievances against the newcomers. Opinion at Aden was if anything more solidly hostile to the Egyptian presence in Somaliland than to the Turkish presence in the hinterland.

For a time the attitude taken in Simla and London was the same as that at Aden. The Viceroy was only slightly less bellicose than the Resident in 1870.[71] In 1874 Argyll pressed the Foreign Office to deal with the Egyptians in the same way as the Turks.[72] But the Foreign Office was even more reluctant to act decisively to protect Somaliland than to protect Aden's Arabian hinterland. The argument was brought forward in 1873 that Egyptian occupation would at least close the coastline to European powers and relieve Britain of the constant worry that their rivals might establish themselves on the route to India.[73] In 1874 this argument was developed and it was pointed out that if Egypt would agree to maintain freedom of trade at Berbera and take over Britain's anti-slave trade commitments on the African coast, Britain would lose nothing and gain much from a continuance of Egyptian rule. By June 1874 this view was strongly held in the Foreign Office. In August the Viceroy, Northbrook, adopted it and a large body of opinion in the Indian Council in

London was also in favour.[74] Salisbury, who succeeded Argyll as Secretary of State for India in March 1874, was the last to be converted, but he too came round in March 1875.[75] The way was then clear for negotiation with the Egyptian Government.

The Khedive was not offered an easy bargain. The British requirements that his new possessions should not be granted away to any other European power may have been easy to concede, but the conditions that he suppress the slave trade and impose no customs duties at the newly developed and expensive port of Berbera were particularly onerous.[76] Yet he had much to gain otherwise from co-operation with the British Government, and even more to lose by refusing it.[77] In August 1877 the deal was concluded and the Khedive signed a Convention which fully secured British interests, including the continuation of cheap provisions for Aden.[78]

How was it that the British Government signed away one source of Aden's supplies on the Somali coast while retaining so tight a grip on the other in Arabia, together with extensive tracts of economically useless territory? Why were not the differences with the Turks settled in the same give-and-take fashion as those with the Egyptians? There is no simple answer to these questions but the difference in the course of events on either side of the Gulf of Aden was not purely accidental. As far as the conscious formulation of British policy was concerned, the parting of the ways can first clearly be discerned at a meeting of permanent officials of the Foreign and India Offices held on 2 June 1874.[79] There, the whole problem of Turkish and Egyptian encroachment was fully discussed, and the upshot was a decision that the *status quo* should be maintained in the Aden hinterland but that, with regard to the Somali coast, only a digest of Britain's treaty rights there should be sent to the Khedive's government. One reason for the difference in emphasis was the simple fact that the Egyptians were in, whereas the Turks had been pushed out. But much was also due to the able advocacy of Sir Bartle Frere, who was not only very well informed on Middle Eastern questions, but was also sensitive to the underlying forces beneath the immediate situation. Behind Frere's contention that the Khedive should be allowed to extend his rule while the Turks should be stopped lay a wide reassessment of Britain's whole strategy with regard to the routes to India.[80] He stated more clearly what others were uneasily beginning to suspect, namely that the old Palmerstonian policy of protecting India's western frontier by maintaining the integrity of the Ottoman Empire was becoming outworn and inadequate. For purely internal reasons Egypt and Turkey were drifting apart. That was clear. The question was, should Britain continue her traditional policy of seeking to arrest the

process. Since the beginning of 1873, when he had had an encouraging interview with the Khedive on his way to Zanzibar,
Frere's answer to this was 'no'. From then on he sought to convince
all those concerned with the making of Britain's Middle Eastern
policy that Turkey 'is a dead body and no good can come from tying
it to the living body of Egypt'. In Egypt, Frere saw 'a genuine move
toward western civilisation', in Turkey he saw none. Therefore
Britain should back the Khedive against his master, and as Egypt
could be regarded as a reliable state it could be entrusted with the
protection of the African coasts of the Red Sea.[81]

While Frere was thus mapping out a new strategy for India's
western defence to replace Outram's now out-dated programme,
the Turks and Egyptians, by their actions in East Africa and Arabia,
were confirming many of his arguments. Turkish evasions, duplicity
and obstinate adherence to theoretical claims over Arabia were a
source of constant irritation to British officials. Aden was the worst
case, but similar things were happening in the Persian Gulf. To
Frere and Badger, who were sniffing at the cold breezes of pan-
Islamism blowing from Istanbul, these and other evidences
of Muslim revivalism added up to something dangerous. Others,
such as Aitchison of the Indian Government's Foreign Department,
added up the same sum and came to a different and less alarming
answer.[82] But the Porte's constant harping on the theme of the
Sultan-Caliph's religious claims to all Arabia as 'the cradle of Islam'
caused a definite hardening of attitudes in London between May
1873 and May 1874. After an acrimonious discussion of the respective
fates of 'Abdallah Muhsin al 'Abdali, detained at Aden despite the
Turkish claim that he was their subject, and the leaders of the 'Alawi
and 'Amiri tribes, held by the Turks despite the British claim that
they were protected, a long and menacing despatch was sent to
Istanbul in April 1874. The Turkish claim to the suzerainty
of Arabia was dismissed as unhistorical and then, noting the pan-
Islamic utterances of officials at the Porte and in the Yemen, the
despatch went on to point out that claims to religious hegemony
had often been used in the past by those who sought to dismember
the Ottoman Empire itself.[83] Suspicion of this curious type of Turkish
religious nationalism was now gaining ground and fears of its effect
on the internal situation in India were now being expressed.[84]
Not only would the Ottoman Empire make a weak and unreliable
ally, there was now a growing feeling in British circles that a Turkish
presence in South Arabia might come to represent a political threat to
India in its own right. On the other hand the Egyptian handling of
British protests at their encroachments in the Gulf of Aden was
suave and conciliatory.[85] The fact that several of the Egyptian

commanders on the spot were Europeans made for easier relationships. At home the Khedive was running a secular state, his Chief
Minister, Nubar Pasha, was a Copt, and his claims were phrased
in terms of commercial values and strategical requirements which
were understandable in London.[86] While the Porte was flirting with
Britain's eastern rivals, the Russians, the Khedive intimated in
1873 that he would be glad to disembarrass himself of his former
friends the French. All this was promising, all this suggested the
existence of firm foundations on which a more permanent Egyptian
friendship could be based. Finally in 1875 was added the more
material guarantee of a strong financial tie. In that year both the
Ottoman Empire and Egypt sank into bankruptcy and while the
British Government did nothing to save its old friend the Sultan,
Disraeli bought up the Khedive's Suez shares at a price above their
original value.[87] A fortnight before this transaction the Consul-
General at Cairo had been ordered to begin the negotiations which
led up to the Somali Coast Convention.[88]

Thus the decisions which brought about the creation of a diplomatic Protectorate in all but name over Aden's Arabian hinterland
and the temporary abandonment of the sphere of influence on the
opposite coast formed an integral part of a wider evolution of Britain's
Middle Eastern strategy. The whole trend of British policy in the
1870s was away from the traditional alliance with the Porte and
toward the direct defence of Britain's more restricted commitments.
Turkish failure to pay the interest on the largely British-held debt in
1875 and Gladstone's campaign against the Bulgarian atrocities threw
public opinion behind the shift and gave it added weight. Thus
when the fate of the Ottoman Empire was called in question during
the long diplomatic crisis which centred on the Congress of Berlin
of 1878, the British Government's attitude was very different from
what it had been at the time of the Crimean War. Beaconsfield and
the Queen alone were in favour of pursuing the traditional policy
and they failed to have their way. Instead, no alliance was made
with Turkey, the Porte was given to understand that Britain would
not accord it any general support. On the contrary Britain acted with
the other powers to force an offensive programme of reforms on the
reluctant Sultan and his people. British interests were protected
but not through a Turkish intermediary. Preparation were made
to prevent a Russian descent either on Egypt or on Constantinople,
but a predominant section of the cabinet saw to it that these moves
should not be misconstrued as an attempt to give general backing
to the Porte in its quarrel with Russia. In like fashion the diplomatic
effort to limit Russian advances in Asia Minor was not conducted
in a spirit of friendship with the Porte; it was made with the frank

intention of keeping the Russians as far as possible from the head of the Persian Gulf. Further afield, the Indian Government compensated for Russian advances by marching into Afghanistan and drawing that country more closely into the British orbit. Ottoman integrity could no longer be regarded as sacrosanct after 1878. Britain had complacently participated in the Congress of Berlin, which gave international sanction to the infringement of that principle in the Balkans; Britain herself had taken over Cyprus. Thus the Ottoman curtain which Palmerston had sought to draw across the routes to India had become somewhat tattered by the end of the 1870s, and it was no longer so easy to mask the coasts of the Red Sea and Arabia from European encroachment by an appeal to the sovereign rights of the Porte. All this tended to create an atmosphere favourable to the development of Aden's control over its hinterland; there was therefore little likelihood that the British Government would go back on its decisions of 1873.

Within the hinterland the pace of British penetration was quickening. The Guest House was expanding its activity as tribal chiefs were finding it convenient to pay off their pensioners and stipendiaries in the new coin of letters of recommendation to the Aden Government. The Aden Troop moved more freely in the interior as the superior authorities recognised the need to know what was happening within the now much-widened sphere of British influence. For these and other reasons the 1870s saw the Hawshabi, the Fadli and the 'Amir tribes brought into the same intimate relations with the Aden authorities as the 'Abdali had been in the previous two decades. The 'Abdali seizure of the Za'ida lands in 1868 and their retention thereafter greatly weakened the Hawshabi Sultanate. Like most of the other rulers of the hinterland, the Hawshabi Sultan was heavily dependent for his revenue on land taxes levied on the cultivators of a small area of irrigated land. This provided a stable basis for the more uncertain control which he wielded over the nomad herders who formed the bulk of his tribe. Without it, his authority over the tribesmen would for most purposes be little greater than that which he could command by the strength of his own personality. The loss of his lands therefore and the consequent removal of his capital from the settled cultivated area of his territory swung the balance of power within the tribe heavily against the Sultanate. As time passed and Sultan 'Ali bin Mana remained unable to recover the Za'ida lands, his authority within the tribe steadily waned. He was forced out on to the uncertain and unfamiliar waters of higher diplomacy and these led him first to the Turks at Ta'izz and then, when this proved ineffectual, to the British authorities at Aden. He could expect little sympathy from Aden after calling in the Turks in 1873, and the fact that throughout the rest of the decade he still received a small subsidy from the rulers of the Yemen did not help matters. But the British had always felt that the seizure of the Za'ida lands had savoured of injustice, and these pricks of conscience were felt the more as, after Sultan Fadl Muhsin's death in 1874, 'Abdali influence at Aden began to decline. The new 'Abdali Sultan, Fadl bin 'Ali, was not so well-thought-of, and had it not been for the energetic presence of his uncle Muhammad Muhsin, Lahej would have fallen even further in British estimation, as happened after the latter's death in 1881.[89] By the late '70s the Aden authorities had begun to work seriously for an accomodation. Substantial gifts were accorded to the Hawshabi to prop up his authority, and in July 1881 an agreement was arrived at by which a portion of his lands were returned to the Hawshabi by Lahej.[90] This agreement did not restore the fortunes of the Hawshabi Sultanate. The Hawshabi did not recover all the lands he had lost. The possibility of future blackmail of the 'Abdali was ruled out by a clause restricting the amount of water he could draw from the irrigation system, and the British were brought into the matter by another clause which made them guarantors of the agreement. Most of the land he was assigned had to be distributed among his family and his subjects, and even then the Ahl Yahya, a powerful sub-section whom he had offended during his period of deprivation, were not appeased. He momentarily recovered some authority in the early months of 1881 when he acquired a cannon, but as he failed to find a competent gunner his efforts to rule by bombardment failed and his financial weakness set him on the downward path which led to the ousting of his successor by the 'Abdali Sultan in 1895.

For the Fadli tribe also the 1870s was a time of troubles and of growing British involvement in their internal affairs. The last calamitous five years of Ahmad bin 'Abdallah's rule had weakened the authority of the Sultanate and when he died in 1870 he left behind him a difficult inheritance. Had he also left a clear successor with the ability to command the tribe as he himself had done in his prime, all might still have been well. But he did not. Instead the Sultanate in the midst of its other difficulties suffered from the additional curse of a disputed succession. Two of Sultan Ahmad's sons contended for the turban and Sultan Haydar, a man of mild disposition, was successful. The loser, Sultan Husayn, did not take his defeat gracefully, and this bold and ambitious individual devoted much of his energy to undermining his brother's position. Thus weakened, Sultan Haydar had not the power to win back what the tribe had lost in the aftermath of the British invasions of 1865–6, and in his quarrels with his encroaching neighbours and rebellious tribesmen he tended to lean on the support of the Aden authorities. Before the death of his father, Sultan Haydar had been one of the principal advocates of a settlement with the British. During 1867 he had had an opportunity to become acquainted with their government, as he had remained at Aden for a period as a hostage for the good behaviour of his tribe. He was pro-British and his friendly sentiments were reciprocated by the officers at Aden.

On their side, the British were pleased to find an amicably disposed ruler on their eastern frontier. Then, as periodic visits by the Aden Troop and the Civil Engineer revealed the full extent of the unused agricultural potential of the lands around Abyan, passive friendship quickly changed to active interest in the economic development of the Sultanate. Economic development could not be separated from political change; cultivation of the Wadi Bana could not begin while the Yafi'i and Fadli tribes were locked in bitter disputes over land and water for irrigation. These disputes were of long standing but since 1866 they had been aggravated by the Yafi'i Sultan's raising the annual charge for water from $25 to $100. The Fadli Sultan retaliated by raising the transit dues on Yafi'i goods passing through his territory and this, together with supplementary conflicts arising from the bad relations between the two, led to the complete stoppage of the water supply to the Fadli Sultanate by 1872. At that point Tremenheere, the Aden Resident, determined to intervene. In July 1872 a settlement was arrived at by which the Yafi'i charge for water was reduced to the old charge of $25 per annum, while the Fadli Sultan abolished the system of levying transit dues. The new agreement was underwritten by the Aden Government, which accorded a subsidy of $85 per month to the Fadli Sultan in lieu of his transit dues.[91] Aden was now thoroughly involved, and when the Yafi'i Sultan denounced the agreement in November 1872 his stipend was stopped and the Aden Government adopted a hostile attitude toward him.[92] Desultory hostilities between the Fadli and the Yafi'i dragged on for four more years, the centre of conflict being the Dirjaj area where the Yafi'i, with some 'Awlaqi help, fostered the desire of some Fadli sub-tribes to secede from the Sultanate. The dispute came to an end with further and more decisive British intervention. In 1876 the Aden Resident finally persuaded the Indian Government to give the Fadli Sultan a nine-pounder cannon, and following this a further conference was held and a new agreement on the lines of that of 1872 was arrived at, with the Aden Government acting more positively as the guarantor.[93] Thereafter the exploitation of the lands of Abyan could begin in earnest and the Aden Government from time to time gave a certain amount of financial assistance to those engaged on the development of the irrigation system. During the next twelve years some 1,000 acres of former wasteland were brought into cultivation.[94]

The complex political manoeuvres required to bring about this result involved the British more closely than ever in the domestic affairs of the Fadli Sultanate. Consequently, when in 1877 the long rivalry between the 'loyal' Sultan Haydar and his brother Husayn ended with the former's assassination, the Aden Government took a close interest in the selection of his successor, and an officer was sent to Shuqra to see that the election was properly conducted. Husayn was the most obvious claimant to the turban but he was strongly suspected of involvement in his brother's murder and he was ousted by his own son Ahmad who took over the Sultanate with the support of his uncles Mihdar and 'Abdallah bin Nasir. The Aden Government backed Sultan Ahmad and played an important part in the fight between the two factions which ensued.[95] Ultimately it was the Aden Troop which put an end to Husayn's resistance. Acting in co-operation with a naval vessel, the Troop in 1879 stormed his stronghold at Al Harka, and Husayn was carried off to Bombay, where he remained a State prisoner until 1886. Husayn was ultimately released on a promise to further the interests of Sultan Ahmad and of the British Government. By that time, although no formal Protectorate Treaty was signed until 1890, the Fadli Sultanate was under general British control. The Sultan ruled as much by grace of the Aden authorities as by election by his tribesmen. The Fadli boundary with Lahej was settled in 1881 by British intervention and in 1883 a force of Indian Native Infantry was sent from Aden to protect Fadli territory from invasion by the 'Awlaqi.[96] The 1870s saw the Fadli Sultanate brought as effectively within the Aden political system as Lahej was at the beginning of that decade. Aden had acquired a new and more extensive frontier, one which now touched on that of the Fadli's powerful neighbours – the Yafi'i and the 'Awlaqi. In the meanwhile, further east, other developments were offering Aden an entirely new area of dominion.

CHAPTER VI

The Hadhrami Sultanates
1800–1900

About 250 miles to the east of Aden, along the barren shores of South Arabia, lie the ports of Mukalla and Shihr, the latter an ancient town, the former a comparatively recent creation. Mukalla developed rapidly in the nineteenth century from a collection of temporary huts into a handsome mud-built town with impressive walls, gates and buildings nestling under sheer rising hills along which a string of forts followed the crests and dropped down into the valleys on either flank, rendering the position more or less impregnable. The immediate hinterland of Shihr and Mukalla was little more productive than that of Aden. Apart from an irrigated area around the town of Ghayl almost mid-way between the two, the coastal districts were generally as barren and forbidding as any in the vicinity of Aden. But some three hundred miles to the northward, across the bare back of the Jol Plateau, lay the Wadi Hadhramawt – a comparatively green corridor two to four miles wide running parallel to the coast for almost a hundred miles between massive walls of rock. There, wells and controlled flash floods provided water for cultivation and, where irrigation was successfully conducted, the rich soil yielded three or four crops each year. This provided the economic basis for a city-dwelling people inhabiting towering buildings in a series of towns, of which the chief were Shibam, Saywun and Tarim. In these old centres of population a highly developed Islamic culture was preserved whose roots reached back to pre-Islamic times. The Hadhramawt had always been one of the great centres of learning in the Islamic world, isolated geographically but maintaining through its emigrant sons more extensive contacts with the outside world than its principal rival in South Arabia – Central Yemen. In the nineteenth century, despite political disturbance, this tradition of scholarship was preserved and greatly extended, notably in the city of Tarim toward the eastern extremity of the Wadi. At the western end of this fertile valley two other smaller corridors of cultivation – the Wadi Du'an and Wadi 'Amd –

156

branched southward and south-westward through the Jol to approximately half the distance between the main Wadi and the coast, and
there too men of substance built their great houses and lived a life of
ease and learning on the produce of their estates and personal
fortunes accumulated abroad.

These wealthy districts in the interior were the *raison d'être* for the
ports of Shihr and Mukalla, in the nineteenth century the preferred
gateways from the Wadis to the outside world. The coast-hugging
traffic which had in earlier centuries lent importance to havens and
watering places on the South Arabian coast was losing out as larger
ships sailed with compass and chronometer across the high seas to
their places of destination. The remnants of this formerly lucrative
entrepôt trade was to be found in the slave depots at Shihr and
Mukalla, where between the 1850s and the 1880s slaves from East
Africa were collected and distiibuted to various parts of Arabia. But
under British pressure the slaving period quickly passed and Shihr
and Mukalla were forced back on the exploitation of purely local
traffic.[1] Neither was a natural harbour. The surf beating on their
shores kept all vessels of any size at a distance. Shihr was unsafe in the
south-west monsoon, and the installations for handling goods at
both were rudimentary. But no more was required, for the most
valuable export from the Hadhramawt was not the bulky produce of
the soil but men. As with most parts of South-West Arabia, the
Hadhramawt had a long tradition of sending its sons abroad in
search of a living. But whereas those who emigrated from the Yemen
in the nineteenth century were most often the sons of peasant farmers
ready to engage in any form of work, a large proportion of those who
went off from the Hadhramawt were members of the educated
élite, out to make their fortunes with their brains rather than with
their hands. Not all of course succeeded; among the Hadhrami
community in Zanzibar in the 1870s were to be found butchers,
artisans and small employers of labour in the port.[2] But the proportion of wealthy emigrants from the Hadhramawt was higher than
from other parts of South Arabia and the absolute proportion of the
population which went abroad was also greater. There was also
this further difference, that the Hadhrami generally went further
afield than their Arab compatriots. There had been a Hadhrami
community in Indonesia since the fifteenth century which was
considerably strengthened in the nineteenth, and extended its links
to the rising port of Singapore. There were Hadhramis also in India,
in East Africa and in the Hijaz, where they dominated the commercial
community.[3] Everywhere they were making their fortunes as
religious leaders or in business, politics or military service. Although
the nineteenth century brought hard times to the Arabian Peninsula,

it was a profitable period for cosmopolitan businessmen and financiers in Asia.

Among the most profitable spheres of operations for Hadhrami emigrants in the nineteenth century was the Indian Princely State of Hyderabad. After the annexation of Oudh, the largest autonomous Indian State, Hyderabad had a population of some ten million and an annual revenue of over 2 million pounds in the mid-nineteenth century. It was situated in the central Deccan at about the limit of the Mughal-Muslim conquest, and its Hindu population was ruled by the Muslim Nizam. It had fallen under British influence in the second half of the eighteenth century and by a series of treaties from 1766 to 1800 it was brought into the position of a subsidiary state. Its foreign affairs were controlled by the East India Company and it was forced to maintain at its own expense a large British military contingent over which it had no control. The history of Hyderabad in the nineteenth century was the history of a declining and demoralised state caught in a mesh of obligations to the powerful British Government whose territories surrounded it. Its finances were crippled by the annual payment of a sum which by 1843 had reached £300,000 for the upkeep of the British contingent. The state debt mounted to the equivalent of one years income by 1854 and more than a quarter was owed to the British Government. Certain territories were held in mortgage by the British and to these were added the rich revenues of the Berars, extorted under threat of war in 1853 to secure the payment of British claims. Inevitably the British Resident wielded great power at the Nizam's Court and from 1806 to 1843 the Residents exercised their influence through the agency of a Hindu Chief Minister to the Nizam, who controlled the state machine and who was kept in place in spite of the Nizam's protests by British pressure.[4]

As British and Hindu influence extended throughout Hyderabad in the early nineteenth century, the Nizam, in order to maintain his position, recruited into his army increasing numbers of his tough independent-minded co-religionists from the Arabian Peninsula. The proportion of Arabs in the army of Hyderabad steadily grew, and by 1849 there were over 5,000 of them. From there they struck out into other branches of the country's life. In the chaotic condition of Hyderabad, torn between the British and the Nizam, Hindu and Muslim, law and order was scarcely maintained and justice poorly administered. Until 1872 the Arabs in the Nizam's service were exempt from the ordinary processes of law, their aggressive bearing also brought them to the fore, and Hyderabad notables soon came to realise that they could best protect their interests by engaging bands of Arab mercenaries. By 1854 every man of any substance or

influence in the city of Hyderabad and most of the greater landowners in the districts retained a personal squad of Arab soldiers.
From military service it was but a short step to money-lending and to
the accumulation of estates – in fact to most of the means by which
the British servants of the East India Company had in the eighteenth
century made fortunes and honeycombed the Indian States in which
they found themselves.

The British Government was by no means happy to see the Arabs
of Hyderabad following in the footsteps of their eighteenth-century
British predecessors. The main grievance against them was their
lack of respect for British power. They gave the impression of
invincibility to the local people. They were well armed, turbulent
and adept at street fighting and had no fear of clashing with the
troops of the East India Company. By the middle of the century
they were regarded as a menace, not only to the British position in
Hyderabad but also to the whole structure of British power in India,
for it was believed that in case of trouble on the frontier it would be
necessary to hold back a substantial British force to overawe them.
One report to the President of the India Board in 1854 went so far
as to describe them as 'the greatest thorn in our side in India'.[5]
Various efforts were made to reduce their numbers and bring them
under control. In 1852 a system of passports was introduced at
Bombay to prevent their immigration, in 1864 the Indian Legislature
conferred power on the Executive to assist Hyderabad in keeping
Arabs out, and in 1872 the Hyderabad Government made them
amenable to ordinary Courts of Justice. These measures succeeded to
some extent in curtailing the growth of the Arab community but in
1868 there 'were still nearly 6,000 Arabs in the Nizam's army alone.[6]

A large proportion of the Nizam's Arab soldiers came from the
Hadhramawt and the Aden hinterland. The old trading links
between South Arabia and western India had maintained a steady
flow of adventurers from there to the service of Indian Princes and
in addition to this the principal Arab officers or *jemadars* in the
Nizam's service in the mid-nineteenth century were of South Arabian
origin. This alone could determine the composition of the Hyderabad
army, for a *jemadar* was not just a military commander. In keeping
with the custom of the time, he was entrusted with the duty of raising,
equipping and paying the men under his command. Of course his
choice fell first upon men of his own tribe and homeland. The
Jemadars themselves were men of great power and wealth. The
most outstanding of them in the 1860s, Barak Jung, alias Salah bin
'Umar al Qu'ayti, controlled a force of 1,500 infantrymen and an
estimated personal fortune of £400,000–£500,000 sterling.[7] No
Sultan or chief in South Arabia could command resources to compare

with this. Yet Salah bin 'Umar was but one member of a veritable
dynasty of Arab officers in the Nizam's service. The Qu'ayti family
fortunes had been founded by Salah's father, 'Umar bin 'Awad,
who had emigrated to India in the early years of the nineteenth
century. He first entered the service of a minor Indian Princeling
and after a successful career and a rich marriage with an Indian
heiress, was engaged by the Nizam and rose to the highest rank in
the Hyderabad army. On his death in 1865 he left a considerable
fortune and five sons, of whom Salah was the most prominent in
Hyderabad. Of the four others, one, Muhammad, died in the 1860s,
another, 'Ali, was estranged from his brothers, while the other two,
'Awad and 'Abdallah, formed with Salah an international trium-
virate building the fortunes of the family in India and Arabia.[8] Of
somewhat lesser consequence was the family of 'Abdallah bin 'Ali
al'Awlaqi, another emigrant from South Arabia, and a contemporary
and rival of 'Umar bin 'Awad, who rose to high office under the
Nizam. Something has already been said of this personage in
connection with the affairs of Lahej. In 1856 he negotiated with
the Lahej Sultan for the purchase of Bir Ahmad, and in 1869 his
son Muhsin provided money for the 'Abdali schemes of conquest
in the Hajariya.[9] He was also involved in the 1860s in negotiations
for the purchase of the small port of Bir 'Ali in Wahidi country and
in the same decade turned his attention towards the Hadhramawt.[10]
A third emigrant from South Arabia, Ghalib bin Muhsin al Kathiri,
had a brief but meteoric career in Hyderabad. Arriving at some time
in the early 1840s he stayed little more than ten years, but in that
time he amassed considerable wealth and rose so rapidly as to challenge the position of *jemadar* 'Umar bin 'Awad. Indeed it is said that
the Nizam called on Ghalib bin Muhsin to leave for fear of the
outbreak of open strife between his faction and the followers of the
Qu'ayti in Hyderabad.[11] The involvement of these powerful men
in the politics of the Hadhramawt from the 1840s onward gradually
transformed the situation there, created new combinations of forces,
and introduced new techniques of government and warfare. Their
wide-ranging intrigues, from Hyderabad to Masqat and Istanbul,
brought their geographically isolated homeland into the mainstream
of international politics.

The political situation in the Hadhramawt in the early nineteenth
century was one of confusion and uneasy compromise. The last
government which had succeeded in bringing under one hand the
control of the Wadis and the coast was that of the Kathiri Sultans
in the sixteenth and seventeenth centuries. In the mid-seventeenth
century the Hadhramawt had been brought for a few decades
under Yemeni control, but with the break-up of the Imamate in the

1680s, the Kathiri Sultans had reasserted their independence. Shortly after this event, however, the Kathiri state went into decline, and by the end of the 1720s its authority and disintegrated.[12] This left the Hadhramawt with a thoroughly decentralised form of government, the main elements in which were the old tribal confederations such as the Humum, the 'Awamir and the Ahl Tamim; in the cities, power lay with the various factions of the former Kathiri ruling house, the Sayyids, who exercised a measure of spiritual authority but carried no arms, and a number of families of Yafi'i origin.[13] The Yafi'i had been brought to the Hadhramawt as mercenaries in the sixteenth and seventeenth centuries, mainly from the Upper Yafi'i country north of Aden, and had settled according to their different clans in most of the towns.[14] There is little evidence that even the three main groupings – the Kathiri, the Sayyids and the Yafi'i – combined on any considerable scale before the mid-nineteenth century. Rather the pursuit of power was conducted on a purely local basis by small factions in each town and district. In the early nineteenth century two separate factions of the Yafi'i tribe, the Ahl Barayk and the Kasadi, ruled the ports of Shihr and Mukalla respectively. Inland, various Yafi'i groups were most numerous and powerful at the western end of the Wadi Hadhramawt around Shibam, with Saywun the centre of Kathiri influence and Tarim the main stronghold of the Sayyids, although everywhere the power of the Yafi'i factions was on the increase.

At all times the many little balances of power throughout the Hadhramawt were subject to sudden jolts when wealthy and ambitious emigrants returned and sought to promote the fortunes of their particular family.[15] But the efforts of these returning adventurers were not to be compared with the persevering operations of the Hyderabad Jemadars working the whole apparatus of improved communications – steamships and, after 1870, the telegraph – with intelligence and ability. From the 1840s when 'Umar bin 'Awad al Qu'ayti and Ghalib bin Muhsin al Kathiri began their empire-building in the Hadhramawt from their respective centres at Al Hawta, west of Shibam, and Saywun, in the centre of the Wadi, the shape of politics gradually changed. Professional soldiers began to take over from Hadhrami family heroes. Ghalib bin Muhsin gave a boost to the small-scale slave trade by importing large numbers of Africans to form a reliable slave army, as a supplement to his tribal levies. The Kuwaiti *jemadar* brought in increasing numbers of raw tribesmen from the Yafi'i hills, together with some of his Arab soldiers from Hyderabad and some well-disciplined Indian troops. The numbers involved on either side in the many combats steadily grew from hundreds in the skirmishes of the 1850s to thousands in the full-scale wars of the '6os and '7os. Likewise the casualty lists lengthened from tens to hundreds of men. Matchlocks were replaced by the latest types of musket and by 1860 cannon in considerable numbers were being accurately and effectively used by skilled artillerymen who could blow down defences hitherto regarded as impregnable.[16] The whole nature of the struggle gradually altered from that of a series of local contests to a countrywide war, in which strategic towns and lines of communication took on a new significance. It became increasingly clear that the prize being fought for was control of the whole of the Hadramawt, and control itself meant something more disciplined and thorough than the old idea of vague authority. As the scale of operations extended and the stakes became higher, the nature of the contending parties altered. The Qu'ayti *jemadar*, at first concerned with establishing the fortunes of his own small sept of a Yafi'i clan settled in the Hadhramawt, began to claim that he was fighting for the cause of the whole Yafi'i tribe. Ghalib bin Muhsin on the other hand sought to unite all the Kathiri factions in the face of Yafi'i aggression.[17] Thus these returned emigrants with their wider vision worked to create two country-wide parties contending for supremacy over the whole of the Hadhramawt.

Two decades of desultory warefare between these two principals and various local leaders culminated in 1866, that year of drought and disturbance in South Arabia, with a great struggle for the ports of Shihr and Mukalla. Both these towns were controlled by Yafi'i rulers although this did not necessarily mean that they were closed to the Kathiri. The situation was still fluid at that date and the Kasadi Naqib at Mukalla was as hostile to Naqib 'Ali Naji at Shihr as to any of the parties in the interior. Both coastal rulers profited from the trade in munitions and men to the warring factions in the Wadi. It was only a matter of time however before the powerful military leaders in the interior would attempt to seize the coastline for themselves and starve their opponents of outside aid. In October 1866 this happened when Sultan Ghalib bin Muhsin gathered the Kathiri forces in the Hadhramawt and marched on Shihr. By November that port was in his hands and his army turned westward, beat down the outer defences of Mukalla and penetrated almost to the town itself.[18] The Naqib of Mukalla had not sufficient strength to cope with the Kathiri onslaught alone and he inevitably turned to the Qu'ayti for aid. The Qu'ayti family was well aware of what was at stake. Forces were immediately sent by 'Abdallah bin 'Umar from Shibam to prop up the Mukalla defences, Salah sent large funds from Hyderabad and 'Awad arrived in person from India with arms, ordnance and 1,100 Yafi'i and Indian troops. Arrangements

were also made with the Fadli Sultan to allow 1,500 fighting men
from Yafi'i country to pass through the port of Shuqra to join the host.
By March 1867 some 4,000 men were mustered and these advanced
on Shihr and drove the Kathiri from that town on 30 April 1867.
From there the joint Qu'ayti-Kasadi force launched an attack on
Tarim and Saywun. But this failed, amid bitter recriminations
between the participating parties. The Naqib turned against the
Qu'ayti and the latter had to meet alone a Kathiri counter-offensive
against Shihr in December. This too failed and by the end of the year
the situation had become stabilised with the Qu'ayti now in possession of Shihr, its former ruler, Naqib 'Ali Naji, having been pensioned
off by *jemadar* 'Awad bin 'Umar.[19]

In many ways a turning point in the Qu'ayti-Kathiri wars, the
battle for Shihr in 1866-7 decisively internationalised the struggle
in the Hadramawt. The British Government, in particular, somewhat thoughtlessly allowed itself to become involved. 'Ali Naji,
the displaced ruler of Shihr, had signed an anti-slave trade engagement and this made his fate a matter for British concern. There was
also some anxiety at the pro-Turkish propensities of the Kathiri.
More important than either of these was the fact that Sir Salar Jung,
the Prime Minister in Hyderabad, had asked the Governor of
Bombay to assist the Qu'ayti.[20] The Government of India relied on
Jung to maintain their influence in Hyderabad and in 1867, they
were particularly eager to oblige him as he was under heavy pressure
from the hostile Nizam.[21] No difficulty was made about allowing
armed Hyderabad troops to leave Bombay for service in the
Hadhramawt and much of the artillery, arms and munitions, whose
arrival at 'Awad bin 'Umar's baggage caused a sensation at Mukalla
in January 1867, was issued to him from the Government Arsenal at
Aden.[22]

Once the British Government had intervened on behalf of one side
it was to be expected that the other would look for some counter-
balancing foreign alliance. The Kathiri Sultan was willing to
compete with the Qu'ayti for British support,[23] but his foreign policy
was determined to a considerable degree by his close alliance with
the Sayyids – and of all parties in the Hadhramawt the Sayyids were
foremost in seeking support from the Muslim power of the Ottoman
Sultan. Because of their religious character the Sayydis were less
willing than others to deal with infidel governments. Many Sayyids
both at home and abroad were vigorously xenophobic.[24] They did
not have the same contacts with British India as either the Kathiri
or the Qu'ayti. They were men of peace who did not join the armies of
Indian Princes.[25] Their emigrant sons were traders and colporteurs
in Indonesia, the Yemen and the Hijaz, and in the last two countries,

where few Yafi'i mercenaries were to be found until the end of the nineteenth century, emigrant Hadhrami Sayyids knew and had influence over the workings of the Ottoman administration.[26] In the Hadhramawt the Sayyids had long been hostile to Yafi'i pretensions and for more than fifty years various powerful personalities among them at different times would appear to have given the lead for attacks on growing Yafi'i power. Control of the city of Tarim had been the main bone of contention, but from there the ill-feeling extended to other parts of the country. Matters were worsened by Sayyidly suspicions of Yafi'i collusion with the iconoclastic Wahhabi, whose brief invasion of the Hadhramawt in 1809 and puritanical attack on some religious practices had had a traumatic effect on Hadhrami religious leaders.[27] The Sayyids took the part of the Kathiri in their struggle with the Yafi'i and, although few bore arms, their influence with the tribesmen and their financial resources were of great assistance to their allies. Important also were foreign contacts and it was largely because of their efforts that Ottoman intervention in the Hadhramawt usually took the form of support for the Kathiri.

The first attempt to use Ottoman Arabia as a base for operations in the Hadhramawt had been made in 1850 when a number of irregulars backed by a few Turkish troops mounted an attack on Mukalla. This however was not an official Ottoman enterprise. The Pasha of Hudayda authorised the expedition on his own initiative at the request of a Hadhrami Sayyid, and the attacking force was repulsed by the coastal rulers.[28] Thereafter, no further attempt was made by the Turkish authorities in western Arabia to intervene directly in the Hadhramawt until 1867. In that year 150 Hadhrami notables, mainly religious leaders, petitioned the Sharif of Mecca, and through him the Turks in the Hijaz, to intervene and put an end to the Qu'ayti-Kathiri war. This time the Ottoman response was quite official. A warship was sent to Shihr and Mukalla in August 1867. All parties were notified that the Hadhramawt formed part of the Sultan's dominions and they were called on to resist foreign encroachment on Muslim territory. 'Awad bin 'Umar was most strongly criticised and it was proposed that the disputed port of Shihr, then in Qu'ayti hands, be surrendered to the Turks as part of a general truce. The Turks were playing upon the prevailing enmity between the Qu'ayti and the Naqib of Mukalla, but the medicine they offered was too strong for either. The Naqib had no wish to replace the Qu'ayti by an even more demanding neighbour. He asked that the matter be shelved for the time being and both he and the Qu'ayti sought British protection against Turkish interference.[29]

These developments caused considerable apprehension in Aden and British India. No one wanted to establish a British Protectorate over the Hadhramawt, but neither did anyone wish to see the Turks established there. Representations were made to the Porte and after some discussion it was agreed that both Britain and Turkey should abstain from all interference in Hadhrami affairs, the question of sovereignty being left open.[30] This seemed at a distance to be a straightforward and sensible solution to the difficulty. But it committed the British to a policy which was almost completely unworkable in practice and which led to a whole series of question-able decisions and tergiversations. What exactly did non-intervention mean? Did it mean that the British should prevent all movements of men, arms and even funds from British India, including Hyderabad, to the Hadhramawt? If no controls were imposed the Porte could maintain that the British had broken the agreement. But if British India did put an effective stop to communication between Hyderabad and the Hadhramawt this would be tantamount to imposing a blockade on the Qu'ayti party. This would itself have constituted an intervention in Hadhrami affairs, for by the end of the 1860s none of the contending parties could claim to be independent of some form of aid from emigrant Hadhrami communities.

While it was difficult to forecast whether Qu'ayti or Kathiri would emerge victorious from the confused fighting of the mid-nineteenth century, one result was quite predictable. No matter which side won the victories, the old established authorities con-sistently lost ground to the newcomers from abroad. Party divisions had little to do with this process. Ambitious emigrants struck quite as hard a bargain in terms of titles to land and authority when offering aid to men of their own side as when dealing with anyone else. The Kathiri ruler of Shibam found this when he had sought assistance from his fellow tribesman, Sultan Ghalib bin Muhsin, in 1858, and he finally signed away half his town to his enemy, the Qu'ayti, to escape the clutches of his own overpowerful subject.[31] Naqib Salah bin Muhammad of Mukalla also found to his cost that help from outside did not come as a free gift. When the Qu'ayti helped him rid his town of its Kathiri invaders in 1867, he also tied up the Naqib in a series of agreements which sapped away the financial foundations of the Mukalla state. The host of 4,000 men which marched out from Mukalla to drive the Kathiri from Shihr was a joint Kasadi–Qu'ayti effort. So also were the two further expeditions which marched on Tarim and Saywun. By agreement the Kasadi Naqib undertook to pay half the costs. Of course he did not have the sort of money required at hand, so he gave the Qu'ayti a promissory note. He hoped to recoup his outlay from the revenues of the captured towns which were to be shared between the victors; as the expedition failed he was left only with the debts. Dependent as he was on Qu'ayti aid, he also agreed to recognise the *jemadar's* assumption of the government of the captured town of Shihr and the pensioning off of its former ruler. For the Kasadi Naqib Salah bin Muhammad, the abortive expedition to Tarim was a double defeat, while for the far-sighted Qu'ayti it contained the seeds of future successes.[32] Already in 1868 the *jemadar* was claiming to control the whole Hadhrami coastline.[33] Nevertheless Salah bin Muhammad, with a fine disregard for his serious financial difficulties, went ahead and undertook costly expeditions to subdue the tribes of the Wadi Du'an in an attempt to bring that home of wealthy pensioners under his protection.[34] He was still engaged in that work when he died in 1873 and left to his weak son an empty, disorganised exchequer and mountainous debts.

The time for foreclosure was at hand. On hearing of Naqib Salah's decease, the financier politician 'Awad bin 'Umar hastened from Shihr to Mukalla, and while consoling the new Naqib 'Umar on his bereavement, fomented a revolt in the Wadi Du'an. The Naqib's troops were drained off to the interior to stem the uprising and as they left, the Qu'ayti men quietly infiltrated into Mukalla. The Naqib's officials were bribed, his Yafi'i soldiers suborned, and finally the Naqib was left isolated, except for his loyal slave guard. 'Awad then brought up the question of the unrepaid Qu'ayti loans and the Naqib was forced to sign a Protectorate and Advisory Treaty as complete as any signed by an Asiatic ruler with a European power. In return he was promised help in the Wadi Du'an and remission of most of the state debt.[35]

Mukalla and the coastline were almost within the Qu'ayti's grasp when the whole project broke down owing to the intervention of another imperialist financier from Hyderabad. In 1865, before the Ahl Barayk Naqibs of Shihr had been forced into bankruptcy, 'Abdallah bin 'Ali al 'Awlaqi had purchased from them a tract of fertile land in the neighbourhood of Ghayl Ba Wazir. There he had built what was clearly designed to be the nucleus of an 'Awlaqi state. In that period of frenetic house building in the Hadhramawt, 'Abdallah bin 'Ali had constructed an immense mansion or fortress at Husn Suda' in an unusual style. While most of the soaring houses in the country were loopholed for muskets, Husn Suda' was squat, with rounded towers and embrasures for cannon. It dominated the surrounding country and there could be no doubt that it was not planned merely as a place for retirement. The Qu'ayti did not approve of the 'Awlaqi's empire-building efforts on his own chosen ground, and thus rivalry in the Hadhramawt brought a new acerbity to the competition for office between the two families in Hyderabad, where the 'Awlaqi were the chief Arab challengers to the Qu'ayti.[36] The old Naqib Salah of Mukalla therefore made a shrewd choice when he named Muhsin bin 'Abdallah al 'Awlaqi the executor of his will. Traditional authorities could no longer survive alone in the Hadhramawt, but they could contrive to avoid destruction by exploiting differences between emigrants. It was Muhsin al 'Awlaqi who saved the Mukalla Naqib from the Qu'ayti in 1873. He advanced money to pay the arrears of the Naqib's troops in Du'an.[37] They were then brought back to Mukalla and the tables were turned on the *jemadar*. The latter had to flee from the town and a joint Kasadi–'Awlaqi force pursued him and threatened in December 1873 to occupy Shihr itself. Thereafter, 'Awlaqi money backed the Kasadi cause, and with Kathiri assistance the new Naqib was able to carry on the struggle with the Qu'ayti.[38]

In the war which followed, the Naqib of Mukalla was a weak, dependent and very minor party. The real combatants who fed the flames of conflict were the two principal *jemadars* at the Nizam's Court – Muqaddam Jung, alias Muhsin bin 'Abdallah al 'Awlaqi, and Barak Jung, alias Salah bin 'Umar al Qu'ayti, with the Kathiri standing in the wings hoping to profit from the strife on the coast. In December 1873 the 'Awlaqi made his bid when he struck at Shihr.[39] In the following year the Qu'ayti raised the stakes. Mukalla was almost impregnable by land, its approaches being covered by a series of strongholds which were further extended, fortified and mounted with cannon after the 'Awlaqi's intervention.[40] But at sea it was vulnerable, and the Qu'ayti purchased a steamer at Bombay, armed it with cannon and sent it in 1874 to bombard and seize his enemy's port. Thus began the war at sea. Both sides mobilised armed dhows, blockade and counter-blockade was proclaimed. Every effort was made by both parties to cut off their opponents' supply of arms and money from India.

The British watched all this with growing dismay and concern. 'Non-intervention' was their declared policy, but it was believed by some that the traditional policy of preserving maritime peace in Arabian waters should also be maintained. For the first time since the occupation of Aden this was now being seriously challenged Yet any attempt to stop the war at sea could easily be regarded as interference with Hadhrami affairs.[41] Certainly the various contending parties were quick to appeal to the Ottoman authorities against any British move which seemed not to favour their interests.[42] Here lay a further difficulty. The international situation was becoming much more delicate. From 1872 the Ottoman Government was committed to its new Arabian policy. The whole Peninsula was claimed as a fief of the Sultan. A Hadhrami Sayyid, with a record of anti-British activity in India, was named as Governor of the Hadhramawt, and there were persistent rumours that two Turkish vessels were being equipped for a landing on the South Arabian coast.[43] In the background there was the alarming prospect of factional disputes in Hyderabad being determined by the manoeuvres of European powers. It seemed more necessary than ever to isolate India from the strife in Arabia. But it was still not clear how best this could be done, other than by attempting to make the policy of non-intervention effective.

This meant in theory, neutrality. At Aden, however, the business was seen in more concrete terms and from 1873 until late in the decade of the '70s there was a strong undercurrent of hostility to the Qu'ayti, who was regarded by men like the Resident Schneider, his Assistant Goodfellow, and the Interpreter Salah Jaffer, as the principal source of trouble.[44] Indeed all the British efforts at making non-intervention work had an anti-Qu'ayti flavour about them. Thus in 1874 the Qu'ayti *jemadar's* steamer, sent from India to relieve the blockade of Shihr and to attack Mukalla, was seized under the 1870 Foreign Enlistment Act when it arrived at Aden to coal, and the Indian soldiers aboard her were warned that they would be prosecuted in India if they fought in the Hadhramawt.[45] But no protest was made at the seizure of two of the Qu'ayti's *buglas* by the Naqib, on the grounds that this was merely an incident in the local Hadhrami war with which Aden had nothing to do.[46] The *jemadar* thereupon consulted his Bombay lawyers and set about devising means of sending assistance without breaking the letter of the law. He first attempted to purchase and register a steamer at Goa with the intention of sending it to the Hadhramawt under Portuguese colours, but this was frustrated by British pressure on the Goan authorities.[47] He then bought an old steamer, the *Jawad*, at Genoa and had it despatched via Suez to Shihr. The Qu'ayti, however, though skilful, modern-minded businessmen in other respects, were somewhat out of their depth in dealing with naval matters. The coal depots at Shihr were insufficient to feed the vessel's hungry inefficient boilers and, to Resident Schneider's great delight, the *Jawad* limped back from Shihr and entered Aden harbour on 18 August 1875 in dire need of repair, with its unpaid crew on the verge of mutiny. Schneider immediately impounded it and refused to release it until an undertaking was signed that it would not revisit Shihr. The repair bill charged at Aden amounted to more than half the ramshackle vessel's original purchase price.[48] Within a few months of this incident the Qu'ayti was once more taken to task for seizing one of the Sultan of Masqat's dhows bound for Mukalla. The British refused to recognise his blockade of Mukalla as effective, and ordered him to pay a large sum in compensation.[49] About the same time, with somewhat less justification, pressure was being put on the Fadli Sultan to stop the embarkation of Yafiʻi mercenaries recruited by the Quʻayti.[50]

Meanwhile, from 1874 onward, the British Resident at Hyderabad was making determined efforts to cut off Indian interference in Hadhrami affairs at its source. He pressed the Minister, Sir Salar Jung, to punish the rival *jemadars* if they did not break their connection with the contending parties in Arabia.[51] Relations between the Residency and Sir Salar Jung however had changed radically since the palmy days of 1867 when Aden had helped his friends to take Shihr. In 1869 the old Nizam had died, and Jung was made joint Regent for the Nizam's young successor – a position which gave him practically complete control over the State's affairs. By 1874 he felt himself sufficiently strong to call upon the British Government to surrender control over the valuable Berars to the now solvent Hyderabad Government. The British Residency angrily refused even to pass on this request to the Viceroy, and controversy over the issue created great ill-feeling between the British Government and Jung which lasted until his death nine years later.[52] In 1877 the Viceroy Lytton was sufficiently annoyed to declare that Jung's intrigues were the greatest threat to his Viceroyalty.[53] In such an atmosphere little co-operation was to be expected from Hyderabad toward the solution of the Hadhrami problem. For several months Sir Salar Jung ignored the Resident's hectoring communications concerning the Hadhramawt. Then, on receipt of a particularly indiscreet letter, he acted. He called the Quʻayti and ʻAwlaqi *jemadars* together and imposed on them a settlement which was distinctly favourable to the Quʻayti. This was more than the British had bargained for and the Indian Government found to its dismay that Jung planned to send agents of his own to the Hadhramawt to see that the settlement was carried out. For a Princely State to take such action outside the borders of India was a violation of the central principle of paramountcy, on which the whole British system in India was based. It was also contrary to all the treaties between the Indian Government and Hyderabad. An immediate protest was lodged, in reply to which Jung coolly cited the Resident's letter as authority for the action he had taken. The Viceroy was embarrassed, the Resident at the Nizam's Court was quietly removed to another station, and Jung was informed that what was wanted was not mediation but the cessation of all interference by subjects of the Nizam in Hadhrami affairs.[54] Further attempts were made to stop the remittance of funds for warlike purposes. But the Quʻayti remittances which formed the subject of British protests somehow got through, while the 'Awlaqi effort in the Hadhramawt languished from lack of supplies. [55] By 1876 it was becoming clear that it was more important to act in the Hadhramawt to stop complications in Hyderabad than to act in Hyderabad to stop complications in the Hadramawt. [56]

For some time the Aden Resident had been advocating more decisive intervention. In the summer of 1876 his appeals for positive instructions became more urgent as fighting in the Hadhramawt became more intense. [57] In June a sum of over £6,000 arrived at Shihr from Barak Jung. In the middle of the same month an expedition was despatched to Tarim and half that town was seized by Qu'ayti troops. Toward the middle of August, reinforcements augmented *jemadar* 'Awad bin 'Umar's army at Shihr to some 3,000 men. The *jemadar* marched westward on Ghayl Ba Wazir and took it on 20 August. The Kathiri abandoned the struggle and retreated to the interior. The Naqib's forces fell back on Mukalla, leaving the 'Awlaqi's 1,000 men at Husn Suda' to their fate. Husn Suda' was invested on 26 August, and after two months' siege it surrendered, thereby bringing to an end the 'Awlaqi's hopes of building a state in the Hadhramawt. [58] The Naqib was left face to face with the victorious *jemadar*. By that time, however, the Indian authorities, badgered by Aden and increasingly worried at the prospect of Turkish intervention, had finally decided to take action. In December the Aden Resident went to Shihr and Mukalla and got the two parties to agree to a two-year truce, with an ultimate British mediation of the dispute in mind. [59]

The British were now committed to finding a solution to the quarrels between the Qu'ayti and the Naqib, and for five years they wrestled with the problem, carefully considering the claims of the two parties. [60] Politics were inextricably mixed with legal arguments, and legally the Qu'ayti was in a very strong position. His heavy financial claims on the Naqib could not be overlooked by a government for which fiscal probity was sacrosanct. He also had the Treaty of 1873, with the Naqib's seal affixed, assigning him half of Mukalla and Burum and much besides. Treaties were also the stuff of which British India was built and could not be disregarded either. As against this there was the political fact that the Naqib was in treaty relations with the British and Schneider's actions from 1873 to 1876 had definitely been angled in the Naqib's favour. The Naqib had come to regard the British as his protector and the British in turn tended to look on him as their man. But in 1877 Schneider and Goodfellow left Aden and were replaced by Loch and Hunter, both of whom grew dissatisfied with this alignment. To Loch, more liberal in outlook than Schneider, the Qu'ayti was an efficient progressive man rather than an ambitious upstart, while the Naqib was uneducated and vacillating – a hopeless man to deal with. Jaffer however was still at Aden and the rearguard action by the anti-Qu'ayti, party together with the Indian Government's determination to avoid a forcible solution, resulted in hesitant and indecisive diplomacy.[61] Various formulae were put forward in the hope of reaching a compromise, all of which were rejected by one or other of the parties. By 1881 matters had practically reached deadlock when the Qu'ayti came forward with a new initiative which was likely to prosper in the more liberal atmosphere of Lord Ripon's Viceroyalty.[62] In February, a cousin of the *jemadar*, 'Abdal Habib bin 'Abdallah al Qu'ayti, came from Bombay to Aden and proposed to Loch that the *jemadar* should purchase Mukalla from the Naqib for $300,000. Loch immediately grasped at this as the best possible solution, particularly as the Qu'ayti also offered to accept British control of his foreign relations. Jaffer was sent to Mukalla with three alternative agreements, of which that put forward by the Qu'ayti was one, and the Naqib was induced to sign all three and await the Indian Government's verdict.

At last the long-sought-after compromise seemed to have been reached. But when the Naqib was informed that the Indian Government had chosen the purchase proposal the Naqib withdrew his consent. He claimed that Jaffer had deceived him. Certainly the many years of support he had received from the British Government must have led him to believe that he was safe. Loch however was adamant. At an interview at Aden he told the Naqib that he would be held to his agreement and a warship was sent to Mukalla to enforce it and if necessary to co-operate with the *jemadar* in occupying the port. Unfortunately the *jemadar* was not ready to move on Mukalla and while he mustered troops, the Indian authorities had time for second thoughts. Anti-Qu'ayti feeling surged up at Bombay, the India Government hesitated and decided to withdraw from mediation and let the two parties fight it out. But Loch at Aden held to his purpose. The Naqib gave him ammunition by declaring himself a Turkish subject and calling for Turk support. The Indian Government immediately authorised a blockade of Mukalla. Then there was the fact that at the beginning of the negotiations the Qu'ayti, under British pressure, had abandoned the port of Burum, twelve miles along the coast from Mukalla. The Indian Government recognised that they must restore the *status quo* on withdrawing from the mediation, which meant putting the Qu'ayti back in Burum.[63] This gave Loch just sufficient cards to play out the game. He entrusted the operation of assisting at Burum to Commánder Hulton, a hotheaded naval officer who had already had arguments with the

Naqib and entertained none of his superiors' squeamishness about the use of force. On 2 November 1881, the Assistant Resident left Hulton with his ship lying off Burum, and when contact was next made with him on 11 November it was found that he had secured the surrender of all the Naqib's coastal forts, ending with Mukalla itself on the previous day. Mukalla was immediately handed over to the Qu'ayti who paid a lump sum to provide a pension for the Naqib.[64] Vainly protesting, the Naqib left for Zanzibar; nearly two thousand of his followers left with him and dispersed to various parts of East Africa and Arabia, a large proportion settling at Aden and Lahej.[65]

In this halting and indecisive manner the British became involved in Hadhrami affairs and helped the Qu'ayti to secure complete control of the coast. Once the Qu'ayti was installed, measures were taken to ensure that there would be no further danger of outside interference in Hadhrami affairs. In May 1882 a treaty was signed by which the *jemadar* agreed to accept British advice in dealing with outside powers and not sell or mortgage any part of his territory to anyone other than the British.[66] This treaty was supplemented by a full Protectorate Treaty in 1888.[67] Thus British India secured the limited objectives it sought with regard to the Hadhramawt. The *jemadars* retained their connections with the Hyderabad, but while they were in Arabia they remained within the screen of British paramountcy. A large section of the South Arabian coast was fenced off from the attentions of other powers and while this was the case the British did not care what happened in the interior. No attempt was made to establish relations with the Kathiri. Experience of their strong pro-Turkish propensities during the 1860s and 1870s had in any case prejudiced the British against them, and when in 1884 they asked the Aden authorities what the British attitude would be to a new attack on Shihr, they were smartly informed that a British gunboat would be sent to see that it did not succeed.[68] The Kathiri retained possession of the part of the Wadi Hadhramawt from Shibam eastward, including the towns of Saywun and Tarim, but they were entirely excluded from the coastline, and Qu'ayti territory lay between them and the independent tribes on the Aden side of the Hadhramawt. The Qu'ayti in fact claimed sovereignty over the whole country and, although they were unable to interfere in the Kathiri area, their control of the communications between the Hadhramawt and the rich emigrant communities overseas gave them the whip hand in their dealings with hostile people inland.[69]

Both by its origin and by its close treaty relationship with the British Government, the new Qu'ayti state had the appearance of being more closely under Aden's control than any other Sultanate in South Arabia. But in practice it was too far for Aden to be drawn directly within the orbit of the Aden Government. Its contact with the British was through India and by consent rather than through Aden and by direct British imposition. The *jemadars* were educated in India, their army was organised on Indian lines, the founders of the state, such as ʿAwad bin ʿUmar, showed a distinct preference for India, and the Quʿayti Sultans were more frequently to be found on their estates in Hyderabad than in their possessions in the Hadhramawt.[70] ʿAwad bin ʿUmar's whole approach was that of an Indian. He preferred Indian troops to either Yafiʿi or slave soldiers, and armed the former with rifles while leaving the latter with the inferior matchlock.[71] The port of Mukalla had an Indian flavour about it, the Parsi traders had the ear of the authorities and much Hindustani was spoken in the streets.[72] The Quʿayti were improvers and modernisers, and though good Muslims they were contemptuous of many of the traditional customs and beliefs. They allied themselves with the wealthy, cosmopolitan, returned emigrants in the towns, while they earned the dislike of many of the traditional religious leaders.[73] Trade and cultivation were encouraged. Interference with the communications by the bedawin was ruthlessly put down. The Shaykhs of tribes were bought over with subsidies and by recognition of their absolute control over their tribesmen. Hostages were taken to secure good behaviour.[74] Trade with the interior was carefully channelled through Mukalla, both to increase the revenue of the port and to control the trade in arms, whose spread among the tribesmen was to become the greatest menace to peace and to the strong administration which the Quʿayti were seeking to establish.[75] For this purpose Mayfaʿ on the coast to the east of Quʿayti territory was occupied at the expense of the neighbouring Wahidi, and efforts were made by the usual Quʿayti methods of mortgage and purchase to gain control of all the Wahidi's outlets to the sea.[76] Most of this met with the approval of the British authorities and an easy and cordial relationship of mutual respect grew up between the British and the Quʿayti which lasted up to and beyond the First World War.

CHAPTER VII

Fortress Aden and Rising Commerce

The last quarter of the nineteenth century was a period of increasing anxiety in Britain about problems of imperial defence. It was a period during which the maritime superiority gained during the Napoleonic wars and reinforced by the industrialisation of the first half of the nineteenth century came under serious challenge. Other powers began to acquire the capacity to build fleets and to invade former British preserves around the world by informal means or by outright annexation of colonies. Britain had to look to her defence and to her outposts along the sea routes of the globe. For those who looked at maps – and colonial rivalry was making this a popular pastime – there could be no doubt of Aden's importance in the new state of affairs. After the opening of the Suez Canal in 1869 a tight cluster of sea routes bent southward through the Red Sea and fanned out east, south-east and south-westward from the Bab el Mandeb to British possessions in India, the Antipodes and Africa. To the propagandists of Empire and others generally acquainted with the subject, Aden now ranked among the most important possessions of the British Crown.[1]

Aden's strategic importance was certainly much greater than when it had been a half forgotten appendage of the Bombay Presidency during the days before the Suez Canal project was conceived. But upon closer inspection, the case for regarding Aden as the guardian of the main lifeline of the Empire seemed very much less obvious. Within a few years of the opening of Suez, some defence experts were saying that the Suez route could not be counted on in wartime. Their principal argument was that it could too easily be blocked by sunken ships and this view strongly influenced Admiralty thinking up to and beyond the end of the century.[2] Such a view was further reinforced by the rapid growth of French naval strength in the Mediterranean in the late 1880s and a concomitant development of Russian Black Sea naval power, together with a decline in Turkish capacity to resist a Russian passage through the Straits. Some naval thinkers began to envisage the possibility of a British naval withdrawal from the Mediterranean in time of war. By the 1890s it was generally assumed that wartime communication with India would be main-

174

Above, view from the Tanks, Aden. Below, Ma'alla Wharf seen from the Main Pass, with the Jewish Cemetery in the foreground.

tained via the Cape – hence increased anxiety about the independent Boer Republics – or alternatively by way of the new railway across Canada.[3] The Indian Government continued to cite the tonnage of British merchant shipping using Aden for purposes of fund-raising in London for Aden's defences,[4] but by the end of the century Aden defence plans spoke less of protection of commerce than of sealing off the Red Sea, should the Canal fall into enemy hands.[5]

So the popular writers' new enthusiasm for Aden during the 'age of imperialism' was largely misplaced; in the more secret offices where defence matters were seriously weighed, there was less certainty about Aden's value and in 1903 it was assessed as being of 'very doubtful importance'.[6] It was a second line of defence in case the whole British position in the Middle East collapsed. But it was in no way the key to that position. The Egyptian approach to India was, as always, to be principally secured by naval command of the Mediterranean and diplomatic action in Europe. Between the 1880s and 1904 Britain's naval position in the Mediterranean was uncertain, while the direct British military presence in Egypt after 1882 provided a countervailing guarantee. Aden's true stategic role had not greatly changed from the days when Palmerston said that its possession would 'make us very strong in those parts', except that the areas in which that strength might be effectively exercised was considerably circumscribed by the assignment of parts of the Red Sea and East African littoral to various European powers and the consolidation of Ottoman authority over much of the rest. After Haines's time warships were no longer stationed permanently at Aden, despite the pleas of Outram and his successors. Instead, after the dissolution of the Indian Navy in 1863, an unarmed government steamer was placed there to maintain contact with the adjacent coasts. Two or more vessels of the Royal Navy were always present in the Persian Gulf, but Aden was only visited when political complications in the area absolutely required it.

Nevertheless Aden's seaward defences were substantially improved in the forty years prior to the First World War. In 1876 obsolete weapons were removed from the forts at Ras Morbat and Ras Tarshyne and 9-inch muzzle-loaders were set in their place in temporary positions. Ten years later a further, and this time major, overhaul of the defences was undertaken. At a cost of £213,000 and after three years' labour by a large number of workmen, Aden emerged with 6-inch and 10-inch breech-loaders in disappearing mountings on Morbat and Tarshyne, and five supplementary muzzle-loaders in positions overlooking Telegraph Bay and down among the Hijuff coalyards, where they remained, to the annoyance of the commercial community, until 1907.[7] The masonry of the land-

ward defences, constructed and reconstructed between 1840 and
1870, was regarded as obsolete but left as it was. The fifty-one old
guns pointing landward were scrapped in 1886 and two 7-inch
breech-loaders and a small subsidiary armament were put in their
place. The twelve guns in Front Bay were replaced by two muzzle-
loaders.[8] This re-vamping of the defences could be regarded as
evidence that Aden was being up-graded as a defensive position.
In fact it came about mainly because of the rapid strides made during
this period in military technology, which rapidly rendered older
weapons obsolete and worthless. It came about also because during
most of the period the gunners had the upper hand over the metal-
lurgists; projectiles were devised which could split the best armour-
plate a warship could carry, and hence in duels between ships and
forts it was expected that forts would always win. All harbour
fortresses in the British Empire acquired additional value and Aden
got its new defences, in company with a large number of others,
after general enquiries into Imperial Defences in 1870 and 1881-6,
and after prolonged wrangling between India and the Home
Government over who should foot the bill.[9]

While Aden's defences were being reorganised, those concerned
with the running of the settlement referred to it with increasing
frequency as a 'fortress'.[10] This did not of course represent an entirely
new departure. Aden had always been a well-defended place. But
the word 'fortress', applied principally to the protected area at
Steamer Point, was from the 1880s onward used as something more
than a mere descriptive term. It was a statement of policy. It meant
that military security was given absolute priority over all other
considerations and in this sense it did represent something of an
innovation.[11] When Aden had first been occupied it had been regarded as a centre of commercial influence as well as a military base.
'Commercial Emporium' was the description that had sprung most
quickly to Haines's lips and Singapore had been looked to as the
model. In 1843 the 'emporium' became a 'fortress', and under Ellenborough's influence trade was subordinated to security and dis-
couraged until 1849. Then commerce came back into the picture with
the institution of the free port, although the appointment of Military
Governors after Haines' departure showed a continuing emphasis on
Aden's military rule.[12] The references to the 'fortress' by the more
precise strategical thinkers of the 1880s pushed the balance decisively
in the latter direction. Other, more general changes in attitude
toward problems of trade and Empire in late Victorian Britain
tended to confirm this view of Aden's primary role. The early nineteenth-century notion that free ports, secure under liberal laws,
could alone liberate the productive energies of peoples in surround-

ing countries had by then given way to the less optimistic view that economic development was a matter of railways, heavy investment and direct European control. In addition, Arabia and North East Africa had not justified earlier hopes that they would become significant trading partners for Britain. The most spectacular developments were taking place elsewhere mainly in European settled areas. The hopes upon which the 'commercial emporium' idea had been based had practically vanished and the 'fortress Aden' concept now dominated official vision.

Paradoxically at the very time that Aden's commercial importance was being most heavily discounted, the settlement was entering upon a period of unprecedented business activity. During the last two decades of the nineteenth century, while the administration was seeking to produce a lean, austere, disciplined fortress atmosphere, the exuberant growth of Aden's commerce was defeating many of the Government's efforts in this direction and was changing the morphology of the settlement in ways that made Aden much less easy to defend. The key to Aden's new prosperity was the coal bunkering business and the opening of the Suez Canal in 1869 was one of the conditions for its growth. There was no abrupt increase in the amount of shipping using Aden as soon as the new waterway was complete. But the cutting of the Canal was not the only determinant of Aden's growth. Aden's fortunes were also bound to those of the steamships which it served and steam was still not in a position to displace sail in 1869. Until substantial improvements had been made in engines and boilers, sailing ships still provided cheaper carriage for goods in bulk. These necessary improvements came gradually between 1869, when the compound steam-engine began to tip the balance, and 1885, when the high-pressure steel boiler and triple-expansion steam-engine sealed the fate of the sailing ship.[13] In the meanwhile, the steamer gained ground where speed and regularity counted and the first upsurge of traffic using Aden in the early 1870s represented an increase in the number of mail steamers calling there. In the middle of that decade there was a pause, and then as freighters began to switch to steam, there was a further rise in the late 1870s and early 1880s.[14] By 1883 the coal bunkering business at Aden seemed poised for an even greater boom, when it was suddenly faced with formidable competition from the island of Perim.

Perim, the barren, waterless island at the mouth of the Bab el Mandeb which the British had occupied in 1857, had thereafter been left to the few fishermen and Somali herders who frequented it.[15] The only sign of British occupation was the lighthouse and a small detachment from the Aden garrison. Few thought of making

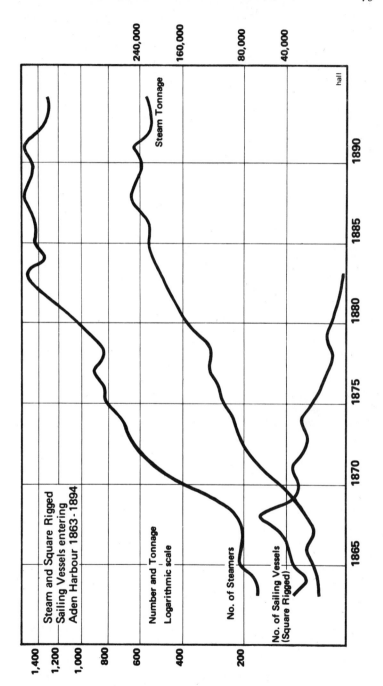

Steam and Square Rigged
Sailing Vessels entering
Aden Harbour 1863 - 1894

Number and Tonnage
Logarithmic scale

No. of Steamers

No. of Sailing Vessels
(Square Rigged)

Steam Tonnage

hall

use of its commodious harbour. In 1859 the Indian Navy suggested that some coals be placed there for the vessels crusing on anti-slavery patrol in the Red Sea, but this was not followed up. Proposals made in 1871 and 1879-80 by an Aden coaling company to start a branch there also came to nothing. Then in 1881, a complete out-sider, Mr. Hinton Spalding of London, was granted permission by the India Office to start a coaling station on the island. With the backing of a number of important shipowners he floated the Perim Coal Company and on 29 August 1883 the first steamer was coaled in Perim Harbour.[16]

That date marked the beginning of a struggle between Aden and Perim for the Red Sea coaling business which was to be waged with varying bitterness until the Second World War. The Perim Company could be regarded as an intruder in more ways than one. The three major coaling firms at Aden were closely linked with two major London coaling brokers possessing interests throughout the world. Their competition with one another never went beyond certain recognised limits.[17] The Perim Coal Company on the other hand was designed to cut out the brokers and several shipping companies had invested money in it for that specific purpose.[18] The Perim Company was therefore not interested in any *modus vivendi* agreement with the Aden companies. It was out to force coaling prices down and the result was an all-out commercial war between the two ports, fought with every weapon the rival parties could dispose of. Coal prices were cut – they fell from 40s. a ton in 1888 to 32s. a ton in 1894, despite rising costs. Bribes to captains were increased.[19] Aden suspected Perim of falsely notifying a cholera outbreak at Aden; Perim suspected Aden of bribing its coolies to desert.[20] Both sus-picions were probably justified. Perim publicised cases of delay at Aden; Aden told insurance brokers that the Perim charges for salvage were extortionate.[21] One Aden company prepared to invade the island and secured a coaling concession for this purpose from the Government; Perim prepared to repel the invaders by altering the position of harbour buoys in such a way as to make life impossible for them. The Aden company withdrew, but petitioned the Government to take over control of Perim's harbour and charge income tax and port dues there. Petitions and counter-petitions were mounted with the support of Lloyd's and various shipping companies, and the India Office was accused of creating a monopoly at Perim 'pernicious to the shipping interests in this country' (i.e. the United Kingdom).[22] Meanwhile all those involved underwent considerable financial strain. Luke Thomas and Company and Cowasji Dinshaw's, foremost in the struggle on Aden's behalf, went through a difficult phase in the late 1880s and were obliged to seek aid from their coaling broker.[23] In the middle '90s it was the Perim Company's turn. The Aden firms resolutely forced prices down and the Perim Company, with its weaker financial structure, finally succumbed at the end of the century, and signalled defeat by turning for aid to one of the London coaling brokers.[24] Thereafter the cut-throat competition ceased and gave place to more gentlemanly solicitation of custom.

This bitter commercial battle could not have been waged for so long had the general market not been buoyant. What happened in fact was that Perim creamed off the new custom which would other-wise have gone to Aden. At the end of the century coal issues at Aden were somewhat higher than they had been in 1885 despite the fact that Perim held approximately a quarter of the market.[25] There had been a time, however, when the prospect at Aden looked very bleak indeed. During the first seven years of competition Perim's business increased by leaps and bounds while Aden's rose slowly and then began to decline. In the late 1880s some of the Aden companies' oldest customers were beginning to drift away. At that stage Perim was in a very strong position. Suggestions were even put forward in some quarters that it be made a fortified coaling base.[26] It was marginally closer to the shortest shipping routes – a captain sailing for Pointe de Galle, the next stop in Ceylon for ships bound for all points east, could cut two miles from his journey by stopping at Perim.[27] The island was entirely geared to coaling operations – the harbour, roads, coolie lines – all were laid out for this sole purpose. No other interests or activities were permitted to hamper the single function of the settlement.[28] The lack of water was no more a drawback than at Aden. Both ports supplied water from condensers to the ships, since at Aden water from the Shaykh 'Uthman wells was considered too brackish for the purpose.[29] The Perim Company also secured the lion's share of the salvage business, owing to its proximity to the trickiest waters in the area, and this was a most lucrative sideline whose large profits offset coaling losses in the leanest years.[30]

These were all minor advantages. The single most important factor that drove shipping from Aden to Perim in the 1880s was the fact that Aden's harbour had become unsuitable for bunkering. The broad expanse of West Bay, lying between the promontories of Aden and Little Aden, had the appearance of one of the finest natural harbours in the world. And so it was, until from the 1850s onward the shipyards of the world began to produce iron and steel-built vessels of greater and greater draught. Thereafter the number of cases of vessels grounding in Aden harbour steadily mounted. By the middle '60s many of the larger steamers did not enter the bay at all. Instead they stood off the port in what was euphemistically called the 'outer harbour' and took in their coal and provisions there. For them Aden was little better than an open roadstead and they were often separated from the coaling bunkers by two miles or more of choppy water. Some idea of the difficulties this created for Aden coaling companies can be gathered from the following graphic description by Cowasji Dinshaw of the coaling of the heavy naval ironclads which escorted the Prince of Wales on his visit to India in 1876. 'The lighters rose and fell violently, striking the ship's side frequently and those in charge expected they would founder every moment. As a consequence the lighters were much injured, the coolies maintained their footing with difficulty, the coal bags could not be thrust through the ports with that celerity which was so desirable. . . .'[31] In that year one-third of all the vessels calling at Aden came no nearer than the outer harbour.[32] The coolies of course thoroughly disliked the dangerous task of going so far out to sea in boats designed for calmer waters. There were frequent strikes, and double pay often had to be offered.[33] By contrast, the deep, well-sheltered harbour at Perim had none of these problems. Ships anchored within a few hundred yards of the coal bunders and bunkering was a comparatively easy and rapid process.[34] It soon became obvious that once Perim had entered the lists, Aden was doomed unless something was done to deepen its harbour.

The trials of ships' captains in Aden's harbour however were minor compared with those of various Aden dredging projects in the shallow waters of Indian finance. Between the first concrete proposal to deepen the harbour in 1859 and the final decision to take action in 1890 lay over thirty years of fruitless but almost ceaseless correspondence between various Government Departments. The figure of Gladstone and his jaundiced view of all Government spending dominated this period. But this was not the only reason why Aden had to wait so long to have its harbour dredged. Nothing better illustrated the anomalous position of Aden in the whole British administrative machine than the difficulty of deciding who should pay for this relatively minor undertaking. Aden was still under the Presidency of Bombay, as it had been in Haines's time. But no Governor of Bombay was willing to spend capital sums on anything but the maintenance of the section of the Bombay army which garrisoned the port. Aden served the purposes of British rather than Indian foreign policy and as for the port, the shipping which used it was far more British than Indian.[35] Thus the dredging project got caught up in the long and inconclusive arguments as to whether Aden itself should be an Indian or British commitment. In 1861, 1874, 1890 and 1900 proposals were put forward that Aden should be transferred entirely to the Home Government. All of them came to nothing because the Indian Government was not willing to relinquish all control while the British Treasury had no desire to pay the expenses of the settlement.[36] This large undecided issue was never far from people's minds and it bedevilled all discussion of improvements to Aden's harbour. Each Department became so entrenched in its position as to be impervious to all arguments, even such cogent ones as that Aden's new forts were protecting berths which only the smallest ships could use, or that the guns themselves were masked by the shipping lying in the outer harbour, near the limit of their range.[37]

It was left to the actual users of the port to break through this administrative deadlock. Since 1857, the Aden coaling companies and other interested parties had been prodding the Government to take action. When in 1883 the rival coaling station was established at Perim, the Aden business men were driven to take desperate steps. It was all too obvious that the Perim Coal Company had been founded because of Aden's deficiencies. One of the sponsors of the Perim Company was a large shipowner who had complained most vociferously at having to coal his vessels in Aden's outer harbour.[38] In consequence, Luke Thomas and Company of Aden and Cowasji Dinshaw organised widespread agitation in London, Aden, Bombay and Calcutta to force a decision on the Government.[39] The Chairman of the P. and O., the Secretary of Lloyd's, over a hundred ship owners representing a million and a half tons of British shipping, the Bengal, Bombay and the newly founded Aden Chambers of Commerce were all mobilised. Parliamentary questions were tabled, the Secretary of State was importuned and various lobbies were made to ring with protests at Government inaction.[40]

The Government in London was much upset by this. But it is doubtful whether anything would have been done had the Aden companies not devised a way of getting round the financial difficulty. It was discovered that the Aden Port Fund, financed by the dues collected from shipping, had accumulated a substantial surplus. Not enough to carry out a dredging scheme, but sufficient to make a start.[41] The Aden companies therefore concentrated on getting control of these funds into their own hands. They had no faith in the Aden Government's stewardship of the harbour dues – and rightly so. Aden was, as always, starved of money by the Bombay Government, and by various devices the officials plundered the Port Fund to pay for other things.[42] In 1884 the Bombay accountants still had the greatest difficulty in understanding the tortuous nature of Aden finance; the conditions which had driven Haines to wholesale falsification had not entirely disappeared.[43] The Aden companies therefore made their first objective the establishment of a Port Trust as a separate institution with business representation on its Board. This idea ran into some trouble from the advocates of the 'Fortress Aden' concept who frowned on representative bodies in such a strategic and cosmopolitan port.[44] Their reluctance was overcome by pressure in London and in 1888 an Act setting up the Aden Port Trust was passed in Bombay. This was the key victory in the battle to have Aden's harbour dredged. Once a piece of administrative apparatus devoted to harbour interests had been created, everything became easy. The accumulated Port Fund surpluses were used to begin operations in January 1891. Confidence improved, revenue increased and even the Indian Government was willing to lend money to the Aden Port Trust once it saw that by so doing it would not saddle itself with unlimited responsibility.[45] By 1895 the first and most important dredging scheme was complete. Aden began to breathe again, while the Perim Coal Company began to experience severe financial difficulties. In the new century the Port Trust undertook further extensive dredging projects and these were coupled with land reclamation schemes which created much of the present business area of Steamer Point. These efforts saved Aden from the fate of so many of its Red Sea neighbours, including its own original harbour facing Crater town, which had failed to keep abreast of the fast changing times. The dredging and re-dredging of the harbour kept Aden competitive against rivals half way across the globe for the custom of the increasingly long-ranged steamers that could now pick and choose their refuelling depots.

In turn the massive flow of shipping through the port helped Aden gather up the greater part of the commerce in its immediate vicinity. With steamers and colliers putting into port every day for a multitude of destinations there was no shortage of cheap and readily available shipping space for the conveyance of produce to the great markets of the world. The American vessels sitting in the harbour for months accumulating a cargo were a thing of the past. Goods were turned over fast by Aden merchants, and telegraphic communication enabled them to buy and sell at the most profitable price. For Aden was now a station on the main telegraph route between Europe and the east and thus in instant contact with the world's main business centres. The first lines were landed at Aden in 1860. They almost immediately failed and Aden's telegraph service must be dated from 1870 when the first effective lines were laid. In the next two decades the first costly and limited service was enormously improved. Lines north and south were doubled and trebled, branch lines installed and charges fell from pounds to shillings.

These advantages were reinforced by the appearance of coasting

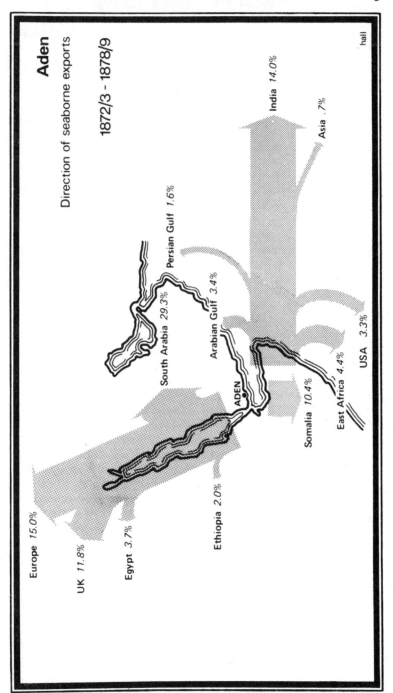

Aden

Direction of seaborne exports

1872/3 - 1878/9

Europe *15.0%*

UK *11.8%*

Egypt *3.7%*

Ethiopia *2.0%*

South Arabia *29.3%*

Persian Gulf *1.6%*

Arabian Gulf *3.4%*

ADEN

Somalia *10.4%*

East Africa *4.4%*

USA *3.3%*

India *14.0%*

Asia *.7%*

hall

steamers linking Aden with other ports along the coast. In 1872 twenty-one steam vessels of 18,411 tons entered Aden from Hudayda and Jedda. Up to eight years later the number had not markedly increased. But in 1893 a hundred vessels of 60,897 tons cleared for those ports and eighty-nine cleared for Zayla and Berbera, with whom there had been no steam communication in the 1870s. The important transformation had taken place in both cases in the 1880s and by the end of that decade most of the steamers were owned by Aden merchants. The Egyptian Government at various junctures in the 1870s and 1890s established steamship companies in an effort to revive the old Egyptian axis of Red Sea commerce. But in the long run victory lay with the practical capitalists at Aden, notably Cowasji Dinshaw. With agents at work in most of the smaller ports bulking goods for dirty puffing little steamers plying regularly alongside the more fitful voyages of the graceful but shabby dhows, which themselves were drawn like magnets in increasing numbers into Aden's commercial field of force, the businessmen at Aden steadily secured a domination over the commerce of the whole area.[46] In the end, Egyptian investments in harbour and other installations in Somalia, Turkish road building and mobilisation of taxable surpluses in the Yemen after 1872, Ethiopia's struggles to modernise, all redounded to Aden's advantage and were reflected in the surging commerce in coffee, hides and skins, gum and ivory through the port's warehouses in the last three decades of the nineteenth century. Aden could regard Turkish efforts to divert the landward coffee traffic to their own Yemeni ports with some complacency: by the 1880s it did not matter which port exported Yemeni coffee, the lion's share ultimately found its way to Aden for final shipment.

When one looks at a commodity breakdown of the trade passing through Aden in its heyday the immediate impression is how little had changed. Apart from the decline in the relative importance of coal and garrison supplies such as alcoholic drinks as Aden's entrepôt commerce developed, the only strikingly new feature was the disproportionate growth of the hides and skins export, largely in response to the demands of the American glove-making trade. Otherwise the constituents of a commerce dating back to the seventeenth century were still there; the large piece goods import, still mainly Indian-based although the products were now mostly American and European-made; the old trade deficit with India still existed, while coffee exports to Europe and the United States brought periodical inflows of treasure in the form of Maria Theresa dollars. Grain still came in from India, peaking ominously in famine years such as 1881, 1891 and 1905. Dates from the Persian Gulf maintained

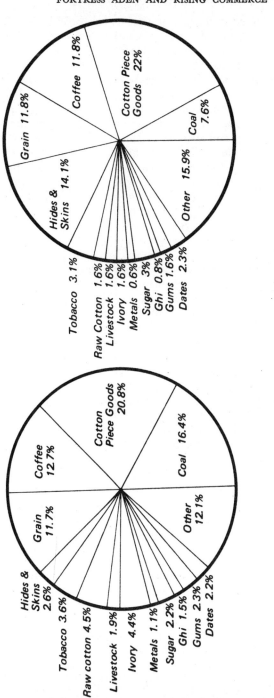

Aden

Imports 1900/01 - 1907/8   By Value

Cotton Piece Goods 22%
Coffee 11.8%
Grain 11.8%
Hides & Skins 14.1%
Coal 7.6%
Other 15.9%
Tobacco 3.1%
Raw Cotton 1.6%
Livestock 1.6%
Ivory 1.6%
Metals 0.6%
Sugar 3%
Ghi 0.8%
Gums 1.6%
Dates 2.3%

Aden

Imports 1872/3 - 1880/1   by Value

Cotton Piece Goods 20.8%
Coffee 12.7%
Coal 16.4%
Grain 11.7%
Other 12.1%
Hides & Skins 2.6%
Tobacco 3.6%
Raw cotton 4.5%
Livestock 1.9%
Ivory 4.4%
Metals 1.1%
Sugar 2.2%
Ghi 1.5%
Gums 2.3%
Dates 2.2%

their position while the consumption of sugar steadily grew. Apart from the massive import of cloth, the commerce was still essentially a matter of exchanging agricultural products. The import of metals and metal manufactures represented an inconsiderable part. It was not a question of an agricultural region being subdued and inundated by the sophisticated products of technologically advanced societies. Nor was it a question of such a region equipping itself with imported capital goods. That was not to come until very much later – until the years before and after the Second World War. At this stage the trade had a traditional flavour – indeed in Aden's hinterland the major change in the nineteenth century was the replacement of raw cotton by the import of cotton twist, involving a transfer of effort from spinning to weaving in the local textile industries in centres such as Lahej and Dali'. The major development was that more of everything was changing hands and it was at Aden that the biggest handfuls of coffee beans, grain and piece goods were to be found.

The bounding expansion of trade gave ample employment to the brokers of every kind that agglomerated in the streets of Aden. At their head stood the old established wealthy English, American, German, French, Italian and Indian firms, with firm business connections in Europe, the United States and Bombay. A typical figure among them was the rich Parsi, Hormusji Dinshaw, who represented commercial Aden on State occasions as the Sultan of Lahej represented the people, or rather the political brokers, of the hinterland. Beneath them stood the smaller fry, the Indian and Arab rank and file in Aden's Chamber of Commerce, whose meetings the managers of the great companies scarcely bothered to attend. Each depended on the patronage or goodwill of those above who controlled access to business and who, until 1905, even owned the wharves across which almost all goods had to pass. Some of the second rank of merchants, mostly Arab dealers in coffee, commanded considerable wealth, although they depended on the firms for a market for their produce. This was not the case with the petty traders who went to the Somali coast peddling goods advanced to them on credit, who were completely dependent on their principals. But they and a mass of small-time brokers, and indeed the whole aggregation of traders in Aden, made a living by forging economic links at an individual level between men from societies that were strangers to one another. Such brokers, middlemen or interpreters were involved in every deal from a £2,000 investment in coffee to the smallest purchase of fowls or provisions. A herd of sheep could be sold four times between the landing place at Ma'alla and the Main Pass gate about a mile off by brokers each promising payment in Crater.[47]

These deals were central to the life of the town; small and large fortunes were made in this way and in most cases repatriated out away from the British-protected, but uncongenial, hurly-burly of the multiracial market place.

With increasing business activity, people flocked into the settlement to seek employment. Between 1881 and 1891, Aden's population increased from 34,860 to 44,079.[48] The newcomers flowed in toward the most active areas on the shores of the western bay rather than to the old town of Crater. In default of better accomodation, they swarmed up the hills behind Steamer Point in caves and temporary mat huts, cluttering up this formerly exclusive residential area. Further down the bay, their mat and reed dwellings mushroomed up around the three hundred and fifty or so small stone houses at Ma'alla. Living conditions were appalling. At Ma'alla in 1881 the reed-built huts averaged just over eleven square yards of living space per person. But in addition to the 2,650 people living in them, a further 780 were without any sort of home.[49] All this was anathema to the now 'fortress'-minded Government officials. Gone were the days when Haines had counted each new immigrant as a triumph for his policy. Now Government with its 'fortress' policy regarded every additional inhabitant as a nuisance and a further mouth to feed in time of siege. The presence of so many footloose nameless 'vagrants' crowding close to military installations was seen as a grave security risk and there was anger at the constant reappearance of unauthorised reed huts masking the guns at Hijuff and the Point. And so sporadic efforts were made between 1880 and 1900 to clear the western area of Aden of all but the most essential personnel.

The biggest scheme for doing this was undertaken in 1881 and involved the purchase from the Sultan of Lahej of all the land at the head of the bay, including the wells at Shaykh 'Uthman. In 1882 work began on the construction of a new town at Shaykh 'Uthman, some five miles from the port. One hundred and fifty houses, a school and a dispensary were erected at government expense and low rents were charged to attract settlers. Simultaneously measures were taken to drive the surplus population from Steamer Point. Mat and reed houses were torn down, heavy municipal taxes were imposed, a register of population was begun and a pass system controlling entry to the 'fortress' area instituted.[50] These measures however were only partly successful. The population of Shaykh 'Uthman certainly rose – from 600 in 1881 to over 7,200 ten years later. But the population of Aden was not reduced. Those expelled from Steamer Point in 1882 came seeping back in various ways toward the centres of employment along the western bay until it was as overcrowded as before. With the prevalent system of casual labour, men could not afford to be far from call and Shaykh 'Uthman, where the rate of unemployment was notably higher than at Aden, was too far.[51] Even the members of the substantial floating Somali community who were more associated with the livestock trade near the head of the bay than with the coaling activity further out, found Shaykh 'Uthman inconvenient and drifted back to their old haunts at Ma'alla.[52]

Stern measures were taken from time to time by Government to repel these invaders of its fortress. The pass system was rigorously enforced and became 'an instrument of great tyranny' in the hands of the police. Coffee shops were closed down to disperse those who congregated round them. Reed and mat huts were ruthlessly torn down as fast as they sprung up. The officials themselves character-ised the steps they took to exclude people as 'very harsh'.[53] They were nevertheless unsuccessful; the pass system was evaded, the denizens of the demolished huts turned up again in masses in the small overcrowded houses at the Point, to pose a further threat of epidemics.[54] The closed coffee shops were replaced by others and the old order was restored.[55]

The character of Aden's labouring population was such that in case of conflict between Government dictates and market pressures the latter would almost inevitably win. On average, labourers stayed no more than three or four months in the settlement before returning to the interior. Even among the Arab shopkeepers, a substantial proportion stayed for no more than six months at a time. The application of a pass system to such an amorphous body of men was almost bound to break down. And since a quarter of those living at the Point were prepared to go without any shelter, control of habitation was little more effective. On the other hand, since most of these seasonal immigrants came with the object of securing employ-ment and earning what they could as quickly as possible, the labouring population responded with exceptional flexibility to economic demand. Aden firms were seldom short of hands. There seemed to be an endless reservoir of labour. During the 1880s the Government engaged over a thousand men to work on the forts, and hundreds more were recruited to build Shaykh 'Uthman and to lay out new salt pans at the head of the bay. At the same time the boom in coal bunkering and commerce was creating further job opportuni-ties. Labour was also recruited in the Aden market for Perim and for construction work on the Somali coast. Yet, throughout the decade, the scale of wages for unskilled men remained remarkably stable. Indeed the scale of wages remained roughly constant at Aden over a much longer period and was substantially the same in 1914 as it

had been in the 1840s.[56] An increased demand for labour did not
improve the workers' bargaining power because there were always
more applicants than jobs. The pool of unemployed did not diminish
because more men were always ready to come down from the hills
of the Yemen and the Protectorate if the opportunities of employment increased. The *muqaddam* system and its ramifications ensured
that the supply of labour responded comparatively smoothly to the
demand. In the 1880s, labour contracting became a well-organised
and profitable business and the government was besieged by
applications from contractors to export workmen to Djibouti, to
Somalia, to East and Southern Africa.[57] At Aden each large employer
had his chief *muqaddam* or *syrang*, and he in turn had several sub-
muqaddams who brought men forward, paid their wages, rented
accommodation for them, and saw that they were fed. At all points
these contractors exacted remuneration for their services, and it
was they who issued the wage to the workers, less the various deduc-
tions. The *muqaddam* himself had to preserve his credit with the
employer and to do this he had to give advances to labourers whose
earnings fell through lack of work. This was how the pool of instantly
ready, under-employed men was maintained. The *muqaddam* could
suffer financially when labour was scarce during the planting season
in the interior. In June, workmen flooded out homeward to tend their
farms and the market remained tight until October. During that
time the coolies were in a better bargaining position. Men would
refuse to risk the long hazardous journeys to coal ships in the outer
harbour. Strikes were frequent and there was a particularly bad
bout of industrial unrest in 1882 when the Egyptian expedition
brought an unusually large number of ships to the port in the middle
of the 'off season'.[58] At these times the *muqaddam* bore the brunt of
the difficulties; he usually had to pay out a larger proportion of the
coolies' wages to keep them at work and satisfy the employer.[59] For
the rest of the year however labour was docile and the super-
abundance of willing hands did much to enable Aden to maintain
its competitive position *vis-à-vis* other bunkering ports.

These arrangements suited the coaling companies and mercantile
firms very well.[60] They were however regarded with rather less
enthusiasm by the government officials, some of whom regarded
the *muqaddams* as parasites who battened on the workers and deprived
them of their rightful wage.[61] Several efforts were made by Government during the 1880s to break the *muqaddam* system in certain
sectors of the labour market. All failed except a scheme for the
direct payment by the employers of the coal coolies on Perim
island.[62] The efforts that were made were symptomatic of a new,
more general, official concern about workers' conditions at Aden.

The Government was beginning to take an almost impartial attitude toward labour questions. The magistrates intervened to settle labour disputes by a rudimentary form of arbitration and they did not always decide in the employer's favour, even when the largest and most respectable firms were involved.[63] In Haines's day, the Political Officers and the businessmen had formed a single, close-knit community. But there was much less evidence of this by the 1880s. The ever-changing Government personnel were becoming functionally separate from the commercial element and to a certain extent hostile to it. The officials belonged to the larger 'official' society of India and Britain and quickly responded to the new ideas of administration and social reform which were flowing through it. In the late nineteenth and early twentieth centuries, the idea that the state should intervene to promote social welfare was gaining ground in Britain and India, and this had its effect at Aden. At the same time the growing estrangement between British authority and the nationalistic Indian bourgeoisie weakened former bonds of sympathy. In any case the policy of shifting Aden's population out of the 'fortress' brought officials into closer touch with what went on in the slums and coffee houses around the port. But, while worthy of note, this shift in the official attitude did not issue in any very substantial benefits for port labour at large. The Government pressured certain employers into providing accommodation for their workmen. But this improvement was more than outweighed by the hardships which resulted from the periodic purges of the working population in the fortress area.[64] The population of Aden was far too mobile and unsettled to be amenable to the then prevailing methods of administrative control, and practically every Government attempt to alter the pattern of economic and social life in the port petered out in failure.

Government action in the field of education had a somewhat greater impact on the life of the community. It began in 1856 through the initiative of G. P. Badger, who hoped to build up a College of Arabic learning at Aden which would radiate its influence throughout the hinterland, bring the sons of Chiefs into closer contact with the British and train Arab administrative staff. A school was established and it ran for two years. But the scheme was premature. It was heavily criticised in India, where the whole idea of state sponsored education was a controversial topic at that time. In any case sufficient Arab pupils could not be found to realise the original plan. The school was dubbed a 'seminary for the education of camp followers' and was closed.[65] For eight more years the only education at Aden was that afforded by the traditional schools attached to the mosques and synagogues, where twenty to thirty fee-paying students would gather round a teacher and learn by rote passages from their respective books of religion. Then in 1866, during the constructive period of Merewether's Residency, a new attempt was made. One school offering an English education under an Indian headmaster and another mainly concerned with Qu'ranic studies were quietly set up and financed partly from Government and partly from municipal funds. From then on the system expanded slowly. In 1879 a second Arabic school was established at Ma'alla and in 1880 a third at Steamer Point.[66] In the next decade two Catholic Mission schools were set up to give instruction in English. The Government schools widened their curriculum to include book-keepking and the Arabic schools reduced the amount of Qur'anic study and supplemented it with modern utilitarian subjects at elementary level. By 1897, when grants in aid of private schools had been introduced, there were 1,768 pupils receiving instruction of all types at Aden. Of these 256 attended the Government Arabic school, which was now sufficiently secular in its outlook to attract Jewish pupils. A further 88 attended the Government English schools. This, for a late nineteenth-century port with a large floating population among its 40,000 to 50,000 people, was a fairly creditable performance. But the vision of the earlier projectors, such as Badger and Merewether, who had hoped to draw the hinterland peoples into the Aden schools, was not realised. In 1896, less than half the students in the Government establishments were Arabs and only sixteen Arabs attended the English-language schools. The ethnic composition of school classes reflected that of the settled population of Aden itself and the educational system ran along conventional lines as a service to the community within the limits of British control.[67]

Generally speaking, the business boom at Aden in the four decades prior to the First World War did not serve to knit in the settlement with its hinterland as the smaller wave of prosperity after the middle of the century had done. Aden's landward trade did not dramatically increase during this period. The centres of fodder production for the port moved gradually outward from the Fadli country in the 1870s to the Lower Yafi'i country in the 1890s.[68] and more vegetables and provisions were imported from Abyan, Lahej and the grain-growing areas beyond Dali'. Aden's economic influence still expanded in the hinterland but did not keep pace with the great strides being made in the port itself. On the other hand Aden began to grow out of the traditional framework which had for so long been familiar to the neighbouring tribes. The old town of Crater was now just one of a group of communities scattered round the Peninsula. The new port in western bay and its grid-iron satellite at Shaykh 'Uthman, stood self-confidently outside the walls which for centuries had sheltered Aden merchants from outside attack. These settlements ignored the interior and geared their life to the steady procession of steamers passing through the harbour. It is true that the visitor from the hinterland would have heard more Arabic spoken. In the 1890s almost half Aden's population was Arab – a striking change from the position at the middle of the century when the Arabs formed less than a quarter of the community and were greatly outnumbered by the Indians.[69] But the accents he would have heared would not have been those of the immediate hinterland. The bulk of the migrant labourers at Aden, who formed a large part of the 'new' Arab population, came in from the Hajariya, Baydha and other parts of the Yemen highlands, rather than from the less populous areas within the British sphere of influence.[70] During this period the economic and social links between Aden and the hinterland became of less importance than the purely political connection. Trade and politics became less closely integrated and in Aden the British authorities became concerned less with keeping the landward trade routes open than with obtaining an internationally recognised frontier which would more directly secure the hinterland of the fortress and the entrepôt.

CHAPTER VIII

Anglo-Turkish Relations and the Delimitation of the Yemen Boundary

The removal of the Turkish troops from Lahej in December 1873 did not effect a permanent settlement of Aden's frontier with the Yemen. Indeed, as far as the Turks were concerned, there was no frontier to settle. The Turkish attitude was that the whole Peninsula formed part of the Sultan-Caliph's historic possessions and the Pashas of the Yemen and of the Hadhramawt divided between them the control of all South-West Arabia. The Ottoman Government showed no willingness to accept the British thesis that the nine tribes in Aden's hinterland were independent. Concessions made on specific issues took the form of favours granted to a friendly power without prejudice to the Porte's claim to ultimate sovereignty, and the Turkish Government duly protested at any British interference in the internal affairs of the hinterland tribes which came to its notice. Even Aden's purchase of Shaykh 'Uthman from the Sultan of Lahej was made the subject of a diplomatic note. The Turks gave no sign that they were prepared to compromise on general principle. Indeed, if anything their opinion on the matter tended to harden during the 1870s and 1880s. Under Sultan 'Abd al Hamid II pan-Islamic ideas became dominant in governing circles and, in addition to this, suspicions grew that the British were fostering incipient Arab unrest in the Sultan's dominions. These suspicions had little basis in fact, for the British carefully avoided any deliberate involvement in the intrigues of Arab critics of Ottoman rule. A request for British aid from Yemeni rebels in 1877 was left unanswered, and similar movements elsewhere in the Arab world were handled with equal caution. But Britain's general posture in the Middle East at the time, her interests in southern and eastern Arabia and Mesopotamia, her support for Midhat's reforms in Iraq, and her position in Egypt after 1882 lent colour to the Sultan's fears. British appeals on behalf of Aden chiefs could easily be represented as part of a general plot to suborn the Sultan's Arab subjects and they therefore usually met with a cold reception.

The authorities in London for their part were not eager to press for

a decision on the sovereignty question. The Foreign Office in
particular had no wish to damage its influence at the Porte by an
attempt to settle a matter so low on its order of priorities as the status
of the Aden tribes. Moreover, the religious twist which the Sultan
gave to his claims brought into operation that underlying fear of
offending the religious susceptibilities of non-Christian, especially
Muslim, peoples which so strongly affected British attitudes to
international politics after the Indian Mutiny. From time to time
the British Ambassador at Istanbul was instructed to protest at
cases of Turkish encroachment on the independence of the tribes.
But these protests were seldom pushed forward vigorously enough to
produce redress. A proposal brought forward in 1882 to delimit the
frontiers of the nine tribes as a means of preventing future dispute
was dropped when the Porte showed no interest. An alternative
scheme for establishing a British Protectorate in South Arabia, drawn
up by the Government of India as early as 1873, was allowed to make
the rounds of Government Departments being refined and modified
for a period of fifteen years, without any action being taken on it.[1]
From 1875 onwards London took care to avoid allowing Aden disputes to complicate relations between Britain and the Ottoman
Empire, which in any case and for other reaons were seldom very
satisfactory.

Despite this forbearance, even London was not prepared to accept
a *de facto* establishment of Ottoman control in Aden's immediate
neighbourhood and the Aden question might have caused severe
conflicts between the British and Turkish Governments had the
Turkish authorities in the Yemen remained as aggressive after 1875
as they had been during the period when they were establishing
their rule in that country. Fortunately this was not the case. The
Governors-General of the Yemen after 1875 were more concerned
with maintaining peace and balancing their budgets than with
taking on new commitments. The barren territories of the nine Aden
tribes beyond the fertile plateau were not worth the cost of administration and therefore hardly interested the economy-minded men at
San'a'. Moreover, in 1877 the Turks jettisoned their alliance with the
Lahej Sultan's old enemies, the Dhu Muhammad and Dhu Husayn,
as part of a general administrative reform, and thereby eased relations in that quarter. The British found in the late 1870s and 1880s
that for the most part, a mildly unsatisfactory state of affairs could
be maintained by direct dealings on an *ad hoc* basis with the authorities in the Yemen, and crises such as that of 1873 did not recur.[2]

The sovereignty question might have been left in this state of
realistic ambiguity for an indefinite period had the British and
Turks alone been concerned, and had other European powers not

appeared upon the scene. This was still very much how matters stood up to 1882. Until then, Britain had seldom been greatly worried by the idea of direct European intervention in South Arabia. The British position there was screened at a distance by Egyptian and Ottoman claims to the Red Sea littoral and the suzerainty exercised by the Sultans of Zanzibar over the East African coast. The nearest active European possession was the small French island of Réunion, in the southern Indian Ocean. But in August 1882 Gladstone's government occupied Egypt, and that act was followed by a whole chain of disturbing events in the Red Sea area, most of which were menacing to Britain's influence in Aden's neighbourhood. Once in Egypt the British could neither get out nor regularise their position there. They were more or less at the mercy of the European powers on the Egyptian Debt Commission, notably the displaced and embittered French and the *tertius gaudens*, Bismarck, who used the '*baton Egyptien*' to extort diplomatic concessions elsewhere.

The Ottoman Sultan was deeply offended and highly suspicious of British intentions while at the same time being afforded multiple opportunities of injuring Britain by the exercise of his remaining rights over the Egyptian Khedivate. Thus crippled diplomatically, London had to face the further problems raised by the Mahdist rising in the Sudan in 1883, and forced Egypt to abandon its costly establishments on the Red Sea coast. The whole western flank of the Red Sea was thereby exposed to European encroachment. Already the Anglo-Egyptian Somali Coast Convention of 1877 had worn rather thin, owing to the refusal of the Porte to ratify it and the establishment of an Italian settlement at Assab in 1880. But now Egypt was too weak to pose a serious threat. Inevitably France stepped in and exploited her twenty-year-old claims to the island of Obokh to establish control over the adjacent Dankali and Somali coasts in November 1884. Gladstone's government could do no more than acquiesce, and seek to circumscribe the effect of the French moves by establishing a Protectorate over the sources of Aden's supplies on the coastline between Zayla and Cape Guardafui.[3]

This was not the end but the beginning of European encroachment on Britain's Middle Eastern sphere of influence. There followed the sudden rush by European powers to acquire paper claims to African territories, usually described as 'the scramble for Africa', and South Arabia was close enough to that scene of diplomatic action to feel some of its effects. Bismarck's *Schutzbrief* of 3 March 1885 brought Germany into East Africa, and the first casualty was Britain's friend, the Sultan of Zanzibar, who lost his claims to the African interior. London saw to it that the Sultanate itself was safeguarded, for its demise would not have been well received at Masqat. But as it was British prestige among the Arabs suffered a heavy blow. In October of the same year, the Germans approached even closer to Aden when they began intriguing just south of Cape Guardafui at the Somali town of Alula, where the disgruntled refugees from the Hadhrami wars had taken up residence.[4]

French and German excursions to the Arab coast at Shaykh Sa'id in the Bab el Mandeb also gave cause for concern.[5] The air became hot with annexations, protectorates, and rumours of both. No sphere of informal influence seemed safe without some diplomatic document to back it up. So in February 1886, the Government of India came forward with its long-considered comprehensive scheme for securing South Arabia by a series of protectorate treaties. Not just the flanks of the Aden position, but the whole coastline from the Red Sea to the Persian Gulf, including the politically-sensitive spots at Masqat and the Hadhramawt, were involved.[6]

Part of this Indian scheme was put into operation immediately in April 1886, when a treaty of protection was negotiated with the Sultan of Qishn and Socotra.[7] This was the obvious place to start, for Socotra was as it were the bell-wether of British intentions in the Gulf of Aden area. It had been briefly occupied in 1835 as a coaling depot for the mail steamers, but quickly abandoned due to sickness among the garrison. In 1876 when the first effects of the opening of Suez were felt, Socotra was made the subject of a 'no sale or mortgage' treaty with its ruler.[8] Now the 1886 Protectorate Treaty with Socotra was to set the pattern for those to be negotiated later with the potentates on the South Arabian coast.[9] Being an island situated in a diplomatic no-man's-land almost midway between Arabia and Africa, Socotra was particularly vulnerable to land-grabbing European states.[10] On the other hand, its remoteness from Arabia's main political centres set it further from the sphere of Ottoman sensitivity. This last was a point of considerable importance, for while Socotra was brought under British protection immediately, the rest of the Indian Government's Protectorate scheme was delayed by fears of a possible Turkish reaction.[11]

During 1886 and 1887 the British Government had to handle all matters relating to the Ottoman Empire with the utmost caution. The Sultan still had more than a local nuisance value, and during the 1885 Penjdeh crisis he had shown that he could block British moves against Russia by closing the straits to British warships. Britain's Middle Eastern interests were challenged on all sides and her diplomatic isolation left her a prey to her enemies. Salisbury, who replaced Gladstone at the head of affairs, saw that each issue could not be dealt with separately. Lesser interests were strictly

subordinated to the greater and the negotiation of the Aden Protectorate treaties came low in the order of priorities. Since the Franco-
Prussian war, Russia was regarded as a more dangerous rival than
France – the Persian Gulf approach to India was therefore more in
need of protection than that by the Red Sea and the Red Sea route
itself was more effectively guarded by the British presence in Egypt
than by the Aden base. Beyond this lay the even more vital questions
of the balance of power in the Mediterranean and in Europe itself.

Salisbury's government had in effect two possible courses of action
open to it. The first, strongly advocated in 1886 by Lord Randolph
Churchill, was to accept that the Ottoman Empire was moribund,
do a deal with Russia at the Porte's expense and safeguard the
routes to India by direct British action. The second was to continue
to rely on the Sultan as the guardian of those routes and seek the
support of the powers of the Triple Alliance who, because of Austria's
Balkan interests, were committed to the preservation of Ottoman
integrity.

Salisbury never clearly chose between these two possibilities but
up to the spring of 1888 he leaned more heavily towards the second
scheme of action. During 1887 he signed the two Mediterranean agreements which drew Britain closer to the Triple Alliance and committed the country to a modified form of the principle of Ottoman
integrity. With the diplomatic currency thus earned, it was hoped
that the Porte could be pressured into regularising Britain's position
in Egypt, and Sir Henry Drummond Wolff was twice sent to Constantinople to secure this object. The negotiations were complex and
protracted, and while they continued, the South Arabian Protectorate scheme was held in suspense, for fear of upsetting the
Sultan.[12] But when the Drummond Wolff mission failed, owing to
French and Russian pressure at the Porte, Salisbury began to veer
in a new direction. There was no clear-cut change of policy – that
was not Salisbury's way – but he began to re-emphasise new options
at the expense of old. In August 1887 he told the German ambassador
that 'British interests may become directed not towards the Straits
and Constantinople but rather on the Euphrates, the countries
between Egypt and India and the security of the Persian Gulf.'
The South Arabian Protectorate scheme was back in play.[13]

There was a further delay while the second Mediterranean
agreement of December 1887 was being contracted, but by March
1888 the major pieces on the board had so been manoeuvred and
protected that Salisbury felt free to pick up a few pawns, and orders
were sent to Aden to go ahead. The treaties were aimed not against
the Porte but against other European powers.[14] Coastal chiefs, some
of whom had never been subject to Ottoman pressure, were called

upon to sign, not those in the interior who had suffered most from
Turkish encroachment. Salisbury even hoped to conciliate the
Sultan by inserting a clause saving his religious rights, and when
Aden said this was not possible, he tried to cancel the whole operation.[15] But his telegram failed to arrive in time to stop the Resident
who was already off along the coast busily signing treaties with the
most accessible coastal chiefs. Once begun, the operation could not be
stopped, and in the following year the other potentates on the coast
were brought within the system. Aden traditions were thus maintained
and once again a decisive step was taken by men on the spot before
their action could be countermanded from above.[16]

This did not exhaust the full Protectorate programme which the
Indian authorities had set before the Home Government in 1886.
The Indian scheme had been based on the nine tribes mentioned in
the 1873 notification to the Porte, and covered the interior as well as
the coast. It provided for the further signature of treaties with the
landlocked Hawshabi and 'Alawi; the independence of the Upper
Yafi'i and Upper 'Awlaqi was to be sustained, while the 'Amir of
Dali''s territory was to be regarded as dispensable – a sop to be
offered to the Porte in return for the recognition of British control
elsewhere. The rationale behind the whole arrangement was that it
would first of all seal off the coast against other powers, secondly
secure Aden's sources of supply and thirdly set a barrier against
Turkish expansion toward the Hadhramawt and Masqat, without
undertaking commitments in areas too remote from British power.
The first of these objectives was secured by what was done in 1888
and 1889. Thereafter, with European intervention thus warded off,
the problem was reduced once more to pre-scramble dimensions.
The continuation of the programme depended on the simple calculation whether protectorate treaties with the interior states would
curb or encourage Turkish hostility and expansion. It also depended
on how far Salisbury and the London Government were prepared
to go along the path leading to partition of the Ottoman Empire.
Salisbury's estimation of the value of Ottoman integrity waned very
gradually from the 1880s onwards; in the early '90s an atmosphere
of caution still prevailed in London, and the Indian Government
confined itself to clarifying the extent of potential commitments
by setting up a geographical survey of the Aden hinterland, with a
view to determining where the boundaries of the various tribes
lay.[17]

In the last resort the strongest pressure for a renewal of British
expansion came from changing conditions in South Arabia itself,
rather than from an alteration in the general Middle Eastern balance
of power. While the broad lines of the future Protectorate were being

planned in Simla and London, for the first time since the British occupation of Aden something of a social and political revolution was beginning to take place among the tribes of the hinterland.

To understand what was happening there in the 1880s and 1890s it is necessary to look critically at what was meant by the word 'tribe'. This was the term used by the British to describe the political systems which confronted them when they went beyond the walls of Aden. This was how the powers of the interior were always spoken of up to 1873, and after the 1873 notification to the Porte it became politically necessary to continue to refer to the 'nine tribes' as such, for their claim to individual identity and independent existence was, as it were, the title deed upon which the sphere of British influence was based. And after all, this was how the Arabs, being members of a society in which social position at all levels was pre-eminently determined by a man's agnatic descent, usually described their individual affiliation to outsiders.

But in many cases the use of the word 'tribe' and 'chief' was quite misleading. The most obvious example of this was to be found in the case of the so-called 'Amiri tribe' in the north-west corner of what was later to be the British Protectorate. The British description of the 'Amiri as a 'tribe' of whom the 'Amir was the 'chief' tended to obscure rather than illuminate the social and political realities in that part of Aden's hinterland. One could justly speak of an 'Amiri 'clan', that is, the fairly numerous descendants of the seventeenth-century founder of the ruling house who elected successors to the title of 'Amir from among their number. But that was clearly not what the British meant when they referred to the 'Amiri. The "Amiri tribe' was supposed to indicate the political unity situated in a large tract of territory extending several miles on either side of the Wadi Hardaba and reaching northward almost to the gates of the Turkish town of Qaʻtaba.[18]

No such political or administrative unity in fact existed. Something over two-thirds of the population of this area belonged to a number of largely autonomous clans or sections inhabiting the slopes of the Jihawf and Mafari mountains to the west and south of the town of Daliʻ, and the Radfan and Halmayn ranges to the south and east. Some of these clans were semi-nomadic, but the majority lived in small villages of 100 inhabitants or less, herding their animals or cultivating the small strips of watered land scattered thinly between the ranges of barren mountains. For most purposes they were independent. They owned and worked their own land and disputes among them were settled by their own Shaykhs or Aqils according to customary law. A third or less of the population lived in the more sizeable villages on the fertile plateau to the north of

Dali' town, which itself had a population of over 2,000. Some of these tribesmen were affiliated to neighbouring clans. But in general, those on the plateau were of mixed origin – immigrants from other areas, peasant subjects of the 'Amir, and a substantial community of Jews, many of whom were engaged in the forty or more weaving establishments to be found there. Here lay the material basis of the 'Amir's power, for in the 1880s roughtly 70 per cent of his revenue came from land. Some came from share croppers whose land he partly owned. Among the unwarlike people of the plateau the 'Amir could rule effectively, collecting fines and market dues and exercising civil and criminal jurisdiction. Beyond the plateau, on the other hand, his writ ran but fitfully. In part, what authority he exercised over the various clans derived from their need for an arbitrator and judge to settle the multifarious feuds and quarrels which arose among them, although here he was in competition with the influential Sayyids of Al Dhubayat, whose religious and pacific character fitted them also for this role.[19]

More important was the 'Amir's command of wealth and his ability to mobilise mercenary troops, which in turn derived from his control of the rich lands on the plateau. The 'Amir's relationships with the clans were as varied as the clans themselves. There is some evidence that a number of them were brought into a dependent and tribute-paying relationship to the 'Amir by his ability to offer relief during years of famine. More usually the clans were made to recognise the 'Amir's leadership by the use of force or the offer of protection. In one case the 'Amir had acquired the right to oppose the clan's election of its Shaykh, but most of the clans admitted only a general suzerainty. The 'Amir's authority outside the settled districts of the plateau was essentially ephemeral and it had no real legitimacy other than a certain marginal respect for an old-established lineage and the personal power and ability of each individual 'Amir.[20]

In this regard the system at Dali' was not vastly different from that obtaining in other parts of Aden's hinterland. The Hawshabi, 'Abdali and Fadli ruling lineages were scarcely older in origin than that of the 'Amir, and the degree of their identification with the people they claimed to rule, as measured by the extent of participation in the election of the chief, was hardly any wider. The ruling houses among the Yafi'i and 'Awlaqi were much more ancient but everywhere the power of the Chief depended principally upon his control of the wealth derived from the settled and mixed populations in the severely restricted areas of well-watered land. For this reason the most tightly organised political system in Aden's immediate hinterland was the 'Abdali Sultanate with its extensive cultivated lands in the Wadi Tuban, plus the wealth which the Sultans were able to derive from the port of Aden.[21] At the other end of the scale was the 20,000 strong Subayhi 'tribe', scattered in small villages and hamlets across an area roughly 100 miles long by 30 miles wide between Lahej and the Bab el Mandeb.

The Subayhi 'tribe' existed in little more than the name which others ascribed to those who lived in that barren territory. There was no ruler among them powerful enough to represent even a simulacrum of political unity. Some vestiges of paramountcy did indeed attach to the Shaykhdom of the comparatively large Mansuri section, in that election to that title required the approval of other Subayhi clans. But the Mansuri Shaykhs were as powerless beyond their own section as any other of the Subayhi Shaykhs. The other Shaykhs themselves were by no means supreme even within their own small sections. They had not the ability to speak singly on behalf of their people with outsiders, and both the Aden and Lahej governments took care to secure the signatures of up to ten or more of the leading men of each section with which they negotiated agreements.[22] Yet these 'sections' grouped no more than a few hundred fighting men each, and many of them were subject to fissure. These communities in fact bore some of the features of a segmentary society – each household tending to break up on the death of its current head. Many of the sections were nomadic, others lived in *kutcha* houses grouped round a few stone dwellings in some of the fertile pockets to be found in what was for the most part an empty widerness.[23] Fissiparous tendencies were built into the whole structure of these communities and the ecology of the area encouraged rather than checked them. The one element of stability, one might say, was the network of trade routes, stretched like taut wires across the area between the settled communities of producers in the Yemen and consumers in Aden and Lahej. The businessmen at either end were hostile to disorder and by their choice of transporters they could exercise an influence favourable to the creation of permanent structures of authority among the normally turbulent Subayhi communities.

Trade however promoted stability only so long as the Subayhi were engaged in bringing *qat* and coffee from the Yemen highlands to Lahej and Aden. In the 1880s a new type of commerce developed which, far from preserving order, acted as a most powerful social solvent. This was the trade in arms, in the so-called 'weapons of precision' which represented a revolutionary advance on the old Arab matchlock. The guns imported were not the famous Winchester repeaters which did such destruction on the American prairies, but the equally deadly though less glamourised Le Gras, Remington and Martini-Henry rifles, which caused war and disorder and sounded the knell of traditional societies over wide areas of

Africa and Asia in the last two decades of the nineteenth century.[24] They came into South-West Arabia through the small island of Obokh on the Dankali coast where French arms merchants were established in 1880, and later through the neighbouring French port and colony of Djibuti. Djibuti was built upon the arms trade and while each new re-equipment of European armies threw new stocks of cheap weapons on to the market, the profits to be earned by shipping them to eager buyers in Arabia were so great for Djibuti merchants, that all efforts by the major powers – Britain, Turkey, Italy and even France herself – to stem the traffic ended in failure.[25] Since the trade was almost entirely contraband it is impossible to arrive at even approximate figures of the number of weapons brought into Arabia. It can be estimated however that the imports into Djibuti were of the order of tens of thousands in the 1880s and of over a hundred thousand per annum during several years in the 1890s and early 1900s. The bulk of these went to Ethiopia but a substantial proportion found its way to Arab ports, from the Hijaz to Ras Fartac, where Djibuti's sphere ended and that of the Masqat arms centre began.[26]

These new weapons began to appear in the Aden hinterland and the Yemen from 1880 onward. By 1886 the Subayhi had substantial numbers of rifles, in 1893 the 'Abdali were believed to be well equipped and some had reached the Hawshabi.[27] In 1897 the Fadli were using Martini-Henry rifles as well as matchlocks.[28] By 1895 it was estimated on good authority that all but two or three of the Subayhi sections were fully armed, and this was corroborated in 1900 by the report of a military expedition into Subayhi territory which stated that every man capable of bearing arms carried a rifle.[29] By 1902 the new weapons had reached the 'Awdhali and both branches of the 'Awlaqi tribe, while the Sultan of Mukalla was desperately trying to control their import into Wadi Du'an and the Hadhramawt.[30] According to one report the illegal import of rifles into the Yemen increased tenfold between 1891 and 1895. By the turn of the century the people of the Ibb district who had still been using spears in 1891 were receiving rifles from the Tihama ports.[31] Only in remote areas such as Ma'rib in the East were the traditional dagger and sword still used in 1904.[32] During the thirty-year period from 1880 to 1910 the traditional tribesman with his dagger at his belt and a slow match for his matchlock bound round his turban was replaced by the now familiar figure of the Arab with his faithful rifle slung across his shoulder.[33]

The effect of this trade in rifles upon the loosely organised Subayhi society was devastating. Their territory became one of the main centres of the traffic, for it was close to Djibuti and beyond the reach of the Turkish and British authorities who were most interested in stopping the flow of arms. Between 1881 and 1886 the Sultans of Lahej, who were quick to cut in on a business which offered such handsome profits, sought to control the trade through Subahyi country. In 1881 they secured British recognition of their suzerainty over the area, the tribesmen were cowed by a vigorous expedition in 1882 and garrisoned forts were established astride the main trade routes.[34] But in 1886 there was a general uprising by the Subayhi who were by then formidably armed with rifles, and the Sultan could do no more than withdraw his garrisons with the help of fifty cavalrymen from Aden. This episode cost the Sultan the loss of Aden's backing. The Subayhi were once more recognised by the British as independent and the 'Abdali were quite unable to reimpose their rule for the rest of the century.[35]

The withdrawal of 'Abdali power removed the last guarantee of order and hastened a general *sauve qui peut* in Subayhi country. Regular commerce was now replaced by fitful and confused smuggling activities which tended to produce not order but anarchy. The arms were brought by small, fast, former slaving vessels from Tajura and dumped now at one, now another of the small havens on the coast which were scarcely worthy of the name of port.[36] Some of the places used, being of little value formerly, in effect belonged to no one and there were frequent struggles to control them. Men and sectional groups, who traditionally would have had no part in the organisation of trade, profited by contraband, and the possession of the new weapons gave them the power to defy their social betters. By the end of the century many of the *ra'iyah* class – those landless men of subordinate status who formed about a half of the Subayhi population – had acquired rifles and were using them to assert their independence. This development in its turn caused a further decline in the cohesiveness of Subayhi society by weakening those more powerful families whose revenues from *ra'iyah* cultivators had accorded them a position of leadership in their sections.[37] Power gradually slipped from their hands and as it did so, the leaders of those familes became increasingly eager to place themselves under the protection of Aden or Lahej, to secure themselves against their neighbours and their own people.[38]

While the arms traffic tended to dislocate the existing order, the new weapons themselves directly attacked South Arabian society at its weakest point. Injuring and maiming had always been fertile causes of dispute among the warlike tribesmen and the mechanisms for settling the conflicts which arose, especially as between sections and tribes, were inadequate. In some cases, compensation for an injury or murder could be made by a money payment. But in many others there was no alternative but recourse to a blood feud between the families of killer and victim. The range and accuracy of the rifle multiplied the occasions for dispute. It was no longer necessary to confront one's enemy with dagger or sword; he could be shot from behind from a distance of five hundred yards or more. Each killing produced a blood feud and society was rent by ever-widening and more complex hatreds.[39] And so a deepening stain of blood spread out from the Subayhi and other ports, up the valleys of the Aden hinterland and out across the mountain ranges, in the wake of the vigorous trade in arms.[40]

The Subayhi were not the only people to be affected in this way. In most parts of the Aden hinterland, social cohesion was more or less undermined by the consequences of the spread of new weapons. And paradoxically, these modern implements tended to threaten most those sectors of society which seem at first sight to be the most potentially modern in outlook, that is the leaders of the wealthier and more peaceably-inclined settled communities. In the last two decades of the nineteenth century all the chiefs responsible for the peace of the trade routes were finding increasing difficulty in coping with the rifle-bearing tribesmen of the semi-independent sections within the sphere of their authority, and all except the 'Abdali were in a state of very marked decline. The arms influx however was not the only cause of the growing weakness of the Dali', 'Alawi and Hawshabi rulers. They suffered also from the effects of the longer-standing encroachment by their more powerful neighbours, notably the Turks and the Sultans of Lahej.

From this point of view the 'Amirs of Dali' were particularly badly placed, for the fertile nucleus of 'Amiri power was not screened from Turkish Yemen by barren wastes. Dali' lay immediately adjacent to another fertile area under Ottoman control and in 1873 the Turks overran the 'Amir's lands, and thereafter were reluctant to abandon them and the revenues they afforded. Their incursion was facilitated by the fact that they arrived on the scene when a dispute for succession to the chieftaincy was in full swing.[41] They backed the pretender to the title against the recently installed chief, 'Ali Muqbil, whom the British had already recognised, and the latter was first ousted, and then imprisoned when he appealed to Aden. Aden protested and 'Ali Muqbil escaped toward the end of 1873. But he was not reinstated as 'Amir until 1876, when the Turks had fallen out with their own protégé.[42] Even then the 'Amir did not recover his former power, for the Turks altered their policy from indirect to a more direct system of rule. Their previous arrangement of working through the 'Amir had evidently failed – the first of 'Ali Muqbil's Turkish-backed rivals had been killed on a tax-gathering expedition, the second absconded when called upon to perform the same duty.[43] After 1878 the Turks worked through lesser shaykhs of sections and others of their own creatures who were supported by the presence of Turkish regular troops and artillery.[44] Indeed a tone of impatience and hostility to traditional chiefs in general began to enter into their statements about that time and pan-Islamic appeals were directed at the mass of the people, emphasising individual loyalty to the Sultan-Caliph.[45] Meanwhile the ʿAmir lost much of the land which had constituted the material basis of his power. By 1880 he was hemmed in to the districts in the south and east of the Daliʿ plateau and despite aid in the form of cannon and ammunition from Lahej and Aden, his ability to control the semi-independent mountain clans inevitably waned.[46] His only hope for survival lay in co-operating and acting as the agent of those who had sapped his independent authority and the ʿAmir Shayaf bin Sayf, who took office in 1886, managed to come to an understanding with the Turks which gave him peace within his restricted area of influence, although it did not win back all that his predecessor had lost.[47]

The plight of the Hawshabi Sultans was little better than that of the Daliʿ ʿAmirs. They suffered more from ʿAbdali than from Turkish encroachment. But the effect on the fortunes of the Sultanate was the same. In 1868 they had lost their valuable Zaʾida lands to Lahej. They recovered them by agreement in 1881 but in 1885 they were definitively transferred to the ʿAbdali, this time by deed of sale and for a sum equal to less than one year's revenue.[48] Thereafter the Hawshabi Sultan's income from land sank to small proportions. He became heavily dependent on subsidies from both the British and Turkish governments, both of whom offered him subsidies and *ad hoc* payments.[49] By 1893 the Hawshabi's income from these extraneous sources amounted to more than half the total value of his previous revenues. The Sultans thus became less and less dependent for their earnings upon the performance of traditional functions within their own society and, not unnaturally, they devoted a smaller proportion of their diminished budgets to customary payments to individuals and groups within their area of authority. The members of the Hawshabi ruling family received less from the Sultan's coffers than before and the semi-nomadic tribes to the eastward, notably the powerful Dhambari, were particularly neglected.

Failure to pay the customary douceurs to the Dhambari threatened the most important traditional source of revenue still remaining to the Hawshabi Sultans – namely transit dues levied on caravans trading along the routes northward and westward from Aden to the Yemeni highlands. If the Dhambari were not induced by bribery or other means to allow free passage along the route to Dali' they could very easily paralyse all traffic there and, as arms seeped through to them from the coast, their power to do this was proportionately enhanced. By the middle 1880s this predictable consequence of Hawshabi decline was clearly taking place. The Dhambari took matters into their own hands and the Hawshabi was forced to take steps in 1887 to open a new route to Dali' further to the westward – away from Dhambari depradations and closer to Turkish-occupied territory.[50] About the same time the Hawshabi moved his capital, once situated in his Za'ida lands, from Al Raha in the east to Musaymir in the west, near the new route and the cultivated lands of the 'Amri people, which still afforded the Sultan a small revenue from direct taxation.[51]

The 'Amir of Dali' experienced similar difficulties with the turbulent Qataybi who were neighbours of the Dhambari to the north on the Radfan range. Along the whole route the links between the semi-nomadic tribesmen in the remoter areas and the traditional guardians of trade were being weakened by the latter's decline. In addition the landward commerce between Aden and the Yemen was no longer expanding – that is, in its legitimate branches. The coffee traffic was returning to the traditional outlets on the Yemeni coast as the Turks improved roads, established peace and developed the port of Hudayda. The trade which continued was subjected to periodic disruption by the Turkish authorities, who raised duties at their frontier posts and on occasion prohibited trade with the Aden hinterland altogether. Arms smuggling of course could pay large profits. But the proceeds of this contraband traffic did not necessarily fall into the hands of the chiefs. Generally speaking, the yield from transit dues rose slowly in the last quarter of the nineteenth century, while the expense of maintaining peace on the roads in the face of rifle-equipped tribesmen mounted rapidly.[52]

At the end of 1886 the Hawshabi Sultan increased his transit dues to pay the soldiers required to ward off Dhambari incursions and within a matter of months all the other chiefs – the 'Amir of Dali', the Ba'ishi Shaykh of Khuraybah, the 'Alawi Shaykh and the Sultan of Lahej followed suit.[53] In December 1888 the British intervened in an attempt to stabilise the rates. A ten-day conference attended by all interested chiefs was held at Musaymir and a general agreement was arrived at, laying down a table of maximum charges for each territory. This however only provided a fixed point of reference for future discussions. Otherwise it was worthless, for a joint offensive against the Radfan tribes, which had also been agreed upon at Musaymir, never materialised.[54] Attacks on caravans by the Subayhi, as well as by the Radfan clans, continued, and each chief protected his section of the route as best he could, with very occasional British support and at the expense of various supplementary levies on the trading caravans.

In the 1890s the major political trends in Aden's hinterland which were already clear in the 1880s became even more marked, and substantial alterations in the traditional structures became possible. It was evident that the wealth and power deriving from sedentary populations was becoming concentrated in the hands of the Turks in Yemen on the one hand and the Lahej Sultans on the other. At the same time, the Turkish Government, with its new ideas on centralisation, was sedulously undermining the existing society by offering places of prestige to formerly inconsequential men in the new political and social status system which it was creating.[55] The small chiefdoms were gradually squeezed out and all came to realise that their survival depended on their adhering to one or other of the major powers in the area – the Turks, the Sultan of Lahej or the British. Their predicament explains their increasing willingness, if not eagerness, to seek British protection, and there is no reason to suppose that they did not seek Turkish protection also.[56]

By 1893 the Hawshabi Sultan's position had become desperate. From the west and north, two of the Turks' upstart tax-gathering administrators – Shaykh Nasir Muqbil of Mawiyah and Shaykh Zendani of Jihawf, were encroaching on what little land was left to him.[57] To the south, the Lahej Sultan barred the way to any compensating increase in his revenue in that direction. The Sultan was forced to raise what he could from those who remained under his control and this led to an outcry against his tyrannical and illegal exactions and appeals by his victims to the Sultan of Lahej and Shaykh Nasir Muqbil.[58] Finally, a way out was offered him by the Ottoman Tobacco Company, which was anxious to prevent infringements of its lucrative tobacco monopoly in the Yemen. The Company offered the Hawshabi a substantial subsidy and the backing of the Turkish Government if he would co-operate. The deal was closed and in 1894 the Sultan agreed to the erection of a Turkish customs post at Al Anad, near the 'Abdali border and close to the bifurcation of the routes from Lahej north and west to the Yemen highlands.[59] By this move the Company hoped to set a curb on the large contraband traffic.

But the Company's hope was the smuggler's fear and those who profited from the clandestine trade in tobacco could not be expected to sit idly by as the barrier was erected. Among those concerned was the Lahej Sultan,[60] and he could count on British aid, for the Aden Government too, although for different reasons, was not prepared to allow the Turks to establish themselves at this focal point in Aden's hinterland.[61] Formal protests were made to the Government of the Yemen and to the Hawshabi Sultan, and when these produced no result the 'Abdali Sultan took action. In May 1894 he raised a large force of 'Awlaqi, Subayhi and other mercenaries and, with the assistance of shells and rifles issued from the Aden arsenal, he drove the Hawshabi Sultan from his lands.

The Hawshabi's weakness was fully exposed. Few were prepared to sustain him and the leading tribesmen and members of the Hawshabi ruling house agreed to elect the 'Abdali as their Sultan.[62] For a year the amalgamation of the two Sultanates held. But during this time the 'Abdali's position weakened. His resources were strained by his efforts to keep the Dhambari and Qataybi in check – a task which he necessarily inherited from his unfortunate predecessor.[63] The former Hawshabi Sultan remained recalcitrant and the 'Abdali was forced to imprison him – an act which did not commend itself to the Hawshabi tribesmen.[64] Moreover, the Aden Government was not wholly happy at the implied disappearance of one of the nine tribes whose independence it was their policy to preserve. The 'Abdali was forced to take a step backward and a compromise was arrived at in 1895. The Hawshabi Sultan was reinstated but his election was made dependent on 'Abdali consent. His taxation rights over the 'Amri people were transferred to Lahej, as were the moneys collected from transit dues in Hawshabi territory and the stipend from the British, which was now augmented to $130 a month. From these, the 'Abdali Sultan undertook to pay to the Hawshabi his various entitlements at appropriate times, after satisfying those with claims to certain customary payments from Hawshabi revenues.[65] In other words the Hawshabi was Sultan in little more than name, since he was entirely dependent financially upon his neighbours.

While recognising his dependence on the 'Abdali, the Hawshabi Sultan also signed a Protectorate Treaty with the British on 6 August 1895. During the three previous weeks his two neighbours to the north and east – the 'Alawi Shaykh and the Lower Yafi'i Sultan – had similarly bound themselves to Britain. The 'Alawi Shaykh had been suffering from much the same pressure as the Hawshabi.[66] and when Turkish agents first offered him an agreement and then sought to suborn his relatives, he turned to the British for protection and financial aid. The Lower Yafi'i Sultan had also received offers from the Turks and there also the British pushed forward to forestall encroachment by their rivals.[67] From the British point of view this new advance into the hinterland was justified by the recent deterioration in Anglo-Ottoman relations and a further evolution of the 'Eastern Question'. While negotiations were proceeding in the

Aden hinterland, Salisbury was again making grumbling noises in London about the early demise of the 'sick man of Europe'.[68] The dynamic situation in South Arabia combined with a shift in great power diplomacy in Europe to determine this new expansion of Aden's commitments in the hinterland. The Protectorate agreements more closely defined the rules of the game of Anglo-Turkish rivalry; they did not arrest the forces of change in the hinterland itself. There they merely involved Aden more closely with the old forces of order at a time of increasing political uncertainty.

Among the forces of order, the most prominent was the Lahej Sultanate, still comparatively weak in fighting manpower, but still strong in the subtlety and adaptability of its ruling family. Its strength in the latter respect was greatly enhanced in March 1898 by the accession of Sultan Ahmad Fadl, second son of Sultan Fadl Muhsin who had so greatly promoted 'Abdali interests in co-operation with the British in the 1860s and 1870s. Like his father, Ahmed Fadl was a man of great ambition and remarkable political acumen. Like his father too, he had a command of English, understood the methods of British administration, and made the exploitation of his connection with Aden the keystone of his policy. He came to power with the help of the Aden Interpreter, Muhammad Salah Jaffer, who was paid handsomely for convincing his superiors of Ahmad Fadl's prior claims to the turban.[69] But within a short space of time Sultan Ahmad Fadl became impatient of Jaffer's mediation. He mounted a great attack on the Interpreter toward the end of 1899 with the co-operation of the Hawshabi, Fadli, 'Awlaqi and 'Alawi rulers – an attack which coincided with the arrival of a new Political Assistant to the Resident, Major Abud, who was out of sympathy with most of his predecessors' policies.[70] Jaffer was first suspended from duty in December 1899 and then in March of the following year he was convicted of intrigue, extortion, indebtedness and misuse of office and dismissed.[71] Jaffer's fall left a serious gap in the Aden Government's information service.[72] For several crucial months the British officers had perforce to turn to Ahmad Fadl for guidance about the state of hinterland politics. Thereafter Aden's Arabic Department gradually recovered, but close co-operation with the Lahej Sultan continued as a matter of policy. In 1901 he was chosen to attend the Delhi Durbar of Indian Princes. In the following year he was appointed a K.C.S.I. and in 1903 he was again at Delhi for the Proclamation of King Edward VII as Emperor of India.[73] From his accession in 1898 to his death in 1913 he was treated by the British almost as if he were the paramount ruler in the hinterland.

For Ahmad Fadl, the first fruits of his close alliance with the British were Aden's support for his policy in the Subayhi country.

Sultan Ahmed Fadl of Lahej.

On his accession the Aden Government still regarded the Subayhi as independent of Lahej. This was the policy laid down in 1886, and it was rigidly ahdered to. Persistent 'Abdali efforts to subdue their troublesome neighbours had found no favour at Aden. Indeed, in 1894, one 'Abdali initiative in this direction was met with menacing words from the Resident and a demand for immediate retraction. It was therefore surprising, and a mark of the confidence which Ahmed Fadl quickly won at Aden, that four months after his election the Aden authorities agreed to allow him to occupy the Subayhi coastline and establish his control over the trade from there inland.[74] In the following year they went further and not only helped him with ammunition to subdue the inevitable Subahyi rising, but sent the Aden Troop to assist him in direct defiance of specific instructions from India. Distant Simla was not carried away by Aden's new enthusiasm for promoting 'Abdali interests and pointed out that only fourteen years before it had been decided that the Subayhi should be treated as independent.[75] The Acting Resident was promptly removed for his unauthorised services to the 'Abdali.[76]

The assistance which Ahmad Fadl received from Aden in regard to Subayhi matters was welcome and timely, for it helped to promote the much wider aims which were clearly revolving in the Sultan's fertile mind. Control of the Subayhi country would have given Ahmed Fadl control also over the greater part of the arms trade. His venture into the territory of his dangerous neighbours was closely linked with the decree forbidding arms smuggling which he issued at Lahej immediately he was chosen as Sultan.[77] He wanted to gather the traffic in weapons into his hands as quickly and effectively as possible and he was evidently prepared to invest substantial sums in order to do so. For at that particular time the stakes involved had become higher than ever before. With the control of the arms trade in his hands, a man could not only speak with authority in the Aden hinterland, he could also claim a say in the growing political debate in the whole of the Yemen and beyond that, in the Arab speaking world.

The Yemen was now stirring restively after twenty-six years of Turkish rule. During that time, roads had been built, trade developed, peace had been imposed over much of the country, and latterly a start had been made with the construction of modern schools and hospitals.[78] The people had been brought under the rule of foreigners, and foreign troops, often with strange habits and customs, had been billeted in many parts of the country. At the same time traditional political structures had been severly interfered with; some heads of clans became tax-gathers, only to be swept out of office when a new Governor-General arrived with new plans for the country. With each change of Turkish policy and personnel, newly created indigenous authorities found their positions placed in jeopardy.[79]

A constant stream of ideas about pan-Islam and the Arabs' place in the governmental system poured into the Yemen from Sultan 'Abd al Hamid's bureau of Arab 'experts' at the Yildiz Palace and stirred up an intellectual ferment.[80] Many were attracted by the new Ottoman ideas, but inevitably a native brand of political reasoning emerged and combined with the simmering revolt in the semi-conquered north of the country to produce an explosive mixture. Imam Muhammad ibn Hamad al din produced the Yemeni antithesis to the Ottoman pan-Islamic thesis. In 1891 he challenged Sultan 'Abd al Hamid's claim to the Caliphate on the grounds that he was not a descendant of the Prophet, opposed the more orthodox Islamic Shari'a law to the modernising Turkish Qanun, and launched attacks on the religious deviations of Turkish personnel.[81] A revolt in 1891–2 was suppressed with difficulty, and during the rest of the decade the country remained disturbed. A widespread famine in 1898 undermined the Ottoman regime and a large part of northern Yemen rose around the Imam's banner in revolt against their Turkish masters.[82]

Sultan Ahmad Fadl was in a position to afford considerable support to the Imam and to sway the fortunes of the struggle between the rebels and the Turks. His influence in South Arabia could affect the political attitudes of such warlike tribes as the Yafi'i and the 'Awlaqi. These tribes had by now assumed importance in the struggle for power in the Yemen, for in the serious 1891–2 uprising many of them had served as mercenary auxiliaries to the Ottoman forces, and since then the Turkish Government had made a number of efforts to win them over.[83]

The Sultan could also of course influence Aden's attitude and he acted as a point of contact between the Imam and the British. During 1899 Zaydi agents made a number of visits to Lahej and toward the end of the year Ahmad Fadl transmitted to Aden a definite proposal from the Imam, offering a partition of his territory (by which the Imam no doubt meant the whole of South-West Arabia including Aden) in return for British protection.[84] This was considered in Britain and India but it was decided that the traditional policy should be followed and no attempt be made to undermine Turkish authority. Nevertheless Ahmad Fadl returned to the charge in 1901 with the suggestion that the British should drive the Turks from the Yemen and promote Arab independence. Once more he received a rebuff from the cautious Indian authorities.[85] There still remained the other services Ahmad Fadl could offer to the Imam. In particular he could greatly assist the Imam's insurgent forces by organising the supply of the weapons which could put them on a par with their rifle-equipped opponents.[86] The Imam had his own sources of supply but during the years 1899–1900 he was particularly dependent on the flow of arms from the south, since he had been temporarily dispossessed of his principal smuggling port at Medi in Northern Yemen.[87]

This was Sultan Ahmad Fadl's opportunity and it was worth his while to make the greatest efforts to monopolise the arms traffic in all the territories within his reach. There were problems in getting the shipments across the border into Turkish-controlled territory. Once beyond British-protected limits, the onward movement of the goods was dependent on the venality or disloyalty of the subordinate Ottoman personnel. Happily for the Sultan, these qualities were widespread among the Turkish and more particularly the Arab officers in the *Vilayet* of Yemen. But when the stakes were so high and the profits so large (tobacco smuggling was also involved) disagreements could occur. In 1900 such a disagreement, which was to have the widest consequences, did occur between the Lahej Sultan and Muhammad Nasir Muqbil, the Yemeni Shaykh who ruled a large district centring on Mawiya and adjacent to Hawshabi territory. Prior to 1900 there had been considerable rivalry between Lahej and Mawiyah. The Hawshabi Sultanate had been a bone of contention between them and in 1894, when the 'Abdali had mounted his assault on the Hawshabi Sultan, the latter had entrusted the defence of his interests to the Shaykh of Mawiyah in return for the promise of half his revenues.[88] The 'Abdali won the day and the Mawiyah Shaykh seemed to accept his defeat without rancour and with some flexibility. But the possibility of a renewal of the contest between the two trading centres of Lahej and Mawiyah remained.

In March 1900 Shaykh Muhammad Nasir Muqbil erected a fort at Al Darayjah on the Hawshabi border astride the main trade route from Lahej to the Yemen highlands. This was an unfriendly act. It was clearly designed to stop the smuggling trade and this was gall and wormwood to Sultan Ahmad Fadl who had just refused an offer of a subsidy from the Ottoman Tobacco Company to check the extensive and profitable contraband in that commodity.[89] Fortunately, however, Nasir Muqbil had constructed his checkpoint on a piece of land which, according to the British Survey map, was within Hawshabi territory. Consequently, when direct remonstrances by the 'Abdali and Hawshabi failed to budge him, Sultan Ahmad turned to the Aden Government and asked for protection under the 1895 treaty. The matter was taken up with the Turkish authorities, who denied all knowledge of the fort and promised

withdrawal for British limits. On the spot, Nasir Muqbil lost the
support of the local Turkish authorities. In May he abandoned Al
Darayjah and in June his forces were defeated by a Hawshabi force
conducting a flag march in the district.[90] Then the pendulum
swung once more. Nasir Muqbil regained Turkish favour; in the
autumn he began collecting crops from lands claimed by the
Hawshabi and by December 1900 he was back at Al Darayjah, with
the assistance of Turkish regular forces.[91]

The Shaykh however had now gone too far. By re-occupying a
fort which the Turks had abandoned after a British protest, he had
violated the rules of the game as it was usually played between Aden
and San'a'. Moreover, the British were by this time in no mood to
tolerate any irregularities. Since Ahmad Fadl's accession, the Aden
authorities had been listening to a steady stream of anti-Turkish
advice from their friend at Lahej and, after Jaffer had been put out of
the way, late in 1899, the message came over in clearer tones.[92]
Things were changing in other ways in Aden. The number of
European troops had been augmented and the military men had
started to agitate for a sanatorium on the Dali' Plateau to alleviate
the boredom and escape the heat that gave Aden so bad a reputation
in military circles.[93] This humanitarian scheme would have required
some revision of the policy laid down in 1888 of sacrificing the 'Amir
to the Turks in return for recognition of the British protectorate.
So there was one influential body of men in Aden and India who
were against pandering to the Ottoman authorities.

Further away, in Calcutta, the aggressive Lord Curzon had
recently taken office as Viceroy; he was an administrator, rather than
a diplomat, and did not like untidy boundaries. Curzon's ideal
boundary was a clear line upon a map which would enable him to
say that all on the one side belonged to his own state machine while
the rest was left to the other fellow. The equivocations and ambiguities, the intrigues and divided loyalties, the limitations of control and
overlapping of authorities that was the reality of Aden's protected
hinterland rendered him impatient rather than cautious. He had
little respect for the Turks and he was ready for a quarrel. The Al
Darayjah trouble, however, only caught the corner of his energetic
eye; at this early stage of what was to grow into a long and serious
contest with the Porte over Aden's boundaries, it was the Foreign
Office in London which initiated action.[94]

By this time those concerned with Imperial policy were less fearful
of offending Ottoman susceptibilities. The Near East was not the
storm centre of world diplomacy that it had once been. Britain was
more concerned with the Cape route to India and the state of affairs
in Central and Eastern Asia. The Ottoman Empire's internal

weaknesses and dissensions and the shift in Russian expansion eastward along the line of their new Asiatic railways lessened the value of
the Sultan's dominions as a shield for India.[95] Ottoman stock was in
decline and Britain's case over Al Darayjah seemed impressively
watertight, in that the Porte had practically admitted that the fort
lay in British-protected territory.[96]

The news of Nasir Muqbil's reoccupation of Al Darayjah was
therefore universally ill-received by the British authorities. In
February 1901 the British Ambassador warned the Porte that action
would be taken on the spot if their troops were not withdrawn. Still
the troops remained and in July, after a typical piece of escalation
along the long line of executive processes between London and Aden,
400 men of the Aden garrison, supported by a mountain battery,
moved out against the new fort. The Turks held their ground and
when the British guns opened fire on 27 July, 350 Ottoman regulars
fired back. A brief cannonade followed during which Shaykh Nasir
Muqbil's auxiliaries fled and left the Turks to fight alone. The
latter were out-gunned by the British and after suffering about a
hundred casualties they withdrew and the men of the Aden garrison
blew the fort to the ground.[97]

The Al Darayjah incident had important repercussions within and
beyond South Arabia. It showed that the British were in earnest
about protecting Aden's hinterland. The Sultan of Lahej was
vindicated although he had his reservations about the way his
heavily armed friends had handled the matter. He would have
preferred to bribe Nasir Muqbil out in his own way.[98] However,
events had shown that he had backed the right horse and he had
reason to congratulate himself. In the other camp there was confusion and alarm. Nasir Muqbil was accused of misleading his
superiors and once more he fell from favour. Rumours circulated
that the British were about to invade the Yemen, which was not
surprising considering Sultan Ahmad Fadl's general views and
conduct.[99] A subjunctive understood as an indicative, one of the
Sultan's hopes understood as an actuality, would have sufficed to
give the impression that his British allies were indeed going to
liberate the Yemen from the Turks. For a few days in July and
August the Turks concentrated forces at Mawiyah to meet the British
threat.[100] Tension mounted and the 'Amir of Dali' joined the fray
by hoisting the now powerful British flag in disputed land and
appealing to Aden when the Turks cut it down. Then assurances
came, calmer counsels prevailed and in order to prevent a recurrence
of the trouble the Porte proposed to the British that a commission be
set up to demarcate the frontier.

This proposal was very well received in London. Aden frontier disputes were a constant headache to the officials at the Foreign and India Offices. With the unpredictable shifts in tribal politics, these disputes often obtruded themselves upon Whitehall at inconvenient moments when more important matters were under discussion. And when trouble arose, especially at Dali', it often led to inter-departmental and other misunderstandings because of the undefined nature of the boundary and the vagueness of British commitments there. If British *meum* and Turkish *teum* in South Arabia could be clearly laid down, one branch of British diplomacy would be rendered more exact and straightforward for the future.[101] The Indian Government too was happy at this hopeful result of their action at Al Darayjah. The Viceroy liked the idea of delimitation as much as did the men in London. But his attitude was somewhat different from theirs. While the home officials were hoping to add one more chapter and close a difficult file. Curzon was looking forward to building another section of India's northern wall, and he wanted it built as strongly and as far away from his vital defence centres as possible.[102] In October 1901 however, there was no disagreement between London and Delhi as to the next step; both were equally eager to take up the Turkish offer. A joint commission was set up, Colonel Wahab, who had made a geographical survey of the hinterland in 1891–2, was named the chief British Commissioner and in February 1902 the Turkish and British officers met to begin their work at Dali' where the position of the frontier was most in doubt.

Then trouble began. The Turkish Commissioners prefaced their work by laying claim to the whole of South Arabia. As far as they were concerned, the Commission was not demarcating the Empire's frontier; it was carrying out one of those frequent Ottoman internal 'reforms' at the behest of and in co-operation with one of the Euro-pean powers. With regard therefore to the 'Amir's territorial claims, he was entitled to nothing for which he did not hold an Imperial *firman* granted by the Porte. In these circumstances the Commission could not even begin its work, and the Turks further circumscribed the activity of the British Commissioners by occupying a number of villages on the Dali' plateau and preventing them from communica-ting with the people in the Turkish-occupied part of the disputed territory.[103] While the two parties to the Commission were at loggerheads, the subject of the inquiry, that is the 'Amir, suffered. For many years he had lived in a no-man's-land between Aden and Turkish Yemen, now leaning one way now another. The then ruler, 'Amir Shayaf bin Sayf had been on reasonably good terms with the Turks since he had given some of their officials shelter and assistance during the 1891–2 rebellion. During the 1890s he had been able to recover some of the rights and territories which his incompetent predecessor had lost, although some parts of the fertile land on the plateau remained under general Turkish control.[104] Now, with demarcation in the offing, the ambiguities and nice balances of local politics had gone and he was unequivocally thrown back on the less valuable part of his dominions which the Turks did not claim. By shifting away from the Turks to the British and bringing down a delimitation commission upon himself, he had managed to get into an unenviable position, although he hoped ultimately to make great gains with British help. It was not long before he began telling the British to recover his lands for him – and of course he put his claims as high or even higher than the evidence would stand – or leave him to make his peace with the Turks.[105]

So, within days of the beginning of the Boundary Commission's work, London's hope that the Aden frontier question would soon be settled began to fade. At the same time, serious differences developed between London and Delhi concerning the method of handling the negotiations and the ultimate objects to be achieved.[106]

The differences arose partly from the ambiguity of British policy toward the question of Dali''s status. In 1873 the 'Amiri had been one of the 'nine tribes' whose independence the British Government had asked the Porte to respect and since then, representations had been made on various occasions on their behalf. On the other hand, Captain Hunter of the Aden Residency had suggested in 1880, during the 'Amirate of the weak and unpopular 'Ali Muqbil, that Dali' was worthless to Aden and recommended that the Turks be allowed to continue to absorb the 'Amir's territory. In 1888 the Government of India adopted as their official policy the idea that Dali' should be regarded as a bargaining-counter to be sacrificed to the Turks in return for recognition of the rest of the Protectorate. This did not quite mean that Dali' was to be immediately abandoned;[107] until serious negotiations began the potential discard was still to be held in the British hand. But it did mean that Residents were somewhat slower to protest at Turkish action there and refrained from making representations about those of the 'Amir's lands which were considered to be irretrievable.[108]

When the Boundary Commission was set up therefore, the British could have pursued two possible courses of action. They could have abandoned the 1888 policy completely and, reverting to the 1873 notification, demanded from the Turks all that their protégé, the 'Amir, could claim as his. Alternatively they could have seen this as an opportune moment to buy Turkish recognition of the Protectorate at Dali''s expense.

As it happened, the basis upon which the British opened their negotiations was largely determined by the circumstances in which the negotiation itself arose. The Turkish proposal that the boundary should be delimited had followed a diplomatic exchange concerning the Al Darayjah incident and a further dispute over the Dali' area in which the British Government had decided to take its stand on a map drawn up by Colonel Wahab in 1891-2, during his survey of the Aden hinterland. This map therefore was taken as the starting point and the British Commissioners were instructed to delimit the boundary in accordance with it.[109]

Unfortunately the 1891-2 map was itself ambiguous. Wahab had marked no line upon it, but in his accompanying report he had outlined in general terms where the limits of the 'Amir's possessions had then lain. Since the survey was compiled at about the nadir of the 'Amir's fortunes, the limits which Wahab there described represented a considerable withdrawal from what the 'Amir had held when the Turks had first appeared on the South Arabian scene in 1872; they would also have left the reigning 'Amir with something less than what he had actually possessed in 1901 when negotiations with the Turks began, and very much less than what he expected his powerful allies to secure for him. The officials in London, who were still thinking largely in terms of the 1888 policy, regarded such a result with equanimity.[110] This was the sort of compromise or bargain they were prepared to strike. They expected to find the Turks in a co-operative frame of mind and hoped to settle the matter quickly in a spirit of give and take.

That however was decidedly not the view of the Aden authorities, who were in an aggressive mood. Nor was it that of Lord Curzon in Delhi. He saw the matter in terms of the 1873 notification. He was not prepared for 'give and take'. He believed that the Government should adopt a tough line with the Turks and force them to recognise the 'Amir's independence. In his opinion that was the only language they would understand and firmness had to be used from the start.[111]

He had already agreed that the delimitation should be carried out in accordance with the 1891-2 survey map and this certainly put him at a disadvantage in arguing with the men in London. But since the map had no line marked on it, there was some room for manoeuvre and Curzon exploited this. He first suggested that the limits of the survey and not any line within the map should be regarded as the true boundary of the 'Amir's territories and London acquiesced. Then when the Commissioners found the difficulty of applying the formula on the ground, they quickly decided to plead for more. The 'limits of the survey' could only refer to the edge of the hachuring on the map which meant that the 'Amir got the occasionally subordinated men of the hachured hills and

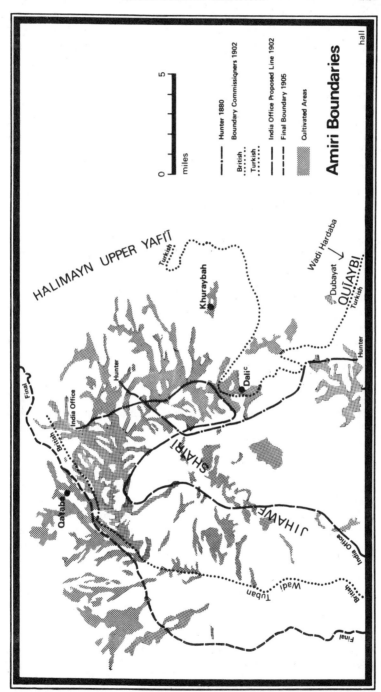

Amiri Boundaries

lost the more valuable subjects of the unmarked plains. To rectify this, Wahab proposed a new line flung further out in to the plain, countering the Turkish claim that pushed the 'Amir into the hills. The Resident, Maitland, supported this and Curzon, notwithstanding the previous discussions on the subject, threw his whole weight behind the new proposal.[112] The former Interpreter, Jaffer, was blamed for having deceived the British officers about the location of the 'Amir's boundary. He was made the scapegoat and as the argument developed the Aden officials tried to throw upon him the responsibility for the whole British policy of 'Amiri abandonment during the twenty years between 1880 and 1900. They even went so far as to suggest that he had been a Turkish agent.[113]

In London this tergiversation was regarded as little short of sharp practice and the officials there brusquely called the Resident back to the original line.[114] A tone of acrimony entered into the correspondence that flew back and forth between London, Aden and India as the India Office tried to hold the Resident in, while the Viceroy urged him forward. Curzon quickly lost patience with London's intervention. He bombarded the Secretary of State with private and public communications urging his point of view and dropping heavy hints that if the London Government wanted to run Aden policy they could pay for it.[115] No one in London wanted to assume the financial burden of Aden's transfer and the Secretary of State, Lord George Hamilton, who never really understood the issues,[116] would not go all the way with the officials on the Indian Council in their opposition to the powerful Viceroy, Apart from this, the other department of government concerned, the Foreign Office, veered round toward a sterner attitude. The extremism of the pan-Islamists at the Yildiz Palace who were pressing intransigence on the Porte bulked larger in their view than the extremism of the Proconsul at Simla. In July, the India Office tried to break out of the stalemate at Dali' and get the Commission back to its work of finding where existing frontiers lay by ordering it eastward to demarcate the Upper Yafi'i border, But this initiative came to grief.

The Turks said the Upper Yafi'i were not among the nine tribes, refused to let the British Commissioners go there and spread violent pan-Islamic propaganda in their prospective path.[117] Stalemate was reached once more and Curzon took another step forward by demanding the negotiation of protectorate treaties with the tribes of the north-east to facilitate the Commissioners' passage.[118] By this time the India Office's cautious counsels were at a discount. At an inter-departmental meeting held at the Foreign Office in August, the Resident carried through the Commissioners' advanced Dali' line as the new basis for negotiation. Sir William Lee Warner from the

India Office could do no more than have the Resident's demand for the immediate use of force deferred, pending the outcome of further pressure at the Porte.[119] The British Ambassador at Instanbul was instructed to seek satisfaction in stronger terms and Captain Fitzmaurice, the First Dragoman at the Embassy, was sent to Aden to add his knowledge of Turkish politics to the British Commissioners' acquaintance with the local scene, and to see that the strong words spoken at the Porte were adequately heard by its agents on the spot.[120]

Thereafter, all depended on what the Turks would do. They procrastinated and made partial concessions. The Porte adopted a more or less conciliatory tone but the men on the frontier stood their ground. By January 1903 it was clear to the British that they were getting nowhere and by focusing attention on Turkish obstinacy, the Secretary of State was able to make the reluctant Indian Council and the cabinet agree to the application of pressure while steering discussion away from the thorny problem of Britain's own policy toward the frontier.[121] On 13 January 1903, 400 infantry and four guns joined the Commissioners at Dali', and at the beginning of the following month a special force named the 'Aden movable column' was organised. By early March the Aden Column numbered 2,200 troops with two mountain batteries while the 1,400 men of the Aden garrison stood in reserve. The thousand or so Turkish troops on the Dali' frontier were now outnumbered. Behind them, the 30,000-strong Turkish VII corps stationed in the Yemen, was tied down by the rebellion in the north of the country, which had by this date reached dangerous proportions. The British forces gathered at Aden were therefore quite capable of driving the Turks from the positions they occupied and would have been ordered to do so had the British Cabinet not drawn back at the last moment from making war in an area remote from the main centres of British power.

Instead it was decided to strike at the safest point – at sea. In February, information was received that Turkish reinforcements were on their way from Syria to the Yemen. Two cruisers were immediately despatched to Aden and the Porte was warned that His Majesty's Government could not allow Turkish troops to be sent to the neighbourhood of the territories in dispute. What was really meant was that the desperately needed reliefs for the army fighting the Imam would be held up until Sultan 'Abd al Hamid chose between giving way on the frontier question or suffering the total loss of the Yemen to the insurrectionary forces. By mid-March the Sultan had made his choice. He had hoped to appeal to the Powers against Britain, but his involvement in Macedonian difficulties made this impossible, and after a desperate argument with his

Ministers he gave way on all points. The Dali' plateau was evacuated and a detachment of British troops moved in. The most obstructive of the Turkish Commissioners was removed and punished. The Upper Yafi'i were recognised as independent and interference with them ceased. The way was open for the peaceful continuation of the Commissioners' work.[122]

Thus Curzon was proved right. Stern measures had, as he had predicted, forced the Turks to climb down. He had won the battle of wills and he exploited Ottoman weakness and London's discomfiture to go somewhat beyond the claim represented by Wahab's 1902 line. The 'Amir's territories were therefore rounded off with a few extra districts which were defensible in military rather than in documentary terms.[123]

The Viceroy's victory was also the victory of all those who had advocated a strong anti-Turkish line. At the local level this meant victory above all for Sultan Ahmad Fadl of Lahej, whose assessment of the balance of forces was also proved correct in the face of all those doubters and waverers among the Arabs who had believed the Turks to be the stronger party. It had seemed in early 1902 that the Sultan and his friends had nearly ruined themselves by appealing to the British. In the spring of 1903 things looked very different. Not that Ahmad Fadl was entirely satisfied with what had happened. He did not like to see British troops staying too long in the hinterland and more especially he did not like British officers roaming about trying to find out some of the secrets of hinterland politics of which he would have preferred to be sole purveyor. But the British forward movement in the hinterland was in many senses an 'Abdali forward movement and the Sultan was able to exercise very considerable influence over the shaping of relations between the British and the potentates in the whole Upper Yafi'i—Upper 'Awlaqi–Bayhan area, which was opened up by the withdrawal of the Turks at Dali'.[124]

Since 1901 the Sultan had been introducing various of these personalities to the Aden Residency and while the inter-departmental and diplomatic struggle was proceeding in India and Europe, he and his agents, the Jifri Sayyids, were deep in intrigue with those who had for long had various types of contact with the Lahej Sultanate.[125]

All this work came to fruition in the spring of 1903 when the balance in the hinterland swung in favour of the British. Chiefs, small and great, some of whom had been hanging back or who had even been hostile, then responded to invitations from Aden to negotiate.[126] London wanted no protectorate agreements with the people of this area.[127] They wanted only to prevent the Turks moving toward the politically-sensitive Hadhramawt, and the Porte gave assurances on this point. But Aden and India wanted protectorate treaties and in May 1903, on the authority of ambiguous instructions issued by London,[128] provisional agreements and compromising negotiations were entered into which made it exceedingly difficult to stop short of establishing a protectorate over all the area within the boundary set by the limits of the 'Amiri, Upper Yafi'i, Upper 'Awlaqi and Bayhan districts. The Government of India did not stop short, London's now feeble protests were brushed aside and in the twelve months following May 1903 a series of protectorate and semi-protectorate agreements and treaties were made with most of the various chiefs who were believed to possess authority within the limits of the Government of India's South Arabian claims.[129]

It would be a mistake to infer that these agreements endowed the British Government with any real authority over the people with whom they were signed. In the case of the Yafi'i the phrase 'His Majesty extends his gracious favour and protection etc. . . .' was omitted because the formula was too reminiscent of agreements of a really protectorate nature signed between the tribesmen themselves. The dispensing of presents and the award of subsidies played an important part in the negotiations – so much so that some sceptics said that those who signed were motivated entirely by greed and that the scraps of paper were regarded merely as an easy way of getting money from the Aden Treasury. It would however be equally mistaken to regard the signing of the treaties as a 'non-event'. The British at Aden were anxious to secure as few treaties as possible – their ideal was a single treaty with one representative from the whole of Upper Yafi'i. This was bound to throw an apple of discord among the tribesmen since it raised the very important question of who, in their loosely structured society, was qualified to speak for his fellows – a question very seldom posed in that remote land. A number of the men who negotiated with the British were quite clearly power-seekers, and such motives, compounded with pro- and anti-Turkish feeling and the other factors already mentioned, made the 1903 treaty negotiations a matter of real political import for the people concerned. They were attended by much internal strife. The nominal Sultan of the Yafi'i was temporarily deposed for going to Aden. Members of the disappointed party attacked and were repulsed by the troops escorting the British Boundary Commissioners.[130] The treaties were certainly meaningful even though their meaning might not have been quite the same in the Aden hinterland as in the chanceries of Europe.

In the meanwhile the delimitation of the 138-mile boundary proceeded with reasonable speed after the main trial of strength had occurred. In May 1904 the Commissioners finally withdrew to

Perim and to Turba on the coast opposite after a last gruelling piece
of work in Subayhi country at its hottest. They produced an agreed
line for the whole frontier from Upper Yafiʿ in the north-east to
within a short distance of Shaykh Saʿid and the coast in the south-
west. The centre of operations was then transferred to Istanbul,
where the British Ambassador was entrusted with the work of bargaining some small concessions in Subayhi country for recognition
of a line due north-east from Upper Yafiʿ to the desert and securing
the formal conclusion of the whole agreement. The Porte however
proved to be remarkably unco-operative at this late stage. They
first sought to reopen the whole question of the north-east and south-
west frontiers, which had already been largely agreed upon by the
Commissioners. Then they sought to insert a clause excluding both
British and Turkish troops from the Aden hinterland. Negotiations
were stretched out over another year and a diplomatic deadlock was
only broken by another naval visit to the Yemen coast in the spring
of 1905, when Turkish troops were being sent in to stem the high
tide of Yemeni revolt.[131]

Finally on orders from the Porte the Turkish Commissioner
signed a *procès-verbal* on 20 April 1905, giving satisfaction on most
of the outstanding points, and the work was brought to a conclusion.
This was regarded as a sufficient diplomatic document and no
further steps were taken when the Sultan refused to ratify the agree-
sent signed by his officials according to his government's orders.[132]

CHAPTER IX

Non-Intervention in Peace and War
1905-1919

In a statement in the House of Lords in March 1903 when the diplomatic crisis over delimitation was at its height, the Foreign Secretary, Lord Landsdowne, explained the limited nature of British objectives in Aden's hinterland. 'We have never desired to interfere with the internal and domestic affairs of the tribes,' he said.[1] All Britain wished was that they should not be interfered with by any other power. The statement was made in good faith and represented the Foreign Office and indeed the British Cabinet view of what Britain's policy should be in the enlarged Protectorate. But of course it was impossible to send over 2,000 troops to Dali', conduct searching investigations into the political rights of various parties in the hinterland and form relations with a multitude of men who claimed political leadership, without interfering with the internal affairs of the tribes. Even the simple matter of maintaining communications between Aden and the force on the Dali' plateau entailed interference in the most sensitive matter of control of the trade routes. Inevitably the Radfan tribes attacked the link between Lahej and Dali' up the Hardaba valley, and they were only temporarily silenced by a punitive expedition in the spring of 1903[2]. They persistently cut the telegraph line until in July of the same year it had to be rolled up and replaced by a heliograph.[3] Nevertheless the road itself was protected and a string of posts were garrisoned by British troops from 1903 to 1907.

When delimitation was completed, the problem of policing the border remained. So also did that of maintaining contact between Aden and the border areas. It could be argued that there was no point in setting a ring fence around Aden's hinterland if nothing were done to see that it was respected. It could be argued too that frontier incidents would recur, to the detriment of Anglo-Turkish relations, if nothing were done to prevent tribesmen on the Aden side from quarreling with their neighbours across the boundary. The India Office, while still protesting against any interference in the internal affairs of the tribes, accepted these arguments and in 1904

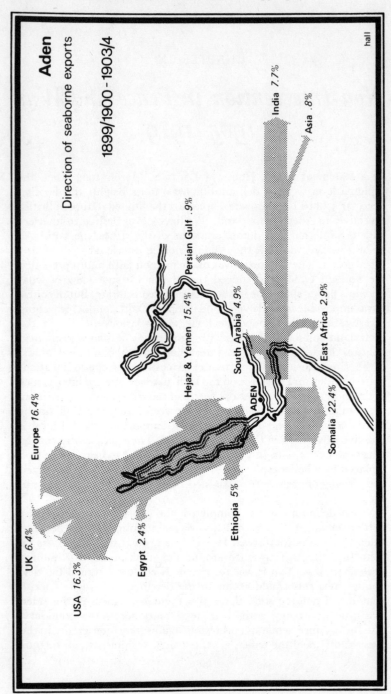

Aden

Direction of seaborne exports

1899/1900 - 1903/4

UK 6.4%

USA 16.3%

Europe 16.4%

Egypt 2.4%

Ethiopia 5%

Hejaz & Yemen 15.4%

Persian Gulf .9%

South Arabia 4.9%

ADEN

East Africa 2.9%

Somalia 22.4%

India 7.7%

Asia .8%

hall

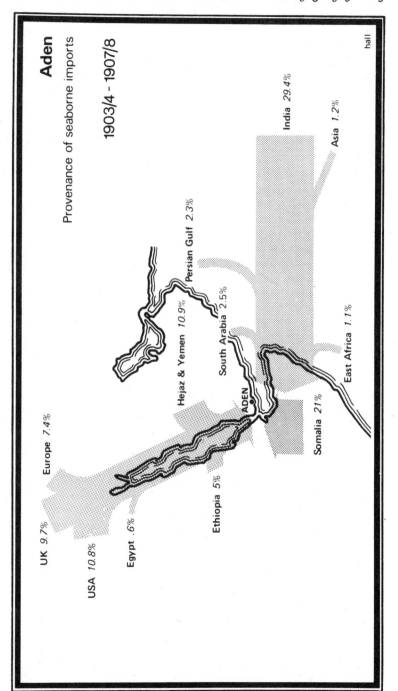

Aden

Provenance of seaborne imports

1903/4 - 1907/8

hall

India 29.4%

Asia 1.2%

Persian Gulf 2.3%

Hejaz & Yemen 10.9%

South Arabia 2.5%

East Africa 1.1%

ADEN

Somalia 21%

Europe 7.4%

Ethiopia 5%

UK 9.7%

USA 10.8%

Egypt .6%

an agreement was made with the 'Amir of Dali' by which he undertook to control his tribesmen and protect the roads in return for a
substantial subsidy toward the upkeep of a standing force of 50
soldiers.[4] In addition a British Political Officer was stationed at Dali'
with a personal escort of 50 troops and the backing of a force of nearly
1,000 infantry. So, while non-intervention was the policy, in practice
the British were heavily involved in tribal politics and very soon
discussion developed in Aden about methods of political control.[5]

Extensive contact with the people of the hinterland was gradually
producing at Aden an awareness of the complexity of South Arabian
society. No rigorous sociological analysis was undertaken; the
'Handbook' still described the people tribe by tribe on a historical
rather than an analytical basis.[6] But more was now known of the
limitations upon the power of the chiefs and the general lack of social
and political integration. In any case, bitter experience showed that
the British were faced with a real choice of policies. They could either
continue to back the chiefs whom they had selected, or who had been
presented to them; or they could attempt to deal directly with the
extended families and smaller clan units.

The latter policy found its strongest advocates in the Aden Secretariat. There, the Curzonian ideas of bureaucratic, developmental
administration ran most purely, and ambitious little Curzons had
appeared, sorting out office procedure, improving records, conducting inter-departmental correspondence and building paper
empires including the Arabic Office, which had fallen into the
Secretariat's maw after Jaffer's destitution.[7] The Sultan of Lahej,
abreast as always of latest developments in Aden, paid them the
compliment of trying to remove the Office Superintendent by intrigue.
The Secretariat's attitude to tribal policy, however, only reflected a
mood which was to be found well beyond the walls of that building
during the early years of the twentieth century and which concerned
matters of more general import than who should rule what in the
Protectorate. Aden was now a bustling port, with strong defences, a
garrison double the nineteenth-century size, a powerful modern-
minded commercial community and improved facilities of every
kind. And Aden itself fed on the trade and ideas of a developing world
where massive investment in railways, mines and commercial
agriculture was taking place and where agents of expanding imperial
powers could more easily speak of progress and development since
such aspirations struck sympathetic chords in the hearts of so many
far-seeing Asians and Africans.

The time had come, it seemed, for Aden to expand its amenities
and extend its prosperity into the neighbouring country. The
Aden garrison insisted on having its healthy hill station at Dali'.[8]

The Residency and the government of Bombay backed up a plan worked out by Cowasji Dinshaw and Sultan Ahmad Fadl for a railway from Aden to Lahej and beyond,[9] and a number of new projects were initiated: a dispensary was temporarily sited in the 'Amir's country; a plan was brought forward to set up a college for the sons of hinterland chiefs; a suggestion was made that tribesmen be recruited into a special force to police the Protectorate;[10] small grants were made to assist agricultural development at Lahej. The civil service at Aden was expanded to handle an increase in business.[11] Out of these elements, a completely new policy of development and social welfare for all could have been evolved. Some indeed did point out the inter-connections between these various items and the benefits they would confer on the people of the hinterland in general.[12] But to attribute them to 'policy' would be to do less than justice to the power and multiple motivation of the drives behind each. In sum they stemmed from the now large and thrusting community at Aden which embodied the new ideas then current in India and elsewhere. Curzon himself, though no doubt with his tongue partly in his cheek, said that he would find it difficult to prevent the schemes being put into operation.[13]

The schemes were however stopped by action from London. The authorities there had never fully consented to the measures taken in the Aden hinterland between 1902 and 1905 and the extension of commitments they entailed. As in 1873, when the list of nine tribes was first drawn up, an immediate Turkish threat had stampeded London into far-reaching decisions about the degree of territorial protection Aden required. Few had wanted to carve out a new slice of empire and fewer still wanted to govern the districts they had acquired. The Secretary of State, Lord George Hamilton, was the chief defender of Curzon's forward policy but even he came to disapprove of what was being done, and before he left office a tone of irritability had crept into his correspondence with the Viceroy on Aden questions.[14] Yet it was Hamilton who had got the Cabinet to take the crucial decision to threaten the Porte in February 1903, and the Cabinet only agreed to this measure in the belief that by so doing it would avoid having to take direct military action to remove the Turks from Dali'.[15] Hamilton had also had to intervene personally to induce the members of the Indian Council to agree to the despatch of reinforcements to Aden in the spring of 1903, and this was only effected after a bitter struggle. The majority of the officials at the India Office opposed almost every forward step advocated by the Government of India, and the Foreign Office was no less hostile.[16]

The best informed and most influential member of the India Office's Political Committee, William Lee Warner, put his view of the matter succinctly when he said 'we no more want Dali' than we do Cadiz outside Gibraltar'.[17] The defeat of their views left these men angry and resentful,[18] so much so that their opposition to the measures being taken became overlaid with personal antipathy toward all those connected with the miserable business of delimitation. In the summer of 1903 their anger flared briefly when Maitland, the Aden Resident, engaged in a quarrel with the British Boundary Commissioners. London sent a stern rebuke to Maitland and would have recalled that arch advocate of the forward policy, had Curzon not spoken up on his behalf and protected him from their ire.[19] For the rest, they reluctantly and critically acquiesced in the working out of the delimitation programme but they remained ready to change the tune when opportunity offered.

Their chance came in 1906 when the Liberal Party won a sweeping victory at the polls and displaced the Conservative Ministry. The new Secretary of State for India was the radical, Lord Morley, who was bent on switching the emphasis of Indian policy from administrative to political reform. He was less concerned with what was to be done than with who was to do it, and he had the good fortune to be able to embark on his reforming work in co-operation with a newly appointed Viceroy, Lord Minto, who was not yet himself committed to any other line of action. In India this partnership produced the Morley-Minto reforms – an important though gradual move in the direction of self-government.[20] At Aden they stopped and even reversed the tendency to expansion begun by Curzon.

In normal times Aden policy was left unaffected by Governmental changes in Britain. As an outpost of the Bombay Presidency under the control of the Government of India, it was administratively too remote to concern anyone but 'Indian experts', defence planners and the representatives of shipping interests. But the clash with the Ottoman Government had made Aden news, its affairs had been discussed in Parliament, and there had been much well-informed criticism of the Government's policy.[21] In any case, Aden could scarcely escape mention in the broader debate concerning the foreign policy of the Empire which was then reaching a climax in Britain. In the House of Commons there was a clamour among the newly elected radical and Labour members for a cut in the country's imperial commitments. From other quarters the Government was under pressure to improve the defensive efficiency of the Empire by resolving its Asiatic differences with Russia as it has already in 1904 settled its African and other colonial differences with France. The possibility that this involved aligning Britain with one of the power blocs in Europe was already half accepted when the Liberals came to office.[22] Accepted too was the complementary naval strategy of concentrating the fleet in home waters.[23] Thus, as the paramountcy of power politics in industrial Europe with its immense and growing armaments gradually prevailed, the importance of local and independent protection of imperial posts like Aden correspondingly declined.

Morley moved with these new pressures. Indeed, if anything, he moved ahead of them. If reform of India's internal policy was his first concern, the overhaul of India's foreign policy came a close second. He was an advocate of a Russian agreement, he soon became suspicious of Germany – the two normally went together – and in regard to frontier policy he warned Minto against 'anything that looks like expansion, extended protectorates, spheres of influence, and so forth'.[24] Morley was not long in office before he teamed up with the critics of the previous Government's foreign policy among the officials of the India Office.[25]

Of these, William Lee Warner, formerly Secretary of the Political Committee and now a member of the Indian Council, was the most outstanding. He was formidably well acquainted with all that had been said and done about Aden and the hinterland. He had all the paradoxes, non sequiturs and discreditable shifts in past policy at his finger tips and he was a man who was accustomed to speaking out his mind; he was a firm and undeviating proponent of the pre-1900 view of Aden's role. With the Liberals in power, Lee Warner's star was once more in the ascendant. When Morley got down to studying the Aden papers in April 1906, Lee Warner was close by his side and the new Secretary of State's hair was soon standing on end at what he discovered.[26] On 4 May a long despatch was sent to the Government of India calling for a complete change in policy. The railway and the army sanatorium schemes were ruled out, the troops were to be withdrawn from the hinterland and no military operations were to be conducted beyond a ten-mile radius from Aden without the express permission of the Secretary of State. The Political Agent at Dali' was also to be withdrawn when the Viceroy saw fit and all new treaty-making was forbidden. Frontier questions were to be handled through diplomatic channels in Europe and not by action on the spot.[27]

The men in India had been expecting something of this sort. Sombre warnings had been reaching them from London since the new Ministry had come to power and some of the men of the 'forward' school had changed their tune accordingly. Recommendations were couched in much more 'non-interventionist' terms, though without too severe a modification of their expansionist substance.[28] But India evidently did not expect anything quite so pointed, direct and effectively comprehensive as Morley's despatch. They reacted

sharply to his attack on so many of their pet schemes. On 9 August
a full rejoinder was drawn up and despatched over the signatures of
the Viceroy and the whole of his Council.[29] The limitations of what
was meant in India by 'non-intervention' now became clearer. What
was understood by 'intervention' there, was direct rule – what the
Governor of Bombay colourfully decribed as 'the immediate
introduction of a perfected civilisation, as exists in British India'.[30]
The suggestion currently sponsored by the Aden Resident for dealing
directly with the minor Shaykhs in the Aden hinterland, was therefore
rejected by the 'non-interventionist' India government, as was a
related tendency to proliferate punitive expeditions.[31] But this was
as far as they would go. They wanted to back up the authority of the
major chiefs with subsidies and with the assistance of the Daliʻ
Political Agent. They wanted to develop a system of tribal levies to
police the frontier. They wanted to suppress the arms trade and were
prepared to occupy the Subayhi roadstead of Ras al Arah in order
to do so. They wanted the railway at least as far as the southern
border of the ʻAmir's territory, and above all, the military men
wanted their sanatorium at Daliʻ and put forward all manner of
arguments in support of it.[32] The despatch closed on an ominous
if not menacing note. In effect the Government of India said that
if the home government wanted to run Aden in their own way they
should take over full financial and political responsibility for the
settlement.

This trump card had been played with effect in Curzon's time. But
much had changed since then. Minto was not, like Curzon, a Cabinet
Minister; he did not even belong to the governing party and could
not hope to undermine such a powerful man as Lord Morley. The
Liberal Ministry was in a commanding position at home and very
different from the weak and divided Conservative government
Curzon had had to deal with during the disputes over demarcation.
So the Secretary of State made only a few concessions. He wrote
mollifying letters to the Viceroy and the Governor of Bombay
explaining his point of view and he delayed the withdrawal of the
Political Agent and Daliʻ troops for the duration of a serious diplomatic crisis which had blown up over hostile Ottoman activity on the
Egyptian frontier at Akaba.[33] But the official answer of the 5 October
to the Government of India's protest despatch was uncompromising
in tone. It tore aside the veils of ambiguity which had hitherto
shrouded the altering nature of British activity in the hinterland.

The propping up of the ʻAmir of Daliʻ was described as a curious
interpretation of the principle of non-interference in tribal affairs.
Why, it was asked, should Aden mediate in tribal disputes which had
regulated themselves for the past fifty years? Delimitation had been

undertaken only to facilitate diplomatic discussion with the Porte. Far from creating new obligations it should assist the Aden Government in returning to the policy of 'inactivity'. Thus the India Office arrived back at its original interpretation of the purpose of demarcating the frontier. The new course which British policy had taken since 1902 was negatived, and the despatch quoted with approval Salisbury's view that the 'occupation of Aden derives its main importance from its relation to the general foreign policy of the Empire'. It was not to be regarded as another province of British India.[34]

The India Office's October despatch insisted strongly upon matching practice with principle, especially with the generally-agreed principle of non-intervention. In fact it contained its own fair share of doubtful logic and it did less than justice to the Government of India's arguments. But these very defects lent it greater weight. It showed clearly that the India Office was as unreasonably determined on cutting commitments as India had formerly been on expansion. By aiming ahead of its target it was more likely to hit it. This became clear in the months that followed, for India offered a stubborn though passive resistance to the execution of the new policy. In October 1906, the Secretary of State ordered the withdrawal of the Dali' troops to India by the next relief; they did not actually go until the following January.[35] The railway scheme for which in 1905 the Resident had said the Sultan of Lahej would require a compensating subsidy, became in 1907 the Sultan's own project, which the Government could hardly frustrate. The Secretary of State however did frustrate it by refusing to allow the construction of any line on Aden territory whether the Sultan wanted it or not.[36] As for the Dali' Political Agent, he was the last evidence of the forward policy to go. He remained on the plateau with an escort of 300 British troops for a full year after London had called for his removal. The India Office persistently pressed its point and by the end of September 1907 he too had gone, and the British stance in Aden's hinterland was forced back toward what it had been before the Al Darayjah incident and demarcation.[37]

The hinterland itself could not be decreed out of existence by London's fiat. Nor could the posts which the British troops had constructed inland for their protection and the various treaties and stipendiary obligations which the Aden Government had lately undertaken. The posts had to be handed over to someone and the stipends could not be cut off. So, British activity in the hinterland altered and became more subdued but it could not return completely to the *status quo ante* demarcation. Moreover the Aden Government had a clearer idea of how Arab society worked and it could now pursue a more coherent and purposeful course of action within the limits laid down by London.

For most of the period up to the First World War, Aden's policy was very much that of Major (later Lieut.-Col.) H. F. Jacob, Political Officer at Dali' from 1904–7 and at Aden from 1910–17.[38] Well before the fever of Arabophilia of the 1920s, Jacob sensed the new national self-consciousness welling up within the Arab world and sought a solution to Arabia's problems in terms of its own special and particular culture and political forms. His sympathy lay with what was specifically Arab rather than with what was universal in the hinterland and necessarily this made him more anxious to conserve what existed than to work for radical change. His general approach was however well attuned to the prevailing requirements of British policy under the 1906 Liberal government, and in the rather bitter faction-fighting between officials and military men at Aden between 1904 and 1907 it was Jacob who came to the top and won the ear of the higher authorities.[39] In his own words Jacob's aim was 'to win over a democracy to its recognised (figure) heads'.[40] In practical terms this meant close co-operation with his friend the Sultan of Lahej, of whom others at Aden were on occasion severely critical.[41] He treated Sultan Ahmad Fadl as the premier chief in the hinterland and, although he did not go so far as to channel all relations with other hinterland rulers through the 'Abdali, he consulted him in regard to the major political questions which arose.[42] While Jacob's views prevailed at Aden the interests of the already powerful Lahej family were well looked after, and 'Abdali influence continued to spread in the hinterland.[43]

The other major chiefs, and this meant, above all, the chiefs who had signed the various protectorate treaties, were also accorded special treatment by the Aden Government. Contact with tribesmen was channelled through them and, much to the disgust and anger of many tribesmen, only those who received a recommendatory letter from the appropriate chief were welcomed and entertained at the Aden Government Guest House – an institution which was now more active than ever before.[44]

All this was very much a continuation in a more sophisticated and active way of what had been done before demarcation. And in one other important respect British policy returned to previous lines, although here it was local pressures as much as conscious design that was the determining factor. Since the 1880s Aden had been issuing rifles and ammunition to approved potentates in the hinterland, especially the Sultans of Lahej, and in 1897 these arms issues had been liberalised to enable British protégés to keep ahead of those with access to smuggled weapons.[45] During the period of delimitation and the contemporaneous disturbances in Somaliland, however, serious attention had been given to the whole question of arms availability. When British soldiers were being shot at with contraband rifles this matter assumed a different and more serious guise. In 1906 a radical proposal was put forward to occupy the Subayhi coast, stamp out smuggling and disarm the tribesmen, as the Turks were trying to do in the Yemen. But this was over-ruled. Instead an intermittent and rather ineffective naval blockade of the coast was established, in co-operation with other powers. This was very much a second-best arrangement, and since it was recognised that the flow of arms could not be staunched, the Aden arsenal continued to issue rifles and munitions in competition with the smugglers so that the arms in the hinterland would become British rather than French and dependent on ammunition from Aden rather than elsewhere.[46] Of course the method of issuing arms was modelled upon the system of paying subsidies and making presents. They went in the first instance to the chiefs, indeed many of the presents to the chiefs took the form of rifles and ammunition rather than cash. In this way Aden hoped to control the whirlwind of arms importation without stopping it.

The policy of supporting the hinterland chiefs was not very successful. The 'Abdali Sultan certainly continued to extend his authority at the expense of other traditional protectors of the trade routes. The 'Alawi Shaykh became heavily dependent upon his aid in arms and ammunition. 'Alawi transit dues were collected at Lahej from 1908 onward and in 1909 the 'Abdali temporarily purchased the 'Alawi's lands to secure closer control of the roads. The 'Abdali also purchased land in Subayhi country and resumed his efforts to control that turbulent area.[47] The general disintegration of society nevertheless went on apace. The Radfan tribes took up their attacks on the Hardaba road with increased vigour after the withdrawal of the Political Officer from Dali'. Sultan Ahmad Fadl could not bring them to heel and his peace-making efforts and those of the Aden Residency were hampered and frustrated by the difficulty of finding any man who could speak for more than a handful of his fellows.[48] In Subayhi country plundering on the roads and internecine strife reached new levels of severity.[49] Every month in 1908 new outrages were perpetrated against Lahej people, against the Sultan's agents, against tribes in Turkish territory, and against Sayyids, who were normally immune from attack.[50] At Dali' the 'Amir, despite aid in arms and ammunition from Lahej and the Turks, quickly lost control of the situation as the hill tribes rose in revolt and strife appeared within the ruling family itself.[51] the Yafi'i and the Fadli fell upon one another in 1908 and the joint efforts of the

Sultans of Lahej and Mukalla and the Resident in Aden produced an uneasy settlement only after the greatest difficulty.[52] The illegal arms trade was not stopped by Aden's decision to compete. It became more active than before, and in 1911 the Resident asked for a naval vessel for the special duty of checking its proliferation.[53] There could be no doubt that South Arabian society was on the move; whether or not the changes being wrought were beneficial to anyone was more open to debate.

What was happening in the Aden hinterland was but a pale and distorted reflection of what was occurring elsewhere in the Middle East at this period. Throughout the area the pace of reform and modernisation was quickening as the twentieth century began. Egypt and the Sudan had emerged from their financial and political problems of the 1880s and 1890s and were moving towards economic, administrative and educational integration.[54] The Ottoman Empire, despite the in many ways reactionary rule of Sultan Abd al Hamid II, was moving in the same direction, as railway construction got under way, the financial and legal organs of centralised government developed and the products of the new schools and the increasing importance of the press made their impact.[55] At the same time each dose of innovation warped existing political institutions, while the uneven response of the Empire's diverse provinces weakened people's loyalty to the state itself. In effect, modernisation was attended by a mounting degree of political fluidity at every level. Sultan 'Abd al Hamid evidently hoped that loyalty to the Caliphate and the idea of pan-Islam would secure the legitimacy of Ottoman rule. But in the early twentieth century other formulae were being put forward, ranging from the secular ideas of the Young Turks, who were themselves still undecided on the crucial question of centralisation, to the religious appeal of the Wahhabi Ibn Sa'ud and the separatist aspirations of the Armenian communities.[56] Wherever unusually close contact between formerly distant people took place, a variety of attitudes varying from repugnance to a feeling of common purpose was produced.[57] Nothing was more certain than political uncertainty itself.

There were very evident signs of this in the Yemen, where the first twelve years of the twentieth century were marked by some remarkable reversals of political fortunes and frequent alterations in the general aspect of government. Warfare between the Turks and various rebel forces was fluctuating but continuous. In the autumn of 1902 the Turkish troops were driven back until they held only the south, the coast and the vital Hudayda–Manakha–San'a' axis in the centre. From the spring of 1903 to the autumn of 1904 there was a détente toward the end of which the Turks, profiting from a succession dispute on the death of the old Imam Hamad al din, pushed back gradually into lost territories. Then in November 1904 the revolt was renewed under the new Imam Yahya and by January 1905 the Ottoman position was critical, with the Hudayda–San'a' road cut and San'a' itself invested. In March 1905 the Turks attempted to recover the capital but their troops had to be directed southward to counter inroads made there by Imamic forces.

In July a new effort was made with Anatolian regiments in place of the ineffective and disloyal reservists from Syrian Arabia who were going over in increasing numbers to the Arab Imam.[58] The offensive was attended with immediate success. The tough new troops stormed through to San'a' and recaptured the greater part of the province. Only the Imam's redoubt at Shahara in the far north stood out. But in trying to reduce Shahara in the autumn of 1905 the Turkish commander met with a crushing defeat, and he retired exhausted to San'a', forfeiting many of his previous gains.[59]

In the meanwhile the Ottoman Government made several efforts at conciliation. The Arab advisers to the Sultan at Constantinople were constantly putting forward new formulae designed either to take the wind out of the insurgents' sails or to end the revolt by according a measure of self-government to such acknowledged leaders as the Imam, within the Ottoman system. In 1899 the Turks attempted reform, and in the summer of 1902, and again in 1905 and 1907, they attempted negotiation. None of these initiatives succeeded.[60] The Imam's advisers and supporters were too intransigent; Sultan 'Abd al Hamid II baulked at any real decentralisation of authority within the Empire.[61] Then in 1908 the Young Turk revolution took place and brought to power a regime which at first wavered in the direction of the policy of unity in diversity.[62] This willingness to experiment removed one obstacle to agreement in the Yemen; the fact that the province was costing the Empire some 10,000 casualities and £500,000 per annum encouraged earnestness in negotiations.[63] A new Governor-General was despatched to San'a' and within a few days of his arrival he negotiated a settlement with the Imam.[64]

The agreement between the two parties was ill kept. The ink was hardly dry on the document when the Imam sought to open relations with the British and asked them for arms and munitions and other forms of support. On the Turkish side the deposition of 'Abd al Hamid in 1909 and the anti-Arab outlook of the nationalist Turkish government during the next four years did not improve relations.[65] The Imam profited from Ottoman disarray to grasp at more territory in 1909. In 1911 he launched a full offensive against the occupying forces, and the Turks, swinging once more in the direction of conciliation, were forced to buy peace by making further and wider concessions.[66]

From the point of view of relations between the controlling authorities in the Yemen and the peoples of the Aden Protectorate, however, the 1908 agreement between the Turks and the Imam marked an important turning-point. In 1902, 1904 and 1905, Imamic forces had briefly appeared on the Protectorate's frontiers.[67] After 1908 a whole section of the border fell under Imamic control. The administrative capital at Ta'izz in Southern Yemen and its dependencies reaching north to Nawa opposite Yafi'i country remained in Ottoman hands, but north and eastward from there the country was within Imam Yahya's sphere, and the adjacent areas under British protection began for the first time to feel the full weight of his influence.

For the British this created a new situation and one which was none too welcome. Lee Warner and the India Office officials had for long been fearful of the consequences of the breakdown of Turkish authority in the Yemen. While many of Curzon's persuasion looked on the Ottoman Sultan as the main obstacle to the consolidation of the British position on the strategic Arabian periphery and talked blandly of the decline of his 'rotten Empire', Lee Warner saw the matter in quite a different light. A despatch from the Ambassador at the Porte in October 1902, which suggested that the Yemen revolt might set off a political convulsion throughout Arabia, provided him with his cue. In a long memorandum which received the approval of the Permanent Under-Secretary and three influential members of the Indian Council, he warned that the fall of the Turks in the Yemen would remove a neighbour amenable to diplomatic control and expressed the fear that a Mahdi would emerge and threaten the protected Aden chiefs.

The fear of a Mahdi was never far from the minds of the men in London in the ensuing years.[68] The news of the arrival of Imamic forces on Aden's frontiers in the summer of 1907 was therefore received with considerable alarm. Urgent orders were sent to India to get the Political Agent out of Dali' as quickly as possible. All communications with the Imam's agents was forbidden. The policy of non-interference with hinterland affairs was given a further twist – above all there was to be no meddling in matters which concerned the insurgent religious leader in the Yemen.[69] The steady decline in Turkish fortunes there was watched with unenthusiastic resignation.[70] It was attended by an adjustment in the spirit though not in the letter of British policy. The fact that the Ottoman Government could no longer control events in a considerable part of South

Arabia was understood and taken into account. The lines which Turks and British had jointly drawn on the maps were recognised to be only lines. But they were still regarded as having diplomatic value. They represented internationally authenticated claims which could be appealed to and enforced at a later date. In 1913, an Ottoman offer to ratify the 1905 *procès-verbal* recognising Aden's Protectorate boundaries, was still regarded as of sufficient value for London to accept it as an item in a general deal between the two powers.[71]

In the meanwhile the chiefs in the Protectorate accommodated themselves in various ways to the changing situation. Sultan Ahmad Fadl of Lahej never regarded his special relationship with the British as precluding any contacts with outside powers; indeed if anything he seemed to use it to meddle the more effectively with matters outside his domain. When an Egyptian newspaper criticised him for subservience to the British he noted with annoyance in the margin that he had signed no Protectorate treaty – which curiously enough was technically correct.[72] In 1905 he made a secret treaty with Imam Yahya and thereafter afforded him assistance in various ways.[73] Some form of understanding between the two rulers continued up to 1915, when the Imam reportedly protested to the Turks, and certainly sent his condolences to the 'Abdali Sultan, when Ottoman forces occupied Lahej.[74]

The 'Abdali, however, was not in direct contact with districts under Imamic rule. The Turks never relinquished control of the country opposite the Subayhi and Hawshabi territories and in consequence Lahej was shielded from what might have been embarrassingly close dealings with the Imam. Such was not the case, however, with the outlying areas of the Protectorate on the north-east.

The Imam's occupation in 1909 of Ma'rib, which had never been under proper Turkish control, brought Bayhan within range of his influence, and the activity of his agents in that area caused a good deal of uneasiness among the Protectorate chiefs indirectly affected.[75] In 1912, after the Turco-Imamic agreement of the previous year, pressure became more marked and more widespread as a further section of the frontier reaching west to Qa'taba was assigned by the Turks to the Yemeni leader.[76] The Sharif of Bayhan, a treaty chief, feared that he would be made the object of an Imamic attack, and 2,000 rounds of ammunition were issued from the Aden armoury to enable him to protect himself. To the west, the Imam's agents soon became involved in the maelstrom of Dali' politics.[77] Report had it that the weak 'Amir declared himself the son of the Imam by beat of tom tom. He denied this to the Aden Resident but the 'Amir's perennial dependence on outside support would suggest that that descendant of Imamic officials had returned in some way to his forbears' allegiance. In any case an emissary of the Imam was at Dali' in January 1912 and at the end of that month letters were despatched from the Imam's headquarters to the Qataybi and 'Alawi Shaykhs, the Hawshabi and Lower Yafi'i Sultans, and the chiefs of the Upper Yafi'i. At this stage the Imam was apparently seeking nothing more than a general acceptance of his authority. What he asked from the chiefs did not go beyond what he had been accorded by the Turks in the 1911 agreement in their own sector of the Yemen – namely acceptance of his religious suzerainty and payment of the Islamic tithe. The need for Muslim unity was part of his argument, the rest stressed his ancestral claims to Southern Arabia and called on those holding documents from his predecessors to renew their allegiance to the central Yemeni authority.

Among the Upper Yafi'i there was once more a flurry of political activity in reponse to this new invitation to regularise their relationship with the world beyond their land. In April 1912 some of the Yafi'i leaders were in conclave at Aden weighing up the British factor; Shaykh 'Ali Muhsin Askar, a prominent figure among the powerful Mawsatta section of the tribe, met an Imamic emissary at Dali'; the advice of the Mansabs at 'Aynat in the Hadhramawt – the traditional religio-political advisers to the Yafi'i – was sought. All watched carefully the Imamic moves in the direction of the small but fertile settled areas of Nawa and Rabayatayn on the northern border of the Yafi' area, whose taxable lands provided a regular source of income for some of the more prominent Yafi'i leaders. The Imam however was apparently aiming at securing his ends in Upper Yafi' by diplomacy rather than by force. In reply to Yafi'i questioning he set out his programme of peace, Muslim unity and the vindication of his ancestral claims. He refused stipends and said that if invited by the Yafi'i he would nominate chiefs over each section of the tribe to collect taxes. Reports reaching the British at Aden suggested that this latter proposal greatly annoyed the Yafi'i. But another report that all but one faction in the tribe had replied to the Imam's letters suggests that the Imam's offer of external support for a new authority structure in the area, together with his other proposals, were not unattractive to some among the Yafi'i. The result was a new bout of intrigue and counter intrigue, and the Yafi'i, together with a number of others in the Protectorate, were still jockeying for position between the Imam, the Turks and the British when the First World War broke out.[78]

*   *   *

The outbreak of war loosened many of the restraints on the political and military activity of the various contending forces in South-Western Arabia without radically changing their comparative strength and composition. The Aden garrison was reinforced within days of the Ottoman Empire's entry into the struggle, although no attempt was made to occupy the Protectorate. As far as Britain was concerned, the diplomatic front line in the Middle East had moved northward beyond Aden in pre-war days. The same Liberal government which had hemmed in the Aden Resident with restrictive instructions and avoided conflicts with Turkey over Protectorate boundaries, spoke firmly and was prepared to take military measures when the eastern frontier of the Egyptian defensive bulwark was in question or when the exposed British positions in the strategically vital Persian Gulf area were threatened by Ottoman encroachment. Aden had become a rearguard position in time of peace; it was not likely that it would become a spear-head in time of war. Indeed the main concern of both British and Turks appears to have been to use South-West Arabia to draw enemy forces away from the really vital theatres of operations. The war therefore was fought out there with little more than the peace-time establishments on either side. It was a war in which each side sought to mobilise the largest possible support from the local Arab population against its adversary.[79] It was a war which naturally tended toward stalemate since victory could easily become more costly in new commitments than defeat.

Britain's main weapons in the struggle were those which she had already been using widely in the Protectorate, namely money, arms and the promise of escape from Turkish rule. She also had command of the sea which made interference possible along all the coastal districts of the Arabian peninsula. As for the Turks, they had a preponderance of troops in the locality and they could count on the still vigorous appeal of Islamic solidarity and the fear of an infidel invasion of Arabia.[80]

The key to the situation was the Imam. Had he decided to rise against the Turks, their situation in South-West Arabia would have become precarious indeed. Various efforts were therefore made to contact him and bring him into the British camp both through his friend the Sultan of Lahej and through the Sharif of Mecca.[81] Prior to the war it had been the Imam who had made vain overtures to Aden when he had been at odds with the Turks. But now that the British had something to offer, the Imam fought shy. There were various reasons for this. Like most Arabs, including those responsible for the Arab Revolt, the Imam did not want to substitute British for Turkish rule. It was understood in Aden that he feared that a British attack launched against Shaykh Saʿid in November 1914 to break up a concentration of Turkish troops and destroy the fort, indicated an intention on Britain's part to extend its control in south Arabia.[82] Had he heard something of the proposals circulating at Aden after 1915 for the creation of a British-protected buffer state in the area of Ibb, he would have believed no doubt that his suspicions were confirmed. In the Yemen moreover, the ideas of secular nationalism based on a consciousness of ethnic difference were much less well formed than in other parts of the Arab world. Religion was still more important than race and the idea of Muslim unity had a stronger hold. Imam Yahya himself wrote a poem extolling the idea of Pan-Islam and during the Italo-Turkish war of 1911–12 he had assisted the Turks against their non-Muslim enemies. Opposition to Turkish rule was stronger among the leaders of the tribal confederations who were impatient of all centralised governmental control, than among the educated classes. Among the latter the spirit which had led the notabilities of San'a' to welcome the Turks in 1872 had not entirely evaporated. In more developed parts of the Arab world and among Arabs competing for office at the centre of the Empire, Turkish rule meant conscription and high taxation and could be represented as a block on progress. In the Yemen however, Ottoman troops were still the best guarantee of order and stability. Certainly, men like the Imam did not want an order which was imposed from Istanbul, but if the Turkish garrison could be made to act as an organised body of efficient mercenaries imposing an order of the Imam's dictation, its presence would not be without advantages.

The firman of September 1913 had not put the Imam in a position to dictate. Southern and Western Yemen remained within the Turkish sphere and a Turkish garrison was placed in the Imam's capital. But the Imam had full authority in the North and East of the country and within the area of Turkish control he had power of appointment over the judges who administered the Shari'a law. Perhaps more important than the formal text of the agreement was the spirit in which it was worked. Among those on the Ottoman side who had been responsible for the negotiation of the agreement was the founder of the Al Ahd party of Arab nationalists and the agreement itself was very much in line with that political group's conception of the Empire as an Austro-Hungarian-type dual system, allowing the fullest autonomy to Arab constituent states but retaining unity for purposes of foreign affairs and defence.[83] This was the spirit in which the agreement was conceived; it was also the spirit in which it was carried out. The Ottoman Governor of the Yemen from 1913 to 1919, with but a short break in 1915, was Mahmud Nadim Pasha, another of those who had negotiated the agreement and a man who remained throughout his career on the best terms with the Imam.[84] With Mahmud Nadim in control, the Imam's interests were safeguarded throughout the Yemen and he was given the opportunity to build up and strengthen his rule in his own domain. Such a system could not but appeal to a far-seeing politician of the Imam's type with the enduring patience that usually marks those who deal in dynastic claims and historical rights to semi-religious authority. The Imam was not likely hastily to abandon so favourable a position because a war had broken out in Europe. While the war lasted British efforts to win him over failed.

The British therefore had to fall back upon an alliance with Sayyid 'Idris, an insurgent leader in the 'Asir district. Sayyid 'Idris was one of the more prominent of those religious personalities which foreign rule and civil strife tended to thrust up in South-West Arabia. Acting as a mediator between Turks and tribesmen and between feuding clans, alternately leading tribal revolts and making propaganda for Ottoman rule, Sayyid 'Idris had become a figure of importance in the early twentieth century, eclipsing some of the older families such as the Sharifs of Abu 'Arish in the 'Asir area. His rise had been meteoric but for that very reason his power was fragile. The base of his authority was no wider than the pivot of the balance between the Turks and tribes that he controlled. Before the outbreak of the war he had become wholly committed to an anti-Turkish course of action. During the Italo-Turkish war of 1911–12, he had taken the Italian side, received Italian assistance and thus completely compromised himself in Ottoman eyes. The 1913 agreement between the Turks and the Imam with whom Sayyid Idris competed for influence over the tribes in Northern Yemen, represented another obstacle to a *rapprochement* between him and the Turks. He was therefore open to offers of alliance from anyone who could enable him to sustain the 'Asiri revolt with imports of arms. The British for their part were aware of his shortcomings as an ally. They knew of the negative character of his authority, they realised that the Imam was potentially the stronger ruler and could do them more harm on the frontiers of the Aden Protectorate. They were alive to the risk that an alliance with 'Idris might complicate their relations with the Imam. But the fact that 'Idris, unlike the Imam, controlled a stretch of coastline meant first of all that his revolt could more easily be sustained and secondly, that by sustaining him the hostile area from which attacks might be mounted against communications in the Red Sea would be reduced.

Steps were therefore taken at an early stage to provide him with arms and money – this was an obvious military measure to take. The negotiation of a treaty alliance on 30 April 1915, however, was something more than a purely military measure. The treaty had a military content in that 'Idris engaged himself to pursue the war against the Turks with vigour, and to attack the Imam too if he entered the war on the Turkish side. But the treaty was largely a political document. It involved a permanent commitment to 'Idris which would outlast the war and was therefore indicative of the growing assumption that the war would bring an end to Ottoman rule in the Arabian Peninsula. The scramble for influence that this could entail was already dimly foreseen and the treaty was at least in part designed to avoid the recurrence of the comings and goings between the Italian colony of Eritrea and the Yemeni coast on the other side of the Empire's Red Sea lifeline, which had become uncomfortably frequent during the Italo-Turkish war of 1911–12. The simultaneous occupation of the island of Kamaran which hugs the coast of northern Yemen and which had hitherto been administered internationally as a pilgrim quarantine station had a similarly ambivalent significance.[85] It transferred a potential base from Turkish to British control while at the same time forestalling any possible Italian claims. In 1917 a further step was taken to seal off Arabia when an additional treaty was signed with Sayyid 'Idris, recognising his claim to the newly conquered Farasan islands, on condition that he agreed not to hand them over to any third power.[86] From the point of view of preserving the safety of the sea route the alliance with Idris could be regarded as a shrewd move. It also made a contribution to the military situation on land, since Idris used the large subsidies and gifts of arms he received to tie down a considerable number of Turkish troops which might have been used against Aden or in Palestine. But it was later to prove a serious liability when the problem of reaching a political settlement in South-West Arabia came to be discussed at the end of the war.

While pursuing these intrigues with the Arab powers in the Yemen, the British took up a largely defensive stance in the immediate neighbourhood of Aden. There they hoped to keep the Turks at arm's length rather than use the tribes of the Protectorate and Southern Yemen as a battering ram against their enemies. As in pre-war days, the Sultan of Lahej was the main medium of communication between Aden and the people of the area. The 'Abdali was pro-British to the extent that he ignored and encouraged others to ignore the Ottoman call to *jihad*. But he was not anxious to attack the Turks either and would have preferred to remain neutral. So long as Aden worked through Lahej, which was the only major chiefdom apart from the semi-dependent Hawshabi Sultanate and the Dali' 'Amirate which bordered on Turkish rather than Imamic territory, there was little hope of striking at the enemy across the Protectorate border. The first initiative which gave promise of a more active policy in Southern Yemen came from beyond the confines of the Protectorate. On 17 December 1914 the Shaykh of Mawiyah, Muhammad Nasir Muqbil, wrote to the Resident proposing an offensive and defensive alliance with the 'Abdali Sultan which would draw in other Protectorate chiefs. The Government of India promptly approved this arrangement, provided that British assistance took the form of arms, munitions and money, and did not involve the despatch of troops. But Aden took some time to close the deal. The 'Abdali Sultan was reluctant to move and before an agreement was concluded recognising the Shaykh's independence and offering him a subsidy of 75,000 rupees payable through the 'Abdali Sultan, Turkish and Imamic troops crossed the Dali' border and secured the submission of the 'Amir. The agreement with Muhammad Nasir Muqbil became a dead letter; the Shaykh dared not move and as Turkish troops pushed into his area in force he co-operated with them in subduing the Dali' area.[87]

There followed a general deterioration of the situation as far as the British were concerned. By the middle of June a large Turkish force had concentrated at Mawiyah, whence it could strike at several parts of the Protectorate. The Turkish Governor, Mahmud Nadim, who worked with the Imam and therefore proceeded circumspectly in dealing with Lahej, was temporarily displaced by more hasty men. Tentative efforts by the Ottoman officials to secure 'Abdali co-operation gave place to more peremptory summons to him to join the Ottoman camp. As in 1873 the old points of difference between him and the Hawshabi were brought up and there was menacing talk of re-transferring the Za'ida lands. Finally towards the end of June 1915 the Turks crossed the border at Al Darayjah and gathered to them the Hawshabi Sultan, sundry Subayhi with grievances against Lahej, and various other disgruntled elements from Yafi' and elsewhere, who had been non-recipients in the pre-war distributions of loaves and fishes by the Aden Government. By 3 July there was no doubt that this polyglot collection of some six thousand embittered men and Turkish regulars had Lahej as its objective. Lahej and Aden were in considerable confusion. British support had been withheld until the last moment while the 'Abdali spun his diplomacy finer and finer in an attempt to stave off a trial of arms.[88] Now a force culled from the Aden garrison and ironically named the 'Aden Movable Column' began its approach march from Aden as the first skirmishes were taking place between an 'Abdali covering force and the Turkish army, within a few miles of the Sultan's capital.

Battle was joined on the 4 July, or rather it would be more proper to say that desultory and uneven combats began on that day between

some British units and the advancing Ottoman forces on the outskirts
and within the town of Lahej. The main British force never went
into action and the defence of Lahej was one of those fiascos in which
armies are defeated by their own poor organisation, rather than by
the efforts of the enemy. It is difficult to believe that 'the terrific heat'
during a dawn march from Shaykh 'Uthman to Lahej was a major
factor, as has often been suggested. More important was the breakdown in transport. One section of the force was rushed forward in
cars requisitioned for the purpose in Aden to improvise a holding
operation while the rest of the column came up. Nine or ten of these
got through but the rest stuck in the sand and had to be abandoned.
The result was that only some two hundred and fifty men and a
ten-pounder battery actually reached Lahej. The rest of the force
fell into confusion and the Arab camel drivers with most of the stores
broke and fled. By the evening of 4 July, although the troops in
Lahej were still holding their positions, the Commander's attention
had switched from defending the 'Abdali capital to preventing the
disintegration of his column. Something like panic seems to have
seized those in command. On 5 July the column was bundled back
to Bir Nasr, a well six miles south of Lahej, leaving behind two
ten-pounder guns, several machine guns and three quarters of the
ammunition. The next day the retreat continued precipitately to
Shaykh 'Uthman and thence to Aden, where a line was drawn up
at the Khormaksar isthmus to receive the anticipated assault on the
port, while frenzied preparations were made to abandon Crater and
make a final stand round the coaling station at Steamer Point.[89]

The exaggerated fears of the Aden command were hardly justified.
It is very unlikely that the Turks had any intention of attacking Aden
itself. Nor, had they done so, would they have had much hope of
success, since the garrison was at least equal in strength to the
Turkish regulars and the flanks of their position were covered by four
warships. Lords Kitchener and Curzon in London rightly ascribed
the defeat to incompetence and dismissed the Resident, transferring
his command to General Younghusband who arrived at Aden from
Egypt on 16 July.[90]

Immediately after the latter's arrival the reports from Aden took
on a calmer tone. Younghusband had no doubt of his ability to
repulse the Turks. But he objected to the Viceroy's instruction that
he should reoccupy Lahej and restore British prestige. As far as he
was concerned, Aden was a 'sideshow' in the war. If Lahej were
occupied it would have to be garrisoned and that would lock up a
brigade of precious troops which could be better used elsewhere.[91]
Younghusband's view received support in London and so, when his
reinforcing brigade arrived at Aden on 20 July it was immediately

launched against the Turks at Shaykh 'Uthman, drove them with ease from that position, but pursued them no further than five miles along the road to Lahej. Shaykh 'Uthman was garrisoned, since Aden was dependent upon its wells for water.[92] Reconnaissance parties secured command of the territory between there and Lahej and scored a number of successes over Turkish troops. But the project for recovering Lahej itself was persistently deferred.[93] Aden was secure. Both British and Turks accepted the military stalemate; the British had not the resources to waste on an attack on Lahej, the Turks were not strong enough to take Aden. Food and fodder began to come in once more despite the Turkish presence at Lahej. The amount of Aden's landward trade of course fell and exports to the interior reached minimal proportions, but imports to Aden from inland never sank below half of the average during the pre-war decade.[94]

Although food prices rose seriously during the war, despite the Government's efforts to control them, the settlement never suffered real privation and it is doubtful whether enemy occupation of part of the interior was more responsible for the price rise than the general inflation caused by the war, especially in view of the fact that Western Arabia as a whole had been for some time a net importer of foodstuffs from India and Egypt.[95] From the point of view of the efficiency of the coaling station the most serious development during the war was the drying up of the ever plentiful supply of labour. For the first time since the 1840s there was a real shortage of coolies at Aden, and a corresponding important rise in wage rates.[96] Nevertheless Aden was able to meet the demands placed upon it by the stream of troopships and other merchant vessels which passed through the port during the war years.

CHAPTER X

Diplomacy and the Search for Stability

The First World War ended with British and Turkish troops still in the same positions they had taken up in 1915. Aden had played a rather inglorious role in the struggle on land[1] and had scarcely contributed more to the war at sea. The nearest Aden had come to seeing naval action had been when in the first months of the war the German commerce raider *Koenigsberg* had cruised off the Hadhrami coast, prior to ending its days in an East African river.[2] After that, no enemy vessel came within a thousand miles of the base and while the port provided services for the stream of ships passing up and down the Red Sea, Aden's naval facilities were mainly used to sustain the blockade of the Yemeni coast – Perim being a scarcely less valuable forward base.

The war was won in the Middle East by the armies operating from bases in Egypt and Mesopotamia and after the war the main line of defence for Britain's Middle Eastern interests lay along the Cairo–Baghdad axis, protecting the Canal at one end and the oil fields of Persia and later Iraq at the other.[3] By then the Ottoman Empire had gone and the intricate balance of interests and rivalries at the Porte, which had hitherto screened the route to India at a distance, was no longer operative. Instead, Britain had established her predominance in Egypt by Protectorate and prevented Egyptians from speaking to other powers at the Peace Conference. To the eastward, Egypt's land frontier in Palestine and Britain's interests in Iraq were protected by internationally recognised mandates. Behind this diplomatic front line lay the Arabian Peninsula and it was assumed that that area lay entirely within the British sphere. The importance of British interests there, Britain's treaty relations with so many of the Arab rulers and the long exercise of influence in various parts of the Peninsula were regarded as sufficient justification for the exercise of some form of suzerainty. On the other hand, in the new post-war world, only France among the allied powers was considered to be a serious potential rival, and France, apart from having no obvious interest in challenging the British, had during negotiations in 1916 and 1917 to some extent recognised Britain's special position in that part of the Arab World.[4] Italy, with her possessions on the opposite coast of the Red Sea, was known to be interested, but Italy had never been regarded as more than a second-rate power which had entered the Red Sea area on British sufferance, and would only be able to go as far as Britain would let her. Mussolini's activity was later to modify this estimate, but at the end of the war Italy was not regarded as a rival worthy of serious consideration. Prior to the Peace Conference, a British Monroe doctrine for Arabia was spoken of in London, and although no British mandate for the area was finally obtained, it was assumed that Britain would have a more or less free hand in the Peninsula; British policy during the inter-war period toward Arab rulers and toward Aden itself can only be understood in this context.[5]

The exclusion of other powers from Arabia, and from its coastline in particular and the containment of Arab nationalism represented the sum total of British objectives in the immediate post-war period. As yet, oil had not been found in the Peninsula and Britain's concern was still the traditional one of securing the routes to India and keeping other European nations at a distance from Britain's eastern preserves. There was no need to go beyond a 'dog-in-the-manger diplomacy' stance. Indeed there were very good reasons for not going on to assert some form of positive control over Arab countries. The strength of Arab xenophobia, whether in the form of Islamic exclusiveness or nationalist sentiment, was well recognised in official circles in Britain and India. The danger of offending Arabs by too much interference in their affairs was fully appreciated and it was believed that the exercise of any but the loosest hegemony would be counter-productive in terms of Britain's principal objectives. On the other hand it was not thought wise to leave the Arabs entirely to themselves. Arab nationalism in the Peninsula and Arab unity were neutral, as far as British interests were concerned. But the creation of broader unities on an Arab linguistic or Islamic basis would affect other British positions in the Middle East and India. So a scheme was devised by which Britain would work in concert with the forces of Arab nationalism, consolidate Anglo-Arab friendship and maintain an influential position in the Arab world. Britain's policy was to be to encourage the improvement of the existing states in Arabia by the offer of financial subventions to the various rulers, to limit the importation of arms by direct action and by international agreement, to encourage the peaceful resolution of disputes between rulers by mediation and by manipulation of subsidies and arms control and to work toward a confederation of all the principalities in the Peninsula.[6] These were the main lines of Britain's 'liberal' and 'non-interventionist' programme for Arabia, and during the inter-war period serious efforts were made to carry it out – with decreasing success as British tax-payers refused to continue the subsidies and as other powers broke through the British monopoly of military aid.[7]

Aden occupied a very rearward position in this whole defensive system. In pre-war days, even though it stood well behind the main bastion in Egypt, its frontier with the Turkish Yemen had endowed it with a certain diplomatic immediacy to the sensitive international nexus at the Porte. Now that too had gone, and its strategic function as a defensive bulwark for India had considerably diminished in importance. During the inter-war period, Aden was mainly spoken of as an 'imperial outpost' with emphasis upon its coaling and communications facilities. The reasons given in the 1839 Parliamentary Papers for its seizure were unquestioningly accepted as sufficient.[8] Indian defence planners were particularly disenchanted and in 1920 the Indian Commander-in-Chief gave his jaundiced view that 'as long as we command the Indian Ocean, Aden is in no danger, and if we do not I cannot see that it is of any use to us'.[9] This statement threw doubt on Aden's value as a naval base. One cannot say that it was generally accepted but these pessimistic remarks were not met by any countervailing enthusiasm elsewhere, and little was done to modernise the settlement's seaward defences. British Aden was accepted because it was there and because there was no reason to give it up. The port afforded valuable facilities to trade and shipping – although Perim was performing the same function equally well as far as coal-burning steamers were concerned – but from the point of view of general military strategy the possession of Aden afforded few advantages which were not already amply secured in other ways or in other places.

In the immediate post-war period and indeed for nearly a decade afterward, few dispassionate appraisals of Aden's strategic worth were made. Throughout that period the administrative problem of determining to which department of Government responsibility for Aden should be assigned bulked so large in the minds of officials that opinions on all other matters relating to the settlement were coloured by men's attitudes to this single all-pervading issue. The transfer of Aden from the Indian to the British Government had been the subject of frequent fruitless discussions during the previous seventy years.[10] Owing to the settlement's indeterminate position halfway between India and the British Goverment's defensive dispositions in the Mediterranean, this matter had been constantly taken up, and, owing to the financial and administrative complications involved, as constantly dropped. But during the war a decisive step was taken. In 1917, the Government of India, recognising its inability to provide the forces for the expedition to Lahej which it believed to be essential, transferred military control to the War Office and control of Protectorate affairs to the Foreign Office.[11] The arrangement was temporary and the transfer incomplete, since India retained control of affairs within the settlement itself. But the question had now been raised in such a form that it could not once more be pigeon-holed and forgotten. Aden had been wrenched from its Indian moorings, and for the next twenty years it drifted uncomfortably and uncertainly in the rock-strewn waters of administrative reorganisation, before being placed firmly under the control of the Colonial Office in 1937. During the intervening period it was the subject of incessant bureaucratic wrangling between different departments of Government, which broke through from time to time into the columns of newspapers and on to the floor of the House of Commons and representative assemblies in India.[12]

The main disagreement was inevitably over the division of costs. Aden served both imperial and Indian interests and therefore a balance had to be struck between the financial responsibility of each government. Indian officials, with their own budgets to prepare, were only prepared to relinquish control at a price; it was up to the appropriate department of the London Government, equally concerned about its estimates, to try to meet that price.[13] This exercise should not have been beyond the bargaining skill of either side – there was a useful precedent in the decision of 1900 on the sharing of the cost of the garrison and defensive works and this was used as a basis for negotiation. But the total expense of Aden's defence was more difficult to compute after 1918 than had been the case at the turn of the century. It depended upon a whole series of political and military variables which so complicated the question that no agreement could be reached between Whitehall and Simla for nearly ten years. Aden's security was inextricably bound up with the state of Britain's relations with the Protectorate tribes, with the Imam in the Yemen, and ultimately with all the rulers in the Arabian Peninsula. Every fluctuation in British prestige, and every change in the political scene in those areas, affected the estimate of the strength of the garrison required at Aden. The vigour and direction of British policy in the Middle East as a whole also had direct significance, for Aden could be as well defended by political manipulation in other parts of the Peninsula as by the presence of troops in the settlement itself. In this way the question of Aden's cost became administratively linked with the even thornier question of how postwar subsidies to Arab rulers should be apportioned between Britain and India – that is until the policy of subsidising Arab rulers on a large scale was dropped.

Administrative efficiency was not improved by the fact that in London these matters were being handled by a constantly changing body of officials. During the war, Aden affairs were dealt with by the India Office, the Service Ministries and the Foreign Office, with the High Commission in Egypt acting as a co-ordinating agency. After the war, the picture was further complicated when the Middle East Department of the Colonial Office began to struggle its way into existence, drawing all the strings of Middle Eastern policy into its hands.[14] At one point the question had become so muddled that the Prime Minister himself did not know who was responsible for Aden, and gave the wrong answers when questioned in the House of Commons.[15] The Cairo Conference of March 1921, which straightened out so many other confused areas of British policy, failed to solve the riddle of Aden's cost and the settlement's administrative future. The London Cabinet decided that Aden should be transferred to Colonial Office control *in toto*, provided that India would agree. But the Colonial Office could not meet the price asked. India did not agree and so Aden remained half in and half out – the Protectorate under the Colonial Office and the rest still ruled from India through the Government of Bombay.

The appearance of the Colonial Office on the scene made it even more difficult to reach agreement with India on Aden's future. The Colonial Office was not popular in India. It was directly involved in the bitter dispute over the position of Indians in Kenya, and was regarded by the Indian public as the main proponent in Britain of racialist policies. Indians therefore became alarmed when they realised that they were being asked to transfer Aden to that department of the British Government. They expected to see their people's interests in Aden disregarded and Indians excluded from business opportunities, civil service places and influence with Aden's Government. Apart from these political overtones, the Indian commercial community at Aden was rich and powerful enough and sufficiently alarmed to make its views heard in the Legislative Council at Bombay.[16] Such opinions could not be ignored. London now had to contend with an India which, as a result of the Montagu-Chelmsford reforms, had a sufficient measure of self-government to make it no longer possible for the British officials to have the sole and final say in how funds should be spent and government run. If nothing more, this stiffened official Indian resolve in negotiation. In Bombay, the existence of hostility to the Colonial Office as a very lively political issue introduced a further and serious obstacle to agreement.

None of this was entirely unprecedented. Aden's whole history since 1839 had been marked by administrative confusion and complication. But during the 1920s these problems assumed a scope and intensity far beyond previous experience, and the whole conduct of government at almost every level was affected. In London, whenever Aden affairs came under discussion, the consideration of policy was either warped or entirely paralysed by the necessity to secure the agreement of a multiplicity of offices. In Aden, officials were constantly baulked by lack of funds, and as they watched other areas under British control going forward during the post-war period of development while Aden stood still, they felt that they were being neglected, and relations between them and the superior authority at Bombay became conspicuously sour.[17] On all sides there was a general feeling of dissatisfaction.

More serious than the day-to-day irritations was the effect of administrative uncertainty upon the formulation of plans for Aden's future. During the post-war period, British imperial interests in other parts of the world were being clothed in new and hopefully more acceptable garments of gradual constitutional advance, and more liberal political relationships with local peoples. Nationalism was regarded as a rising force to be reckoned with and possessions were being assigned to what was hoped to be the appropriate nascent nation and set upon a longer or shorter ladder of constitutional progress. But this could not be done with Aden while it remained part of a tug-of-war between the London and Indian Governments. As was often the case in the inter-war period, what seemed at first sight to be a purely administrative problem involved choices of great long-term political importance. Aden could of course have become an outlying military base attached to an increasingly independent India, although there was little pressure even from India for such a solution. The officials in charge of Indian defence were not interested, and only a very few Indian politicians envisaged Aden as making a permanent contribution to India's military power.[18] In London on the other hand the view was firmly held from the early 1920s that Aden was an Arab town in an Arab land and that the destiny of its people lay with Arabia and not with India.[19] Efforts were made to build up a feeling of local identity among the people of Aden to counter the claims of Indian politicians, and some despair was expressed at the lack of political consciousness on the part of the Arab populace of the settlement.[20] The census reports became more concerned with demonstrating the size of the Arab element in the population than with the traditional problem of the homeless and 'vagrants' in the fortress. Transfer to the Colonial Office with its Middle Eastern interests and its Arabophil personnel represented a vital part of this process of weaning Aden away from India and setting it in an Arab context. But while the settlement remained under the baleful scrutiny of the Bombay Legislature the building of an Arab

Aden could hardly be begun. This was one of the main reasons for the hatred of Bombay to be found among officials concerned with Aden affairs, whose desires were becoming an increasingly important determinant of policy.[21] Clear-cut long-term political objectives were an essential requirement for the members of the rapidly growing British bureaucracy whose planning propensities abhored uncertainty. The same administrative drive which had lain behind Curzonian assimilation of Aden to India was now geared to the policy of an Arab Aden. Over and above this desire for tidy development it was clearly realised that Britain could more easily maintain control of the Aden base if it were held separate from an India now moving steadily toward independence. This matter became urgent at the end of the 1920s when discussion of constitutional reforms in India began. In 1932 Aden was removed from the purview of the Bombay Legislative Assembly and made a Chief Commissioner's Province under direct control of the Viceroy, ostensibly on administrative grounds.[22] In 1937, complete transfer to the Colonial Office was effected, this time after a clear statement that the British Government was unwilling to share control of the imperial base or anything pertaining to it with an independent Indian administration.[23]

While the future of the settlement was caught in this administrative tangle, the situation in the Protectorate during the post-war period was almost equally productive of controversy and uncertainty. The first steps after the withdrawal of the Turkish troops from Lahej were straightforward and decisive enough. As all were painfully aware, Britain had failed during the war to protect directly those rulers with whom treaties of protection had been concluded in pre-war days. The Aden authorities were therefore disposed to overlook the fact that many of them had actively co-operated with the Turks during the war, and treaty relations and stipends were renewed without overmuch enquiry into the wartime conduct of their recipients.[24] Loyal friends, on the other hand, were well rewarded. In particular Sultan Sir 'Abdalkarim Fadl of Lahej, who had fled to Aden and remained there with his followers throughout the war, was reinstalled in his capital with British aid; his rivals in the 'Abdali family, who had tried to induce the Turkish Commander to have one of his relations elected Sultan, were brusquely set aside.[25] Friendship with Lahej was made the linchpin of British policy in the Protectorate in a more ostentatious and unambiguous fashion than in pre-war days. In February 1919 a treaty was signed placing a number of the Subayhi Shaykhs under 'Abdali suzerainty, and their pre-war stipends from Aden were now made payable through the Sultan.[26] The Hawshabi also, who had enthusiastically taken part in the sack of Lahej in 1915, was firmly told that he must make his peace with the 'Abdali before being received by Aden, and in due course he sank once more into his pre-war position of dependence on his more powerful neighbour.[27] Backing up these negotiations was a powerful British force stationed in 'Abdali territory. When the main body withdrew in March 1919, it left behind it a small garrison to protect a newly built military railway extending from the wartime terminus at Shaykh 'Uthman to Lahej. These measures, together with the raising in 1918 of a force of local levies called the Yemen Light Infantry, and a projected college for the sons of chiefs, represented the fulfilment of a major part of the abortive forward programme of 1905, which had never been forgotten and which had cropped up from time to time when officials in wartime Aden mused about what should be done when the fighting ended.[28]

But if the plans of 1905 for more intensive activity beyond Aden had not been forgotten, neither had the 1906 hesitations concerning the geographical scope to be given to British action in Aden's hinterland. While expeditions for the recovery of protected lands were being planned at Aden during the war, and while, therefore, military considerations entirely outweighed the political, the gravest doubts were cast upon the value to Aden of Dali', and indeed of all the lands beyond Hawshabi territory. The possession of Lahej could putatively have added to the defensive strength of Aden but a force in the Dali' mountains would have served no purpose and merely invited an enemy attempt to cut its communications.[29] On the other hand, covetous eyes were cast on Shaykh Sa'id, commanding part of the Bab el Mandeb strait, and also on the Ta'izz area of Southern Yemen, where it was calculated that an independent buffer state which had friendly relations with the British at Aden would add considerably to the security of the base.[30] The latter seemed the more feasible because of Aden's friendly contacts with the Shaykh of Mawiyah in the early months of 1915, and both ideas were taken so seriously that in wartime treaties and communications with Arab rulers such as Sharif Husayn and Sayyid Idris, all references to Aden's post-war boundaries were left studiously vague.

The British therefore approached the question of Aden's boundaries with open minds and the fact that all Arabia was initially regarded as an exclusive British sphere at the end of the war was an added reason for flexibility. By the summer of 1919, British thinking had crystallised into three major alternatives. The first was that later given publicity by Colonel Jacob in his *Kings of Arabia*, published in 1923.[31] It involved the abandonment of the whole Protectorate to the Imam apart from Aden's immediate, defensible hinterland, notably Lahej. In the light of later events such a policy could be regarded as one of surrender. In the context of the time, Jacob's lifting of the bars of the Protectorate cage was intended as much to allow the British to fly out as to let the Imam in, and by the time he published his views Jacob was already involved in attempts to float a company which would secure in the Yemen the sort of commercial concessions his contemporary Philby acquired in Sa'ud's Arabia. The other alternatives considered could therefore be regarded as less ambitious. One was to negotiate with the Imam for his recognition of the 1905 boundary. The other was to ignore him and consolidate the Protectorate by more intensive administrative and other action. For ten years after the war, British policy was to waver between these alternatives, as efforts were made to produce an arrangement offering some hope of stability and certainty in the matter of Aden's landward defence.[32]

Aden's defence however was not the main priority in the immediate post-war period. In those heady days of victory all attention was devoted to making the whole Peninsula an exclusive British sphere and Aden's boundary was a purely local problem, which figured only in relation to the specific terms that might eventually be offered to the Imam. It was fear of Italian intrigue rather than anxiety about Aden's boundary that prompted the first post-war efforts to negotiate at San'a'. In January 1919 Imamic emmissaries arrived at Aden with letters to the French, Italian and American Consuls, as well as to the Resident himself, requesting representation at the Peace Conference. The envoys were bundled back to the Yemen. Their request for representation was placed on a par with similar demands by Egyptian and other nationalists; their contacts with other powers were regarded as little less than subversive.[33] The Imam was informed a few weeks later that the matter of his representation at Paris 'had been disposed of'. Yet it had not been entirely 'disposed of', because the Italian delegates spoke privately to their British counterparts at Paris about it, and articles in the nationalist press in Italy indicated that attempts to secure recognition of an exclusive British sphere in the Yemen would not go unchallenged. So London decided to occupy the diplomatic vacuum on the ground by sending a mission to open negotiations with the Imam.[34]

The man to be negotiated with, however, was full of suspicions about British intentions. During the war the Imam had been aligned with the Turks, while the British supported his deadliest enemy, Sayyid Idris, and the war between Turkish and British principals was intimately associated with the struggle between their local associates. In early 1918, as Turkish financial strength waned, the countervailing tide of British gold washed up through Idrisi hands until, to the Imam's alarm, it reached the vital Hashid and Bakil confederations.[35] October brought the armistice between British and Turk but not the end of fighting in the Yemen. The British could not persuade Sayyid Idris that the war was done;[36] indeed for him it had just begun; he used the £10,000 a month received from Britain to hustle his way forward with arms and diplomacy into the vacuum left by the Turkish defeat. Zaraniq tribesmen too, who had no love for Imamic rule, received British arms, though not formal British recognition.[37] The Imam, hoping at least to rescue something from the disaster by seizing Turkish assets and turning his former masters into mercenaries, sought to obstruct the evacuation of Turkish troops.[38] Here again he ran into conflict with Britain for whom the first priority was to rid the Peninsula entirely of the Turks. A British force seized Hudayda toward the end of 1918 to facilitate the exit of Turkish soldiers and by February 1919 most of them had gone.[39] Whatever its motive, the occupation of Hudayda was seen by the Imam as an indication of British aggressive intentions and the treatment of his envoys shortly after did nothing to dispel such an impression. In January 1919 he retailed to a meeting of Yemeni Shaykhs gloomy prophesies of a period of British rule in the Yemen, and urged all to renew their Islamic solidarity.[40] In the ensuing months, further British actions tended to confirm the Imam's fears. Despite the War Office's anxiety to evacuate its men, the battalion of British troops was kept on at Hudayda until the Imam had 'come to heel'.[41] Other forms of pressure were maintained, including the wartime blockade of the Yemeni coast which, with its various exceptions in favour of British friends, continued to operate to the Imam's disadvantage until August 1919.

The Imam was wrong about British territorial pretensions. It had been decided that no further acquisitions were required in Western Arabia and a self-denying agreement by France rendered otiose the original plan to seize Shaykh Sa'id.[42] Nor were the authorities in London generally ill-disposed toward him. Earlier ideas about making Sharif Husayn the suzerain of the Peninsula had been relegated to a second line in British thinking by 1919, and dealing with each small Shaykh individually was yet more firmly eschewed. In March 1919 it was agreed that Britain's 'non-interventionist' policy in Arabia should be operated by recognising only 'overlords' and mediating between them in the interests of Arab unity. The Imam, along with Sharif Husayn and Ibn Sa'ud, was designated as one of those 'overlords', while his rival, Idris, was unenthusiastically included in their ranks, in accordance with treaty obligations rather than out of any conviction as to the permanency of his rule.[43] The ultimate aim therefore was to encourage Imamic control over the whole of the Yemen outside the Aden Protectorate and the Idrisi's wartime haunts. The Imam for his part, was expected to channel his relations with European powers, his procurement of arms and military skills, through Britain, and accept British mediation of disputes with his neighbours in the Peninsula. The general formula lay close to what the Imam was presumed to hope and expect; the major difficulties were expected to arise over boundaries, those with the Idrisi, who had no political *locus standi* in the Imam's eyes, being seen as the major stumbling block. The Aden boundary was not expected to create much difficulty.

Colonel Jacob was the principal figure on the British side in the negotiations that ensued. He had maintained contact with the Imam through his 'Abdali friends, was regarded as the expert on Yemeni affairs and, after soliciting and receiving a letter of welcome from the Imam, was entrusted with the command of the ill-fated mission that left for San'a' in August 1919. Jacob had with him an autograph letter from King George V to reassure the Imam of the British view of his status, but otherwise he was ill-provided with the means to negotiate. Part of the blame for this lay with Jacob himself, for his own vague and oracular utterances had at various times traversed the whole gamut of possible policy alternatives without clearly choosing between them. Before the war his prescription for the Protectorate was 'support the chiefs'; in 1919 he said it had failed and spoke instead of railways, schools, tribal levies and broad contact with the mass of the population. That, said a Foreign Office official, meant 'consolidation of the Protectorate'. Not at all, Jacob unconvincingly replied, he stood as always by the motto 'hands off direct administration'. His views on the Yemen were quite as confusing. He strongly maintained that the Imam was the man to back and that too much had been made of Shafi'i–Zaydi differences. But he insisted equally strongly that any treaty with the Imam should contain a clause conditioning British support on the Imam's conciliation of his Shafi'i subjects. As for the Protectorate boundary, his pronouncements could have meant several different things. Beneath all this lay a strong tendency to see issues in terms of personalities, much as Haines had done. Much like Haines, whom he certainly admired, Jacob also wanted a free hand to arrive at an arrangement that would fit in best with the constellation of personal friendships he had built and was building.[44] As things turned out, his desire was apparently fulfilled, for in the pressures and confusions of European peace-making, he was sent with instructions that had no great meaning. The object of his mission was simply to provide evidence of British negotiation with the Imam so that the Italians at Paris could be persuaded that only the British should negotiate with the Imam! Otherwise all options were to be kept open and Jacob was supposed only to reassure the Imam about British intentions and explore his views.[45] Confused from the start, the mission set off along the route between Hudayda and San'a' that had become the focus of the struggle for power in the Yemen between Imamic, anti-Imamic and opportunistic forces of every kind. Like those of not a few other venturers into areas of post-war chaos, Jacob's efforts came to naught. He was stopped at Bajil by Shaykhs who wanted no British contact with the Imam and was held there, virtually a prisoner, while his quicksilver mind schemed out new combinations, envisaging a Shafi'i political grouping in western Yemen, with possible Turkish involvement. He was finally released after aerial intervention, and returned utterly discredited in the sharper eyes of the men in Whitehall.[46]

British impotence in the face of tribal hostility during the three months of Jacob's incarceration took the shine off Britain's world war victory and amply demonstrated the dangers of a more ambitious policy in the Yemen. By the end of October those in charge had washed their hands of the Yemen and were using any available means to release the mission, without regard to the effect they might have upon the future internal organisation of the country.[47] This meant, in effect, a return to the wartime posture of securing only what was strategically essential and easy to defend by direct action. It meant also the re-emphasis of a policy which had always been a major irritant in Anglo-Imamic relations, namely friendship with the Imam's enemy, Sayyid Idris. Britain's wartime subsidies to Idris had been brought to an end in June 1919, but arms shipments continued on a limited scale. In August 1919, when Jacob had been sent to San'a', another mission had been sent to the Sayyid to reassure him that his interests would not be neglected. Since the former failed and the latter succeeded, Britain continued its pro-Idrisi alignment despite reservations about the intrinsic strength of that ruler's position. Sayyid Idris controlled a substantial coastline, his territory was at once more accessible and more strategically vital than the interior, and to ensure his continued friendship, the Foreign Office decided in December 1920 to permit him to occupy Hudayda on the evacuation of British troops from that port.[48] This was another and a most serious rebuff to the Imam, which resulted in a further deterioration in relations.

While the general relations between the Imam and the British were thus going from bad to worse, misunderstandings over the Aden hinterland had already reached the stage of armed conflict. As always, Dali' was the first to suffer from disagreement between Aden and San'a'. In January 1919 Zaydi troops gave assistance to 'Amir Nasr of Dali', and immediately the opposing group in that faction-ridden area rushed to Lahej for aid.[49] After a year of desultory intrigue the alliances were reversed, 'Amir Nasr sought the support of Aden and was promptly deposed by the Zaydi. His opponents rallied to the Imamic cause and the British promised him support in arms and money against the invaders.[50] The reversal of alliances at Dali' coincided with more serious Zaydi incursions elsewhere. Large bodies of Zaydi troops now moved into the Protectorate from bases near Ta'izz and Mawiyah which had fallen under the Imam's control in October. Upper Yafi' was also attacked and the territory of the Hawshabi Sultan invaded. The Sultan of Lahej became thoroughly alarmed, and 'Abdali alarm sounded the tocsin at Aden. In January 1920 large quantities of arms and ammunition were issued to all in the Protectorate who wished to defend themselves. The Lahej railway was extended to near the 'Abdali frontier at Khudad.[51] The Resident went up in person with a force into 'Abdali territory, and a strong protest was sent to San'a'. These measures set a term to Zaydi encroachment and for the rest of 1920 there was sporadic fighting on the confines of the occupied area in the Wadi Hardaba between the Imam's soldiers and British-armed tribesmen, who were fighting either to maintain their independence or simply to feed themselves in that time of famine from imposts on the valuable Yemen coffee trade which was temporarily diverted to Aden for want of another outlet.[52]

The tribesmen pushed the Zaydi back, but not out of such places as Dali', and after a brief new foray in September 1921 into the sensitive Subayhi country, then under 'Abdali control, a major second round was fought in the winter of 1921 to 1922, when farmers, taxmen and highway robbers went out once more to gather in their respective harvests. Between January and March 1922 Zaydi soldiers were active all along the frontier line from Subayhi to Dali', and threatened 'Abdali positions in Hawshabi as well as Subayhi country. Once more dismay spread among those who relied on British backing to maintain their independence from Zaydi control, including the now agitated and always influential Sultan of Lahej. This time, however, the Aden authorities were ready and willing to take more effective counter-measures than before. The usual issues of rifles and ammunition to anti-Zaydi tribesmen were made on a sufficiently liberal scale to enable the Qataybi in particular to make headway against the invaders. Over and above this, Aden for the first time made extensive and, as it proved, decisive use of a new arm of war. In October 1921 a flight of R.A.F. aircraft had arrived just too late to deal with the Yemeni incursion of September. In February 1922 they were ready for action, and after protests and warnings to the Imam, they bombed the headquarters of the

Zaydi commander who was directing the troops in Hawshabi and Subayhi country.[53] The planes were preparing for further action against Dali' when they were called away to take part in a campaign in Somaliland which they did with outstanding success. What they had already done, however, was enough. The Imam's men had no protection against air attack, and were forced to withdraw from Hawshabi country. The local balance of power swung in favour of the Protectorate tribesmen and, although they were unable to recover Dali', they were able to force the Zaydi to relinquish their recent gains. For the next year Aden was reasonably content with affairs as they stood and believed that the combination of air power and tribal resistance would suffice to keep the Imam at arm's length.

If Aden could defend itself there was little need for a treaty with the Imam. That at least was how the Aden authorities tended to see the matter after March 1922. It helped them to sustain the point of view with regard to the Aden frontier that they had persistently held since the end of the war. Aden wanted to retain the Aden frontier as it had been in 1905, and was unwilling to see the slightest modification. But while the Resident felt increasingly secure behind his planes and tribes, the men at the Colonial Office were exposed to the ever colder post-war winds of austerity blowing from India and the Treasury. Stalemate in Aden's hinterland was not enough; a substantial reduction of the garrison was what was really required to resolve the difficulty with India over Aden costs. There was, moreover, considerable dissatisfaction in London at a state of affairs in which Britain remained in a state of semi-belligerence with one of the major powers in Arabia, over a stretch of territory which the Service Chiefs believed there was little hope of recovering. The unsettled situation in the Yemen offered an invitation for other European powers to exploit the breach and upset things in Britain's Arabian preserves.

In March 1921 the meeting of Middle Eastern experts at Cairo had proposed offering the Imam a treaty, recognising his claims down to the frontiers of Lahej. The Resident managed to fend this off but the proposal came forward once more in the spring of 1922. The authorities in London had by then come to the conclusion that the proper strategy to follow was to do a deal with the Imam at the expense of the untrustworthy and undefendable Protectorate chiefs, get him to recognise Aden and Lahej as British, and bring him into Britain's orbit by making Aden his principal trading outlet.[54] The Resident was told to look again at the question of how much of the hinterland was needed for Aden's defence. The Resident dustily replied that the 1905 line was the most suitable. This was not the sort of answer London wanted, as the Permanent Secretary at the

Colonial Office pointed out. The military men in London were
practically unanimous in the opinion that Daliʿ and the distant
mountains could not be defended.[55] But, as in 1873, London had
let the time pass when a compromise could be made. With the clash
of arms in the neighbourhood of Lahej, party lines had hardened in
the hinterland. The Resident needed his tribesmen to maintain his
defensive system, and he in turn could not go back on his recently
assumed commitment to them. In July the Resident came to London
and successfully defended his position at a further meeting of the
Middle East Committee. It was decided that no compromise should
be made at the tribes' expense. In any case, as the Resident pointed
out, long discussions between Aden officials and an Imamic envoy
in the autumn and winter of 1921 had shown that the Imam was
much more interested in ousting Britain's ally Sayyid Idris from
Hudayda than in making gains in Aden's hinterland. Hudayda held
the key to the whole Tihama, which the Imam was most anxious
at this stage to wrest from his rival's hands. The Imam was well aware
that Britain could determine the Idrisi's fate. So were the Aden
authorities, and forced to choose between Idris and the Protectorate
tribesmen, they proposed that the former be bribed out of Hudayda
and that port given to the Imam.[56] To this the London authorities
reluctantly agreed, and preparations were being made to carry the
measure through when the principal object of the transaction,
Sayyid Muhammad al Idris, who had built the fortunes of his house,
died. In theory the Idrisi's death simplified matters for there was a
current of opinion in London that Britain's wartime treaty obligations to the father did not automatically carry over to his sons. But
in practice, the confused period that followed under his weak successors was deemed to be a bad time to broach so delicate a matter.
Before any decisive steps were taken Idrisi power was being torn to
shreds by Ibn Saʿud and the Imam and Tihama affairs evolved
toward a new equilibrium without any decisive British intervention.

Meanwhile the shape of the Middle East was steadily changing,
new patterns were crystallising out of the confusion of the war's
aftermath and the shape of the new forces which were to guide the
destinies of the area was becoming clearer. In November 1922 the
Ottoman Sultanate was abolished and in March 1924 the Caliphate
followed in its wake. The Islamic world and within it the Arab world
was henceforth an acephalous body and this required at least some
theoretical adjustments. Although Imam Yahya had robustly
asserted his independence of the Sultan, the Ottoman Caliphate had
offered the Yemenis, including the Imam, some semblance of
Islamic solidarity and order in the face of infidel encroachment.
Now the reality of Islamic and Arab disarray could no longer be

avoided while the challenging possibility of the emergence of a new leadership in Arabia aroused temptations and fears.[57] In the Fertile Crescent and Iraq the broad lines of the European mandatory and treaty regimes had been laid down by 1922 and the extent and limitations of the European states' power and objectives had become plain after the revolts, incursions and ripostes of the three previous years. In the Peninsula Ibn Rashid was eliminated by Ibn Sa'ud in 1921, and by the end of 1923 the Hashemite Kingdom in the Hijaz was also clearly doomed. Ibn Sa'ud and the fundamentalist Wahhabi Ikhwan emerged as the dominant power and the only other state which existed in the Peninsula other than by virtue of British protection was the Imamate of Yemen. The Yemen was beginning to look more and more like an island in a Wahhabi sea which threatened to engulf it by intrigue all round its restricted periphery.

The Yemen's predicament *vis-à-vis* the other forces operating in the Arab world possibly offers a partial explanation of the new tone and direction which the Imam's activity in southern Arabia began to assume between 1922 and 1925. Up to 1922 Zaydi pressure had been heaviest on the western and north-western borders of the Aden Protectorate, and could to a considerable extent be regarded as a mere extrapolation of the process of bringing adjacent areas in the Yemen under Imamic rule. There was even doubt in some cases as to whether encroachment was authorised from San'a' or whether it arose solely from the agressiveness of local commanders. In 1922 and 1923, however, the weight of the Yemeni thrusts began to shift from the west to the north-east border of the Protectorate, and military moves were backed by broader and more decisive political initiatives. Growing signs of Imamic interest in the Hadhramawt, as well as in the Yafi'i and other tribes of the east, from mid-1922 onward, culminated in a Zaydi advance to Baydha in June 1923, and the issue of a manifesto to the peoples of the Protectorate and the Hadhramawt outlining the Imam's programme. This latter document represented a curious blend of pan-Islamic and Arab nationalist ideas. On the one hand it looked to the past rather than the future. The fourteenth *hijra* century (which began in A.D. 1882) had been, the Imam said, a period of Muslim decline, and the Muslims were now no longer the honoured ones of the world. He attributed this to their disunity, and heavily stressed the necessity of returning to the unity of early Islam. Unity was to be found by a return to the fundamentals of religion – people must 'cease traversing the wrongful and misleading ways which lead us away from (God's) way, as directed by the Koran', Having spoken of the plight of Islam in general, the manifesto turned to the state of the Arabs in particular – the men through whom God caused the elevation of Islam, those who because they were unitarians in every respect had succeeded in conquering and occupying most parts of the world. They, more than anyone, ought to unite. And then the Yemen – it was one territory, with one people, one religion and one language; among the different sections of the population there was no difference except – and here was a point upon which the Imam strongly insisted – except for those who did not know the Shari'a and its clear and vast ways. Beyond the Yemen the Imam was not seeking authority or fiscal control, but merely wished to unite the Muslims; he would leave each country under its own rulers. Nor did he anticipate opposition from Britain in this, he asserted, for Britain also wished to see the unity of the Arabs. Although the administrative content was on the one hand less modern and on the other more Arab, this was the Ottoman pan-Islamic strategy in a refurbished guise and the conferment of swords and robes of honour on co-operating chiefs which went along with the manifesto made the resemblance to Ottoman methods more complete.[58]

There was a further slant to the Imam's circular letter which gave it a particular and specific significance. The descendants of the Prophet were singled out for special mention, and while the Imam addressed himself to all, he addressed himself more specifically to those men 'who are particularly honoured with the sense of precedence and reverence'. Various *hadiths* were cited referring to this theme, including the Prophet's words: 'I am leaving behind me the Holy Book of God and my descendants, and so long as you hold fast by them you shall never go astray'. The Imam himself was of course one of these sheet anchors of Islam, as were a good number of the learned men around him who had monopolised so many of the most important positions in the post-war Yemen. But these words were calculated also to strike sympathetic chords in some very troubled hearts in the Hadhramawt.

For some ten years the traditional social dominance of the Sayyids in the Hadhramawt had been under fire and by 1923 the dispute over the degree of respect which should be accorded to that class of descendants of the Prophet had reached violent proportions. Those who challenged the social and political position of the Sayyids came mostly from the rising class of wealthy tribesmen who, like many of the Sayyids themselves, had made their fortunes in Indonesia and the East Indies. The quarrel had first broken surface in Indonesia in 1905 with a controversy over the Islamic legality of a marriage between the daughter of a Sayyid and a Muslim who did not belong to the Sayyidi class. The question had serious social implications, since marital restrictions of this kind were one of the main props of the system of social differentiation in the Hadhramawt. At first the

Sayyids had the best of the argument since they possessed a quasi monopoly of Islamic learning. But in 1914 the Sayyids' opponents secured an effective intellectual leader when Ahmad Surkati, a modernising Sudanese teacher recruited by the Sayyids for their schools, was asked by them to state his view on this crucial issue. Surkati spoke against marital restrictions, was disowned by the Sayyids and at once taken up by the other party. The anti-Sayyid group, or 'Shaykhs' as they may be called, threw their weight and money behind Surkati. One of them was reputedly the wealthiest man in Batavia, and with the help of their enthusiasm and financial support a new organisation, the Irshad society, was formed in 1915 to promote Surkati's socially subversive opinions. Schools were founded in Indonesia and the Hadhramawt and efforts were made to root out Sayyidi influence in the Hadhrami communities at home and overseas. The Sayyids reacted strongly to all this. There were riots in Batavia in 1916. In the bitter polemics that followed, the Irshadis were accused of undermining religion and propagating bolshevism, while they in turn sought to disprove the authenticity of some Sayyidi genealogies. Ink and money flew fast and freely as each side fought over these deeply-felt matters of religion and social status.[59]

The conflict shook the whole Hadhrami body politic and drew in all who were in any way connected with that part of the world. The contesting parties sought to mobilise the Cairo press, the Quʿayti and Kathiri authorities, the turbulent semi-independent tribes, the British and Ottoman Governments and, later, the various rulers of Arabia. Each and all of these could in one way or another affect the course of the struggle. If ideas were to be propagated the consent of Governments in the Hadhramawt had to be obtained; if the people of the Hadhramawt were to be won over, both sides had to look to that crucial strategic factor in all Hadhrami disputes – the lines of communication between the homeland and the fields of fortune overseas. During the First World War the Sayyids were more successful than their adversaries in the game of politics. They had the support of the powerful coastal Sultanate of Mukalla through one of their number who was Wazir to the Sultan. They also had the support of the British Government, since the latter kept in line with Mukalla and was angered by Irshadi support for the Ottoman cause. So the Sayyids could move freely while their enemies were baulked at Mukalla and Batavia, where the British authorities did nothing to help them against the Dutch Government's anti-Arab immigration regulations.[60] But by 1922 the Sayyids had become dissatisfied with the performance of their friends. The Quʿayti Government began to waver and in 1924 swung over toward the other side.[61] The

British, relieved from the strain of war, were casting aside the categories of 'enemy' and 'loyal friends' and were less committed to their Sayyidi allies.[62] At the same time the Sayyids were seeking more decisive outside support, since their enemies were making headway among tribesmen beyond the reach of the Governmental authorities they could influence. In 1922 some even talked of seeking armed British intervention.[63] For the Imam of the Yemen here was a plum ripe for the picking. The Hadhramawt was rich – rich in wealth and, which was perhaps even more important to a man of Yahya's style, rich in talent and learning. Some of the Sayyids had already appealed to him by 1923 and if he had any doubts about supporting them rather than their opponents these would have been dispelled by the knowledge that the Irshadis were cultivating Ibn Saʻud, whose Wahhabi ideas, especially on the crucial matter of veneration for saints and Sayyids, accorded well with their own.[64]

This then was the further meaning of the Imam's manifesto of June 1923 and it was one which boded ill for British interests. The Aden Protectorate, as it had emerged in the years from 1873 to 1905, was not simply a means of keeping potentially hostile powers at a safe distance from the Imperial base. Since the 1870s Britain had been concerned at Turkish meddling with the Hadhramawt because of the latter's connection with Hyderabad. The preoccupation with the north-east frontier during delimitation (1902–5) and the negotiation of its north-eastern extension to the desert in 1914 owed much to the lively continuance of those fears. After 1923, with the fall of the Caliphate, this particular threat ceased to have the same meaning as before. But other preoccupations still remained. The South Arabian coastline was still regarded as strategically important to the extent that there was anxiety that it should not be allowed to fall into the hands of any other major power.[65] The best way of keeping other powers off this coastline facing India was by supporting the rule of the Mukalla Sultans who were in treaty relations with the British Government. This policy had served Britain well during the world war. While others had given aid to Britain's enemies, the Sultan of Mukalla had staunchly stood by his alliance and in return had received a loan of Rs.400,000.[66] Co-operation between Mukalla, the Sayyid party and the British had produced the Quʻayti–Kathiri Treaty of 1918, which established on paper Quʻayti suzerainty over the inland Kathiri Sultanate, and a British Protectorate over all.[67] British assistance was given to Mukallan agriculture and the Sultan in return had helped resolve a troublesome dispute between members of the ruling house at Lahej. Britain's good offices were invoked to settle a dispute over the succession to the Sultanate following the death of Sultan Ghalib of Mukalla in 1922. Relations between Aden and Mukalla were of the best.[68] No one wanted to see this agreeable arrangement replaced by the strange and unpredictable rule of Imam Yahya.

Yet in the autumn of 1923 it seemed that something of this sort was imminent. If the Imam could have pushed aside the tribal pawns on the desert edge to the North-East of the Protectorate he would have been able to put his hands on one of the major pieces in the game of Arab politics. There was not a great deal that Aden could do to stop him. Troops certainly could not be sent from the Aden garrison to the remote areas affected. Nor could the Bristol fighters of the R.A.F. Flight go there – their range fell very short of such an undertaking. Stop-gap measures had to be used until the defensive system of the west could be extended eastward to cover the threatened area. The Baydha Sultanate, which lay within the line conceded by the Ottoman Government in 1914, was first supported, then, in 1924, abandoned to the Zaydi.[69] To the eastward however, Bayhan, which commanded an important route into the Hadhramawt, was given extensive and continuous aid. In July 1923, 10,000 rounds of ammunition were issued to the Sharifs who had a Protectorate Treaty with Britain, followed by a flood of military assistance which totalled 126 rifles and 226,000 rounds by April 1925, considerably more than was given to any group of similar size elsewhere in the Protectorate.[70] When Baydha was invaded in strength by the Zaydi in September 1923, and alarm spread to the crescent of tribes from Upper Yafi' through Fadli country to the 'Awdhali and up to the Upper 'Awlaqi, further arms issues were made to those who were deemed to be most immediately threatened. The tribes could not be relied upon as an entirely effective shield, for they were riven by internal differences which could easily be exploited. They needed some stiffening and that Aden sought to provide in December 1923 by despatching a ship to reassure the Fadli Sultan at Shuqra and by constructing a landing strip in Fadli country from which air operations could be extended up to 'Awdhali country.[71] Efforts were also made to promote tribal unity in the face of the Zaydi threat. Long and patient negotiations were conducted with the leaders of the Upper Yafi' sections to this end during 1924 and 1925, using the offer of large arms issues as bait, though with very limited success.[72] Aden's main weapon was still the supply of arms, and these were issued on a massive scale. During 1924, 479 rifles were sent up and more than a million rounds of ammunition.[73] This, and the usual uncertainties of tribal politics, kept the battle swaying back and forth in the Baydha area throughout 1924. But officials in Aden and London were not very happy about the state of affairs and while this went on further efforts were made to come to an agreement with the Imam.

After some six years of desultory negotiations during which several draft texts had been examined and various discussions held, one might have expected that just about all that could be said about Anglo-Imamic relations had been said and that both sides would have concluded that their interests were hopelessly incompatible. But their interests were not necessarily incompatible, and it was this that made the negotiations so tantalising. British policy toward the Yemen retained its initial post-war ambiguity. Colonel Jacob may have been out, as far as the civil servants in the Colonial Office were concerned, but he was still shouting vociferously from the sidelines. From time to time the political heads of the Office listened to what he had to say, especially when the official approach seemed to be leading nowhere. And although the officials with their long memories could always use past proofs of Jacob's diplomatic inability to disqualify him as an adviser, his ideas had a ring of truth about them which could not be entirely ignored. Questions in the House of Commons as to why Britain had no commercial treaty with that important segment of the Arabian Peninsula could be embarrassing, and became more so after 1926, when first Italy and then the Soviet Union successfully negotiated such agreements with the Imam.[74] Within the Office, the idea of penetrating Yemen commercially had never been abandoned and the draft treaties of the 1920s were stuffed with clauses designed to make this feasible. But the officials were not prepared, as Jacob was, to buy their way in at the expense of making Aden's security dependent on the Imam's goodwill. On the other hand, their criticisms of what the Resident thought Aden's security required continued up to 1928. In 1923 they asked again for a more flexible approach to the question of the Protectorate's status and Aden had to fight for the pre-war line once more.[75] So the British position was not fixed, there was room for manoeuvre and some modifications were made, such as the dropping in 1923 of the clause giving Britain a special position in the Yemen *vis-à-vis* other powers. It was a general characteristic of British foreign policy in the 1920s to pursue the path of moderation and to believe in the possibility of negotiated solutions, and successes elsewhere buoyed up hopes that the Yemeni problem also could be satisfactorily resolved. But this same preference for compromise ensured that Aden's vigorously expressed views would never be discounted and therefore that the full Jacob programme could never be adopted.

Herein lay the tragedy of the negotiation, for while the Imam on his side was prepared to go a good way to meet the British, what he was prepared to offer overlapped only with the Jacob programme and did not reach the centre of the British negotiating position. This could be seen in the draft that he put forward in July 1924 after a further round of discussions at Aden during the previous January. He required a general recognition of his claim to his ancestral lands without specifying what they were, but in regard to 'the country south of the province of Yemen', that is the Protectorate, he only offered certain concessions in regard to the way he would administer the area over which he still claimed ultimate sovereignty. He undertook to leave the coastal states from Lahej to Mukalla inclusive and the lands of the Hawshabi and Yafi'i tribes under their rulers, with the single proviso that they act in accordance with the Islamic Shari'a. He would neither garrison nor send troops into their territory. Elsewhere – that is, in Dali' and other parts of the Protectorate – he proposed to rule directly, although using the Shafi'i and not the Zaydi interpretation of the Shari'a. The coastal states could continue their friendly relations with the British Government but would be responsible to the Imam 'in matters of the country and its affairs' – possible a reference to the power struggle in the Peninsula.[76] Thus the Imam was prepared to share influence in the Aden hinterland and coastal Hadhramawt with the British Government. He was not prepared to compromise on sovereignty. The formula was nearly identical with that put forward by the Colonial Office in 1921.

Was it simply a coincidence that the Imam had struck upon an arrangement which had been seriously considered earlier by the British Government? It is difficult to believe that it was. Imam Yahya had already shown himself to be a supple, patient and, despite his rigid adherence to his large theoretical objectives, a thoroughly practical negotiator. During the long dialogue he had conducted with the Ottoman Government between 1905 and 1913 he had talked and prodded and waited until the combination of forces in the Yemen and Istanbul turned in his favour, and finally concluded a satisfactory bargain with the parties most friendly to himself. He no doubt expected to repeat this performance with the British and his intelligence system, based on leakages from the Aden Secretariat, prolonged discussions conducted by emissaries at Aden, contacts with such men as Jacob and the European experience of his Turkish adviser Ragheb Bey, enabled him to see a good way into the minds of the other side. But not far enough. There are various indications that he overestimated the role of personality in the making of British policy and expected changing personnel to bring about dramatic changes in Britain's attitude.[77] It is highly doubtful that he imagined the real workings of the Colonial Office where the colourful characters – the Churchills and Lawrences – of the early post war-days had been replaced by the grey committee-men with their accumulating bundles of past papers, as British Middle Eastern policy passed from its constructive to its administrative phase. He could hardly

have envisaged the sheer immobility engendered by Aden's inter-
departmental status and the crucial role Aden officials were able to
play in the formulation of policy. Had he done so he would not have
sought to circumvent Aden as he tried to do in July 1924, when he
wrote directly to the King.[78] Had he done so he would perhaps have
realised that the pin-pricks on the frontier were counter-productive
in the sense that they made Aden more dependent on the tribes for
the organisation of defence and hence more committed to perpetuating their independence of his rule. Aden's commitment to the
tribes had already reached such a point by 1924 that compromise
was no longer possible, and those who participated in the discussions
thereafter were little more than actors in a drama whose scenario
had already been written.

' This became clear in January 1926 when Sir Gilbert Clayton was
sent to San'a' to make a serious attempt to come to an understanding with the Imam. The Clayton mission followed upon clashes
of arms on Aden's north-east frontier in July and October of 1925
between Zaydi troops and tribal (mainly 'Awdhali) forces fighting
under British air cover.[79] There had been two battles, one in July,
the other in October, and their upshot was that the Zaydi eastward
advance through 'Awdhali country had been stemmed, but the
fertile 'Awdhali tribal lands on top of the precipitous Khor al Awdhilla
had been lost, largely owing to the inability of the Bristol fighters
to operate effectively so far from their new base at Shuqra. Aden
was left with a new set of impoverished allies on its hands and with
some doubts about the efficacy of its defensive weapons. Hence the
renewed enthusiasm there and in the Colonial Office for negotiation.[80] But there was little left to negotiate with. When entrusted
with his appointment, Sir Gilbert Clayton was told that there were
only a few outstanding points to clear up.[81] But as he went through
the papers he realised with dismay that the gap between the British
and the Yemeni position was so great that his mission was almost
foredoomed to failure. The British draft he was given to work with
had been drawn up in the autumn of 1924 when Hudayda was
still in Idrisi hands. Since then the Imam had recovered that port
without British help or hindrance and therefore Britain had nothing
to offer in return for the Yemeni recognition of the Protectorate
frontier and treaties that the 1924 draft required.[82] Clayton therefore
had to rely upon his own considerable negotiating skill, the value
to the Imam of British friendship at a time when his relations with
Ibn Sa'ud were strained, and the veiled threat of reprisals if no
agreement was arrived at.

As it turned out, the negotiations at San'a' were lengthy, exhaustive
and not entirely unprofitable. After several days of preliminary

skirmishing during which the Imam discovered that Clayton had not come to hand over the Protectorate to him, the two men got down to serious business and devised a new basis of discussion which opened up at least the possibility of a temporary agreement. The new basis, which Clayton put forward on his own initiative, represented essentially an agreement to avoid the issue of the Protectorate's ultimate destiny while both sides disengaged from the area for the time being. Neither side was to renounce or to require recognition of its claims but both would sign a general treaty of friendship providing for commercial and military co-operation on a footing of equality and mutual advantage. Within this framework active discussions proceeded between the British and Yemeni delegations with regard to subsidiary points such as the degree of British military presence in the Protectorate to be permitted, the provisions to be made for security of trade routes, when and how much of the Protectorate Imamic troops would evacuate and the degree of recognition the Imam would accord to the existing treaties between Aden and the tribes. Difficulties over the last two points finally led to the breakdown of the talks; the Imam would not evacuate Dali' and refused to recognise the treaties. Clayton was insistent on both and thus the discussion ended. As it was, the Imam had gone further to meet the British than public opinion in San'a' would allow. When he presented a sketch of what he proposed to do to an assembly of notables he came under strong criticism. Learned men insisted on historic claims. Interested Governors protested at withdrawal from areas adjacent to their commands. The lesson Clayton drew from his experience was that the anti-foreign party in San'a', rather than the Imam, represented the real obstacle to agreement and in consequence that Britain should firmly defend its position in the Protectorate against further weakening encroachment either by a military expedition or by continuous promotion of tribal cohesion.[83]

Thus once more the sphinx's riddle of the Protectorate status had not been solved and the struggle between Zaydi encroachers and Aden-backed tribes was resumed. This was a particularly unhappy outcome of efforts to reach agreement and one is tempted to ask at this stage whether the sphinx's riddle had an answer and if so what it was. Were the tribes of South Arabia really the Imam's unwilling subjects or were they not? Unfortunately an answer to this question is not so easily given. One way of seeking an answer would be to examine the response of tribesmen to specific Imamic overtures. If one takes the attempts at the imposition of Zaydi rule over various parts of the Protectorate between 1919 and 1925 as useful examples, one must conclude that they were met with hostility but not with universal hostility. If one then asks whether one class of society was favourable while another was hostile, the reply is equally confusing – the 'Amir of Dali' was in both categories at different times. So, in a more subtle fashion, was the Sultan of Lahej. Certain sections of the Radfan tribes opposed the Imam, others on occasion accepted his authority. One may then shift the argument on to another level and ask whether the Protectorate tribesmen had any common pre-dispositions which would have led them to take a different attitude to the Imam's rule from that of the people in the Yemeni highlands who had already accepted it. A number of British officials said that they had. They said that being Shafi'i the tribesmen were opposed to a regime based on Zaydi principles. [84] Jacob however said this was not the case, that the difference was slight and could easily be sur-mounted. [85] One could point also to the the the fact that there were many other Shafi'i, notably in the Tihama, who had already accepted the Imam's authority, albeit reluctantly. Furthermore, the Imam in his manifesto of June 1923 had offered concessions on this point, with his proposal to appoint Shafi'i Hakims in Shafi'i areas. On the other hand the very fact that the Imam offered such a concession was itself evidence that he anticipated general objections to his rule on these grounds, and it is open to doubt whether his offer really affected tribal attitudes. It is likely that as far as most tribesmen were con-cerned, the Shafi'i-Zaydi question was merely a cover for their unwillingness to have any sort of courts imposed upon them. To say this is in fact to say that tribal resistance to Imamic rule amounted to little more than a preference for parochialism; that it implied not so much a refusal to enter the modern world of integrated states under the Imam's auspices, as a refusal to enter the modern world under any auspices at all. One cannot describe the Imam's Yemen in the 1920s as a modern state, but it was certainly a more integrated entity than the tribal confederations of the Protectorate and there was between the two what one might term a modernisation gap across which tensions were bound to develop. [68]

This means that serious discontinuities were very likely to emerge and that the onus lay upon the Imam to avoid or mitigate this. One way in which this could be done was by evoking a sense of con-tinuing historical indentity which would transcend temporary differences, and this was the method which the Imam principally used. The main burden of his case was his ancestral claim to Aden and the Hadhramawt; an argument for present in view of previous sovereignty. Such an approach however suffered from serious weak-nesses. Since identity was seen not in terms of affinity between the peoples concerned but in terms of a presumed common allegiance to the holder of the Imam's office, it was difficult to avoid the fact that the Imam's rule had not been exercised in most of the area of

the Protectorate since the early eighteenth century, and that the
ending of the Imam's authority had been the outcome in most cases
of rebellion, rather than of voluntary withdrawal. Such an awkward
fact could perhaps have been explained away had it been possible
to bring people to reject the interim period as being without historical
value. But the tribesmen of the Protectorate were not disposed to
blot out from their minds this part of their past. The memory of the
removal of Zaydi rule had a strong grip upon the popular mind in
most parts of the Protectorate outside Dali', there were historical
works available to document it, and the publication of *Haddiyat
al Zaman fi akhbar al Muluk Lahej wa 'Adan* – the story of the 'Kings'
of Lahej and Aden, by Ahmad Fadl al 'Abdali in 1931, must be
regarded as a form of counterblast to the Imam's historical propaganda, although it was equally aimed at the British.

This leaves the argument of coercion, that is, whether the Imam
could enforce acquiescence during the transitional period of integration into the political and administrative system of the Yemen. In
all likelihood the Imam could have forced most of the tribes to
accept his rule had the British not given them assistance against him.
At least he would have been able to occupy the principal fertile areas
and from thence exercised increasing influence over tribes dependent
on them. But without the acquiescence of the British, who had the
means to counteract the Imam's superiority in military equipment,
the tribesmen could not be overawed. Herein lay the relevance of
the prolonged Anglo-Imamic negotiations to the general political
evolution of the area. The tribesmen failed to unite in the face of
Zaydi encroachment, but most of those who opposed Imamic rule
sought Aden's assistance and thus made Aden into the focus of an
artificial unity for the purpose of resistance to the San'a' government.
British military weakness and inability to deal single-handed with
Yemeni thrusts ensured that the relationship between Aden and the
tribesmen was not one-sided. And so the British were not external
to the process of consolidating opposition to Zaydi encroachment
in the Protectorate area. They were part of it. Given tribal resistance
and British dependence on the tribes, a Protectorate antithesis to
the Imamic thesis began to emerge and with it a nexus of interests
involved in South Arabian or South Yemeni separatism.

CHAPTER XI

Air Power and Expansion

'Protectorate' is an ambiguous term. Essentially it belongs to the language of international diplomacy and defines an area over whose external relations the protecting power has exclusive control. In practice, however, and in common parlance by the early twentieth century, the word had come to be used as a euphemism for 'colony', and implied full control over internal as well as external affairs in the protected area. In the first sense the Aden Protectorate was built up between 1886 and 1918. In the second sense it did not emerge until the 1930s and 1940s, and in some parts, notably Upper Yafi' had still not emerged by the time of the British withdrawal in 1967. The Aden Protectorate as an administered territory was set up so late as to represent something of an anachronism – a new colonial conquest secured at a time when most parts of the then British Empire were beginning to move along the path towards responsible government and independence. One can hardly explain the new growth of British activity in Aden's hinterland during this period, after so many years of quiescence, in terms of some new drive for empire in Britain. During the early years of expansion in the 1930s, the dominant note in Britain was anti-imperialist and anti-militarist. Parliamentarians and public were generally hostile to the idea of extending Britain's overseas possessions, and absolutely opposed to paying for anything of the kind. Such attitudes were underpinned by the continuing shift in emphasis in defence matters from the world to industrial Europe -- a trend which had begun in pre-war days and which was largely confirmed by wartime experience. Had Parliament and the British public had anything to do with deciding whether the Aden Protectorate should be made effective or not, it is likely that they would have obstructed such a development or vetoed it altogether. But they were seldom asked. The Aden Protectorate like so many parts of Arabia under British control in the inter-war period was a bureaucrats' empire, planned by experts and administered by officials working here and there in co-operation with the semi-bureaucratic servants of large concessionary companies, which themselves were linked in one way or another with Government. There were few missionaries, private traders or journalists to urge

276

Government forward or hold it back or to transmit private reports and organise lobbies at home. Anyone who did not conform to the official line was liable to be squeezed out and the major determinant of policy was therefore the ideas flowing within the official system rather than those operating outside it. If one seeks some general explanation for the extension of British imperialism from Aden to the

Lieut.-Col. Sir Bernard Reilly, K.C.M.G., C.I.E., O.B.E., Resident at Aden 1931–7 and Governor 1937–40.

more distant lands of the Protectorate, it is to Schumpeter's rather than to Hobson's or Lenin's model that one must look.[1]

The main architect of the effective Protectorate, if any one man can be so described, was very much an official's official. Sir Bernard Reilly as acting Resident 1925–6 and as Resident, then Chief Commissioner and finally Governor between 1931 and 1940, presided over Aden's fortunes during the crucial period of expansion, and effectively laid down the broad lines along which the Protectorate was to develop from then onward. Sir Bernard Reilly was a dedicated professional who had followed his father into the Indian Army at the age of twenty and transferred to the Indian Political Service in 1908. Practically his whole life was devoted to Aden affairs. He first came to the settlement in the aftermath of the Curzonian period of expansion and worked as magistrate in the Arab town of Shaykh Uthman. He remained in Aden throughout the war, went with the Jacob mission to the Yemen in 1919 and spent months in patient negotiation with the Imam's representatives in Aden between 1921 and 1923. By the middle 1920s he was already beginning to speak on political matters with the authority of long experience, and when he became Resident in 1931 he was the longest-serving official on the Aden staff. No Resident since Haines had had such a long acquaintance with Aden prior to taking office; no one other than Haines held the highest post at Aden for as long as Reilly was to do. In ordinary circumstances Reilly would have had little chance of becoming Resident at all. In former days the post of Resident had gone to senior members of the Indian military establishment, while Reilly on appointment was a mere Lieutenant-Colonel. But in the days of the awkward India–Colonial Office dyarchy Reilly was an eminently suitable compromise candidate.[2] His heart was with the Colonial Office but his badges of rank were Indian. His selection avoided an unpleasant clash between the two administrations over whose man should get the post, and so officials on either side had reason to be grateful to him for his very existence, which provided them with a way out of an impasse.

His appointment was of a piece with the rest of Reilly's career at Aden. His special talent lay in oiling the wheels of the administrative machine. He knew how to delegate responsibility and to utilise the special abilities of those who worked under him while retaining control over the broad lines of policy. In a settlement where, since the beginning, there had been constant backbiting and intrigue among the British official staff, his careful tact and discretion won him the respect and affection of almost all his small band of colleagues. Over and above this, Aden officials had reason to like him because their interests and his were alike. He stood for expansion. Within Aden itself he had seen the effects of Curtis's slashing cuts in staff in 1912 and was determined to restore the administrative services to Curzonian levels. In the Protectorate he wanted a return to the policy of peace and social welfare abandoned in 1906. All this involved the creation of opportunities for men at Aden to exercise their talent for rule. Reilly enlarged the staff, took Aden out of the doldrums and substituted forward movement for the old circular diplomacy of the 'fortress' period.

It is not then so surprising that he was popular at Aden, although his predecessor, Maitland, had in similar circumstances between 1901 and 1905 achieved a quite opposite result. What is really rather difficult to explain is how Reilly was able to sell his policy of expansion to superior authorities who had no ambitious plans for Aden's future. Part of the explanation is that by the mid-1920s the Colonial Office had become exhausted by the effort of trying to extricate Aden from the administrative morass in which it was foundering. Even the civil servant's faithful standby – past papers – did not help because they said so many conflicting things. Most bureaucracies have an inherent preference for imposing patterns and eschewing ambiguity.[3] And so, men in London began to listen more attentively to Reilly's quiet, but firm and persistent voice, coolly repeating certain simple, straightforward and basically attractive ideas. Britain must honour her treaty commitments in the Protectorate; the 1905 boundary must be respected; Aden must be emancipated from Bombay's inhibiting control; and – after signature of the 1934 treaty of San'a' – peace must be kept on the Protectorate roads in accordance with that treaty.[4]

These ideas seemed on the face of it unadventurous enough. Indeed they were thoroughly conservative in form, harking back as they did to the work of the early years of the century and, in the case of road security, to the time of Haines and his successors. And there was nothing of the swashbuckling empire builder in Reilly's approach. He avoided the limelight, did not dramatise his work, seldom if ever engaged in abstract speculation about ultimate goals and objectives. He remained a little-known figure outside official circles even after his successful negotiation of the 1934 treaty with the Imam had won him a knighthood. Reilly was more or less absent from the minds of the great in Britain and so was his emergent empire. This was as he liked it; his style was to tone down all discussions and get his superiors to allow policies to emerge from the facts of the immediate situation.

Herein lay the key to his success, for the facts of the situation were changing dramatically in Aden's favour and making expansion possible as it had never been before. The most striking new fact was the emergence of air power as a new determinant of military fortunes in South-West Arabia. Previous technical innovations in weapons production had sapped but had not completely undermined the ability of men in the Arabian Peninsula to defend themselves. The introduction of fire-arms in the sixteenth century had placed them at a temporary disadvantage but they had soon succeeded in acquiring and learning to use these arms themselves, and with that, Ottoman rule had soon come to an end. In the nineteenth century the rifle and the mountain gun had again briefly swung the balance. But once again the problems of procurement and acquisition of skills were not too serious and by the end of the First World War they had been largely surmounted. The aeroplane however was a rather different proposition. It could penetrate the most inaccessible fastnesses and was especially effective in semi-desert areas where it could easily pin-point its targets. It was also expensive and difficult to purchase and required a pool of technically-trained men to maintain it which could hardly be produced by a society which sought to avoid contact with modern science. Yemen had had difficulty in finding artillerists. It

A Fairey 'Panther': the weapon that so dramatically changed the balance of power at Aden.

had even greater difficulty in finding aircraft mechanics, and for want of them the Imam's purchase of two aircraft from Italy in 1927 yielded him few advantages.[5] The tribes of South-West Arabia were in an even worse position. They had been able to buy rifles; the purchase of aircraft was quite out of the question and without them they were more or less at the mercy of outsiders. Thus the invention of the aeroplane finally destroyed the military basis of South Arabian isolationism. Henceforward the association of the people of South-West Arabia with larger political systems outside the area lay in the logic of history.

The British had been using aircraft since 1915 to bolster up the military defences of Aden and the results of their efforts against Yemeni encroachments have already been referred to.[6] In the

early 1920s however the British were only experimenting with the
weapon. In the highest quarters there was but limited confidence
in its efficacy and the other Service departments in London sought
to disprove its worth in order to divert what little money there was
available for defence into their own rather than the infant Royal
Air Force's coffers.[7] The turning-point came after the failure of the
Clayton mission to San'a' in 1926. That shook London's confidence
in the ultimate success of diplomatic action. To complicate matters,
other governments were now interfering in the affairs of South-West
Arabia. Hardly had the residual danger of Turkish intrigue been
scotched by the Lausanne Treaty of 1923 than first the Italian and
then the Soviet Governments opened relations with the Yemen.
Soviet Russia represented little danger to British interests, but the
Italians, with their Colony of Eritrea facing the Yemen across the
Red Sea, proved troublesome neighbours. They began to ask
embarrassing questions about the status of Kamaran Island which
Britain occupied but did not claim, and since 1922 they had been
involved in supplying arms to the Imam.[8] Thus the British monopoly
over Arabia's foreign relations was broken and it became more
difficult to put diplomatic pressure on the Imam. Hopes of persuading
him to withdraw from the Aden Protectorate faded and London
began to consider more seriously the question of how the Yemeni
soldiers could be forced back. The matter was referred to the War
Office and the army chiefs came back with the alarming estimate
that the operation would need a full infantry division at a cost of over
a million pounds.[9] Such a bill was unacceptable at that time of
financial stringency, and had the War Office been the only offerers
in the field, that would have been that. But at this point the Air
Ministry stepped in. They claimed to be experts in the business of
small-scale wars, after some notable successes in Somaliland and
Iraq. They were looking for opportunities to expand their vote by
substituting their own units for existing army garrisons in Colonial
territories and had had their eye on Aden for some time as a likely
place to take over. Now they came forward with a very attractive
offer. If Aden were transferred to them and made an air command
they guaranteed to deal with both its landward and part of its seaward
defence with one squadron of twelve bombers, an armoured car
section and a body of local levies. In other words they proposed to
extend to Aden the system which had proved so successful in Iraq
and other parts of the Middle East and they estimated that the full
cost would be about £100,000 less than the existing military establishment at Aden. This was much to the liking of the Treasury. The
Army tried to defend its wicket by heaping incredulity upon the
scheme but the Air Ministry had bought off the other Service

Department by withdrawing their objections to the Navy's scheme for the defence of Singapore and so was able to carry the day.[10] In 1927 the Air Ministry assumed responsibility for the defence of Aden. In April 1928 a squadron of bombers duly arrived from Iraq to take over from the single flight of aircraft which had been there since 1920 and over the next two years the two battalions of British and Indian troops which had formerly composed the garrison were withdrawn.[11]

This change in military control was of crucial importance for the future of Aden. For the systematic use of the new air weapon not only made expansion possible, it absolutely required expansion for its most efficient use. While Aden relied for its defence upon the natural advantages of its position and the superior firepower of its garrison and fixed armaments it was unsound strategy to fritter away the available forces on the defence of any part of the interior. Indeed immediately before the Air Force stepped in, the Government in London had all but decided to abandon to the Imam all but Aden's immediate hinterland.[12] But when the defence of the settlement depended upon the ability of aircraft to bomb an incoming enemy into retreat, the military command wanted as much room as possible to deploy the air weapon and as much prior warning as possible of an enemy advance in order to maximise the period of air attack. If the enemy were allowed to come to close quarters, aircraft would become ineffective and Aden with its small military garrison would be at his mercy. The new strategic doctrine of airpower therefore transformed the role of the Protectorate in British thinking. Dali' was no longer an indefensible outwork retained only for political reasons; it was now the first line of Aden's defence. And so also with other outlying areas in the Protectorate; if they were sacrificed to the Imam the new defensive arrangements would become less viable and the costly military garrison would have to be reinstalled. An intelligence network had to be established in the Protectorate to give warning of attack and this meant pushing political officers into the most remote areas. The armoured cars and the levies were not to sit behind Aden's walls where they would have been comparatively useless; they were expected to work in the Protectorate, building up a light defensive screen for use in conjunction with the air arm.[13]

The air system of defence also required a multiplicity of landing grounds to serve the comparatively short range aircraft of those days.[14] These were established in various parts of Aden's hinterland during the following decade to ensure the defence of the settlement. Others were cleared for use along the coast to the eastward, in the territories of the Sultan of Mukalla, in the Mahra Sultanate and in the lands of the Sultan of Masqat. They formed part of the air link between Aden and Iraq which was assiduously developed during the eight years after Aden became an air command. In 1932 the Air Officer Commanding at Aden met his opposite number from Iraq with a flight of aircraft in the Sultan of Masqat's territories, and four years later the first scheduled flights between the two bases began.[15] This represented a further development in the logic of the new air strategy for now Aden could be rapidly reinforced from the Royal Air Force's principal bases in the Middle East and was linked in with the other recently established imperial air routes reaching on to India and the East. The whole shape of imperial defence was changing. Air routes were replacing sea routes as defensive arteries, along which military units could be shuttled back and forth, especially in the Middle East where the Air Force was in control, and the security of landing grounds and airfields was coming to equal in importance the protection of naval bases and harbours.[16] In the new strategy Aden was still rather out on a limb; the main centres were still to the northward in Egypt and Iraq. But after the Second World War when the British were driven from those forward positions, Aden was to become their residuary legatees and take over the control of the whole Middle Eastern defensive network.

The Air Force's take-over of Aden's defence was accompanied by a stiffening of the British attitude toward the Imam. When tax-gathering time came round again for the people in the Yemeni controlled Dali' area in the spring of 1928 and the usual disputes and difficulties arose, the British moved more quickly than usual to the support of their adherents. On 8 February 1928 the 'Alawi and Qataybi Shaykhs, both British allies, were arrested for recalcitrance by Yemeni soldiers. Protests and ultimata were ussued from Aden and from 21 to the 23 February Yemeni positions in Dali' were bombed.[17] Still the Shaykhs remained in captivity, and London now decided to follow the Air Force's doctrine that aircraft knew no boundaries and demonstrate to the Imam that the British machines could strike at will at Yemeni territory.[18] Dali' was again attacked and for five days at the beginning of March the Yemeni head-quarters at Qa'taba, just across the border, was bombed. This brought on the most serious crisis in Anglo-Yemeni relations since 1922. Questions were asked in the House of Commons whether Britain was at war with Yemen and the same question was asked in many places in South-West Arabia.[19] The Imam began to talk angrily of an all-out attack on Aden, the Yemeni army was expanded and forces began to concentrate on the frontier at Mawiyah. At the same time diplomatic activity moved into high gear, a truce was arranged and Major Fowle the Acting Resident at Aden went with the Sultan of Lahej to treat with a representative of the Imam at Ta'izz. Aden was prepared for a rectification of the boundary which would have transferred to Yemen the people of the Jabal Jihawf and beyond, who had long been disloyal to the 'Amirs of Dali'. The Imam for his part released the captive Shaykhs. But London now pushed for a settlement of the larger issue of the Yemeni occupation of the Dali' plateau, and on this point the Imam refused to budge.[20] The informal talks at Ta'izz broke down and London authorised further air action while mobilisation went on in the Yemen and the people of Lahej began to flee to Aden in anticipation of hostilities.[21] For three weeks machines from Aden attacked selected targets in the Yemen and gradually this air offensive began to swing the balance of power in Aden's favour.[22] The increasing restiveness of the Tihama tribes posed a threat to the Imam's rear, and although Aden refused direct aid to dissidents there, the movements of aircraft were well calculated to encourage their revolt.[23] In the neighbourhood of the Protectorate border, Zaydi troop concentrations were broken up by air attack before they could begin their march. All this put heart into the Protectorate tribesmen and at the end of the first week of operations the Qataybi took a post which had been held by the Imam's troops for eight years. This tribal success and the onset of bad weather switched attention from targets in the Yemen to Dali' itself, which had hitherto been regarded as too strong to take. A force of tribesmen was gathered together and with a British Officer maintaining radio contact, an air and ground assault was launched against Dali' on 14 July which in two days resulted in complete success. A landing ground was hastily constructed, and with air support tribesmen drove off two counter-attacks during the subsequent month. At this point the Imam called a halt and issued orders to his forces to make no further attempts to cross the frontier. Thus Dali', which had been more or less under the Imam's control since the Ottoman departure, was brought back into the Protectorate and the former Turkish boundary was more or less restored in the north-west, leaving only part of 'Awdhali territory further to the eastward still to be recovered.

The Air Force had largely proved its point that aircraft could defend Aden at minimal cost. But not entirely so. Sceptics still maintained that it could not defend the settlement if thousands of Protectorate tribesmen decided to advance on Aden with Yemeni support.[24] The problem of internal Protectorate security still remained, indeed it bulked larger in British minds now that the Settlement was being steadily stripped of its ground forces. The success of the operations against the Imam's forces however made this problem easier to solve and in the euphoria following the recovery and consolidation of Dali' a great conference of Protectorate chiefs was called at Lahej in the first week of April 1929 to promote general solidarity among the tribesmen against Yemeni encroachment.[25] The conference was carefully prepared by the Aden officials and was intended to represent a new departure in British policy toward the hinterland. Words like 'darbar' and 'indirect rule' were bandied about and the acceptance of their applicability meant that the banner of 'Colonial administration' had been raised. The Protectorate was to be an administered protectorate and not an area of diplomatic manoeuvre. This was portentous for the future. For the present the 'liberal' policy of home rule and limited British involvement in internal tribal matters was still uppermost. This meant support for the *status quo*, for what was assumed to be the established order of the power of the chiefs. In fact, their power was indirectly augmented. They were given pride of place at the conference and efforts were made to whittle down their 'retinues' – that is all the others who thought they should have a say and a share of the pickings. For the future it was hoped that the visits of the chiefs to Aden would be more frequent and that less should be seen of their followers. Accordingly, the money allotted for entertainment of the latter at Aden was cut. Issues of arms to friendly tribesmen were also drastically curtailed, a measure which bore most heavily on the smaller groups.[26] In January 1929 the Subayhi rose in protest and were promptly brought to heel by air action. It was hoped that the chiefs would be able to settle the prevailing inter-tribal disputes at the conference and the ultimate aim laid down was a federation of all the chiefs of the western Protectorate to maintain solidarity against Yemeni encroachment and ultimately to bring about a more peaceful order in the whole area.[27] If the status of all chiefs was to be enhanced, one chief, namely the Sultan of Lahej, was singled out for advancement beyond all the rest. He was called on to preside at the conference. It was hoped that he would preside also over mediatory committees which might be set up to settle inter-tribal disputes. The First Assistant Resident, Major Fowle, maintained that Aden should pursue continuously and judiciously a policy of aggrandisement of the 'Abdali Sultan, and this was indeed done for several years following the conference, at the expense in particular of such tribes as the Subayhi.[28] Lahej got advanced military equipment and military advice from Aden when other groups were getting nothing and the Sultan benefited from transit dues on the large but faltering through trade from Aden to the Yemen.[29] As on previous occasions the 'Abdali ruling family profited most from British attempts to act more positively in the Protectorate.

While the Aden political officers were cajoling chiefs and trying to remould the old political system, mainly through its accepted processes, another set of officers was hard at work building a new organisation with men selected for their personal prowess and ordered along disciplined lines, with a chain of command through which were transmitted orders and not advice. The Aden Protectorate Levies was raised in 1928 as part of the new defence scheme to replace the last battalion of British troops which left Aden in 1929. It was not the first such force that the Aden Government had organised. In the last year of the war a body of men called the First Yemen Infantry had been formed, only to be disbanded when peace came. The only link between the Yemen Infantry and the Levies was one of personnel. Both were recruited by Colonel M. C. Lake and there was therefore a considerable carry-over of men from the one force to the other. There was a bias toward the fighting men of the east, notably the 'Awlaqi and 'Awdhali, in recruitment for both bodies.[30] When the Yemen Infantry had been raised, many of those groups in the western parts of the Protectorate who might have furnished volunteers were under fairly close Turkish control. As for the Upper Yafi'i, who had traditionally competed with the 'Awlaqi in providing mercenary soldiers, whether in India, the Hadhramawt or the Yemen, they had sent a contingent of 900 volunteers a few weeks too late, when all the places had been filled.[31] When the Levies were being recruited, the previous links with the east and lack of contact with other groups ensured a continuance of the 'Awlaqi preponderance. Apart from this particular bias there was a yet more evident and inevitable general bias toward the recruitment of men from the fighting tribes – men of the Sayyidi class of course would never join and there was scant enthusiasm for such a profession among the more settled citizenry and their ruling houses. The existence of the Levies therefore opened up a whole new range of contacts between British officers and sections and groups in South Arabian society hitherto scarcely known to the Aden administration. And the atmosphere in which those contacts were made was very different from that in which the Political Officers manoeuvred and bargained with the chiefs. In the Levies, officers and men were engaged in a joint endeavour, working within a single system, teaching and learning to apply order and method to the traditional art of South Arabian warfare and building up a feeling of comradeship in shared adventure.[32] For recruits with ability there was a ladder which led to the commissioned ranks – the first such opportunity within a British system accorded to men from the Protectorate. Friendships were forged in the Levies which were to mitigate many mutual suspicions and open the way to broader contact between the Aden administration and South Arabian society in a way which no paper policies could have done.[33] Not that the Levies were in origin or form a political instrument. Unlike the various other forces which mushroomed in the ensuing twelve years – the Tribal Guards, the Government Guards, the Hadhrami Beduin Legion and so on[34] – the Levies were trained along conventional British military lines for organised warfare in defence of the Protectorate as a whole and not to perform semi-political duties within it. But the very existence of the body and the personal relationships it produced opened new channels of communication which were to have a profound influence on the general aspect of Aden's relationship with the hinterland.

These new developments in the British outlook on Protectorate affairs were backed up by a deliberate attempt to reorient the town and port of Aden towards the hinterland.[35] Slowly the Colonial Office view that Aden should be treated as an Arab town and not as an outwork of India began to bear fruit. As the fortress mentality was discarded, Government schemes which tied Aden more closely to its hinterland were regarded with greater favour. In 1928, Sir Stewart Symes, the first Colonial Office-appointed Resident, put forward a scheme for extending Aden's medical services to the hinterland. The civil hospital was expanded and people from the Protectorate were encouraged to attend.[36] The private Keith Falconer Mission which had been running a dispensary in Aden was encouraged to extend its work inland. It undertook a training scheme for dispensers from the Protectorate and in 1937 established a dispensary in Dali'. The Air Force also contributed to this medical work as a deliberate policy and brought back serious cases from remote areas for treatment in Aden. The scale of operations was small – the civil hospital in 1936 still had no more than two doctors and the Keith Falconer Mission had a similar establishment – but what they did was appreciated, since curative medicine was one of the few things that South-West Arabia at that time was eager to have from outsiders. In 1932 the Sultan of Lahej established a dispensary in his capital with an Indian doctor providing similar services, mainly to the people of his state.[37]

Sir Stewart Symes hoped also that the improvement of Aden's educational facilities would ultimately benefit the people of the interior. In fact those facilities were, and for some time remained, rather unimpressive. In the early '30s there were less than a thousand pupils in three government and six aided primary schools and about two hundred pupils in three government Anglo-Vernacular secondary schools.[38] In the late 1930s less than five per cent of the slender annual budget was being spent on education. Instruction was given in the vernacular except for the final three classes where English was

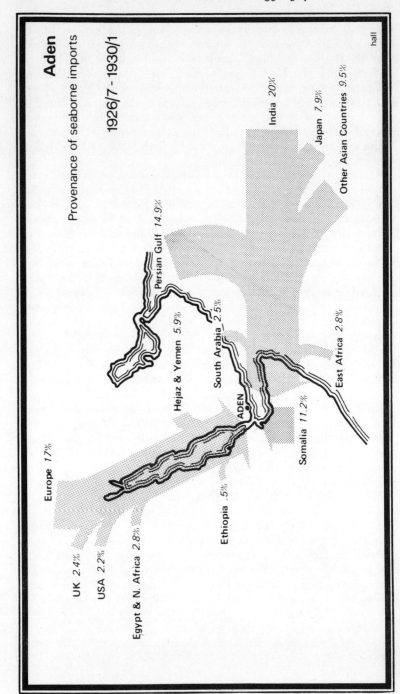

Aden

Provenance of seaborne imports

1926/7 - 1930/1

Europe 17%

UK 2.4%

USA 2.2%

Egypt & N. Africa 2.8%

Persian Gulf 14.9%

Hejaz & Yemen 5.9%

South Arabia 2.5%

Ethiopia .5%

ADEN

Somalia 11.2%

East Africa 2.8%

India 20%

Japan 7.9%

Other Asian Countries 9.5%

hall

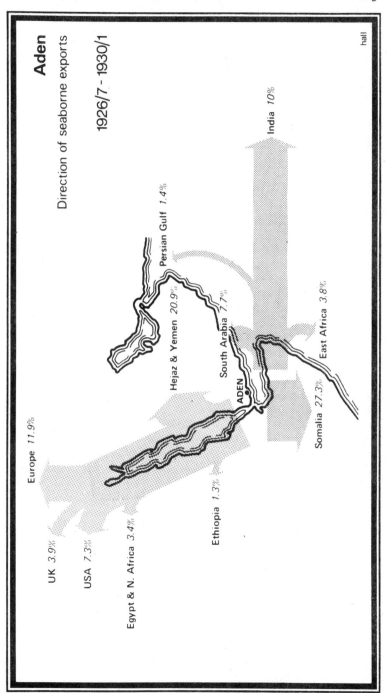

Aden

Direction of seaborne exports

1926/7 - 1930/1

hall

UK 3.9%

USA 7.3%

Egypt & N. Africa 3.4%

Ethiopia 1.3%

Europe 11.9%

Persian Gulf 1.4%

Hejaz & Yemen 20.9%

South Arabia 7.7%

ADEN

India 10%

East Africa 3.8%

Somalia 27.3%

introduced along with commercial subjects. During this period, however, there was a significant shift in the composition of the school population. More Arabs were now being brought within the ambit of this modern educational system where, although they were still under-represented by comparison with other communities, such as the Indians and Jews, they had by 1936 become the predominant group in the male school population. Small as it was, the Anglo-Vernacular school, with five graduate and three other teachers, maintained high standards and by 1935 was largely supplying the demand for clerks in the settlement. From these small beginnings a more Arab-oriented civil service began to emerge, and with it a small group of men with a modern education was formed. In 1937 this was followed up by the establishment of a college for the sons of chiefs, with the direct object of producing men versed in more modern methods of administration to fill key positions in the Protectorate.[39]

A more immediate impact was made by the reorganisation of the police force – a body which consumed a much larger proportion of Aden's budget and which was a much more prominent feature of the essentially 'law and order' government of the settlement than any of its social welfare branches. The Aden Police had, since its establishment by Haines in 1840, been an exclusively Indian organisation, recruited in India and run on Indian lines.[40] This was regarded as unsatisfactory by the Colonial Office, on grounds of expense at least, and from 1928 onward, against the stiffest opposition from the Bombay Legislative Council, which treated the orientation of the police force as a key issue, a policy of Arabisation was undertaken.[41] At first only the armed police was affected. It was so much expanded to fill the gap left by the withdrawal of the military garrison that it became in effect a new and separate organisation. The Colonial Office paid part of its cost and therefore had a more effective say in determining its composition. It was intended to be a para-military force rather than a constabulary and so the qualifications for admission could more easily be met by uneducated men from the Protectorate. By 1931 there were 112 Arabs on the strength and in the following year these men proved their worth by stolidly and impartially maintaining order during three days of Arab–Jewish rioting – the first that Aden had experienced.[42] After 1937 when the settlement's last links with India were broken and it became a colony, the same policy of Arabisation was applied to the Civil Police, and its composition gradually changed. Arabisation in the case of the police meant recruitment from the Protectorate rather than from Aden itself. As with almost every other military or para-military body recruited in the 1930s, the nucleus of the Armed Police was taken from the Aden Protectorate Levies, with the same predominantly 'Awlaqi-'Awdhali mixture as was to be found there. And the Civil Police was quite naturally recruited first from the ranks of the Armed Police, thus perpetuating the bias. The men of the more distant parts of the Protectorate were much more heavily represented in the police than among the general populace of Aden Town.

In Aden town the population was continually being swelled by the now traditional immigration of seasonal and semi-seasonal labour from the Yemen. The war, which had brought a large influx of Indian troops and their followers, while incoming Yemenis had found their passage hampered, had temporarily swung the balance towards the Indians. But in the inter-war period the pendulum swung heavily back the other way and the final departure of the Indian garrison in 1929 gave it a further push. The total population between the wars exceeded by some twenty per cent the number reached in the period 1891–1914.[43] Business was brisk in the 1920s. The pre-war entrepôt trade revived with a boom in 1920, then levelled out at slightly above the pre-war rate. Hides, skins, and coffee once more poured out and cotton goods (coming increasingly from Japan rather than India and elsewhere) poured in. The saltpans and the tobacco factories were active and in 1932 they were supplemented by soap manufacture. Then came the slump, first felt in 1929–30, followed by further losses in the next five years until the value of the trade flow had sunk below wartime levels. Aden's bunkering business on the other hand fared rather better in the 1930s than in the 1920s. In the first decade after the war, Aden was faced once more with competition from Perim, to such a degree that between 1923 and 1927 Perim was putting more coal aboard passing vessels than Aden.[44] Once again Aden was suffering from the shallowness of the harbour and the increasing draught of more modern ships. The Port Trust however took the matter in hand with greater promptitude than in the 1880s. At the end of 1928 dredging work began and by 1930 the harbour had berths available for the largest ships.[45] An oil-bunkering depot had also been established in 1920 and from 1924 onward Aden could afford to watch some of her former customers going to Perim to coal, for the island had hardly any share in the fast-growing oil fuel business.[46]. It was with oil that the future lay as became suddenly and devastatingly clear when the depression struck shipping in 1929–30. The older coal-burning steamers were immediately axed from the world's fleets. The coaling business collapsed and with it went Perim. Aden on the other hand weathered the storm. With a slight and temporary setback in 1930, the number of oil-burning vessels using Aden steadily mounted throughout the depression years, and even the coaling business got a bonus from the bankruptcy of Perim after 1935. By the time the war broke out, Aden was primarily an oil-bunkering port in a world of mainly oil-fired ships. It was also now closer than any other major bunkering station to the cheapest supply of fuel in the Persian Gulf. Perim was the first competitor to fall; others at a greater distance were soon to follow suit as the full extent of Aden's geographical and other advantages became effective.

Thus Aden's continued prosperity was assured and on the basis of the thriving bunkering trade the economy of the town began to diversify. Aden became less a town of coal heavers and camp followers and more a place where man engaged in a variety of trades. More men were drawn into engineering workshops to handle shipping repairs and to service the increasing number of motor vehicles which had first appeared before the war and which had so multiplied as to require bituminised roads by 1931.[47] In 1926 a small electric power station was set up at Hidjuff. In 1934 it expanded and in the following year electricity was supplied to Shaykh 'Uthman.[48] The substitution of piped water from bore wells for scarce and expensive supplies from condensers between 1931 and 1935 further altered the Aden scene. It was coupled with an overhaul of the sanitary arrangements which until then had been deplorably inadequate.[49] Aden was gradually acquiring the ever more elaborate amenities that marked a modern town even before its take-over by the Colonial Office in 1937 released further funds for improvements. Each step forward widened the range of services as against the old staple industries of Port and garrison, and each major public works undertaking brought into employment a new wave of migrant labourers.

Despite the efforts of the Government, Aden was not becoming more integrated economically with its hinterland. If anything, as the settlement changed with the world urban industrial society of which it was a part, the gap between it and the hinterland grew rather than diminished. The trade which linked Aden with the hinterland affected a proportionately smaller section of the community as other branches of activity developed. In 1937 the landward imports to the settlement were much as they had been in the time of Haines. *Qat*, firewood and fodder still bulked large and the contribution of fruit, vegetables and livestock had only marginally grown.[50] India was still providing a substantial part of the settlement's provisions.[51] Moreover, the landward trade suffered disproportionately from the 1930s slump; while Aden's total trade fell to about 60 per cent of its 1920s value, its landward trade fell to less than half that of the pre-depression period.[52] Political problems complicated those produced by the fall in the price and demand for primary products.

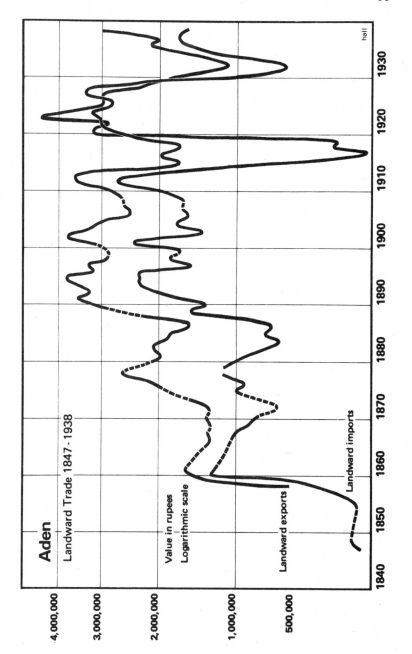

Aden

Landward Trade 1847 - 1938

Value in rupees
Logarithmic scale

Landward exports

Landward imports

hall

Those who controlled the hinterland trade routes expected constant returns from dues, whatever the state of the market, and when they did not receive them there were outbreaks of violence.[53] The roads became increasingly unsafe in the early 1930s, disputes of all kinds reached a new climax, and to add to all these troubles, the Imam decided in 1932 to close the road to Aden, thus cutting off some of the most lucrative transit traffic and causing confusion among those in Aden and Lahej who organised and profited from the Yemen trade.[54]

The Imam's trade boycott represented another feint in the long sparring match between Aden and the Yemen. Since 1928 negotiations of one sort or another had gone on without cease. Contacts had been maintained through letters and through Imamic emissaries, through accredited British agents and through private persons, through the American Consul at Aden and through the Italians at Eritrea, and through visiting Yemeni personalities in Egypt and Ethiopia. Drafts and counter-drafts of proposed treaties went back and forth, mainly based on the two themes of a simple frontier standstill agreement and a broader and more general treaty between Britain and the Yemen. Negotiations were kept turning over, speeded up or broken off as each party sought tactical advantages.[55] Certain underlying conditions remained constant, namely the refusal of the Imam to renounce his ultimate claim to Aden's hinterland and the refusal of the British Government to give up its treaty rights and hand over the hinterland to the Imam's control. Certain other underlying conditions encouraged attempts at compromise. Both parties remained weak in the face of internal resistance to their rule while the power across the border was hostile. Although Aden did not encourage revolt in the Imam's territories, rebellious tribesmen in south western Yemen took advantage of any clash between the Imam and the British. Likewise the British had to handle disorderly elements and plunderers on the roads with care for fear of driving them over to the Yemen.

On broader grounds both parties stood to gain from friendly relations. The Foreign Office was uneasy at the possibility of other powers gaining significant influence in the Yemen and thus affecting the situation elsewhere in Arabia;[56] the Imam was painfully aware that his neighbour Ibn Sa'ud derived considerable advantage from his friendship with the British Government. While the frontier difficulties continued, Britain refused to allow the Imam to purchase British arms, while Ibn Sa'ud did not suffer from this disability. On the other hand these factors making for compromise were of varying importance. The danger of friction with Italy was considerably reduced by an agreement made in 1927 providing for consultation between the two Powers on Arabian questions.[57] This diminished the risk of European involvement in the disputes between Ibn Saʿud and the Imam. It also diminished Britain's potential usefulness to the Imam in any conflict with his neighbour, for Britain could not act freely or for example transfer Kamaran and other coastal islands either to the Imam or to Ibn Saʿud without bringing Italy into the affair. The failure of the Italians to make any notable progress in the xenophobic Yemen and indeed the failure of most other outsiders to get any sort of footing there tended to allay Foreign Office fears – after all British policy was to keep others out of the Yemen rather than to push British influence in, and if the Imam maintained his complete independence there was no need for a treaty to bind him to do so.[58]

As for internal conditions in the Yemen and the Aden Protectorate, the disadvantage of having no settled understanding gradually swung to Aden's side after 1930 as the Imam settled his southern provinces, and unrest in certain areas of the Protectorate became more irksome to the Aden Government. The areas that worried Aden most after 1928 were Bayhan and ʿAwdhali. Both were strategically placed with regard to the Hadhramawt, and the Hadhramawt's importance to Britain was greatly enhanced as the coastal air defence route to the East was established. In addition the increasing numbers of ʿAwdhali and ʿAwlaqi in the ranks of the Aden Levies and the Armed Police kept the fate of the ʿAwdhali's Yemeni-occupied upland fields constantly before the notice of British officers and involved the Aden administration more closely in the severe internal disputes which split the ʿAwdhali people. Fear about the 'loss of British prestige' arising from failure to protect treaty rights against Yemeni encroachment was now coming to mean more precisely the loss of face of British officers before their ʿAwdhali and ʿAwlaqi colleagues and soldiers. Yemeni inroads into Subayhi country for example began to dwindle into comparative insignificance as Zaydi money and intrigue brought into question the allegiance of Aden's main recruiting grounds in the East.[59] The R.A.F. was less worried than the political men and the Air Ministry in London seldom had a good word to say for negotiation with the Imam. The ideas of heavy retaliation, deep penetration and concentrated bombing were gaining around among the airmen. As applied to South Arabia this meant a shift in emphasis from co-operation with tribal forces against limited objectives, to independent action by bombers against the main Yemeni centres. The Air Ministry was confident that it could adequately defend the Protectorate and was suspicious of any treaty terms which might inhibit their future action.[60] While the R.A.F. was developing this more extreme doctrine, the Aden administrators like Reilly began to appear more and more in the guise of moderates. By 1933 they had come to believe that Britain definitely had something to gain by concluding a treaty with the Imam;[61] they were annoyed by the trade boycott, saw the obstacle Imamic hostility presented to the peaceful economic and social development on which they had set their hearts and hoped that a negotiation backed by force could rid them of the increasingly dangerous 'Awdhali problem. As they watched the desultorily deteriorating relations between the Imam and Ibn Sa'ud, their hopes of bringing the Imam to terms rose, fell and rose again. On the other side the Imam came to realise that he could get no better bargain than that offered by the Aden authorities, that airmen could be worse than political officers and that the growing Sa'udi threat made an accommodation with the British essential.

It was on this basis that the Anglo-Yemeni Treaty of 1934 was negotiated. During 1933 worsening relations between the Imam and Ibn Sa'ud on the one hand and a deterioration in the 'Awdhali situation on the other drove the two sides closer together. In June the Imam offered a set of proposals which came close to what the British Government would accept and in August at a meeting of the Committee of Imperial Defence in London it was decided that the time was ripe to send Reilly to San'a' to negotiate an agreement, while separately requiring the evacuation of 'Awdhali territory under threat of air bombardment.[62] At the end of November the Imam indicated that he would welcome a British mission led by Reilly, and on 15 December the Chief Commissioner left Aden for the Imam's capital. The discussions were conducted in a friendly atmosphere, but there was very hard bargaining over the text of the treaty and especially over the ownership of frontier locations and the affiliations of border sub-groups. The latter represented the main substance of the agreement for the treaty, as far as it treated of the Protectorate, amounted to no more than an agreement to let the existing situation stand for the next forty years. In place of the many drafts bandied back and forth over the previous sixteen years in which all manner of different formulae had tried to reconcile British and Imamic claims, the 1934 treaty simply said that the two parties 'agreed to maintain the situation existing in regard to the frontier on the date of .. signature..'. What the frontier situation was to be on the date of signature caused the greatest wrangles for the question of the 'Awdhali evacuation came in here. After a threat to break off the negotiation Reilly was able to induce the Imam to evacuate sixty-four 'Awdhali and eight Dali' villages still in the hands of Yemeni forces, and on this basis the treaty was signed. The primacy of the frontier problem over all other aspects of Anglo-Yemeni relations was highlighted by Britain's agreement not to ask to send a permanent representative to the Imam's capital. The appointment by both sides of frontier officers who would seek the solution of any disputes which might arise was regarded as sufficient. The British Government was not enthusiastic about sending a representative to San'a', since it would encourage other powers to do likewise. In like fashion no great effort was made to secure large trade concessions; there was no enthusiasm now for British commercial penetration of the Yemen. The British Government was content to leave the Yemen in its isolation, and here they saw eye to eye with the Imam and his advisers, who wanted nothing more.[63]

What the Imam got from the treaty was an assurance of British friendship. The British Government formally recognised his independence which, although it was no longer a serious issue, was nevertheless a point gained. More importantly, it brought the period of hostility between the two Governments to an end which had the immediate effect of removing the British embargo on arms. Without the treaty the Imam would not have had the thirty-five armoured lorries he had ordered before negotiations began, which reached him through Aden after Sa'udi forces had occupied his port at Hudayda.[64]

The Aden authorities for their part were freed from the uncertainties which the unsettled frontier produced both in the Protectorate and in the formulation of policy. The trade boycott was lifted and the movement of commodities between the Imam's territories and the Protectorate revived. Reilly made much of this aspect of the agreement. He noted that he had found that peace was better kept in the Yemen than in Aden's hinterland and that the Imam had complained and made disparaging comments on the insecurity of communications in the Protectorate. 'Peace on the roads' now became the slogan of the Aden Government – a slogan which could be said to have the Imam's approval, which should commend itself therefore to even the most circumspect officials in London and which could easily be represented as the absolute minimum that a progressive government could require in the territories for which it was responsible. Under this slogan of 'peace on the roads', the structure of law and order government was steadily erected piece by piece in the Protectorate in the ensuing years.[65]

Promptly on Reilly's return the process of opening the roads began. The Aden Government had already in 1931 declared its intention of maintaining road security; now swift action was taken to show that that declaration would be made effective. In February 1934 the Bakri sub-tribe, which interfered with a caravan moving down the Wadi Hardaba, were immediately bombed and in the following month a bombing campaign started against Qataybi plunderers which lasted sixty-seven days, and ended with their agreeing to a fine and the surrender of hostages.[66] These demonstrations frightened other potential disturbers of the peace for a time. But by now Aden realised that bombing was not enough. It had been done before and had produced a temporary lull, after which trouble always recurred. There were too many reasons for men to plunder – falling trade, the threat of lorries to many tribesmen's livelihood, the diversion of traffic to the new motor road constructed by the Sultan of Lahej between his capital and Ta'izz in 1934, the periodic recurrence of famine, as in 1937, and the welter of blood-feuds which produced a divided and disorderly society rich only in thieves and men of violence.[67] Aden knew that it was essential to follow up the bombing, which none liked, with such other measures as could be taken within the framework of the existing policy of non-interference in internal affairs. The power of the chiefs was therefore further strengthened. The Lahej Sultanate's army was reorganised by British officers and re-equipped with modern weapons, including machine guns.[68] This was the start. In the next five years similar forces mushroomed all over the Protectorate under British auspices financed with British money. A number of attempts had previously been made over the years at Dali' to provide the 'Amir with a disciplined body of men. Now, starting with the Hawshabi and 'Awdhali in 1934 and Fadli and Dali' in the following year, Tribal Guards were organised under British supervision around nuclei of ex-Levies N.C.O.s for most of the rulers in the Aden hinterland.[69] By 1937 even this was not regarded as enough, and a new control body, the Government Guards, was raised, as a temporary measure in the first instance, to back up the Political Officers and hold the ring while the system of Tribal Guards was developed and consolidated. The Aden staff responsible for Protectorate affairs was enlarged in 1934 by the appointment of another Political Officer. This official was assigned to no particular area of the Protectorate; he was expected to tour, to assist the measures taken to strengthen the existing authorities, to watch and to report on infringements of road security. The man chosen for this task was a vigorous army officer, R. A. B. Hamilton, who had already gained considerable knowledge of tribal politics through three years' command in the Levies, and it was not long before he shifted from watching to taking independent action.[70]

Hamilton was most active in those fringe areas where the jurisdiction of the recognised chiefs was weakest. Where the Mawiyah–Lahej road reached across wild country to the east of the now

pitifully weak Hawshabi's capital at Musaymir, where the Dali'
road plunged down through the inhospitable Radfan mountains
under the eyes of the powerful Ja'ud and Qataybi confederations,
and in the remoter Subayhi deserts, Hamilton did his most effective
work. It was work of conciliation as well as of control, for while he
sought out and attacked with air and ground forces those who
plundered travellers or sought to block the roads, he also established
closer contacts between Aden and the larger tribal confederations
like the Qataybi and the Ja'ud, and sought to reassure them that the
extension of the British-backed peace did not mean their subjection
to neighbouring chiefs. In 1938 he also tried with temporary success
to stop feuding over a large area of Subayhi country by bringing
in his newly formed Government Guards to exploit the effect of an
especially prolonged bombing campaign in that area. Constantly
on the move, knotting and unknotting local alliances and intrigues,
shoring up one authority here, encroaching on another there,
Hamilton never had time to impose any very permanent pattern
on the relationships between men and groups on the roads fanning
westward and northward from Aden to the Yemeni border.[71]

In the Fadli Sultanate, however, Hamilton and other officers
made British control felt in a much more continuous fashion. There
the Sultan was weak; two important routes from Yafi'i and from
'Awdhali and the east debouched toward the sea; the land was
potentially rich but remained poor, while Yafi'i and Fadli quarrelled
over payment for the waters which could have fertilised the fields.
The origins of the Fadli–Yafi'i dispute stretched back into the
nineteenth century, to the time of Merewether's expedition and
beyond. In the 1930s it was as lively as ever and Aden hoped that
the Lahej Sultan would be able to solve it by his mediation.[72] The
'Abdali wrestled with the problem in vain and in the summer of 1934
Aden officials began wrestling at his side with little more success.
It was an 'internal affair' between the tribes, not a matter of road
security, and therefore outside Aden's then normal terms of reference.
Reilly felt he could not impose a settlement.[73] But Hamilton could
pursue those who carried the quarrel on to the road and after an
agreement had been reached and signed by Fadli and Yafi'i Sultans
under the Resident's auspices in September 1934, he did so with the
greatest vigour.[74] In July 1935 the Ahl Haydara Mansur, a sub-
section of uncertain allegiance who had desultorily defied the Fadli
Sultan for more than sixty years, murdered six Lower Yafi'i
travellers. A heavy fine was imposed upon them and exacted under
threat of air bombardment.[75] In November of the same year another
of the Fadli's 'dissident' sub-tribes, the powerful and turbulent
Marqashi, narrowly escaped a heavy bombing for trying to exact

their annual blackmail from the Fadli Sultan – and through him from the Abyan cultivators. In July 1936 a section in the similarly 'dissident' Dathinah area were forced by air demonstrations to pay a fine for misdeeds through their Fadli overlord. November 1936 saw the Ahl Haydara Mansur fined again, this time to the point of total ruination, for robbery on the Aden road and defiance of their Sultan. A year later after yet another incident, the reluctant Fadli Sultan was pushed to establish his authority in the Ahl Haydara Mansur's hometown of Dirjaj while R.A.F. planes watched from above.[77] By the end of 1937 few could have doubted in Abyan that it was the British Government and its political officers who were maintaining order and that the Fadli Sultan had become little more than their agent in this respect.

Further east, the chiefs were still very far from becoming British agents, although British strength was beginning to be felt in their countries too. The 'Awdhali Regent, who ruled on behalf of his infant nephew after murdering the previous Sultan, could still look British officers in the eye. They were painfully aware of their failure to protect his land from Yemeni incursions between 1925 and 1934 and felt a debt to those 'Awdhali authorities who had refused to go over to the Imam. The 'Awdhali were favourites of the Protectorate administration. Their leaders had been given arms and money to sustain their fight with the men across the border and after 1934 the Regent got his Tribal Guards and air assistance against those who defied his authority.

Beyond 'Awdhali, the 'Awlaqi confederation and Bayhan still seemed remote. To the 'Awlaqi Sultan and many of those around him, their relationship with the port of Aden was little different from what it had been a hundred and more years before – that of the distant but powerful and menacing blackmailer and his rich merchant clients. But things were changing quickly. The large numbers of 'Awlaqi in the Levies bore witness to another sort of British activity. The network of landing grounds was extending eastward, and with them came the aircraft, the R.A.F. Intelligence Officers and the patron of the 'Awlaqis on the Aden Protectorate staff – Colonel Lake.[78] At first these men came in the guise of travellers and guests. But forceful interventions around the edges of the 'Awlaqi territory began to give them a somewhat different character. In 1935 air demonstrations forced a dissident Aqil back under the 'Awdhali Regent's control and dealt with a case of robbery in Bayhan.[79] In June 1936 an example was made of a section of the Lower 'Awlaqi, who challenged a Political Officer's right to move freely in their country. Twenty-three aircraft from three squadrons flew up from Aden and blockaded them for seven days until they surrendered to the Political Officer and paid a fine.[80] In 1938 aircraft moved up again to Shabwa beyond Bayhan and helped Hamilton and two hundred and fifty locally-raised men to push back a Yemeni incursion and establish a temporary peace. The east was also gradually feeling the pressure of Aden's hand.[81]

Thus in the western Protectorate the Political Officers were gradually coming to represent new nodes of authority, aiding the power of some, and cutting into the area of control of others of the recognised chiefs. Which received one treatment and which another depended very much on the personal predilections of the Political Officer concerned. Hamilton and the Sultan of Lahej did not like each other, but Hamilton was not the Aden Government.[82] Aden still more or less followed the policy of 'Abdali primacy and the Sultan of Lahej alone of the Protectorate rulers served with the Resident, the Air Officer Commanding and their advisers on the Protectorate Affairs Committee, which informally decided where and what was to be done in the Protectorate after the discontinuance of the Lahej Conferences in 1934.[83] The 'Abdali Sultan still negotiated and mediated outside his territory with Aden's blessing and co-operation – in Fadli country, on the Dali' road, in Upper Yafi'i. His army gave him added strength and some shrewd purchases of land in Abyan in 1934 and 1935 diversified his income.[84] As for the other chiefs, they too were deliberately strengthened by the Aden Government. The final abolition in 1937 of recommendatory letters and ammunition issues stopped the old system by which Adens' largesse reached the tribesmen through the chiefs. Instead, the money involved – which had come to represent a substantial proportion of some rulers' budgets – was assigned to specific projects for improving and developing the chief's administration, notably the establishment, equipment and payment of Tribal Guards.[85] The role of the chiefs was changing, or being changed, as fast as Aden's new initiatives could outpace their absorption by 'corruption' and other ways into the traditional pattern. The chiefs too (that is, those closest to Aden) were becoming nodes of authority in a patchwork system of British-imposed order which was slowly and falteringly becoming the pattern in Aden's hinterland.

It was in the Hadhramawt, however, that the greatest progress was made, for there was a stronger desire for peace and already powerful Arab authorities ready to organise it.[86] There too, people had a livelier sense of the necessity of introducing modern education to keep Hadhramis abreast of educated Indonesians and Egyptians.[87] The progressive Irshadi movement had lost none of its vigour; it was actively spreading its ideas of social reform among the remoter tribesmen. And in competition with the Irshadi the more progressive

leaders among the Sayyidi class were anxious to spread their influence
within and beyond the Wadis and draw all within the circle of
ordered and progressive government. Most of the returned and
visiting emigrants from the Far East, whatever their persuasion,
were anxious for the ending of the feuds which made life unsafe
throughout the area and hampered the introduction of modern
amenities. But unfortunately the cleavages within this group,
especially over the position of the Sayyids, had produced a deadlock
which paralysed much of their effort. Indeed the competition of the
two parties for the control of uncommitted tribesmen tended to
exacerbate strife as each sought in the end to arm themselves and
their allies against their rivals.[88] The alliance with the Qu'ayti
Sultanate remained the linchpin of the Aden Government's policy,
and as the tempo of that policy quicked with the building of a chain
of landing grounds through the Hadhramawt toward the Persian
Gulf, the links binding Aden and Mukalla drew tighter. Most of
the desirable sites for airstrips lay in Qu'ayti territory and the
Sultan made agreements with other chiefs to secure control of those
not already in his dominions.[89] Aden was therefore more than ever
committed to working with the Mukalla Sultan and since, during
the crucial period when Aden was pushing its tentacles eastward, the
Sultan was closely linked with the Sayyidi party, Aden became pro-
Sayyid too. After refusing to take sides in 1932, Aden gave way to
Qu'ayti pressure and turned definitely against the Irshadi in the
following year. The British Consul-General in Java, much against
his will, was instructed to obstruct the movement of members of the
party to the Hadhramawt. In the following year, worldwide British
contacts were used to frustrate the shipping of Irshadi arms through
the Wahidi port of Bir'Ali to the Wadis of the interior.[90]

Thus the warring groups of reformers and the Aden Government
were as it were drawn towards one another. The uneasy balance of
power tempted both Sayyids and Irshadi to seek foreign intervention in their isolated homeland; Britain's strategic interests made
a British presence more strongly advisable. In 1933 Reilly visited
the Wadi and was received by the heads of both parties. In 1934
and 1935–6 Harold Ingrams, then an officer on the Aden Protectorate staff, made an extensive survey of the social and economic
conditions thioughout the area.[91] This survey became the basis for
a policy of intervention – and intervention came dramatically with
the bombing in February 1937 of the villages of a small sub-tribe in
the mountains between Shihr and Tarim. The sub-tribe had
committed the double offence of interfering with road security and
firing on the British flag, for they had attacked a British engineering
officer who had been sent to examine a major road building project.

The officer had been sent with just such an eventuality in mind, for the Hadhrami needed no advice on road construction but did need protection for their skilled men from armed raids by badawin. The incident was exploited to the full. After four days the offenders saw they were powerless against aircraft. Ingrams had them surrender ceremoniously to himself and the Kathiri Sultan at Saywun and pay a substantial fine,[92] and the occasion was taken to call for a general peace between all feuding parties. The work others had been doing in the same direction, notably Sayyid Bubakr al Kaff, who had been dispensing money on all sides to draw the tribesmen together, and who could now claim to have the British at his back, since it was his road between Shihr and Tarim that had been protected, now came to fruition. Within a few weeks over a thousand truces were signed, followed shortly by several hundred more. This was 'Ingrams Peace' – a three-year truce which ended the uncontrollable war that had torn the disintegrated society of the Hadhramawt. It halted the creeping paralysis of spreading feuds, which cut family from family and not only brought death to many but narrowed and impoverished the lives of the living. The feud had locked warring neighbours for months or even years in their tall climbing Wadi houses yards apart. It had huddled traditional markets into cramped protected spaces away from the sights of gunmen on the towering cliffs above. It had hounded labourers from their fields, and the fields and trees themselves were threatened with retaliatory destruction by methods so common that their names found their way into treaties – names which happily fell out of the vocabulary with the onset of peace and were forgotten by the rising generation.[93]

Peace was the first step to progress, the second was the establishment of an acceptable and effective administration to guarantee the continuance of that peace. This was the step that was most difficult to take in the Aden hinterland: in those parts of the Hadhramawt under Qu'ayti control the British did not need to take it. A new treaty was made in 1937 by which the Sultan agreed to take British advice on matters not related to religion.[94] The reigning Sultan had no need of British advice. Sultan Salih was a vigorous decisive statesman and man of letters who like most of his predecessors was bent upon reform and the introduction of systematic, disciplined, bureaucratic administration along the British-Indian lines he knew so well.[95] What he got from the treaty was a guarantee of British support against vested interests which would oppose change and the guarantee of continuity of administration. He wanted his son to succeed him and the British guaranteed that. He also wanted his work to be maintained during his periods of absence when he went to manage his interests in Hyderabad. That too the

British provided by the creation of the office of Resident Adviser to which Ingrams was appointed. Ingrams and his successors kept watch in Mukalla when Sultan Salih was away and in 1938 this arrangement was reinforced by the establishment of a State Council on which the Resident Adviser and other British officers served.

On this basis the reform programme got under way. The first key measure was the overhaul of the Sultan's armed forces – the Yafi'i mercenaries and the slave guard. These had become an encumbrance; militarily they were ineffective, politically they were a source of intrigue. The Yafi'i in particular had become little more than a privileged group of moneylenders and politicians who underpinned the old order. With British advice and assistance, the paper soldiers among them were eliminated and the rest were re-embodied as the Mukalla Regular Army under experienced Indian officers with a clear chain of command and specific functions to perform. By 1939 the Mukaila Regular Army was an efficient fighting force of 400 men with artillery and mortars and was providing garrisons for forts in outlying areas where previously there had been no government presence.

A second set of key measures was the reorganisation of the State's finances. In 1938 the old system of farming the customs was brought to an end, an Indian customs clerk with long experience in British Somaliland was brought in and a systematic reorganisation took place. The general finances were then dealt with by a British officer and trained clerks recruited to provide continuity. The taxation system was considered and reconsidered from the point of view of efficiency and equity as between different classes of the community and improved systems were gradually introduced. The finances of the State rapidly improved under this treatment and larger funds were made available for various forms of development. The central and local administration was improved along the same lines. Recognised procedures were established, a registry of documents was set up and at all stages and levels clerks and administrators with modern education and training were recruited. To supply the men needed, the educational system was reformed. A Sudanese teacher from the Bakht al Ruda College in the Sudan became Director of Education and after some initial resistance in regard to this now most delicate of subjects, he managed to introduce new systems of instructions which more or less secured the support of all parties. Ghayl ba Wazir became an important educational centre and men capable of efficiently filling posts in the new army and administration began to flow from the reformed Qu'ayti schools. On the economic side, Sultan Salih sought the advice of the Aden Director of Agriculture and introduced new strains to improve the tobacco crop which constituted the State's main export. He constructed a new road across the Jol from Mukalla to Wadi Du'an and beyond. He introduced electric light at Mukalla. He took steps to control the arms trade throughout his dominions. Within three years of the establishment of the peace the Qu'ayti state had taken a long stride along the path to modernity. The Resident Adviser had needed to do little other than offer encouragement and support.[96]

Beyond Qu'ayti territory however the situation was very different. In the Wadi and in the Wahidi Sultanates along the coast[97] the situation resembled that in parts of the western Protectorate. Although the communities in the Wadi were rich with emigrant gains and the houses of the great families large and well-appointed, there was no single authority capable of imposing order. The Kathiri Sultan had not the resources of his Mukalla neighbour. He had no seaport and hence no customs revenue. In the 1930s the Kathiri Sultan had little independent income and was dependent on subventions from men who were wealthier than himself. His slave guard was ill-paid, unruly and scarcely under his control. The Sultan could scarcely maintain his authority in his own capital at Saywun. His influence over the rest of the territory he claimed was very slight. Real power lay in the hands of men with money and the will to use it for political purposes. Most prominent among these was Sayyid Bubakr bin Shaykh al Kaff, of the wealthy al Kaff family. He subsidised the Kathiri Sultan and was therefore the most powerful man in the State. But he was not the only power in the Wadi. To the west of Saywun, his powerful rival and bitter enemy, 'Ubayd bin Salih bin Abdat, ruled like an independent potentate in the town and district of Al Ghurfa, controlling twenty-one forts scattered round the area, as well as the strong walled town of al Ghurfa itself. At the other end of the Wadi, a separate branch of the Kathiri Sultan's family ruled Tarim in conjunction with the wealthy Sayyidi citizens of that town, who were disposed to reject the Sultan's claim to even the loosest suzerainty over them. Outside these centres and the Qu'ayti possessions west of Shibam, al Kaff and bin Abdat, as the most prominent men in the Sayyidi and Irshadi parties, vied for the control of uncommitted and potentially dangerous tribesmen. After 1937 a certain stability was produced by the truces and that stability among the tribesmen was maintained by a number of 'peace boards' which were established to maintain the peace and settle disputes. But these peace boards did not constitute a regular government. Above all, as far as the British were concerned, they had no treaty. The treaty ruler was the Kathiri Sultan and therefore only his authority could be used as the nucleus for the development of a recognised administration. For this reason, if for no other, the

Resident Adviser was tied to al Kaff and the Sayyidi party, for al Kaff controlled the Kathiri, and without the Kathriri the British had no stable position in the Wadi. Ingrams was a strong advocate of the system of working through the local authorities and preserving as much as possible of what was traditional in Hadhrami Arab society. In any case he had little choice but to do so if he were not to use much more force than the then British policy would have allowed. Hadrami society was intensely xenophobic and intensely suspicious of British intentions. On all sides there was evidence that the British presence was resented, even though the peace Ingrams had brought was highly appreciated.[98] The conditions upon which British intervention was tolerated by a substantial section of the people was that it was sponsored by the influential al Kaff, a well recognised pillar of Hadhrami Muslim society. Ingrams was therefore tied to al Kaff and with some misgivings about interfering in what he thought was a religious dispute, he acted against the Irshadi elements when they sought to gain control of the al Kaff-dominated peace boards.[99]

By 1940 when the three-year truce ran out, hardly any progress had been made in the matter of building up a regular administration in the Wadi. The Kathiri Sultan was as weak as ever and efforts to set up a disciplined Kathiri Armed Constabulary came to grief in the face of opposition from the Sultan's slave guard, and the reluctance of the ruling family itself to embark upon reform.[100] Moreover when the time came for the renewal of the truces it seemed that even the peace itself was in danger, for bin Abdat indicated that he would work against the re-erection of a system which had worked against his interests. Bin Abdat began to build his own system of truces, his own peace, in competition with the new ten-year truces Ingrams and al Kaff were trying to negotiate. Clashes began to occur in 1939 between tribesmen paid by bin Abdat and the opposing forces. Intrigue was widespread and the some of the displaced Yafi'i mercenaries from Mukalla showed signs of alignment with the Irshadi party. Many of the tribesmen outside the main towns were dissatisfied with some of the aspects of the peace and there was a certain feeling that the justice of corrupt Shari'a courts was no better than the justice of the rifle. All this aided bin Abdat's cause.[101]

A showdown became inevitable and, as Hitler's armies marched into France, an operation was hastily mounted to deal with bin Abdat before aircraft were taken from Aden to fight in other theatres. The operation was only partially successful. Vincent bomber blew down the walls of al Ghurfa, but the Mukalla Regular Army and other hastily assembled forces were not prepared to make the assault. Bin Abdat's old friends, the Humumi tribe on the plateau south of the Wadi, made diversionary attacks and prevented an effective blockade of al Ghurfa from being established. Bin Abdat surrendered to the bombing and engaged some of his Singapore property as security for future good behaviour, but his power had by no means been broken.[102] When Italy entered the war in June and shifted Aden's eyes and her aircraft to the defence of Somaliland and eventually Aden itself, against Italian planes, Bin Abdat began his intrigues once more with very considerable success. Al Ghurfa continued to defy the British throughout the war years and while he remained unsubdued, Tarim also maintained its independence and refused to come under the Saywun administration. The Kathiri Sultanate remained a paper province, weak in the face of over-mighty subjects, unable to discipline its own police force or to secure an adequate revenue.

More notable progress was made among the badawin tribesmen, especially in the north and west. There the chosen instrument of control was a new semi-military force, the Hadhrami Beduin Legion.[103] Formed at the beginning of 1949 the Legion was organised on the lines of its counterpart in Jordan, wearing a similar uniform and officered at the outset by Arab and British personnel drawn from the parent force. Its object was educational and political as much as military. Boys were recruited from the more influential tribal families and during their four-year service they went through a thorough training of character and intellect as well as military method. In 1943 the strictly educational branch was hived off into a separate cadet school for badawin and other boys which soon began to provide administrators as well as recruits for the Legion. Through the Beduin Legion the Resident Adviser and his staff were able to establish direct contact with the tribesmen, its garrisons kept the peace in the remoter areas and the soldiers helped in settling disputes among their relations. Above all the Legion provided the Residency with a force under its direct control and in 1941 Ingrams brought a body of Legionaries into the Wadi to police the roads around Saywun. This however was not very congenial to the men of power in the Kathiri Sultanate. Even al Kaff looked askance at the presence of the Legion and this tended to complicate Ingram's relationships with others in the area.[104] In the early 1940s the Legion and its British controllers were still far from strong enough to secure a mastery of the situation. The involuted intrigues continued, the administration made little progress and in the Hadhramawt as in the Aden hinterland the tempo of the 1930s was not sustained into the next decade. Large gains in terms of general peace had been made but they were not being effectively consolidated at any considerable speed.

In many ways the period between 1941 and 1944 represented a

turning-point in the process of British expansion. The first wave
had more or less spent itself with the establishment of a roughly
effective system of road security in Aden's immediate hinterland and
a substantially strengthened Qu'ayti Sultanate in the Hadhramawt.
A second wave was gathering as the number of Political Officers
grew from two in 1934 to twelve in 1941, backed by an increasing
number of technical men and a force of Government Guards which
now numbered 200.[105] As these men went about their tasks relations
between them and the chiefs they were advising tended to deteriorate.
The chiefs for the most part did not want to become the administrators the Political Officers were trying to make of them. That was
not how they understood their role in society. Nor did they have
much sympathy for the schemes of social betterment – the dispensaries, schools and agricultural improvements – they were
constantly advised to introduce; their thoughts did not run along
those lines. And so by 1941 the patience of some of the Political
Officers began to wear very thin.[106] The deposition of the Fadli
Sultan for 'misrule' (this was his real offence despite official reference
to his interference with road security) might have opened the
floodgates, had the Governor of Aden, then Sir John Hall, not
stepped in with a restatement of the old policy of respecting the
chiefs' authority.[107] While the Political Officers were eager to move
forward, some of the men of influence in the Protectorate became
wary of British penetration. And across the border there was rumbling
disapproval from the Imam, whose forces clashed with the British
in the remote oasis of Shabwa north of Bayhan in 1938. The Imam
resented the extension of British influence in that area: it brought
the British close to areas toward which Sa'udi influence reached.
He also objected to the moving of Hadhrami forces to the town of
Al Abr on the route from the Yemen to the Hadhramawt. Attempts
were made to come to terms but met with little success, and the
Imam's officers in Baydha began to intrigue with the 'Awlaqi and
other peoples of the east to counteract British penetration there.
In fact after 1941, contacts between those tribes and Aden became
less frequent.[108] When the Governor told his officers to respect
chiefly sovereignty, he also stopped further movement in the direction of the Dathina area, which could have brought about further
British involvement in 'Awlaqi politics. Hall's more general 'non-
intervention' instruction itself tended to tie the Protectorate staff's
hands in its dealings with that area as a whole.

But opinion in official circles gradually swung over to the side of
those who wanted to extend the British peace from the roads to the
tribal areas. Knowledge of South Arabian society steadily accumulated and as it did the very limited character of the chiefs' power in

the circumstances of the time became more fully exposed. More characters were brought onto the scene – the 'Aqils of the tribal sections, the heads of extended families and the unarmed ra'iyah cultivators.[109] It was gradually impressed on the official mind that Britain had a 'responsibility' (the magic word for charming subventions out of the British Treasury) toward these people as well as toward the chiefs. The 'responsibility' consisted not simply in offering protection from the Imam, although that was stressed too on the grounds that all were Shafi'i, but also in providing the basic amenities of a modern society that no Colonial Government could withhold.

Not all saw things in this light. There were still those who did not want to push too fast, did not want to change the traditional character of Arab society, did not want to offend the Imam, and saw that innovation would not in the end win Arab friendship. But the men with these ideas were becoming fewer and less influential at Aden. In the clash of the Second World War, of modern tanks and planes and guns, the vision of an isolated, romantic, unchanging Arabia was receding, along with the aristocratic and atavistic attitudes in Europe that had so often nurtured it. More impatient men were forcing their way forward, men who girded at chiefly 'misrule', men who tended to see in the Protectorate something of a class conflict between 'feudal' chiefs and the oppressed ra'iyah and poorer tribesmen. Traditional Arab pejorative references to 'oppressors of the poor' became a catch phrase on their lips, and a justification for more radical initiatives. These men wanted more rapid change, if not a complete overhaul of policy, and a declared alliance with the poor against all chiefs, including the greatest chief of them all – the Imam himself. Behind them stood the solid weight of the British technical advisers of every sort who eschewed politics and wanted to get on with their respective jobs. In London, where Reilly's experienced voice at the Colonial Office carried the greatest weight, their views were heard with sympathy although their more extreme counsels were rejected on grounds of moderation. After 1942 it became clear that Britain was winning the war. The flush of victory began to be felt in Whitehall, and Britain's victory over the Axis powers in the Middle East was already more complete than anywhere else. The area was left clearly in British hands, and this removed a lot of the complications which might otherwise have held back further expansion.[110]

While the debate on policy was swinging back and forth in Aden and London nature took a hand in South Arabia and produced conditions which gave the expansionists a heaven-sent opportunity to carry through their plans. In 1943 the rains failed over a wide area of South-West Arabia, and there followed a drought and harvest failure which, like that of 1867, shook all the traditional institutions in the area. Men poured in to Aden from the famine-stricken Yemen in the summer months. Many of the Jews among them were ultimately swept off by Zionists to Palestine; their Arab confrères were left to subsist on the charity of the government and private persons. By the end of the year evidence of unrest and serious protest at the Imam's regime had appeared and in 1944 numbers of political refugees fled to Aden and began to agitate for a change of regime in their homeland. The Hadhramawt was even more severely affected, for the drought followed upon the Japanese occupation of South-East Asia and the halting of those remittances which had been the lifeblood of the wealthier families, and through them, of countless others in the Wadis and on the coast. The harvests failed, money to maintain the normally substantial imports of foodstuffs was no longer forthcoming and the camels who carried the food across the wide expanses of the Jol to the Wadi began to faint and die for lack of fodder. In June 1943 an estimated twenty deaths a week from famine were occurring in the Wadi. A famine relief scheme was mounted and the Resident Adviser set up grain distribution centres for the tribes, using the Hadhrami Beduin Legion to administer them. But transport costs in the Hadhramawt kept the price even of famine relief food very high. Conditions improved with the harvests later in the year but in 1944 there was famine once more as Hadhrami society could no longer afford its normal imports. Further famine relief measures were set on foot. Grain was flown in to the Wadi by R.A.F. aircraft and the British Government made a gift of £318,000 available for immediate and long-term relief measures.[111]

The famine in the Hadhramawt decided the policy issue in favour of the expansionists at Aden. Whether or not the people wanted improved social services in normal times was arguable; there was no need to make a case for saving them from death by starvation. With the British Government's grant, the Political Officers now had at their disposal funds equal to half the estimated annual value of remittances to the Hadhramawt in pre-war years. While the wealthy Hadhrami had become poor, the Residency was suddenly rich. The money was used partly to provide cheap issues of food but partly also to set on foot public works such as the construction of the Nuqra dam and other irrigation schemes to succour those the great families could no longer afford to employ and solve the long-term problem of food deficiency.

Famine relief work received little assistance and a good deal of obstruction from the established authorities. The Tarim community in 1943 refused to allow a grain distribution centre to be established in their town – they did not want to let the Hadhrami Beduin Legion in. Bin Abdat at al Ghurfa was as recalcitrant as ever, excluding famine relief services from his lands, firing on a surveying officer who approached too close and levying heavy tolls on relief goods passing though his territory. This was too much for those in charge of relief operations. The obstruction offered by these men was seen as clear evidence of that callous indifference toward the suffering of the poor of which the Political Officers had suspected them all along. In December 1944 an ultimatum was sent to bin Abdat, and when he did not comply, he was decisively crushed by a powerful force of Aden Levies, Mukalla Regulars and British and Indian troops equipped with armoured cars, brencarriers, artillery and mortars in March 1945.[112] This blow resounded throughout the Hadhramawt, and the Kathiri administration was now established on a firm footing. Tarim as well as al Ghurfa was brought under Saywun, the boundarise between the Qu'ayti and Kathiri Sultanates were more clearly defined, and a more effective system of taxation was devised. The year 1945 saw an easing of the food situation, although the threat of famine continued to hang over the Hadhramawt until 1950. Agricultural experts put great effort into improving the yields of Hadhrami farms. The Nuqra dam was completed in 1947, advances were made to farmers, new crops and new strains were introduced and in 1948–9, when another drought required an airlift to prevent famine, an extensive pump scheme was introduced, with central workshops to maintain its services.[113] Meanwhile a number of the impoverished Sayyids, who had in former palmy days held aloof from government, were induced to enter the educational service and devote their talents to the improvement of state primary and secondary schools.[114] When the last threat of famine had dispersed the greater part of Hadhrami society had been drawn within the ambit of the reformed and more efficient Qu'ayti and Kathiri states. Political activity was also beginning to shape itself to the new context. The old politics of raising tribesmen, seizing forts and blocking roads was giving place to quarrels between the Kathiri and Qu'ayti bureaucracies over boundaries and functions and to struggles for places in the administration, as more Hadhrami with the required qualifications came from the new schools. In December 1950 a sign of the dawn of a new political era came with the upheaval at Mukalla over the Sultan's appointment of a Residency-backed Sudanese candidate to the key office of Qu'ayti State Secretary. A recently formed body calling itself the Hizb al Watani – the National Party — organised a great protest demonstration and in the subsequent riot sixteen persons were killed and twenty-four wounded. The question of who should control the administration, not altogether absent in the years before 1937, was now becoming the most important question of the day.[115]

In the rest of the Protectorate the drought and famine of 1943 also marked a turning-point in British policy. The war and the troop concentrations in Aden had posed the problem of agricultural production before the drought occurred. When famine struck, the Government jostled private Arab enterprise aside. As food prices soared in Aden and food and fodder became scarce throughout the Protectorate, the Lower Yafi'i Sultan was forced to yield control of the potentially fertile land in Abyan which he had failed to develop. On 23 June 1943, the British Agent for the Western Protectorate (a post created in 1942) moved in with three Political Officers and a section of the Government Guards. A 'Khanfar Development Board' was set up under British management, backed by British loans. Work was started on irrigation works and some 600 acres of land were distributed to farmers who were to pay half their crop as rent to the Sultan, from whom the Board was to recover the capital advanced. During its four years of operation the Khanfar scheme opened up 5,000 acres of new land for cultivation by the use of traditional Arab methods of irrigation.[116]

Further eastward, in the Lower 'Awlaqi Sultanate at Ahwar, where there was a substantial cultivable area, a somewhat weaker dose of the same medicine was administered. In June 1943 a Political Officer and a section of Government Guards was sent in to stop the feuds in the area. In August more Government Guards followed, a start was made with the organisation of Tribal Guards and a drive to develop agriculture was set on foot. By the autumn of 1943 the new 'forward' policy had gathered momentum throughout the Protectorate and on the 20 September, fifty Government Guards were moved up to the threatened frontier area of Bayhan, where feuding was paralysing economic activity. The feuds were stopped. The Sharif of Bayhan, who stood out from his fellows primarily if not solely because his predecessors had maintained treaty relations with the Aden Government, was made chief and the nucleus of an ordered administration, complete with the treasury devoted to state purposes, was set up. Peace was established, markets reopened, trade revived, and with the funds available a new school and dispensary were established. Bayhan soon became the showplace of the benefits of ordered administration and its ruler one of the favourite sons of the Aden Government.[117]

The results of the frenetic activity in the second half of 1943 strengthened the resolve of the Political Officers and impressed the Colonial Office in London. In March 1944 the idea of establishing regular administration in tribal areas was approved. There were still some reservations however about the role the Political Officers should play. The bogey of 'direct rule' still haunted the corridors of

the Colonial Office. Something more than lip service was still paid
to the notion of 'Arab independence'. The treaties were still regarded
as the basic justification for the British presence in the Protectorate
and the independence of the treaty chiefs had to be respected. So it
was decided that the new expansionist wine should still be poured into
old bottles and further progress was sought through the negotiation
of 'advisory treaties' and the establishment of state treasuries whose
finances were open to British scrutiny and partly assigned to the
maintenance of Tribal Guards and social services.[118] In this way
the Aden Government hoped to reconcile its duty toward treaty
chiefs with its responsibility toward the mass of South Arabian
society. With support from London, the 'forward policy' men were
now definitely in the saddle and the Sultan of Lahej, as sensitive as
his predecessors to the shifting breezes blowing through Aden
offices, declared himself in favour of policies which he had influen-
tially obstructed just two years before. Before the Political Officers
could do it for him, he began to build his own schools, train his own
administrators and develop his own health services.[119]

The momentum of the forward movement was sustained. By
September 1944 the Sultans of Fadli and Lower 'Awlaqi and the
'Amir of Dali' had signed advisory treaties.[120] In the following
year, when staff shortages were overcome, a regular administration
was set up in the Fadli Sultanate with central services and offices
in charge of the several districts. The fertile Dathinah area to the
eastward was penetrated by a motorised column in June 1944 to
stifle some of the feuding there. In mid-January 1945, Indian troops
were sent in and a garrison of fifty Government Guards established.
In October, armoured cars made another visit and further truces
were signed. Gradually, order was imposed in this area, where
various sub-sections had been constantly at feud. Dathinah did not
fit into the pattern of treaty chiefdoms, for the suzerainty which the
Fadli Sultan had exercised over some of the sections now lay in the
distant past while the more recent claims of the Upper 'Awlaqi
Sultan to a certain blackmailing suzerainty were regarded as
unacceptable. And so, when the time was ripe, a new type of administration was set up in 1947 with a governing committee representing
the various tribal sub-sections as the controlling body for the team
of officials who collected the taxes and administered the funds of the
increasingly prosperous Dathinah treasury.

North from Aden a new attempt was made to solve the intractable
problem of establishing a satisfactory system of government for the
'Amirate of Dali'. In October 1945 the 'Amir ,who had been spending
much of his time in Lahej, was induced to return to his capital and a
number of Lahej-trained clerks went with him to help establish a

regular administration. Old political problems remained, notably the 'Amir's unsettled quarrel with the Sha'iri co-occupiers of the Dali' Plateau. Even the presence of British amoured cars could not prevent it flaring up again and again, and the mass emigration of the Shairi to the Yemen in July 1946 after the 'Amir had tried to remove their Shaykh, gravely upset relations between the 'Amir and the British. In September a new settlement was made by the Political Officer. The Shairi were brought back, but relations between the 'Amir and the British deteriorated to the point where in 1947 he had to be replaced. While these difficulties were being experienced in Dali', the Radfan tribes remained unabsorbed in any of the administrative groups in the Protectorate. In 1947 the Qataybi, after seven years of quiescence, began plundering traffic on the Hardaba road and air action was taken against them, followed by the establishment of a Government Guards garrison at Thumayr to prevent further incursions. To the west, in Subayhi country, the tribesmen were handled with greater success and two administrations were set up, one under British, the other under 'Abdali auspices, which maintained order and permitted the extension of educational and medical services. Gradually the tide of ordered administration washed up and around areas still unclaimed. In 1951 the last major grouping, apart from the Upper Yafi'i, which had stood out for traditional government were drawn into the net, when the Upper 'Awlaqi Shaykhdom opted for a British-organised administrative system.[121]

The new institutions that were being established throughout the Protectorate required money to operate them. The schools, dispensaries and above all, the officials and the police forces had to be paid for. The money in most cases came in the first instance from the Aden Government. But the object of the treasury system was that each chiefdom should ultimately become self-supporting. It was therefore not surprising that the fastest progress, apart from the special case at Dali', was made where the land was comparatively rich and where there was room for economic development whose results could, at least for a time, win popular support for the new regime and sugar the pill of increased and more effective taxation. Such was the case in the Dathinah area, in Ahwar, in parts of the Wahidi Sultanate and in the 'Awdhali Sultanate whence the export of vegetables to the Aden market reached the rate of three tons per day in 1944. Such above all was the case in the Abyan area which straddled the Fadli and Lower Yafi'i Sultanates. There in 1947 the Khanfar Development Board gave place to a much larger organisation – the Abyan Development Board – which with the help of a substantial loan from the British Government undertook a series of major irrigation works which by 1954 had brought some 45,000 acres of new land into cultivation. The principal crop grown was cotton which put cash into the hands of the farmers and into the hands of the treasuries of the Fadli and Yafi'i states. Abyan became prosperous, it could afford medical services, schools and roads which other parts of the Protectorate could hardly equal and a settled integrated community rapidly emerged.[122]

Abyan was unique. But in its own way, every administrative area in the Protectorate was unique, usually isolated from its neighbours by physical distance or by contrasting conditions. Although in 1950 the area of authority of most chiefdoms had been greatly extended and transformed by comparison with what had obtained ten years earlier, the Protectorate was still a patchwork of different forms of government whose diversity defied any single simplified description. However, in the western Protectorate, as in the Hadhramawt, certain underlying formative factors were now emerging. The various administrations, whatever their character, and their various supporting organisations, were becoming the most important fact of Protectorate life. For those who wanted status and something more than a life devoted to subsistence agriculture or nomad herding, an official post or a place in one of the armed forces now offered the most likely and the most promising way forward. By the late 1940s even the small administration at Bayhan employed over fifty officials of all grades. In 1954 the Abyan Board employed 150 salaried staff of whom over a hundred were local men. In 1950 eighteen of the twenty-three officers in the Government Guards were Arabs and nearly 600 found employment in the other ranks. In addition the various Tribal Guards, almost entirely under Arab command, mustered between them over 800 men in the same year. Both of these forces had grown rapidly since 1940 and were still growing and offering increasing employment and expectations of promotion. The Protectorate Office also offered places of outstanding power and responsibility. From the 1930s Arabs had been associated in one way or another on a footing of near equality with the British Political Officers who were pushing into the Protectorate. In the forward movement after 1943, Arab Assistant Political Officers formed the backbone of the new administrations.[123]

At the start these men were recruited from those who had risen through the military organisations, notably the Aden Levies, and also from such Aden families as the Jaffers who had long provided political clerks for the administration. But as time went on an increasing number were the products of the Aden and Protectorate schools where boys were seeking an education with a view to just such a career. The turning-point in education came significantly in the years 1943–4. Up to then boys of other nationalities still outnumbered Arabs in the Aden schools. The college for the sons of chiefs, founded in 1935 with two masters and an ex-Levies usher to form future administrators, had scarcely grown, and still registered just over thirty pupils.[124] Then suddenly Aden and Protectorate boys began to flock to the schools, a large bulge appeared in the lower classes, school facilities became inadequate and the pressure grew as those in the upper forms left before completing their education to take up posts offered them in Aden and the Protectorate. A new bureaucratic class was in the making and the best brains in the Protectorate were being drawn into and becoming committed to the new system – although not necessarily to its British creators.[125]

In the Protectorate, the chiefdoms still existed. They were the governments of recognised traditional rulers. But a constant winnowing was going on among those rulers. They were pushed forward and strengthened, or pushed aside, deposed or otherwise silenced, according to the criteria of administrative efficiency and loyalty to the British. While others were becoming administrators by training, the members of ruling families were being made so by a process of, as it were, natural selection. Where other methods failed, the old British principle of constitutional monarchy usually served the purpose. By 1950 an increasing number of administrations were being endowed with state councils of one sort or another and if the Sultan Chairman did not satisfy, power could be transferred into the hands of a 'managing director' chosen from among men of proved efficiency. By 1950 there was little that was 'feudal' in the Protectorate administrations, if that ambiguous word were given the connotation of 'traditional'. Autocracy was prevalent but it was seldom the autocracy of men who had an ancient title to rule. There was inevitably a bias toward those families which had by custom provided candidates for the Sultanate but then this was just one among many biases in recruitment resulting from British favouritism. The earlier contact of some geographical areas with the British administration, earlier educational opportunity and the many other unevennesses to be expected in a society undergoing rapid and piecemeal change under foreign auspices were of almost equal importance.

It was British power that had historically created the new regimes and underpinned those which were still insecure. There could be no doubt of that. To the degree that extension of administration into fringe areas required good political management it could be said that it was based on consent, but the existence of the administrations themselves was scarcely subject to such consent. They were there because they had been historically put there and they continued to function by their own momentum and by the will of the Aden Government. The administrations, though bearing a simulacrum of formal independence through the old treaties, were quite definitely under British control. As the organisation developed, the British Political Officers came back from pioneering work among the tribesmen, handing over administrative functions to Arab assistants and the local authorities. But they remained omnipresent in general supervisory capacities. Their position was consolidated by membership of the various state councils, the Abyan Board, and by their preponderance in the technical services. Above all they were able to control the financial lifeblood of the system, no longer as in the first phase of the forward movement of the middle 1940s by the crude method of actually distributing the pay of the Tribal Guards, but by more sophisticated although no less effective means. And generally speaking, almost all the administrations were dependent in one way or another on the munificence of the British Government, and a continued acceptance of Whitehall's dictates was the price they had to pay to achieve their goals.

CHAPTER XII

Apogee and Evacuation

During the two decades after 1934 the British were in command of the processes of change in South Arabia. They initiated most of the major alterations in the relationships between men and groups of men. Their military presence dominated wartime Aden and Britain's war effort created work in town and port for those who flocked there in search of employment. Government action during this period dominated Aden's economic life more obtrusively than at any time since the earliest years of British rule. Wartime economic controls, some of which persisted until the early '50s, regulated the movement of goods and shipping through the harbour. The government-controlled food market strove to maintain stable prices for provisions. In the Protectorate, the spreading tentacles of colonial administration upset tribal society as it had never been upset before. After 1950 British activity in Aden and the Protectorate continued with sustained intensity. But it was gradually overtaken and finally engulfed by other dynamic forces, some of them set off by an initial British impetus, others operating independently and, especially in the political sphere, in vigorous conflict with British efforts.

From the Second World War onward, economic activity at Aden advanced by great leaps and bounds, interspersed with brief pauses when expansion slowed but did not stop. The basis of Aden's prosperity was the surging growth of its bunkering business. The large growth of traffic between the expanding oilfields of the Persian Gulf and oil-hungry Europe redounded to Aden's benefit. So did the general rise in world trade which brought more and larger ships to Aden for refuelling. By comparison, the entrepôt trade was of declining importance. When post-war economic controls were relaxed in 1954 other Red Sea ports began to ship an increasing proportion of their exports direct to their various destinations; the development of their harbour facilities gave continuing force to this trend.[1] Aden merchants still dealt largely in commodities from Somaliland, Ethiopia and the Yemen but they were increasingly aware that this business could not last and were unwilling to invest substantially in its problematical continuance. Bunkering however was recognised as having a rosy future, and as Aden outstripped port after port, becoming by 1958 the busiest harbour in the world after New York, those concerned with the management of the Colony's affairs confidently poured funds into the development of its installations and services. Investment was encouraged also by the fact that, alone in the Middle East, Aden was held under outright British sovereignty. For larger investors, especially British investors, this offered an escape to apparent long-term security and simplicity from the increasing uncertainty of agreeements with nationalistically-inclined independent states.

In an atmosphere of complacent self-confidence the rocks and sand of Aden were mastered and moulded to productive purpose. At the end of the war the main landmarks of man's endeavour were still mostly those that had been put there in the nineteenth century. Playfair's and Merewether's work was still much in evidence – the barracks facing Front Bay, the Anglican church on the hill in Crater, the fortified bridge gate at Main Pass, the Tanks which every visitor was advised to see. The threefold division of the town, with the European residences clutching the hills above the coalyards and shops at Steamer Point, the low-built houses against the quays at Ma'alla, and the grid-iron pattern of shops and houses in Crater, were roughly as they had been eighty years before. To the northward lay the separate town of Shaykh 'Uthman to which little that was permanent had been added since it was laid down in the 1880s. The airport runway, lying across the Khormaksar isthmus, had been built in the inter-war years and had been enlarged and surrounded by a complex of military and other buildings during wartime. But this was the only major twentieth-century addition to Aden's ecology, apart from the oil tanks for bunker fuel. The Aden of 1945 would still have been quite familiar to anyone who had seen it in the late nineteenth century. In the next twenty years, however, great changes were wrought. In 1952 an oil refinery began to mushroom out of the emptiness at Little Aden across the bay. By July 1954 it was delivering oil to ships while work continued on a new town around it, which established entirely new standards in residential accommodation.[2] The workers' houses were far superior to the barrack-like dormitories which Aden employers had on occasion grudgingly provided for 'coolies'. The senior staff housing was lavish in modern conveniences by comparison with what officials and businessmen had previously enjoyed at Aden. Prompted by the refinery example and by a new outlook on social welfare, the government made an effort to improve amenities in Aden itself. Sixteen hundred modern flats for workers were erected at Ma'alla which quickly grew during the late 1950s into a town rivalling Crater in size and outstripping it in modernity.[3]

There, and at the Khormaksar isthmus, senior staff housing was built, first to accommodate the growing number of officials, and later for the families of armed forces personnel. In Crater and Steamer Point multi-storied office blocks rose up to dwarf Victorian Aden and make formerly important shopping streets seem like back alleys. In 1945 Shaykh 'Uthman, still something of a distant outpost, was extended, and permanent buildings ate into the fringe of *kutcha* slums, while the latter in turn spread onward and outward into the desert.[4] In 1960 a whole new area was laid out; by 1965 Shaykh 'Uthman had doubled its pre-war size and had acquired its own suburb of Al Mansurah, and a somewhat smaller sister town stood across on the Lahej side of the Colony boundary at Dar Saad. The various centres of settlement at Steamer Point, Ma'alla, Crater, Khormaksar and Shaykh 'Uthman rushed toward one another along the new highways that replaced the old narrow roads until they began to resemble different districts of a single conurbation, whose population grew from 51,500 in 1931 to 80,500 in 1946 and an estimated 225,000 in 1963. The Main Pass gate did not survive the fever of construction and reconstruction. In 1956 the roadway through it was enlarged and ten years later the fortified bridge across the pass had been demolished to make way for the steadily increasing traffic. In 1955 a causeway road plunged out across the head of the bay to speed communication with Little Aden and Shaykh 'Uthman and replace the old isthmus road that had run across the runway of the increasingly busy civil airport. Another enlarged highway swung round the base of the eastern heights between the isthmus and Crater to provide a more effective access to the old town where its second gate had stood. A series of dredging programmes deepened the harbour for larger vessels and threw up spoil for new land reclamations along the shore.[5] Water schemes enlarged the output of the Shaykh 'Uthman wells and then brought a new supply from Lahej. Electricity supplies were expanded and re-expanded to meet the needs of the Colony and its immediate hinterland. The construction of schools, dispensaries and hospitals went on apace to cater for the expanding population and to provide a more extensive service in keeping with the improved standards at which the Colony's government now aimed.

All this constructional effort of itself contributed much toward the dynamic aspect that the Colony assumed during this period. During the twenty years after 1945, between a sixth and a quarter of Aden's workforce was engaged in building construction. At its peak in 1953–4 refinery construction alone accounted for 11,000 out of something over 40,000 workers employed in the Colony. This represented more than three times the number then registered as engaged in employment around the port. Never from 1952 onward did the number of port workers exceed the numbers engaged in construction.[6] The bulk of those who rebuilt Aden were casual labourers from the Yemen and the Protectorate, following in the footsteps of so many of their predecessors who had gone to Aden to work for a period and go home. Like their predecessors, they gathered around the coffee shops, slept in the open or squatted in *kutcha* huts and caves around the settlement. But this apparent continuity with the past concealed the fact that the character of Aden's working population was steadily changing. The bulk of seasonal labour was now involved in the process of adding to Aden's material capital; it was no longer engaged in the continuing business of heaving coal around the wharves and on to ships. Masses of cheap labour had formerly been the tool which with Aden did its daily, labour-intensive work; now it was becoming peripheral to the activity of a more sophisticated economy.[7] The installations that the seasonal labourers erected were rapidly making Aden a place where raw muscle counted for less than a mixture of capital and skills.

Before the outbreak of the Second World War the diversification of employment at Aden had already begun. After the war this process gathered momentum and had already progressed so far by the early 1950s that the final demise of the great old coaling business passed almost without notice. Oil bunkering required comparatively little labour. On the wharves at Ma'alla, Aden's imports and exports were now handled by cranes and other mechanical equipment as well as by stevedores and dockers. In the streets, the rough carts, laden with goods and pushed and pulled by gangs of straining labourers were becoming a less familiar sight, and by the 1960s what had formerly been the stuff of Aden's life had become a degrading anachronism to which nationalists pointed with abhorrence. New permanent jobs were created at the refinery where 2,500 men found work from 1954 onward. Small industries and services such as the garages serving the extremely high concentration of motor vehicles in the Colony and other technical workshops expanded their workforce alongside the stagnant old coffee and gum cleaning concerns, the salt pans, and the hides and skin treaters. There was a steady expansion in the retail business selling to visiting ship's passengers, who from the 1950s onward avoided mounting sales taxes in their own countries by buying goods in Aden's free port. The most rapidly expanding area of employment, however, was provided by the government and the armed services. Practically every department of government multiplied its personnel during the twenty years after the end of the war to cope with the growing size of the Colony and the extended scope of government activity.[8] During the 1960s the build-up of British military strength associated with the transfer of Middle East Command to Aden produced a further demand for local labour. On the eve of the British evacuation, the government and the armed forces were by far the largest employers of labour and Aden had become once more what it had been in the times of Haines – first and foremost a garrison town and military base.

All this was very different from the pre-war picture. The permanent population had formerly been predominantly a community of dealers; shopkeepers with or without their families retailing to traders and visitors from the hinterland, coffee-house keepers and labour contractors who battened on seasonal labour, old families such as the Jaffers who hung on the fringes of government, offering their services as interpreters and middlemen.[9] A multitude of cash nexuses held the amorphous society together. The big foreign firms, such as Besse, founded in the 1890s, Cowasji Dinshaw, Luke Thomas and Cory's dating from earlier in the nineteenth century, dealt with the ships and Aden's more distant customers. In Aden they dealt with Arab and other brokers who in turn engaged workmen or retailed goods. Aden indeed consisted of a hierarchy of brokers from the heads of the foreign firms to the lowest workman or child who offered his labour or hawked in the streets.[10] It was essentially a bourgeois society at the mercy of virtually uncontrolled (except for the war period) and often uncontrollable market forces.[11] Speculators, hoarders and price rings frequently sent commodity and foodstuff prices rocketing up and down while moneylenders and dealers dampened the effect of this for the rest of the population at a price which included a claim to social leadership. Acquisitive individualism was mitigated only by ethnic and other local solidarities formed outside rather than within the town.[12] It was not surprising that such a community was politically docile and lacking in civic concern. Aden was the 'resort for traders' that British policy had originally intended it should be, with low taxation and a regime which offered opportunities to all who did not challenge British power.[13] Ultimate responsibility for Aden's fate rested with the colonial power and bourgeois Aden was content to leave it thus. The Legislative Council established in 1947 was expected to advise only about eleemosynary matters and these remained its principal concern for its first ten years and more.[14]

Most of Aden's citizens still accepted these facts up to 1950, and when they thought of politics they tended to look to the destinies of places other than their place of work. During and after the

Second World War the first and most active political groupings to emerge in Aden were concerned with political reform in the Yemen, in India, in Palestine, in the Hadhramawt, practically anywhere but Aden. During the 1940s an Aden-based organisation called the Free Yemenis became the main focus of opposition to the Imam's rule. It was involved in the assassination of Imam Yahya in 1948 and in the abortive attempt to remove Imam Ahmad in 1955.[15] At Aden, Yemeni factions could indulge in political discussion more openly than at home, and amateurs among the shopkeepers and workers had a chance of sharpening their wits against the professional politicians who occasionally visited Aden to cultivate support for the regime in the Yemen, or who fled thence as refugees. The Indian community provided another focus of political life, *sotto voce* while the British Raj continued, more openly after 1947 when Indian officials in Aden could speak without endangering their jobs. A Muslim Association was formed in 1947 by members of the Muslim Indian community, which had always numerically outweighed the Hindus in Aden.[16] The issues it was first concerned with were Kashmir and the situation in Hyderabad, the latter being of special concern to Arab members of the Association, who saw their brothers streaming through Aden as refugees after the Indian take-over in 1948. The Palestine question stirred especially strong feelings. Assertiveness among Aden's Jewish population, the flying of Zionist flags on V.E. day, the flow of Jewish migrants through Aden from the Protectorate and the Yemen during and after the war, and other incidents, lent an immediacy to a problem which affected the whole Arab world. There had been a brief anti-Jewish riot in 1931; in 1947 there was a violent flare-up which resulted in over a hundred deaths, the declaration of a state of emergency and a decision by the British Government to station British troops permanently at Aden to maintain internal security. The Palestine question had a serious effect on British prestige in Aden and the hinterland. Since the 1930s it had become a favourite topic of discussion by those who wished to embarrass the British and cast doubt on their wisdom and integrity. The 1947 incident found government policy at odds with the whole Arab community, including those who manned the police forces, and the authorities were compelled to reveal the iron fist of British power within its usual velvet glove of tact and diplomacy. For a brief period the even tenor of Aden's life of tacit political compromise was disturbed, until the departure of the bulk of Aden's Jews removed the immediate irritant, leaving only the memory of the trauma.[17]

While the old Aden of shopkeepers and contractors was being jolted into sporadic political life from different sides, an entirely new type of community was beginning to emerge as occupational patterns altered. The first symptom of change was the awakened interest in modern education in the middle 1940s. The sons of old families and more recent immigrants then began to realise that there were other ways of making a living in Aden than labouring or buying and selling. Businesses and Government became anxious to recruit clerks and skilled men to fill posts in offices and workshops. As time went on the demand for men with such qualifications became almost insatiable. The expansion of Aden's schools, which before the war had been regarded largely as a social welfare measure, became an urgent economic need after 1945.[18] And despite a steady expansion of the school population, the establishment of a Technical Institute at Ma'alla in 1950 and Aden College in 1952, employers could never find enough suitable applicants. Boys were attracted away to well-paid jobs before their schooling had ended, attempts were made by the Refinery, the Port Trust, by Besse and by the Administration to upgrade staff through in-service training, some posts were filled by intelligent men with no paper qualifications, and still there were not enough.[19] The growing number of schools required teachers and they too had to be found in the overtaxed market for educated men. Some two thousand immigrants were brought in, mainly from India, to fill the gap.[20] But after 1955 government policy and local protests restricted the recruitment of this type of immigrant. Temporary cut-backs in Aden's general employment after the completion of the refinery in 1954–5 and during the closure of the Suez Canal in 1956–7 had little effect on the demand for experienced and trained men.[21] The revolution in Aden's employment pattern went on regardless of such temporary economic ups and downs. The numbers involved may not have been large in relation to the total working population. In 1961, out of a registered 49,569 workers, only 3,538 were listed as being in clerical employment, and 6,361 more were classed as craftsmen and artisans.[22] But their presence had a significance out of proportion to their numbers. Although they could command comparatively high wages, these men did not have the freedom of a shop-keeper or petty contractor. They were mostly the employees of large organisations, integrated as subordinate personnel into an industrial society whose higher echelons were almost exclusively manned by Europeans or Indians. Their careers were tied up with scholastic qualifications, conditions of service, service and company rules, rates of promotion, competition for jobs with expatriate and other rivals, housing and the cost of living, the policies of the organisations to which they belonged and, above all, the policies of the Colonial government which was now concerned with every aspect of education, labour conditions, immigration and welfare. The new men's relationship with the Europeans at Aden was not one of buying and selling but of alternate individual command and collective negotiation. Europeans, Indians and Arabs had never been so closely tied on such a permanent basis and there was the constant grating of mutual incomprehension, harshness, mistrust and uncertainty as the new society emerged. Despite the government's emphasis on the 'neutral' subjects of science and technology and its careful recruitment of supposedly 'safe' teachers from Jordan or the Sudan, students in Aden's schools were soon alive to the political movements in the Middle East and the world at large and were discussing nationalist ideas hostile to the existing regime in Aden. In 1946 the students struck in protest that the anniversary of the founding of the Arab League was not made a public holiday.[23] This was symptomatic of the development of political consciousness among the steadily increasing student population.

The 1940s and early 1950s were a transitional period during which the old shopkeeping Aden remained dominant but suffered some nasty blows. In 1948 there was a wave of labour unrest in the port. Its origins lay in the wartime and post-war price inflation which made it difficult for the average worker to survive on the wages he received. But the situation was much worsened by a quarrel that developed between the traditional private employers of labour and the government and semi-public institutions. In July 1948 a Government Commission of Inquiry (the Corney Commission) recommended that inflation be offset by a general increase in the emoluments of all public employees, backdated to the beginning of 1946. These recommendations found their way into the press and at once the employers fell into disarray. Private business, realising that they would have to follow the Government's lead, objected to the form and detail of the proposed award and secured a suspension of action while discussions proceeded. The workers however had also read of the Corney proposals and quickly became impatient at this procrastination. On 1 August, the floating craft workers struck, and extracted an interim award from the Port Trust. A month later workers at the B.P. oil depot secured a similar douceur. Other commercial concerns and the Government itself also had to follow with concessions. Meanwhile, discussions about the main award went on slowly until November. By then the workers had once more lost patience and the B.P. employees struck, followed by Cowasji's and Cory's men. The port was paralysed, 850 men came out, and the original dispute was soon overlaid by other grievances as attempts were made to negotiate. Three weeks went by before the men were induced to return by the promise that all workers would receive the full extent of the award to the government employees.

The 1948 strikes revealed the weakness, indeed the virtual absence of any system of industrial bargaining recognisable as such to those accustomed to handling these matters in more developed parts of the world. The management of B.P. raised its influential voice in protest and the Colonial Office, which now had a powerful section concerned with labour affairs, was determined that something decisive should be done. The breakdown had been produced partly by the inability of the different managements to agree on a consistent policy. But as the debate proceeded, the antediluvian system of labour organisation at Aden with its *muqaddams* and *Syrangs*, its labour brokers and casual labourers, was brought into the limelight to be ridiculed by Colonial Office officials, Oil Company personnel managers and reforming labour advisers alike. Since the late nineteenth century, government officials had looked askance at Aden's labour brokers and the private employers who sponsored them, but had neither sufficient will nor sufficient means to do much about them. Now they had both. The Colonial Office under a Labour Government was more anxious than ever to bring about improvement in the industrial field. The peculiarities of the British colonial system of government normally set close limits to metropolitan interference, but a breakdown such as that of 1948 provided a way in. One of the first results of the 1948 strikes was the establishment of a Labour Office at Aden and the appointment of a Labour Officer. From this small beginning, the Labour and Welfare Department steadily grew over the next ten years and became one of the most active innovating agencies of the Aden Government. It was dedicated to the modernisation of Aden's industrial relations, the fostering of trade unions and the abolition of the old *muqaddam* system. It had the support in the first instance of the Port Trust and B.P. It drew on the aid of the British Trade Union movement which, through the Labour Department of the Colonial Office, provided moral support and expert advice. It had the patronage of Sir Tom Hickinbotham, who spoke for reform as Chairman of the Port Trust, and who then became Governor of the Colony for the period 1951–6. Against this combination the supporters of the old system, strong as they were in the commercial world, could only fight a delaying action. When, in 1954, the B.P. refinery began permanent operations with its 2,500 workers, recruited without recourse to the usual *muqaddams*, mostly housed by the firm, provided with medical services and other amenities and directly paid what was in the Aden context a good wage, the balance of forces swung heavily against those who opposed change.[24]

The next wave of labour unrest which hit Aden in 1956 represented in many ways the turning-point between the old society and the new. The demands of workers were concerned with improvements in living standards and conditions of employment rather than with increased wages alone. The refinery and the Port Trust had established norms which others were anxious to attain. A 48-hour working week, annual leaves, sickness pay and free medical attention were among the improvements that the strikers secured as a result of their action. Once more the men on the floating craft were in the forefront of the fight, followed by dock labour. On this occasion, however, the work stoppage was on a far larger scale than in 1948. The disputes spread from the port to practically all the major employers of labour in Aden. At the peak, in March to April 1956, more than 7,000 men were involved, and during the course of the trouble there were two serious clashes between workers and police.[25] The nature of worker organisation was also very different from what it had been before. In 1953 the Labour Department had still been ruefully reporting that workpeople 'have little conception of labour organisation or of collective bargaining'. In that year however three trade unions were already registered. At the beginning of 1956 there were eight workers' unions; at the end of the same year there were twenty-four involving some 4,000 men.[26] The unions were dominated from the start by the new men in the offices and workshops who had gradually been coming to the forefront of Aden's life.[27] They were not the spontaneous creation of Aden's labouring classes. The lower-paid workers had grievances and aspirations, but could not provide the leadership to negotiate complex deals with managements. Nor were the labour brokers capable of filling the breach – this was not their line of business and they fell into the background, harried by the clerks and other junior professional men who called for the dissolution of the *muqaddam* system. Within a short time the *muqaddams* were only able to survive by assuming a position subordinate to the new labour leadership.[28] The clerks, intellectuals and educated craftsmen were the men of the hour. They offered their services to the workers first of all as members of the radical United National Front and later, when employers refused to negotiate with politicians, in the guise of trade union leaders. Success bred success. The ability of the new young men to extract large concessions from management by the use of the strike weapon convinced workers that they were the men to follow. The trade union movement went from strength to strength; by 1959 more than 15,000 men were unionised, by 1963 trade union membership exceeded 22,000 – more than one-third of Aden's working population other than domestic servants.

Strikes occurred with increasing frequency and every employer
who was susceptible to pressure was squeezed to grant the maximum
benefits to his personnel.[29] Trade union leaders became prominent
and popular men in Aden society, negotiating with employers,
haranguing and organising workers, consulting with the Government
about labour and welfare matters.

The rise of the young professionals was not regarded by all the
members of Arab society with equal favour. At least one group was
jealous of the sudden popularity they had acquired, and especially
disliked their claim to political leadership. This group comprised
Aden's traditional political families – the Hassan 'Alis, the
Luqmans, Mackawis and others, long resident in the Colony and
interlinked by family and other ties. These families had provided
brokers of a special type, men whose business it was to mix commerce
and politics, seeking the right formulae for reconciling the British
administration with Arab society inside and beyond the Colony.
They were political specialists, ready to adapt their methods to
changing times. The Jaffer dynasty had played a notable role in
the nineteenth century, and their spiritual descendants in related
families helped found Aden's first newspaper, with some government
aid, in the middle 1940s, again mediating between government and
Arab public opinion, moving forward but not so far as to lose touch
with what advanced British thinking might be prepared to concede.[30]
These families belonged to Aden and felt that Aden belonged to
them. No doubt Aden was a British colony, that was a factor to be
reckoned with. But that did not mean that on another plane the old
political families did not feel themselves to be in some sense in
charge. In human terms, Aden's colonial government represented a
kaleidoscope of changing British faces, apart that is, from the very few
who found promotion in Aden and not in other parts of Britain's
empire. Did Aden belong to this multitude of passers-by or to the
families who spent their lifetimes studying the quirks and shifts in
the Aden scene? As each British newcomer came and fumbled with
the complexities of public policy, Aden's professionals smiled,
weighed him up and fitted him into the appropriate place on the
chessboard. Should he have recourse to them for information they
were ready to open to him the arcana of the accumulated family
knowledge – their own image of Aden's reality. This was their line
of trade, as so many Aden dealers had their specialities. They
expected in return to be consulted and to wield their traditional
continuing influence over the administration. A government which
left them out of account would be resented; so also would any new
political group which invaded their special field and tried to oust
them from their place. If the young clerks and professionals stuck

to trade unionism well and good. They could be weighed up and added to the galaxy of forces to be controlled. But the supple old political managers did not want new men, especially those who spurned or disregarded their advice, to step in and supplant them.[31] Nor did they hold much brief for those who called for the complete overthrow of British rule. Until British power began visibly to crack in the 1960s they regarded such programmes as unrealistic. What they hoped for was gradual political advance by negotiation and in 1956 the goal of the Aden Association, which broadly reflected their interests, was self-government for Aden within the Commonwealth, a formula which would institutionalise their mediatory position at a higher level than before.[32]

The Aden Association might have been tailor-made to act as a partner to a reforming British colonial government. One might say indeed that the lines of flexibility and inflexibility in Britain's post-war colonial policy created the niche into which the Association's politicians fitted. Aden officials looked to them as the representatives of the people of Aden, consulted them informally and conceived of political concessions in terms of widening the area of participation by these 'responsible' men in government through the Port Trust, the township authorities and the Legislative Council. Colonial policy on the industrial front however created another niche of a different kind into which the young clerks who assumed the role of trade union leaders more or less fitted during the formative years of the labour movement. They were employees, they were able to secure the confidence of the workers as a mass, and were best qualified to establish a bureaucratic union machine in continuous negotiation with management, which was how the colonial government hoped that labour relations would ultimately be conducted. But to the dismay of the authorities, the trade union leaders constantly tended to go beyond the area of competence assigned to them. They were expected to conform to the British pattern of a trade union movement which stuck to industrial bargaining and did not directly engage in politics. This they never did. Those who led the unions had first of all been concerned with politics. They had only abandoned their label as leaders of the young and radical United National Front as a tactical manoeuvre to secure control of the workers' movement, but never abandoned their political ideas and aspirations. The leadership of the Aden Trades Union Congress, which was formed in 1956, interlocked with that of the U.N.F. Despite the efforts of the Labour Department and visiting British Trades Unionists, political objectives continually reappeared at the side of industrial grievances in trade union demands.[33] The very form of the unions, which began as 'house unions' gathering together the whole, predominantly Arab staff from office to workshop in a block against expatriate management and supervisory personnel, underlined the nationalist character of the movement.[34] Their constant concern with the exclusion of expatriates from employment and from the colony reflected the clerks' fears of Indian competition for desirable posts, rather than communal rivalry between Arab and Somali labourers. This was another area in which politics and industrial relations overlapped. It was an area around which trade union propaganda was built up most vigorously at an early stage. By 1958 the Aden T.U.C. had virtually taken over the political stage from its moribund partner the U.N.F., and had become the main focus of radical nationalism in Aden.

There was little hope of meaningful negotiation about politics between the colonial government and the young radicals of the U.N.F. and T.U.C. during the 1950s. British policy, as stated by Lord Lloyd, the Colonial Secretary, to the Legislative Council in 1956, did not even envisage the eventual self-government which the moderate Aden Association asked for.[35] The ending of British rule at Aden figured in the U.N.F.'s programme from the very start. They also advocated the absorption of Aden and its Protectorate into the Yemen and, although this was not a feasible programme for immediate action while the utterly un-radical Imam Ahmad ruled across the border, it postulated an ultimate destiny for the colony which was quite at odds with British long-term thinking at practically every stage. The Aden administration therefore preferred the more comfortable company of the old Aden political managers. This entailed a certain inconsistency in their general stance toward the Arab community. On the industrial front they supported the new against the old. On the political front they maintained the old against the new. When members were nominated to deliberative bodies other than those concerned with labour and welfare in the colony they were chosen from among the elderly and the bourgeois. Management and commerce were represented on the Municipal and Legislative Councils; labour was not. When the first elections were held, in 1949 for the Municipal, in 1955 for the Legislative Council, the vote was given to the Aden-born, and British subjects long resident in Aden, a formula which included Indians and Somalis but excluded immigrant Yemenis. Property and age qualifications for candidates and voters were also calculated to exclude the young trade unionists and their supporters.[36] All this fitted with the classic British pattern of constitutional evolution, general British beliefs about the nature of trade union organisation and an, at first sight, logical policy of distinguishing between floating and stable, foreign and Commonwealth elements in the population.

In practice it emphasised and prolonged the division between what was old and what was new in the character of the community. Elected Legislators and trade union leaders depended on what were in the main different constituencies. They were soon at loggerheads with one another. In 1956 the Legislative Council asked for an inquiry to determine how far strikes were politically motivated. In January 1959 the T.U.C. organised a boycott of the Legislative Council elections. In 1960 the Legislative Council passed the Industrial Relations Ordinance which restricted the right to strike and imposed compulsory arbitration. By the end of that year 'death to the Legislative Council' had become one of the T.U.C.'s main political slogans.

While the Aden scene was changing with increasing rapidity during the 1950s, the tempo of events in the Protectorate was mounting too. The 'forward movement', which had begun during the Second World War, continued to advance in surges as funds and staff were forthcoming and as hesitations and fears of Yemeni inteference and opposition waned.[37] The period between 1951 and 1954 saw further large strides made on all fronts. New administrative organisations were established in the pacified 'Awlaqi country. Roads were extended eastward and northward. Existing administrations were purged of tribal placemen and the savings pumped into new social welfare schemes. Agricultural development was pressed ahead, especially at Abyan, where new land was brought under tillage, the cotton acreage extended and ginneries built. Immigrant farmers, most of them from the lowest classes of South Arabian society, flocked into the comparatively prosperous towns and villages of Abyan whose population swelled tenfold in seven years.[38] The Abyan Development Board, managed by expatriate personnel, presided over this development and accumulated marketing profits which were used to support similar progress elsewhere in the Protectorate, at Ahwar, Dathinah, 'Awdhali country and Lahej. In Abyan itself, the British-advised administrations of the Fadli and Yafi'i states were rich with the rents paid by sharecroppers who farmed the extensive state lands. They financed educational and health services on a scale which no other Western Protectorate states could match.

Improved communications, education and commercial agriculture were changing the whole aspect of Aden's hinterland. A more integrated society was beginning to emerge and the vision of those most actively engaged in this dynamic process widened as each forward step seemed to open up new and more exciting possibilities. The British officials became increasingly impatient of the existing fragmented administrative structures. They wanted an escape from the unnecessary duplications and parochial corruption of the chiefdoms. The 'forward policy' men had lost none of their hostility to chiefs and ruling clans, whom they still regarded as selfish and oppressive clogs on the wheels of progress.[39] They needed a more powerful central organisation to pool resources and finance large-scale development. The formula for this was Federation, and in January 1954 a proposal for the creation of a Federation of the States of the Protectorate was put before a gathering of chiefs.

The 1954 scheme for Federation was mostly of a piece with the rest of careful British 'forward policy' diplomacy. It did not seem to involve any very radical changes initially. The power of the British Agency was to be somewhat increased and that of the chiefs somewhat reduced.[40] In compensation, there was to be a shadowy Council of Rulers and some rulers were to be nominated to the central Executive and Legislative Councils which were to assist the Governor in controlling the re-vamped administration of the British Agency – an arrangement which harked back to the Sultan of Lahej's membership of the pre-war Committee for Protectorate Affairs.[41] But the scheme contained endless ambiguities in terms of the timing of measures and their relationship to Protectorate political realities, ambiguities, most of which the Governor alone was empowered to resolve.[42] The Governor was likely to become the 'honest broker' of the new state, while the rulers would dance attendance on him to secure their share of the loaves and fishes Federation would create. Beyond that, the Governor had it in mind to shift power right out of the chiefs' hands in the long run and transfer it to elected representatives of the people. Progressive men would be brought forward and the politics of the Protectorate transformed by careful British management. The bait was tempting to some; it offered to a chosen few, power far beyond what they had previously exercised. But there was one major defect. By speaking of a Federation and making the Governor its head, the proposal stated publicly and clearly what had hitherto been fudged and hidden under the *ad hoc* and the piecemeal. It set out in a constitutional document the awkward fact that the independent-minded men of Aden's hinterland had somehow been caught up in a British-directed system of administration. There were a number of men and groups in the Protectorate who saw the value of forming larger political entities in South Arabia. Some progressive men in the Hadramawt had proposed an amalgamation of the two Sultanates there in 1946. The South Arabian League had been formed in 1951 with the promotion of unity as one of its principal objectives. But political integration raised the question of the identity and the control of the new states. The Hadhrami movement had foundered on this issue, the Shaykh party seeing amalgamation as a device for extending Sayyidi power. The South Arabian League was beset with similar difficulties over the relationship to the Yemen and the role of the 'Abdali ruling family. None of these forward-looking men wanted a Federation under a British head. On the contrary, the South Arabian League aimed at emancipation from British control. When the Federation proposal was put to the rulers, those who wanted unity joined with the intransigent advocates of chiefly autonomy in rejecting it. Popular protest, expressed in more strident tones, and the hostile reaction of Egypt, the Yemen and the Arab World in general, indicated that it would be dangerous to proceed any further.[43]

The Federation proposal of January 1954 marked the turning of the tide in the Aden Protectorate. Already, strong forces were gathering against British rule. Advancing technology, which had carried the British forward in the inter-war period, now reversed its role. Where aircraft had enabled centralised military power to to penetrate the furthest fastnesses, radio now strode out to catch at the thoughts of men in inaccessible towns and hamlets and bring them into contact with broader movements beyond their parochial world. Political broadcasting to South Arabia had begun on the eve of the Second World War with German and Italian propaganda, followed by the B.B.C.'s efforts to counter it. This was but a crude prelude to what was to come later. It enlivened political discussion among a limited and already well-informed public in the most populous centres but that was all. The broadcast word only became a powerful political instrument in the 1950s and then it did so with the suddenness and force of a revolution. At almost the same time as Cairo Radio began to speak in the tones of revolutionary Arab nationalism, the development of cheap, transportable transistor radios created a mass audience among the poor and the remote.[44] Men who had long lived in isolation now found a common political language and a breathtaking, liberating community of sentiment with multitudes in their own land and across the Arab World. They soon began to echo Cairo's charges of colonialism. Aden's government had to try to meet this challenge but it was ill-equipped to do so. The Aden Information Office had been allowed to run down after 1945 until by 1952 it had almost ceased to exist. In 1954 it was brought back to life, a broadcasting station was opened and in 1956 its service was hurriedly extended, although it remained even technically no match for the Voice of the Arabs.[45]

Even with the best equipment, the British administration had little hope of competing with Egypt in the field of propaganda. It had no ideas to offer which could compare with Cairo's resounding appeals to Arab brotherhood and denunciations of colonialism.

The idea that Britain had obligations toward those with whom she had signed treaties could still pass muster in the legalistic context of international discussion but it was not the stuff out of which political slogans could be made. The Protectorate in such terms was an essentially negative entity. But to speak more positively would necessarily emphasise the fact of British tutelage. Even talk of progress toward self-rule conflicted with the idea that the treaty rulers were theoretically self-governing. The administration could not effectively use the radio to propagate broad and general ideas of political integration. Instead, broadcasting became one of the principal means by which popular sentiment was galvanised against British rule. As radios poured into Aden in a mounting flood throughout the 1950s and early '60s, the legitimacy of the British presence was steadily sapped away.

The general and growing dislike of foreign rule and interference was magnified and embittered in many cases by more immediate and personal grievances. Throughout the Protectorate important groups of rifle-carrying tribesmen had traditionally supplemented their meagre incomes by levying tolls or transporting goods by camel across the barren wastes they inhabited. Motor roads and lorries represented an invasion of their territory and a threat to their livelihood. In many cases the administration sought to cushion the effect of this by prohibiting the carriage of certain goods by lorry and continuing the collection of tolls.[46] Such measures were, however, regarded as temporary and whenever possible the lorry operators, most of them Adenis or other city men, were given free scope. In the 1920s and 1930s the Subayhi were squeezed out of the Yemen traffic in this way. In 1928 a road was pushed through to Dali' and thereafter the men of Radfan had to fight to retain their livelihood.[47] In the 1930s the roads from the coast to the Wadi Hadhramawt menaced the tribes on the Jol; in the 1940s further roads and famine relief measures pierced more holes in their former monopoly.[48] The same decade saw traffic opened through Fadli to 'Awdhali country, and as the lorry-borne export of vegetables and fruit got under way as a substantial scale in the 1950s tribesmen along that line had to stand by and watch processions of strangers' vehicles pass freely over routes where formerly each caravan had had its local guide. In 1951 new roads were thrust through from the coast to 'Awlaqi country against the protests of local people and under the protection of detachments of Government Guards. Another group thus saw their territorial independence invaded. Within two years they had become 'dissidents'.[49]

Other members of the tribesman class, who could traditionally pride themselves on being less badly off than some of their neighbours, were affected in other ways by the multifarious changes that were taking place. During the war years, Wahidi country lost substantial numbers of its lower classes who had formerly cultivated it for the profit of their betters. Some of the slave farmers were sold by their famine-stricken masters. Many of the weavers emigrated to Shaykh 'Uthman and Dar Saad to sell in the Aden market, which was temporarily starved of Japanese textiles. Wahidi *ra'iyah* joined the general rush of such men from uncompetitive farming areas toward the new lands at Abyan.[50] Dali' lost a substantial section of its taxable population when most of its Jewish weavers and artisans answered the call of Israel between 1945 and 1949. There were of course compensations for at least some of the tribesman class. Wherever the Agricultural Officers sank bore-wells, set up irrigation systems or developed new crops, those fortunate enough to have claims in the newly fruitful lands, or the ready cash to buy them, secured fresh sources of unearned income.[51] There were places to be had and stipends to be secured from the growing state administrations. For others again there was the possibility of joining the Tribal Guards, the Government Guards, the Protectorate Levies, the Aden Police or seeking employment in Aden where government and semi-public institutions, such as the refinery, were eager to place Protectorate recruits.[52] But this was different from living off traditional rents and tolls. These were the more assailable gains secured in a lottery whose most glittering prizes went to those who stood closest to the British-controlled administration. In taking them up a man entered a new world subject to the vagaries of British interference, administrative rules and, in the case of the Protectorate forces in the early '50s, falling real wages,[53] Government action was impinging at a multitude of points on the lives of many of the important tribesman class in South Arabian society and many among them had good reason to feel dissatisfied with its results. The backward were being hustled out of their old ways. Those who sought new opportunities found themselves beset on all sides by evidence of British interference and control. Their plight was beginning to resemble that of those who inhabited the new bureaucratic Aden.

As for the mass of settled cultivators, those in Abyan, in 'Awdhali country, Ahwar and some parts of the Hadhramawt could be said on the whole to have gained from the changes made. Life was more peaceful, the fear of famine had receded, there were growing possibilities of education, medical services were becoming more widespread and new crops earned more. But whatever material benefits they had received they could still as tenants, and often heavily indebted tenants, feel a sense of relative deprivation as others benefited even more than they from the new-found prosperity.[54] Above all, there was the sight of the well-heeled expatriate administration of the Abyan Board to excite envy and from 1954 onward the Yafi'i Na'ib Muhammad bin Idris focused popular attention on the Board's doings. The whole establishment and its accumulating reserves were of course maintained from the proceeds of marketing the crop, and this was brought home to farmers when in 1955 Lahej began cotton-growing on a large scale with Abyan developed seed, and paid a much higher price to the producers. The British controlled Abyan Board had to bow to popular clamour and raise its own price. From then on, relations between the Abyan administration and the farmers, which had never been good, were overlaid with distrust and further mutual incomprehension.[55] The lost profits of Abyan became a handy plank in every anti-British platform and the most materially successful development scheme in the Protectorate became politically a liability.

Violent resistance to innovation was nothing new to the Aden officials. They were inured to the hostility of road bandits and other disturbers of the peace and accepted them as inevitable.[56] While the administration could deploy overwhelming military force, these and other violent protests of the desperate and the angry could be mastered by the time-worn technique of aerial bombardment supplemented by increasing use of local ground forces. Behind the bombers and the Government Guards stood the strength of British power in the Middle East, which at the end of the war was greater than it had ever been before. Italian competition had been eliminated and, for a brief period, the other world powers were prepared to recognise British pre-eminence in the region. This did not last long. In a few dramatic years after 1950 Britain was harried out of her Egyptian base, challenged in Oman[57] by Sa'udi Arabia and defeated in the Suez débâcle. Arab nationalism, Russian rivalry and American criticism hacked great gashes in Britain's privileged position. The decline in Britain's power was brought home to the Aden administration by the actions of the neighbouring Yemen. In 1949 the Imam had recoiled from a fort on the Bayhan frontier after British air action and in 1950 his representatives concluded a *modus vivendi* agreement in London, much in the spirit of the 1934 pact.[58] Then the Yemeni attitude began to change. The 1950 agreement was not effectively carried out. Yemen became a haven for Protectorate rebels and from 1952 onward, with a few tactical pauses, the Imam's agents actively fostered unrest in the Protectorate.[59] British protests were rejected in the language of Arab nationalism amid appeals to the Arab League, the United Nations, the British and world press and public opinion. In private negotiation, the Imam's claims to the Protectorate were reiterated in a tone of increasing expectation that their early fulfilment had become a matter of practical politics.

The simultaneous upsurge of these forces in the middle 1950s dramatically altered the whole aspect of affairs in the Protectorate. At first resistance took the conventional form of sniping by Rabizi tribesmen at convoys sent to supply the garrison of the fort established in their territory in November 1953.[60] This had been anticipated. The administration had expected them to resist the effort to dominate their land and end their opposition to the forward movement in 'Awlaqi country. What was not anticipated was the tenacity of Rabizi resistance which was sustained by issues of arms from the Yemen. The situation was further complicated by additional outbreaks of violence, also Yemeni backed, in Bayhan, 'Awdhali country and Lower 'Awlaqi. All this represented a magnification of previous problems connected with the imposition of a British-directed peace-keeping administration within the Protectorate. The enemies of the new order had previously been terrorised into submission or picked off one by one; now, partly through Yemeni prompting, partly through the general growth of anti-imperialist sentiment, their activity assumed a self-confidence and co-ordination which taxed the small Protectorate forces to the limit. Strained thus at the periphery, during 1954 and 1955 the administration also had to face the first manifestations of serious unrest at the heart of the British system. In Lahej and Abyan the South Arabian League mobilised anti-British sentiment among townsmen and farmers. The 'Abdali and Lower Yafi'i authorities became less willing to co-operate with British officials. In Aden itself the League was busy and there the strands of protest in the Protectorate inter-laced with political agitation by the rising youth of the city. From Aden and Lahej nationalist ideas were carried back to the Protec-torate by schoolteachers and by the very soldiers of the Aden Levies who were despatched from their Aden depot to quell the insurgents in the more backward districts. Disaffection among the underpaid Levies reached serious proportions during 1954 and 1955. A whole detachment mutinied while on duty in Upper 'Awlaqi, hundreds deserted, others obeyed orders with reluctance. By the summer of 1955 it seemed that the whole system of British control was sagging toward collapse.

The whirlwind of opposition brought about a complete rethinking of the British position in the Protectorate. The forward policy as a whole was abruptly stopped. The further penetration of Upper 'Awlaqi was abandoned and a general disengagement from the remoter areas of the Protectorate was ordered. Garrisons were retained in a few key forts which could be supplied by air but the road patrols and convoys were discontinued. British troops were drafted in to extricate the most beleaguered garrisons. The Aden Levies were drawn back to their Aden depot for retraining and re-equipment under a more effective cadre of British officers. The pay and conditions of both Levies and Government Guards was raised far enough to restore morale and encourage new recruits to join. There was a return to more extensive use of air bombardment as a method of control despite growing reservations about its more disruptive effects. The administration reverted also to the long-abandoned policy of arms issues to control the situation on the frontier. The Yemeni supply of weapons to dissidents was countered by British issues of arms through Protectorate chiefs, notably the Sharif of Bayhan and the 'Awdhali Sultan. The measured diplomatic and military manoeuvres of British and Yemeni authorities along the frontier gave way to a free-for-all of shootings, forays and petty intrigues back and forth across the border by their local agents. Gradually the British-assisted chiefs gained the upper hand and the danger of Yemeni subversion was averted. At the expense of a general deterioration in law and order the Protectorate Government managed to ride out the storm.[61]

The events of 1954–5 effectively destroyed the long-term credibility of the British regime in the minds of acute observers. The Imam and the Protectorate rulers in different ways intimated to Aden officials that they did not expect British rule to last.[62] The policy of disengagement encouraged the belief that the British were withdrawing, as they were simultaneously withdrawing from their base at Suez. The major questions that now loomed up were not whether the British would hand over power but how much, when, and to whom. Among the various candidates for the succession, the Imam of the Yemen, persistently referring to his ancestral claims, appeared the most formidable to those responsible for British policy. His demands were the most familiar, and it was estimated that he had the greatest power to enforce them, as his interference was taken to be the cardinal reason for Protectorate dissidence. In London there was some advocacy of wide concessions such as the handing over of all but Aden's immediate hinterland to the Imam.[63] But the British Government was not prepared for such a leap in the dark. Instead, piecemeal efforts were made to improve Anglo-Yemeni relations. Britain and the more conservative elements in the Yemen had an evident common interest in maintaining the political *status quo* in South-West Arabia in the face of growing radical nationalism and this factor operated at various junctures between 1955 and 1962. Whenever Yemeni conservatism felt itself unduly threatened, olive branches were sent to Aden and these usually elicited a friendly British response.[64] Thus Anglo-Yemeni relations became a matter of more or less British interference in the more sensitive areas of the Protectorate, more or less Yemeni support for dissidents, more or less British pressure on Yemeni refugees and the Free Yemeni movement in Aden – a subtly played out game whose ground rules never changed.

The alternative to agreement with the Imam seemed to be negotiation with the rulers of the Protectorate, who figured more largely on the scene now that the policy of disengagement and the devolution of frontier defence gave them more freedom of action. After the abandonment of the British project for Federation in 1955, it was hoped that the chiefs might coalesce of their own accord into a friendly federation and stabilise Aden's hinterland. Among the rulers, the main support for Federation came from the 'Abdali ruling house, fertile as ever in supple political leadership. The Sultan, 'Ali 'Abd al Karim, had pleased many British officials by his zeal for domestic reform and when the federation idea was first mooted in Aden, Sultan 'Ali was an obvious candidate for a leading position in any new arrangement.[65] But 'Ali 'Abd al Karim had discarded none of the traditional 'Abdali determination to keep the British at arm's length, despite his willingness to sign an advisory treaty. Furthermore, he became heavily involved with the South Arabian League which advocated the incorporation of Aden in any new South Arabian State. This was at variance with the then British policy, and there was a gradual deterioration in Anglo-'Abdali relations after 1955.[66] Sultan 'Ali made no secret of his admiration for the rising power of Gamal 'Abd al Nasser and demonstrated his alignment by recruiting Egyptian schoolteachers for 'Abdali schools. He also came to be suspected of collusion with the Imam and with Yemeni supported dissidence in the Protectorate. The weight of opinion among British officials swung against him while 'Ali himself, striving to maintain contact with a League that was moving to the left, gravitated towards a position of outright opposition to British rule.

As 'Ali fell from favour, his rival rulers in the more backward areas of the north-east, Sharif Husayn of Bayhan and Sultan Salih al 'Awdhali, became more congenial company to the British administration. These men had been too localistic in outlook to be enthusiastic about federation, but they were stalwart in defence of the frontier against Yemeni raids. Gradually a new grouping of forces began to crystallise in the Protectorate – a grouping which, as always in the past, was mainly due to 'Abdali initiative. In their campaign for unity, Lahej and the South Arabian League, while issuing nationalist propaganda and seeking to create a broadly-based movement, had built up a political coalition by specific intrigue along old lines, gathering notabilities, rulers and factions in the various parts of the Protectorate into their camp. The rival notabilities, rulers and factions, in each case, inevitably began to gravitate toward one another and toward the British administration, in self-defence. The Lahej–League thesis produced an anti-'Abdali antithesis. Finally, the news of the formation of the United Arab Republic of Egypt and Syria and Yemen's adhesion to form the United Arab States, coupled with the rumour that Sultan 'Ali would abrogate his British Treaty and take Lahej into the union, brought the 'Abdali's disparate enemies to the point of fusion. In the spring of 1958 the rulers of Bayhan, 'Awdhali, Fadli, Lower Yafi'i, Dali' and Upper 'Awlaqi, came forward and proposed that their states should form the nucleus of a British backed Federation.[67] There could be no mistaking the anti-'Abdali character of the new combination – every individual had been directly affected by Sultan 'Ali's intrigues during the previous three years. The alliance was cemented almost at once by a British occupation of Lahej and the subsequent deposition of Sultan 'Ali. The rupture of the hundred-year-old alliance between the British and the house of 'Abdali in Aden hinterland affairs marked in many ways the end of an era. Other radical changes in the politics of the area were already in the offing.

After three years of indecision the British Government had made its choice. In February 1959 the Federation of Arab Amirates of the South was inaugurated as an autonomous entity subject to British advice and guaranteed by a British defence treaty.[68] It was an arrangement which conformed to the realities of the British predicament in South Arabia, although much less to the realities of the world on the eve of 1960. Since the whirlwind of 1955-6 the considerable persuasive powers and special expertise of British Political Officers had turned from securing acceptance of innovation to shoring up existing structures. Administration had given way to politics and in this field the colonial officials were limited by their inability to make any mass ideological appeal which could compete with that of their nationalist opponents. They had to make do with older methods of political management, concentrating on the particular rather than the general, winning over traditionally distinct individuals and groups by bribes and administrative favours. Their new-found allies (criticism of 'oppressive chiefs' had perforce gone by the board)[69] were in a somewhat similar situation. Broadcasting, education and general social integration cut into and rendered otiose the chiefs' traditional functions of interpreting a wider world to their parochial followers. Men like the Sultans of Lower Yafi'i and Upper 'Awlaqi, who in a sense stood for their tribal people, could retain some legitimacy in such a situation but these men held aloof and the rulers who were involved in the political game, either on the side of the Federation, or, like Sultan 'Ali, against it, found themselves regarded with increasing jealousy and scepticism.[70] The federal rulers, like the Political Officers, were confined mostly to the increasingly anachronistic methods of piece-meal bargaining with the hierarchies of a social system that was passing away.[71] It was this political style rather than the status of the rulers, most of whom, to borrow the colourful phrase of a Yemeni official were British selected chiefs 'of the day before yesterday', that warranted the use of the word 'feudal' as a description of the Federation, although the associated extension under its auspices of the old fief-holding land tenure in settled districts lent added meaning to the term.[72] Federal rule consisted of an amalgam of autocratic commands through British-created administrative structures, and political manipulation of traditionally-determined social mechanisms. As time went on and British money and skills were poured liberally into the system, the first feature tended to overshadow the second. The Federation never assumed an effective political identity. It remained what it had been at the start, an aggregation of interested individuals and groups, united not so much by a positive fellow-feeling as by fear of common enemies. This was reflected in the Federal constitution, which left the rulers as absolute as ever in their home districts, appointing delegates to a Federal legislature and sharing between them the Ministries and rotating Chairman-ship of the executive Council.

The most enthusiastic supporters of the Federation were the officials of the Protectorate administration. It provided them with escape from the tortuous diplomacy and uncertainties of the previous four years to the clear paths of administrative building toward discernible goals. It meant the resumption of the 'forward move-ment' in a new context under the Federal umbrella and with sub-stantial funds provided by the British Government. A new capital for the state was erected at Al Ittihad just beyond the Aden border, new vigour was breathed into the educational, medical and agricul-tural services, the construction of strategic roads was undertaken and, above all, the security forces were greatly expanded with an increasing proportion of Arab officers. The Government Guards which, together with the various Tribal Guards became the Federal Guards in 1959, trebled in size from under 1,000 to over 3,000 men between 1956 and 1961. In the latter year the Aden Levies were also built up to a strength of 3,000 and transferred to the Federation as

the 'Federal Army'.[73] New recruitment continued thereafter and
these wholly British-paid forces continued to grow out of all proportion to the small and poor state of less than a million souls they
were supposed to serve.[74] British-subsidised schemes of various
kinds produced a new wave of innovations and this lent a factitious
dynamism to the Federation which temporarily concealed but did
not remedy its underlying political fragility.

Almost as soon as the Federation was formed the question whether
Aden should be incorporated in it was broached. From a geographical, economic and administrative point of view Aden's exclusion
would have been an anomaly. From a political point of view, the
separation of head from body made no better sense. Aden with its
schools, its press and its political parties, generated political ideas
which emanated outward into the Protectorate. The South Arabian
League had wanted Aden as part of a South Arabian union so that
its politically-mobilised inhabitants could give force to the nationalist
movement in the hinterland. The promoters of the Federation,
looking across at the city from their growing offices at al Ittihad,
saw Aden as a place where opposition to their new state could organise and express itself under the shelter of the Colony's laws. The
focal point of that opposition was the leadership of the Aden trade
unions which still had their niche in the Colony's political and
administrative structure and were therefore able to continue an
open and meaningful existence. The trade union leaders were as
critical of the Federation as they were of the Legislative Council
and made no secret of the fact that they would act against its
interests if ever they got to power.

For its part, bourgeois Aden and the politicians it had elected
in 1959 to represent its interests, regarded the possibility of
joining the Federation with divided counsels. On the one hand they
were tempted to ally with the enemies of their enemies. On the
other, they feared that Federal poverty would be financed from
Aden's wealth, that Federal autocracy would disrupt the freedoms
of Aden's money-making life. They found too, when negotiations
got under way in 1961, that the Federal team was forcing Aden
toward a subordinate role in the union, setting it more or less on a
par with the tribal states. This was too galling for some of the Aden
political class whose forbears had interpreted the wishes of British
Aden to all the Protectorate chiefs. Like Sultan 'Ali of Lahej, they
expected to lead, as they had always done in the past.[75] The reversal
of fortunes left them muttering in opposition. In the last resort the
merger was carried through by an act of British will. Aden's hesitations were bought off with promises of subsidies and the assignment

of Colony security to the Governor. The Legislative Council was blackmailed by making advance toward self-government conditional on acceptance of the merger.[76] Under these conditions the Council voted Aden into the Federation on 27 November 1962 by a narrow majority, with the concurrence of those in the city who opposed the rising radical tide in South-West Arabia generally and feared the faceless, property-threatening Aden mobs.[77]

With Aden's inclusion in the Federation, the whole structure of Britain's relations with South Arabia was apparently clarified and simplified. Of Britain's former dependencies only the Qu'ayti and Kathiri states, which still hoped to find oil, and Upper Yafi'i, whose links with Aden had always been tenuous, remained outside the Federation by 1965. Instead of the multiplicity of diplomatic relationships with Protectorate rulers, with political groups in Aden, with the Yemen and with Egypt, Britain was now committed to a defence pact with a single political entity which had been promised ultimate independence and which in turn had guaranteed the continuance of the British base. But political and administrative simplicity had been won at a considerable price. Within British official circles, the path to Federation was bestrewn with discarded policy alternatives. Many of the advocates of other solutions, of negotiation with the South Arabian League, with the Yemen, with Egypt and with the Aden Trade Unionists as well as those who would have preferred a separately developing, Singapore-like Aden, remained unplacated. With troubled minds and frayed tempers, they watched with a critical eye the performance of the aggressively determined protagonists of the Federation policy, who by this stage had become perilously few in number.[78] Outside the Government offices, criticism mounted in the British press, Parliament and the Trade Union movement. Journalists witnessed the violent protests in Aden that accompanied the passing of the Federation bill through the Legislative Council. In November 1962, the opposition Labour Party in Britain formally declared itself against the merger of progressive Aden with the 'feudal' Federation.[79] Thenceforward the Federation's fortunes were tied to those of the governing Conservative Party, with consequent effects on its ultimate credibility. To make matters worse, a thoroughly divided Britain was called upon to justify its policies before the bar of world opinion. During the merger negotiations discontented Aden politicians appealed to the United Nations to intervene.[80] The question was taken up by the Committee on Colonialism and from then on all that the Federal and British authorities did was subject to the baleful scrutiny of that hostile body. Its criticisms were much more difficult to meet than the charges of border violations which the Yemen had from time to time brought before the United Nations. The political weakness of the British-backed Federation was fully exposed.[81] It became evident that the United Nations would never accept it as representative of the people of South Arabia, and with that the possibility of sheltering the British base behind an eventually independent and internationally recognised Federation began to recede.

While the general political bases of Britain's hundred-and-twenty-year-old position in Aden were crumbling away, British military forces were rumbling into the town in unprecedented numbers. At last Aden was being made into a first-class British military base. In 1960 it was made the headquarters of Middle East Command and thereafter it came to be regarded as the pivot of British defence in the Middle East, with the dual role of defending the oil-rich dependencies in the Persian Gulf and acting as a staging-point toward the other major East of Suez base at Singapore. The number of British soldiers in the garrison had been steadily mounting since 1957, and in 1964 a full brigade of troops was brought in from Kenya. Aden was subjected to a final British invasion. Except for periods of crisis and war, Aden had never before been called upon to harbour so many British troops. Nineteenth-century Aden had seldom had more than two thousand British and Indian soldiers stationed in the settlement. For much of the twentieth century there had only been a few hundred men of the Royal Air Force. Now, soldiers, sailors and airmen poured in with their wives and families. By 1964 there were eight thousand members of the armed forces, not counting their dependants. Added to the supervisory personnel of the Refinery and the expanded Government Departments, they made Aden more British than it had ever been before. The base dominated Aden's life in the 1960s, initiating a variety of new building projects, creating new demands for consumer goods, and employment for up to 20,000 Arab workers.[82] Talk of forthcoming independence sounded hollow and unreal to those who saw this influx of foreigners into a city they were beginning to regard as their own. The weight of military might also hung heavily on those who were planning Aden's fate. The Ministry of Defence had its own exigent ideas about how much security the base required.[83] Military chiefs in Aden had professional ideas about internal security operations which did not always correlate well with the delicately diplomatic methods that had been used in creating and maintaining British Aden.[84]

During late 1962 and 1963 forces built up on either side for a final climatic struggle. The gathering of pro-British groups in Aden and South Arabia under the Federal umbrella was matched by an

unexpected solidarisation of their various opponents. A week before
the Aden Legislative Council opted by a narrow majority for merger
with the Federation, the old Imam Ahmad died and on the day of the
Legislative Council vote his son and successor, Badr, was swept away
by a republican revolution. The greatest 'chiefdom' of all was thus
overthrown and a tremor passed through the whole of South-West
Arabia. The position of chiefs and Sayyids was everywhere shaken
and the revolution in the Yemen was followed by minor anti-Sayyid
revolutions in certain parts of the Hadhramawt.[85] The men of the new
order in Aden were jubilant. Some who had been active in Aden
politics went off to become Ministers in Republican Yemen, others
went there to open up businesses. Those that remained behind
strengthened their resolve to destroy the Federation, remove British
control and unite Aden with its revolutionary neighbour. While the
old Imam Ahmad had still lived his dual policy of hostility to British
rule in the protectorate and ultra conservatism in the Yemen had
confused and complicated the political scene in South-West Arabia.
Now the revolutionary régime in the Yemen, bound in close alliance
with President Nasser's Egypt and with the revolutionary forces in
Aden removed much ambiguity and uncertainty. The British
Government's decision under pressure from Federal Ministers to
refuse recognition to the new régime in the Yemen and the Federal
Government's alignment with counter revolutionary Imamic forces
reinforced this polarisation.[86]

     In the new and harsher climate the nationalist movement in Aden
and the Protectorate began to change its shape. The initiative passed
from the hands of the older political managers of the South Arabian
League to the younger and more radical activists who formed the
'National Liberation Front' in June 1963. Throughout the autumn
preparations were made for a violent struggle and in October the
N.L.F. proclaimed a revolutionary struggle against the Federal
régime.[87] In Aden revolutionary words flowed faster and more
turbulently around the backstreets. In the hinterland, especially in
areas close to the Yemen border, a well-directed stream of weapons
ran through the hands of N.L.F. organisers towards tribesmen in the
hills, and sporadic clashes occurred.[88] The flash-point came with a
grenade attack on the High Commissioner, Sir Kennedy Trevaskis, at
Aden airport in December 1963. The High Commissioner escaped but
his deputy was killed as he shielded his chief from the blast. Trevaskis,
who was the main architect of the Federation, struck back with
vigour. A state of emergency was proclaimed throughout the whole
Federation. The leaders of the People's Socialist Party, which since
1962 had been the main organ of nationalist opinion in Aden, were
thrown into detention. At the end of the month a major operation was

launched with three battalions of the Federal Army against in-surrectionaries in the Radfan mountains.[89] During the next year the application of emergency regulations stifled protest in Aden. But on all other fronts the Federation fought a losing battle. Bourgeois Aden was alarmed and alienated by the application of Protectorate authoritarianism to the city.[90] The use of such methods under the eyes of the international press against men like the P.S.P. leader, 'Abdallah al Asnag, who had already cut a figure for themselves on the world scene, contributed further to the discredit of the Federation idea in the United Nations and in Britain. The invasion of Radfan brought no political dividends: rather the reverse. In March, the Federal Army had to be pulled out and in the following month a new effort was made with mainly British troops. A quick little muscle-flexing operation was expected. Instead, the Radfan marksmen, defending their rugged homeland, turned out in strength and drew in the greater part of the disposable force at the Aden base and, with it, a good deal of the *raison d'être* of the base itself. The British and Federal armies forced their way into the fertile heart of Radfan during the course of the year, but at enormous financial and political cost.[91]

Meanwhile, the Federal Government stood up badly to the political strain. British tutelage became more obtrusive as the war was being fought. Among the rulers there was a certain loss of nerve as the stakes were piled up beyond what they could comprehend or control. The Federation's ramshackle political machinery was inadequate to the tasks of administrative expansion and political manoeuvre in war conditions.[92] In London, the Conservative Ministry wavered back and forth under the pressure of controversy and adverse publicity until its fall in October 1964. The Labour Government which succeeded it was determined upon a change of policy. Within a few weeks of coming to power the new Colonial Secretary, Anthony Greenwood, removed Trevaskis from his post as High Commissioner and thus ended any hope that the Federation would survive along existing lines.

The advent of the Labour Government gave a new shape to British policy in Aden. Commitment to the Federation gave way to a more studied regard for underlying British interests.[93] The base was to be retained, but only if it did not involve tying down British forces in support of an unpopular local regime. The Colonial Secretary's main task therefore was to concoct a more popular government for South Arabia. Counting upon the good relations members of the Labour Party had maintained with 'Abdallah al Asnag and the P.S.P. while in opposition. Greenwood set about transforming the existing Federal regime by creating a unitary form of government which would reduce the power of the rulers, and by calling a round table conference out of which it was hoped a broadly-based government would emerge. But the time for this form of negotiation had passed. On the surface it appeared that Greenwood's diplomacy was successful in that he got the agreement of both the Federal ministers and 'Abdallah al Asnag to the broad lines of his programme. But while he was engaged in these discussions in Aden at the end of November, violent demonstrations were exploding in the city. During the next month grenade attacks against British servicemen began: Aden was erupting into sporadic violence and British-imposed order was beginning to break down. In February 1965 the N.L.F., which was now pushing itself to the fore in competition with 'Abdallah al Asnag's trade union-based organisation, threatened to kill anyone who attended Greenwood's constitutional conference.[94] Disputes also arose concerning the agenda for the conference, and finally it had to be cancelled. In March 1965 Greenwood tried to move toward a more broadly-based regime from another angle. 'Abd al Qawi Mackawi, a front figure for the P.S.P. in the Aden Legislative Council, was made Chief Minister in place of the pro-Federal Baharoon. With a representative of the nationalists thus placed in the heart of the Federal system, the British Government began to manoeuvre toward further constitutional reform.

But Mackawi proved a wrecker rather than a negotiator. Outside the Council, violence continued; the press of bourgeois Aden now fearfully toed the nationalist line, and the elected members voted unanimously in April for the suspension of the state of emergency and the implementation of the 1963 United Nations resolution, which had called for immediate elections throughout the Federation on the basis of universal suffrage and the grant of independence.[95] The Aden delegates walked out of the Federal Council and in July 1965 Mackawi checkmated another British initiative by banning the entry of two Commissioners appointed by the British Government to draft a new constitution. In August Greenwood made one more attempt at negotiated constitutional reform by convening a working party of Federal ministers and representatives of all political parties, except the prescribed N.L.F., in London. But this too failed, owing to controversy over the security of the base and the form elections should take in the rural areas.[96] This phase of British policy was brought to an end by the dismissal of Mackawi in September and the reversion to Crown Colony Government in Aden in the face of continuing urban insurgency.

During the next three months London came round to the view that the base had become untenable and in February 1966 it was

announced that Britain would abandon it by 1968.[97] From then on
the principal object was to withdraw British troops in good order and
to prepare a viable successor government. Efforts were made to
open up further negotiations to this end, but the initiative had by
this time passed from British hands. The legitimacy of British rule
had long disappeared. With the declaration that Britain would
hand Aden over, the network of personal relationships, promotion
prospects, feelings of professional duty and expectation of political
gain which still bound many individuals to the government machine
began to fray. During late 1965 and early 1966 a number of key men
in the Police Special Branch were assassinated. By mid-1966 the
British authorities had come to regard the Civil Police as unreliable.[98] Disaffection spread to the very heart of the administration
and the Federal armed forces. The financial and technical aspects
of British administration still went forward. Army engineers were
building and tarring roads northward and eastward of Aden as
fast as those mining them would permit.[99] Schools were being
constructed while students spent an increasing amount of time striking in protest at British rule. Money and training officers were
poured in during 1966 to expand the Federal Army to ten battalions
while many of the soldiers strengthened their affiliations with the
nationalist organisations. An influx of British and newly-trained
Arab civil servants passed more and more files to each other at Al
Ittihad along corridors echoing with political emptiness. The
contracts for construction of new married quarters for British
servicemen were scarcely complete when the decision to withdraw
was taken.

By contrast, purposeful politics were now being pursued elsewhere,
in Ta'izz, in the Radfan hills, the cotton fields of Abyan, and the
offices and backstreets of Aden. There the struggle to create a new
Arab government for South Yemen was being fought out. During
1966 practically all the principal opponents of British rule, ranging
from deposed Sultans who retained links with some of their erstwhile
colleagues in the Federal Government, to Mackawi, 'Abdallah
al Asnag and the men of the N.L.F., were gathered together in the
broadly-based Front for the Liberation of South Yemen. The
Front had the support of Egypt and was recognised as the principal
nationalist body by the U.N. Committee on Colonialism. But it
lasted only as long as the well-organised activists in the N.L.F. felt
the need of international assistance and the services of prominent
negotiators such as Mackawi and al Asnag in the fight against the
isolated and retreating British regime. At the end of the year, the
N.L.F. definitively broke off from the main body, turning its guns
against its rivals and securing its own funds by blackmailing mercan-

tile Aden. The battle against British forces and the anti-colonialist dynamic then gripping South Arabia, put a premium upon an intransigent appeal to all those who had lost most or benefited least during the period of British rule, and to those lowest down on the new competitive promotional ladders which bureaucratic Aden and the Protectorate administration had created. The men most willing to fight were the disherited tribesmen of the hills, sons of indebted *ra'iyah* cultivators, the lower ranks and most recent recruits in the forces and government service – the educationally backward and unskilled Protectorate rather than the relatively privileged Aden. It discounted not only the Federal Government but also deposed rulers, ministers who had resigned, the South Arabian League, senior officers in the Federal forces, most notably the 'Awlaqi, and even the Aden nationalist politicians and trade union leaders who, though persecuted by the Federal Government, had yet from time to time found favour in British eyes. The political climate changed with incredible swiftness in a radical direction and many of the adherents of F.L.O.S.Y., which had seemed to be the acme of nationalism in early 1966, assumed the guise of a doomed political generation by the second half of 1967. The action of Egypt and of the United Nations, once so important, became increasingly irrelevant, and in March 1967 a visit by a delegation from the Committee on Colonialism to Aden ended in fiasco.

The British could in no way control this whirlwind of nationalist revolution or influence the choice of their successors. The best they could do was to conduct a fighting retreat. During their last year of tenure, the British security forces, blinded by lack of information, desperately tried to maintain a semblance of order along the main highways.[100] In June 1967 they drew back from the hinterland into Aden and at once the N.L.F. took over and was accepted by the garrisons of the Federal Army. In July they had to face a mutiny in the Federal Army and Police which came within an ace of provoking a major conflict between British and Federal forces. All round them the battle for supremacy between the N.L.F. and F.L.O.S.Y. raged sporadically into gun battles in the streets while both sides sponsored demonstrations and launched periodic terrorist attacks on British personnel to point up their nationalist legitimacy. In September F.L.O.S.Y. was finally driven from the field and the Federal Army in Aden declared for the N.L.F. Meanwhile, the evacuation of British troops and the removal of the base had been under way since June, with British servicemen operating the strike-bound port. The progressive abandonment of section after section of the Aden conurbation took the form of a military withdrawal in the face of the enemy. Finally only a tight perimeter round the airfield and the barracks remained and on 29 November 1967 the last men were flown out by helicopter to a naval task force assembled in the harbour, and Aden was handed over unconditionally to the victorious N.L.F.

So ended the hundred and twenty-eight years of British rule in Aden. Its evacuation sounded the death knell of British dominion in the Middle East and also closed an epoch in the history of the city. For a thousand years or more, Aden had essentially belonged to the wealthy merchants of the world, be they South Yemeni or foreign, while the people of its hinterland watched with jealous and poverty-stricken eyes from beyond its gates. The British period of mercantile rule had differed somewhat from that of earlier periods. British Aden had never until its last years been a prepossessing town. Within its protective shell of imposing fortifications, it straggled untidily across the mountains and along the foreshore, its low-profiled, tentacular appearance corresponding with the diversely engaged acquisitiveness of its inhabitants who gathered in wealth to embellish their homes in the Hahdramawt or the Yemen, Bombay or London, Massachusetts or the French Riviera. The Karimi merchants and others in mediaeval times had often been agents for principals in Cairo or elsewhere, but no previous generation of traders had created so little of beauty in the town, although one could scarcely have expected those who handled raw skins, cheap textiles and coal in the 'cinder heap of the world' to match the efforts of dealers in fragrant incense and spices, silks, jewels and luxury articles of every kind. British Aden was an outpost of a world commercial and industrial society concerned with the production and exchange of low-cost goods in mass and reflected its most unlovely aspects until that society found the means to its own amelioration. When it did, the days of British Aden were numbered. Modern, bureaucratic, technological society, and the ideas flowing through it, were hostile to the old fragmented social structures and the multitude of brokers, interpreters and political managers who profited from their discontinuities. In the last thirty years of British rule, the Colonial Government acted as the agency of these new forces, jostling the mercantile city and knitting together the peoples of the hinterland until embarrassing questions were asked about the reasons for its own presence. The initiative then passed to the leaders of the national revolution whose attitudes coincided with those of reforming British officials in more ways than either would have cared to admit. The reconquest of Aden in the 1960s by the men of the hinterland did not represent another of those subjugations of the city by its tribal neighbours which had heralded disaster in the past. It represented a revolution in a roughly-knit society comprehending all of South Arabia which was now predominantly urban in character and attitudes. The new leaders took over a considerably damaged inheritance for, apart from the dislocation caused by the revolution itself, the winding up of the base and simultaneous closure of the Suez Canal knocked away the two main props of British Aden's prosperity. There remained however, a greater abundance of local skills and resources, better attuned to the needs of a wider world, than at any time in the past. And Aden was still a place of great potential strategic value – greater indeed than when engulfed in a broader British power system stretching from Egypt to India, as it had been from 1882 until the Second World War. Aden could still expect to profit from that position so long as the Great Powers of the world were convinced that they could serve their national interests by deploying force beyond the borders of their own states.

Notes

CHAPTER I

1 *The Times* (11 March 1839), p. 4, column c (27 March 1839), p. 3, column e. *Bombay Times* (20 February 1839), p. 113.

2 H. Wilberforce Bell, 'The Romance of Aden', *Journal of the Royal Central Asian Society* (Vol. 10, 1923), p. 149.

3 H. Salt, *A Voyage to Abyssinia* (London, 1814), p. 114.

4 Abyan was clearly a rich cultivated area in Rasulid times. See J. W. Redhouse (trans.), *The Pearl Strings: a History of the Rasuliyy Dynasty of Yemen by Aliyy ibn al Hasan al Khazrijiyy* (London, 1906–18, Vol. III, Part I, pp. 278, 280–1 and *passim*. I have been unable to determine when cultivation declined at Abyan. Aden secured provisions from the Berbera coast in the early sixteenth century but the ruler of Khanfar appears to have been a powerful man in the third decade of the seventeenth century. Abyan probably declined at the same time as Aden – in the sixteenth to seventeenth centuries.

5 J. Ryckmans, 'Petits royaumes sud-arabes', *Muséon* (Vol. LXX, 1957), p. 76.

6 C. Préaux, *L'Empire royale des Légides* (Paris, 1939), p. 362.

7 C. W. Van Beek, 'Frankincense and Myrrh in ancient South Arabia', *Journal of the American Oriental Society*, Vol. LXXVIII, No. 3; Préaux, op. cit., pp. 359–64.

8 T. Frank, *An Economic Survey of Ancient Rome*, 1938, Vol. 4, part 2, pp. 344 ff.; H. von Wissman, 'Himyar, Ancient History', *Muséon* (Vol. LXXVII, 1964), Parts III and IV, pp. 446–7; Ryckmans, op. cit., *Muséon* (Vol. LXX, 1957), p. 86.

9 I follow the chronology of this period set out by the Ryckmans school. Cf. J. Pirenne, 'La date du périple de la Mer Rouge', *Journal Asiatique*, 1961, p. 441; A. G. Loundine and J. Ryckmans, 'Chronologie des rois de Saba et Dhu Raydan', *Muséon* (Vol. LXXVII, 1964), Parts III and IV; J. Ryckmans, 'De quelques dynasties Sud-Arabes', *Muséon* (Vol. LXXX, 1967), Parts I and II. The account in these paragraphs is largely based on these works, and especially on H. von Wissman's article, 'Himyar, Ancient History', in *Muséon* (Vol. LXXXVII, 1964), Parts III and IV.

10 F. P. Albright and R. L. Bowen, *Archaeological Discoveries in South Arabia*, (Baltimore, 1958), pp. 65–80.

11 Wissman, op. cit., *Muséon* (Vol. LXXVIII, 1965), pp. 492 ff.; Ryckmans, op. cit., *Muséon* (Vol. LXX, 1957), p. 88.

12 See C. L. Geddes, 'The Yu'firid Dynasty of San'a' ', Univ. of London, Ph.D. thesis, 1959).

13 Wissman, op. cit., shows how under the later rulers of Saba and Dhu

Raydan tribal differences played an increasing role in the determination of political events. The prevalence of rural insurrection and autonomy is clear throughout the history of Yemen, from the Yu'firids to the Ottomans in the sixteenth century and beyond.

14 The 'Jerusalem' *Bible* (Paris, 1956) situates the frequently cited 'Eden' of Ezekiel 27.23 on the middle Euphrates, and opines that 'Sheba' as opposed to 'Seba' refers to a Sabaean colony in north Arabia. Pp. 352 and 1165.

15 Miss Pirenne, in her *Le royaume Sud-Arabe de Qataban et sa datation* (Louvain, 1961), p. 174, says: 'Nous estimons en effet qu'aucun texte, avant le *Périple*, ne cite "Arabie Heureuse" ni "Aden".' In another publication of the same year Miss Pirenne dated the *Periplus of the Erythrean Sea* at A.D. 210 or 221 (*Journal Asiatique*, 1961, pp. 441 ff.). Even the 'Arabia Eudaemon' of the *Periplus* is not necessarily Aden. H. Ingrams in *Arabia and the Isles* (London, 1942), expresses some doubts about the description in the *Periplus* of Aden's water supply. I also find it difficult to see where the abundant good water came from and the *Periplus*'s picture of the village of 'Arabia Eudaemon' hardly fits with the reality of Aden's dramatic scenery. See W. H. Schoff (trans.), *Periplus of the Erythrean Sea* (London, 1912), p. 32. Qana' (Husn al Ghurab) is more aptly described as being closed in by a cape – such a description would have been even more appropriate – in the case of Aden. The distance from the Bab el Mandeb given by the *Periplus* points to the vicinity of Aden as the location of Arabia Eudaemon, but if Von Wissman is correct in identifying Pliny's 'Messalum' with Am Assala in the Abyan area – which the Fadli Sultan (Aden Records, A4A, Vol. 3) claimed in 1872 had been the outlet for Yafi'i' trade since time immemorial – that could possibly be the place referred to by the *Periplus*, and it could also be the 'Arabia Emporium' of Ptolemy, whose map does not show the Aden–Little Aden promontories, which appear conspicuously on maps by later cartographers, and places Arabia Emporium on the re-entering coastline to the east of Aden. There are indications that seafaring merchants of the incense-trade period were less security-conscious than their spice-trading successors. The incense-trading port at Qana', for example, which fell out of use about the seventh century, does not seem to have had a wall. See D. B. Doe, 'Husn al Ghurab and the site of Qana' ', *Muséon* (Vol. LXXIV, 1961), p. 191. In such circumstances, Aden's defensive advantages would have been less attractive. The rivalry for the eastern trade between the Roman and Persian empires which became particularly intense in the sixth century, leading as it did to military campaigns in South-West Arabia, must have put a premium on military security. Cf. G. Hourani, *Arab Seafaring* (reprint Beirut, 1963), p. 43. D. B. Doe, who suggested to Wissman the identification of Am Assala with Mesalum, calls it, in his *Southern Arabia* (1971), p. 144, a 'mediaeval town'. But it was still a well-built place in 1867 when the British sacked it. There is an etching of it then in the *Illustrated London News*, 1867. Furthermore it figures prominently on a Map accompanying the 1907

354   ADEN UNDER BRITISH RULE 1839-1967

edition of Hunter and Sealey's *Arab Tribes in the Vicinity of Aden* and on
that map is an entry further south at the estuary of the Wadi Hasan
marked 'Old Asala'. *This* was probably the mediaeval town whose
memory apparently remained fresh in the 1870s when the information
on which the map was based was compiled.

16 Al Tabari (trans. Zotenberg, Paris, 1958), Vol. II, p. 161.

17 *Encyclopaedia of Islam*, new ed. (London, 1960), pp. 180–1.

18 C. L. Geddes, op. cit., p. 7.

19 G. Wiet, *L'Egypte Arabe* (Cairo, 1937), p. 167.

20 Hourani, op. cit., p. 79; Abbass Hamdani, 'The Fatimid–Abbassid
conflict in India', *Islamic Culture* (Vol. XLI, 1967), No. 3.

21 H. C. Kay, *Yemen, its Early Mediaeval History* (London, 1892), p. 5;
K. M. Setton, *History of the Crusades*, Vol. I, p. 96; S. D. Goitein, 'Letters
and Documents on the Indian Trade in Mediaeval Times', *Islamic
Culture* (Vol. XXVII, 1963), No. 3, pp. 188 ff. W. J. Fischel, 'The
Spice Trade in Mameluke Egypt', *Journal of the Economic and Social
History of the Orient* (Vol. I, April 1958), Part II, p. 160; Goitein, 'The
Beginnings of Karimi Merchant Trade to the East'; *Encyclopaedia of
Islam*, 'Aden'; H. T. Norris and F. W. Penhey, *An Archaeological and
Historical Survey of the Aden Tanks* (Aden, 1955), pp. 3–4.

22 R. J. C. Broadhurst (trans.), *The Travels of Ibn Jubayr* (London, 1952),
p. 61; S. D. Goitein, 'Two eye-witness Reports of an Expedition by the
King of Kish [Qays] against Aden', *Bulletin of the School of Oriental and
African Studies* (Vol. XVI, 1954, p. 247; Redhouse, op. cit., Vol. I,
pp. 196–8, Vol. II, pp. 240, 255 and 272.

23 D. MacPherson, *Annals of Commerce, Manufacturers, Fisheries and Navigation* (London, 1805), pp. 141, 174 and 490; *Islamic Culture* (Vol. III,
1963), Part I, pp. 271 and 274–5.

24 A. Kammerer, *La Mer Rouge, l'Abyssinie et l'Arabie depuis l'antiquité*
(Cairo, 1929–52), Vol. III, Part III, pp. 3–4.

25 25 Ibid., Vol. I, pp. 273–4, Vol. II, pp. 118–20 and 266. Darrag,
L'Egypte sous le règne de Barsbay 1422–38 (Damascus, 1961), p. 197.

26 Kammerer, op. cit., Vol. III, Part III, pp. 166 ff.

27 Redhouse, op. cit., Vol. III, Part II, pp. 109, 139, 244–6, 274–5, 314–17.

28 Darrag, op. cit., p. 233; E. Ashtor, 'The Karimi Merchants', *Journal
of the Royal Asiatic Society* (1956), Part I, p. 46; Redhouse, op. cit.,
Vol. I, p. 317.

29 Redhouse, op. cit., Vol. III, Part I, p. 316, Vol. II, p. 14; Kammerer,
Vol. III, Part III, p. 173; cf. the evidence of ninth-century decline of
city culture in the Yemen in N. A. Faris (trans.), *Al Hamdani: Antiquities
of South Arabia* (1938).

30 Redhouse, op. cit., Vol. III, Part I, p. 244; Kammerer, Vol. III, Part
III, p. 167.

31 Redhouse, op. cit., Vol. III, Part I, pp. 167, 238, 275, 281 and 283;
Vol. II, p. 18.

32 Darrag, op. cit., pp. 215, 227 and 230.

33 G. P. Badger (ed.), *Ludovico di Varthema, Travels in Egypt, etc.*, Hakluyt
Society, (London, 1863), p. 63.

34 G. W. F. Stripling, *The Ottoman Turks and the Arabs 1511–1574* (Illinois, 1942), p. 23; D. Barbosa, *The Book of Duarte Barbosa* (London, 1918–21), Vol. I, p. 57.

35 R. B. Sergeant, *The Portuguese off the South Arabian Coast* (Oxford, 1963), pp. 14–21.

36 F. Braudel, *La Méditerranée et le monde méditerranéen a l'époque de Philippe II* (Paris, 1966), p. 181 and pp. 425–30.

37 T. Frank (ed.) *An Economic Survey of Ancient Rome* (Oxford, 1959), Vol. II, p. 345; Kammerer, op. cit., Vol. III, Part III, p. 6, cites reports of forty or fifty sail of pirates off Aden in the thirteenth century, some of them carrying six to eight hundred men. When the rulers of Dhufar pillaged the people of the Hadhrami coast in the late thirteenth century, the latter were outraged and said that the 'Lords' of India, China and Persia had never done this sort of thing (Redhouse, Vol. I, p. 193). It is likely that those 'Lords' confined their activities to the seaways only, controlling and taxing the shipping.

38 Sergeant, op. cit., p. 29.

39 Braudel, op. cit., pp. 424 and 431–4.

40 E. D. Ross, 'The Portuguese in India and Arabia', *Journal of the Royal Asiatic Society* 1922.

41 C. Ansaldi, *Il Yemen nella storia e nella legenda* (Rome, 1933), p. 153.

42 Sir W. Foster (ed.), *The Journal of John Jourdain 1608–1617* (Cambridge, 1905), pp. 75 ff. and 351; C. Beckingham, 'Dutch Travellers in Arabia in the seventeenth century', *Journal of the Royal Asiatic Society* (1951), pp. 71 and 79; B. S. Ingrams, *Three Sea Journals of Stuart times* (London, 1936), p. 120.

43 J. de Laroque, *Voyage to Arabia Felix . . . also a narrative concerning the tree and fruit of coffee . . .* (London, 1732), pp. 309–27.

44 H. E. Jacob, *Coffee: the Epic of a Commodity* (London, 1935), pp. 69, 71 and 102.

45 Jacob, op. cit., pp. 69 and 128.

46 S. J. Shaw, *The Financial and Administrative Development of Ottoman Egypt, 1517–1798* (Princeton, 1962), p. 104.

47 Braudel, op. cit., pp. 434–6 and p. 441.

48 Sir W. Foster, *The Red Sea and adjacent Countries at the Close of the Seventeenth Century . . .* (London, 1949), pp. 173–4.

49 From P. Masson, *Histoire du commerce de Marseille*, Vol. V, pp. 388, 560 and 589, and Foster, op. cit., pp. 62 and 78, it would appear that the northward flow of coffee was maintained by two fleets, one based at Mocha and other Yemeni ports, which plied to Jedda, and an Egyptian fleet of larger vessels operating between Suez and Jedda, bringing grain to Jedda for the Holy Places and taking coffee back to Suez. The Suez fleet declined in size and efficiency during the course of the eighteenth century. The number of ships involved was estimated at 20–25 by Ovington in the 1690s, 40 by Daniel around 1700, 20–25 according to Masson around 1715, about 30 at some unspecified time in the early eighteenth century by Venture de Paradis. He said that in 1761 only seventeen of the original thirty were left and that by 1791

all those large vessels of up to 1,000 tons burthen had been lost and had not been replaced by ships of comparable size. Daniel commented (Foster, op. cit., p. 62) that from Suez to Jedda was carried little but provisions and pieces of eight.

50 This description of the organisation of the trade is drawn in the main from the reports of the East India Company factors at Mocha in the early eighteenth century. That coffee was always paid for with cash is clear from their reports and is stated also by W. Milburn, *Oriental Commerce, or The East India trader's Complete Guide* (London, 1825), p. 65. See India Office Records, Egypt and Red Sea, Vol. 1–3 *passim*. A useful summary is contained in Egypt and Red Sea, Vol. VI, pp. 33 ff. Bombay Political Consultation, 10 July 1801, Remarks on the trade to the Gulfs collected from among natives of Bombay. See also Beckingham, op. cit., *Journal of Royal Asiatic Society* (1951), pp. 79, 80 and 170; Sir W. Foster (ed.) *The Journal of John Jourdain* . . . (Cambridge, 1905), p. 95. H. R. Scott, *Surat and the English* (London, 1915), pp. 7–20.

51 D. Macpherson, *Annals of Commerce etc.*, Vol. II, p. 299. India Office Records, Egypt and Red Sea, Vol. III, p. 333. Thomas Mathieson to Govt. of Bombay, 8 April 1771.

52 J. Biddulph, *The Pirates of Malabar* (London, 1907), p. 26. The great Surat ship did not travel in convoy like the others; it carried 80 guns and was in effect a treasure-bearing man-of-war of the first rate.

53 M. E. Wilbur, *The East India Company and the British Empire in the Far East* (Stanford, 1945), pp. 186–9; see also East India Company Factory Records, *passim*. Biddulph, op. cit., pp. 3–13.

54 Sir W. Foster, *The Red Sea and adjacent Countries at the Close of the Seventeenth Century* (London, 1949), p. 175; P. Gosse, *The History of Piracy* (London, 1954), pp. 236–8; N. Williams, *Captains Outrageous* (London, 1961), p. 178.

55 The main sources for this statement are the figures given in S. J. Shaw, op. cit., pp. 105 and 106; Foster, op. cit., p. 73; India Office Records, Egypt and Red Sea, Vol. VI, pp. 299 ff.; ibid., Vol. I, No. 29, Report on coffee trade 20 July 1721; No. 123, Report on coffee trade 1723; No. 201, Report on coffee trade 27 July 1726; Vol. II, Collection 42, Report on coffee trade 9 August 1731, 15 August 1732, 4 July 1733; Egypt and Red Sea, Vol. VI, p. 299, Home Popham to Wellesley, 26 June 1802. All the figures cited in these reports have to be treated with caution. Even the reports on the coffee trade from Mocha are subject to the reservation that they indicate figures for the main coffee season while the export northward continued throughout the year. The impression that emerges however is clear, namely that the bulk of the coffee went north and that only in the early eighteenth century, when European demand was rising fast and no alternative source had been found, did the southward export amount to more than half that northward and then only during one or two years.

56 Foster, *Journal of John Jourdain*, p. 173; Egypt and Red Sea, Vol. I,

No. 178, Cowan to Court of Directors, 25 August 1725, British Museum Addl. MSS. 26602, folio 4; beyond the wholesale buyers and sellers there was a number of Arab middlemen who took goods on credit for sale in the local markets and bulked the coffee for sale to the dealers. For finance of Indian imports see Egypt and Red Sea, Vol. VI, Bombay Political Consultation, 10 July 1801, p. 33, Remarks on the trade to the Gulfs collected from among the natives of Bombay.

57 Egypt and Red Sea, Vol. I, No. 140, Factors to Court of Directors, 12 July 1724.

58 Egypt and Red Sea, Vol. I, p. 9, Factors to Court of Directors, 25 July 1720.

59 Egypt and Red Sea, Vol. VI, Bombay Political Consultation, 10 July 1801, Remarks on trade, etc. . . . Throughout the eighteenth century there was a tendency to export cheaper and cheaper piece goods from India and China, evidently designed for the mass market in the Yemen, not the choice cloths imported in the early seventeenth century for a privileged few. These imports competed in the markets with locally produced textiles made from local and imported cotton and imported silk thread. B. M. Addl. MSS. 26602, Captain Samuel Wilson (5 June 1799), report of mission to San'a', folio 4. In the early eighteenth century Lahej produced a large amount of cotton for local use and imported some as well. Foster, *Journal of John Jourdain*, pp. 77 and 82.

60 Foster, *The Journal of John Jourdain*, p. 75. A. S. Tritton, *The Rise of the Imams of Sana'a'* (London, 1925), p. 12.

61 Tritton, op. cit., pp. 8, 91, 93 and 104.

62 Ottoman Yemen was run from Egypt and most of the occupying troops came from the Mamluq army there. S. J. Shaw, op. cit., pp. 4 and 184–5.

63 Tritton, op. cit., pp. 93 and 106; A. Kammerer, *La Mer Rouge, L'Arabie et l'Abyssinie depuis l'antiquité*, Vol. II (Cairo, 1929–52), p. 399. *English Factories in India*, 1624–9, p. 351, 1634–6, p. 300, 1637–41, pp. 39–40.

64 Aden Secret Letter (A.S.L.) 147 of 23 February 1902, Documents appended to proceedings of demarcation commission. The 'Amir of Dhali' submitted a document dated Muharram 982. (April–May 1574) confirming him in his possessions and entitling him to 1½ dollars per camel load and 30 ounces of gold per month from the guarded city of Dhamar. These concessions were extended by a further agreement of 15 Rabi' al Awwal 1029 (20 February 1620), a moment of crisis for the Ottomans in south-west Yemen, when they accorded 'Amir Ahmad bin 'Amir Sha'fal al Sha'fali the import and export duties of Mocha and Aden in addition and 30 *haraf* of gold from Ta'izz. See also A.S.L. (23 December 1902), Appendix 2. In 1605 the Ottomans authorised the Shaykh of Shairi to collect tolls.

65 The 'Amir of Dhali' and the ruler of Khanfar who controlled Aden were at odds with one another. Cf. Tritton, op. cit., p. 104.

66 This however was the major explanation current at Aden in 1802 for the decline in the port's commerce. Home Popham, who spent

much time with the Sultan of Aden's son, gave this explanation to Wellesley in his letter of 26 July 1802 (Egypt and Red Sea, Vol. 6). It was that while the Ottomans favoured the port, its trade had been ruined under the Imam's rule when the latter invited the principal chief allied to the Sultan to his Court and killed him, whereupon the chief's adherents dispersed and plundered so indiscriminately that the planters could send no more coffee by that route and sent coffee to Hudayda instead.

67 In 1702 Yafi'i coffee was being offered for sale at Aden. B. S. Ingram, op. cit., pp. 120ff.; Laroque considered purchasing coffee at Aden in 1709 but transferred to Mocha because the better grades of coffee from Bayt al Faqih were available there. Aden could provide coffee from San'a' and one other district. Laroque, op. cit., p. 102.

68 B. S. Ingram, op. cit., Laroque, op cit., pp. 47 and 52–6. H. Salt, *A Voyage to Abyssinia* (London, 1814), pp. 106–10; Aden Records, F1A, Vol. I, Memoir by Haines on Aden (1835).

69 B. H. Vlekke, *Nausantara, a History of the East Indian Archipelago* (Cambridge, Mass., 1945), p. 180.

70 E. Jacob, op. cit., p. 216; Masson, op. cit., pp. 465–6.

71 From Bal Krishna, *The Commercial Relations between India and England 1601–1757* (London, 1924), Ovington, Laroque, Salt, and the volumes in the Egypt and Red Sea series. One can arrive at the following rough series of prices in $ for the Mocha *bahar* of 280 lb. 1696 – $30, 1709 – $43, 1711 – $55–67, 1712 – $68–70, 1717 – $83–98, 1718 – $101, 1721 – $115, 1723 – $190–200, 1726 – $67, 1756 – $28, 1802 – $29, 1803 – $36, 1805 – $46, 1809 – $64.

72 The date for Aden's independence from the Imam's rule is given as 1728 in Hunter and Sealey, *Arab Tribes in the Vicinity of Aden* (Bombay, 1909); this is based on the dates Haines took from the Lahej records. K. Niebuhr, *Travels through Arabia and other Countries in the East* (London, 1792), p. 48, gives the date as 1730. But in Egypt and Red Sea, Vol. 2, Page and Beresford to Court of Directors (1 July 1733), it is stated that the Imam gave the province of Udayn to his rebellious brother on condition that he restore to the Imam's rule the towns of Lahej and Aden which had been taken from him 'last year' by the Yafi'i.

73 P. Masson, *L'histoire de l'établissement français dans l'Afrique barbaresque* (Paris, 1903), p. 601; Egypt and Red Sea, Vol. 3, Thomas Mathieson to President of Bombay (8 April 1771).

74 V. T. Harlow, *The Founding of the Second British Empire*, Vol. I (Oxford, 1952), Chapter 1.

75 H. L. Hoskins, *British Routes to India* (Cambridge, Mass., 1928), Chapter 1.

76 Hoskins, op. cit., Chapter 2.

77 Aden Records (A.R.), F1A, Vol. I, Murray to Govt. of Bombay (4 October and 10 December 1799), Hoskins, op. cit., pp. 60 and 65.

78 Hoskins, op. cit., pp. 70 ff.

79 Cf. C. Northcote Parkinson, *War in the Eastern Seas* (London, 1954).

80 India Office Records, Range 419/40, pp, 252 ff.; Bombay Commerce Reports 1802-3, 1803-4; ibid., Range 178, Vol. 16, folio 184, Report (26 August 1806). There was great alarm at these developments in Bombay. It was alleged that most of the Arab ships were navigated by Frenchmen.

81 S. E. Morison, *The Maritime History of Massachusetts* (Boston, 1941), p. 92.

82 Egypt and Red Sea, Vol. 6. The exchange of correspondence in this collection and the memoranda it contains are a case study in the methods of peaceful penetration and the building up of political power by the use of both mercantilist and non mercantilist commercial activity. See also George, Viscount Valentia, *Voyages and Travels to India, Ceylon, Abyssinia and Egypt in the years 1802, 1803, 1804, 1805 and 1806* (London, 1809); and H. Salt, op. cit. The last two authors were actively engaged in carrying on where Home Popham left off. India Office (I.O.) Home Miscellaneous Series 497/4 Board of Trade to East India Company (17 December 1807), advocating the opening of English trade to North East Africa, and B. M. Addl. MSS. 19347 Belzoni to Valentia, Aden (15 March 1809).

83 Valentia, op. cit., Vol. 2, pp. 378-427; Salt, op. cit., p. 106; B. M. Addl. MSS. 19347, folios 35 and 105; Egypt and Red Sea, Vol. VII *passim*; H. F. Jacob, *Kings of Arabia* (London, 1923), p. 28.

84 Valentia, op. cit., Vol. 2, p. 400; C. R. Low, *A History of the Indian Navy* (London, 1877), Vol. 2, p. 30.

85 C. U. Aitchison, *A Collection of Treaties, Engagements and Sanads relating to India and neighbouring Countries: Persia, the Arab Principalities in the Persian Gulf and Oman* (Calcutta, 1865 ed., Vol. VII, p. 301); Egypt and Red Sea, Vol. VI, Home Popham to Wellesley (26 July 1802).

86 See J. B. Kelly, *Britain and the Persian Gulf* (Oxford, 1968), Chapter IX.

87 B.S.L. (1820-7), Govt. of Bombay to Secret Committee (9 August 1820); Egypt and Red Sea, Vol. VII, Salt to Dart (28 February 1821) enclosing Bruce to Salt (20 January 1821); Aitchison, op. cit. (1865 ed.), Vol. VII, p. 302.

88 Low, op. cit., Vol. I, p. 478.

89 H. L. Hoskins, op. cit., Chapter VI *passim*.

90 B.M. Addl. MSS. 27674, Memorandum on the Wahhabi by Sir C. Colville (1828).

91 Egypt and Red Sea, Vol. VII, Report by Salt on Egyptian army (20 January 1824).

92 M. O. Tamisier, *Voyage en Arabie; séjour dans le Hejaz, campagne d'Asir* (Paris, 1840).

93 Low, op. cit., Vol. 2, p. 29; F.O. 78/2753, memorandum on the status of the countries of South-West Arabia (14 November 1843); F.O. 78/3185 Mackenzie to Johnstone (1 January 1837). P. E. Botta, *Relation d'un voyage dans l'Yemen* (Paris, 1841), pp. 9-10.

94 F.O. 78/2753, memorandum (14 November 1843), summarising British transactions with Muhammad ʿAli in this regard over the previous ten years.

95 Egypt and Red Sea, Vol. VI, Home Popham to Wellesley (15 September 1801), Governor-General to Govt. of Bombay (27 November 1801), transmitting instructions to Popham. In 1843 the Court of Directors of the East India Company doubted whether the Sultan of Aden was fully independent. India Office MSS. Eur. F.78/38 'Aden bundle'.

96 Egypt and Red Sea, Vol. VII, Salt to Strangford (7th December 1822), Salt to Dart (9 June 1825).

97 F.O. 78/3815, Mackenzie to Johnstone (1 January 1837), enclosed in Johnstone to Palmerston (4 July 1837), Palmerston to Campbell (4 August 1837, 12 May 1838, 24 May 1838, 8 June 1838, 25 July 1838).

98 Hoskins, op. cit., pp. 210 ff. See also India Office Home Miscellaneous 838, Hobhouse to Auckland (1 April, 13 June and 30 August 1837).

99 *Parliamentary Papers*, 1839, Vol. XL, p. 37 (Correspondence relating to Aden).

100 G. Waterfield, *Sultans of Aden* (London, 1968), p. 55; *The Times* (22 August 1840), p. 3. There was little contemporary discussion in the press until well after the event. Even *The Times*, which suported the move, was uneasy at the method of acquisition. *Blackwood's Magazine* in 1843 was hostile and expressed these sentiments in stronger terms.

101 Low, op. cit., Vol. II, p. 112.

102 Low, op. cit., Vol. II, p. 70; F.O. 78/3185, Campbell to Palmerston (23 February 1837); Hobhouse at first preferred Perim to Aden. I.O. Home Misc. 838, Hobhouse to Grant, 4 December 1837; Indian Secret Letter 55 (28 March 1872), enclosing collection on British relations with Socotra.

103 Low, op. cit., Vol. II, p. 70, Hoskins, op. cit., p. 189 and footnote 20.

104 B.S.L. (5 May 1839), memorandum by Farish on correspondence relating to Aden (25 March 1839). Bombay Secret Consultation (4 April 1838), minute by Governor of Bombay (26 March 1838) on proceedings leading up to Haines's mission to Aden. See also A.R. FiA, Vol. II, p. 170.

105 *Parliamentary Papers*, 1839, Vol. XL, pp. 49 ff.; *The Times* (22 August 1840), p. 3; A.R., FiA, Vol. I, p. 199, Haines to Malcolm (6 July 1837) and Minutes.

106 *Dictionary of National Biography:* Sir Robert Grant.

107 I.O. Home Misc. 841, Auckland to Hobhouse (5 August 1837).

108 I.O. Home Misc. 836, Grant to Hobhouse (27 June 1836); Home Misc. 841, Auckland to Hobhouse (19 December 1837).

109 I.O. Home Misc. 836, Grant to Hobhouse (27 June 1836). The rapidity with which the *Hugh Lindsay* arrived on the scene of disturbances at Mangalore in 1837 was considered by Grant a good example of the sort of advantages to be expected from steam vessels. Ibid., Grant to Hobhouse (28 April 1837).

110 I.O. Home Misc. 838, Hobhouse to Auckland (1 April and 30 August 1837); ibid., 841, Grant to Chairman of Secret Committee (17 August 1837).

111 I.O. Home Misc. 841, Grant to Chairman of Secret Committee (17 August 1837); Grant to Hobhouse (17 August 1837); Bombay Secret Consultation (4 October 1837).

112 *Parliamentary Papers*, 1839, Vol. XL, p. 51; Govt. of India to Govt. of Bombay (16 October 1837).

113 Egypt and Red Sea, Vol. VI, Home Popham to Wellesley (26 July 1802); Valentia, op. cit., Vol. II, p. 391; Salt, op. cit., p. 111; J. R. Wellsted, *Travels in Arabia*, London 1838, Vol. II, pp. 410 ff.; Egypt and Red Sea, Vol. VII, Hutchinson to Warden (27 March 1822). Hutchinson said that the Sultan had made an arrangement with the Turks that they occupy the fort on the beach while he retained the gate and civil and military jurisdiction in the town. The Sultan was prepared to risk losing Aden through this arrangement because of the overriding necessity of securing protection from his neighbours. See also ibid., Salt to Strangford (7 August 1822). Salt said that the Sultan asked him to establish a British factory at Aden in 1810. The Sultan's fear of his neighbours was well grounded. The Fadli attacked and plundered Aden in 1835. Wellsted, op. cit., Vol. II, p. 410.

114 S. D. Goitein, Two eye-witness reports of an expedition by the King of Kish (Qays) against Aden', *B.S.O.A.S.* (Vol. XVI, 1954), pp. 247 ff.

115 A full description of the negotiations that ensued is to be found in Waterfield, op. cit., pp. 37–69. Waterfield outdraws the main features of the negotiation very effectively. However, he presents Haines as a straightforward man carrying out his superiors' orders to take full possession of the town. I have a different opinion of Haines's character and I believe it was he who was principally responsible for reducing the range of options open to him. 'Occupation' was a flexible and ambiguous term in early nineteenth-century India. It did not necessarily mean, as Haines insisted it did, outright control of the town and the citizens living in it. The Governor-General had instructed 'peaceful occupation' of a coal depot only. Haines did not act according to the letter or the spirit of that instruction.

116 *Parliamentary Papers*, 1839, Vol. XL, pp. 52 ff.; Haines to Superintendent of Bombay Marine, (20 January 1838) and enclosures.

117 See K. Ballhatchet, *Social Policy and Social Change in western India* (London, 1961).

118 There was some doubt subsequently as to the British title to Aden R. H. Thomas, *Treaties, Agreements and Engagements between the East India Co. and Native Princes, etc. in western India 1851–3*, pp. 282–3, cited the bond of 22 January and the note of 23 January making the British claim that of sale as well as conquest. C. U. Aitchison, however, produced the definitive statement in the 1865 edition of his *Treaties and Engagements* (Vol. VII, p. 268) where he referred to the British claim as conquest only, the purchase element being discounted.

119 *Parliamentary Papers*, 1839, Vol. XL, p. 53. A.R., F1A, Vol. I, p. 80, Haines's political report on Aden, No. 2 (3 February 1838).

120 Bombay Secret Proceedings, Bombay Secret Consultation (4 April

1838) and enclosures. Ibid., minute by Grant (26 March 1838) and by Farish (29 March 1838).

121 Home Misc. 841, Grant to Hobhouse (20 May 1838).

122 Home Misc. 838, Hobhouse to Grant (10 May 1838). Subsequent private letters from Hobhouse to Grant (21 May and 9 June) also urged the immediate occupation of Aden.

123 B.M. Addl. MSS. 46915, Palmerston to Hobhouse (27 August 1838 and 14 December 1839), Home Misc. 838, Hobhouse to Palmerston (29 August 1838), ibid. 841, Carnac to Hobhouse (5 October 1839). R. J. Gavin, 'Palmerston's policy toward the East and West coasts of Africa', (Univ. of Cambridge Ph.D. thesis, 1959), pp. 55 ff.

124 Home Misc. 839, Hobhouse to Melbourne (23 December 1838).

125 B.M. Addl. MSS. 46915, Palmerston to Hobhouse (1 January 1839).

126 Hobhouse had trouble with the Secret Committee over the matter in May 1838 and there was a rather sharp exchange of letters between him and the Court of Directors in the autumn of 1839. The Court correctly suspected that there had been serious irregularities in the manner in which the crucial decisions had been made but they could not get the relevant secret correspondence to prove their point. Home Misc. 838, Hobhouse to Grant (10 May 1838); I.O. Political and Secret Home Correspondence 1839, Court of Directors to India Board, (6 September 1839), India Board to Court of Directors (9 September 1839); India Office MSS. Eur. F.78/38 Wood Papers, 'Aden bundle'; I.O. Home Correspondence Board and Individuals 1836–50, Melville to W. B. Baring (3 November 1842). East India Company officials still referred in 1849 to the 'unjust seizure' of Aden. See Boards Collections 118095, Minute on Despatch to Bombay (30 May 1849).

127 Home Misc. 838, Hobhouse to Melbourne, 26 October 1838, recommending Carnac. B.M. Addl. MSSS. 46915, Palmerston to Hobhouse (14 December 1839) on hearing of Carnac's doubts, Palmerston clearly indicated that had he known of them earlier he would have opposed his appointment. Carnac said that Aden was not acquired when he was on the Secret Committee, Home Misc. 842, Carnac to Hobhouse (31 January 1840). This was a quibble. Carnac held that post when the important decisions were being taken. But that he should have made that remark indicates that the consultation that should have taken place between the India Board and the Secret Committee had been defective to say the least.

128 Bombay Secret Letter (B.S.L.) 16 (27 August 1838) enclosing Govt. of India to Govt. of Bombay (2 July 1838). The Governor-General had previously said that it was neither 'expedient nor proper' to take Aden just because of the *Duria Dowlat* incident. Bombay Secret Letter (30 November 1837) enclosing Govt. of India to Govt. of Bombay (16 October 1837).

129 B.S.L. 16 (27 August 1838) enclosing India Board to Govt. of Bombay (30 May 1838).

130 Home Misc. 838, Hobhouse to Grant (9 June 1838).

131 Waterfield, op. cit., pp. 55–8.
132 Low, op. cit., p. 29.
133 Waterfield, op. cit., Chapter VII, gives a good account of the proceedings at Aden between October 1838 and January 1839.
134 B.S.L. 1 (2 January 1839) enclosing Haines to Willoughby (17 November 1838).
135 Waterfield, op. cit., pp. 70–2.
136 Home Misc. 841, Farish to Hobhouse (25 February 1839).
137 Cited in *Parliamentary Papers*, 1839, Vol. XL.
138 Home Misc. 841 and 842, Carnac to Hobhouse (5 October and 26 November 1839, 31 January, 27 April and 21 May 1840).
139 A. H. Imlah, *Lord Ellenborough* (Cambridge, Mass., 1939), p. 79; Indian S.L. 27 (9 April 1843).
140 Broadlands Papers, Hobhouse to Palmerston (3 April 1847).

CHAPTER II

1 Waterfield, op. cit., p. 79; B.S.L. 21 (25 February 1839), memorandum on the occupation of Aden; B.S.L. 124 (22 November 1839), Govt. of Bombay to Haines (26 November 1839).
2 B.S.L. 108 (29 September 1839), Haines to Govt. of Bombay 18 (8 August 1839) and enclosures; B.S.L. 124 (22 November 1839) and enclosures.
3 B.S.L. 14, undated, of 1840, Haines to Govt. of Bombay 8 (18 December 1840), Capon to Military Adjutant-General (2 March 1840), Govt. of Bombay to Capon (23 March 1840), Home Misc. Series 839, Hobhouse to Auckland (4 July 1840). Waterfield op. cit., pp. 113–18.
4 B.S.L. 70 (31 August 1841), Haines to Govt. of Bombay 70 (28 July 1841), B.S.L. 142 (2 December 1846), Haines to Govt. of Bombay (24 September 1846), Govt. of India to Govt. of Bombay (5 November 1846), B.S.L. 69 (6 August 1847) and 85 of (1 October 1847).
5 Home Misc. Series 853 Hobhouse to Hardinge (7 January 1847) Home Misc. Series 846, Labouchere to Hobhouse (22 April 1849), enclosing extract from letter by Bowring (2 February 1849).
6 Home Misc. Series 854 Dalhousie to Hobhouse (20 January 1848).
7 This was most clear in the disputes of 1839–41, but the disputes of 1846 and 1847 also arose out of Haines's attempts to put business in the way of his protégés. Tyrannous conduct by subordinates was openly referred to in B.S.L. 14, undated, of 1840, Capon to Milty. Adjutant-General (2 March 1840), B.S.L. 70 (31 August 1841), Haines to Govt. of Bombay 70 (28 July 1841). In the latter reference was made to a letter in the press by 'Phile Amicron' who was, Haines believed, an officer of the garrison. Anonymous threatening letters (not from the military officers) to Haines were quite common. See Elphinstone Papers, Coghlan to Elphinstone (27 July 1857).
8 B.S.L. 14 (1840) Capon to Adjutant-General (18 February 1840).

9 B.S.L. 70 (31 August 1841), Haines to Govt. of Bombay 70 (28 July 1841) and Governor's undated minute.

10 B.S.L. 14 (undated of 1840); Haines to Govt. of Bombay 6 (16 February 1840).

11 B.S.L. 18 (1840); Haines to Govt. of Bombay 8 (18 December 1840). B.S.L. 85 (1 October 1847), Haines to Govt. of Bombay 45 (15 July 1847).

12 Home Correspondence 1873, G. P. Badger to Under-Secretary of State for India (5 April 1873).

13 B.S.L. 84 (4 July 1839), Haines to Govt. of Bombay 14 (9 June 1839), East India Company Registers, 1829 to 1836, A.R., FlA, Vol. I. Haines Memoir on Aden, 1835.

14 B.S.L. 1 (2 January 1839), Haines to Govt. of Bombay (12 December 1838), B.S.L. 20 (30 April 1840), Haines to Govt. of Bombay 13 (19 March 1840), B.S.L. 19 (27 March 1841), Haines to Govt. of Bombay 2 P (29 February 1841), A.R., A1A, Vol. 142, pp. 40(b) and 16(b). Evidence at Haines trial.

15 B.S.L. 51 (16 April 1839), Haines to Govt. of Bombay 54 and 55P (10 April 1839), B.S.L. 109 (3 October 1839), Haines to Govt. of Bombay 3 (1 September 1839).

16 A.S.L. 16 (28 August 1854) Outram to Govt. of Bombay 119 (10 August 1853), Appendix to Enclosure B, Inquiry by the Revd. G. P. Badger into the laws and customs of the Arabs in the vicinity of Aden. In a somewhat unreliable report, a French visitor remarked that in 1838 Haines could not speak Arabic and the negotiations with Lahej were conducted through Mulla Jaffer, A(rchives) des A(ffaires) E(trangères) (Paris), Mémoires et Documents, Asie 26, Mission de M. Alciate de Grilhon dans Yemen. But in 1840 Haines used his knowledge of Arabic to outdo Capon, who spoke only Hindustani.

17 B.S.L. 51 (16 April 1839), Haines to Govt. of Bombay 42P (28 February 1839), A.S.L. 14 (11 December 1843).

18 A.S.L. 2 (10 February 1842).

19 A.S.L. 7 (14 June 1844).

20 Enclosure to B.S.L. 11 (28 February 1840), Haines to Govt. of Bombay 6 (1 February 1840).

21 Enclosure to B.S.L. 104 (31 December 1840), Haines to Govt. of Bombay 75 (28 November 1840).

22 Enclosures to B.S.L. 14 (undated) of 1840 Capon to Haines (19 February 1840). Enclosures to B.S.L. 20 (30 April 1840), Haines to Govt. of Bombay 13 (28 February 1840).

23 Waterfield, op. cit., pp. 67–8.

24 Enclosure to B.S.L. 14 (1840) Capon to Haines (19 February 1840). Jaffer had a powerful faction at Aden composed mainly of men from Mocha. B.S.L. 14 (1840) Capon to Milty. Adjutant-General (2 March 1840), enclosing Capon to Haines (19 February 1840).

25 A.S.L. 9 (11 May 1845) enclosing Haines to Govt. of Bombay 23 of (28 April 1845).

26 Enclosure to B.S.L. 4 (29 January 1840), Govt. of Bombay to Milty.

Adj.-General (30 November 1839), Enclosure to B.S.L. (30 September 1840), Haines to Govt. of Bombay 26 (10 September 1840).

27 A.R., A1A, Vol. CXLII, Haines trial, p. 50 (B); Haines to Cruttenden (10 April 1853). Haines had known Cruttenden for nine years before he appointed him.

28 Haines's secretiveness led to a misunderstanding with the military commander in 1844 who found some inconsistencies in the information Haines was giving him. A.S.L. 14 (11 November 1844), Haines to Govt. of Bombay 70 (23 October 1844), Enclosures to Bombay S.L. 79 (28 September 1844), Garrison Cmdr. Aden to Milty. Adj.-Genl. Bombay (9 August 1844).

29 Enclosure to B.S.L. 6 (3 January 1841), Haines to Govt. of Bombay 42 (23 December 1840).

30 Enclosures to B.S.L. 51 (16 April 1839), Haines to Govt. of Bombay 50P (8 March 1839), Govt. of Bombay to Haines (9 April 1839).

31 A.S.L. 15 (11 December 1844) enclosing Haines to Govt. of Bombay 77 (24 November 1844), Survey of house construction at Aden.

32 Enclosures to B.S.L. 19 (27 March 1841), Haines to Govt. of Bombay 2P (29 February 1841), the case of the expulsion of two Frenchmen for traducing Jaffer and suggesting that he took bribes for the grant of liquor licences.

33 Enclosures to B.S.L. 14 (1840), Capon to Bombay Milty. Secretary (18 February 1840). Enclosure to B.S.L. 20 (30 April 1840), Sayyid Zayn bin 'Alawi al 'Aydarus to Govt. of Bombay (29 February 1840). Sayyid Zayn said that Jaffer cast doubt on his character as a true Muslim.

34 Enclosure to B.S.L. 42 (25 May 1841), Hamerton (Zanzibar) to Govt. of Bombay (25 February 1841).

35 Enclosure to B.S.L. 14 (1840), Capon to Milty. Secretary Bombay (18 February 1840).

36 *Parliamentary Papers*, 1839, Vol. XL, p. 49, Deposition by Sayyid Nur al Din bin Jamal (1 August 1837).

37 Enclosure to B.S.L. 51 (16 April 1839), Sultan Muhsin Fadl to Governor of Bombay (16 March 1839), B.S.L. 60 (8 May 1839), Baillie to Govt. of Bombay (4 April 1839), enclosing Sultan Ahmad al Fadli to Governor of Bombay (19 March 1839), Aden Merchants to Governor of Bombay (12 April 1839).

38 The quarrel with Baillie arose out of Jaffer's breaking the usual rule that all visitors surrender their arms on entering Aden by permitting a number of chiefs to retain their arms. This was done on Haines's orders but Haines had neglected to inform Baillie, the Military Commander, and Baillie, evidently already nettled by Jaffer's pretensions, immediately protested. The quarrel with Capon arose from a search of the Arab town for unlicensed liquor shops by the military authorities. Jaffer immediately got up a deputation to protest to Haines, as he evidently regarded the Arab town as his own private preserve. The dispute quickly developed into a concerted attempt by practically all the military officers in the garrison to break Jaffer's power.

39 This incident must have decidedly weakened Haines's influence at Bombay. Enclosures to B.S.L. 42 (25 May 1841), Hamerton to Willoughby (25 February 1841), Haines to Govt. of Bombay 66 (24 March 1841), Govt. of Bombay to Haines (20 May 1841).

40 Captain Moresby said that the quarrel with Sharif Husayn of Mocha arose entirely from the latter's dislike of 'Abd al Rasul. Haines said that this was not the case and strongly urged the Bombay Govt. to seek the restoration of all 'Abd al Rasul's property confiscated by Sharif Husayn. Until 1840, 'Abd al Rasul had been Agent at Mocah for the French as well as the British Government, but this did not deter Haines from putting complete trust in him.

41 Enclosures to B.S.L. 35 (20 June 1840), Haines to Govt. of Bombay 32 (2 June 1840), A.S.L. 3 (11 March 1844), Haines to Govt. of Bombay 18 (2 March 1844).

42 A.R., FIA, Vol. I. Haines Memoir on Aden 1835.

43 A.S.L. 1 (11th January 1843) enclosing Haines to Govt. of Bombay 93 (29 December 1842).

44 B.S.L. 51 (16 April 1839), Report by Captain Foster on Aden Defences (30 March 1839), Enclosure to B.S.L. 20 (30 April 1840), Haines to Govt. of Bombay 13 (28 February 1840). The two mosques still intact were the 'Aydarus mosque and the Masjid al Suq.

45 B.S.L. 20 (30 April 1840), Haines to Govt. of Bombay 13 (9 March 1840).

46 B.S.L. 51 (16 April 1839), Foster's report (30 September 1839).

47 Both Mocha and Hudayda had large numbers of this type of hut. The town of Shuqra was entirely built in this fashion except for two major buildings.

48 A.S.L. 10 (15 October 1842); J. P. Malcolmson, 'An Account of Aden', *Journal of the Royal Asiatic Society* (Vol. VIII, 1846), p. 286.

49 A.S.L. 8 (8 July 1843), Haines to Govt. of Bombay 53 (19 June 1843), Enclosure to B.S.L. 121 (15 October 1846), Haines to Govt. of Bombay 47 (2 September 1846), Haines used convict labour to clear the streets.

50 A.S.L. 15 (11 February 1844), enclosing Haines to Govt. of Bombay 77 (24 November 1844), Survey of House construction at Aden.

51 A.S.L. 13 (31 August 1845), enclosing Haines to Govt. of Bombay 7 (20 August 1845).

52 A.S.L. 13 (10 October 1844). The old Arab and Jewish quarters of approximately equal size remained throughout the 1840s.

53 Up to 1845 the main means of communication between the two parts of the settlement was by sea. B.S.L. 104 (31 December 1840), Supt. of Indian Navy to Govt. of Bombay (28 November 1840). J. P. Malcolmson, 'An Account of Aden', *Journal of Asiatic Soc.* (Vol. VIII, 1846), Cruttenden, however, who was in charge of the coal depot, used horses to go back and forth. A.S.L. 8 (8 July 1843), Haines to Govt. of Bombay 53 (19 June 1843).

54 A.S.L. 10 (10 October 1842), Haines to Govt. of Bombay No. 7 (7 October 1842).

55 B.S.L. 144 (2 December 1846), Enclosure 30, Memorandum on housing

at Steamer Point Aden, and Haines to Govt. of Bombay (20 April 1846). Six army officers, the Chaplain, the Camp Surgeon, Captain Luke Thomas of the P. and O. and Haines himself had houses on Ras Morbat in 1846. The French Consul at Jedda, visiting Aden in 1847, mentioned a fine road leading from Main Pass to the coal depot and Haines's house on the Point. A.E.E. Politique, Turquie (Djeddah) Fresnel to Ministre des Affaires Etrangères (24 March 1847). Haines had first established himself in the former Sultan's Palace in Crater, Parbury, *Handbook for India and Egypt, comprising the narrative of a journey from Calcutta to London* (London, 1841), p. 222.

56 See below, p. 80.

57 A.S.L. 1 (28 January 1849), Haines to Govt. of Bombay 11 (24 January 1849). A police post was set up at the Point in June 1848 in view of the increasing population there. A.S.L. 11 (29 July 1848), Haines to Govt. of Bombay 11 (4 June 1848).

58 A.A.E. Mémoires et Documents, Asie 26, Capitaine Guérin to Ministre de la Marine et des Colonies (18 April 1852).

59 *Parliamentary Papers*, 1851, Vol. XXI, Select Committee on Steam Communication with India, etc., Question 6236.

60 B.S.L. 51 (16 April 1839), Foster's report on the Aden defences (30 March 1839).

61 Enclosure to B.S.L. 84 (4 July 1839), Haines to Govt. of Bombay 13 (9 June 1839).

62 B.S.L. 55 (19 August 1840), minutes by Carnac (9 June 1840), by Farish (11 June 1840), Carnac (18 June 1840) and 27 June 1840), by Farish (4 July 1840) and Govt. of Bombay to Military Board (26 June 1840). Enclosures to B.S.L. 66 of 1840, undated, minutes by Farish (14 August 1840), by Carnac (19 August 1840), by Anderson (26 June 1840), Govt. of Bombay to Military Board (25 August 1840). Enclosures to B.S.L. 20 (30 April 1840), Haines to Govt. of Bombay 7 (16 February 1840).

63 B.S.L. 66 of 1840, Capon's report on the state of Aden Defences (24 July 1840).

64 B.S.L. 66 of 1840 Extract of Proceedings in the Military Department (24 July 1840), Foster's Recommendations. Foster had previously suggested a system of defences primarily designed to repel a seaward invasion and this plan had provided for the abandonment of Aden town and the construction of an entirely new fortress at Steamer Point. This plan was opposed by Haines and was turned down in favour of the construction of defences to repel an invasion by land whch in the summer of 1839 seemed the more immediate threat. Enclosures to B.S.L. 5a (16 April 1839) Foster's first Plan (15 March 1840) envisaging a landward defence, Enclosures to B.S.L. 69 (28 May 1838), Foster's second plan envisaging seaward defence (15 May 1839), B.S.L. 84 (4 July 1839), Haines to Govt. of Bombay 14 (9 June 1839).

65 A Special Committee was set up in December 1842 to inquire into the subject and all work on forts and barracks was suspended pending its report. In April 1843 Lord Ellenborough criticised the findings of this

Committee and Bombay's recommendations in I.S.L. 27 (9 April 1843). When Lord Hardinge replaced Ellenborough in the following year, he too, though favourable to the construction of both seaward and landward defences and less sceptical of Aden's value than his predecessor, entered into a long battle with the Bombay Government which wanted to make Aden as powerful a fortress as Gibraltar. Home Misc. Series 854 Hardinge to Hobhouse (7 July 1847), Enclosures to B.L.S. 135 (16 November 1846), memorandum on Aden's defences by Hardinge enclosed in Govt. of India to Govt. of Bombay (14 October 1846). The defences were still incomplete in 1851 and the East India Company was reluctant to spend any more money on them. Home Misc. Series 846, Hardinge to Hobhouse (14 May 1851).

66 Enclosure to B.S.L. 101 (27 August 1846), Haines to Govt. of Bombay 40 (15 August 1846).

67 B.S.L. (16 April 1839), Govt. of India to Govt. of Bombay (20 and 25 March 1839).

68 B.S.L. 51 (16 April 1839), Haines to Govt. of Bombay 8 (25 February 1839) and 42P (28 February 1839).

69 B.S.L. (30 September 1840) enclosing Haines to Govt. of Bombay (13 July 1840), and statement by Herah Priya and others.

70 A.R., AlA, Vol. LII, p. 238. See also *Bombay Geographical Journal* (1849–50), pp. 129–30.

71 H. Salt, op. cit., p. 106; B.S.L. 85 (1 October 1847), Haines to Govt. of Bombay 44 (29 July 1847).

72 M. Guillain, *Documents sur l'histoire, la géographie et la commerce de l'Afrique orientale* (Paris, 1856), Part II, pp. 481–8.

73 A.R., AlA, Vol. LXXI, p. 497 and Vol. LXXIV, p. 473.

74 A.S.L. 8 (30 April 1848) enclosing Cruttenden to Haines (4 April 1848), B.S.L. 77 (30 September 1840) enclosing Moresby to Haines (24 August 1840).

75 A.A.E. Mem. et Docs., Asie 26, Capitaine Guérin to Ministre de la Marine et des Colonies (18 April 1852).

76 R. J. Gavin, 'Palmerston's policy toward the east and west coasts of Africa', (Ph.D. thesis, Cambridge 1959), Chapter 3.

77 A.S.L. 3 (11 March 1844), Haines to Govt. of Bombay 18 (2 March 1844).

78 Haines sought to encourage permanent settlement at Berbera but when he found in 1845 that Shermarki's towers were causing violent disputes he asked Shermarki to remove them. B.S.L. 84 (4 July 1839) enclosing Haines to Govt. of Bombay (9 June 1839); A.S.L. (5 June 1843), enclosing Haines to Govt. of Bombay 49 (29 May 1843); A.S.L. 13 (10 October 1844), A.S.L. 15 (29 October 1845) enclosing Haines to Govt. of Bombay 54 (18 October 1845).

79 A severe faction fight broke out in 1842–3 which was to determine the alignment of forces in Somaliland for more than twelve years, A.S.L. 1 (11 January 1843), 4 (26 March 1843) and 15 (11 December 1844).

80 A.R., Vol. XXXVII, p. 13 and Vol. LXVI, p. 741.

81 A.S.L. 8 (8 July 1843), Haines to Govt. of Bombay 6T (4 July 1843).

82 Value of total trade (import and export):

	rupees		rupees
1843–4	1,586,560	1850–1	2,114,851
1844–5	1,755,167	1851–2	5,032,228
1845–6	2,308,140	1852–3	5,873,897
1846–7	2,329,660	1853–4	6,171,001
1847–8	2,383,486	1854–5	6.764,530
1848–9	2,172,856	1855–6	6,613,479
1849–50	2,369,683	1856–7	8,824,825

Sources: AlA, Vol. L, p. 515, AlA, Vol. LVIII, p. 506, AlA, Vol. LXXI, p. 499, AlA, Vol. XCIII, p. 417; R. L. Playfair, *A History of 'Arabia Felix' or Yemen* (Bombay, 1859).

83 B.S.L. 137 (16 November 1846), Haines to Govt. of Bombay (30 November 1846).

84 In 1850 Haines noted a steady increase in American imports and exports Aden Records AlA, Vol. LXXXIX. By 1852 French, American and Hamburg vessels had entirely abandoned Mocha. AlA Vol. CX, p. 347. Haines induced the French house of Vidal Frères to establish itself at Aden and this firm began to import cargoes of coffee from Hudayda in 1852. A.A.E. Mems. et Docs., Asie 26 etc., Capitaine Guérin to Ministre de la Marine et des Colonies (18 April 1852).

85 A.R., FlA, Vol. CXLII, p. 21 Cruttenden's evidence at Haines's trial.

86 A.R., AlA, Vol. L, p. 518 and Vol. LVIII, p. 506.

87 B.S.L. unnumbered (30 September 1840); Haines to Govt. of Bombay 47 (6 August 1840), B.S.L. 97 (30 November 1840), Haines to Govt. of Bombay 72 (5 November 1840).

88 B.S.L. 76 (31 October 1843), memorandum by Governor of Bombay, (21 October 1843), quoting Haines to Govt. of Bombay (4 July 1843).

89 In 1838, La Place of the *Artemise* said that Mocha was a shadow of what it had been in 1808, A.A.E. Mems. et Docs. Asie 26, etc., Rapport du Commandant La Place sur Moka et la commerce de l'Arabie. Téhenne in 1842 said that Mocha had been in decay for fifty years. Ibid., Rapport de Capitaine de Corvette Téhenne sur Moka, etc., 1842. In 1846 heavy coffee purchases by Americans gave a fillip to Mocha's commerce, A.R., AlA, Vol. LVIII, p. 506. In 1849 Mocha yielded $20,000 revenue as compared with $80,000 at Hudayda. A.S.L. 6 (2 July 1849), Haines to Govt. of Bombay 30 (13 June 1849).

90 B.S.L. (30 April 1840), Haines to Govt. of Bombay 44 (27 June 1840).

91 They waited from January to June. A.S.L. 2 (27 January 1848), A.S.L. 11 (29 July 1848), Haines to Govt. of Bombay 39 (22 June 1848).

92 B.S.L. (30 September 1840), Haines to Govt. of Bombay 46 (23 July 1840), Sherjebi asked for arms secured on the coffee sale, A.S.L. 5 (13 May 1842), Haines to Govt. of Bombay 36 (2 May 1842), A.R., AlA, Vol. 71, p. 499.

93 B.S.L. 6 (4 February 1850), Haines to Govt. of Bombay (15 January 1850), B.S.L. Haines to Govt. of Bombay (14 April 1850).

94 A.S.L. 11 (26 October 1842) enclosing Haines to Govt. of Bombay 35 (24 October 1842).

95 Cf. note 89 above. Mems. et Docs., Asie 26, Capitaine Téhenne, Rapport sur Moka, etc., 1842.

96 *Parliamentary Papers* 1851 Vol. XXI, Questions 6236, 6243. At Haines's trial it was estimated that the Aden Treasury disbursed between £100,000 and £120,000 per annum.

97 That is, up to 1851; see note 82 above.

98 See chart on p. 57 and A.R. AlA, Vol. LVIII, p. 501; Vol. LXXI, p. 497.

99 The Commissariat had to be on good terms with all at Berbera because of its heavy purchases. A.S.L. 8 (30 April 1848), Cruttenden to Haines (4 April 1848) all Aden's fresh meat came from there. Ibid., Haines to Govt. of Bombay 22 (5 April 1848).

100 In 1847 coasting craft were heavily engaged in transporting lime for use on the defences, A.R. AlA, Vol. LXVI, p. 741. See below Chapter V, p. 144.

101 Home Misc. Series 846, Labouchere to Hobhouse (22 April 1849) enclosing extract of letter from Bowring (20 February 1849).

102 B.S.L. 42 (21 May 1841), Haines to Govt. of Bombay 29 (18 April 1841), 'enormous' profits were made by the monopolists. It was again a monopoly in 1844. A.S.L. 15 (11 December 1844), Haines to Govt. of Bombay 9 (22 November 1844).

103 A.S.L. 15 (11 December 1844), Haines to Govt. of Bombay 9 (23 November 1844). At that time Haines proposed to break up the monopoly by auctioning and dividing it. The *qat* monopolist could dictate prices to the traders coming in from the Yemen.

104 For this dispute see I.O.R. Board's Collections 105617 and 110767 of 1847.

105 A.S.L. 1 (11 January 1843), Haines to Govt. of Bombay 93 (29 December 1842), Report on Census.

106 A.R. AlA, Vol. XVIII, p. 202.

107 B.S.L. 135 (16 November 1846), Hardinge's Memorandum on Defences (10 October 1846), A.S.L. 1 (28 January 1849), Haines to Govt. of Bombay (24 January 1849), A.R. AlA, Vol. 200 pp. 18–24; Rhodes House Library, Gen. Mansfield to Sir Bartle Frere (7 December 1862).

108 A.R. 1849 and 1856 Censuses.

109 A.R. AlA, Vol. XVIII, p. 202, 1842 Census. In March 1839 there had been more women than men. B.S.L. 51 (16 April 1839), Haines to Govt. of Bombay 45P (5 March 1839), Report on Census.

110 A.R. AlA, Vol. CII. Haines to Govt. of Bombay 8J (24 April 1851).

111 A.R., 1856 Census.

112 A.R., 1849 Census.

113 B.S.L. 14 (undated, 1840). Adjt.-Genl. of Army to Govt. of Bombay (18 March 1840) enclosing Capon to Adjt.-Genl. (2 March 1840).

114 A.S.L. 10 (27 May 1845), Haines to Govt. of Bombay 2 (17 May 1845), A.S.L. 12 (2 September 1848), Haines to Govt. of Bombay 11 (4 June 1848), A.R., AlA. Vol. CII, Haines to Govt. of Bombay 8J (24 May 1851).

115 B.S.L. 84 (4 July 1839), Haines to Govt. of Bombay 13 (9 June 1836).

B.S.L. 42 (21 May 1841), Haines to Govt. of Bombay 29 (18 April 1841), Govt. of Bombay to Haines (20 May 1841).

116 B.S.L. 51 (16 April 1839), Haines to Govt. of Bombay (10 April 1839).

117 The Parsi community at Aden was from the outset closely connected with the garrison. There were no Parsi names on the list of Aden Residents in 1839. They came to Aden after the occupation in the wake of the army and probably were mostly engaged in providing services for the troops. In 1846 they began to move into the gum, hides and coffee trade and they seemed to be the only members of the commercial community with large enough capital at that date to buy the cargoes of American ships (A.R. AlA, Vol. LVIII, p. 506). The Parsis headed the list of Aden residents who signed the address to Haines in 1854. (*Bombay Times* Overland Survey of Intelligence (31 July to 29 August 1854)). Among those who signed was one 'Cowasji Dinshawji', the founder of the still prominent firm of Cowasji Dinshaw Bros. at Aden. See also the history of Cowasji Dinshaw Bros. in *Port of Aden Annual* 1956, and A. de Gobineau, *Trois ans en Asie 1855–1858* (Paris, 1859), Chapter V. Cf. D. A. Farnie, *East and West of Suez* (Oxford, 1969), pp. 37–8, on the role of Bombay Parsis.

118 J. P. Malcolmson, 'An Account of Aden', *Journal of the Asiatic Society*, Vol. VIII, 1846, p. 286.

119 In 1843 Haines pressed the Commissariat to buy grass and timber from Arab merchants at Aden. A.S.L. 6 (11 May 1843), Haines to Govt. of Bombay 37 (24 April 1843); Haines also tried to force the Executive Engineer to employ his labourers through 'Ali Bubakr; A.R., AlA, Vol. LVIII, p. 473, Haines to Govt. of Bombay 107 (5 December 1846). Captain Kilner, the Executive Engineer, tried to change the policy of the Public Works Department to exclude Haines's friends and this caused the furious disputes between him and Haines in 1846 and 1847. Haines seized every opportunity to criticise the Engineer's work and ruin him in the eyes of his superiors after the altercation over the labourers. B.S.L. 69 (6 August 1847) and 85 (1 October 1847).

CHAPTER III

1 F. M. Hunter and J. Sealy, *An account of the Arab tribes in the Aden Hinterland* (1886 ed.), p. 10. B.S.L. 84 (4 July 1839) enclosing Haines to Govt. of Bombay 40P (23 February 1839) and B.S.L. 51 (16 April 1839) enclosing Haines to Govt. of Bombay 51P (15 March 1839).

2 At some time in the recent past the Fadli had seized control of the sea coast near Aden from the Yafi'i. A.R., A4B/7, Report on Yafi'i bani kasad, 1903.

3 Cf. the description of rulers' powers in D. Ingrams, *Survey of the Economic and Social Conditions of the Aden Protectorate* (Asmara, 1949).

4 Belhaven, *The Kingdom of Melchior* (London, 1949), Chapters II and III.

5 B.S.L. 11 (28 February 1840), Haines to Govt. of Bombay 79 (4 December 1839).

6 B.S.L. 51 (16 April 1839) enclosing Haines to Govt. of Bombay 8 (25 February 1839); B.S.L. 84 (4 July 1839) enclosing Haines to Govt. of Bombay 15 (11 June 1839); B.S.L. 109 (3 October 1839) enclosing Haines to Govt. of Bombay 22 (13 September 1839).

7 B.S.L. 11 (28 February 1840) enclosing Haines to Govt. of Bombay 79 (4 December 1839).

8 B.S.L. 51 (16 April 1839) enclosing Haines to Govt. of Bombay 51P (15 March and 10 April 1839).

9 This is the impression given by G. Waterfield in his *Sultans of Aden* (London, 1968).

10 B.S.L. 84 (4 July 1839) enclosing Haines to Govt. of Bombay 15 (11 June 1839); B.S.L. 124 (12 November 1839) enclosing Haines to Govt. of Bombay (20 October 1839).

11 B.S.L. 1 (1 January 1840) enclosing Haines to Govt. of Bombay 33 (11 December 1840); B.S.L. 11 (28 February 1840) enclosing Haines to Govt. of Bombay (1 February 1840).

12 B.S.L. 20 (30 April 1840) enclosing Haines to Govt. of Bombay 24 (31 March 1840); B.S.L. 35 (20 June 1840) enclosing Haines to Govt. of Bombay 32 (20 June 1840); B.S.L. (30 September 1840) enclosing Haines to Govt. of Bombay 46 (23 July 1840) and 47 (6 August 1840).

13 B.S.L. 124 (12 November 1839) enclosing Haines to Govt. of Bombay 72 (20 October 1839); B.S.L. 97 (30 November 1840) enclosing E. Haines to Govt. of Bombay 72 (9 November 1840).

14 B.S.L. 20 (30 April 1840) enclosing Haines to Govt. of Bombay 24 (31 March 1840).

15 B.S.L. (30 September 1840) enclosing Haines to Govt. of Bombay 46 (23 July 1840).

16 These attacks are well described in Waterfield, op. cit., Chapters 11 and 13.

17 B.S.L. 11 (28 February 1840) enclosing Haines to Govt. of Bombay 4 (1 February 1840); B.S.L. 4 (29 January 1840) Asst. Surgeon Malcolmson to Medical Board Bombay (19 October 1839); nearly two-thirds of the 24th Regiment at Aden had scurvy.

18 B.S.L. 35 (20 June 1840) enclosing Haines to Govt. of Bombay 32 (2 June 1840); B.S.L. 50 (23 July 1840) enclosing Capon to Haines (15 June 1840); J. P. Malcolmson, 'An Account of Aden', *Journal of the Asiatic Society*, Vol. VIII.

19 B.S.L. 11 (28 February 1840) enclosing Govt. of Bombay to Haines (26 February 1840).

20 I.O. Home Misc. Series, Hobhouse to Carnac (4 April 1840).

21 B.S.L. 70 (30 August 1841) enclosing Haines to Govt. of Bombay 71 (2 August 1841). The incident is still remembered among the Fadli, and I was given an account of it at Zinjibar in 1959 by the then Fadli Naib, Ahmad bin 'Abdallah.

22 B.S.L. 70 (30 August 1841) enclosing Haines to Govt. of Bombay 78 (15 August 1841).

23 B.S.L. 94 (24 November 1841), Haines to Govt. of Bombay 105 (30 October 1841); A.S.L. 2 (10 February 1842) enclosing Lt. Christopher to Haines 3 December 1841.

24 A.S.L. 2 (10 February 1842) enclosing Haines to Govt. of Bombay 10 (31 January 1842); A.S.L. 8 (10 August 1842).

25 A.S.L. 1 (10 January 1842) enclosing Haines to Govt. of Bombay 1 (4 January 1842).

26 A.S.L. 5 (13 May 1842), 10 (15 October 1842), 12 (11 November 1842) and 13 (11 December 1842).

27 A.S.L. 1 (10 January 1842) enclosing Haines to Govt. of Bombay 1 (4 January 1842).

28 A.S.L. 12 (11 November 1842) enclosing Haines to Govt. of Bombay 42 (1 November 1842); A.S.L. 1 (11 January 1843) enclosing Haines to Govt. of Bombay 52 (17 December 1842), 57 (21 December 1842) and 62 (28 December 1842); A.S.L. 2 (11 February 1842) enclosing Govt. of Bombay to Haines (20 December 1842), Haines to Govt. of Bombay 10 (3 February 1842); B.S.L. 124 (22 November 1839) and enclosures.

29 A.S.L. 2 (11 February 1843), enclosing Haines to Govt. of Bombay 10 (3 February 1843), and Muhsin and Ahmed to Haines (20 January 1843); A.S.L. 3 (1 March 1843) enclosing Haines to Govt. of Bombay 15 (28 February 1842); B.S.L. 42 (21 May 1841) enclosing Haines to Govt. of Bombay 33 (30 April 1841).

30 B.S.L. 18 (17 February 1844) enclosing Haines to Govt. of Bombay 92 (13 October 1843) and Cruttenden to Haines (24 August 1843). The Sultan claimed that he had been encouraged to enter Aden and negotiate in January 1843 because he saw Cruttenden waiting to receive him at the Gate.

31 B.S.L. 18 (17 February 1844) enclosing Haines to Govt. of Bombay 92 (13 October 1843) and 100 (19 October 1843). Govt. of Bombay to Haines 125 (17 February 1844).

32 The Governor-General ordered the renewal of the agreement in November 1843 but Haines held up renewal for three months. B.S.L. 84 (30 November 1843) enclosing Govt. of India to Govt. of Bombay (18 November 1843) Haines to Govt. of Bombay (1 November 1843); A.S.L. 1 (11 January 1844) and 3 (11 March 1844) enclosing Haines to Govt. of Bombay 18 (2 March 1844).

33 A.S.L. 6 (11 May 1843) enclosing Haines to Govt. of Bombay 37 (24 April 1843).

34 A.S.L. 13 (31 August 1845) enclosing Haines to Govt. of Bombay 47 (20 August 1845).

35 C. Webster, *The Foreign Policy of Palmerston*, Vol. II, p. 705.

36 A.A.E. Turquie Alexandrie, Vol. IX, Cochelet to Soult 161 (16 January 1840) and 168 (26 February 1840); B.S.L. (1 January 1840) enclosing Haines to Govt. of Bombay 31 (19 November 1839); B.S.L. 11 (28 February 1840) enclosing Haines to Govt. of Bombay 5 (1 February 1840); B.S.L. 20 (30 April 1840) enclosing Hodges to Carnac (17 March 1840).

37 B.S.L. 75 (29 September 1840), Sharif Husain to Govt. of Bombay 3 September 1840.

38 A treaty was signed with Sharif Husayn himself in 1840 but the India Board refused to ratify it. B.S.L. 97 (30 November 1840) enclosing Govt. of Bombay to Govt. of India (12 November 1840) and Hobhouses's comment. F.O. 78/2753 Memorandum on Ottoman rights in Arabia (14 November 1843) and Queen Advocate's decision (15 May 1844); B.S.L. 76 (31 October 1843). Minute by Governor of Bombay and collection of correspondence on Sharif Husayn's case.

39 B.S.L. 77 (30 September 1840) enclosing Haines to Govt. of Bombay 25 (28 August 1840).

40 B.S.L. 19 (27 March 1841) enclosing Haines to Govt. of Bombay 12 (25 February 1841). He may even have exceeded his instructions. Fresnel, the French Consul at Jedda, said that the British provided the Imams with money and munitions for use against Sharif Husayn, A.A.E. Politique, Turquie, Djeddah, Fresnel to Ministre des Affaires Etrangeres (27 March 1848).

41 B.S.L. 6 (31 January 1841) enclosing Haines to Govt. of Bombay 3 (3 January 1841). B.S.L. 42 (21 May 1841) enclosing Haines to Govt. of Bombay 33 (30 April 1841). B.S.L. 70 (31 August 1841) enclosing Haines to Govt. of Bombay 72 (6 August 1841). A.S.L. 5 (13 May 1842) enclosing Haines to Govt. of Bombay 3C (2 May 1841). A.A.E. Mems. et Docs., Asie 26, Tehenne to Ministre de la Marine et des Colonies (4 March 1842), said that the Imam was constructing a road from Ta'izz to Aden to let cannons up and coffee down.

42 B.S.L. 34 (19 May 1843) enclosing Govt. of India to Govt. of Bombay (1 May 1843).

43 A.S.L. 3 (11 March 1842) enclosing Haines to Govt. of Bombay 24 (6 March 1841); A.S.L. 5 (13 May 1842) enclosing Haines to Govt. of Bombay 3C (2 May 1842).

44 A.S.L. 9 (7 August 1844) enclosing Haines to Govt. of Bombay 49 (29 July 1844); A.S.L. 11 (8 September 1844) enclosing Haines to Govt. of Bombay 52 (22 August 1844).

45 B.S.L. 79 (28 September 1844) enclosing Commander British Forces Aden to Adjutant-General (9 August 1844), Haines to Govt. of Bombay (30 August 1844), and Governor's Minute, B.S.L. 97 (30 November 1844), Haines to Govt. of Bombay 71 (23 October 1844) and comment; A.S.L. 11 (8 September 1844) enclosing Haines to Govt. of Bombay 52 (22 August 1844); B.S.L. 97 (30 November 1844) enclosing Haines to Govt. of Bombay 71 (23 October 1844); A.S.L. 14 (11 November 1844) enclosing Haines to Govt. of Bombay 73 (26 October 1844) and 76 (1 November 1844).

46 A.S.L. 1 (10 January 1845) enclosing Haines to Govt. of Bombay 95 (31 December 1844); A.S.L. 2 (28 January 1845).

47 A.S.L. 2 (28 January 1845), B.S.L. 12 (28 February 1845) Haines to Govt. of Bombay (30 January 1845), Cmdr. of British Forces Aden to Milty. Adjt.-Genl, Bombay (30 January 1845) and Bombay minute.

H.M.S. *Serpent* left for Aden on 22 February 1845. There were 1,500 men in the garrison at the time. On 27 February H.M.'s 94th Regiment arrived to replace H.M.'s 17th Regiment and this meant a double garrison for a short period while the changeover was taking place.

48 A.S.L. (10 January 1845), A.S.L. 6 (26 March 1845), A.S.L. 7 c12 April 1845), A.S.L. 8 (29 April 1845).

49 B.S.L. 106 (15 September 1846) enclosing Haines to Govt. of Bombay 32 (30 August 1846), B.S.L. 101 (27 August 1846) enclosing Haines to Govt. of Bombay 40 (15 August 1846). Arnaud said that the Sayyid was a native of Senaar in the Sudan. Mems. et Docs. Asie 26, Arnaud's report (26 April 1847).

50 Haines said that Sharif Husayn supported the Sayyid (B.S.L. 106 [15 September 1846] enclosing Haines to Govt. of Bombay 32 [30 August 1846]). But Haines tended to see Husayn's hand behind every anti-British plot. Arnaud said that Husayn held aloof having seen the effect of Faqih Sa'id's populist uprising (Arnaud's report [26 April 1847]).

51 B.S.L. 101 (27 August 1846) enclosing Haines to Govt. of Bombay 30 (15 August 1846). B.S.L. 106 (15 September 1846) enclosing Haines to Govt. of Bombay 44 (26 August 1846) and Haines to Govt. of Bombay 32 (30 August 1846); B.S.L. 123 (15 October 1846) enclosing Haines to Govt. of Bombay 40 (29 September 1846).

52 B.S.L. 106 (15 September 1846) enclosing Haines to Govt. of Bombay 32 (30 August 1846); B.S.L. 114 (1 October 1846) enclosing Haines to Govt. of Bombay 44 (26 August 1846); B.S.L. 130 (2 November 1846) enclosing Haines to Govt. of Bombay 62 (16 October 1846); B.S.L. 137 (16 November 1846) enclosing Haines to Govt. of Bombay (30 October 1846); B.S.L. 148 (2 December 1846) enclosing Haines to Govt. of Bombay (16 November 1846); cf. J. Christie, *Cholera Epidemics in East Africa* (London, 1876). Another religious leader rose up in Central Yemen in 1843 and renewed the fervour of the Bani Yam adherents of the Isma'ilite sect of Islam. They dominated the Jabal Harraz area from then until 1872. Sayyid Isma'il was killed in 1848 in a quarrel with a *badu* shaykh (A.S.L. 12 [2 September 1848]). The harvest failed in Yemen in 1846–7.

53 B.S.L. 106 (15 September 1846) enclosing Minute by Governor of Bombay (9 September 1846); B.S.L. 123 (15 October 1846) enclosing Minute by Governor-General (21 September 1846); I.O. Home Misc. 853 Hobhouse to Hardinge (7 January 1847).

54 B.S.L. 162 (27 August 1845) enclosing Haines to Govt. of Bombay (28 July 1845); B.S.L. 130 (2 November 1846) enclosing Haines to Govt. of Bombay 62 (16 October 1846) and Minute by Governor of Bombay (1 November 1846).

55 A.R., A1A, Vol. LXXIII, p. 130, Haines to Govt. of Bombay (8 January 1848).

56 B.S.L. 62 (27 March 1845) enclosing Haines to Govt. of Bombay (28 July 1845).

57 A.R., A1A, Haines to Govt. of Bombay (8 January 1848). The Chiefs
   involved were those of 'Abdali, 'Aqrabi, Fadli and Hawshabi.
58 A.S.L. 5 (10 March 1848) enclosing Haines to Govt. of Bombay 21
   (31 March 1848).
59 A.S.L. 2 (27 January 1848) enclosing Haines to Govt. of Bombay 7
   (25 January 1848). Husayn had been weakened by a long struggle with
   "Ali Humayda the Chief of Bajil in 1847 (Arnaud's report [26 April
   1847]).
60 Periodical reports in Aden Secret Letters throughout 1848 and 1849
   tell the tale of this struggle, also Arnaud's reports in A.A.E., Mems et.
   Docs., Asie 26. C. U. Aitchison, *Treaties, Engagements and Sanads*, etc.
   (1929 ed.), Vol. IX, p. 38.
61 A.S.L. 1 (9 January 1848) enclosing Haines to Govt. of Bombay 2
   (4 January 1848).
62 A.S.L. 5 (10 March 1848) enclosing Haines to Govt. of Bombay 13
   (29 February 1848); A.S.L. 6 (10 April 1848) enclosing Haines to
   Govt. of Bombay 15 (12 March 1848).
63 Vegetables had been grown for some time in experimental gardens
   with convict labour at Aden. Malcolmson, 'An account of Aden',
   Journal of the Asiatic Society (Vol. VIII, 1846), p. 285.
64 In July 1847 a Lahej merchant undertook to supply all the Engineer
   Department's needs of grass at low prices. Haines stopped this by
   forbidding the sale of grass at the Aden wall thus making it compulsory
   to buy in the open market in Aden town. He did this because he said he
   did not want to leave Aden entirely dependent on the then vacillating
   Sultan of Lahej for its provisions. B.S.L. 85 (1 October 1847) Haines
   to Govt. of Bombay 45 (15 July 1847) and enclosures.
65 A.S.L. 6 (10 April 1848) enclosing Haines to Govt. of Bombay 15
   (12 March 1848).
66 A.S.L. 16 (27 December 1848) enclosing Haines to Govt. of Bombay
   73 (17 December 1848) acknowledging receipt of instructions.
67 I.O. MSS. Eur. F.78/38, Sir C. Wood to Governor-General (9 December 1854); ibid., F.78/28 Elphinstone to Wood (16 January 1855).
68 A.S.L. 6 (10 April 1848) enclosing Haines to Govt. of Bombay 15
   (12 March 1848).
69 A.S.L. (29 July 1848) enclosing Haines to Govt. of Bombay 47 (15
   July 1848) and 47 (27 July 1848); A.S.L. 15 (28 November 1848);
   A.S.L. 16 (27 December 1848) enclosing Haines to Govt. of Bombay
   74 (27 December 1848).
70 A.S.L. 1 (28 January 1849) enclosing Haines to Govt. of Bombay 9
   (20 January 1849) and 12 (28 January 1849); A.S.L. 9 (7 August 1844)
   enclosing Haines to Govt. of Bombay 49 (27 July 1844); B.S.L. 92
   (5 August 1846) enclosing Haines to Govt. of Bombay 24 (15 July
   1846).
71 Practically the whole ruling family was struck by the disease. In May
   Dr. Vaughan, the Surgeon at Aden, was sent to Lahej to vaccinate
   against smallpox. A.S.L. 5 (29 May 1849) enclosing Haines to Govt.
   of Bombay 28 (25 May 1849).

72 A.S.L. (29 May 1849) enclosing Haines to Govt. of Bombay 28 (25 May 1849)

73 A.S.L. 16 (28 August 1854), Appendix B to Outram's Report.

74 The question in dispute was whether or not the 'Abdali Sultan retained rights over the 'Aqrabi. Most authorities agree that the 'Aqrabi Shaykhs had made themselves independent of the 'Abdali in the 1770s. See F. M. Hunter, *Arab Tribes in the Vicinity of Aden*. Haines at one time referred to him as the 'Aqrabi 'Sultan' (A.S.L. 3 [11 March 1842]). Nevertheless the 'Abdali had forced the 'Aqrabi to pay a share of the old tributary blackmail to the 'Awlaqis at the same time as the 'Uzaybi sub-chief who was clearly an 'Abdali dependent. B.S.L. 69 (6 August 1847) enclosing Haines to Govt. of Bombay 44 (15 July 1847).

75 Haines in 1853 maintained that the 'Aqrabi, having paid tribute to Lahej for 'more than a century' was not independent (B.S.L. 37 [23 May 1853] and enclosures). But in 1854 he said that they were independent but tribute-paying up to 1852 when presumably Haines, believed they had been subjected to Lahej (A.S.L. 3 [5 February 1854]).

76 A.S.L. 9 (6 October 1849) enclosing Haines to Govt. of Bombay 51 (28 September 1849); A.S.L. 10 (29 October 1849) enclosing Haines to Govt. of Bombay 53 (21 October 1849); A.R., AIA, Vol. XCII, p. 107, Haines to Govt. of Bombay (15 March 1850).

77 A.S.L. 9 (6 October 1849) enclosing Haines to Govt. of Bombay 51 (28 September 1849); A.S.L. 16 (28 August 1854) enclosing Outram to Govt. of Bombay 119 (10 August 1854).

78 A.R., AIA, Vol. XCII, p. 145, Haines to Govt. of Bombay (27 July 1850); ibid., p. 155, Haines to Govt. of Bombay (27 August 1850); ibid., p. 165, Haines to Govt. of Bombay (29 September 1850); ibid., p. 169, Haines to Govt. of Bombay (14 October 1850); ibid., p. 181, Haines to Govt. of Bombay (27 November 1850); B.S.L. 11 (17 January 1851) enclosing Haines to Govt. of Bombay 63 (28 December 1850); B.S.L. 12 (3 February 1851) enclosing Haines to Govt. of Bombay 2 (14 January 1851).

79 A.R., AIA, Vol. CI, p. 7, Haines to Govt. of Bombay (27 January 1851).

80 A.R., AIA, Vol. CI, p. 151, Haines to Govt. of Bombay (11 December 1851); A.S.L. 16 (28 August 1854) enclosing Outram to Govt. of Bombay 119 (10 August 1854). Haines reported as a success the fact that an attempt had been made to poison one of the murderers. B.S.L. 103 (3 December 1852) Haines to Govt. of Bombay (14 November 1852).

81 A.R., AIA, Vol. CI, p. 68, Haines to Govt. of Bombay (25 August 1851); ibid., p. 92, Haines to Govt. of Bombay (2 September 1851).

82 A.R., AIA, Vol. CI, p. 59, Haines to Govt. of Bombay (24 July 1851); ibid., p. 69, Haines to Govt. of Bombay (25 August 1851).

83 I.O. Home Misc. Series, Falkland, the Governor of Bombay, wrote of the Fadli's 'scurvy conduct' – Falkland to Broughton (24 June 1851); see also correspondence noted in A.S.L. 16 (28 August 1854), Outram to Govt. of Bombay 119 (10 August 1854).

84 The President of the India Board, Lord Broughton (formerly Sir J. Hobhouse), warned Falkland against action at Aden on 7 August 1851.

Falkland was not pleased at this but obeyed instructions – Falkland to Broughton (1 and 24 September and 1 and 10 October 1851). See A.R., A1A, Vol. CVIII, p. 155, Haines to Govt. of Bombay (28 November 1852) on agricultural difficulties. The rise of the 'Abdali ruling house was producing widespread protest at Lahej.

85 A.R., A1A, Vol. CI, p. 91, Haines to Govt. of Bombay (2nd September 1851) enclosing Sultan Ahmad al Fadli to Sultan 'Ali, undated.

86 A.R., A1A, Vol. CI, pp. 127 and 129, Sultan 'Ali to Haines (20 October 1851), Haines to Sultan 'Ali (21 October 1851); I.O. Home Misc. Series 841.

87 See report of these proceedings compiled by Outram and Badger and enclosed in A.S.L. 16 (28 August 1854). We see here the origin of the 'Abdali ruling family's dominance at Lahej, cf. A. M. A. Maktari, *Water Rights and Irrigation Practices in Lahej* (Cambridge University Press, 1971), p. 67.

88 A.R., A1A, Vol. CI, p. 139, Haines to Govt. of Bombay (15 November 1851); ibid., p. 143, Haines to Court of Directors (26 November 1851).

89 A.R., A1A, Vol. CVIII, pp. 55, 103, 111, 155 and 161, Haines to Govt. of Bombay (11 July 1852), Sultan 'Ali to Captain Haines (20 August 1852), Haines to Govt. of Bombay (14 September 28 November,, and 14 December 1852).

90 A.R., A1A, Vol. CVIII, p. 99, Haines to Govt. of Bombay (27 August 1852); B.S.L. 17 (1 March 1853) enclosing Haines to Govt. of Bombay 60 (11 February 1853); B.S.L. 20 (14 March 1853) enclosing Haines to Govt. of Bombay 78 (28 February 1853).

91 On 28 May a load of fodder cost 12 Rs., on 14 June 1853 the same load cost 1 R. B.S.L. 42 (2nd July 1853) enclosing Haines to Govt. of Bombay 32 (14 June 1853); A.S.L. 1 (5 January 1854).

92 B.S.L. 42 (2 July 1853) enclosing Haines to Govt. of Bombay 32 (14 June 1853); A.S.L. 1 (5 January 1854).

93 A.S.L. 1 (5 January 1954) and A.S.L. 3 (5 February 1854).

94 A.S.L. 3 (5 February 1854), Haines to Govt. of Bombay 13 (January 29 1854). The 'Aqrabi elders refused to have one of Sultan 'Ali's brothers as their ruler. A.S.L. 7 (7 April 1854), Clarke to Govt. of Bombay 39 (31 March 1854). Haines's promise was made in writing and sent to Sultan 'Ali at Lahej. Haines got the 'Aqrabi to agree to the truce by threatening to destroy Bir Ahmad there and then. Haines had no authority to issue either the promise or the threat.

95 A special tax was imposed on water to support the Hiswah garrison in 1852. A1A, Vol. CVIII, p. 100, Haines to Govt. of Bombay (27 August 1852). Haines had difficulty in preventing coffee being held up at Lahej to force up the Aden price. B.S.L. 37 (23 May 1853) Haines to Govt. of Bombay 26 (13 May 1953). He had to act quickly also to prevent Lahej from monopolising Aden's vegetable supply in April 1852. A1A, Vol. CVIII, p. 37, Haines to Govt. of Bombay (25 April 1852).

96 B.S.L. 2 (3 January 1853), Haines to Govt. of Bombay 66 (14 December 1852). A.R., A1A, Vol. CVIII, p. 10. Haines to Govt. of Bombay (27 January 1852). Ibid., p. 87, Haines to Govt. of Bombay (27 July

1852) – Haines ignored 'Aqrabi pleas to have their bandar reopened while they were hostile to Lahej. He acted again in May 1853 to secure the fort at the Hiswah from attack. A.S.L. 16 (28 August 1854), Badger's Report.

97 AR, AiA, Vol. CI, p. 1, Haines to Govt. of Bombay (14 January 1851).

98 *Bombay Telegraph and Courier*, 31 July 1854. A deficiency of 20,000 Rs. had been discovered in 1847 but Haines had managed to cover up on that occasion. A.A.E. Mems. et Docs., Asie 26, Arabic. Capitaine de Vaisseau Guérin to Ministre de la Marine et des Colonies (18 April 1852).

99 *Bombay Telegraph and Courier* (31 July 1854) Report of Trial. I.O. MSS. Eur. F. 78/28 Elphinstone to Wood (14 January and 14 February 1854).

100 See F. J. Goldsmid, *James Outram: A Biography* (London, 1883), Vol. II, Chapter III.

101 MSS. Eur. F. 78, Letter Book IV, Wood to Elphinstone (24 February 1854).

102 MSS. Eur. 78, Letter Book IV, Wood to Elphinstone (8 February 1854).

103 MSS. Eur. F. 78/28 Elphinstone to Wood (14 January 1854), ibid., Letter Book IV, Wood to Elphinstone (24 February 1854).

104 MSS. Eur. F.78/28, Elphinstone to Wood, 14 March and 14 April 1854, ibid., Letter Book IV, Wood to Elphinstone, 8 June, 24 June and 25 November 1854.

105 *Bombay Times Overland Summary of Intelligence* (31 July to 29 August 1854), Report of Trial. Differing rates of exchange made the discounting business a profitable one. Maria Theresa dollars could be bought 2 per cent cheaper at Bombay than at Aden. Rupees at Aden were also at a discount of 3-4 per cent. B.S.L. 35 (30 April 1841), Haines to Govt. of Bombay 21 (26 March 1841). The annual turnover at Aden on Government account exceeded £100,000.

106 *Bombay Times Overland Summary of Intelligence* (31 July to 29 August 1854), Report of Trial.

107 A.R., AiA, Vol. CXLII, Haines's Trial, Evidence.

108 A.R., AiA, Vol. LXLI, Minute by Acting Chief Secretary to Bombay Govt. (19 March 1854).

109 I.O. Records Elphinstone Papers, Coghlan to Elphinstone (23 December 1854).

110 A.S.L. 16 (28 August 1854), Badger's report.

111 I.O. Home Correspondence 1873, Revd. G. P. Badger to Under-Secretary of State for India (U.S.S.I.) (5 April 1873).

112 B.S.L. 18 (29 February 1844), Haines to Govt. of Bombay 92 (13 October 1843), Evidence of 'Muhammad Kaisee' and 'Amar Eghori'.

113 *Bombay Telegraph and Courier* (31 July 1854) Report of Trial.

114 A.R., FiA, Vol. CXLII, Haines's Trial, Evidence.

115 A.R., AiA, Vol. CXLVII, Aden Trade Report 1850.

116 A.S.L. 13 (June 1854). Haines's rumoured partnership with Aden merchants was a standing joke among the officers at Aden. He also received money from Vidal of Marseilles, an old schoolfellow and

friend of his, to purchase coffee at Aden. Cruttenden's Memorandum
for private circulation in Elphinstone Papers, MSS. Eur. F.87, Box 7D,
Cruttenden to Lumsden 23 April 1854.

117 *Bombay Telegraph and Courier* (31 July 1854), Report of Trial.
118 I.O. Home Correspondence 1873, Badger to U.S.S.I. (5 April 1873).
119 *Bombay Telegraph and Courier* (31 July 1854) Report of Trial, Taylor's
speech for the defence.
120 MSS. Eur. F. 78/28, Elphinstone to Wood (14 March, 14 April and
10 May 1854) and Memorandum (6 April 1854).
121 MSS. Eur. F. 78/28, Elphinstone to Wood (14 April 1854).
122 *Bombay Telegraph and Courier* (31 July 1854), Report of Trial.
123 *Bombay Times Overland Summary of Intelligence* (31 July to 29 August
1854), *Bombay Telegraph and Courier* (31 July 1854). The Army Commander-in-Chief was hostile to Haines. Outram Papers, Holland to
Outram (28 August 1854). MSS. Eur. F. 78/. Letter Book IV, Wood
to Elphinstone (24 May 1854).
124 MSS. Eur. F. 78/28, Elphinstone to Wood (30 August 1854).
125 He had said he would pay in 1853. A.R., F1A, Vol. CXLII, p. 42,
Haines to Cruttenden (10 April 1853). He made the offer again at
his trial and in October 1854 when Elphinstone reluctantly accepted.
Eur. F. 78/28, Elphinstone to Wood (14 October and 28 November
1854).
126 Haines had accumulated savings of over £10,000. *Bombay Telegraph
and Courier* (31 July 1854), Report of Trial.

CHAPTER IV

1 See Sir F. Goldsmid, *Outram: A Biography* (London, 1881), Vol. II.
2 B.M. Addl. MSS. 38982, Rassam to Layard (24 October 1854),
Captain Eastwick, a Director, was Outram's main backer at the
East India House. Goldsmid, op. cit. He was Dalhousie's Aide-de-
Camp in 1853. Cf. Outram Papers, Adam (Private Secretary to Lord
Elphinstone) to Outram (12 October 1854).
3 Goldsmid, op. cit., Vol. II, pp. 36–7 and pp. 41–2; Bombay Secret
Letter 38 (25 July 1850) and 29 (3 April 1851).
4 Outram Papers, Elphinstone to Outram (11 April 1854).
5 B.M. Addl. MSS. 38775, Outram to Badger (18 November 1854). Cf.
also Elphinstone Papers, Wood (President of India Board) to Elphin-
stone (25 October and 5 November 1854), MSS. Eur. F. 78/28,
Elphinstone to Wood (19 March 1855).
6 Outram Papers Outram to Elphinstone (29 March 1854), Outram to
Adam (13 April 1854). Playfair and Murray; see B.M. Addl. MSS.,
Rassam to Playfair (12 January 1855). I.O. MSS. Eur. F. 78/28,
Coghlan to Elphinstone (11 February 1855).
7 B.M. Addl. MSS. 38775, folios 3, 5 and 13, letters from Outram to
Badger. Outram Papers, Badger to Outram (26 September and 12

November 1857). E. Stock, *History of the Church Missionary Society* (London, 1899), Vol. I, p. 349; *Dictionary of National Biography*: G. P. Badger; *The Times* (1 November 1872), Sir John Kaye's address to Royal Geographical Society.

8 Outram Papers, Outram to Elphinstone (12 August 1854), B.M. Addl. MSS., Rassam to Layard (24 October 1854).

9 B.M. Addl. MSS., Rassam to Layard (25 March 1857), Outram Papers, Badger to Outram (26 September 1857). Cf. Elphinstone Papers, Correspondence between Coghlan and Elphinstone.

10 Cf. H. L. Hoskins, *British Routes to India* (London, 1928) and C. W. Hallberg, *The Suez Canal: its History and Diplomatic Importance* (New York, 1931), pp. 118–19.

11 Cf. D. Johnson, *Guizot: Aspects of French History* (London, 1963), p. 285 and Chapter 6, *passim*.

12 Broadlands Papers, Hobhouse to Palmerston (6 April 1847). Wood, who succeeded Hobhouse at the India Board, was sceptical about French designs in the Red Sea. His view, like that of Gladstone was that if the French wished to interfere with the line of communication with India they could more easily do so in the Mediterranean. Cf. Elphinstone Papers, Wood to Elphinstone (24 April 1854). Wood regarded Aden as of importance for the influence it gave in South Arabia as well as because it was a staging post on the way to India. Outram Papers, Wood to Outram (24 April 1854). He was therefore concerned that the Aden Government should pursue a peaceful policy toward its neighbours.

13 Hallberg, op. cit., pp. 106–14.

14 Outram Papers, Dalhousie to Outram (11 March 1854), Goldsmid, op. cit., Vol. II, pp. 93–4.

15 Hallberg, op. cit., pp. 118–19.

16 R. J. Gavin, 'Palmerston's policy toward the East and West coasts of Africa 1830–1865' (Univ. of Cambridge Ph.D. thesis, 1959), p. 123

17 Hallberg, op. cit., p. 155.

18 Hallberg, op. cit., p. 143

19 Hallberg, op. cit., pp. 144–5.

20 Outram Papers, Outram to Wood (8 July 1854). Aden was regarded as a safeguard against a French *coup de main* in Egypt mounted from the south. Indian S.L. 17 (24 June 1859), Outram's Memorandum (13 June 1859), Canning's Minute (23 June 1859), Indian S.L. 22 (1 September 1859), Outram's Memorandum (15 August 1859). See also Badger Papers.

21 See T. E. Marston, *Britain's Imperial Role in the Red Sea Area 1800–1878*, pp. 223–7. Marston's account is correct in that it emphasises the strategic motivation. But the idea of occupying Perim was mooted earlier than 1856 the discussion of how it should be done advanced *pari passu* with the development of the Suez scheme and finally Coghlan had to act precipitately because of a fear that the French would forestall him. Marston, op. cit., pp. 223–7, rightly rejects the many apocryphal stories which grew up around this incident based on the fact that a French frigate arrived at Aden simultaneously with the departure of the

British sloop charged with the duty of occupying Perim. But he also rejects the authentic story of the occupation given by Coghlan in C. R. Low, *History of the Indian Navy* (London, 1877), Vol. II, p. 384, which is corroborated by other more contemporary evidence in much of its detail. Playfair in his 'Reminiscences', *Chambers Journal* (6th Series, 1899), p. 97, also rejected the apocryphal accounts, by that time well embroidered and put into print, but he did not deny Coghlan's story. See also J. S. King, *A Descriptive and Historical Account of the British Outpost of Perim in the Straits of Bab el Mandeb* (Bombay, 1877).

22 A.S.L. 11 (10 July 1857), Coghlan to Govt. of Bombay 88 (July 4 1857). F.O. 78/3815, Bulwer to Malmesbury (11 May and 6 July 1859, Cowley to Russell (25 May 1860).

23 Enclosures to B.S.L. 1863–9, Enclosure 5 to B.S.L. 4 (23 June 1863), Coghlan to Govt. of Bombay (23 January 1863) and S.S.I. to Coghlan No. 1 (24 December 1862).

24 J. D'Arcy, *La France et l'Angleterre: cent années de rivalité coloniale: l'Afrique* (Paris, 1900), pp. 365–7.

25 B.M. Addl. MSS. 38985, Rassam to Layard (23 February 1857) heard that the Pasha of Hudayda was furious on learning of the occupation and wrote straight to Istanbul.

26 B.M. Addl. MSS. 38989, Rassam to Layard 1 April 1859. C. R. Low, *History of the Indian Navy*, Vol. II, pp. 388–9.

27 G. Douin, *Histoire du règne du Khédive Isma'il* (Cairo, 1933), Tome III, p. 250.

28 See J. R. Hooker, 'The Foreign Office and the Abyssinian Captives', *Journal of African History* (II, 1961); Aden Administration Reports (A.A.R.) (1869 Report).

29 Outram Papers, Badger to Outram (19 December 1859), A.S.L. 16 (26 August 1856).

30 Elphinstone Papers Coghlan to Elphinstone (25 November 1858).

31 Elphinstone Papers, Coghlan to Elphinstone (24 August 1856), Norris and Penhey, op. cit; A.R., A1A, Vol. 172, p. 291, and Vol. 200, p. 97.

32 A.A.R. (1866–7 and 1867–8). The Church was consecrated in December 1871 by the Bishop of Bombay, Indian S.L. 212 (3 October 1872) Aden Newsreport 25 (8 December 1871). C.O. 846/3, Return of Works and Buildings (31 July 1939).

33 Condensers were first suggested by Coghlan in 1857 (A.S.L. 17 [10 October 1857], Coghlan to Govt. of Bombay 121 of [9 October 1857]) with the object of bringing down the exorbitant price of water. The tanks, wells, Government and P. and O. condensers, together with camel-borne supplies, were insufficient in 1863 to keep prices below starvation level. Letters from Aden etc. 1863, Merewether to Govt. of Bombay 73 (2 October 1863). In 1868 six new sets of condensers were ordered. A.A.R. (1869).

34 During a drought in 1857 prices rose to 4 Rs. per 100 gallons and on occasion as much as 5 Rs. was paid. Elphinstone Papers, Coghlan to Elphinstone (9 October 1857). In 1863 water from the Government condensers sold at 7 rupees per 100 gallons and Shaykh Uthman

water at 8 Rs. per 100 gallons. The average daily wage of a coal coolie
in the middle decades of the nineteenth century was 4 annas.

35 Letters from Aden, etc. (1863) and 64, Merewether to Govt. of Bombay
80 (17 October 1863), 83 (2 November 1863) and 108 (17 November
1864). MSS. Eur. F. 78/74, Merewether to Wood (30 October 1865).
By 1870 the price of water had been brought down to 1 rupee per 100
gallons, Indian S.L. 95 (9 June 1871), Memorandum by Merewether
(24 November 1870).

36 Letters from Aden, etc., 1865, Merewether to Govt. of Bombay 78
(17 June), 102 (17 July), 84 (24 June 1865), 131 (September 18 1865),
125 (31 August 1865), 116 (16 August 1865), 111 (1 August 1865). At
the beginning of August 9 lb. of *jowari* could be bought for one rupee,
at the end of the month only 8 lb., MSS. Eur. F. 78/4, Merewether to
Wood (30 August 1865).

37 R. L. Playfair, *History of Arabia Felix or Yemen and an Account of the British
settlement at Aden* (Bombay, 1859), p. 11.

38 Aden Records, A1A, Vol. 173, p. 321, Administration Report 1866–7.

39 See A.R., A1A, Vol. 199, pp. 463 and 457, Vol. 323, p. 187. A.A.R.
(1866–7). Indian S.L. 212 (3 October 1872), Tremenheere to Govt. of
Bombay 186/1327 (25 August 1871) enclosing Prideaux's report on
Aden landward trade.

40 A.A.R. (1866–7).

41 A.R., A1A, Vol. 198, p. 65, Coghlan to Govt. of Bombay (8 July 1857).

42 Enclosure to B.S.L. 4 (29 January 1840), Assistant Surgeon Malcolmson
to Medical Board, Bombay (19 October 1839).

43 A.R., A1A, Vol. 174, pp. 49–51, Vol. 836, p. 783.

44 A.R., A1A, Vol. 578, p. 98.

45 A.A.R. (1882–3).

46 A.A.R. (1881–2).

47 A.R., A1A, Vol. 323, p. 173, A.A.R. (1866–7).

48 Outram Papers, Elphinstone to Outram (19 July 1854).

49 A.A.R. (1869).

50 A.R., A1A, Vol. 198, p. 65, Coghlan to Govt. of Bombay (8 July 1857),
R. H. Thornton, *British Shipping*, Cambridge 1959, p. 45.

51 A.A.R. (1869). A.R., A1A, Vol. 198, p. 65, Coghlan to Govt. of Bombay
(8 July 1857).

52 Indian Political Letter 48 (22 March 1872) enclosing Tremenheere to
Govt. of Bombay 187/1328 (25 August 1871).

53 A.R., A1A, Vol. 171, p. 245. A.S.L. (1857), Coghlan to Vernon Smith
(17 July 1857), Cambridge University Library MSS. E 909, folio 9,
Badger to Wood (31 December 1861).

54 A.A.R. (1884).

55 Letters from Aden, etc., Merewether to Govt. of Bombay 111 (1
August 1865).

56 *Bombay Telegraph and Courier* (10 April 1854), p. 677.

57 *Port of Aden Annual* (1954–5), p. 30.

58 See above page 61, and Enclosures to B.S.L. 42 (21 May 1841), Haines
to Govt. of Bombay 29 (18 April 1841).

59 Indian Political Letter 48 (22 March 1872). Tremenheere to Govt. of Bombay 187/1328 (25 August 1871).

60 Letters from Aden, etc., Merewether to Govt. of Bombay 47 (18 April 1866).

61 Elphinstone Papers, MSS. Eur. F. 87 Box 6D, Coghlan to Elphinstone (29 March 1857). Aden Administration Report 1875–6. Aden Secret Letters 1863–70, Russell to Govt. of Bombay 1083 Pol. (6 September 1870), enclosing Hassan 'Ali Rajab 'Ali to Russell (6 September 1870). Home Corresp. F.O. to I.O. (7 April 1891), Note by Rastem Pasha (28 March 1891).

62 F. M. Hunter, *The Aden Handbook* (London, 1873), list of prominent Aden citizens and their offices.

63 A.A.R. (1882–3 Report). Also Aden Municipal Records File 627/525, Historical Resumé of Aden Municipality (1936).

64 A.R., A1A, Vol. 195, p. 15, and Vol. 758, p. 97.

65 A.R., A1A, Vol. 578, p. 115.

66 A.R., A1A, Vol. 533, p. 483, Vol. 788, p. 303, Vol. 985, p. 420, A1A 20/30/259.

67 Elphinstone Papers, Coghlan to Elphinstone (24 November and 12 December 1855).

68 Outram Papers, Badger to Outram (26 September 1857), B.M. Addl. MSS. 38984, Rassam to Layard (12 March 1856).

69 B.M. Addl. MSS. 38984, Rassam to Layard (12 March 1856), 38989, Rassam to Layard (26 January 1863), A.R., A1A, Vol. 533, p. 503, Memorandum (18 November 1868).

70 A.R., A1A, Vol. 172, pp. 18–27, Vol. 758, p. 97.

71 A.S.L. 3 (24 February 1857), Coghlan to Govt. of Bombay 22 (23 February 1857), B.M. Addl. MSS. 39115, Merewether to Layard (25 June 1865), A.A.R. (1866–7), Indian S.L. 212 (3 October 1872), Tremenheere to Govt. of Bombay (15 April 1872).

72 A.R., A1A, Vol. 172, pp. 118 and 250.

73 A.R., A1A, Vol. 165, p. 161.

74 A.R., A1A, Vol. 172, p. 291, A1A, Vol. 165, p. 161 and Vol. 200, p. 97.

75 A.R., A1A, Vol. 758, pp. 97 and 125.

76 A.R., A1A, Vol. 578, pp. 98–105.

77 A.A.R. (1881–2), A.R., A1A, Vol. 612, p. 267, Vol. 696, pp. 177 and 267.

78 B.M. Addl. MSS. 38983, Rassam to Layard (23 January 1855).

79 Elphinstone Papers, Coghlan to Elphinstone (24 August 1855).

80 Outram Papers, Badger to Outram (26 September 1857, 12 November 1857, 19 December 1857), Elphinstone Papers, Coghlan to Elphinstone (2 May 1859). A.R., A1A, Vol. 312, p. 389, Badger to Forbes (7 June 1861) and p. 395, Coghlan to Forbes (8 September 1861).

81 B.M. Addl. MSS. 38984, Rassam to Layard (24 May 1855).

82 For list of Badger's publications, see *Dictionary of National Biography*.

83 Enclosure to Indian Secret Letter 69 (15 July 1873), Sayyid 'Alawi to Tremenheere (8 May 1871).

84 Elphinstone Papers, Coghlan to Elphinstone (24 August 1855).
85 Elphinstone Papers, Coghlan to Elphinstone (25 February, 30 March 1856).
86 B.M. Addl. MSS. 38775, Outram to Badger (18 November 1854), cf. Outram Papers, Clarke to Outram (3 August 1854), A.S.L. 6 (23, March 1854) enclosing Clarke to Govt. of Bombay (23 March 1854) A.S.L. 7 (7 April 1854) enclosing Clarke to Govt. of Bombay 39 (31 March 1854).
87 A.S.L. 14 (20 July 1854) enclosing Outram to Anderson (12 July 1854).
88 A.S.L. 14 (20 July 1854) enclosing Outram to Anderson (12 July 1854) and Sultan Ahmad Abdallah to Clarke (1 April 1854). A.S.L. 16 (28 August 1854) enclosing Outram to Anderson 119 (10 August 1854), Appendix B. Badger's memorandum on hinterland policy.
89 Outram Papers, Outram to Wood (8 July 1854), Outram to Lowe (23 August 1854), A.S.L. 15 (6 August 1854) enclosing Outram to Anderson 114 (26 July 1854). Lord Dalhousie described Clarke's efforts as 'melancholy specimens of political imbecility', B.M. Addl. MSS. 38775, Outram to Badger (18 November 1854).
90 R. L. Playfair, *History of Arabia Felix*, pp. 171–5; C. U. Aitchison *Treaties, Engagements and Sanads . . .* (1865 ed.), Vol. VII, p. 269; F. M Hunter, *Arab tribes in the vicinity of Aden*, pp. 8 and 9.
91 Elphinstone Papers, Coghlan to Elphinstone (25 December 1856).
92 A.S.L. 1 (25 January 1857), B.M. Addl. MSS., Rassam to Layard (23 February 1857).
93 A.S.L. 7 (25 April 1857), Coghlan to Govt. of Bombay 44 (10 April 1857).
94 Elphinstone Papers, Coghlan to Elphinstone (27 November 1854, 11 February, 27 March, 24 April, 27 July, 3 August, 24 August, 21 September, 27 October and 27 November 1855). A.S.L. 1 (10 January 1856), Coghlan to Govt. of Bombay 1 (10 January 1856), A.S.L. 2 (26 January 1856), Coghlan to Govt. of Bombay 17 (25 January 1856), A.S.L. 4 (27 February 1856), Coghlan to Govt. of Bombay 31 (26 February 1856).
95 I.S.L. 188 (9 September 1870), Sultan Fadl Muhsin to Sir Seymour Fitzgerald (28 March 1870).
96 A.S.L. 26 (26 December 1856), Coghlan to Govt. of Bombay 187 (25 December 1856).
97 A.S.L. 26 (26 December 1856), Coghlan to Govt. of Bombay 187 (25 December 1856).
98 Elphinstone Papers, Coghlan to Elphinstone (27 April 1857), A.S.L. (10 May 1857), Coghlan to Govt. of Bombay 84 (26 June 1857). Cf. Playfair, op. cit., p. 34.
99 A.S.L. 7 (25 April 1857), Coghlan to Govt. of Bombay 44 (10 April 1857), A.S.L. 26 (26 December 1856), Coghlan to Govt. of Bombay 187 (25 December 1856).
100 Elphinstone Papers, Coghlan to Elphinstone (11 January 1857).
101 A.S.L. 7 (25 April 1857), Coghlan to Govt. of Bombay 44 (10 April 1857).

102 Elphinstone Papers, Coghlan to Elphinstone (24 August 1855) and postscript (28 August 1855).

103 A.S.L. 7 (25 April 1857), Coghlan to Govt. of Bombay 44 (10 April 1857) and 48 (12 April 1857).

104 A.S.L. 7 (25 April 1857), Coghlan to Govt. of Bombay 44 (10 April 1857).

105 A.S.L. 3 (24 February 1857), Coghlan to Govt. of Bombay 22 (23 February 1857) and Elphinstone Papers, Coghlan to Elphinstone (13 December 1856).

106 A.S.L. 7 (25 April 1857), Coghlan to Govt. of Bombay 44 (10 April 1857), 48 (12 and 24 April 1857). A.S.L. 8 (11 May 1857), Coghlan to Govt. of Bombay 67 (8 May 1857).

107 A.S.L. 7 (25 April 1857), Coghlan to Govt. of Bombay 44 (10 April 1857).

108 Elphinstone Papers, Coghlan to Elphinstone (25 July 1857 and 16 February 1858).

109 A.S.L. 10 (10 June 1857), Coghlan to Govt. of Bombay 73 (25 May 1857), A.S.L. 11 (10 July 1857), Coghlan to Govt. of Bombay 84 (26 June 1857) and 91 (9 July 1857).

110 Elphinstone Papers, Coghlan to Elphinstone (9 June 1857), A.S.L. 17 (10 October 1857), Coghlan to Govt. of Bombay 121 (9 October 1857), Outram Papers, Badger to Outram (26 September and 12 November 1857).

111 Elphinstone Papers, Coghlan to Elphinstone (16 February, 19 March 1858), A.R., A1A, Vol. 226, p. 117, Coghlan to Govt. of Bombay (24 February 1858).

112 Rassam said of Coghlan that the great difference between him and Outram was that if Outram thought a thing right he did it, while Coghlan believed that nothing could be done right unless the Directors were first consulted. B.M. Addl. MSS. 38984, Rassam to Layard (12 January 1855).

113 Elphinstone Papers, Coghlan to Elphinstone (19 March 1858 and April 1858).

114 Elphinstone Papers, Coghlan to Elphinstone (2 July 1858).

115 Elphinstone Papers, Coghlan to Elphinstone (14 February 1858).

116 I.S.L. 69 (15 May 1873), Badger to Tremenheere (15 April 1871).

117 Goodfellow was backed by relations in Bombay (B.M. Addl. MSS. 38989, Rassam to Layard [26 January 1863]), Merewether was also a man of mainly local fame. In 1866 Goodfellow began to speak of 'contemptible savages' in referring to the Fadli (Letters from Aden, etc. 1866, Goodfellow to Govt. of Bombay 88 [2 July 1866]). This tone of impatient superiority had been steadily creeping into the language of Aden officials since Coghlan's departure. It had not been detectable before.

118 Elphinstone Papers, Coghlan to Elphinstone (27 July 1856).

119 B.M. Addl. MSS. 38997, Badger to Layard (24 February 1865) complained that Merewether made insufficient use of 'native agency', in this case no doubt meaning Sayyid 'Alawi. Badger to Layard

(1 April 1868) referred to Merewether as 'one of the Jacob school who despises diplomacy'.

120 See I.S.L. 95 (9 June 1871) for a repetition of Merewether's ideas in Goodfellow's Memorandum (23 October 1870).

121 A.S.L. 13 (20 May 1863), Coghlan to Govt. of Bombay 33 (18 May 1863), Letters from Aden, etc., 1863, Coghlan to Govt. of Bombay 26 (17 April 1863) and Merewether to Govt. of Bombay 47 (2 July 1863).

122 Letters from Aden, etc., 1863, Merewether to Govt. of Bombay 47 (2 July 1863), 53 (17 July 1863) and 63 (17 August 1863) – the Sayyids of Wahut who customarily turbanned the Lahej Sultans refused to turban Sultan Fadl Muhsin, and other Sayyids had to be asked. B.M. Addl. MSS. 39114, Rassam to Layard (23 June 1865), Memorandum of Rassam's services. I.S.L. 212 (3 October 1872), Tremenheere to Govt. of Bombay 104/754 (11 May 1871), notes that Fadl Muhsin was always the intermediary between Sultan 'Ali and the British – a fact well authenticated in Coghlan's correspondence.

123 I.S.L. 212 (3 October 1872), Tremenheere to Govt. of Bombay 13/34 (20 January 1872) enclosing Prideaux's Report on Arab tribes I.S.L. 188 (9 September 1870) enclosing Sultan Fadl Muhsin to Sir Seymour Fitzgerald (28 March 1870). Letters from Aden, etc., 1863, Merewether to Govt. of Bombay 57 (1 August 1863).

124 The famine in the Aden hinterland in 1859 was sufficiently severe for Coghlan to find it necessary to send dates and rice to succour the Fadli tribe (Elphinstone Papers, Coghlan to Elphinstone [26 July 1859]). Three or four years later, in late 1862 or early 1863, murrain began to appear among the cattle at Lahej; by the summer it was severe and in July a plague of locusts attacked the crops in many parts of the hinterland (Letters from Aden etc. 1863, Merewether to Govt. of Bombay 63 [17 August 1863]). In the spring of 1864 a cyclone struck the Hadhrami coast, causing a landslide and widespread damage in Mukalla and destroying some 170 native vessels (ibid., Merewether to Govt. of Bombay 49 [17 June 1864]). Smallpox spread through the Tihama in the same year (ibid., Merewether to Govt. of Bombay 1 [January 1 1864]), and by the end of the year grain prices were reaching famine level in all the Red Sea ports (ibid., Merewether to Govt. of Bombay 98 [3 October 1864]). 1865 was the worst year, with murrain still rife among cattle, killing off every beast of draught; there was a prolonged drought and locusts again attacked crops in July (ibid., Merewether to Govt. of Bombay 14 [28 January 1865] and 102 [17 July 1865]). This caused widespread famine in Yemen and the hinterland, followed up by cholera epidemics (ibid., Merewether to Govt. of Bombay 78 [17 June 1865]). 1866 brought some respite, the harvest was good (ibid., Merewether to Govt. of Bombay 165 [27 December 1866]), and in 1870 again there were very good crops of grain, but once more in 1871 there was murrain among the animals at Lahej and in 'Awlaqi country, and cholera at Aden, and famine

and disease in southern Yemen drove people south in search of food (I.S.L. 212 [3 October 1872], Prideaux's report on Arab tribes).

125 I.S.L. 212 (3 October 1872), Tremenheere to Govt. of Bombay, 13/34 (20 January 1872) enclosing Prideaux's Report on Arab tribes. I.S.L. 261 (21 December 1870), Russell to Government of Bombay (20 October 1870) enclosing Qa'id Hasan bin Abu Ra's to Russell (20 October 1870). The claim was correct in Islamic legal theory but did not correspond with South Arabian practice.

126 Approximate figures of landward coffee import to Aden (000 Rs.):

1843/4 9·4	1846/7 11·9	1854/5 219	1858/9 420	1865/6 387
1844/5 6·2	1847/8 12·9	1855/6 268	1859/60 311	1866/7 279
1845/6 8·6	1848/9 6·4	1856/7 185	1860/1 187	1867/8 521

127 I.S.L. 212 (3 October 1872), Tremenheere to Govt. of Bombay 13/34 (20 January 1872) enclosing Prideaux's report on Arab tribes. Tremenheere to Govt. of Bombay 186/1327 (25 August 1871), Prideaux's report on Aden's landward trade.

128 I.S.L. 188 (9 September 1870), Russell to Govt. of Bombay (26 May 1870), Russell mentioned the great check to the coffee trade caused by rising 'Abdali transit dues. Yet he suggested that a payment be made to Sultan Fadl, rather than that pressure be put on him to lower his duties. Letters from Aden etc. 1866, Merewether to Govt. of Bombay 81 (17 June 1866), Sultan Fadl raised his charges to pay for a guard at Shaykh Uthman. There were protests from tribesmen but the British supported him.

129 A.A.R. (1876–7). By that time the Sultan received $8,433 per annum from the aqueduct water.

130 Indian Political Letter 48 (22 March 1872), Tremenheere to Govt. of Bombay 187/1328 (27 August 1871).

131 Luke Thomas Records, Hormusji Dinshaw to Atkinson (15 May 1889).

132 I.S.L. 212 (3 October 1872), Tremenheere to Govt. of Bombay 13/34 (20 January 1872) enclosing Prideaux's report on Arab tribes.

133 I.S.L. 95 (9 June 1871), Memorandum by Merewether (24 November 1870), Letters from Aden etc. 1865, Merewether to Govt. of Bombay 14 (28 January 1865) and 159 (1 November 1865).

134 Letters from Aden etc., Merewether to Govt. of Bombay 80 (17 October 1863) and 83 (2 November 1863,) 10 (18 February 1864) and 108 (17 November 1864), 159 (1 November 1865).

135 Letters from Aden etc., Merewether to Govt. of Bombay 80 (17 October 1863), 10 (18 February 1864), 108 (17 November 1864), 6 (3 January 1865), 17 (17 January 1865), 14 (28 January 1865), 19 (28 January 1865), 49 (2 April 1865), 54 (18 April 1865), 131 (18 September 1865), 181 (18 December 1865).

136 Letters from Aden etc. 181 (18 December 1865), 182 (23 December 1865), 186 (31 December 1865), 1 (9 January 1866), 34 (17 March 1866).

137 Letters from Aden etc., Merewether to Govt. of Bombay 126 (2 October 1866), Goodfellow (Acting Resident) to Govt. of Bombay 26 (18 February 1867) and 64a (24 May 1867).

138 Letters from Aden etc., Merewether to Govt. of Bombay 182 (23 December 1865) and 14 (28 January 1865). A.S.L. 1 (27 January 1863), Honner to Govt. of Bombay 93 (30 September 1862), referred to letter from the Sultan saying that he 'would not search for words to please the *Faranji*'. Rassam refused to receive the Fadli's letters and Merewether continued that practice. Letters from Aden etc., Merewether to Govt. of Bombay 42 (2 April 1866).

139 There can be no doubt that Ahmad bin 'Abdallah had extended Fadli power. He brought the Dathinah tribes under Fadli control – they had formerly been under the Upper 'Awlaqi. In 1837 he had taken over the strip of territory between Yafi'i country and Aden, raised a customs house at Assala and diverted trade to his own port of Shuqra. I.S.L. 212 (3 October 1872), Tremenheere to Govt. of Bombay 13/34 (20 January 1872) enclosing Prideaux's report. Tremenheere to Govt. of Bombay 94/344 (8 May 1872), Letters from Aden and Muscat etc., Merewether to Govt. of Bombay 186 (31 December 1865), 42 (2 April 1866), 34 (17 March 1866).

140 The Hawshabi derived most of his income from his Za'ida lands. I.S.L. 212 (3 October 1872), Tremenheere to Govt. of Bombay 13/34 (20 January 1872) enclosing Prideaux's report. F. M. Hunter and Sealy, *Arab Tribes in the Vicinity of Aden* (1886 ed.), p. 24. Sultan Fadl managed to capture the Hawshabi Sultan, Ali bin Mana, in the July campaign, and forced him to sign a bond transferring Za'ida as a condition of his release. A.S.L. 6 (20 November 1868), Russell to Govt. of Bombay 460 (19 November 1868), A.S.L. 11 (18 December 1868, Russell to Govt. of Bombay 480 (18 December 1868), A.S.L. 1 (1 January 1869), Russell to Govt. of Bombay 2 (1 January 1869).

141 I.S.L. 95 (9 June 1871), Merewether's memorandum (24 November 1870).

142 I.S.L. 23 (25 January 1870), Acting Assistant Resident to Govt. of Bombay 289/1694 (30 October 1869).

143 I.S.L. 188 (9 September 1870), Russell to Govt. of Bombay 236/1343 (26 August 1869) and 327/1915 (24 December 1869). Memorandum by Goodfellow (14 April 1870). Letters from Aden etc., Merewether to Govt. of Bombay 10 (18 December 1864), B.S.L. 4 (23 June 1863) enclosure 3, Coghlan to Anderson (18 May 1863).

144 I.S.L. 188 (9 September 1870), Russell to Govt. of Bombay 236/1343 (26 August 1869). Goodfellow had information that Sayyid 'Alawi received in the form of unsolicited gifts from the 'Aqrabi sums equal to one-third of the price of the 1863 option agreement and of the 1869 purchase.

145 I.S.L. 188 (9 September 1870), Goodfellow's Memorandum (14 April 1870), ·Alawi was the middleman in dealing with the Fadli until 1865, A.S.L. 1 (27 January 1863), Honner to Govt. of Bombay 93 (30 September 1862), Letters from Aden etc., Merewether to Govt. of Bombay 47 (2 July 1863) and 14 (28 January 1865). I.S.L. 69 (15 May 1873), Sayyid 'Alawi to Tremenheere (8 May 1871) – Rassam on his brief return to Aden in 1869 pleaded on the Sayyid's

behalf and Russell promised that he would look into the matter, but
shortly afterward Rassam retired from the service. The field was
left to Goodfellow, who was disliked by all of the Coghlan team.
Badger and Coghlan persistently tried to have the case reopened, but
after four years of agitation the case was finally closed in 1873.

146 I.S.L. 69 (15 May 1873), 'Alawi to Aden Resident (8 May 1871).

147 I.S.L. 188 (9 September 1870), Russell to Govt. of Bombay 236/1343
(26 August 1869), Aitchison (Govt. of India) to Gonne (Govt. of
Bombay) 607P (31 March 1870) pointed out the discrepancies in the
Aden correspondence – the praise for Sayyid 'Alawi in April 1869,
the condemnation of Sultan Fadl in June, then the complete reversal
of opinion in August. Memorandum by Goodfellow (14 April 1870)
explained this. I.S.L. 69 (15 May 1873), Sayyid 'Alawi to Tremenheere (8 May 1871) makes clear that he thought that Goodfellow's
knowledge of Arabic was defective; Coghlan also wrote in disparaging terms of Goodfellow's linguistic ability. Goodfellow and Rassam
had competed for the post of Assistant Resident in 1863; Coghlan had
recommended Rassam because of his fluency in Arabic, and Rassam
got the appointment. Merewether however in 1866 made favourable
mention of Goodfellow's ability as an interpreter. I.S.L. 89 (26
December 1873), Schneider's report on the case (6 September 1873)
decided that Sayyid 'Alawi had made himself the Sultan of Lahej's
lessee in 1853 – Sayyid 'Alawi said that this was a fictitious lease,
although he admitted that the document itself was genuine.

148 I.S.L. 188 (9 September 1870), Russell to Govt. of Bombay 325/1913
(22 December 1869), Govt. of Bombay to Govt. of India 165 (12 May
1870) recommends $5,000. Govt. of India to Govt. of Bombay 1545P
(31 August 1870) refuses, and also refuses the offer of the Hiswah
I.S.L. 168 (17 October 1871), Russell to Govt. of Bombay 158
(18 August 1870) asks again for $5000, Tremenheere to Govt. of Bom-
bay 150/981 (30 June 1871) supports this. Govt. of India to Govt.
of Bombay 2079P (30 September 1871) offers a payment of $2,500.
Indian Political Letter 48 (22 March 1872), Tremenheere 246/1564
(17 November 1871) enclosing Sultan Fadl to Tremenheere (16
November 1871) refuses the money and tries to have the case
reconsidered. Govt. of India to Govt. of Bombay 546P (8 March 1872)
refuses to alter the decision. I.S.L. 172 (2 October 1873), Schneider
to Govt. of Bombay 206/815 (31 July 1873), Sultan Fadl to Schneider
(28 July 1873) accepts the money under protest.

149 I.S.L. 95 (9 June 1871), Tremenheere to Govt. of Bombay 40/286
(23 February 1871). the area in question was that stretching from
Ta'izz to Ibb and including the Hajariya.

150 The Zaydi themselves were comparative newcomers to power in the
Hajariya, the Dhu Muhammad and Dhu Husayn clans had recently
wrested control from the Sharjabi Chief. I.S.L. 8 (18 January 1871),
Russell to Govt. of Bombay 222/1500 (4 November 1870) enclosing
Qa'id Hassan bin Abu Ra's to Russell (2 November 1870), I.S.L.
168 (17 October 1871), Tremenheere to Govt. of Bombay 150/981

(30 June 1871), A.S.L. (1863–70), Russell to Govt. of Bombay 219 (22 October 1870), I.S.L. 212 (3 October 1872), Tremenheere to Govt. of Bombay 69/461 (25 March 1871).

151 I.S.L. 95 (9 June 1871), Russell to Govt. of Bombay 284/1852 (31 December 1870), 40/286 (23 February 1871), I.S.L. 261 (21 December 1870), Russell to Govt. of Bombay 200/1261 (8 October 1870).

152 I.S.L. 261 (21 December 1870), Russell to Govt. of Bombay 167/1059 (2 September 1870), 173/1103 (7 September 1870), 192/1209 (30 September 1870), 216/1433 (15 October 1870), 236/1585 (12 November 1870), A.S.L. (1863–70), Russell to Govt. of Bombay 219 (22 October 1870). Qa'id Hasan told Russell that he could divert the San'a' traffic from Aden without moving from his house. I.S.L. 8 (18 January 1871), Russell to Govt. of Bombay 222/1500 (4 November 1870) enclosing Qa'id Hassan to Russell (2 November 1870), I.S.L. 166 (12 August 1870), Russell to Govt. of Bombay 93/610 (12 August 1870), A.S.L. Russell to Govt. of Bombay 161 (25 August 1870), 193 (1 October 1870), 200 (8 October 1870).

153 I.S.L. 261 (21 December 1870), Govt. of Bombay to Aden Resident (26 October 1870).

154 I.S.L. 188 (9 September 1870), Russell to Govt. of Bombay (26 May 1870), I.S.L. 9 (18 January 1871), Russell to Govt. of Bombay 251/1701 (2 December 1870) asked for $500 per month. I.S.L. 95 (9 June 1871), Tremenheere to Govt. of Bombay 284/1852 (31 December 1870) asked for $800 per month.

155 The French were ousted by the Turks during the Franco-Prussian War. A.S.L. 24/594 (22 April 1876). Cf. also F.O. Red Sea and Somali Coast Confidential Print, Vol. II, p. 44, Memo by Hertslet p.505 and 227 extract from *Le Temps* (13 December 1884) and *Le Soleil* (16 December 1884).

156 I.S.L. 95 (9 June 1871) Wedderburn (Govt. of Bombay) to Secretary, Foreign Department, Govt. of India 1043 (13 March 1871) enclosing Memorandum by Wedderburn (5 July 1870) citing Sultan Fadl to Sir Seymour Fitzgerald (28 March 1870), Memorandum by Good-fellow (23 October 1870) and by Merewether (24 November 1870). Aitchison (Govt. of India) to Acting Secretary Govt. of Bombay 1076P (2 June 1871).

157 A.R., AIA, Vol. 909, pp. 77 and 175, Vol. 533, p. 503, Vol. 312, p. 395, B.M. Addl. MSS. 28988, Rassam to Layard (21 July 1862), Letters from Aden etc., Merewether to Govt. of Bombay 115 (3 December 1865). A.R., AIA, Vol. 490, p. 607, Govt. of India to Govt. of Bombay (12 March 1869).

158 For example the Residents mentioned in their correspondence, visits from the following Chiefs in the year 1871–2:

February 1871	long visit from the 'Abdali Sultan		
February 1871	,,	,,	son and brother of the Upper 'Awlaqi Sultan
February 1871	,,	,,	Wahidi Chief of Husn Ghurab

April 1871	long visit from the Upper 'Awlaqi Shaykh Farid bin Nasir		
July 1871	,,	,,	eldest son of Lower Yafi'i Sultan
August 1871	,,	,,	Sharjabi Shaykh of Hajariya
November 1871	,,	,,	'Abdali Sultan
December 1871	,,	,,	Fadli Sultan's brother
January 1872	,,	,,	'Amir of Qa'taba, ruler of country to Ibb and Jible
February 1872	,,	,,	Hawshabi Sultan
February 1872	,,	,,	Wahidi Sultan 'Abdallah bin Talib
February 1872	,,	,,	'Abdali Sultan

159 A.R., AiA, Vol. 1380, p. 391.
160 A.R., AiA, Vol. 1308, pp. 388–9.
161 Salah Jaffer retired in 1883 and was succeeded by his son, who held this post until 1899.
162 A.R., FiA, Vol. 381, p. 79.
163 A.R., AiA, Vol. 909, p. 83.
164 A.R., AiA, Vol. 533, pp. 503–4, cf. above, p. 125.
165 A.R., AiA, Vol. 909, p. 83.
166 A.R., AiA, Vol. 1308, pp. 388–9.
167 A.S.L. 83 (5 May 1870) enclosing Russell to Govt. of Bombay – referred to the 'Amir of Dhali' as 'with two or three exceptions the most powerful chief of Yemen'. Cf. below, p. 222.
168 Letters from Aden etc., Merewether to Govt. of Bombay 14 (28 January 1865), 28 (18 February 1865).
169 Letters from Aden etc. Govt. of India to Govt. of Bombay (5 May 1865) Merewether to Govt. of Bombay 84 (24 June 1865), 155 (17 October 1865), Govt. of India to Govt. of Bombay 1044 (9 December 1865). MSS. Eur. F. 78/74 Merewether to Wood (30 October 1865), I.S.L. 212 (3 October 1872), Merewether to Govt. of Bombay 45/243 (15 April 1867).

CHAPTER V

1 C. Huber, *Journal d'un voyage en Arabie* (Paris, 1891), p. 746.
2 F.O. Consular and Diplomatic Reports on Trade and Finance No. 1264, Turkey: Jedda Report for 1892.
3 A.S.L. 26 (26 December 1856) and Aden Resident to Govt. of Bombay 183 (11 December 1856).
4 A.S.L., Playfair's 1857 report on Perim. B.S.L. (1863–9), Coghlan to Anderson (29 April 1863).
5 A.R., AiA, Vol. 226, p. 355, Coghlan to Govt. of Bombay (25 September 1858).
6 Letters from Aden, Muscat etc. Merewether to Secretary of State for India 26 (30 October 1863).

7 I.S.L. 72 (19 April 1872) enclosing Aden Res. to Govt. of Bombay 29/96 (8 February 1872).

8 Letters from Aden, Muscat etc., Merewether to Melville (29 October 1863) and Merewether to Secretary of State for India 26 (30 October 1863).

9 See below, Chapter VI.

10 R. J. Gavin, 'The Bartle Frere Mission to Zanzibar, 1873', *The Historical Journal* (No. 2, 1962).

11 R. J. Gavin, 'The Ottoman Re-occupation of Arabia', *History Today*, (November 1963).

12 One may cite the various Mahdist movements in the eastern and western Sudan, the Sanusiya in North Africa, the Mutawwa movements in Masqat and Zanzibar, Wahhabi in India, and Padrists in Sumatra – all very active in this period after 1850.

13 H. K. Nuseibeh, *The Ideas of Arab Nationalism* (New York, 1956), pp. 119ff.

14 Cf. E. E. Ramsaur, *The Young Turks* (Princeton, 1957), pp. 14ff.

15 Gavin, 'The Ottoman Reconquest of Arabia', *History Today* (November 1963).

16 The British Ambassador at Constantinople had expected that they would be withdrawn after the suppression of the 'Asir rising.

17 R. J. Gavin, op. cit.

18 See Gavin, 'The Bartle Frere Mission to Zanzibar, 1873', and I.S.L. 13 (1 March 1872).

19 M. Daud, 'British Policy in the Persian Gulf', (Univ. of London, Ph.D. thesis, 1956) p. 263. I.O. Home Correspondence F.O. to I.O. (17 April, 8 May and 3 June 1871). I.O. to F.O. (9 and 15 June 1871).

20 I.O. MSS. Eur. C. 144 II 9. Northbrook to Rawlinson (17 March 1872).

21 A.R., A4A, Vol. III. Minute by Schneider (1872, undated).

22 F.O. 78/2755, Memorandum by Frere (June 1874).

23 Cf. W. D. McIntyre, *The Imperial Frontier in the Tropics 1865–1875* (London, 1967), pp. 372ff.

24 The disease was not confined to the Gladstone cabinet; Lytton commented acidly on divisions within Beaconsfield's cabinet on matters of Middle Eastern policy. B.M. Addl. MSS. 38969, Lytton to Layard (2 June 1877 and 23 January 1878).

25 The new *Vilayet* system of administration was applied to the Yemen in 1872.

26 I.S.L. 22 (14 February 1873), Aden Resident to Govt. of Bombay (24 January 1873).

27 I.S.L. 141 (1 July 1872), Aden Resident to Govt. of Bombay 92/335 (7 May 1872).

28 I.S.L. 95 (9 June 1871), Aden Resident to Govt. of Bombay 40/286 (23 February 1871).

29 Abstracts of Bombay Proceedings No. 181 (May 1872), Aden Resident to Govt. of Bombay (7 May 1872) and No. 159 (August 1872), Aden Resident to Govt. of Bombay (6 August 1872).

30 F.O. 78/2753, Memorandum by Tenterden (14 November 1873).

31 Abstracts of Bombay Proceedings No. 80 (November 1872), Aden Resident to Govt. of Bombay (26 October 1872).

32 I.O. MSS Eur. C. 144 II 9, Northbrook to Argyll (10 January 1873).

33 P.R.O. 30/29/103, Frere to Granville 18 January 1873. I.O. MSS. Eur. C. II 9, Frere to Northbrook (2 January 1873) enclosing copy Frere to Elliott (Ambassador at the Porte) (2 January 1873), Badger Papers, Cambridge University Library Addl. MSS. 2910, Badger to Kaye (4 January 1873).

34 I.S.L. 6 (10 January 1873) enclosing Govt. of India to Govt. of Bombay, authorising Schneider to warn the Turkish Governor-General to suspend action pending diplomatic discussion. I.S.L. 31 (21 March 1873), Aden Resident to Govt. of Bombay, 60 (19 February 1873), Schneider was able to show Sultan Fadl Elliott's telegram of 30 January 1873, saying that Lahej would not be interfered with. P.R.O. 30/29/102, Elliott to Granville (6 January 1873).

35 T. E. Marston, *Britain's Imperial Role in the Red Sea Area 1800-1878* (Hamden, Conn., 1961), pp. 406-8, gives a detailed account of the negotiations.

36 F.O. 78/2753, Tenterden's Memorandum (14 November 1873).

37 I.S.L. 22 (14 February 1873) and 38 (11 April 1873).

38 Home Correspondence F.O. to I.O. (16 May 1873) enclosing Granville to Elliott (15 May 1873), cited Marston, p. 409.

39 I.S.L. 212 (3 October 1872), Aden Resident to Govt. of Bombay Pol. (15 April 1872), enclosing Prideaux's report on Aden tribes.

40 I.S.L. 37 (22 February 1870), Aden Resident to Govt. of Bombay 35/202 (11 February 1870).

41 I.S.L. 38 (11 April 1873).

42 Prideaux's report on Arab tribes 1871 - the Subayhi.

43 The 'Alawi Shaykh's stipend of $360 per annum had been secured on his behalf from Haines by the then Hawshabi Sultan - Prideaux's report.

44 See text in C. U. Aitchison, *Treaties, Engagements and Sanads, etc.* (1865 ed.), Vol. VII, p. 291.

45 E.g. Sayyid 'Alawi. Texts in Aitchison, op. cit., pp. 275-97.

46 In October 1874, in discussing the general question of Egyptian and Turkish encroachment in the Red Sea, Northbrook the Viceroy, while supporting the idea of recognising Egyptian gains added that 'unfortunately' it was impossible to retract at Aden. Red Sea and Somali Coast C.P., Vol. I, p. 140, Govt. of India to S.S. (9 October 1874).

47 F.O. 78/2753, Tenterden's Memorandum (14 November 1873) contains a fairly full account of the negotiations.

48 Home Correspondence, I.O. to F.O. (20 May 1873) enclosing Resident to Secretary of State (27 May 1873), I.S.L. 67 (4 August 1873), Govt. of Bombay to Govt. of India Tel. (30 May 1873 and 27 June 1873). I.S.L. 84 (23 October 1873), Aden Res. to Govt. of Bombay Tel. (10 October 1873). Despite the Porte's assurances, the Turkish

Governor-General informed Schneider in October that he had annexed Hawshabi country.

49 I.S.L. 67 (4 August 1873), Aden Resident to Govt. of Bombay 25, (17 June 1873) and 26 (25 June 1873).

50 I.S.L. 84 (23 October 1873), Aden Resident to Govt. of Bombay Tel. (21 October 1873).

51 I.O. MSS. Eur. C. 144 II 9, Northbrook to Argyll (23 October 1873), I.S.L. 84 (23 October 1873), Govt. of India to Aden Resident Tel. (23 October 1873).

52 Home Correspondence F.O. to I.O. (31 October 1873) enclosing Aden Res. to S.S. (27 October 1873). I.S.L. 2C (5 December 1873), Aden Res. to Govt. of India Tel. (2 December 1873).

53 He was critical of Granville's policy toward Russia in 1870, on the Alabama question and on general matters of Colonial policy. P.R.O. 30/29/59, Argyll to Granville (24 November 1870, 19 March 1872, 12 November 1869).

54 Argyll rejected Gladstone's analogy with the Gold Coast and said that Aden was necessary for British communication with the East. P.R.O. 30/29/59, Argyll to Granville (29 October 1873).

55 P.R.O. 30/29/59, Argyll to Granville (2 December 1873) enclosing Resident's telegram of (2 December 1873); Granville to Argyll (3 December 1873), Granville to Gladstone (3 December 1873), Home Correspondence F.O. to I.O. (25 October 1873) enclosing Granville to Elliott (25 October 1873).

56 He had not been turbanned in traditional fashion by the Sayyids of Wahut.

57 This was all explained to Elliott, the Ambassador to the Porte, by the Turkish Foreign Minister, who showed him the report from the Governor-General of the Yemen. The Turks made very bitter reference to Sultan Fadl Muhsin, whom they tended to blame for the whole difficulty.

58 The ambitious and energetic conqueror of the Yemen, Ahmad Mukhtar Pasha, had been replaced by Ahmad Ayub at the end of June, but despite Elliott's hopes this hardly affected the increasing Turkish embroilment in the affairs of South Arabia. I.S.L. 67 (4 August 1873), Govt. of Bombay to Govt. of India (12 July 1873).

59 Ignatieff, the Russian Ambassador, had begun to draw the Porte's attention to British activity in South Arabia and at Lahej in late 1872. F.O. 78/2753, Elliott to Granville (1 January 1873). The Turkish Foreign Minister explained to Elliott in October 1873 that the military commanders were difficult to control, see Tenterden's memorandum.

60 F.O. 78/2754, Elliott to F.O. (1 April 1874).

61 Home Correspondence I.O. to F.O. (12 January 1874); Aden Res. to Govt. of Bombay (8 December 1873).

62 A.A.R. for 1873-4 in B.S.L. 4 (25 January 1874).

63 A scheme for a Protectorate over the nine tribes had been drawn up in April of 1873 by the Indian Government. See Marston, op. cit., pp. 410–12. In September the Viceroy began to urge that this scheme

be seriously considered. MSS. Eur. C. 144 II 9, Northbrook to Argyll (15 September 1873). On 13 October Argyll wrote to Granville strongly advocating a Protectorate (P.R.O. 30/29/59) and on 17 October Gladstone passed his comments. A. Ramm, *The Gladstone-Granville Correspondence* (London, 1952), Vol. II, pp. 427-8.

64 A.S.L. 11 (30 January 1875) enclosing 'Ali Muqbil to General Schneider (21 January 1875) and Shaykhs of Dali' to 'Ali Muqbil undated.

65 Red Sea and Somali Coast Confdl. Prints Vol. I, pp. 129-40, Treaty texts in Aitchison, *Treaties, Engagements and Sanads, etc.* (1878 ed.).

66 I.S.L. 104 (10 June 1870), Memorandum by Merewether (June 1869).

67 I.S.L. 104 (10 June 1870) enclosing Westbrook to Aden Resident (15 March 1870).

68 I.S.L. 104 (10 June 1870) enclosing Aden Resident to Govt. of Bombay 51 (4 March 1870) and 47 (25 February 1870). Red Sea and Somali Coast C.P., Schneider to Govt. of Bombay (2 September 1873, 22 October 1873, 26 November 1873, 13 December 1873); A.S.L. 66 (12 November 1875), Newsreport No. 9 (1 March 1876) and No. 6 (22 September 1876), Report by Wodehouse on Berbera (21 September 1876).

69 Russell to Govt. of Bombay (18 August 1870) in I.S.L. 203 (27 September 1870), Red Sea and Somali Coast C.P., p. 54; Memorandum by Tremenheere (13 July 1874), who however did envisage concessions to the Egyptians; Memorandum by Schneider, Schneider to Govt. of Bombay (4 December 1873), A.S.L. 15 (27 February 1875) and 22 (9 April 1875) enclosing Aden Resident to Govt. of Bombay 56 (7 April 1875).

70 I.S.L. 104 (10 June 1870), Aden Resident to Govt. of Bombay 74 (21 April 1870) and Westbrook to Aden Resident (15 March 1870).

71 Red Sea and Somali Coast C.P., Mayo to Secretary of State (10 June 1870) and Argyll's Memorandum (5 August 1870).

72 Ibid., Argyll to Granville (17 January and 3 February 1874).

73 Ibid., Elliott first suggested it on 13 November 1873 to Granville.

74 Ibid., Tenterden to Hamilton (F.O. to I.O.) (21 August 1874), Govt. of India to S.S. (9 October 1874), Stanton (Cairo) to Derby (15 September 1874), F.O. to I.O. (14 October 1874).

75 Ibid., I.O. to F.O. (7 August 1874), the general tenor of this letter was in favour of recognising the Egyptian occupation but Salisbury dissociated himself from its conclusions. Ibid., Salisbury to Derby (23 March 1875) began to change his tone.

76 Ibid., Derby to Vivian (10 November 1875); Egypt in 1878 appealed to Britain to allow the levy of duties at Berbera, Britain refused, Vivian to Derby (25 July 1878).

77 Cf. R. Coupland, *The Exploitation of East Africa* (London, 1939), pp. 281 ff.

78 Red Sea and Somali Coast C.P., Derby to Vivian (31 August 1877).

79 Ibid., p. 55, Memorandum of Conference held at F.O. (2 June 1874).

80 Ibid., p. 55, Memorandum by Frere (27 June 1874), MSS. Eur. C. 144 9.

81 J. Martineau, *Life and Letters of Sir Bartle Frere* (London, 1895), Vol. II,

pp. 75–7, 108–9; Salisbury Papers, Frere to Salisbury (1 December 1875 and 4 February 1877), Frere's Memorandum on Egypt (29 October 1875). See also Frere's article on the Ottoman system in *Quarterly Review* (October 1876), p. 483.

82 MSS. Eur. C. 144 II 9, Northbrook to Argyll (2 January 1874); enclosing Aitchison's Memorandum (30 December 1873) and Eur. C. 144 II 14, Northbrook to Rawlinson (2 January 1874).

83 F.O. 78/4529, Memorandum by Bertie (2 October 1886) referring to Musurus Pasha's note (28 January 1874) and Derby's reply to Locock 100 (4 April 1874).

84 C.U.L. Addl. MSS. 2910, Badger to Kaye (4 January 1873). Indian Pol. and Secret Letters 55 (16 June 1873), Enclosure 3, Frere to Granville (18 January 1873), citing a letter from the Turkish Governor-General to Shaykhs in the Aden neighbourhood.

85 Marder, op. cit., pp. 472–8.

86 Red Sea and Somali Coast C.P., Vivian to Granville (22 September 1873).

87 D. C. Blaisdell, *European Financial Control in the Ottoman Empire* (New York, 1929), p. 80. In October 1875 the Ottoman Goverment defaulted on its debt payments, on 26 November 1875 Beaconsfield bought the Suez shares.

88 Red Sea and Somali Coast C.P., Derby to Vivian (10 November 1875).

89 Hunter and Sealy, *An Account of the Arab Tribes in the Vicinity of Aden* (Bombay, 1909), pp. 10–11, 46 and 160.

90 A.R., A4A, Vol. 18, pp. 637, 476 and 566, 'Ali bin Mana to Loch (April, August and 26 December 1881).

91 I.S.L. 212 (3 October 1872), Aden Resident to Govt. of Bombay Pol. (15 April 1872) enclosing Stevens to Tremenheere (25 March 1872); A.R., A4A, Vol. 3, Tremenheere to eldest son of Yafi'i Sultan (25 March 1872), Tremenheere to Fadli and Yafi'i Sultans (30 March 1872) – threatening to break off relations if they do not agree to mediation. I.S.L. 212 (3 October 1872), Aden Resident to Govt. of Bombay 94/344 (8 May 1872), details of agreement.

92 A.R., A4A, Vol. 3, Yafi'i Sultan to Tremenheere June 1872. I.S.L. 15 (24 January 1873) enclosing Aden Resident to Govt. of Bombay 246/897 (12 November 1872).

93 A.S.L. 28 (7 May 1875), A.A.R. (1875–6) in B.S.L. 36 (28 July 1876), A.S.L., Aden Newsreport No. 12 (23–29 March 1876), A.S.L. 49/1164 (21 July 1876), detail of agreement. A.A.R. (1876–7) in Bombay Political Letters 86 (18 July 1877).

94 A.R., A4A, Vol. 18, Memorandum (19 June 1881), Report by Jaffer (25 March 1881). In 1888 Sultan Husayn bin Ahmad brought 5 sq. miles under cultivation. A4A, Vol. 5, p. 628, undated, Report by Muhammad Salih Jaffer. Hunter and Sealy, op. cit., p. 39. In 1872 the Fadli constructed bunds each year a short distance up Wadi Bana' from Mussana to irrigate the plain west of Tiran; Sultan Ahmad's works were at Al Khawr. I.S.L. 212 (3 October 1872), Aden Res. to Govt. of Bombay Pol (15 April 1872).

95 A.S.L. 28 (9 November 1878), enclosure B. Loch to Hunter (10 September 1877).

96 Hunter and Sealy, op. cit., pp. 37–8.

CHAPTER VI

1 J. R. Wellsted, *Travels in Arabia*, Vol. II, pp. 434–5. Marston, op. cit., p. 220. A.S.L. 13 (20 May 1863), Bombay Political Letter 8 (1 February 1873), Prideaux's report on Mukalla and Shihr.

2 J. Christie, *Cholera Epidemics in East Africa* (London, 1876), pp. 329–30.

3 See Van den Berg, *Hadhramawt and the Arab Colonies in the East Indian Archipelago* (Bombay, 1887). Marston, op. cit., p. 265. H. St. J. Philby, *Arabian Highlands* (New York, 1952), p. 574.

4 C. U. Aitchison, *A Collection of Treaties, Engagements and Sanads, etc.*, (1878 ed.), Vol. V, pp. 131ff. McAuliffe, *The Nizam – the Origin and Future of the Hyderabad State*, pp. 27ff.

5 I.O. Library – Sir R. Temple, 'Report on the Administration of the Government of H.H. the Nizams in the Deccan' (1868), pp. 21–5. I.O. MSS. Eur. F. 78/38, Major Moore to Sir C. Wood (6 January 1854).

6 Sir W. Lee Warner, *The Native States of India* (London, 1910), pp. 240–1. Aitchison, op. cit., p. 131, Abstracts of Bombay Proceedings May 1872, No. 4 and Supplement to July Abstracts.

7 Sir R. Temple, op. cit., p. 26.

8 A.S.L. 73 (20 October 1876), Memorandum by F. M. Hunter on Hadhramawt and Hyderabad; Salah al Bakri, *Tarikh Hadhramawt al Siyasi* (1956 ed.), p. 121, note 1; Salah al Bakri, *Fi Janub al Jazirat al 'Arabiyah* (1949) pp. 175–6.

9 Al Bakri, op. cit., p. 183, A.S.L. 73 (20 October 1876) Memorandum by Hunter; A.S.L. 4 (27 February 1856), Aden Resident to Govt. of Bombay 31 (26 February 1856).

10 A.S.L. 126 (2 October 1866).

11 Sa'id 'Awad ba Wazir, *Tarikh al Jazirat al 'Arabiyah*, pp. 268–9, Al Bakri, Fi Janub al Jazirah, p. 166.

12 Al Bakri, op. cit., pp. 139–40.

13 Ba Wazir, op. cit., p. 267; Wellsted, op. cit., pp. 442 and 449. When it suited them the Naqibs of Mukalla claimed the protection of the Sultans of Masqat in matters relating to trade and foreign relations, cf. A.S.L. 28 (9 November 1878) and F.O. 84/1212, Coghlan to Govt. of Bombay 18 May 1863. The major divisions here are inevitably oversimplified, there was much interlocking between them and the groupings themselves did not cohere. For an analysis of Hadhrami social and political structures see A. S. Bujra, *The Politics of Stratification* (Oxford, 1971).

14 Salah al Bakri, *Tarikh Hadhramawt al Siyasi*, pp. 96–7.

15 Salah al Bakri, *Fi Janub al Jazirah*, pp. 140 and 142; Ba Wazir, op. cit., p. 266.
16 I am indebted to Sayyid Salah bin 'Ali al Hamidi for information concerning Ghalib bin Muhsin. Both sides used slave soldiers extensively. For the use of cannon cf. Al Bakri, op. cit., p. 128.
17 Cf. Al Bakri, pp. 145–6.
18 A.S.L. 139 (2 November 1866), Al Bakri, op. cit., pp. 177–9.
19 Al Bakri, op. cit., pp. 180–1, 186 and 190–1. Hunter, *Arab Tribes in the Vicinity of Aden*, pp. 126–8. Bombay Political Letter 8 (1 February 1873). Prideaux's Report on Mukalla and Shihr. I.S.L. 185 (9 September 1870) Memorandum by Barak Jung enclosed in Salar Jung to Hyderabad Resident (12 February 1870).
20 I.S.L. 185 (9 September 1870) enclosing Salar Jung to Hyderabad Resident (30 November 1866).
21 I.O. MSS Eur. F. 86/81, Sir R. Temple's Diary 1867, cf. Indian Pol. and Secret Letter 62 (26 October 1874) and Minute by O. T. Burne.
22 I.S.L. 185 (9 September 1870), Govt. of Bombay to Hyderabad Resident (18 December 1866). Bombay Political Letter 8 (1 February 1873), Prideaux's report on Mukalla and Shihr. A.S.L. 73 (20 October 1876) Hunter's report on connections between Hyderabad and Hadhramawt. Cf. Al Bakri, op. cit., p. 180.
23 A.S.L. 154 (4 December 1866). I.S.L. 104 (10 June 1870) enclosing Aden Resident to Govt. of Bombay 64 (31 March 1870), A.S.L. 10 (16 January 1873).
24 Cf. Marston, op. cit., p. 265 and references cited.
25 W. H. Ingrams, *Arabia and the Isles* (London, 1942), p. 172. F. Stark, *The Southern Gates of Arabia* (London, 1936), p. 121.
26 E.g. the remarkable career of the 'Alawi Sayyid Fadl, appointed Governor of the Hadhramawt 1876 by the Ottoman Government, helped in 1878 to establish a Government in Dhufar, becoming finally one of the chief advisers to Sultan Abd al Hamid II. Certain Hadhrami Sayyids asked Muhammad 'Ali of Egypt to take over the Hadhramawt. Ba Wazir, op, cit., pp. 267–8.
27 Ba Wazir, op. cit., pp. 267–8. Al Bakri, op. cit., pp. 152 and 150–1.
28 Marston, pp. 152–3. Al Bakri, op. cit., p. 160.
29 A.S.L. 103 (10 August 1867) and 113 (17 September 1867), Secret Home Correspondence F.O. to I.O. (19 October 1867) enclosing Barron to Stanley (5 October 1867).
30 I.S.L. 104 (10 June 1870), Govt. of India to Govt. of Bombay 799P (15 July 1870).
31 Al Bakri, op. cit., pp. 128–9.
32 The texts of these agreements are in A.S.L. 28 (9 November 1878), Appendix K. Agreement between Jemadar 'Awad bin 'Umar al Qu'ayti and Naqib Salah' bin Muhammad al Kasadi (24 Ramadhan 1283/30 January 1867). Appendix L. Agreement between the same (6 Jumad al Awla 1284/5 September 1867).
33 B.S.L. 1 (11 April 1868), enclosure 5. Aden Resident to Govt. of Bombay 180 (20 February 1868).

34 A.S.L. 11 (23 February 1874) enclosing Naqib 'Umar bin Salah to Resident Schneider (16 February 1874).

35 A.S.L. 32 (19 May 1873), 55 (30 September 1873), 61 (30 October 1873) and 73 (3 December 1873) which contains text of treaty signed between the Jemadar and the Naqib (3 Rajab 1290/27 August 1873). A.S.L. 28 (9 November 1878) Naqib 'Umar bin Salah to Sultan of Muscat (30 Jumad al Awal 1878). Salah al Bakri, *Tarikh Hadhramawt al Siyasi* (1936 ed.), Vol. II, pp. 5-7.

36 A.S.L. 73 (20 October 1876), Hunter's Memorandum gave 1861 as the approximate date of the 'Awlaqi's purchase of Husn Suda'. Al Bakri, *Fi Janub al Jazirah* pp. 183 and 185.

37 A.S.L. 69 (3 October 1876) enclosing Naqib 'Umar to Major Goodfellow (11 Ramadhan 1293/30 September 1876).

38 A.S.L. 11 (23 February 1874).

39 A.S.L. 69 (3 October 1876), Awad bin 'Umar to Goodfellow (9 Ramadhan 1293/30 September 1876).

40 A.S.L. 83 (29 December 1876).

41 Hunter, op. cit., p. 129. A.S.L. 26 (30 April 1875) citing Govt. of India to Govt. of Bombay 418P (13 February 1874). I.S.L. 136 (28 June 1875).

42 A.S.L. 39 (14 November 1874), 13 (2 March 1874). I.S.L. 84 (25 April 1874). A.S.L. 30 (26 May 1876) enclosing Naqib to Schneider (1 May 1876).

43 I.S.L. 18 (14 July 1871). A.S.L. 10 (16 January 1873).

44 A.S.L. 26 (30 April 1875), 73 (20 October 1876). Captain Prideaux, however, was pro-Jemadar, A.S.L. 26 (30 April 1875), Prideaux to Schneider (26 April 1875).

45 Hunter, op. cit., p. 129.

46 A.S.L. 24 (9 May 1874).

47 Hunter, op. cit., pp. 129-30. A.S.L. 26 (30 April 1875).

48 A.S.L. 47 (28 August 1875), 59 (16 October 1875).

49 A.S.L. 26 (30 April 1875) enclosing Schneider to Jemadar (17 April 1875). On the other hand the Naqib's blockade of Shihr was regarded as effective – A.A.R. (1873-4) in B.S.L. 4 (25 January 1875).

50 A.S.L. 33 (3 June 1876). A.S.L. 45 (11 July 1876) enclosing Naqib to Goodfellow (25 June 1876).

51 I.P. & S.L. 215 (4 December 1874), Resident at Hyderabad to Sir Salar Jung (9 May, 30 July, 5 August and 30 October 1874).

52 G. Geary, *Hyderabad Politics* (Bombay, 1884) pp. 9ff. I.P. & S.L. 62 (26 October 1874).

53 R. P. McAuliffe, *The Nizam – the origin and future of the Hyderabad State* (London, 1904), p. 35, cf. E. H. Thornton, *Sir Reginald Meade*, pp. 279ff. Jung was troublesome mainly because he had numerous influential sympathisers in England. His case raised serious controversy about the British attitude to progressive administrators in Princely States which was not without bearing on the dispute between Qu'ayti and Kasadi on the Hadhrami coast.

54 I.P. & S.L. 73 (31 March 1876) and enclosures.

55 I.P. & S.L. 39 (11 September 1876), Resident at Hyderabad to Govt.

of India 47 (23 June 1876), I.S.L. 8 (16 March 1877), Resident at Hyderabad to Govt. of India 126a (4 December 1876).

56 Minute by O. T. Burne on Aden Secret Letters 27 and 28 (7 and 9 November 1878).

57 A.S.L. 33 (3 June 1876) and 61 (19 September 1876).

58 A.S.L. 61 (19 September 1876) and enclosures, A.S.L. 78 (14 November 1876), I.S.L. 8 (16 March 1877), Hyderabad Resident to Govt. of India 126a (4 December 1876).

59 A.S.L. 67 (3 October 1876) I.P. & S.L. 39 (11 September 1876) enclosing S.S. to Govt. of India (18 May 1876) and Govt. of India to Govt. of Bombay (4 August 1876), A.S.L. 83 (29 December 1876).

60 See Hunter, op. cit., pp. 131–44.

61 A.S.L. 34 (25 September 1877) and Minute; A.S.L. 43 (1 December 1877) and 44 (15 December 1877), 28 (9 November 1878) and 32 (29 November 1878) show the course of the debate which turned as much on the interpretation of the situation as on enunciation of policy.

62 Ripon adopted a friendly attitude to the Qu'ayti's friend Jung in contrast to Lytton's bitter dislike of the Hyderabad Minister. Schneider's outlook was similar to Lytton's, while Loch's was closer to that of the new Viceroy.

63 I.S.L. 146 (30 October 1881) and enclosures illustrate the rather turgid diplomacy.

64 Hunter, op. cit., p. 143.

65 I.S.L. 66 (14 July 1882).

66 Hunter, op. cit., pp. 169–70.

67 Ibid., pp. 186–7.

68 Ibid., p. 123.

69 Aitchison's Treaties (5th ed. 1930), Vol. XI, pp. 157–9. Cf. al Bakri, *Fi Janub al Jazirah*, pp. 202–4.

70 Hunter, op. cit., p. 145. A.R., A4A, Vol. VII, p. 3, Newsreport (April 1896), A.S.L. (1902), Maitland to Jenkins Private (1 March 1902).

71 Indian Secret Records Register No. 2780 (1905), S.N.O. Aden to C.-in-C. East Indies (26 December 1905).

72 T. Bent, *Southern Arabia* (London, 1900), p. 75.

73 Ibid., p. 115.

74 I.S.L. Reg. No. 2780 S.N.O. Aden to C.-in-C. East Indies (26 December 1905), A.S.L. 320 (31 January 1900).

75 Ibid. and Aden Monthly Memoranda (April, June and July 1910).

76 Hunter, op. cit., pp. 146–7, A.R., A4A, Vol. VII, pp. 77 and 121.

CHAPTER VII

1 J. C. Parkinson. *The Ocean Telegraph to India* (London, 1870), p. 152; A. M. Murray, *Imperial Outposts* (London, 1907), p. 40 and F(oreign) O(ffice) C(onfidential) P(rint), 8767, S.S. to Govt. of India (4 May 1906), enclosed in I.O. to F.O. (7 May 1906). A.R., A1A, Vol. 1046/463, Aden Resident to Govt. of Bombay 154 Marine (14 May 1888).

2 Speech by Sir Garnet Wolseley (2 March 1877), *Journal of the Royal United Service Institute*, Vol. XXI. *Parliamentary Papers*, 1900, Vol. XXIX, Royal Commission on Indian Expenditure; Q. 6549, Evidence of Milty. Secty. to Govt. of India, Q.14850, Evidence of Lord Brackenbury, Member of Colonial Defence Committee.

3 A. J. Marder, *British Naval Policy, 1880–1905*, (London, 1941), pp. 224–6.

4 I.S.L. 79 (26 May 1891), *Parliamentary Papers*, 1896, Vol. XVI, Appendix 48, *Parliamentary Papers*, 1900, Vol. XXIX, Q. 6537.

5 P.R.O. Cab. 11/78, Defence Scheme for Aden 1901.

6 Cab. 1/4, Report by Northcote on Aden (9 April 1903).

7 The guns installed in 1876 had lain rusting for five years before being mounted. W. H. Russell, *The Prince of Wales' Tour in India* (London, 1877), p. 95. I.O. Records, Ad. IIIa, A.A.R. (1876–7); Cab. 11/78, Report on Aden Defence (1886), Defence Scheme for Aden (1895 and 1907).

8 P.R.O. Cab. 11/78 Report on the Defences of Aden (1886).

9 Marder, op. cit., pp. 3–10, and Chapter 6. India Office MSS. Eur. F. 114/5/1, Report by Colonel Jervois on the Defence of Bombay, Aden and Perim (1870). *The Times*, (London, 26 January 1888), Address by Lord Brassey to London Chamber of Commerce. P.R.O. W.O. 32/91/7519, Memorandum on Aden Defences; *Parliamentary Papers*, 1896 Vol. XVI, Appendix 48. The matter was discussed throughout the 1870s also but no decision was arrived at owing to financial stringency. See Jervois MSS. Eur. F. 114, 5/1; Public Works Proceedings Bombay (1870); A.A.R. (1873/4, 1875/6).

10 I.O.R., Aden IIIa, A.A.R. (1881–2).

11 I.O. MSS. Eur. E. 243/4, Reay to Cross (19 November 1886).

12 See I.O.R., Boards Collections, Vol. 2395, No. 128734. Secretary to Govt. of India to Secretary to Govt. of Bombay (30 September 1848) and minute by J. E. D. Bethune (18 July 1849).

13 See G. S. Graham, 'The Ascendancy of the Sailing Ship', *Econ. Hist. Review*, Vol. IX (2nd series), p. 74.

14 Ad. IIIa, A.A.R. (1872–3 to 1896–7).

15 H. Spalding, *Perim as it is* (London, 1890).

16 F.O. 78/1478, Commodore Edgell to Admlty. (19 January 1859); Luke Thomas and Co., Records, Capt. Luke Thomas to Cowasji Dinshaw (11 December 1879); I.O. Political Home Correspondence, (1893), No. 32, Memorandum by Wollaston on the situation at Perim.

17 Luke Thomas Records, Cowasji Dinshaw to Atkinson (9 February 1879).

18 H. Spalding, op. cit.

19 Luke Thomas Records, Atkinson to Vidal (Aden Manager) (18 October 1888), Contracts were made for 1888 at 41s. for Cardiff and 40s. for Newcastle coal, by November the current price had been reduced to 39s. and 38s., Atkinson to Vidal (30 November 1888); Atkinson to Vidal (10 October 1890), the 1891 contracts were got out at 37s. and 35s; Atkinson to Vidal (4 December 1891), the 1892 contracts were made at

a maximum of 32s. Luke Thomas Records, Cowasji Dinshaw to Atkinson (12 February, 14 April, 22 May, 5 and 18 July 1890).

20 Ibid., Hormusji Dinshaw to Atkinson (9 October 1890). Spalding, op. cit.

21 Pol. Home Corresp. (1893), No. 32, Wollaston's Memorandum; Luke Thomas Records, Atkinson to Cowasji Dinshaw (6 March 1889). Pol. Home Corresp. (1893), No. 32, Wollaston's Memorandum, attached correspondence, Secretary of Lloyd's to Secretary of State (16 December 1892). The Secretary of Lloyd's addressed fourteen letters to the I.O. on this topic between August 1890 and March 1893.

22 Luke Thomas Records, Copy of Circular to Ships' Captains issued by Manager, Perim Coal Co.; Spalding, op. cit.; *The Syren and Shipping* (17 March 1900). Luke Thomas Records, Atkinson to Vidal (8 August 1890).

23 Luke Thomas Records, Cowasji Dinshaw to Atkinson (18 July 1890), Luke Thomas and Co., Annual Report for 1888.

24 Luke Thomas Records, Perim Coal Co. Annual Reports (1893–8), Atkinson to Aden Manager (22 January 1900).

25 Cab. 11/78, Aden Defence Schemes; *Parliamentary Papers*, 1896, Vol. XVI, Appendix 48.

26 Marder, op. cit., p. 224; Col, Nugent, 'Imperial Defence Abroad'; *J.R.U.S.I.* (1884); H. Spalding, *Perim as it is*, (London, 1890). Political Home Corresp. (1893), No. 32, Wollaston's memorandum outlines the discussions between the Admiralty, War Office and India Office on this subject in 1883, 1885 and 1886.

27 Luke Thomas Records, Distance Charts compiled by J. A. Burness.

28 India Office, Revenue, Statistics and Commerce Dept. No. 2256 (1884), Lt. Williams to First Asst. Resident, Aden (18 March 1884), Abstracts of Bombay Proceedings (1889), Aden Resident to Govt. of Bombay 504/853 pf. (1 March 1889).

29 Cab. 11/78, Defence Scheme for Aden (1907).

30 Political Home Correspondence (1896), No. 1011, Correspondence relating to Perim, Secretary of Lloyd's to S.S. (15 July 1896). Luke Thomas Records, Perim Coal Co. Reports (1890–9).

31 Bombay Administration Report (1863–4), pp. 134–42. I.O. Records, Public Works, Old Series, Vol. I, No. 5, Aden Resident to S.S. (24 March 1876) enclosing letter from Cowasji Dinshaw.

32 Ad. IIIa, A.A.R. (1875–6), A.R., A1A, Vol. 814, p. 929, P. and O. Agent to Aden Resident (22 March 1879). In 1877–8 only 372 out of 920 came in.

33 Luke Thomas Records, Atkinson to Vidal (3 July 1891).

34 H. Spalding, *Perim as it is*.

35 Part of the prolonged discussions is summarised in a lengthy precis compiled by the Government of Bombay in August 1884. I.O. Public Works Records 1884, Reg. No. 1887. Part can also be found in Public Works Old Series, Vol. I, No. 5.

36 I.S.L. 19 (20 March 1874); Salisbury Papers, Frere to Salisbury (29 June 1876); I.O. MSS. Eur., Lansdowne Correspondence with

S.S. (January–December 1890). Cross to Lansdowne (28 March 1890). Letters to India, S.S. to Govt. of India 16 (11 July 1890); I.S.L. 79 (26 May 1891); *Parliamentary Papers*, 1896, Vol. XVI, Appendix 48; *Parliamentary Papers*, 1900, Vol. XXIX, Questions 14, 849 and 995. Sir Bartle Frere and Lord Salisbury were the main advocates of transfer.

37 A.R., AIA, Vol. 1056, pp. 448–51, Civil Engineer to Aden Resident (10 May 1883).

38 This was Messrs. Henderson and Co., of Glasgow, cf. Public Works Records (1883), Reg. No. 1263, P. Henderson and Co. to Secretary of State (13 July 1883); H. Spalding, *Perim as it is*, list of shareholders in the Perim Coal Co.

39 Luke Thomas Records, Atkinson to Vidal, various letters (March–December 1888).

40 Public Works Records (1885), Reg. No. 75, 603, 751 and 755; Public Works Records (1888), Reg. No. 565, 913, 1026, 1340 and 1900.

41 Public Works Records (1885), Reg. No. 649, Shipowners' Memorial (16 April 1885) contains this suggestion.

42 Public Works, Old Series, Vol. I, No. 5. This allegation was brought forward by the P. and O. Co., in 1874, and there is much in the methods of administration at Aden to bear it out, e.g. the payment of the whole establishment of the trade registration department from the proceeds of the Port Fund after 1871 – A.R., AIA, Vol. 578, p. 115.

43 I.O. MSS. Eur. E. 243/55, Reay to Cross (6 May 1889).

44 I.O. MSS. Eur. E. 243/48, Reay to Cross (13 September 1886); A.R. AIA, Vol. 1056, pp. 449–51, Aden Resident to Govt. of Bombay (14 May 1888).

45 A.R., AIA, Vol. 1056, p. 613, Aden Resident to Govt. of Bombay (21 March 1890).

46 I.O.R. Official Publications 66 (1966), Aden Trade and Navigation Returns (1885–6 to 1893–4).

47 See F. M. Hunter, *An Account of the British Settlement of Aden in Arabia* (1877, reprinted 1968), pp. 268–9; *Parl. Papers*, 1905 (163), p. 11.

48 Census Returns in A.A.R. (1883–4 and 1892–3).

49 A.R., AIA, Vol. 901, p. 551, report on living conditions in Ma'alla.

50 A.A.R. (1880–1 and 1881–2), Hunter and Sealey, *An Account of the Arab Tribes in the Vicinity of Aden* (1885 ed.), p. 12.

51 A.A.R. (1892–3), report on the 1891 Census, 77 per cent of males living in Aden had employment, but only 66 per cent of males in Shaykh 'Uthman. These employment figures are probably too high, since it was dangerous for a man to admit he had no job, given the government attitude to what was termed 'vagrancy'. But the lower employment rate at Shaykh 'Uthman is nevertheless clear.

52 A.R., AIA, Vol. 1092, p. 292, Vol. 1155, p. 219.

53 A.R., AIA, Vol. 923, p. 457, Stace to Messageries Maritimes Agent (15 January 1883). Ibid., Vol. 1125 p. 163, Directive by General Jopp (28 September 1891); Vol. 1039 p. 684; Vol. 1336, p. 139; Vol. 1155, p. 255.

54 Ibid., Vol. 1155, p. 283.

55 Ibid., Vol. 1151, p. 81. Govt. of Bombay to Govt. of India (13 July 1906) in I.O. to F.O. (11 October 1906); I.O. Pol. and Secret Records (1921), Reg. No. 57069, report on vagrant and houseless population (1 November 1921).

56 The rate per day was 5 annas in 1846, A.R., A1A, Vol. 58, p. 473, Haines to Military Board (2 September 1846); it was 5 annas in 1888, ibid., Vol. 1025, p. 129; in 1914 the rate was 5–7 annas per day, Aden Administration Report (1914). The daily rate doubled during the war years, Aden Administration Reports, (1915–21), as a result of the massive rise in the cost of provisions.

57 I.O. Records, Monthly Memoranda from Aden (April 1908); Pol. and Secret Records (1900), Reg. No. 41, Aden Res. to S.S. 66 (2 March 1900); A.R., A1A, Vol. 1201, p. 542, Vol. 1209, p. 165, Vol. 1241, pp. 241 and 257, Vol. 1378, p. 1.

58 A.R., A1A, Vol. 1039, pp. 321 and 684, Vol. 1120, p. 667; Revenue Statistics and Commerce Records (1884), Reg. No. 2256, Aden Resident to Govt. of Bombay (5 May 1884).

59 A.R., A1A, Vol. 1155 p. 120, Memorandum by Vidal on labour troubles at Aden (June 1891).

60 A.R., A1A, Vol. 1068, p. 187, Petition by Luke Thomas and Co., Aden Coal Co., and Cowasji Dinshaw Bros. (24 July 1889).

61 A.R., A1A, Vol. 1155, pp. 120 and 283; Revenue Stats. and Commerce Records (1884), Reg. No. 1764, Hunter to Govt. of Bombay, enclosing report by Lt. Walsh on coolie disturbances at Perim (18 July 1884).

62 E.g. A.R., A1A, Vol. 1058, pp. 669–75, Memorandum by Assistant Resident Stace on the case of a labour contractor deported for extortion in the building trade, November 1889. The man was eventually allowed to return. A.R., A1A, Vol. 1193, p. 325, cites another case of a contractor who was found by Government in 1889 to be extorting 20s. to 30s. per voyage from men engaging as firemen. He was removed and a Government Registrar of Firemen was put in his place. In 1895 it was discovered that the contractor was still securing money from prospective firemen. The Government therefore decided to cut its losses and abolished the office of Registrar, thus restoring the former moderately corrupt situation. But in 1900 it was found that the displaced Registrar had continued to batten on aspiring seamen and receive money from them. Government intervention had in fact worsened the lot of the firemen. For Perim see Revenue Stats. and Commerce Records (1884), Reg. No. 1764, Hinton Spalding to S.S. (4 September 1884).

63 Revenue Stats. and Commerce Records (1884), Reg. No. 2256, Aden Resident to Govt. of Bombay (5 May 1884). The sanctions involved were loss of business for the company and deportation for the coolies. A.R., A1A, Vol. 1329, p. 325. Cowasji Dinshaw's request to prevent the despatch of coolies to Djibuti on 28 September 1900, was refused on the grounds that the coolies would stay of their own volition, were it not for the fact that 'they are not so well off here as they might be'.

64 The 'fortress' policy often clashed with the humanitarian policy of con-

structing labour lines. A.R., A1A, Vol. 1336, p. 305, Vol. 1366, pp. 129 and 139, Vol. 1403, p. 253.
65 I.O. MSS. Elphinstone Papers, Coghlan to Elphinstone (25 February and 30 March 1856), and (12 November 1858); *The Friend of India* newspaper (17 May 1856). I.O.R. Aden Administration Report (1859–60), in Collections to Bombay unanswered Letters.
66 A.A.R. (1882–3), summary of educational progress.
67 A.A.R. (1896–7).
68 I.S.L. 141 (16 July 1895), Enclosure 4, Annexure A, Note by Muhammad Salah Jaffer (17 March 1895).
69 Comparative figures in A.A.R. (1892–3).
70 Cf. A.R., A1A, Vol. C 53, p. 235; H. F. Jacob, *Kings of Arabia*, p. 83.

CHAPTER VIII

1 I.S.L. 68 (11 August 1873) and 10 (6 February 1874).
2 See Memorandum by Bertie (2 October 1886) in F.O. 78/4529, and A.S.L. (1877–86).
3 A. Ramm, 'Great Britain and the Planting of Italian Power in the Red Sea, 1868–85', *English Historical Review* (1944), p. 211.
4 F.O.C.P. 5243, I.O. to F.O. (22 October 1885).
5 Red Sea and Somali Coast C.P. 1884; Malet to Granville (31 August 1884); Wyndham to Granville (22 November 1884); Lyons to Granville (16 December 1884); I.O. to F.O. (2 February 1885). The Turks occupied and fortified Shaykh Sa'id in 1885–6.
6 F.O.C.P. 5399, I.O. to F.O. (15 September 1886). F.O.C.P. 5331, Kimberley to Viceroy (26 March 1886).
7 F.O.C.P. 5331, Kimberley to Viceroy (26 March 1886). Text of treaty in F. M. Hunter, *Arab Tribes in the Vicinity of Aden*, p. 170.
8 F.O.C.P. 3568, Salisbury to Viceroy (10 January 1876), A.S.L. 7 (5 February 1876).
9 F.O. 78/4529, Minute by Pauncefote and F.O. letter to I.O. (19 November 1887).
10 Between the signature and ratification of the Protectorate Treaty Socotra was visited by German vessels. A.S.L. 50/2732 (31 December 1886).
11 F.O.C.P. 5399, F.O. to I.O. (15 December 1886).
12 F.O. 78/4529. The scheme was sanctioned reluctantly in May 1887. Cross to Dufferin (5 May 1887), but nine days later the F.O. called for the suspension of the operation during the Drummond Wolff negotiations, F.O. to I.O. (14 May 1887).
13 F.O.C.P. 5587, I.O. to F.O. (15 September 1887), F.O. to I.O. (19 November 1887). Salisbury asked Cross to bring the matter before the cabinet in October 1887. I.O. MSS. Eur. E. 243/17, Cross to Reay (27 October 1887).
14 This was explicitly stated in Salisbury's letter to the I.O. (19 November

1887) in F.O. 78/4529. It was feared at the F.O. that if the treaties were negotiated piecemeal the French would move in, as in West Africa, and seek a *quid pro quo* for their withdrawal. Cf. I.O. MSS. Eur. E. 243/48 Reay to Cross. (13 September 1886 and 26 November 1886); 243/51 Reay to Cross (16 January and 4 June 1888); 243/17, Cross to Dufferin (17 November and 1 December 1887), Cross to Reay (16 December 1887). For December delay see F.O. 78/4529, White to Salisbury 375 (10 December 1887) and Minutes.

15 MSS. Eur. E. 243/17, Cross to Dufferin (23 November 1887); 243/18 Cross to Dufferin (27 April 1888). Also F.O. 78/4529 Dufferin to Cross, private (2 April 1888) and I.O. to F.O. (2 July 1890).

16 F.O. 78/4529 I.O. to F.O. (3 July 1890) and enclosures.

17 I.S.L. 25 (4 February 1891) enclosing Govt. of India to Govt. of Bombay (2 February 1891); F.O. 78/4529, I.O. to F.O. (18 March 1891).

18 By the 1880s the British were aware of their original mistake but continued to refer to the 'Amir's 'subjects' since it was convenient to do so. Cf. A.S.L. 37/1853 (21 September 1886), in which the Resident refers to the Amir's people as 'merely a congeries of semi-independent tribes who attach themselves to the nearest powerful chief'.

19 See A.S.L. (30 March 1880) enclosing Resident to Govt. of Bombay, 89/491 (30 March 1880) and Hunter's report (24 February 1880) – the first detailed British description of the Dali' area.

20 A.S.L. 138 (16 December 1902), Wahab's memorandum on the 'Amir's boundary and Appendix of documents, also G. Wyman Bury, *The Land of Uz* (London, 1911).

21 Cf. F. M. Hunter, *An Account of the Arab Tribes in the Vicinity of Aden* and D. Ingrams, *A Social and Economic Survey of the Western Aden Protectorate* (Asmara, 1949).

22 Hunter and Sealey, *An Account of the Arab Tribes in the Vicinity of Aden,* (1909 ed.), pp. 20–6, 'The Subayhi', pp. 161 and 227. Treaties and notes on the various Subayhi notables in Appendix E, pp. 340–56.

23 Cf. Hunter and Sealey, op. cit., pp. 270–82, Appendix C, list of places in the interior of Arabia visited by the Aden Troop (1874–5).

24 Ordinary muskets were imported into Aden in the 1870s but none paid much attention to the movement of these less deadly weapons. Cf. Aden Secret Letter 279 (24 December 1870). The matchlock could be a very inefficient weapon. The tribesmen on the Qa'taba Damar road in 1891 preferred to use spears. (W. B. Harris, *A Journey through the Yemen* [London, 1893], p. 217). In like fashion Angoni warriors in East Africa preferred the assegai to the mid-century musket.

25 F.O.C.P. no. 1651, enclosure in no. 1, Ferris to Gomer (23 October 1895); H. de Monfried, *Pearls, Arms and Hashish* (London, 1930), pp. 106–9, 153 ff. I.S.L. 52 (28 March 1894). The Turks patrolled the coast in the 1890s but failed to check the expansion of the trade, see I.O. Home Correspondence, F.O. to I.O. (30 March 1894) enclosing Currie to Kimberley 121 (21 March 1894).

26 R. Pankhurst, 'Firearms in Ethiopia', *Ethiopian Observer*, Vol. VI, No. 2.

27 I.S.L. 52 (28 March 1894) enclosing Resident to Govt. of Bombay, (22 December 1893).

28 T. Bent, op. cit., p. 401.

29 I.O. Home Correspondence, Aden Resident to Govt. of Bombay 387 (16 November 1895) enclosing statement by interpreter aboard H.M.S. *Brisk*. A.S.L. 438 (15 December 1900), Report by Aden Jemadar.

30 A.R., A4A, Vol. II, p. 153, notes of an interview between Resident and Fadli Sultan (12 April 1902).

31 *The Times* (20 November 1895); Harris, op. cit., p. 217. The other principal destination of Djibuti arms was Ethiopia, but by 1894 the market was saturated (F.O.C.P. 6567, Phipps to Kimberley [12 October 1894]). Nevertheless arms still poured into Djibuti, especially after the 1893 re-equipment of the French army released large new stocks of second-hand rifles (F.O.C.P. 6176, I.O. to F.O. [4 November 1891], Stace to Cromer [31 March 1893]). In 1891 Stace on the Somali Coast said (ibid., Stace to Hardinge [10 September 1891]) that the only obstacle to the Arabs receiving arms was their poverty. All the evidence points to the 1890s as the beginning of really large-scale arms smuggling into the Yemen. Djibuti rifles were pouring into the Imam's port of Medi in 1902 and the Imam had a personal force of 2,000 soldiers, fully equipped with magazine rifles, by that date. (A.S.L. 95 [3 September 1902].) By the turn of the century the tribesmen in southern Yemen were already heavily armed with the new weapons. (I.O. Home Correspondence, Reg. No. 2471, Bunsen to Lansdowne [20 July 1902] enclosing report by Turkish doctor on the situation in southern Yemen.)

32 A.R., A4B, Vol. XXI, Report by Warneford.

33 I.O. Pol. and Secret Memoranda E. 55, Military Report on the Aden Protectorate, p. 86.

34 I.O. Records, Ad. IIIa. A.A.R. (1883), Hunter and Sealey, *An Account of the Arab Tribes in the vicinity of Aden* (1885 ed.), p. 12. For Abdali activity on the boundary of Subayhi country, see F.O. 78/4529, Memorandum by Bertie (2 October 1886). A.R., F1A, Vol. CXLII.

35 I.O. Records, Ad. IIIa, A.A.R. (1892-3); A.S.L. (18 August 1886) enclosing Aden Resident to Govt. of Bombay (14 August 1886). F.O. 78/4529, I.O. to F.O. (2 July, 1890), enclosures 19, 27 and 28. The defeat of the 'Abdali in 1886 was still celebrated in Subayhi popular songs some twenty years later, G. W. Bury, *The Land of Uz*, pp. 15 and 80.

36 I.O. Home Correspondence, Aden Resident to Govt. of Bombay 387 (16 November 1895) enclosing statements by Somali interpreter aboard H.M.S. *Brisk* and Ahmad Ibrahim Warsangali, *Nakhoda* of a Somali *sambuk*. A.R., A4A, Vol. X, p. 6, Resident to Govt. of Bombay, No. 264 (31 August 1898), enclosing report by Jaffer on Subayhi arms trade.

37 I.O. Pol. and Secret Memoranda E. 55, Report on Military situation in Aden hinterland (1915), pp. 136-54. Cf. R. A. B. Hamilton's derisive reference in 1949 to the once powerful 'Atafi Shaykhs as 'a small family

of half-destitute goat-keepers'. Belhaven, *The Kingdom of Melchior* (London, 1949), p. 2.

38 A.R., A4A, Vol. VII, Monthly Report for 1895.

39 Cf. Report in I.O. Pol. and Secret Records, Aden Monthly Memorandum (February 1908) that feuding was accelerating social disintegration in Subayhi country.

40 For a graphic description of the effects of the blood feud, see Belhaven, *The Uneven Road* (London, 1955), pp. 75–6. The advent of rifles intensified feuding but society had been by no means peaceful before. In 1865 Merewether commented on Aden's hinterland, 'every man and boy is armed . . . every man's hand is against his neighbours'. A.S.L. (1863), etc. Resident to Govt. of Bombay 14 (28 January 1865).

41 I.S.L. 212 (3 October 1872) enclosing Resident to Governor of Bombay 9 (13 March 1872) and 13 (10 April 1872). Aden Records, A4A, Vol. III, Muthanna Musa'ad to Schneider and reply (16 May 1872). Muthanna Musa'ad to Tremenheere (22 May 1872); A.S.L. 70 (27 November 1875).

42 A.S.L. 11 (30 January 1875), 19 (19 March 1875), 46 (25 August 1875), 70 (27 November 1875), 32 (3 June 1876), 51 (28 July 1876), 55 (12 August 1876), 56 (26 August 1876), 70 (12 October 1876), and (30 March 1880), enclosing Report by Hunter (24 February 1880).

43 A.S.L. (30 March 1880) enclosing Hunter's report (24 February 1880), A.S.L. 51 (28 July 1876).

44 A.S.L. 21 (27 May 1880). The Turks dealt separately with the Sha'iri and the people of Jabal Jihawf, both of which groups were claimed by the 'Amir. See A.S.L. 138 (6 December 1902). Wahab's Memorandum and Appendices.

45 Cf. Izzet Pasha to Hunter (28 October 1884), referring to the 'savage Yemenis' in A.S.L. 22 (19 November 1884), and Izzet Pasha to Blair (4 November 1884), referring to savage Yemeni chiefs in A.S.L. 23 (24 November 1884). Governor-General Ahmad Feizi Pasha to Aden Resident (9 December 1885), referring to barbarian bedawin at Dali' in A.S.L. 2/15 (5 January 1886); also Governor-General to Resident (26 February 1886), referring to 'Amir's government as uncivilised, and Proclamation to the Sha'iri people in A.S.L. 12 (16 March 1886). Turkish ill-treatment of prominent personages was the occasion for the 1891 revolt in the Yemen, see G. B. Rossi. *Nei Paesi d'Islam* (Rocca San Casciano, 1897), pp. 229–30.

46 A.S.L. (30 March 1880), enclosing Hunter's Report of 24 February 1880 and map. A.S.L. 7/317 (17 February 1885) enclosing report on 'Amiri losses, 26 January 1885. Cf. Manzoni, *Il Yemen; Tre Anni Nel Arabia Felice* (Rome, 1884), p. 59, description of area controlled by the Turks at Qa'taba.

47 I.S.L. 25 (4 February 1891), Resident to Govt. of Bombay 391 (7 October 1889), Aden Secret Letters, Reg. No. 49, Creagh D.O. to Lee Warner (20 December 1899) and enclosures gives a summary of Turco-Dali' relations.

48 For 1881 Agreement see Hunter and Sealey, *Arab Tribes in the Vicinity of Aden* (1886 ed.), p. 24.

49 A.R., A4A, Vol. XV, p. 98, report by Jaffer (13 January 1894).

50 A.S.L. 15 (8 July 1890).

51 The Hawshabi attacked the 'Amri tribesmen in 1888 – no doubt to enforce the payment of increased taxes. A.R., A4A, Vol. XX, Report by Jacob on Hawshabi relations with the 'Amiri people (18 January 1906).

52 In 1903 it was estimated that a third of the 1,800 Qataybi fighting men were equipped with rifles, and some 1,000 of the Radfan tribesmen were believed to have breechloaders. A.S.L. (5 December 1903) enclosing report on operations in Qataybi country.

53 A.R., A4A, Vol. XV, p. 120, 1894, Memorandum on transit dues.

54 A.R., A4A, Vol. VII p. 113, Newsreport (December 1895). Ibid., Vol. XV, p. 130, Jaffer to Sealey (1 May 1894).

55 Cf. the many offers such as that made by Shaykh Nasir Muqbil to the Sayyids of Al Dubayat in 1902 offering them respect and honour from the Muslim Turks instead of the lack of consideration they could expect from a Kafir government which would not recognise their religious importance. A.S.L. 84 (31 July 1902). Medals and honours were widely bestowed by the Turks – indeed this tampering with the status system was the main weapon in their political armoury.

56 E.g. I.O. Home Correspondence Telegram from Viceroy (1 April 1893) concerning the Hawshabi Sultan's desire for a protective treaty.

57 A.R., A4A, Vol. XV, p. 98, Report by Jaffer (13 January 1894).

58 A.R., A4A, Vol. XV, Report by Jaffer 136 (8 August 1894).

59 A.R., A4A, Vol. XV. p. 225, Fadl bin'Ali to Jopp (13 January 1895).

60 Cf. A.R., A4A, Vol. XV, pp. 388–9, Fadl bin'Ali to Jopp (10 December 1893).

61 Sultan Ahmad Fadl later accused the Resident of having actually proposed verbally to the Lahej Sultan that he should attack the Hawshabi. Ahmad Fadl to General Mason (23 July 1905) (A.R., A4A, Vol. XX). This can neither be disproved nor verified, but the Aden Government certainly backed Lahej strongly in the matter and would have given larger support for military operations had the Indian Government permitted them to do so. Cf. A.R., A4A, Vol. XV, Minute by Sealey on letter from Fadl bin 'Ali (24 May 1894),and p. 237, note of interview between Resident and Fadl bin 'Ali (13 January 1895).

62 A.R., A4A, Vol. XV, p. 166, Report by Jemadar (12 July 1894).

63 He claimed he had spent MT$100,000 on establishing his position as Sultan of the Hawshabi. A.R., A4A, Vol. XV, p. 185, Fadl bin 'Ali to Jopp (25 July 1894).

64 A.R., A4A, Vol. VII, p. 2, Monthly Report (April 1895), Fadl bin 'Ali to Jopp (7 May 1895).

65 A.R., A4A, Vol XV, Sultan Fadl bin 'Ali al 'Abdali to Resident, 3 June 1895. This system was still in operation in 1905. A.R., A4A, Vol. XX, notes of interview between Hawshabi and General Mason, 10 June 1905 and Sultan Ahmad Fadl to Mason, April 1905.

66 A.R., A4A, Vol. VII, pp. 113 and 131. Newreports (December 1895 and January 1896). The 'Alawi Shaykh was also raising transit dues and discontinuing customary stipends. See also Hunter and Sealey, *Arab Tribes in the Vicinity of Aden* (1907 ed.), pp. 75–6.

67 I.S.L. 141 (16 July 1895) and enclosures.

68 J. A. S. Grenville, *Lord Salisbury and Foreign Policy 1895–1902*, (London 1964), Chapter II.

69 A.R., A1A, Vol. 1286, p. 3.

70 Abud successfully urged a change of policy toward Dali' upon the Resident at the end of 1899. A.S.L., D. O. Creagh to Lee Warner (20 December 1899) and enclosures, also A.R., A1A, Vol. C21, Letter No. 347 (18 November 1899), Resident to Govt. of Bombay in Abud's hand. Abud later urged the view that Jaffer was a Turkish agent, A.R., Vol. C29, p. 321.

71 I.O. Pol. and Secret Records, Register No. 1149. I.S.L. 6080 (11 August 1900) enclosing Aden Resident to Govt. of Bombay 63 (3 May 1900) and Bombay Resolution (11 August 1900). A.R., F1A, Vol. 381, contains details of the case. See comment on Jaffer in Creagh, op cit., p. 210.

72 A.S.L. 59 (22 August 1901); Creagh, op. cit., p. 216.

73 The Governor of Bombay pleaded for a K.C.S.I. for the Sultan in 1900 for 'delicate work that cannot be spoken of'. I.O. MSS. Eur. F. 123/27, Northcote to Hamilton (7 March 1900).

74 A.R., A4A, Volume XI, p. 271, Statement by Muhammad Mas'ud Jablis (19 April 1898), ibid., Vol. 10, p. 3, Resident to Govt. of Bombay 249 (14 August 1898) I.S.L. 42M (26 October 1899), enclosing Resident to Govt. of Bombay 22 (1 September 1899). I.O. Pol. and Secret Records, Reg. No. 1196, I.S.L. 151 (25 October 1900) enclosing Aden Resident to Govt. of Bombay 316 (7 September 1900).

75 I.S.L. 51M (28 December 1899).

76 I.O. MSS. Eur. F. 111/160, Curzon to Hamilton (17 January 1901).

77 A.R., A4A, Vol. VII, Resident to Govt. of Bombay 249, Pol. (11 August 1898).

78 *The Times* (25 August 1891), p. 3, A.R., A4A, Vol. II, p. 221; I.O. Pol. and Secret Records, Reg. No. 15, A.S.L. 25 (16 January 1900) and enclosures and Reg. No. 29, A.S.L. 41 (8 February 1900).

79 A.S.L. 57 (21 October 1899) and enclosures, I.O. Pol. and Secret Records, Reg. No. 29, A.S.L. 41 (8 February 1900), Reg. No. 41, A.S.L. 75 (8 June 1901), Reg. No. 36, A.S.L. 74 (23 April 1902). Cf. I.O. Pol. and Secret Records, Reg. No. 3565, F.O. to I.O. (24 August 1906) enclosing report by Richardson on Yemen situation (30 June, 1906).

80 Berard, *Le Sultan, l'Islam et les Puissances* (Paris, 1907), pp. 31–4.

81 I.O. Home Miscellaneous, F.O. to I.O. (23 April 1892), *The Times* (29 October 1891), p. 3.

82 See W. B. Harris, *A Journey through the Yemen* (London, 1893), I.O. Home Correspondence F.O. to I.O. (7 December 1891), enclosing report by Military Attaché (14 November 1891); *The Times* (19 and 20 November 1895). I.O. Home Correspondence, F.O. to I.O. (27

June, 18 July and 5 October 1898; 23 March, 19 May, 6 June, and 27 July 1899) and enclosures.
83 Cf. A.R., A1A, Vol. C37–8, p. 273. I.S.L. 141 (16 July 1895) enclosing Resident to Govt. of Bombay 59 (28 November 1894) and 3 (30 January 1895).
84 A.S.L. 10 (10 April 1899) and 48 (5 December 1899) enclosing Resident to Govt. of Bombay 69 (5 December 1899).
85 A.R., A4A, Vol. II, p. 131, notes of an interview between the Aden Resident and the 'Abdali Sultan. The 'Abdali harboured the ex-Mutasarif of Ta'izz – a strongly anti-Turkish Arab from Damascus. In 1902 the 'Abdali was once more visited by an Imamic agent, A.S.L. 85 (27 July 1902), Wahab's diary (15 July 1902).
86 Both G. B. Rossi, *Nei Paesi d'Islam*, p. 232, and C. Ansaldi, *Il Yemen*, p. 165, say that in 1891 and 1907 the Yemeni rebels were receiving arms from Aden. During the 1891 rebellion it was believed that arms were smuggled in tobacco packages from Aden to Hudayda and toward the end of that year the Controller of customs at the latter port was arrested for alleged complicity in the traffic. I.O. Home Miscellaneous, F.O. to I.O. (27 September and 1 December 1891, 17 May 1892). Up to 1910 suspicions persisted that arms were reaching Yemen by this route. The other route was direct from Lahej or Subayhi to purchasers at Mawiyah or elsewhere beyond the border. The Turkish Government accused the Sultan of Lahej of complicity in the trade in 1895 and produced some evidence in support of their allegations (I.O. Home Correspondence, F.O. to I.O. [14 September 1895]). The trade in lead and sulphur was quite legal and the Sultan imported large quantities of these through Aden. In 1902 the Sultan openly avowed his interest in the traffic to the Aden Resident. (A.R., A4A, Vol. II, Sultan to Resident, [10 June 1902]). The Resident asked him to desist but without avail (I.O. L/P and S/10/33 Govt. of Bombay to Govt. of India [5 March 1906]). Indeed the Sultan spoke as if he were doing the British a service by smuggling arms and ammunition to the Imam. A reliable report in 1910 indicated that rifles were regularly smuggled in large numbers from Obekh, opposite Djibuti, to Ras al Arah on the Subayhi coast where the import was controlled by a clerk from Lahej and thence to Lahej or Ma'alla (I.O. L/P and S/10/34 C.O. to F.O. [20 August 1910]). The Sultan was only interested in checking Subayhi smuggling in competition with his own. See also I.O. Records L/P. and S/10/32 No. 2726, S.N.O. Aden to C. in C. East Indies (28 January 1905) complaining at Resident's reticence in face of clear evidence of Lahej-directed Arms smuggling at Ras Imran. There is also a clear record of a trade in rifles from Lahej to the borders of the Hadhramawt (A.R., A4A, Vol. I, p. 51, notes of an interview between first Assistant Resident and Shaykh of Hawra [13 December 1903]).
87 I.O. Pol. and Secret Records, Reg. No. 29, A.S.L. 41 (8 February 1900).
88 A.R., A4A, Vol. XV, Report on 'Abdali operations (18 June 1894).
89 F.O. 416/3 p. 20, Aden Resident to Govt. of Bombay (10 April 1900)

enclosing report by H.M. Abud (12 March 1900), on occupation of Darayjah. The Turkish Government attempted in vain to secure British assistance against tobacco smuggling (I.O. Home Correspondence, F.O. to I.O. [4 November 1897]). Aden's landward export of tobacco rose from 278,921 lb. in 1892–3 to 3,142,608 lb. in 1897 (I.P.S.L. 128 [8 September 1897] enclosing Resident to Govt. of Bombay [3 June 1897]). The fact that the Ottoman Government estimated Yemeni consumption at $3\frac{1}{2}$ million lb. while less than half a million lb. went through Turkish customs, and that this entailed a loss of £T100,000 to the exchequer, gives an idea of the scale of possible profit. For the Turkish approach to Lahej see I.O. Pol. and Secret Records No. 11, A.S.L. 13 (8 January 1900).

90 F.O. 416/3, pp. 50, 52 and 54, Salisbury to O'Conor (7 May 1900), O'Conor to Salisbury (14 and 19 May 1900); Aden Records, A1A, C22, pp. 17, 85, 157, 189 and 199–200.

91 A.R., A1A, Vol. C22, pp. 229 and 267.

92 A.S.L. 11 (10 April 1899); A.S.L. 48 (5 December 1899).

93 This scheme was mooted by the Resident, Major-General Creagh, in Aden Resident to Govt. of Bombay 347 (18 November 1899), enclosed in A.S.L. (15 December 1899). One of the regiments at Aden in 1901 had in fact been sent there for misbehaving itself in Burma. I.O. MSS. Eur. F. 111/160, Curzon to Hamilton, (31 July 1901), see also Ronaldshay, *Lord Curzon of Kedleston* (London, 1928), Vol. 2, pp. 72–3.

94 I.O. MSS. Eur F. 111/160, Viceroy to S.S. (31 July 1901).

95 J. A. S. Grenville, op. cit., Chapter XIII.

96 F.O. 416/6, no. 69, Lansdowne to Anthropoulo Pasha (29 July 1901).

97 It was the F.O. which initiated the demand for action but the subordinate authorities were eager to press forward rather than to hold back and this led to the clash of arms. I.O. MSS. Eur. F. 111/160, Curzon to Hamilton (31 July, 7 August and 22 August 1901). See Correspondence in F.O. 416/6, especially 102, I.O. to F.O. (7 August 1901) and enclosures, no. 4, enclosing Govt. of India to Govt. of Bombay (11 June 1901), and no. 58, S.S. to Viceroy (17 July 1901), and Viceroy to S.S. (24 July 1901) – the I.O. first heard of the action from the newspapers.

98 A.S.L. 101 (22 August 1901). Report by Major Davies, Aden Records, A1A, Vol. C22, p. 475.

99 See the anxious communications from the Ottoman Government in F.O. 416/6, especially nos. 64, 65 and 68.

100 A.S.L. 61 (31 August 1901).

101 Pol. and Secret Records, Reg. No. 2299, note by Lee Warner on Aden Demarcation, (18 June 1902). Lee Warner's and Lyall's Minutes on A.S.L. 46 (15 December 1899) and Lee Warner's Minute on A.S.L. 49 (29 July 1901). I.O. MSS. Eur. F. 111/162, Hamilton to Curzon (5 June 1903).

102 Cf. I.O. MSS. Eur. F. 111/530, 'Summary of the principal events of the Viceroyalty of H. E. Lord Curzon of Kedleston in the Foreign Department, Vol. III, 'Aden and Dependencies'.

103 Ibid.
104 I.O. Records Home Correspondence, Reg. No. 2420, note by Maitland (28 July 1902), A.S.L. 138 (16 December 1902), Appendix I to Wahab's Memorandum on 'Amiri boundary, Items 11 and 12.
105 Pol. and Secret Records, Reg. no. 2420, note by Maitland (28 July, 1902), A.R., A1A, Vol. C29, p. 407.
106 Since 1900 the officials in the India Office had been urging caution, especially in regard to the 'Amiri area. Cf. Minutes on A.S.L. (19 March 1900).
107 The Aden Residency as late as 1895 however interpreted it to mean something very close to this, I.S.L. 141 (16 July 1895), enclosing Jopp to Govt. of Bombay 33 (22 March 1895) Jopp to Govt. of Bombay (11 November 1895). Jopp's view was based on the advice of Sealey who had been in Aden for eighteen years and had seen the 'Amiri abandonment policy begin. The Memoranda by Hunter and Schneider (28 September and 1 October 1885) (I.O. Records Pol. and Secret Memoranda B. 30), upon which the Govt. of India's policy was based, recommended simply abandoning the 'Amir.
108 The Govt. of India (29 March 1888) ordered that diplomatic pressure in respect of Dali' should be relaxed. These instructions were not carried out fully by Aden Residents, A.S.L. (15 December 1899), enclosing Creagh to Govt. of Bombay (18 November 1899), but cf. Aden Records, A4A, Vol. VII, pp. 32, 52, and 160. Newsreports (May and August 1895 and March 1897) for clear cases of Residency restraint.
109 Pol. and Secret Records, Reg. No. 2299, note by Lee Warner on Aden Demarcation (18 June 1902).
110 Ibid.
111 I.O. MSS. Eur. F. 111/530, Summary of the principal events and measures of the Viceroyalty of Lord Curzon, Vol. III, 'Aden and Dependencies'.
112 A.R., A1A, Vol. C29, p. 383, Maitland to Wahab (11 May 1902).
113 A.R., A1A. Vol. C28, Wahab to Maitland (19 January 1902); A.S.L. 29 (11 March 1902). Pol. and Secret Records, Reg. No. 2420, Memorandum by Maitland (29 July 1902). The Jaffers in fact had been quite out of sympathy with the policy. See A.R., A4A, Vol. V, p. 628, Jaffer's report on relations with tribes (1888) and I.S.I. 141 (16 July 1895), Aden Resident to Govt. of Bombay 33 (22 March 1895), Annexure A. Memorandum by Jaffer. The 'Amiri abandonment policy was initiated by F. M. Hunter, see Pol. and Secret Memoranda B. 30 – Memorandum regarding relations with the tribes in the hinterland of Aden, by Major F. M. Hunter (29 August 1885).
114 F.O. 416/9, p. 85, Wahab to Govt. of India (7 April 1902); Secty. of State to Maitland (28 April 1902); p. 93, Secty. of State to Aden Resident (12 May 1902); p. 166a, Aden Resident to Secty. of State and Secty. of State to Aden Resident (18 May 1902); p. 173, Secty. of State to Aden Resident (23 May 1902); Aden Resident to Secty. of State (26 and 28 May 1902); I.O. Pol. and Secret Records Reg.

No. 2299, note by Lee Warner on Aden Demarcation (18 June 1902).

115 I.O. MSS. Eur. F. 111/161, Curzon to Hamilton (4 June 1902); ibid., F. 111/162, Curzon to Hamilton (22 and 29 January, 12 February and 19 March 1903); F.O. 416/9, p. 237, Govt. of India to Secty. of State (13 June 1902); F.O. 416/10, p. 117, Govt. of India to Secty. of State (24 July 1902).

116 Cf. his irrelevant remark in Aden Secret Letters 1903, Hamilton to Godley, (12 January 1903), 'how impossible it is to prevent a civilised power encroaching on the spheres of influence of a semi-civilised neighbour' – there was nothing uncontrollable about the forces at work at Aden. He thought the signing of treaties with the Upper Yafi'i 'a rambling side-issue', I.O. MSS. Eur. F. 111/162, Hamilton to Curzon (23 January 1903).

117 F.O. 416/10, p. 43; S.S. to Govt. of India (19 July 1902); F.O. 416/11, Wahab to Govt. of India (22 March 1903).

118 F.O. 416/10, p. 117, Govt. of India to S.S. (24 July 1902).

119 F.O. 416/10, p. 82, Memorandum of Interdepartmental Meeting (6 August 1902). The weakness in the I.O.'s position with regard to the Dali' line was that it was based on Wahab's 1891–2 survey, which was not designed to demarcate the border but only to effect a geographical survey of the British sphere as far as he was able. To this extent the survey was useful as an indicator of the area at that time lying within the 'Amir's power, but as the edge of the hachured map was taken as the edge of the 'Amir's territory, the 'Amir's land ended with the hachuring, leaving the 'Amir the hills and the Turks the unhachured, cultivated plateau.

120 F.O. 416/10, p. 135, Lansdowne to Bunsen (18 August 1902).

121 I.O. MSS. Eur. F. 123/67, Memorandum by Sir D. Fitzpatrick on the conduct of the India Council Meeting (28 January 1903).

122 I.O. Pol. and Secret Records, No. 27, Lansdowne to O'Conor (6 April 1903). I.O. MSS. Eur. F. 111/530, Summary of principal events, etc., Vol. III, I.O. MSS. Eur. F. 111/162. Hamilton to Curzon (5 February, 13 February, 5 March, 27 March and 8 April 1903). The Germans advised the Porte to give way – A.R., Vol. C33-VI, p. 105. Military elements in Turkey were against any surrender. A.R., A1A, Vol. C34, pp. 97 and 439. In the following year the Porte was further embarrassed by the necessity of sending troops to hold back 'Abdal 'Aziz Ibn Sa'ud in central Arabia. Cf. H. St. S. Philby, Sa'udi Arabia, p. 245. F.O.C.P. 8377, No. 114, O'Conor to Lansdowne (21 April 1903), F.O.C.P. 8399, No. 196.

123 I.O. MSS. Eur. F. 111/530, Summary of principal events, etc., Vol. III. Cf. A.S.L. 138 (16 December 1902), Wahab's Memorandum on the 'Amir's boundary and Appendix of documents.

124 The more so since these negotiations were conducted by the Resident at Aden and not, as one might have expected, by the Boundary Commissioners then on the borders of Upper Yafi'i. This led to a most acrimonious correspondence between the Resident and the Commissioners, for the Resident withheld the London instructions to move into

Yafi'i country until he had completed his personal negotiations with the Yafi'i leaders. See F.O.C.P. 8399, No. 62, Wahab to Govt. of India (26 June, 1903), No. 86, S.S. to Resident (21 July, 1903), No. 102, Wahab to Govt. of India (10 July 1903) and No. 187, Maitland to Govt. of Bombay (10 July 1903). The role of Lahej can be perceived in Maitland's remark in the last mentioned despatch 'the Commission have never understood the Yafi'i or how to deal with them . . . the Residency has better sources of information and greater experience in dealing with the tribes'. See also ibid., F.O.C.P. 8377, No. 117, Aden Resident to Govt. of India (26 April 1903). Information, including private minutes by Assistant Residents, leaked from the Aden Secretariat to Lahej. See Aden Records, 30/30/1/270, p. 491.

125 A.S.L. 32 (23 March 1901), Lahej reported Turkish intrigues in the north-east to the Aden Residency. A.R., A4A, Vol. II, p. 189. Note on interview between Resident and 'Abdali Sultan (14 February 1903). F.O.C.P. 8561, Mason to Govt. of India (13 May 1905) enclosed in No. 13. A.S.L. 128 (22 November 1902) enclosing Wahab's diary (14–19 November 1902).

126 I.O. Pol. and Secret Library, F.O.C.P. 8399, No. 62, enclosing Wahab to Govt. of India (26 June 1903). Some of the lesser Yafi'i potentates had made earlier offers to sign treaties. See A.S.L. 92 (10 August 1902), 93 (18 August 1902) and 104 (27 September 1902).

127 A.S.L. (1903). Minute by Lee Warner (12 January 1903) countersigned by five other members of Indian Council. Memoranda by Sir W. Lee Warner and Sir D. Fitzpatrick (19 and 20 January 1903) on Resident's telegram (15 January 1903). I.O. MSS. Eur. F. 123/67, Memorandum by Fitzpatrick (28 January 1903); for the Prime Minister's and Foreign Secretary's attitude, see I.O. MSS. Eur. F. 111/162, Hamilton to Curzon (14 January 1903), and Curzon to Hamilton, (14 May 1903). I.O. Records Home Correspondence, F.O. to I.O. (25 August 1902).

128 I.O. MSS. Eur. F. 111/162, Curzon to Hamilton (14 May 1903). The London Government, that is the Prime Minister and the Foreign Secretary, authorised treaties of friendship solely in order to allow the Boundary Commission access to Yafi'i territory and provided that all other means of effecting this had failed. F.O.C.P. 8377, No. 42. Secretary of State to Govt. of India (9 January 1903). Maitland the Resident contended that delimitation would be impossible without them, ibid., F.O.C.P., 8378, No. 91. Aden Resident to Govt. of India, 18 April 1903, but this was not the opinion of the Commissioners themselves and was at variance with the conclusions of a discussion held between Resident and Commissioners at Dali' on 22 March. F.O.C.P., 8399, No. 62, Wahab to Govt. of India (26 June 1903). The Resident's conduct on this occasion led to the violent quarrel between him and the Commissioners mentioned above.

129 F.O.C.P. 8377, No. 124, I.O. to F.O. (28 April 1903); F.O.C.P. 8399, No. 202, enclosing Govt. of India to Aden Resident (23 August 1903).

130 G. W. Bury, *The Land of Uz*, pp. 28ff., contains a good account of Yafi'i negotiations. See also correspondence F.O.C.P. 8399 and 8400, the full summary of the negotiations is in F.O.C.P. 8400, No. 13, enclosure 1, Maitland to Govt. of Bombay (2 August 1903). Texts in Hunter, op. cit., pp. 207–21.

131 R. Bidwell, *The Affairs of Arabia 1905–1906* (London, 1971), Vol. I, Part 1 p. 86, Lansdowne to Townley (7 February 1905); ibid., Part 2, p. 7, F.O. to Admiralty (3 March 1905); p. 20 Fitzmaurice to O'Conor (12 March 1905), p. 21, O'Conor to Lansdowne (14 March 1905), p. 34, O'Conor to Lansdowne (14 March 1905) and enclosures.

132 Bidwell, op. cit., Part 3, p. 115, Lansdowne to O'Conor (3 May 1905); ibid., p. 64, Fitzmaurice to Govt. of India (30 April 1905) enclosing text of *procès-verbal* (20 April 1905) and final report; Part 6, p. 23, O'Conor to Grey (7 February 1906), p. 51, I.O. to F.O. (28 February 1906).

CHAPTER IX

1 *Hansard*, 4th Series, Vol. 120, Col. 548, Lansdowne's reply to question by Lord Reay (30 March 1903).

2 F.O.C.P. 8399, July–December 1903. Aden Resident to Govt. of India (27 and 28 May 1903) and report by Col. Warneford.

3 I.O. Pol. and Secret Memoranda E.82, Field Notes on the Aden Protectorate, 1917.

4 Text in Hunter and Sealey, *Arab Tribes in the Vicinity of Aden* (1909 ed.), pp. 222–3.

5 F.O.C.P. 8984, I.O. to F.O. (11 October 1906), enclosing Govt. of Bombay to Govt. of India (13 July 1906), summarises much of the discussion.

6 Cf. Hunter and Sealey, *Arab Tribes in the Vicinity of Aden* (1886 and 1909 eds.).

7 The following figures give an indication of the growth of business in the Secretariat:

Year	Letters Inward	Letters Outward
1886	1,153	3,382
1896	1,571	4,649
1904	3,384	5,645
1905	5,750	5,844

In 1904 the work of the Secretariat was departmentalised into four branches – General, Confidential, Arabia and Registration. In the same year the system of drafting office minutes was taken over by the office from the Resident and his Assistants, the systematic registration of correspondence was begun and the office records were overhauled and indexed. In 1905 a new First Assistant Resident extended this work of reorganisation and the amount of business substantially increased. In 1906 an administrative expert was called in from Bombay to enquire into office arrangements and as a result of his work there was a substantial increase in the office establishment. The tendency to elaboration and expansion continued until 1914 when another expert from India, Curtis, did for the office what Morley had done for the emerging Protectorate in 1907; thereafter administrative expansion was checked and indeed reversed. (Aden Records File 30/30/I, pp. 260, 263, 267 and 269, 30/30/II, 521ff. and 470–88.) The Arabic Office became a branch of the Secretariat Office on Jaffer's destitution in 1900. In 1904 it was fully incorporated into the Office and brought under the Office Superintendent, to the annoyance of the Sultan of Lahej and the Arab clerks.

8 Cf. Sir G. Arthur, *Life and Letters of Lord Kitchener* (London, 1920), Vol. II, pp. 261–2.

9 I.O. MSS. Eur. B. 159, Reel 675, Lamington to S.S. (18 February 1903, 8 April 1905), Lamington to Viceroy (11 April 1905).

10 C.O. M(iddle) E(ast) C(onfidential) P(rint) 52 Reilly to S.S.C. (19 September 1934) on college for sons of chiefs. I.O. MSS. Eur. B. 159/2, Lamington to S.S. (11 April 1907); I.O. Pol. Secret Memoranda B. 216, Memorandum by Jacob on hinterland policy (9 September 1915).

11 Lamington Papers, I.O. MSS. Eur. B. 159, Reel 675, Lamington to S.S. (12 January 1906).

12 Cf. Lord Northbrook's Confidential Memorandum (9 April 1903), Cab. 1/4, 332. This was criticised as untimely however, by both Hamilton and Curzon. I.O. MSS. Eur. F. 111/62, Hamilton to Curzon (15 May 1903), Curzon to Hamilton (4 June 1903).

13 I.O. MSS. Eur. F. 111/162, Curzon to Hamilton (4 June 1903).

14 Cf. Correspondence in I.O. MSS. Eur. F. 123/72 and I.O. MSS. Eur. F. 111/162, Hamilton to Curzon (3 June 1903, 23 July, 30 July and 20 August 1903). For conflicts between Curzon and the Home Government see Ronaldshay, *Lord Curzon of Kedleston*, Vol. II, pp. 238ff. and *passim*.

15 I.O. MSS. Eur. F. 111/162, Hamilton to Curzon (5 February, 13 February and 15 May 1903).

16 Ronaldshay, op. cit., Vol. II, p. 238; I.O. MSS. Eur. F. 111/162, Godley to Curzon (21 January 1903), Hamilton to Curzon (23 January 1903).

17 I.O. Home Correspondence, Memorandum by Lee Warner on F.O. to I.O. (5 November 1902).

18 Cf. I.O. MSS. Eur. F. 123/67, Memorandum by Sir D. Fitzpatrick for Lord George Hamilton (28 January 1903).

19 For the Resident versus Commissioners dispute, see F.O.C.P. No. 8399, especially no. 62, Warner to Govt. of India (26 June 1903), and no. 86 enclosure 2, S.S. to Aden Resident (21 July 1903).

20 Lord Morley, *Recollections* (London, 1917); M. N. Das, *India under Morley and Minto* (London, 1964). S. R. Wasti, *Lord Minto and the Indian Nationalist Movement* (Oxford, 1964), however, credits Minto with the initiative.

21 *Hansard*, 4th Series, Vol. 120, cols, 544–8, Vol. 124, col. 791, Vol. 130, col. 552, Vol. 131, col. 853, Vol. 136, col. 17, Vol. 149, cols. 229ff.

Some of the questions asked were evidently inspired by dissident officials.

22 See G. Monger, *The End of Isolation* (London, 1963).
23 See A. J. Marder, *From the Dreadnought to Scapa Flow* (London, 1961), Vol. I, Chapter III.
24 Lord Morley, op. cit. p. 169.
25 I.O. MSS. Eur. B.159, Godley to Lamington (6 April 1906).
26 Cf. Sir H. Barnes's criticism of Lee Warner's activities in I.O. Pol. and Secret Memoranda B. 158, notes by Lee Warner and Barnes on Aden policy; I.O. MSS. Eur. B. 159/3, Morley to Lamington (12 April, 1906, 4 May 1906); I.O. Records Home Miscellaneous 864, Diary of F. A. Huntzell, P.S. to Lord Morley (18 December 1906).
27 Bidwell, op. cit., Part 7, p. 26, Morley to Govt. of India (4 May 1906).
28 I.O. MSS. Eur. B. 159/1, Godley to Lamington (6 April 1906); ibid., Reel 675, Lamington to Viceroy (29 January 1906); I.O. MSS. Eur. B. 159/3, Morley to Lamington (16 February 1906); I.O. MSS. Eur. D. 573/1, Morley to Minto (23 March and 3 May 1906).
29 F.O.C.P. 8984, Viceroy in Council to S.S. (9 August 1906) in I.O. to F.O. (11 October 1906).
30 I.O. MSS. Eur. B. 159, Reel 675, Lamington to Viceroy (2 May 1906); cf. discussion of policy in R. Ritchie, Relations of the British Government with the tribes of the Aden Hinterland (19 March 1906), I.O. Pol. and Secret Memoranda B. 155.
31 I.O. MSS. Eur. B. 159, Reel 675, Lamington to S.S. (7 March 1906); cf. Bidwell, op. cit., Part 2, pp. 98–108, I.O. to F.O. (18 April 1905) and enclosures. The Bombay Government rejected the local political officer's criticism of the 'Amir of Dali''s weakness on the grounds that the government had a 'treaty with the 'Amir who is the *de facto* head of his tribesmen, subjects and dependencies', p. 104, Govt. of Bombay to Aden Resident (25 November 1904). The whole matter is discussed fully in I.O. Pol. and Secret Memoranda B. 155. Memorandum by Ritchie, Relations of British Government with the tribes in the Aden Hinterland (19 March 1906).
32 G. Arthur op. cit., Vol. II, p. 262.
33 I.O. MSS. Eur. D. 573/1, Morley Papers, Morley to Minto (29 June 1906). For the Akaba crisis, see G. Monger, *The End of Isolation*, pp. 296–7 and Lord Lloyd, *Egypt since Cromer*, Vol. I, pp. 41–5.
34 F.O.C.P. 8984, S.S. to Govt. of India (5 October 1906).
35 F.O.C.P. 8984, S.S. to Govt. of India (3 October 1906). I.O. MSS. Eur. B. 159/1, Reel 675, Lamington to Viceroy (9 October 1906). F.O.C.P. 9050, Govt. of India to S.S. (16 January 1907).
36 Bidwell, op cit., Part 6, pp. 43–51, Mason to Govt. of Bombay (19 November 1905) and enclosures. F.O.C.P. 8984, Govt. of India to S.S. (9 August 1906) in I.O. to F.O. (11 October 1906). F.O.C.P. 9305, Govt. of Bombay to Govt. of India (3 July 1907), S.S. to Govt. of India (27 September 1907) in I.O. to F.O. (30 September 1907).
37 F.O.C.P. 9305, S.S. to Govt. of India (25 July 1907), in I.O. to F.O. (27 July 1907), I.O. Pol. and Secret Records, Reg. No. 1951, monthly summary (September 1907).

38 For Jacob's career see I.O. Lists, 1913 and 1921.

39 H. F. Jacob, *Kings of Arabia*, p. 88; I.O. MSS. Eur. B. 159/2, Lamington Papers, Reel 675. Lamington to S.S. (7 March and 2 May 1906).

40 A.R., FıA, Vol. 430, p. 573, Memorandum by Jacob (21 January 1906). I.O. Pol. and Secret Memoranda B.216, Memorandum by Jacob on political policy in Aden hinterland (9 September 1915). The bracketed insertion is Jacob's.

41 In particular he took the 'Abdali's side in his 1905 dispute with the Hawshabi Sultan who was trying to assert his independence of Lahej. Aden Records, A4A, Vol. 20, report by Jacob on differences between 'Abdali and Hawshabi (24 July 1905), Jacob to Hancock and Hancock to Jacob (20 November 1905). Memorandum by Jacob on 'Amiri relations with the 'Abdali and Hawshabi (18 January 1906), printed in Bidwell, op. cit., Part 6, pp. 83–6. G. Wyman Bury in *Panislam* (1919) levelled some scathing criticisms at this policy.

42 H. F. Jacob, *Kings of Arabia*, pp. 88–9; I.O. Pol. and Secret Records, Monthly Memoranda from Aden (March and April 1908). cf. F.O.C.P. 8767, I.O. to F.O. (24 May 1906) enclosing Mason to Govt. of Bombay (28 October 1905) and Ahmad Fadl to Mason (29 January 1906).

43 For example in 'Awlaqi country, through the Al Jifri family.

44 Jacob, op. cit., p. 85; A.R., FıA, Vol. 430, p. 563, Memorandum by Jacob (21 January 1906); C.O. M.E.C.P., No. 8, report by Colonel M. C. Lake on Upper and Lower Yafi'i (8 January 1926).

45 I.P.S.L. 71 (25 May 1897) and enclosures.

46 Lamington Papers, Reel 675, Lamington to Viceroy (6 November and 2 November 1904 and 26 May 1906). I.O. Records L/P and S/10/33. Govt. of India to I.O. (2 January 1908), enclosing Govt. of Bombay to Govt. of India (5 March 1906); ibid., Memorandum by Hancock (3 June 1907); L/P and S/10/34, Minute on Reg. no. 3845. I.O. MSS. Eur. F. 111/530, Summary of Principal Events, etc., Vol. III.

47 I.O. Pol. and Secret Records, Monthly Memoranda, Aden (March 1908, July and August 1909).

48 I.O. Pol. and Secret Records, Monthly Memorandum, Aden (July 1908).

49 F.O.C.P. 8984; Govt. of Bombay to Govt. of India (13 July 1906) in I.O. to F.O. (11 October 1906). I.O. Pol. and Secret Records, Monthly Memoranda (1908, 1909, 1910). In February 1910 the 'Abdali Sultan said that he would no longer report the many outrages. In March 1910 plundering spread to the outskirts of Shaykh 'Uthman.

50 I.O. Pol. and Secret Records, Monthly Memoranda, Aden (1908).

51 I.O. Pol and Secret Records, Monthly Memoranda, Aden (December 1908, January, February and July 1909; June, August, October 1910; June 1911).

52 I.O. Pol and Secret Records, Monthly Memoranda from Aden (April, May, July, August, September and October 1908).

53 A.S.L., Resident to Govt. of Bombay, C42 (2 February 1908), I.O. Pol. and Secret Records, Aden, Monthly Memoranda (April and June 1908). I.O. Pol. and Secret Records, Monthly Memoranda from Aden

(March 1911). The naval patrol was partially effective, see H. de Monfried, *Pearls, Arms and Hashish*, p. 153.

54 C. Issawi, *Egypt in Revolution* (Oxford, 1963), Chapter II.

55 B. Lewis, *The Emergence of Modern Turkey* (Oxford, 1963), Chapter VI. Z. Y. Hershlag, *The Modern Economic History of the Middle East* (Leiden, 1964), Part 3.

56 Lewis, op. cit., pp. 197ff. and 209.

57 Cf. the Imam of Yemen's objections to the Turks' lack of religion, to rule by Kurds and Ethiopians, to the enhanced consideration given to Christians and Jews, and to the officials having 'insulted and degraded the noble, until posterity was corrupted'. Bidwell, op. cit., Part 5, pp. 47–50. Drummond Hay to O'Conor (20 October 1905) enclosing Muhammad Yahya Hamad ad din to Muhammad Effendi al Harin. This letter nevertheless professed loyalty to the person of the Sultan-Caliph, its main stress was on Ottoman neglect of the decendants of the Prophet – i.e. the Sayyids.

58 F.O.C.P. 8548, Maxwell to O'Conor (22 April 1905), O'Conor to Lansdowne (28 April 1905); I.O. Pol. and Secret Corresp., Reg. No. 3307, I.O. to F.O. (20 July 1906), enclosing O'Conor to Grey (1 July 1906); E. Jung, *La revolte arable* (Paris, 1906), p. 15.

59 I.O. Pol. and Secret Corresp., Reg. No. 3565, report by Richardson on the Yemen (1 November 1905, 30 June 1906) in O'Conor to Grey (21 August 1906). British Naval Intelligence Handbook: *Western Arabia and the Red Sea*, 1945 ed., pp. 287–8.

60 Cf. I.O. Home Corresp., F.O. to I.O. (21 April and 3 May 1893) and enclosures. Aden Secret Letter 10 (17 January 1900) quoting *Overland Mail* report 29 September 1899). In July 1902 a mission offered the Imam a measure of recognition in return for his aid against the British. Aden Secret Letter 95 (3 September 1902). I.O. Pol. and Secret Records, Reg. No. 2803, F.O. to I.O. (5 November 1902) enclosing memorandum by Weakley (18 September 1902); Reg. No. 2833, F.O. to I.O. (7 April 1905) and enclosure; Reg. No. 2857, F.O. to I.O. (14 April 1905) and enclosures, Reg. No. 3308 (25 August 1905) and enclosures, especially report by Richardson (15 July 1905); Bidwell, op. cit., Part 8, pp. 4–5, Surtees to O'Conor (1 July 1906); Reg. No. 3567, F.O. to I.O. (24 August 1906) enclosing report by Richardson (30 June 1906); Reg. No. 1951, Aden Monthly Memorandum (September 1907); C.O. 725/4 Jacob to Col. Office (22 June 1922) enclosing Jacob to Allenby (16 February 1920), report on his mission to the Yemen.

61 Cf. H. Saab, *The Arab Federalists of the Ottoman Empire* (Amsterdam, 1958), p. 192.

62 Cf. E. Jung, *La revolte arabe*, p. 23.

63 I.O. Pol. and Secret Records, Reg. No. 1951, Aden Monthly Memoranda (A.M.M.), September 1907. The Yemen losses were one of the main grievances of the Turkish army against 'Abd al Hamid's regime, cf. E. E. Ramsaur, *The Young Turks* (Princeton, 1957), p. 119, n. 65.

64 I.O. Records, A.M.M. (February 1909).

65 I.O. Records, A.M.M. (1909), Lewis, op. cit., pp. 214–15. Z. N. Zeine,

Arab–Turkish Relations and the Emergence of Arab Nationalism, pp. 78–80. Cf. H. Saab, op. cit., pp. 217–22. The agreement was rejected by the Turkish Parliament and did not come into force until 1912 when the Chamber was dissolved. It was sanctioned in 1913, when the Committee of Union and Progress turned back toward Sabah al din's programme of decentralisation, and Turco-Arab relations began to improve. C. Ansaldi, *Il Yemen nella storia e nella legenda*, p. 168; M. Khadduri, 'Aziz Ali Misri and the Arab Nationalist Movement', *St. Antony's Papaers*, No. 17, Oxford 1965, F.O.C.P. 10376, Lowther to Grey (21 April 1913).

66 I.O. MSS. Eur. F. 111/530, Summary of Principal Events, etc., Vol. 3; F.O.C.P. 8548, O'Conor to Lansdowne (4 April 1905); I.O. Pol. and Secret Records, Reg. No. 2833, F.O. to I.O. (7 April 1905) and enclosures.

67 I.O. Home Corresp., F.O. to I.O. (5 November 1902) enclosing O'Conor to Lansdowne (21 October 1902), Memorandum by Lee Warner. Minutes by Sir J. Westland and Sir A. C. Lyall of Indian Council. Further note by Lee Warner for Indian Council and Minutes by Sir A. Godley, Sir A. C. Lyall and Sir D. Fitzpatrick. Lee Warner made the same point at the inter-departmental conference on Aden Demarcation on 6 August 1902 – P. and S. Records, Reg. No. 2803. This somewhat modifies the otherwise acceptable impression of the general British attitude to the Ottoman Empire during the twentieth century conveyed in the article by A. Cunningham 'The Wrong Horse – A Study of Anglo-Turkish relations before the First World War', in *St. Antony's Papers*, No. 17, Oxford, 1965. Cunningham tends to stress the Eurasian at the expense of the Arabian content of the bundle of British interests in the Ottoman Empire.

68 I.O. Records, Home Corresp. Reg. No. 2781, Minute by Lee Warner on F.O. to I.O. (27 February 1905), and on F.O. to I.O. (1 April 1905). A message from the Imam to the King in the autumn of 1905 was left unanswered. Lord Cromer advised quiescence at Aden to avoid suspicions that Britain intended to move upon the Holy Places, Morley Papers: Morley to Minto (27 July 1906), Morley to Kitchener (23 August 1906), quoted in Arthur, op. cit., Vol. II, p. 261.

69 F.O.C.P. 9305, Secretary of State to Govt. of India (25 July 1907), in I.O. to F.O. (27 July 1907); S.S. to Govt. of India, (1 August 1907), in I.O. to F.O. (12 August 1907); Govt. of India to Secretary of State (28 August 1907) and S.S. to Govt. of India (29 August 1907), in I.O. to F.O. (2 September 1907).

70 Cf. the Govt. of India's attitude to rumours of Italy's intention to establish a Protectorate over the Yemen. I.O. Pol. and Secret Records, Aden Monthly Memoranda (February 1912). Turkish activity in the Persian Gulf, especially in connection with the Baghdad Railway scheme was however regarded in a somewhat different light. See B. C. Busch, *Britain and the Persian Gulf 1894–1914*, (Berkeley and Los Angeles, 1967), Ch. X.

71 F.O.C.P. 10401, Govt. of India to S.S. (4 September 1913), in I.O.

to F.O. (8 September 1913). Text in *British Documents on the Origins of the War*, Vol. X, Part 2, p. 340.

72 H. F. Jacob, *Kings of Arabia*, p. 87.

73 I.O. Pol. and Secret Memoranda B. 216. Memorandum by Jacob on hinterland policy (9 September 1915). It is very likely that the 1905 agreement with the Imam had some bearing upon the then current dispute between the 'Abdali and the Hawshabi. Sultan Ahmad Fadl mentioned to Jacob the receipt of letters from the Imam (A.R., A4A, Vol. XX, Ahmad Fadl to Jacob [2 July 1905]). These letters may well have contained the secret treaty of which Jacob only heard in 1915. H. F. Jacob, op. cit., p. 91, denied the Turkish allegations that Lahej sent arms, but admitted that the 'Abdali smuggled a minting machine to the Imam, p. 105. Ahmad Fadl acted as a mediator between the Turks and the Imam in 1911 (Jacob, op. cit., p. 103) and as a channel of communication between the Italians and the Imam, F.O.C.P. 10401, Lowther to Grey (1 August 1913). In 1908 Imamic emissaries were collecting subscriptions for rebel funds at Aden and Lahej, I.O. Records, A.M.M., June 1908.

74 Jacob, op. cit., pp. 102 and 112. I.O. Pol. and Secret Memoranda, B. 231; Memoranda by Jacob in G.O.C. Aden to Govt. of India (13 May 1916).

75 In April 1909 the Resident interviewed and gave a non-committal reply to one of the Imam's emissaries, who had asked for arms and ammunition against the Turks, because it was feared that if no reply were given the Imam would make reprisals against Bayhan. I.O. Records, A.M.M. (March, April and May 1909).

76 I.O. Pol. and Secret Records, A.M.M. (February 1912).

77 The 'Amirs of Dali' had been in touch with the Imams at least since 1902 if not before, see A.R., A1A, Vol. C29, pp. 21–3.

78 I.O. Pol. and Secret Subject File, 137/1904, Parts I and II, Aden Protectorate, especially Reg. No. 2746, Govt. of Bombay to Govt. of India (17 May 1912); Reg. No. 2711, Aden Resident to Govt. of Bombay (23 May 1914).

79 Cf. E. Macro, *Yemen and the Western World* (London, 1968), p. 40.

80 Pan Islamic sentiment had been strong in the Yemen during the Italo-Turkish war of 1911–12.

81 I.O. Pol. and Secret Memoranda B.227, Brig.-Gen. Walton to Govt. of Bombay (14 March, 1916) enclosing report by Jacob, 'The Present Situation in our Hinterland and beyond the Border' (10 March 1916).

82 For this incident see Macro, op. cit., p. 40; I.O. Pol. and Secret Memoranda B. 231, G.O.C. Aden to Govt. of India (13 May 1916) enclosing memorandum by Jacob.

83 M. Khadduri, 'Aziz 'Ali Misri and the Arab Nationalist Movement, *St. Antony's Papers*, No. 17 (Oxford, 1965).

84 Macro, op. cit., pp. 48–9.

85 M.E.C.P. 22, Memorandum on Kamaran Island (15 July 1927).

86 C.O. 13698 Aden Res. to Secretary of State (21 March 1922) enclosing Memorandum on relations with Sayyid 'Idris.

87 I.O. Pol. and Secret Memoranda, No. 296, Memorandum on British commitments to the Shaykh of Mawiyah. Ibid., No. 231, enclosure 1, note by Colonel Wauhope (Wahab) R.E. on boundary of Aden Protectorate.

88 I.O. Pol. and Secret Memoranda B.216, Memorandum by Jacob on policy in the hinterland (19 September 1915). Ibid., B.264, notes on the political situation in the Aden hinterland, 27 August, 1917. G. W. Bury, *Panislam* (London, 1919), p. 42. Bury believed that over-reliance on 'Abdali diplomacy was one of the main reasons for the defeat.

89 P.R.O. Cab. 37/131/99, G.O.C. Aden to C.G.S. India (7 July, 1915) and Political Resident Aden to C.G.S. India (8 July 1915), Jacob, *Kings of Arabia*, p. 65.

90 P.R.O. Cab. 37/131/16 and 17, Viceroy to General Younghusband (14 July 1915), Memorandum of Cabinet discussion (15 July 1915).

91 P.R.O. Cab. 37/131/22, Younghusband to C.G.S. (16 July 1915).

92 P.R.O. Cab. 37/131/32 and 38, G.O.C. Aden to C.G.S. (21 and 22 July 1915).

93 *The Times* (5 July 1916), p. 7; (2 August 1918), p. 6. P.R.O. Cab. 24/26/G.J. 2072, Memorandum by G.I.G.S. (19 March 1917).

94 Aden Landward trade (£'000):

Year	Imports	Exports	Year	Imports	Exports	Year	Imports	Exports
1903/4	212	79	1909/10	170	110	1915/16	107	50
1904/5	198	100	1910/11	186	124	1916/17	132	7
1905/6	181	103	1911/12	231	162	1917/18	128	1
1906/7	149	91	1912/13	239	185	1918/19	105	16
1907/8	165	99	1913/14	173	149	1919/20	295	125
1908/9	157	94	1914/15	137	120	1920/21	171	198

Source: C.O. 725/4

95 See A.A.R. (1914–21).

96 Aden Chamber of Commerce Report, 1921, Appendix, Secretary of Chamber of Commerce to Secretary of Port Trust (21 October 1916); estimates of average wage rates in A.A.R. (1914–21). The labour shortage continued until 1922.

CHAPTER X

1 The populace of Aden acclaimed the Turkish Commander when he came in to surrender at the close of hostilities. *Journal of the Royal Central Asian Society* (Vol. X, 1923), p. 149.

2 Sir J. S. Corbett and Sir H. Newbolt, *Naval Operations* (*History of the Great War based on official documents* (London, 1920–31), Vol. II., p. 280.

3 Cf. *J.R.U.S.I.*, Vol. LXVII, p. 259.

4 *Documents on British Foreign Policy*, 1st Series, Vol. IV, No. 405, notes of Anglo-French meeting (23 December 1919); ibid., Vol. XIII, No. 267, Vansittart to Young (21 June 1920).

5 I.O. Pol. and Sec. Memoranda B. 621. Foreign Office Peace Conference Memoranda; Cab. 24/72, Imperial War Cabinet Resolution (20

December 1918); *Documents on British Foreign Policy*, 1st Series, Vol.
VIII, No. 250, Memorandum on future control of the Middle East
(17 May 1920). The pre-Conference policy was not to bring the
Arabian Peninsula within the scope of the conference at all, to avoid
even the minor trammels of a mandate. During the conference, Allenby
in Egypt began to plead for a mandate to facilitate negotiations with
the Yemen, but fear of Italian demands for a *quid pro quo* and the force of
inertia resulted in the persistence of the more ambiguous original policy.
See correspondence in F.O. 371/4212, collection 36308.

6 Cf. I.O. Pol. and Sec. Memoranda B. 621, F.O. to Sir R. Wingate
(4 February 1918) and ibid., B. 367, F.O. to Allenby (24 May 1919)
'Documents on British Foreign Policy', 1st Series, Vol. IV, No. 253,
Allenby to F.O. (28 May 1920).

7 Cf. *J.R.U.S.I.* (Vol. LXXII, 1927), pp. 644 ff., on the operation of the
arms convention.

8 C.O. M.E.C.P. 22, p. 57, Symes to S.S. for Colonies (9 December 1929).

9 Sir F. B. Maurice, *The Life of Lord Rawlinson* (London, 1928), pp. 284–5.

10 See above, Chapter VIII, n. 114, and Chapter VII, p. 182.

11 Cab. 24/26, G.T. 1643, Extract from 7th meeting of the Mesopotamia
Administration Committee (21 July 1917).

12 *The Times* (27 March 1922), p. 6.

13 C.O. 725/4, Report by Meinertzhagen on cost of Aden garrison and the
Govt. of India's offer (15 June 1922).

14 *Hansard*, Vol. 130, col. 1378, and Vol. 136, col. 572, Ormsby Gore's
questions (21 June and 15 December 1920); C.O. 725/4, Cabinet
Paper by Duke of Devonshire (December 1922). See A. S. Klieman,
The Foundations of British Policy in the Arab World (Baltimore, 1970),
p. 88.

15 *Hansard*, Vol. 138, col. 1409, Lloyd George's statement (28 February
1921) and ibid., col. 2009, Lloyd George's reply to Glyn (3 March 1921).

16 *Hansard*, Vol. 156, cols. 1143 and 1152. *Proceedings of Bombay Legislative
Council* (26 March 1927).

17 *Journal of East India Association* (1941), p. 75. Sir Tom Hickinbotham,
Aden (London, 1958), p. 23. The tale of Bombay's neglect of Aden is
taken up in most of the books published about the town written since
the Second World War.

18 Cf. the prejudiced, but on this point not inaccurate, account by W. G.
King in *Indian Empire Review* (Vol. IV, 1935), p. 107.

19 *The Times* (27 March 1922), p. 6.

20 M.E.C.P. 22, p. 57, Symes to S.S.C. (9 December 1929).

21 Hickinbotham, op. cit., pp. 22–4, indicates how British officials encouraged the growth of self-conscious, anti-Indian sentiment among
the Arabs in Aden at this stage.

22 'Report on the Indian Constitutional Reform Committee', Vol. III,
p. 149, Record IX, memorandum by Sir Pheroze Sethna. The military
and political administration of Aden was transferred to the C.O. in 1927,
leaving control of civil affairs in the settlement under Bombay.

23 Ibid., memorandum by S.S.I. (20 November 1933); draft instructions

to the Governor and C.-in-C. of the Colony of Aden, H.M.S.O., Cmd. 5227 (1936).

24 E.g. the Fadli Sultan, who accepted a Turkish stipend during the war, although their forces never reached his territory.

25 F.O. 406/42, Aden Resident to Foreign Office (3 January 1919) enclosing Aden Newsletter (A.N.) (November and December 1918).

26 F.O. 406/42, A.N. (31 March 1919).

27 F.O. 406/42, A.N. (November and December 1918 and January 1919). In 1922 300 Lahej troops enforced the election of Muhsin bin 'Ali Mana as Hawshabi Sultan. C.O. Reg. No. 46815, A.N. (5 September 1922).

28 H. F. Jacob, *Kings of Arabia*, pp. 270–1 and 275; I.O. Pol. and Secret Memoranda B. 231, Memorandum by Jacob enclosed in G.O.C. Aden to Secretary to the Govt. of India (13 May 1916).

29 Jacob in a memorandum on the Yemen written in 1930 cited the view of Sir Mark Sykes, put forward in 1915, that the whole Protectorate should be ceded to the Imam leaving a small buffer state or cordon round Aden (M.E.C.P. 34). In a despatch to the Secretary to the Government of India (13 May 1916), the G.O.C., Aden, said bluntly that he did not see why Dhali' had ever been taken. (I.O. Pol. and Secret Memoranda B. 231). The same opinion was expressed by Col. Wauhope (Wahab) who had commanded the 1902–4 Boundary Commission in a 1916 note on the boundary of the Aden Protectorate (ibid.).

30 I.O. Pol. and Secret Memoranda B. 231, G.O.C. Aden to Secretary to Govt. of India (13 May 1916) enclosing Memorandum by Jacob; F.O. 406/40, Memorandum on certain conditions for a settlement in Western Asia by D. G. Hogarth, Arab Bureau, Cairo (20 November 1918).

31 Jacob, op. cit., p. 243.

32 The alternatives were spelt out in a memorandum by H. Young on a draft treaty with the Imam (14 May 1919), F.O. 371/4212, Reg No. 36308/76578.

33 F.O. 406/42, A.N. (31 March 1919); see also C.O. 725/4 for Jacob's criticism of the Resident's action (22 June 1922).

34 F.O. 371/4212, Reg. No. 36308/76653, Curzon to Balfour (31 May 1919); ibid., 75276, Rennel Rodd to Curzon (9 May 1919) and minutes; 74580, Balfour to Curzon (19 May 1919).

35 F.O. 371/4212, Reg. No. 36308/65064, memorandum by Jacob.

36 Ibid., 92981, minute of interview with General Stewart (23 June 1919).

37 F.O. 406/42, Aden Newsletters (January and March 1919).

38 F.O. 371/3416, Reg. No. 191505, D(irector) of M(ilitary) I(ntelligence) to Balfour (19 November 1918).

39 Ibid., 206674, Rear-Admiral, Egypt, to Admiralty (15 December 1918).

40 F.O. 406/42, Aden Newsletter (January 1919).

41 F.O. 371/4212, Reg. No. 36308/53210, D.M.I. to Foreign Office (4 April 1919); ibid., 40937, Milne Cheetham to Curzon (11 March 1919);

50317, Allenby to Curzon (12 April 1919); 65064, Jacob's memorandum 73188, War Office to G.O.C., Aden (12 May 1919).

42 F.O. 371/4212, Reg. No. 36308/102388, minute by H. Young (15 July 1919). Various suggestions about the occupation of Salif, opposite the island of Kamaran, then in British hands, circulated in Aden and Cairo, but were not sanctioned by London.

43 Ibid., Reg. No. 36308, minute by Young (7 March 1919), 55445, Allenby to Curzon (7 April 1919), 75632, Curzon to Allenby (24 May 1919); see 78462 for an outburst by Young against Sayyid Idris (26 May 1919).

44 F.O. 371/4212, Reg. Nos. 36308, 65604, 76508 and 98000, memoranda by Jacob on future of the Yemen (April 1919), by Young on Jacob's draft treaty (14 May 1919), by Jacob on Young's comments, 19 June 1919, and minute by Young.

45 Ibid., No. 75633, Eyre Crowe to Curzon, (17 May 1919) and minutes; 75632, Curzon to Allenby (24 May 1919); 79665 Curzon to Allenby (30 May 1919) and minutes.

46 C.O. 725/4, Jacob to S.S.C. (22 June 1922) enclosing his report to Allenby on his mission, (16 February 1920) and marginal note on this; C.O. file no. 46003/25, minutes by Young and Shuckburgh on Resident to Secretary of State (30 September 1925); Jacob, op. cit., p. 53.

47 F.O. 406/41, Cheetham to Curzon (22 September and 27 October 1919).

48 F.O. 406/44, Curzon to Aden Resident (13 December 1920). Hudayda was handed over to a local committee which accepted Idrisi rule immediately after the British departure. C.O. Reg. No. 10410, A.N. (17 February 1921).

49 F.O. 406/42, A.N. (November and December 1918 and January 1919).

50 C.O. Reg. No. 57193, Resident to S.S.C. (9 December 1925).

51 M.E.C.P. 22, p. 168, note on the Lahej Railway.

52 F.O.406/43,Resident to High Commissioner, Cairo (7, 15, and 23 April 1920). The Resident refused to negotiate with the Imam until the Protectorate was evacuated and sent Imamic emissaries back in April 1920. For famine in Radfan see C.O. 725/1, No. 23166, Resident to S.S. (27 April 1921) enclosing memorandum on Zaydi incursions into Radfan.

53 C.O. 725/1, No. 48116, Resident to S.S. (26 September 1921); No. 54073 Resident to S.S. (30 October 1921); C.O. 725/3, Nos. 6972 and 12022, A.N. (31 January and 28 February 1922).

54 C.O. 725/1, No. 37933, Resident to S.S. (15 July 1921); ibid., No. 48116, minute on Resident to S.S. (26 September 1921); C.O. 725/3, No. 18356, minute by Shuckburgh on Resident to S.S. (15 April 1922); F.O. 371/7707, No. 5475, C.O. to F.O. (27 May 1922); ibid., 6016, minutes of a meeting of the Middle Eastern Committee (2 June 1922).

55 C.O. 725/4, C.O. to War Office (20 June 1922), enclosing correspondence with the Resident and minute by Shuckburgh.

56 C.O. 725/4, Minutes of meeting of the Middle East Committee (28 July 1922) and Resident to Acting Resident (17 August 1922); details

of discussions between the Imam's representative, Qadi al Arashi, and Major Reilly in F.O. 371/7707, No. 7423.

57 See Sir T. W. Arnold *The Caliphate* (London, 1965), pp. 163-84 and 205 ff.; E. Kedourie, *The Chatham House Version* (London, 1970), Chapter VII. King Husayn tried to win the support of Lahej for his claim to Arab leadership. C.O. Reg. No. 23842, A.N. (30 April 1924).

58 C.O. 725/5, No. 4202, Resident to S.S. (2 August 1923) enclosing Imam's Manifesto (19 June 1923); ibid., No. 50511, A.N. (30 September 1923); the Imam had already written in 1922 to the rulers of the Hadhramawt claiming that region as his – F.O. 29733/22, Consul-General, Batavia, to F.O. (11 May 1922). But the 1923 initiative was more sophisticated and was backed up by military moves.

59 For an analysis of this conflict see A. S. Bujra, 'Political conflict and social stratification in the Hadhramawt', *Middle East Journal* (July and October 1967), Vol. III, No. 4, and Vol. IV 4, No. 1; additional information can be found in I.O. Pol. and Secret Records, Reg. No. 7616, Schrieke to Arnold (30 July 1920) and Lee Warner to S.S. for India 15 July 1920; H.K., 'La presse musulmane aux Indes Néerlandaises', *Revue du Monde Musulmane* (August 1921), p. 124.

60 I.O. Pol. and Secret Records 1740/1915, Appendix II to Eastern Report No. 39; F.O. to Allenby (4 June 1919) and to Milner (9 June 1919) ending embargo on Kathiri remittances; Lee Warner to F.O. (3 March 1919) enclosing report on the Hadhramawt. I.O. Pol. and Secret Records 7616/1920, Lee Warner to F.O. (15 July 1920) said that the British Consul-General in Batavia was responsible for Britain's wartime alignment with the Sayyid party.

61 Cf. copy of Irshad letter enclosed in Lee Warner to F.O. (15 July 1920). In 1924 Sayyid 'Abd al Rahman al Kaff gave up his farm of the Mukalla customs on behalf of the Sultan as a result of pressure from the Sayyid party. C.O. Reg. No. 22347, Resident to S.S. (30 April 1924).

62 In December 1920 the British Consul-General in Batavia informed the Irshad party that in future they would have no difficulty in securing passports. H.K., op. cit., *Revue du Monde Musulmane* (August 1921).

63 F.O. 29773/22, Consul-General, Batavia, to F.O. (11 May 1922).

64 F.O. 29773/22, notes by 'Ali bin Ahmad enclosed in Consul-General, Batavia, to F.O. (11 May 1922).

65 I.O. Pol. and Secret Records, Reg. No. 1740/1915, F.O. to I.O. (17 April 1919).

66 C.O. 725/6, No. 22347, Resident to S.S.C. (30 April 1924).

67 The treaty was signed after an abortive attempt by the Kathiri, in alliance with the Irshadi and the Humumi tribe, to break the Qu'ayti control of the coastline at Shihr, which was being used to prevent the Irshadi moving freely between the interior and the sea. I.O. Pol. and Secret Records 1740/1915, Consul-General, Batavia, to Balfour (12 January 1918); ibid., Lee Warner to F.O. (3 March 1919); text of treaty in D. Ingrams, *Survey of Social and Economic Conditions in the Aden Protectorate* (Asmara, 1949).

68 C.O. 725/5, No. 26526, Resident to S.S.C. (16 July 1923).

69 C.O. 725/6, No. 29804, Aden Newsletter (31 May 1924).

70 C.O. 725/5, No. 35494, Resident to S.S.C. (14 July 1923).

71 C.O. 725/5 and 6, Nos. 55868, 4331, and 5603, A.N. (6 November and 31 December 1923) and Resident to S.S.C. (23 January 1924).

72 C.O. 725/6, No. 1573, Resident to S.S. (22 December 1924), M.E.C.P. No. 8, report by Colonel M. C. Lake on Upper and Lower Yafi' (8 January 1926); a further vain attempt to unify Upper Yafi' was made in 1930 – A.R., A2B7, 592/113.

73 C.O. 725/7, No. 21274, Resident to S.S. (29 April 1924) enclosing details of arms issues 1920–5.

74 *Hansard*, Vol. 187, cols. 850 and 1181; J. C. Hurewitz, *Diplomacy in the Near and Middle East 1535–1956* (Princeton, 1956) Vol. II, pp. 146 and 177 – texts of treaties between the Yemen and Italy (2 September 1926) and the Soviet Union (1 November 1928).

75 C.O. 725/5, No. 43154, Resident to S.S. (29 August 1923).

76 C.O. 725/6, No. 38336, Acting Resident to S.S. (31 July 1924), enclosing Imam's draft treaty.

77 Cf. C.O. 725/1, No. 32475, his letters to Scott and Barrett (21 May 1921) in Resident to S.S. (30 June 1921). The first indicated that the Imam believed that Scott's predecessor, Stewart, had been a major obstacle to agreement. The second referred to the public notifications that Britain had no territorial ambitions in Arabia.

78 C.O. 725/6, No. 35767, Acting Resident to S.S. (17 July 1924) enclosing Imam's letter to the King (3 July 1924). A reply was sent to the Imam to indicate that the Resident and not Jacob was the man to negotiate with.

79 C.O. 725/7, No. 23893, A.N. (30 April 1925); the Zaydi incursions into 'Awdhali cultivated lands began in February 1925.

80 C.O. 725/7, Nos. 34206, 34208, 45664, 49109, 51525, 37215; A.N. (27 July 1925), Resident to S.S. (15 July, 7 October, 30 October and 4 November 1925), minute by H. Young on Resident to S.S. (12 August 1925); by now, however, it was realised that Britain had few bargaining counters left, and there was increasing talk of forcing the Imam to the table, see minutes on Resident to S.S. (5 August 1925).

81 M.E.C.P. No. 10, S.S.C. to Clayton (18 November 1925).

82 The British Govt. finally abandoned the Idrisi and stopped supplying them with arms and ammunition in March 1925. C.O. 725/7, No. 13965, S.S. to Resident (27 March 1925). On the same day as this instruction was issued, the Imam's forces entered Hudayda in the wake of the Idrisi's collapsing authority, ibid., No. 17698, A.N. (31 March 1925).

83 These negotiations are discussed at length in Sir Gilbert Clayton, *Arabian Diary* (ed. R. O. Collins) (Berkeley and Los Angeles, 1969), pp. 189–271; the texts of the drafts and counter-drafts exchanged are at pp. 280–99, Appendices III–VIII.

84 Cf. Belhaven, *The Kingdom of Melchior* (London, 1949), p. 3; Sir Tom Hickinbotham, *Aden*, p. 62; Sir B. Reilly, *Aden and the Yemen* (London, 1960), pp. 15–16.

85 H. F. Jacob, *Kings of Arabia*, pp. 242–3.

86 Cf. the Imam's references to the 'Awdhali as 'vagabonds' and 'badawin', to their 'lack of wisdom' and 'savage nature' reported in Resident to Secretary of State (1 September 1925). Zaydi officials were still treating Protectorate rulers with similar contempt in the 1950s, see K. Trevaskis, *Shades of Amber* (London, 1968), p. 102. There was a notable difference between this and the human respect involved in the later nationalist appeal to Arab brotherhood.

CHAPTER XI

1 J. A. Schumpeter, *Imperialism and Social Clases.* J. A. Hobson, *Imperialism: a Study*, (London, 1902). V. I. Lenin, *Imperialism, the Highest Stage of Capitalism.*

2 Cf. correspondence in M.E.C.P. 22, p. 63, I.O. to C.O. (23 January and 7 April 1928); C.O. to I.O. (31 August 1928); C.O. to Resident (14 December 1928).

3 Cf. the chorus of relief and enthusiasm in the C.O. on receipt of a co-ordinated programme of development submitted by Sir Stewart Symes in 1929. C.O. 69289/29, Minutes on Symes to S.S. (30 January 1929).

4 Cf. Reilly's exchanges with the C.O. during 1931 in M.E.C.P. No. 34.

5 The Imam reportedly had six machines in 1927 but the two Italian pilots he had recruited had had no success in training Yemenis to fly. C.O. Reg. No. 48067/27. Note by Major Fowle on the Zaydi Army (13 July 1927); see also F.O. Reg. No. C 69280/29, Hudayda News-report (June 1929).

6 See above Chapter X, pp. 262–3, and E. Macro, *Yemen and the Western World since 1571* (London, 1968), p. 43.

7 Cf. A. Boyle *Trenchard* (London, 1962), Chapters XIV to XIX. The aircraft used against the Turks in 1918 suffered many losses from rifle fire. E. S. Montagu, *An Indian Diary* (London, 1930), p. 376.

8 F.O. 371/7707, F.O. to C.O. (11 January 1922); C.O. 48027/27, Graham to F.O. (13 January 1927). Note of meeting held at Rome (11 January 1927) between Graham, Clayton, Guariglia and Gasparini, see also M.E.C.P. No. 22, pp. 281 ff. C.O. 48067/27, note by Major Fowle on Yemen Army (13 July 1927).

9 S. Symes, *Tour of Duty*, p. 150, quotes the figure of £1 million and a division of troops. S./Ldr. J. L. Vachell ('Air Control in South-West Arabia', *R.A.F. Quarterly*, Vol. II, No. 1, p. 1) said the Aden G.O.C. had asked for an extra Indian division and a squadron of aircraft. F./Lt. F. M. V. May ('Aden Survey Flight', *J.R.U.S.I.*, Vol. LXXX, p. 769) mentions a division and £6–10 million.

10 *J.R.U.S.I.*, Vol. LXXVI, p. 85; A. Boyle, op. cit., pp. 559–71, *passim*; Cab. 24/198; Cabinet Paper 250; Cab. 23/55, Conclusion 9 (6 October 1927); Cab. 24/231. Report by Sub-Committee on the Persian Gulf (31 October 1928).

11 B. R. Reilly, 'Aden and its Links with India', *Journal of East India*

Association (Vol. XXXII, 1941), p. 69; S./Ldr. R. A. Cochrane, 'The Work of the Royal Air Force and Aden', *Journal of the R.U.S.I.* (Vol. LXXVI), p. 88.

12 Cab. 23/54, Cabinet Conclusion (16 December 1926), ordered the Chiefs of Staff to find a way of putting the Aden garrison on to a less costly basis. Cab. 24/188, Cabinet Paper 250, Memorandum by C.I.G.S. (7 January 1927), pointed toward the abandonment of the mountainous interior as the solution and this was repeated by the Foreign Office at a Cabinet Meeting on 4 July 1927 (Cab. 23/55).

13 S./Ldr. R. A. Cochrane, 'The Work of the Royal Air Force at Aden', *J.R.U.S.I.* (Vol. LXXVI, 1930), p. 88. The essence of air control, said Cochrane, was accurate and detailed knowledge of the people. Cf. A. Boyle, *Trenchard*, pp. 452–7, showing how air strategy imposed a similar 'forward' policy in respect of Northern Iraq in 1922–3.

14 The aircraft used were Fairey III Bs and Fs, which were shortly replaced by Vickers Vincents.

15 *Near East and India*, Vol. XLI, p. 333; 'Air Notes', *Royal Air Force Quarterly*, Vol. VI, No. 2; W./Cmdr. J. A. McDonald, 'Some Notes on the Air Route between the Persian Gulf and Aden', Vol. IX, No. 1, p. 44, and 'The late W./Cmdr. A. R. M. Rickards', Vol. X, No. 1, p. 26; F.O. 371/13718, Aden Political Intelligence Summary 147 (2 November 1929).

16 Cf. comment by G./Capt. C. L. Courtney on paper by S./Ldr. Cochrane, *Journal of the R.U.S.I.*, Vol. LXXVI, p. 101. Cf. Cab. 24/198, C.P. 348, Second Annual Review of Imperial Defence by Chiefs of Staff Sub-Committee (1928); Cab. 24/231, Report by Sub-Committee of Committee of Imperial Defence on Persian Gulf (30 October 1928), took up the old fear of a Russian advance on India in a new form and recommended the development of civil air routes on the Persian side of the Gulf and military air routes on the Arabian side as countermeasures.

17 F.O. 371/12999/1927/8, Aden Political Intelligence Summary 59 (18 February 1928).

18 C.O. E. 1184/80/91, S.S. to Resident (2 March 1928).

19 *Hansard*, 4th series Vol. 214, col. 1516, Question by Kenworthy and Statement by Amery. Also col. 1655.

20 C.O. 59312/28, Acting Resident Fowle to S.S. (24 April 1928 and 11 June 1928).

21 C.O. X59312/28, S.S. Tele. to Ag. Resident (15 June 1928).

22 For a description of these operations, see *Hansard*, 4th Series, Vol. 219, col. 1392, Statement by Amery, *The Times* (26 July 1928); S./Ldr. L. A. Cochrane, 'The Work of the Royal Air Force at Aden', *J.R.U.S.I.*, Vol. LXXVI, p. 88; S./Ldr. J. L. Vachell, 'Air Control in South-West Arabia', *Royal Air Force Quarterly*, Vol. II, No. 1; and Belhaven, *The Kingdom of Melchior*, p. 4.

23 See M. W. Wenner, *Modern Yemen 1918–1966* (Baltimore, 1967), p. 74.

24 S./Ldr. J. L. Vachell, 'Air Control in South-West Arabia', *R.A.F. Quarterly*, Vol. I, No. 1.

25 A.R., A2B/592/47, contains a discussion of the objects of this conference. For a description of the conference see Sir S. Symes, *Tour of Duty*.
26 M.E.C.P. 22, Symes to Secty of State for Colonies, (30 January and 18 December 1929), cf. R. A. B. Hamilton, *The Kingdom of Melchior* (London, 1949), p. 29.
27 *J.R.U.S.I.*, Vol. LXXVI, p. 88, M.E.C.P. 22, Symes to S.S.C. (18 December 1929).
28 A.R., A2B/592/15, Minute by Fowle (23 October 1928).
29 Aden Political Intelligence Survey 390 (4 July 1934).
30 M.E.C.P. 46, Champion to S.S.C. (20 June, 1933), C.O. Reg. No. 48060/27 Resident to S.S.C. (22 June 1927) stating that the 'Awlaqi had formed the best company in the Yemen Infantry; M.E.C.P. 34, Acting Resident to S.S.C. (9 October 1931); C.O. 78002/41, Minute by Reilly (16 May 1941).
31 F.O. 406/42, Resident to Curzon (F.O.) (31 March 1919).
32 Cf. R. A. B. Hamilton's tale of his adventures in *The Kingdom of Melchior*, (London, 1949), and *The Uneven Road* (London, 1956).
33 It is significant that one of the most systematic studies of society inAden's hinterland was drawn up by the first commanding officer of the Government Guards. R. A. B. Hamilton, 'The Social Organisation of the Tribes of the Aden Protectorate', *Journal of the Royal Central Asian Society* (Vol. XXIX, 1942, and XXX, 1943).
34 For a list of these forces at one point of time, see Sir B. Reilly, *Aden and the Yemen* (London, 1960), pp. 13–14.
35 M.E.C.P. 22, p. 58. Symes to S.S.C. (9 December 1929). The Resident looked forward to the day when economic development in the Protectorate would integrate it with Aden to form a province, with Aden as its administrative capital and metropolis.
36 C.O. 846/3, A.A.R. (1935/6).
37 A.A.R. (1935/6).
38 A.A.R. (1931/2). There were however nearly 2,000 scholars in other unaided schools.
39 A.A.R. (1932/3, 1935/6, 1937/8, 1938/9 and 1939/40).
40 For a brief history of the police force see A.A.R. (1935/6).
41 M.E.C.P. 22, p. 180, Telegrams, Govt. of Bombay to I.O. (1 June 1928); Viceroy to S.S. India (8 June 1928); I.O. to C.O. (14 February 1929); Viceroy to S.S. India (9 September 1929).
42 Cab. 24/231, C.P. 232, Memorandum by S.S.I. on disturbances at Aden.
43 See comparative figures in *Aden Census Report* (1946).
44 See A.A.R. in C.O. 846/2 and 3 for trade figures. Coaling figures for the period 1904–39 are in the Report of the Aden Port Trust (1939–40), in C.O. 846/3. The tonnage of merchant vessels calling at Aden rose throughout the period 1919–39, apart from brief setbacks in 1922 and 1931–4.
45 C.O. 846/3, Report of Aden Port Trust (1939–40).
46 'Aden's Bunkering Trade', *Port of Aden Annual* (1959–60), p. 43.
47 C.O. 846/1, A.A.R. (1931/2).

48 C.O. 846/2, A.A.R. (1935/6).

49 C.O. 846/1, A.A.R. (1931/2) and C.O. 846/2, A.A.R. (1935/6). The water scheme had been discussed since 1906, Work began in 1931.

50 Trade returns in A.A.R. (1931/2–1939/40) and Aden Port Trust Reports.

51 A.A.R. (1927/8).

52 Aden Port Trust Report (1939/40). Comparison of five year averages 1924/5–1928/9 and 1929/30–1933/4.

53 The trade from San'a' in 1928 paid transit dues at Mawiyah, Musaymir and Lahej. M.E.C.P. 22, p. 171.

54 F.O. 371/15999, Political Intelligence Summaries 275 (19 April 1932), 282 (8 June 1932), 317 (8 February 1933).

55 M.E.C.P. 34, *passim.*

56 This point was also made several times in the House of Commons by Opposition speakers. *Hansard*, Vol. 187, col. 850; Vol. 241, col. 411; Vol. 224, col. 402; Vol. 225, col. 15.

57 C.O. Reg. No. 48027/27, Minutes of meeting between Clayton and Graham and Guariglia and Gasparini (11 January 1927).

58 M.E.C.P. 34.

59 M.E.C.P. 46. Champion (Acting Resident) to S.S.C. (12 July 1933); Reilly Minute on telegram from Champion (14 August 1933); Proceedings of Committee of Imperial Defence meeting (15 August, 1933).

60 Cf. Air Ministry's attitude at meetings of Committee of Imperial Defence (9 July and 14 September 1931). There was however by 1933 some distaste in other than Air Force quarters in Britain at the indiscriminate use of the air weapon, which did not help Britain's case in disarmament discussions in Europe. See M.E.C.P. 46, military appreciation prepared for Committee of Imperial Defence Meeting (15 August 1933).

61 M.E.C.P. 46, Minutes of Committee of Imperial Defence Meeting (15 August 1933).

62 M.E.C.P. 46, Meeting of Committee of Imperial Defence (15 August 1933) and connected papers.

63 Sir Bernard Reilly, *Aden and the Yemen* (London, 1960), p. 18. Text of Treaty and exchange of notes, ibid., pp. 72ff. See also Belhaven, *The Uneven Road*, pp. 100–7; Reilly's report in M.E.C.P. 46.

64 A.R., A4A, 24/31/8/34.

65 C.O. Reg. No. 78481/41, Reilly to S.S.C. (14 February 1940). The theme constantly recurs in Reilly's other despatches and was reiterated by him to the author with much emphasis during a number of interviews in 1959. The advantages of the policy set out here are supplied by the author, Sir Bernard Reilly did not state them. His position was roughly that the policy of expansion was covered by the complaints made by the Imam himself in 1934 about the parlous state of road security in Aden's hinterland. Belhaven says there would have been expansion whether the treaty had been signed or not (*The Uneven Road*, p. 105). But he emphasises the Imam's expressed desire for peace on the

roads as affecting the initiation of the policy (*The Kingdom of Melchior*, pp. 58–9; *The Uneven Road*, pp. 111–21).

66 C.O. Reg. No. 78481/41, Reilly to S.S.C. (14 February, 1940); Aden Political Intelligence Summaries.

67 A.R., A2B/592/5; Aden Political Intelligence Summary 390 (4 July 1934). *R.A.F. Quarterly*, Vol. IX, p. 215.

68 Aden Political Intelligence Summary (A.P.I.S.) 390 (4 July 1934).

69 A.R., A4A/24/12/9/34.

70 Belhaven, *The Uneven Road, passim*, especially Chapter XI; D. Ingrams, *Social and Economic Survey of the Western Aden Protectorate*, pp. 31 and 60.

71 Belhaven, *The Uneven Road*, pp. 114ff., especially p. 139 and pp. 158–71.

72 A.P.I.S. 387 (13 June 1934). In 1924 the Wazir to the Sultan of Mukalla, Sayyjd Husayn al Mihdhar had made an unsuccessful attempt to settle the dispute. C.O. Reg. No. 39449/24, A.N. (31 July 1934).

73 W. H. Ingrams, *Arabia and the Isles* (1966 ed.), Chapter X; A.R., A4A/24/5/6 (31 October 1934).

74 A.P.I.S. 403 (3 October 1934).

75 *R.A.F. Quarterly*, Vol. VII, p. 120.

76 Belhaven, *The Uneven Road*, pp. 155–7.

77 *R.A.F. Quarterly*, Vol. VIII, No. 3, pp. 314 ff.; and Vol. IX, No. 2, p. 215. Belhaven, *The Uneven Road*, pp. 150–5.

78 Belhaven, *The Kingdom of Melchior*, Chapter II.

79 *R.A.F. Quarterly*, Vol. VII, No. 1, p. 120.

80 Ibid., Vol. VIII, No. 1, p. 88; Belhaven, op. cit., Chapters X and XI.

81 Belhaven, op. cit., p. 127 ff.

82 Belhaven, *The Uneven Road*, pp. 116–17, 152–3.

83 A.R., A4A/24.

84 A.P.I.S. 460 (13 November 1935).

85 C.O. 78481/25/43, Report on Upper 'Awlaqi (29 March 1943). The 'Awlaqi were the last to benefit from the system.

86 The best description in English of the bringing of peace to the Hadhramawt is in W. H. Ingrams, *Arabia and the Isles* (London, 1942).

87 C.O. 78332/38, Report on Education in the Hadhramawt (1938).

88 For example, the first man to establish an Irshadi school in Habban in the Wahidi Sultanate, a wealthy merchant from Java was murdered within a few months of the opening of the institution, and this led to severe unrest in that close-built town. A.P.I.S. 407 (31 October 1934).

89 With the neighbouring Wahidi Sultans, for example.

90 F.O. Reg. No. E 2868/868/91, Reilly to S.S.C. (10 May 1933); E 3580/868/91, Reilly to Fitzmaurice, Consul-General, Batavia (15 April 1933); Fitzmaurice to Reilly (1 June 1933); E 6304/6304/91/1932.

91 C.O. 78018/35, Reilly to S.S.C. (17 April 1935) and minutes. C.O. 846/3, Annual Report on Social and Economic Progress of the peoples of the Eastern Aden Protectorate 1939–40.

92 Sir Tom Hickinbotham, *Aden* (London, 1958), p. 157; *R.A.F. Quarterly*, Vol. VIII, No. 3, p. 314; W. H. Ingrams, *Arabia and the Isles* (1966 ed.),

p. 22–3; I am indebted to Sir Bernard Reilly for giving me his personal account of this episode and his reaction to it.

93 Mukalla Intelligence Summary 67 (22 October 1938); D. Ingrams, *Survey of Social and Economic Conditions in the Aden Protectorate*, p. 109; W. H. Ingrams, *Arabia and the Isles*, pp. 240–2; D. Van der Meulen, *Faces in Shem* (London, 1961), pp. 166–7.

94 Cf. H. L. Liebesny, 'Administrative and Legal Development in Arabia: Aden Colony and Protectorate', *Middle East Journal* (Vol. IX, 1955), No. 4, p. 385. D. Ingrams, *Social and Economic Conditions in the Aden Protectorate*, Appendix II.

95 Mukalla Intelligence Summary 58 (25 June 1938), reporting Sultan Salih's public speech announcing reforms on 21 June 1938. Sultan Salih signed the advisory treaty in order to guarantee his son's succession and did so on the understanding that he himself would remain in control and not become a British cypher. W. H. Ingrams, *Arabia and the Isles* (1966 ed.), pp. 24 and 27.

96 W. H. Ingrams, op. cit. (1966 ed.), Introduction, pp. 31 ff. Mukalla Intelligence Summaries 59 (9 July 1938), 73 (3 December 1938), 102 (24 June 1939); C.O. 78291/1939, Ingrams to Aden Political Secretary (15 April 1929). C.O. 846/3, Annual Report on Social and Economic Progress of the People of the Eastern Aden Protectorate (1939–40).

97 An advisory treaty was signed with the ruling Regent of Balhaf in 1938. In 1939 a customs officer was brought in to collect duties and an ex-Aden Levies officer was recruited to organise a force of 49 Tribal Guards. C.O. 846/3, Report on Social and Economic Progress of the people of the Eastern Aden Protectorate (1939–40).

98 The opposition to British rule became clear when censorship of letters was instituted at the outset of the Second World War. Mukalla Intelligence Summary 112 (17 September 1939).

99 Mukalla Intelligence Summaries 74 (11 December, 1938), 77 (31 December 1938). The summary made the curious remark that while wishing to pursue a policy of religious toleration, the Adviser regarded the Shafi'i as the 'established faith' of the country and that therefore the Irshadi-inspired religious disturbance in Gaydun had to be stopped. The British alignment with the Al Kaffs dated back to 1919 when Lee Warner had marked down the Abdat family as anti-British and the Al Kaffs as friendly. (I.O. P. and S. Records Reg. No. 1740/1915, Lee Warner to Curzon [3 March 1919]). Nevertheless both parties had approached Reilly when he visited the Wadi in 1933 and bin Abdat tried to bribe Ingrams to his side in 1940.

100 W. H. Ingrams, *Arabia and the Isles* (1966 ed.), Introduction, pp. 31 ff.

101 C.O. 846/3, Report on the Social and Economic Progress of the Aden Protectorate (1939–40). W. H. Ingrams, op. cit., p. 29.

102 Mukalla Intelligence Summary 108 (19 August 1939); 128 (6 January 1940) and 143 (1 June 1940).

103 A. M. Clark Hutchinson, 'The Hadhrami Beduin Legion', *Journal of the Royal Central Asian Society*, (Vol. LVII, 1950), Part 1, p. 62. W. H. Ingrams, op. cit. (1966 ed.), Introduction, p. 30.

104 Mukalla Intelligence Summary (22 June 1941).

105 See B. R. Reilly, 'Aden and its links with India', *Journal of East India Association* (1941), p. 80; D. Ingrams, *Survey*, etc., p. 60.

106 The principal advocate of more interference was Hamilton; the principal opponents were Lake and Ingrams. See Belhaven, *The Uneven Road*, pp. 245-6; W. H. Ingrams, *Arabia and the Isles* (1966 ed.), p. 16.

107 C.O. 78481/41, J. Hawthorne Hall to S.S.C. (12 September 1941) enclosing minutes of Protectorate Affairs Council (28 July 1941). Ingrams was the leading advocate of caution. Cf. his foreword to the 1966 edition of *Arabia and the Isles*, pp. 7-14 and 16. The main source of criticism of the Political Officers' activity was the Sultan of Lahej. This passage of arms confirmed the opposition between expansionists – especially those with an eastward ('Awlaqi and 'Awdhali) bent – and the house of Lahej. This line of conflict was to remain in Aden politics for many years to come.

108 See E. Macro, *Yemen and the Western World since 1571*, pp. 74-6. W. H. Ingrams, *The Yemen* (London, 1963).

109 Hamilton's 'The Social Organisation of the Tribes of the Western Aden Protectorate' was published in 1942.

110 C.O. 78481/41, 44 and 45, Memoranda by Gent, Blaxter and Reilly (1941), and by Seager (1944); policy despatch by Sir John Hall (9 March 1944) after meeting on 15 December 1943 with Sir Cosmo Parkinson; Note by Reilly (7 February 1945). D. Ingrams, *Survey of Social and Economic Conditions in the Western Aden Protectorate*, W. H. Ingrams, *Arabia and the Isles* (1966 ed.), Introduction, p. 34.

111 C.O. 78002/43, Aden Intelligence Summaries 4 (30 April 1943), 5 (31 May 1943), 6 (30 June 1943), 8 (31 August 1943), 11 (30 November 1943) and 7 (31 July 1943). C.O. 78647/44, Sir J. Hall to S.S.C. (10 and 14 March 1944). D. Ingrams, op. cit., p. 111. W. H. Ingrams, op. cit., pp. 374-7.

112 D. Ingrams, op. cit., p. 28. C.O. 78002/43, Aden Intelligence Summary 12 (31 December 1943); C.O. 78481/44, Aden Intelligence Summary November (1944). C.O. 78484/45, Governor to S.S.C. (16 January 1945) and 'Report on operations undertaken against Shaykh Obeid Saleh bin Abdat of al Ghurfa in Hadhramawt'.

113 *Colonial Reports, Aden* 1946, pp. 59-60 and 1949-50, pp. 69-71. *Annual Report of Aden Protectorate, Department of Agriculture*. Aden Government Printer (1947), p. 5 and (1949), pp. 8-11.

114 D. Ingrams, op. cit., p. 64.

115 *Colonial Reports, Aden* 1949 and 1950, H.M.S.O. (1952), p. 60.

116 Proposals that Abyan should be developed had been put forward as early as 1926. See C.O. 48017/27, Resident to S.S.C. (29 December 1926), enclosing report by Major Fowle on Abyan. Monetary aid for agricultural development in this area had been desultorily given on a small scale by the Aden Government during the nineteenth century. Description of Khanfar development scheme work in *Annual Report, Aden Protectorate Department of Agriculture*, Aden Government Printer (1947).

117 D. Ingrams, op. cit., C.O. 78002/43, Aden Intelligence Summaries
6 (30 June 1943); 9 (30 September 1943); 10 (31 October 1943);
12 (31 December 1943).
118 Text in D. Ingrams, op. cit., p. 178, Appendix IV.
119 D. Ingrams, op. cit., p. 25.
120 C.O. 78002/44, Aden Intelligence Summary 10 (31 October 1944)
Sir B. Reilly, *Aden and the Yemen*, pp. 22–3.
121 Sir Tom Hickinbotham, *Aden*, pp. 116–26.
122 *Colonial Reports, Aden* 1953 and 1954, H.M.S.O. (1956), Appendix I,
p. 104, 'The Abyan Scheme'.
123 *Colonial Reports Aden* 1947, p. 60; 1949 and 1950, pp. 81–1; 1953 and
1954, p. 105; D. Ingrams, *Survey of Social and Economic Conditions . . . ,*
p. 31 n.2.
124 The object of the school was to produce better rulers. Sudanese teachers
were preferred to Egyptians who, it was feared, would introduce
'Egyptian politics' into the Protectorate. See C.O. M.E.C.P. 52,
Reilly to S.S.C. (19 September 1934).
125 D. Ingrams, op. cit., p. 50. In March 1946 the boys at the Government
Secondary School boycotted classes when their request for a holiday
on the anniversary of the foundation of the Arab League was refused.

CHAPTER XII

1 *Aden: Report of the Trade Development Committee on the state of Aden's trade*
(Aden Govt. Printer, 1962).
2 *Annual Report of the Department of Labour and Welfare, 1956 and 1957,*
p. 17.
3 Compare Charles Johnston's description of Ma'alla in 1961 (*The view
from Steamer Point,* [London, 1964], p. 14) with Hans Helfritz's of 1935
(*Le pays sans ombre* [Paris, 1936], pp. 258–61).
4 *Colonial Reports, Aden,* 1949 and 1950 (H.M.S.O., 1951), p. 5.
5 Sir Tom Hickinbotham, *Aden* (London, 1958), pp. 27–8.
6 See figures in Annual Reports of the Department of Labour and Welfare. The Aden Census 1946 stated that the port was still at that date
the largest employer of labour.
7 *Colonial Reports, Aden, 1949 and 1950* could still report that 'mechanisa-
tion is almost unknown and a large labour force is thus employed in
such processes as bunkering coal by hand'. (P. 9.)
8 A. E. S. Charles, *Report of the Adenisation Committee* (Aden Govt. Printer,
1965), p. 10.
9 The comparative employment patterns of the Aden-born and immigrants can best be seen in the 1946 Aden Census Report, Adenis pre-
ponderated in the public service and legal profession, carpentry (the
carpenters were the first to unionise against Italian competition in 1947),
motor transport, general storekeeping, clerks and cashiers and fishing (a
remnant of pre-British Aden). The police force and general storekeeping

438 ADEN UNDER BRITISH RULE 1839-1967

were the main resorts of Protectorate immigrants – the latter being largely Hadhrami. Tailors were mainly Muslim Indians. The food-stuffs trade, coffee-house keeping and, above all, labouring were principally the province of Yemeni immigrants. It was not a matter of Aden-born traders and dealers battening on immigrants and visitors. A large proportion of the business community, whether French, Indian, Greek, British, Yemeni or Hadhrami, had their homes outside the settlement.

10 In 1952 it was estimated that seventy-five per cent of Aden's income tax was derived from the profits of forty to fifty large firms. In 1956 the Aden Merchants' Association of smaller retailers numbered some two thousand – these paid virtually no tax at all. *Aden Colony: Proceedings of the Legislative Council*, Aden Government Printer (Sixth Session) p. 68; (Tenth Session), pp. 162 and 167.

11 Cf. D. A. Sutherland, *Aden Salaries Report* (Aden Government Printer, 1956) paragraph 49; 'Aden's wholesale produce market', *Port of Aden Aden Annual* 1962–3, p. 66. Efforts were made with little success after the war to enforce maximum prices. *Aden Colony: Proceedings of the Legislative Council* (Eleventh Session), p. 34.

12 *Annual Report of the Department of Labour and Welfare 1956 and 1957*, p. 8. Cf. Sir Kennedy Trevaskis, *Shades of Amber* (London, 1968), p. 40.

13 Profiteering by retailers was a recurrent theme in official circles after the war and there can be no doubt that fortunes were made at Aden the largest apparently being that amassed by the house of Besse, which donated over £1 million sterling to St. Antony's College, Oxford.

14 See *Proceedings of the Legislative Council passim* and Hickinbotham, op. cit., pp. 32 ff.

15 E. Macro, *Yemen and the Western World since 1517*, (London, 1968), pp. 78–9.

16 Hickinbotham, op. cit., p. 195. The Muslim Association was originally called the 'Jinnah Volunteer Corps' but gradually became more Arab-oriented.

17 Hickinbotham, op. cit., pp. 82–7.

18 *Colonial Report, Aden, 1947* (H.M.S.O., 1948), p. 7. *Aden Colony: Education Five-Year Plan*, (Aden Govt. Printer, 1949). A sense of economic urgency was by this time beginning to appear, although there was still reference to 'potential demand' and the cultural value of education. See p. 3.

19 Hickinbotham, op. cit., pp. 44–5; *Aden Colony: Proceedings of the Legislative Council* (Sixth Session, January to February 1952), p. 55. (Seventh Session, 1953), p. 3; *Annual Report of the Department of Labour and Welfare* (1955), p. 4; D. A. Sutherland, op. cit., paragraphs 28–30.

20 *Colonial Report, Aden 1949 and 1950*, p. 7.

21 *Aden Development Plan 1965–70*, Aden Government Printer, p. 2. The Suez crisis did however produce temporary unemployment among low-grade clerical workers. See *Annual Report of the Department of Labour and Welfare* (1956 and 1957), p. 4.

22 Clerical Workers: 1955, 1,547; 1956, 1,740; 1957, 2,029; 1960, 3,111; 1961, 3,538. Reports of Department of Labour and Welfare.

23 Following on this strike, Arab students joined with a retired Indian

official to build up a new political organisation. By 1951 Arab League day demonstrations by schoolboys had become an annual event, to the annoyance of the administration. *Proceedings of Legislative Council,* (Sixth Session, 1952), p. 7.

24 Hickinbotham, op. cit., Chapter XI.

25 *Aden Colony Police, Annual Report 1956,* Aden Govt. Printer, pp. 14–15.

26 B. C. Roberts, *Labour in the tropical territories of the Commonwealth,* (London, 1964), p. 69; *Annual Report of the Department of Labour and Welfare* (1956 and 1957), pp. 8 and 39.

27 *Middle East Journal* (Vol. XVI, 1962), No. 4.

28 Trevaskis, op. cit., p. 97.

29 Roberts, op. cit., p. 102.

30 E.g. article by Luqman in *Fatat al Jazirah* (29, April 1951), demanding scholarships, elections to the Legislative Council, revised membership of committees and the appointment of qualified Arabs to senior administrative posts. At this time this statement represented the feeling of the more radical wing of the Adeni group.

31 Cf. Hickinbotham, op. cit., pp. 204 ff.

32 Hickinbotham, op. cit., pp. 195–6.

33 Roberts, op. cit., pp. 99–103, Trevaskis, op. cit., pp. 96–9.

34 Roberts, op. cit., p. 69.

35 Hickinbotham, op. cit., p. 212; B. R. Reilly, *Aden and the Yemen,* (H.M.S.O., 1960), pp. 44–5.

36 Little, op. cit., pp. 62–3.

37 The British Agent for the Western Protectorate, Basil Seager, once a "forward policy" man himself, was outdistanced by the new Governor, Hickinbotham, after 1950. See Trevaskis, op. cit., p. 21.

38 *Colonial Reports Aden, 1953 and 1954* (H.M.S.O., 1956), p. 111.

39 Trevaskis, op. cit., pp. 81 ff.

40 Hickinbotham, op. cit., p. 166. 'In the beginning it was the intention to make the Federal authorities responsible only for customs, communications, education and public health.' Of these the last two were already almost exclusively the concern of the British Agency, Aden had always taken a close interest in roads and had been interfering with customs and tolls since 1873. Trevaskis says (op. cit., p. 44) that the federation proposal 'envisaged a federation in which the member states would surrender most of their powers and responsibilities to a federal government . . .' This may have been the eventual object but the scheme, some of whose details Hickinbotham gives, would not seem designed to bring this about at once.

41 Ibid., Chapter XI, p. 33.

42 Various features of the proposal are to be found in Hickinbotham, op. cit., pp. 165–9.

43 Trevaskis, op. cit., p. 45; Hickinbotham, op. cit., p. 168; Reilly, op. cit., p. 38. The rulers accepted the idea of federation in principle but rejected the specific proposal put before them.

44 Import of radios into Aden: 1956, 13,645; 1957, 14,963; 1958, 18,215; 1959, 46,572; 1960, 86,701; 1961, 137,509. Approximately ten per cent,

of the 1956 import was recorded as being re-exported to the Protectorate. *Aden Colony: Report of the Trade Development Committee on the state of Aden's trade*, p. 9.

45 *Aden Colony: Proceedings of the Legislative Council* (Second Session, 1948), p. 42; (Sixth Session, January to February 1952), p. 31; (Ninth Session, January 1955), p. 14; (Eleventh Session, January 1957), p. 19; G. King, *Imperial Outpost – Aden* (Oxford, 1964), p. 59.

46 There was still a rule at Lahej in 1962 which ensured the carriage of vegetable produce by camel to the Aden border where lorries took over. *Port of Aden Annual* (1962–3), p. 69. Various rules of a similar nature were enforced on roads in the Protectorate at different times when camelmen had to be conciliated.

47 Aden Records, A2B/592/5.

48 One of the three points in a joint petition put to the British Agent at Mukalla by the heads of tribes in the western part of the Eastern Aden Protectorate in 1950 was 'a complaint against truck owners carrying loads which are forbidden by the Government's agreement with the Bedu'. *Colonial Reports, Aden, 1949 and 1950*, p. 61.

49 Trevaskis, op. cit., pp. 51 and 85.

50 *Wahidi Handbook*, Notes by Kennedy.

51 The opening of new land at Khanfar in 1945 produced a scramble in which the Lower Yafi'i Sultan displaced some of his relations in favour of slave cultivators and outsiders. The Jifri Sayyids of Lahej and Yeshbum bought new cotton-bearing lands (Hickinbotham, op. cit., p. 122). The Wahidi State Secretary used his place on the local Agricultural Development Board in the late 1950s to acquire land where bore wells were to be sunk.

52 Without proper statistics one can only guess at the numbers involved. In 1956 something of the order of twenty per cent of the Protectorate's adult male population was employed in Aden, in the security forces and the Protectorate's administrative, agricultural and social welfare services. This proportion must have risen substantially over the following ten years. By 1964/5 Government expenditure in the Protectorate was running at the rate of £12 per head of the population (see *Aden and South Arabia* [Central Office of Information, 1965] p. 22), i.e. not far short of the *per capita* income of some of the poorer countries of the world.

53 Trevaskis, op. cit., p. 86; *Colonial Reports, Aden, 1955 and 1956*, (H.M.S.O., 1958), p. 118.

54 C. Johnston, op. cit., p. 206; most farmers in the Protectorate were sharecroppers and had always been so. See D. Ingrams, *Survey of Social and Economic Conditions in the Aden Protectorate*, p. 111. The administration made sporadic attempts to get a better deal for cultivators such as forcing Hadhrami landowners in 1946 to give sharecroppers three quarters instead of half of the crop yields.

55 Trevaskis, op. cit., p. 118.

56 Cf. Trevaskis, op. cit., p. 19.

57 The Buraimi affair in 1955 was accompanied by Sa'udi pressure on the Aden Protectorate frontiers.

58 Macro, op. cit., pp. 88–94; B. R. Reilly, op. cit., Chapter II.

59 Macro, op. cit., pp. 96 ff.; Reilly, op. cit., p. 38.

60 See Trevaskis, op. cit., pp. 53 ff.

61 David Holden estimates that 100,000 rifles were legally imported into Aden between 1949 and 1964. *Farewell to Arabia* (London, 1966), p. 41. The Government passed legislation at Aden in 1956 increasing the maximum penalty for the unauthorised possession of arms, against the opposition of the unofficial members on the grounds that security might otherwise be threatened. *Proceedings of the Legislative Council* (Tenth Session, November, 1956), especially p. 187. The administration had been trying up to this point to minimise the practice of arms-bearing in the Protectorate.

62 Cf. Trevaskis, op. cit., pp. 64–6, 75, 96, 123 and 132.

63 B. Seager, 'The Yemen', *Journal of the Royal Central Asian Society* (1955), Part III, pp. 227–8; R. W. Sorensen, 'Aden and the Yemen', *Venture* (Vol. X, July 1958), No. 2; W. H. Ingrams, *The Yemen* (London, 1963); cf. Johnston, op. cit., p. 153.

64 Trevaskis, op. cit., p. 150, Johnston, op. cit., p. 80. Cf. Hickinbotham's guarded remarks in *Aden*, p. 172.

65 Cf. Hickinbotham's contradictory comments on Sultan 'Ali, pp. 134 and 234 of his *Aden*. There is some evidence that 'Ali, like his predecessors, sought to play off one British official against another.

66 Trevaskis, op. cit., pp. 91–6.

67 Trevaskis, op. cit., pp. 100–39. In my opinion this was the last occasion on which the Aden administration was faced with a real choice of policies in dealing with nationalist organisations. Once the alliance with the League had been rejected no further really feasible opportunities for compromise were offered. It ensured that there would be an abrupt breach with the past in South Arabia's development rather than a gradual transition.

68 See texts in J. Y. Brinton, *Aden and the Federation of South Arabia*, (American Society of International Law, Occasional Paper, 1964).

69 Trevaskis, op. cit., p. 88.

70 The legitimacy of chiefs was already heavily eroded and may well have gone before radio became a significant factor. Political Officers were perennially surprised at the ease with which rulers were deposed. There is practically no instance of popular resistance to a chief's removal. Cf. Trevaskis, op. cit., p. 21. Even an 'old hand' like Seager expected trouble when Sultan 'Ali's predecessor was removed, but was proved wrong.

71 Cf. the remarks by the Wahidi State Secretary recorded by Johnston, op. cit., p. 78.

72 For the extension of fief-holding see A. M. A. Maktari, *Water rights and irrigation practices in Lahej*, (Cambridge University Press, 1971), p. 11.

73 *Colonial Reports, Aden, 1955 and 1956*, p. 118; Reilly, op. cit., p. 13; G. King, op. cit., p. 63.

74 In addition, the Hadhrami Beduin Legion and the Mukalla Regular Army in the Eastern Protectorate remained unabsorbed and they numbered some 2,000 men, with over 1,000 police to back them up. The population of the Protectorate was estimated at 758,300 at the end of 1960. When British rule ended the armed forces were about 10,000 strong.

75 Cf. T. Little, *South Arabia: Arena of Conflict* (London, 1968); on the Luqmans' role, see Chapter IV.

76 The merger negotiations are discussed in Johnston, op. cit., and Holden, op. cit., Chapter IV.

77 The demonstrations mounted by the Aden T.U.C. from July to September had alarmed the property-holding classes, as had the attacks on pro-Federal religious leaders. Similar fears had been aroused in 1948 during the anti-Jewish riots, when mobs engaged in extensive looting.

78 Cf. Little, op. cit., pp. 95–6; Holden, op. cit., pp. 58–60; Trevaskis, op. cit., pp. 194–5, 200–2, 204–5, 209–10 and 224.

79 Trevaskis, op. cit., p. 173.

80 U.N. Documents, A/AC109/Pet. 24, 36, 37, 38, 39 and 40.

81 E.g. the negative arguments used before the Colonialism Committee by the Secretary-General of the ruling Aden United Party in defence of the Federation which amounted to a claim that they had squeezed more concessions out of the 'imperialists' than their immature and unrealistic opponents.

82 G. King, op. cit., p. 45; when the base was wound up in November 1967 there were 8,500 Arabs directly employed by the base. J. Paget, *Last Post: Aden 1964–1967* (London, 1969), p. 247.

83 Cf. Trevaskis, op. cit., p. 205; G. Robinson, 'A British policy for Aden', *Venture*, Vol. XVII, No. 10.

84 Cf. Trevaskis, op. cit., pp. 207–8; Paget, op. cit., pp. 46, 53, 131–2, 147.

85 A. S. Bujra, 'Political conflict and social stratification in the Hadhramawt, *Middle East Journal*, Vol. IV, No. 1.

86 Holden, op. cit., pp. 57–8.

87 The P.S.P. claimed that the fighting began in Hawshabi in mid-October 1963. U.N. Docs. A/AC109/Pet. 183/Add. 3, P.S.P. petition (23 March 1964); see also A5800/Add. 4*, evidence of U.K. representative, and evidence of Qahtan al Sha'abi (16 June 1965).

88 The cost of a rifle at Aden fell from £100 to £25 in nine months during 1963. Holden, op. cit., p. 63.

89 Trevaskis, op. cit., p. 207; Paget, op. cit., p. 40. The Qataybi had suffered from the abolition of tolls on the Hardaba road in April 1963, part of the general abolition of customs by the Federation. They were also annoyed at their inclusion in the Federation at the behest of the 'Amir of Dali', whose suzerainty they had never recognised. The Qataybi can have needed little outside prompting to engage in revolt.

90 Little, op. cit., pp. 106–7; D. Taverne, 'Aden after the emergency', *Venture*, Vol. XVI, No. 2.

91 See Paget, op. cit., Part I.

92 Cf. Trevaskis, op. cit., Part III, Chapter VI, 'All over bar the shouting', *passim*.

93 Little, op. cit., p. 114.

94 U.N. Docs. A/AC109/L.194. On 24 November 1964 the N.L.F. condemned both Labour and Conservative policies on Aden and described the Aden political parties and the traditional authorities as renegades from the popular will.

95 U.N. Docs. A/RES/1949 (XVIII) (18 December 1963), Resolution. 1949 (XVIII) (11 December 1963).

96 U.N. Docs. A/AC109/L243. Report of the Sub-Committee on Aden (10 September 1965); G. Robinson, 'A British policy for Aden', *Venture*, Vol. XVII, No. 10.

97 *Venture*, Vol. XVII, Nos. 8 and 10; Statement on the Defence Estimates 1966, Part I; *The Defence Review* (H.M.S.O. Comnd. 2901).

98 Paget, op. cit., pp. 134–5 and 164–5.

99 P. C. Shapland, 'The Dhala Road', *The Royal Engineers Journal* (Vol. LXXXIII, June 1969), No. 2.

100 Paget, op. cit., pp. 158 ff.

APPENDIX A

Residents, Governors, etc. of Aden 1839–1967

Captain S. B. Haines, Indian Navy	Political Agent 1839–54
Major-General J. Outram	Political Agent 1854–6
Col. W. Coghlan	Political Resident 1856–62
Major-General R. W. Honner	Political Resident 1862
Col. W. Coghlan	Political Resident 1863
Major W. L. Merewether	Political Resident 1863–7
Major-General Sir E. L. Russell	Political Resident 1867–70
Major-General C. W. Tremenheere	Political Resident 1870–2
Brigadier-General J. W. Schneider	Political Resident 1872–7
Brigadier-General F. A. E. Loch	Political Resident 1877–82
Brigadier-General J. Blair	Political Resident 1882–5
Brigadier-General A. G. F. Hogg	Political Resident 1885–90
Brigadier-General J. Jopp	Political Resident 1890–5
Brigadier-General C. A. Cunningham	Political Resident 1895–9
Brigadier-General O'Moore Creagh	Political Resident 1899–1901
Brigadier-General P. J. Maitland	Political Resident 1901–4
Major-General H. M. Mason	Political Resident 1904–6
Major-General E. De Brath	Political Resident 1906–10
Brigadier-General J. A. Bell	Political Resident 1910–14
Brigadier-General C. H. U. Price	Political Resident 1915
Major-General J. M. Stewart	Political Resident 1916–20
Major-General T. E. Scott	Political Resident 1920–5
Major-General J. H. K. Stewart	Political Resident 1925–8
Lieutenant-Colonel Sir G. S. Symes	Political Resident 1928–30
Lieutenant-Colonel B. R. Reilly	Political Resident 1930–2
Lieutenant-Colonel B. R. Reilly	Chief Commissioner 1932–7
Sir Bernard Reilly	Governor 1937–40
Sir John Hathorn Hall	Governor 1940–4
Sir Reginald Champion	Governor 1944–51
Sir Tom Hickinbotham	Governor 1951–6
Sir William Luce	Governor 1956–60
Sir Charles Johnston	Governor 1960–3
Sir Kennedy Trevaskis	High Commissioner 1963–5
Sir Richard Turnbull	High Commissioner 1965–7
Sir Humphrey Trevelyan	High Commissioner 1967

Aden Population

Year	Arabs	Somalis	Jews	Indians	Europeans	Other	Total
1839 (March)	617	63	574	35			1,289
1839 (October)							2,885
1840 (April)							4,600
1841	7,262		777	207			8,246
1842 (April)	9,078	2,600	1,060	370	⏜		13,108
1842 (November)	12,170	2,050	1,079	481	747		16,527
1849	4,845	2,877	1,150	7,605	778	1,868	19,024*
1856	4,812	2,896	1,224	8,563	791	2,452	20,738*
1867	9,350	3,387	1,275	2,308	49	1,177	17,546
1872	8,241	5,346	1,435	3,589	208	470	19,289*
1881	13,285	9,150	2,121	7,265	2,101	789	34,711*
1891							40,926*
1901	n.a.	n.a.	n.a.	n.a.	n.a.	n.a.	39,986*
1911							42,675*
1921							57,571*
1931	29,820	3,935	4,120	7,387	1,145	331	46,638*
1946	58,455	4,325	7,273	9,452	366	645	80,516*
1955	103,879	10,611	831	15,817	4,484	2,608	138,441

* Including military.

Sources: A.R., Series A1A, Vol. 18, p. 202; B.S.L. (3 October 1839 and 30 April 1840); A.R., Series F1A, Vol. 39; Series A1A, Vol. 461, p. 688; F. M. Hunter, *An Account of the British Settlement of Aden in Arabia* (1877), p. 26; Census of India (1881 ff.), Census of Aden (1946 and 1955).

Aden Total Seaborne Trade: Imports and Exports

Year	Value (Rs.000)	Index 1881/2 = 100	Year	Value (Rs.000)	Index 1881/2 = 100
1843/4	1,587	5	1878/9	29,306	84
1844/5	1,755	5	1879/80	34,050	97
1845/6	2,308	7	1880/1	35,310	101
1846/7	2,329	7	1881/2	34,945	100
1847/8	2,383	7	1882/3	37,827	108
1848/9	2,172	6	1883/4	41,020	117
1849/50	2,369	7	1884/5	36,835	105
1850/1	2,114	6	1885/6	41,290	118
1851/2	5,032	14	1886/7	45,283	130
1852/3	5,873	17	1887/8	49,419	141
1853/4	6,171	18	1888/9	62,327	178
1854/5	6,764	19	1889/90	62,878	180
1855/6	6,613	19	1890/1	60,294	173
1856/7	8,824	25	1891/2	70,016	200
1857/8	11,455	33	1892/3	76,668	219
1858/9	9,069	26	1893/4	76,110	218
1859/60	9,840	28	1894/5	80,789	231
1860/1	9,994	29	1895/6	88,420	253
1861/2	8,259	24	1896/7	88,380	252
1862/3	8,817	25	1897/8	76,714	220
1863/4	12,829	36	1898/9	79,773	228
1864/5	11,315	48	1899/1900	75,446	216
1865/6	12,701	36	1900/01	68,606	196
1866/7	14,271	41	1901/2	86,374	247
1867/8	27,631	79	1902/3	88,904	254
1868/9	22,283	64	1903/4	98,702	282
1869/70	15,543	44	1904/5	86,979	249
1870/1	18,400	53	1905/6	94,048	269
1871/2	20,900	54	1906/7	95,490	273
1872/3	20,555	59	1907/8	86,076	246
1873/4	26,190	75	1908/9	95,362	273
1874/5	30,568	87	1909/10	99,494	285
1875/6	31,609	90	1910/11	101,015	289
1876/7	29,321	84	1911/12	117,882	337
1877/8	29,878	85	1912/13	130,903	375

Year	Value (Rs.000)	Index 1881/2 = 100	Year	Value (Rs.000)	Index 1881/2 = 100
1913/14	123,002	351	1936/27	151,970	435
1914/15	100,224	287	1927/28	171,730	491
1915/16	108,029	309	1928/29	150,888	431
1916/17	148,668	425	1929/30	135,637	388
1917/18	120,023	343	1930/31	102,487	293
1918/19	148,847	426	1931/32	96,928	277
1919/20	198,302	567	1932/33	87,916	251
1920/21	192,378	551	1933/34	86,541	248
1921/22	161,388	462	1934/35	84,770	243
1922/23	139,042	398	1935/36	112,852	323
1923/24	140,130	401	1936/37	110,175	360
1924/25	161,610	462	1937	125,893	360
1925/26	159,360	456	1938	121,602	348

Sources.

1 I.O.R. Aden Records, R/20/A1A, Vol. 50, p. 515, Haines to Govt. of Bombay (20 August 1945).
2 I.O.R. Aden Records, R/20/A1A, Vol. 58, p. 501, Haines to Govt. of Bombay (10 September 1846).
3 I.O.R. Boards Collections, Vol. 2395, No. 128 735 (1850), Govt. of India to Court of Directors (24 September 1850) enclosing Aden Custom House and Trade Reports (1847/8 and 1848/9).
4 I.O.R. Aden Records, R/20/A1A, Vol. 93, p. 417, Haines to Govt. of Bombay (22 July 1850).
5 I.O.R. Aden Records, R/20/A1A, Vol. 199, pp. 45 ff., Report on the Trade of Aden for the official year 1856/7.
6 I.O.R. Aden Records, R/20/A1A, Vol. 265, pp. 12ff., Administration Report for Aden 1858/9.
7 I.O.R. Bombay Unanswered Letters (Political Department), Bombay Political Letter 40 (27 June 1861) endorsing Aden Administration Report for 1860/1.
8 Bombay Administration Reports 1862/3, pp. 44–5; ibid. (1863/4), p. 58, ibid. (1864/5), p. 62.
9 I.O.R. Official Publications (42) 1269, Trade Returns Aden (1867–70).
10 Ibid. (66) 1966, Aden Trade and Navigation Returns (1885/6–1893/4).
11 Account of the Trade of Aden (1901/2–1906/7), Calcutta (1903, 1904, 1905, 1906, 1907 and 1908).
12 Report on the Trade and Navigation of British India for the years ending 31 March 1877, 1881, 1882–1931. (Contain as Appendices Aden Trade Reports.)
13 *Parliamentary Papers*, Vol. XXIX, 1924; Vol. XXV, 1931/2; Vol. XXVI, 1935/6; Statistical Abstracts for British India. (Contain statements of Aden trade totals in Rupees.)
14 Colonial Office Report on the Social and Economic Progress of the People of Aden (1937 and 1938).

Note on Sources

(i) UNPUBLISHED SOURCES

The main sources used for this work were the Aden Records and the materials relating to Aden's history available in the India Office Library and the Public Record Office in London.

The Aden Records are now located in the India Office Library under the classification R/20 Residency Records and are being catalogued by Mrs. Tewson. Some of the older records are in a poor state of preservation and a few of the volumes were lost as early as the beginning of this century. Nevertheless the collection remains the most valuable source for Aden's history. The principal series for the history of the nineteenth century up to 1905 is the series AIA, which contains material relating to all aspects of the town's history which came within the purview of the Residency. The series is catalogued and, although the records as far as 1854 consist of indifferently organised letter books, there are indexes compiled at various times from the middle of the last century to 1905 covering the whole series. The second principal group of documents is the A4A series of Arabic correspondence beginning in the 1870s. This series is less valuable than might be expected. It contained the originals of Arabic letters to and from hinterland personalities, but many of the letters were subsequently repeated in general political correspondence and can be found also elsewhere. The third group is the F1A series which contains the Bombay records relating to Aden which were transferred from Bombay on Aden's becoming a colony. Unfortunately, a severe destruction policy at the time of transfer resulted in the elimination of large amounts of valuable material, and this truncated group of volumes is principally useful for the minutes and memoranda of Bombay officials upon correspondence, much of which is available elsewhere. In Aden there are the records of the Port Trust and the Municipality which contain material relating to the period prior to the founding of those bodies in the 1880s as well as later. I made limited use of these collections, which I found too detailed in content for my purposes. The records of the Aden Chamber of Commerce are disappointingly scanty.

The India Office Records proper contain a mass of relevant documentation. Much of it duplicates what is to be found in the Aden Records but it also contains the documents concerning the formulation of policy during the period when Aden was administered by the Indian Government, and some of the duplicated material, being better preserved, is easier to use in this form than in the Aden

Records. Throughout the period up to the First World War, the series of Aden Secret Letters containing correspondence on major issues and on matters concerning Aden's hinterland, Somaliland and other countries bordering on the Red Sea, communicated direct to the Home Government, provides a continuous commentary on such matters. Further detail for the earlier period is contained in the Bombay Secret Letters series, and, after the 1860s, the Indian Secret Letters series. Apart from these principal collections, Aden affairs found occasional mention in the Public Works old and new series, and Perim affairs after 1881 were predominantly dealt with by the Revenue, Statistics and Commerce Department. Correspondence with other departments of government in London is to be found in the Home Correspondence series, and from 1900 onward much of the political correspondence concerning Aden was printed by the Foreign Office, in the 'Persia and Arabia' and 'Affairs of Arabia' confidential prints. Prior to 1900 a certain amount of such correspondence concerning Aden was printed in the 'Red Sea and Somali Coast' series of confidential prints. During the First World War political and military business concerning Aden was handled through the War Office and Foreign Office; for this period, the well-indexed Foreign Office material in the Public Record Office is the most useful source. From 1921 onward, Protectorate affairs, and from 1937 the whole business of the then Colony, were handled by the Colonial Office and the C.O. 725 series thereafter contains most of the most valuable material, some of it being printed out in the series 'Middle East Confidential Prints'.

In addition to the public records, I made use of certain private collections, notably the Broughton Papers in the Home Miscellaneous series at the India Office Library, the papers of Sir Charles Wood, Lord Elphinstone, Lord Northbrook, Viscount Cross, Viscount Curzon, Lord George Hamilton, Lord Lamington and Lord Morley, all in the European Manuscripts section of the India Office Library. I also consulted the Badger Papers in the Cambridge University Library, the Outram papers in the Royal Military College, Camberley, the Layard Papers in the British Museum, the Broadlands Papers in the National Record of Archives, the Salisbury papers in Christ Church, Oxford and the Granville papers in the Public Record Office. I was also kindly given access to the records of Luke Thomas and Company in London. The material in these private collections helped to throw light on the play of personality in discussion of public policy. The Luke Thomas Records provided a useful insight into the conduct of business at Aden, both by this old firm and the associated Cowasji Dinshaw and Company.

(ii) PUBLISHED WORKS

The following is a list of works cited and consulted which contain significant bodies of material relevant to the history of Aden. It does not pretend to be exhaustive. For further material relating to Aden the reader is referred to Eric Macro's *Bibliography of the Arabian Peninsula* (University of Miami Press, 1958) and the catalogue of the School of Oriental and African Studies which contains the result of Professor R. B. Sergeant's bibliographical work.

Bibliography

Aden: *Annual Reports on the social and economic progress of the people of Aden* (Colonial Annual Reports), 1937, 1938, 1946, 1947, 1948, 1949–50, 1951–2, 1953–4, 1955–6 (London, 1939 and 1948, etc.).
—— *Police Annual Report*, 1947 ff.
—— *Department of Agriculture Annual Report*, 1947 ff.
—— *Report of the Education Department for the period 1946–7* ff.
—— *Annual Report of the Department of Labour and Welfare*, 1953 ff.
—— *Report of the Trade Development Committee on the State of Aden's Trade* (Aden Govt. Printer, 1962).
—— *Report of the Adenisation Committee*, A. E. S. Charles, (Aden Govt. Printer, 1959).
—— *Proceedings of the Legislative Council: Official Report*, (Aden Govt. Printer, 1947–67).
—— *Report on Aden Salaries*, D. A. Sutherland (Aden Govt. Printer, 1956).
—— *Report of the Commission of Inquiry appointed to inquire into the causes of trade disputes which occurred in the Colony during March 1956, etc.* (Aden Govt. Printer, 1956).
—— *Report on Social Conditions and Welfare Service in Aden*, Mohsin H. Khalife (Aden, 1956).
—— *Education Five-Year Plan* (Aden Govt. Printer, 1949).
—— *Development Plan 1965–70* (Aden Govt. Printer).
Ahmad Fadl bin Muhsin at 'Absali, *Haddiyat az Zaman fi akhbar al muluk Lahj wa Adan* (Cairo, 1932).
Aitchison, C. U., *A Collection of Treaties, Engagements and Sanads relating to India and Neighbouring Countries* (Calcutta, 1862–5, 1876–8, 1892, 1909 1931).
Albright, E. P., and Bowen, R. L., *Archaeological discoveries in South Arabia* (Baltimore, 1958).
Ansaldi, C., *Il Yemen nella Storia e nella Leggenda* (Rome, 1933).
Ashtor, E., 'The Karimi Merchants' (*J.P.A.S.*, 1956), Part 1
Ba Wazir, S. A., *Ma'alim Tarikh al Jazirat al 'Arabiyah* (Cairo, 1954).
Badger, G. P., *The Travels of Ludovico di Varthema* (Hakluyt Society, 1863).
Bakri, Salah al, *Tarihk Hadramawt al Siyasi*, 2 Vols. (Cairo, 1956).
—— *Fi Janub al Jazirat al 'Arabiyah* (Cairo, 1949).
Barbier de Meynard, *Notice sur l'Arabie meridionale* (Paris, 1883).
Barbosa, D., *The Book of Duarte Barbosa* (London, 1918–21).
Bent, M. V. A. and J. T., *Southern Arabia* (London, 1900).
Berard, V., *Le Sultan l'Islam et les Puissances* (Paris, 1907).
Bidwell, R., *The Affairs of Arabia 1905–1906*, 2 Vols. (London, 1971).
Botta, P. E., *Relation d'un voyage dans l'Yemen* (Paris, 1841).

Bremond, E., *Yemen et Saoudia* (Paris, 1937).

Brinton, J. Y., *Aden and the Federation of South Arabia* (American Society of International Law, 1964).

Broadhurst, R. J. C. (trans.), *The Travels of Ibn Jubayr* (London, 1952).

Bujra, A. S., *The Politics of Stratification* (Oxford, 1971).

Bury, G. W., *Arabia Infelix* (London, 1915).

—— (A. Mansur), *The Land of Uz* (London, 1911).

—— *Panislam* (London, 1919).

Calwell, C. E., *Handbook of the Turkish Army* (London, 1892).

Caton Thompson, G., *The Tombs and Moon Temple of Hureidha, Hadhramut* (London, 1944).

Charles Roux, F., *L'Angleterre et l'expedition en Egypte* (Cairo, 1925).

Christie, J., *Cholera Epidemics in East Africa* (London, 1876).

Clayton, G. (ed. R. O. Collins), *Arabian Diary* (California, 1969).

Creagh, O. Moore, *Autobiography* (London, 1930).

Darrag, *L'Egypte sous le règne de Barsbay 1422-38* (Damascus, 1961).

Documents on British Foreign Policy, 1st Series, Vols. IV and VIII (1939).

Doe, D. B., *Southern Arabia* (London, 1971).

Douin, G., *Histoire du règne du Khedive Ismail* (Rome, 1933).

El Attar, M. S., *Le sous-développement économique et social du Yemen* (Algiers, 1964).

Encyclopaedia of Islam (1st ed. 1913; new ed. 1960).

England: Colonial Office. *Accession of Aden to the Federation of South Arabia*, Cmd. 1814 (1962).

—— Colonial Office. *Aden Protectorate: Report on the Social, Economic and Political Condition of the Hadhramaut*, W. H. Ingrams, (Colonial No. 123) (1937).

—— Colonial Office. *Report of the Commission of Enquiry into disturbance in Aden, December 1947* (Colonial No. 233) (1948).

—— Colonial Office. *Treaty of friendship and protection between the United Kingdom and the Federation of Arab Amirates of the South, 11 February 1959* (H.M.S.O.) (London, 1959).

Fakhry, A., *An Archaeological Journey in Yemen* (Cairo 1951-2).

Faris, N. A. (trans.), *The Antiquities of South Arabia* (Al Hamdani) (Princeton, 1938).

Farnie, D. A., *East and West of Suez* (Oxford, 1969).

Fayein, C., *Une française médecin au Yemen* (Paris, 1955).

Foster, W., *The Journal of John Jourdain*, Hakluyt Series, Vol. XVI (London, 1905).

—— (ed.), *The Red Sea and the adjacent countries at the close of the Seventeenth Century* (London, 1949).

Geddes, C. L., 'The Yu'firid Dynasty of Sana'a', (Univ. of London Ph.D. thesis, 1959).

Gobineau, A. de, *Trois ans en Asie 1855-1858* (Paris, 1859).

Goldsmid, F. J., *James Outram: A Biography* (London, 1881).

Gosse, P., *The History of Piracy* (London, 1954).

Graham, G. S., *Great Britain in the India Ocean: A Study of Maritime Enterprise 1810-1850* (Oxford, 1967).

Grenville, J. A. S., *Lord Salisbury and Foreign Policy 1895–1902* (London, 1964).

Guillain, M., *Documents sur l'histoire, la geographie et la commerce de l'Afrique Orientale* (Paris, 1856).

Haig, F. T., *Report of a Journey to the Red Sea Ports* (London, 1887).

Hallberg, C. W., *The Suez Canal: Its History and Diplomatic Importance* (New York, 1931).

Hamilton, R. A. B., *Kingdom of Melchior* (London, 1949).

—— *The Uneven Road* (London, 1955).

—— 'The Social Organisation of the Tribes of the Aden Protectorate', *J.R.C.A.S.* (Vols. XXIX and XXX, 1942).

Harris, W. B., *A Journey through the Yemen* (London, 1893).

Heyworth Dunne, J., *Al Yemen: General, Social, Political and Economic Survey* (Cairo, 1952).

Hickinbotham, T., *Aden* (London, 1958).

Holden, D., *Farewell to Arabia* (London, 1966).

Hoskins, H. L., *British Routes to India* (Cambridge, Mass., 1928).

Hourani, G., *Arab Seafaring* (Beirut, 1963).

Huber, C., *Journal d'un Voyage en Arabie, 1883–1884* (Paris, 1891).

Hunter, F. M., *A Handbook of Aden* (London, 1873).

—— and Sealey, J., *An Account of the British Settlement at Aden* (London, 1877).

—— *Arab Tribes in the Vicinity of Aden* (Bombay, 1886 and 1909).

Hurewitz, J. C., *Diplomacy in the Near and Middle East: A Documentary Record*, 2 Vols. (Princeton, 1956).

Ingrams, B. S., *Three Sea Journals of Stuart Times* (London, 1936).

Ingrams, D. I., *Survey of the Economic and Social Conditions in the Western Aden Protectorate* (Asmara, 1949).

Ingrams, W. H., *Arabia and the Isles* (1st ed. London 1942; 2nd ed. 1966).

—— *The Yemen* (London, 1963).

Jacob, H. E., *Coffee: the Epic of a Commodity* (London, 1935).

Jacob, H. F., *Perfumes of Arabia* (London, 1915).

—— *Kings of Arabia* (London, 1923).

Johanston, C., *The View from Steamer Point* (London, 1964).

Kammerer, A., *La Mer Rouge, L'Abyssinie et l'Arabie depuis l'antiquité*, 3 Vols. (Cairo, 1929–52).

Kay, H. C., *Yemen, its Early Medieval History* (London, 1892).

Kelly, J. B., *Britain and the Persian Gulf* (Oxford, 1968).

King, G., *Imperial Outpost Aden* (Oxford, 1964).

Klieman, A. S., *The Foundations of British Policy in the Arab World* (Baltimore, 1970).

Langles, L. M., *Voyage de l'Inde à la Mekke* (Paris, 1797).

La Roque, J. de, *A Voyage to Arabia Felix* (London, 1732).

Lenczowski, G., *The Middle East in World Affairs* (1952).

Lindsay, W. S., *A History of Merchant Shipping*, 4 Vols. (London, 1876).

Little, T., *South Arabia: Arena of Conflict* (London, 1968).

Lofgren, *Arabische Texte zur Kenntnis der Stadt Aden im Mittelalter* (Uppsala, 1936–50).

Lowe, C. R., *A History of the Indian Navy* (London, 1877).

454 ADEN UNDER BRITISH RULE 1839–1967

Lunt, J., *The Barren Rocks of Aden* (London, 1966).
McAuliffe, R. P., *The Nizam – the Origin and Future of the Hyderabad State* (London, 1904).
Macro, E., *Yemen and the Western World* (London, 1968).
Maktari, A. M. A., *Water Rights and Irrigation Practice in Lahj* (Cambridge, Mass., 1971).
Manzoni, R., *Tre Anni nell' Arabia Felice; escursione fatta del Settembre 1877 al Marzo 1880* (Rome 1884).
Marder, A. J., *British Naval Policy 1880–1905* (London, 1941).
Marston, T. E., *Britain's Imperial Role in the Red Sea 1800–1878* (Hamden, Conn., 1961).
Milburn, W., *Oriental Commerce*, 2 Vols. (London, 1813).
Mitchell, C., *Having been a Soldier* (London, 1969).
Monfried, H. de, *Secrets of the Red Sea* (London, 1934).
—— *Pearls, Arms and Hashish* (London, 1930).
Morison, S. E., *The Maritime History of Massachusetts* (Boston, 1941).
(Admiralty) Naval Intelligence Division, *A Handbook of Arabia*, 1917 and 1920.
—— *Western Arabia and the Red Sea* (London, 1946).
Neibuhr, C., *Travels through Arabia and other Countries in the East* (London, 1792).
Norris, H. T., and Penhey, F. W., *An Archaeological and Historical Survey of the Aden Tanks* (Aden, 1955).
Nuseibeh, H. Z., *The Ideas of Arab Nationalism* (Ithaca, 1956).
Paget, J., *Last Post: Aden 1964–1967* (London, 1969).
Parkinson, J. C., *The Ocean Telegraph to India* (London, 1860).
Philby, H. St. J., *Sheba's Daughters* (London, 1939).
—— *Arabian Highlands* (New York, 1952).
—— *Sa'udi Arabia* (London, 1955).
Phillips. W., *Qataban and Sheba* (London, 1955).
Pirenne, J., 'La date du periple de la Mer Rouge', *Journal Asiatique* (1961).
Plas, J., and Gebirke, U., 'Die Aden Grenze in der Sudarabienfrage', *Schriften des Deutschen Orient Instituts* (1967).
Playfair, R. L., 'A History of Arabia Felix or Yemen', *Bombay Records, New Series*, No. XLIX (1859).
Popper, W., *Egypt and Syria under the Circassians* (Berkley and Los Angeles, 1955–7).
Preaux, C., *L'Empire royal des Lagides* (Paris, 1939).
Ramm, A., *The Political Correspondence of Mr. Gladstone and Lord Granville* (London, 1952).
Ramsaur, E., *The Young Turks: Prelude to the revolution of 1908* (Princeton, 1957).
Redhouse, J. W. (trans.), *The Pearl Strings: A History of the Rasuliyy Dynasty of Yemen by Aliyyu ibn Hasan Al Khasrijiyy* (London, 1906–18).
Reilly, B. R., 'The Aden Protectorate', *J.R.C.A.S.* (Vol. XXVIII, 1941), Part 2.
—— *Aden and the Yemen* (London, 1949).
—— *Aden and the Yemen* (London, 1960).

Rihani, A., *Around the Coasts of Arabia* (London, 1930).

Roberts, B. C., *Labour in the Tropical Territories of the Commonwealth* (London, 1964).

Robson, J., *Ion Keith Falconer in Arabia* (London, 1923).

Rodgers, F., *The Journal of Francis Rodgers* (London, 1936).

Romer, C. F., and Mainwaring, *The Second Battalion Royal Dublin Fusiliers in the South African War with a Description of Operations in the Aden Hinterland* (London, 1908).

Ronaldshay, Lord, *Lord Curzon of Kedleston* (London, 1928).

Rooke, H., *Travels to the Coast of Arabia Felix* (London, 1783).

Ryckmans, J., *L'Institution monarchique en Arabie méridionale avant l'Islam, Ma'in et Saba* (Louvain, 1951).

Saab, H., *The Arab Federalists of the Ottoman Empire* (Amsterdam, 1958).

Salt, H., *A Voyage to Abyssinia in the Years 1809–1810* (London, 1814).

Sanger, R. H., *The Arabian Peninsula* (New York, 1954).

Schoff, W. H., *The Periplus of the Erythrean Sea* (New York, 1912).

Sergeant, R. B., *The Portuguese off the South Arabian Coast* (Oxford, 1963).

Spalding, H., *Perim as it is* (London, 1890).

Stark, F., *The Southern Gates of Arabia* (London, 1936).

Stripling, G. W. F., *The Ottoman Turks and the Arabs 1511–1574*, 'University of Illinois, Studies in Social Science', Vol. XXVI, No. 4.

Symes, S., *Tour of Duty* (Toronto, 1946).

Tamisier, M., *Voyage en Arabie, sejour dans le Hejaz, campagne d'Asir* (Paris, 1840).

Thomas, B., *Arabia Felix* (London, 1932).

Toussaint, A., *Histoire de l'Océan Indien* (Paris, 1961).

Trevaskis, K., *Shades of Amber* (London, 1968).

Tritton, A. S., *The Rise of the Imams of Sana'a* (London, 1928).

Valentia, Lord, *Voyages and Travels to India, Ceylon, Abyssinia and Egypt in the years 1802–1806* (London, 1809).

Van den Berg, L. W. C., *Hadhramaut and the Arab Colonies in the East Indian Archipelago* (trans. J. Sealey) (Bombay, 1887).

Van der Meulen, D., *Aden to the Hadhramaut* (London, 1947).

Ward, C. Y., *Gulf of Aden Pilot 1863* (London, 1882).

Ward, M. C. P., *Handbook of the Turkish Army* (London, 1901).

Waterfield, G., *Sultans of Aden* (London, 1968).

Wellsted, J. R., *Travels in Arabia* (London, 1838).

Zeine, Z. N., *Arab–Turkish Relations and the Emergence of Arab Nationalism* (Beirut, 1958).

Index

457

60–2, 64–8, 70–8, 80–6, 90–1, 98,
107, 111–13, 117, 176–7, 182–3,
189, 192, 260, 278–9, 290, 292,
363–8, 371, 376–7, 379–80; negotiates at Aden, 31–2, 35–6, 361;
disputes with colleagues, 41–3,
58; fosters trade, 43–4; his social
theories, 44–5; trial of, 86–9
Hajariyah 51, 55, 60, 64–5, 74, 119,
125–6, 138, 140, 160, 194, 380,
392
Hall, Sir John H., 308
Halimayn Mountains, 201
Hamilton, Lord George, 222, 231
Hamilton, R. A. B., Lord Belhaven,
298–9, 301, 408
Harrar, 52
Hashid 'tribe', 6, 76, 258
Hasan 'Abdallah Katif, 46, 48, 66,
70
Hasan 'Ali Rajab 'Ali, 107, 328
Hawshabi, 66, 119, 122, 140–1, 144,
146, 200, 209–11, 241–2, 246, 271,
299, 395, 410, 420, 423; arms
import to 204; Zaydi incursions,
262–3; Tribal Guards formed,
298; revolt against British rule,
442
Hawshabi Sultans 65, 262, legitimacy, 202; interference with
'Abdali irrigation system, 63, 69,
153; taken under 'Abdali protection (1848), 78; loses Za'ida
lands to 'Abdali, 123–4, 145;
loses stipend for caravan raiding,
124; decline in power 209; falls
under 'Abdali control (1895),
152–3, 207–8, 215 (1919), 256–7;
intrigues with Turks, 139; and
al Darayjah incident, 216
Haydar bin Ahmad al Fadli, 153–5
Hizb al Watani, 311
Hides and Skins, 52, 186, 291, 371
Hijuff, 176, 189, 192
Himyar, 5–8, 64
Hiswah, 49, 80, 84, 87, 113–14,
120, 122, 125, 378–9
Hobhouse, Sir J., Lord Broughton,
33–5, 37, 69, 75, 360, 362, 377

Hostages, 70, 173
Hudayda, 16, 54, 73, 98, 132, 135,
164, 186, 208, 238–9, 264, 297,
358, 366, 369, 382; occupied by
British (1919), 259; handed to
Sayyid Idris, 261; taken by Imam
Yahya, 429
Hugh Lindsay, 27, 360
Humum 'tribe', 161, 306, 428
Hunter, Capt. F. M., 170, 219
Husayn bin Ahmad al Fadli, 153,
155, 397
Husayn bin 'Ali Haydar, Sharif,
44, 54–5, 72–4, 366, 374, 376
Husn Suda', 166, 170
Hyderabad, 126, 133, 158–61, 163,
165–70, 173, 268, 303, 323, 400–1

IBB, 73, 76, 204, 244, 390
Idris, Sayyid Muhammad al, 245–6,
257–9, 261, 264, 429
Incense, 3, 52, 353
India (see also Defence of India;
Hyderabad; Bombay), 3, 7, 9, 11,
21, 27, 32–4, 39, 50, 58, 88,
94, 96, 132–4, 150, 157, 159, 165,
168–9, 173–4, 176, 182, 231, 233,
251, 254, 283, 286–7, 323–4, 351,
355; trade with Red Sea, 17,
23–4, 30, 51, 55, 182, 186, 249,
291–2; routes from Europe, 21–2,
32–4, 93–5, 149, 152, 174, 199,
250, 283; immigrants from to
Aden 49, 324; attitudes to education, 192
India Government of, 38–9, 57, 82,
91, 150, 247, 290, 395–6; attitudes
to Aden's occupation, 35, 37;
attitudes to Aden's commercial
and strategical function, 51, 54,
177; attitude to political expansion, 127, 213–4, 216, 221–2,
224–5, 233–4; role in relation to
other decision-making authorities,
136–8, 144, 183, 218, 222, 231–5;
and formation of Aden Protectorate, 140–1, 144, 196, 198, 200,
222, 225; interest in Hyderabad
and Hadhramawt, 163, 167, 169–

279, 296; indecisiveness; 137–8,
255; opposition to expansion, 82,
129, 148, 196, 219, 220, 222,
224–5, 231–2, 235, 240, 263–4,
282, 346; authorises air action
against Yemen (1928), 284; supports 'forward policy' (1944),
312–13
London Agreement (1950) with
Imam, 336
London coaling brokers, 180–1
Luke Thomas & Co., 49, 180, 183,
322, 367
Lytton, 1st Earl of, 169, 401

MA'ALLA, 103, 107, 110, 147, 175,
188–90, 193, 319–21, 324
Mackawi family, 328, 347, 348
Maghrib, 7, 9, 16, 21, 96
Mahmud Nedim Pasha, 244–5, 247
Mahra, 282
Mail Communication, 21, 26–30,
36, 93, 106, 198
Ma'in, 3, 64
Maitland, Maj.-Gen. P. J., 220,
232, 278, 416
Mamlugs, 11, 15, 19, 25, 357
Manakha, 135, 238
Mandates, 250, 265
Mansurah, al, 320
Ma'rib, 3, 6, 204, 241
Marqashi, 69, 299
Massawa, 96–7
Masqat, 29, 47, 52, 109, 132–3, 136,
160, 168, 198, 200, 336, 393;
air link through, 282; Egyptian
threat to (1837), 27; Indian ship-
ping moves to (c. 1800), 23; pro-
tection sought by Nakib of Muk-
alla, 398; Sultan proposed as
ruler of Aden, 33
Matchlocks, 1, 19, 67, 135, 162, 173,
203–4, 407
Mauritius, 23–4, 106
Mawiyah, 119, 209, 215, 247, 257,
262, 283, 298, 412
Mecca, 12, 15, 96, 133, 135;

Sharifs of, 26, 96, 111, 164, 243,
257, 259
Medi, 215
Mediterranean, 9, 16, 21–2, 24, 32,
38, 133, 174, 176, 199, 252
Mediterranean agreements, 199
Merewether, Col. W. L., 107, 109,
145, 192, 299, 319, 386, 390;
his constructional work at Aden,
99, 102; his thrusting hinterland
policy, 116–18, 122; invades
Fadli Country, 123; forms Aden
Troop, 132
Mesala (see also Assala), 3, 5, 353
Mesopotamia (see also Iraq), 6, 9,
11
Messageries Maritimes, 106
Milne, Capt., 81, 113
Minto, 4th Earl of, 232–4
Montagu-Chelmsford reforms, 254
Morley, John, Viscount, 232–4
Motor transport, 292, 298, 321, 334
440
Muhammad 'Ali Pasha of Egypt,
24, 35, 38, 93–4; British fears of,
30, 32; warnings to, 26–7, 33;
occupies Tihama, 25; relations
with Imams, 25, 72
Muhammad bin 'Idris at Yafi'i, 336
Muhammad Muhsin al 'Abdali, 118,
153
Muhammad Nasir Muqbil, 209,
215–17, 247
Muhsin bin 'Abdallah al 'Awlaqi,
126, 160, 167
Muhsin Fadl al 'Abdali, 43, 76, 77;
attitude to British occupation of
Aden, 30–1, 36–7, 65; attitude
to Haines, 35, 65; attacks and
blockades Aden, 67, 69, family
problems, 66; Haines' view of,
28; intrigues against Mullah
Jaffer, 71; negotiates with Haines,
31–2, 62–3, 70; temporary abdi-
cation, 75
Muhsin Shah Monti, 45
Mukalla, 28, 161, 163, 165, 167–70,
271, 282, 305–6, 398, 428; aspect
of, 156; abortive Kathiri invasion